DATE DUE

DEMCO 38-296

Controversies in Constitutional Law

Collections of Documents and Articles
on Major Questions of American Law

General Editor

Paul Finkelman
University of Akron School of Law

A GARLAND SERIES

Domestic Violence
From a Private Matter to a Federal Offense

Volume 3
The Civil Justice System's Response to Domestic Violence

Edited with an introduction by

Patricia G. Barnes

GARLAND PUBLISHING, INC.
A MEMBER OF THE TAYLOR & FRANCIS GROUP

New York & London
1998

Library of Congress Cataloging-in-Publication Data

Domestic violence: from a private matter to a federal offense / edited
   with an introduction by Patricia G. Barnes.
         p.   cm. — (Controversies in constitutional law)
      Includes bibliographical references.
      Contents: v. 1. Domestic violence: intimate partner abuse —
   v. 2. Crimes of domestic violence — v. 3. Civil justice system's
   response to domestic violence.
      ISBN 0-8153-3063-4 (alk. paper)
      1. Family violence—Law and legislation—United States.
   I. Barnes, Patricia G. II. Series.
   KF9322.D66 1998
   345.73'02555—DC21   98-36905
                                                      CIP

Printed on acid-free, 250-year-life paper
Manufactured in the United States of America

Contents

Mediation

Torts

Insurance Discrimination

Immigrants

Civil Rights

MODEL CODE ON
DOMESTIC AND FAMILY VIOLENCE

CHAPTER 3

CIVIL ORDERS FOR PROTECTION

Sec. 301. Eligible petitioners for order.

1. A person who is or has been a victim of domestic or family violence may file a petition for an order for protection against a family or household member who commits an act of domestic or family violence.

2. A parent, guardian, or other representative may file a petition for an order for protection on behalf of a child against a family or household member who commits an act of domestic or family violence.

COMMENTARY

Subsection 1 broadly defines the class of persons eligible to seek protection from the violence inflicted by family or household members in order to enable courts to effectively intervene in domestic or family violence. Comprehensive inclusion of all those exposed to risk within a family or household gives courts the latitude to construct relief to prevent further abuse and to provide essential safeguards. A person abused by another to whom she or he is related by blood or marriage may petition. Subsection 2 recognizes that children are acutely vulnerable to the trauma of domestic or family violence, whether they are the biological children of the victim or perpetrator or any other children residing with either, the Model Code permits petitioning by a child-victim or by a responsible adult, be it a parent, guardian, or other representative, on behalf of the child-victim. Moreover, the class of eligible petitioners is not limited to those victims currently or formerly residing with the perpetrator. This section also recognizes that the risks posed by perpetrators do not end when victims separate from abusers, but rather that some perpetrators are likely to use more severe violence after the separation or divorce.

Sec. 302. Uniform form required for petitions and orders; required statements in petitions and orders; duty of clerk to provide petitions and clerical assistance.

1. The insert name of appropriate state agency shall:

(a) Develop and adopt uniform forms for petitions and orders for protection, including but not limited to such orders issued pursuant to divorce, custody, and other domestic relations hearings; and

(b) Provide the forms to the clerk of each court authorized to issue such orders.

2. In addition to any other required information, the petition for an order for protection must contain a statement listing each civil or criminal action involving both parties.

3. The following statements must be printed in bold faced type or in capital letters on the order for protection:

(a) "Violation of this order may be punished by confinement in jail for as long as insert time period and by a fine of as much as insert amount."

(b) "If so ordered by the court, the respondent is forbidden to enter or stay at the petitioner's residence, even if invited to do so by the petitioner or any other person. In no event is the order for protection voided."

4. The clerk of the court or other designated person shall provide to a person requesting an order for protection:

(a) The forms adopted pursuant to subsection 1;

(b) All other forms required to petition for an order for protection, including but not limited to, forms for service and forms required by Uniform Child Custody Jurisdiction Act; and

1

(c) Clerical assistance in filling out the forms and filing the petition.

5. Except as otherwise provided in section 305, a petition for an order for protection must be in writing, verified, and subscribed to in the manner provided by state law.

6. All orders for protection must be issued on the form adopted in accordance with subsection 1.

COMMENTARY

Subsection 1 requires that the appropriate state agency promulgate uniform forms for all petitions and orders for protection which are authorized by statute in any family law or domestic relations matter. The agency is, likewise, required to supply the various forms to each court authorized to grant any of the protection orders.

Subsection 2 directs that the form petition require the petitioner to provide notice to the court of all the civil and criminal matters, past and present, involving both parties. With this notice, the court can more readily access court dockets, pleadings or charges and outcomes, including the issuance of any civil protection or criminal restraining orders, the contents of which may be relevant to action taken in the matter currently before the court. This notice will facilitate informed court practice and inhibit the issuance of contradictory court orders.

Subsection 3 is designed to provide the perpetrator of domestic or family violence with clear, unequivocal notice of the potential consequences of violation of an emergency, *ex parte*, or comprehensive protection order. The right of every citizen to due process of law makes it essential that a person against whom an *ex parte* protection order is issued be apprised of the consequences of violation. Beyond this, paragraph (b) of subsection 3, informs the perpetrator that conduct which might otherwise be permissible is precluded by the protection order. This provision gives notice to the respondent, and indirectly to law enforcement officers, that entry into the residence from which the perpetrator is excluded will not be condoned and the order will be valid and enforceable notwithstanding any invitation by the victim.

Subsection 4 enumerates the responsibilities of the person designated by the court to assist petitioners for protection orders. Besides giving petitioners the forms developed by the state agency, the clerk of court must provide all other forms necessary for completion of the application process. In many jurisdictions this may include forms related to service; any form necessary for transmittal of an order to a local or state registry of protection orders; forms related to custody and visitation; forms required by the Uniform Child Custody Jurisdiction Act; and forms related to requests for restitution, child support, and attorney's fees. Court clerks or others providing clerical assistance to petitioners are also charged with helping them complete all forms and file petitions.

Subsection 5 provides that all petitions be written and executed pursuant to state law and creates an exception to the requirement for telephonic orders issued pursuant to the request of law enforcement in section 305. Subsection 6 directs courts to issue orders only on forms developed by the state agency pursuant to subsection 1. The purpose of this section is to underscore the importance of simple, consistent, and comprehensive orders.

Sec. 303. Jurisdiction; venue; residency not required to petition.

1. The court that has jurisdiction over domestic relations has jurisdiction to issue orders for protection.

2. A petition for an order for protection may be filed in the insert county or district:

(a) Where the petitioner currently or temporarily resides;

(b) Where the respondent resides; or

(c) Where the domestic or family violence occurred.

3. There is no minimum requirement of residency to petition for an order for protection.

2

Subsection 1 assigns subject matter jurisdiction in civil protection order matters to the court with jurisdiction over domestic relations proceedings for several reasons. The drafters concluded that the judiciary handling cases constructing family rights and responsibilities after the separation of the parents or dissolution of the marriage should address the issues involved in applications for civil protection orders, especially the vital issue of safety for victims of domestic or family violence and other family or household members.

Subsection 2 provides for personal jurisdiction and venue in any judicial district where a victim may require the assistance of the court in achieving safety. The drafters of the Model Code recognize that the abused person may require the protection of the justice system in locations other than where the acts of abuse occurred. This subsection also establishes venue in the judicial district where the perpetrator resides.

Subsection 3 specifies that residency is immediately conferred upon a party who is present in a district and seeks at least temporary residency therein. Victims of domestic or family violence may relocate for a variety of reasons such as to acquire family and personal support or safe shelter, and should not be limited to legal protection in the district of origin or abuse. Ready access to the courts is necessary for protection of adult and child victims of domestic or family violence so long as such access does not encroach unduly on the constitutional rights of perpetrators.

Sec. 304. Continuing duty to inform court of other proceedings; effect of other proceedings; delay of relief prohibited; omission of petitioner's address.

1. At any hearing in a proceeding to obtain an order for protection, each party has a continuing duty to inform the court of each proceeding for an order for protection, any civil litigation, each proceeding in family or juvenile court, and each criminal case involving the parties, including the case name, the file number, and the county and state of the proceeding, if that information is known by the party.

2. An order for protection is in addition to and not in lieu of any other available civil or criminal proceeding. A petitioner is not barred from seeking an order because of other pending proceedings. A court shall not delay granting relief because of the existence of a pending action between the parties.

3. A petitioner may omit her or his address from all documents filed with the court. If a petitioner omits her or his address, the petitioner must provide the court a mailing address. If disclosure of petitioner's address is necessary to determine jurisdiction or consider venue, the court may order the disclosure to be made:

(a) After receiving the petitioner's consent;

(b) Orally and in chambers, out of the presence of the respondent and a sealed record to be made; or

(c) After a hearing, if the court takes into consideration the safety of the petitioner and finds such disclosure is in the interest of justice.

Subsection 1 expands upon the obligation to provide the court with notice of other civil or criminal proceedings involving the party articulated in subsection 2 of section 302. The duty is defined as continuing and is imposed on both the petitioner and respondent. The duty is operative only during court proceedings related to the protection order. The scope of other litigation or prosecution about which notice is to be given is enlarged. It is not only legal proceedings between the parties; it is all litigation involving either party. The drafters concluded that the court should evaluate the relevance to the protection order deliberations of any civil or criminal case in which either party is involved, rather than articulating a limited list of specific legal actions encompassed within the duty of notice.

The Model Code also requires that a party, who has information which will facilitate identification and review of these other proceedings, furnish that information to the protection order court.

Subsection 2 makes it clear that a victim of domestic or family violence is not compelled to elect a single remedy in law or equity and that the protection order application may proceed to disposition notwithstanding any proceeding or outcome in any other legal arena. It rejects the statutory imposition of preemptive and exclusive jurisdiction by divorce courts contained in some state statutes once a divorce complaint has been filed by either party. The Model Code directs the protection order court to proceed immediately to disposition and prohibits deferral of disposition pending the outcome of other pending litigation between the parties.

Subsection 3 enables the petitioner to omit her or his address from all documents filed with the court in protection order applications in order not to reveal the location of the residence, whether or not it is a shelter for abused family members. The petitioner need not seek court approval for non-disclosure in all protection order documents. However, the petitioner must furnish the court with a mailing address, which need not be his or her residence, so that the court can provide the victim with notice of any proceedings and with copies of all orders issued. To determine jurisdiction or consider venue, the court may order disclosure of the address under prescribed conditions.

Sec. 305. Emergency order for protection; available relief; availability of judge or court officer; expiration of order.

1. A court may issue a written or oral emergency order for protection ex parte when a law enforcement officer states to the court in person or by telephone, and the court finds reasonable grounds to believe, that the petitioner is in immediate danger of domestic or family violence based on an allegation of a recent incident of domestic or family violence by a family or household member.

2. A law enforcement officer who receives an oral order for protection from a court shall:

   (a) Write and sign the order on the form required pursuant to section 302;
   (b) Serve a copy on the respondent;
   (c) Immediately provide the petitioner with a copy of the order; and
   (d) Provide the order to the court by the end of the next judicial day.

3. The court may grant the following relief in an emergency order for protection:

   (a) Enjoin the respondent from threatening to commit or committing acts of domestic or family violence against the petitioner and any designated family or household member;
   (b) Prohibit the respondent from harassing, annoying, telephoning, contacting, or otherwise communicating with the petitioner, directly or indirectly;
   (c) Remove and exclude the respondent from the residence of the petitioner, regardless of ownership of the residence;
   (d) Order the respondent to stay away from the residence, school, place of employment of the petitioner, or any specified place frequented by the petitioner and any designated family or household member;
   (e) Order possession and use of an automobile and other essential personal effects, regardless of the ownership of the essential personal effects, and direct the appropriate law enforcement officer to accompany the petitioner to the residence of the parties to ensure that the petitioner is safely restored to possession of the residence, automobile, and other essential personal effects, or to supervise the petitioner's or respondent's removal of personal belongings;
   (f) Grant temporary custody of a minor child to the petitioner; and
   (g) Order such other relief as the court deems necessary to protect and provide for the safety of the petitioner and any designated family or household member.

4. A judge or other court officer with authority to issue an order for protection must be available 24 hours a day to hear petitions for emergency orders for protection.

5. An emergency order for protection expires 72 hours after issuance.

COMMENTARY

Subsection 1 creates 24-hour access to emergency orders of protection utilizing law enforcement officers as agents for judicial officers who are authorized to issue the order by telephone. In states or jurisdictions where there is a judge on duty 24 hours a day, this section creates an additional Avenue of access to the court. The drafters considered the high risk of continuing violence in these cases when determining the standard of proof of immediate danger rather than imminent or present danger.

Subsection 2 requires an officer to reduce any oral order issued by the court to writing on the prescribed form, furnishing a copy to the petitioner immediately and to the court during its next business day.

The scope of relief authorized in emergency orders for protection in subsection 3 is intended by the drafters to ensure that victims are afforded all the relief necessary to curtail access by a perpetrator to the victim and thereby to safeguard against elevated risk of violence, to accord the victim safe shelter in the family residence, and to inhibit conduct by the perpetrator that jeopardizes the employment and personal support of the victim. It also enables courts to award temporary custody of minor children both to protect the child from violence and to impede abduction by the perpetrator. It permits the court to mandate assistance by law enforcement to the victim for effectuating the terms of the order.

Subsection 4 requires 24-hour access for orders of protection, and invites legislators and courts in every jurisdiction to consider authorizing other court personnel to serve in lieu of the judiciary for purposes of issuing emergency orders for protection.

Subsection 5 limits the duration of emergency orders for protection, thus requiring the victim to file a petition with the court, requesting any or all of the relief enumerated in section 307.

Sec. 306. Order for protection; modification of orders; relief available ex parte; relief available after hearing; duties of the court; duration of order.

1. If it appears from a petition for an order for protection or a petition to modify an order for protection that domestic or family violence has occurred or a modification of an order for protection is required, a court may:

(a) Without notice or hearing, immediately issue an order for protection ex parte or modify an order for protection ex parte as it deems necessary to protect the petitioner.

(b) Upon notice, issue an order for protection or modify an order after a hearing whether or not the respondent appears.

2. A court may grant the following relief without notice and hearing in an order for protection or a modification issued ex parte:

(a) Enjoin the respondent from threatening to commit or committing acts of domestic or family violence against the petitioner and any designated family or household member;

(b) Prohibit the respondent from harassing, annoying, telephoning, contacting, or otherwise communicating with the petitioner, directly or indirectly;

(c) Remove and exclude the respondent from the residence of the petitioner, regardless of ownership of the residence;

5

(d) Order the respondent to stay away from the residence, school, or place of employment of the petitioner, or any specified place frequented by the petitioner and any designated family or household member;

(e) Prohibit the respondent from using or possessing a firearm or other weapon specified by the court;

(f) Order possession and use of an automobile and other essential personal effects, regardless of the ownership of the essential personal effects, and direct the appropriate law enforcement officer to accompany the petitioner to the residence of the parties to ensure that the petitioner is safely restored to possession of the residence, automobile, and other essential personal effects, or to supervise the petitioner's or respondent's removal of personal belongings;

(g) Grant temporary custody of any minor children to the petitioner; and

(h) Order such other relief as it deems necessary to provide for the safety and welfare of the petitioner and any designated family or household member.

3. A court may grant the following relief in an order for protection or a modification of an order after notice and hearing, whether or not the respondent appears:

(a) Grant the relief available in accordance with subsection 2.

(b) Specify arrangements for visitation of any minor child by the respondent and require supervision of that visitation by a third party or deny visitation if necessary to protect the safety of the petitioner or child.

(c) Order the respondent to pay attorney's fees.

(d) Order the respondent to:

(1) Pay rent or make payment on a mortgage on the petitioner's residence and pay for the support of the petitioner and minor child if the respondent is found to have a duty to support the petitioner or minor child;

(2) Reimburse the petitioner or other person for any expenses associated with the domestic or family violence, including but not limited to medical expenses, counseling, shelter, and repair or replacement of damaged property; and

(3) Pay the costs and fees incurred by the petitioner in bringing the action;

4. The court shall:

(a) Cause the order to be delivered to the appropriate authority for service;

(b) Make reasonable efforts to ensure that the order for protection is understood by the petitioner, and the respondent, if present;

(c) Transmit, by the end of the next business day after the order is issued, a copy of the order for protection to the local law enforcement agency or agencies designated by the petitioner; and

(d) Transmit a copy of the order to the state registry.

5. An order for protection issued ex parte or upon notice and hearing or a modification of an order for protection issued ex parte or upon notice and hearing is effective until further order of the court.

6. The designated authority shall provide expedited service for orders for protection.

6

Paragraph (a) of subsection 1 authorizes the *ex parte* issuance and modification of orders for protection. An *ex parte* order can be issued without notice or a hearing only if the court concludes the order is necessary to protect the petitioner. The risks of recidivism and harm are high in the context of domestic and family violence. See also the commentary following sections 202, 203, 205, 207, 208, 219, 220 222, 301, 302, and 305. There is evidence that the safety, if not the lives, of victims would be jeopardized if they were required to give notice and participate in a full hearing before any legal protection is issued. The Model Code thus requires that a petitioner only make a *prima facie* showing that he or she is eligible for protection and that an order is necessary to protect against future violence before issuing or modifying an order for protection *ex parte*. The Code ensures that respondents be accorded due process, notwithstanding the availability of *ex parte* relief. See subsection 1 of section 307. Paragraph (b) of subsection 1 addresses the situation where a respondent elects not to attend a hearing after requisite notice. The Model Code explicitly authorizes *ex parte* issuance of orders as described in section 307 when a respondent has been given notice, while availing the respondent ready access to seek modification of an order should the circumstances later warrant it.

Subsection 2 lists the relief that may be included in an *ex parte* order. Much of the relief is that designed to deny the respondent access to the victim. Because of the significant use of weapons in both non-lethal and lethal assaults by perpetrators of domestic and family violence, the Code contains an option prohibiting the use or possession of a firearm or other weapon. See commentary following section 207.

Subsection 3 specifies the relief courts may award after notice and hearing. First, the court may affirm or supplement the relief granted in any temporary order, as well as order any relief granted in accordance with subsection 2 for a petitioner who has not obtained an *ex parte* order. See commentary following section 401. It also requires a court to deliberate about whether the perpetrator should be accorded visitation based on the risks that the perpetrator may pose to the abused parent or the child. Paragraph (b) gives a court three options: denial of visitation, supervised visitation by a third party who is not the victim, and unsupervised visitation. When any visitation is awarded, a court is to enumerate the arrangements for visitation, including conditions to protect the child and the petitioner. Paragraphs (c) and (d) afford additional economic assistance to a victim for costs incurred as a result the violence and monies necessary to achieve economic stability.

Subsection 4 assigns the court several responsibilities necessary for due process and enforcement. Because law enforcement must be able to reasonably rely on the orders furnished to their agencies or the state registry, it essential that the court employ a reliable system that minimizes exposure of law enforcement to liability. The Code directs courts to oversee these functions.

Subsection 5 provides that an order for protection issued pursuant to section 306 or 307 is in effect until a court modifies or rescinds the order. No time limitations are imposed. This does not preclude a court from fixing review hearings to evaluate the continuing need for an order, nor does it preclude a request by either the petitioner or perpetrator to terminate the order. Subsection 5 departs from the duration strictures found in some state statutes because the risk posed to victims is not time limited or certain. The Code seeks to protect victims for as long as that protection is required, which should be determined by the court after hearing; expiration should not occur as a function of the passage of an arbitrary period of time. This provision also limits the unnecessary demand on court dockets required for reissuance or extension of orders when protection is required beyond the time of automatic expiration. This provision also shifts the burden from the victim to the perpetrator who is responsible for seeking court approval to terminate an order that is no longer essential.

Subsection 6 requires the designated authority to provide service in an expedited manner.

Sec. 307. Required hearings; duty of court when order for protection denied.

1. Except as otherwise provided in subsection 2, if a court issues an order for protection ex parte or a modification of an order for protection ex parte and the court provides relief pursuant to subsection 2 of section 306, upon a request by either party within 30 days after

7

service of the order or modification, the court shall set a date for a hearing on the petition. The hearing must be held within insert number of days after the request for a hearing is filed unless continued by the court for good cause shown. The court shall notify both parties by first class mail of the date and time of the hearing.

2. The court shall set a date for a hearing on the petition within insert number of days after the filing of the petition if a court issues an order for protection ex parte or a modification of an order of protection ex parte, and:

(a) The petitioner requests or the court provides relief in accordance with paragraph (g) of subsection 2 of section 306, concerning custody of a minor child; or

(b) The petitioner requests relief pursuant to paragraph (b), (c), or (d) of subsection 3 of section 306.

Such a hearing must be given precedence over all matters except older matters of the same character.

3. In a hearing held pursuant to subsection 1 or 2 of this section:

(a) Relief in accordance with section 306 is available.

(b) If respondent seeks relief concerning an issue not raised by the petitioner, the court may continue the hearing at the petitioner's request.

4. If a court denies a petition for an order for protection or a petition to modify an order for protection that is requested without notice to the respondent, the court shall inform the petitioner of his or her right to request a hearing upon notice to the respondent.

COMMENTARY

Subsection 1 provides the party who did not initiate the *ex parte* petition for relief or modification with the opportunity to challenge any provision of an order or modified order issued. The respondent, whether the victim or perpetrator, must make a timely request for a hearing on matters in dispute related to subsection 2 of section 306; otherwise, all issues that might have been contested are waived. The Model Code provides 30 days from service to make the request for hearing. This window of time gives the respondent adequate time to prepare the request for reconsideration and enables the moving party to rely upon the order issued at a date certain. Due process is thus afforded both parties. The court is assigned the responsibility for notice of both parties.

However, subsection 2 requires that when a court granting the *ex parte* order or modification awards custody of the minor children to the petitioner, when either party desires respondent visitation with the children, or when the petitioner seeks economic relief, the court must schedule a hearing within a time certain of the filing of the petition for protection or modification. The hearing is to be given precedence on the docket over all other matters except order for protection proceedings previously scheduled.

Subsection 3 reaffirms that the relief enumerated in section 306 may be granted at the hearing, even if neither the petitioner nor the respondent has made application for the specific relief orally or in documents filed with the court. This provision enables the court to issue supplemental relief pursuant to section 306 as it deems the relief is necessary to provide for the safety and welfare of the petitioner and family or household members. It permits the petitioner to request relief without the formality of amending the pleadings. It eliminates the requirement for responsive pleading; requiring only that the respondent request a hearing and allowing the respondent to identify any issues in dispute or relief sought at the hearing itself. If the respondent raise issues or ask for relief not addressed or sought by the petitioner, the court may grant a continuance should the petitioner ask for time to prepare to respond to the matters raised by the respondent.

Subsection 4 requires a court to advise the petitioner of his or her right to request a hearing if the court denies a petition. Notice to the respondent is required.

8

Sec. 308. Effect of action by petitioner or respondent on order.

If a respondent is excluded from the residence of a petitioner or ordered to stay away from the petitioner, an invitation by the petitioner to do so does not waive or nullify an order for protection.

COMMENTARY

This section firmly underscores the principle that court orders may only be modified by judges and rejects the notion that any party, by his or her conduct, can set aside or modify the terms and conditions of any order for protection, even by agreement of the parties. The remedy for the victim or perpetrator seeking to be excused from any provision of an order of protection is to petition for modification pursuant to section 306. Likewise, this section gives unequivocal direction to law enforcement officers that orders for protection are to be enforced as written and that no action by a party relieves the duty to enforce the order.

Sec. 309. Denial of relief prohibited.

The court shall not deny a petitioner relief requested pursuant to section 305 or 306 solely because of a lapse of time between an act of domestic or family violence and the filing of the petition.

COMMENTARY

This section recognizes that a perpetrator of domestic or family violence may pose a risk of violence long after the last act or episode of violence and that an order may be necessary to protect a victim from that continuing or recurrent risk.

Sec. 310. Mutual orders for protection prohibited.

A court shall not grant a mutual order for protection to opposing parties.

COMMENTARY

The Model Code explicitly prohibits the issuance of mutual protection orders. Mutual orders create due process problems as they are issued without prior notice, written application, or finding of good cause. Mutual orders are difficult for law enforcement officers to enforce, and ineffective in preventing further abuse. However, the Code does not preclude the issuance of separate orders for protection restraining each opposing party where each party has properly filed and served petitions for protection orders, each party has committed domestic or family violence as defined by the Code, each poses a continuing risk of violence to the other, each has otherwise satisfied all prerequisites for the type of order and remedies sought, and each has complied with the provisions of this chapter.

Sec. 311. Court-ordered and court-referred mediation of cases involving domestic or family violence prohibited.

A court shall not order parties into mediation or refer them to mediation for resolution of the issues in a petition for an order for protection.

COMMENTARY

This section prohibits a court from ordering or referring parties to mediation in a proceeding for an order for protection. Mediation is a process by which parties in equivalent bargaining positions voluntarily reach consensual agreement about the issue at hand. Violence, however, is not a subject for compromise. A process which involves both parties mediating the issue of violence implies that the victim is somehow at fault. In addition, mediation of issues in a proceeding for an order for protection is problematic because the petitioner is frequently unable to participate equally with the person against whom the protection order has been sought. Also see section 407.

Sec. 312. Court costs and fees.

Fees for filing and service of process must not be charged for any proceeding seeking only the relief provided in this chapter.

COMMENTARY

This section underscores and enhances the public policy position incorporated in many state codes, that victims of domestic or family violence must have ready access to the courts and that access must not be constrained by the economic means of petitioners. The drafters concluded that the determination of indigence by the court or an affidavit of inability to pay fees and costs, required by some codes, unduly burdens victims and court personnel.

Sec. 313. Court-mandated assistance to victims of domestic and family violence.

1. The court system in each jurisdiction shall provide assistance to victims of domestic or family violence. The administrator of the court system may enter into a contract with a private agency or organization that has a record of service to victims of domestic or family violence to provide the assistance.

2. The duties of the provider of assistance include but are not limited to:

(a) Informing victims of domestic or family violence of their rights pursuant to insert state law concerning victims' rights and assisting victims in securing those rights;

(b) Informing victims of the availability of orders for protection and assisting victims in obtaining such orders;

(c) Providing interpreters for cases involving domestic or family violence, including requests for orders for protection;

(d) Informing victims of the availability of shelter, counseling, and other social services; and

(e) Providing victims with safety plans and assisting victims in preparing the plans.

3. The provider of the assistance shall coordinate the provision of services with the providers of programs for victims of domestic or family violence.

COMMENTARY

Subsection 1 requires that the court in each jurisdiction establish an assistance program for victims of domestic or family violence. It may be staffed by court personnel or the court may contract with an organization with expertise in serving victims of domestic or family violence to provide the assistance enumerated in subsection 2. Many court programs that serve victims in protection order cases and in other civil or family law matters are located in community-based agencies. Subsection 2 specifies the minimum of assistance to be rendered. The Code requires the provider of assistance to provide information to victims about legal rights, the protection order process, safe shelter, community services and supports, as well as safety planning to enhance justice system protections. In addition, the assistance program must furnish interpreter services for the hearing impaired and for those who are not able to effectively communicate in English in domestic or family violence cases. Subsection 3 directs the provider of the assistance to collaborate with those other offices or organizations in the community providing domestic or family violence services.

Sec. 314. Registration and enforcement of foreign orders for protection; duties of court clerk.

1. A certified copy of an order for protection issued in another state may be filed in the

10

office of the clerk of any <u>district or family</u> court of this state. The clerk shall act upon the order in the same manner as the clerk acts upon an order for protection issued by a <u>district or family</u> court of this state.

2. An order for protection filed in accordance with subsection 1 has the same effect and must be enforced in the same manner as an order for protection issued by a court of this state.

3. The clerk of each <u>district or family</u> court shall:

(a) Maintain a registry in which to enter certified orders for protection issued in other states that are received for filing.

(b) At the request of a court of another state or at the request of a person who is affected by or has a legitimate interest in an order for protection, certify and forward a copy of the order to that court or person at no cost to the requesting party.

4. A court of this state shall enforce all provisions of a registered foreign order for protection whether or not such relief is available in the state.

COMMENTARY

Subsection 1 explicitly articulates the mechanism for registration of foreign orders for protection. Upon filing, the clerk of court is required to handle the foreign order as he or she would any order for protection issued by a court within the state. Subsection 2 directs courts and law enforcement to fully credit and enforce foreign orders filed with the clerk of court.

Paragraph (a) of subsection 3 requires that the clerk of the designated court keep a registry in which foreign orders for protection are to be registered. Paragraph (b) requires the clerk to certify and forward a copy of the order at the request of a court of another state, or at the request of a person who is affected by or who has a legitimate interest in the order for protection. Copies of orders must be provided to appropriate courts and persons at no charge.

Subsection 4 directs courts to enforce foreign orders as written and for the duration specified even if the state statute where the order is registered provides for more limited relief to residents. The provisions of this section do not relieve any party from the requirements of the Uniform Reciprocal Enforcement of Support Act and the Uniform Child Custody Jurisdiction Act for registration and other matters regarding support and custody.

Sec. 315. State registry for orders for protection.

1. The <u>appropriate state agency</u> shall maintain a registry of all orders for protection issued by a court of this state or registered in this state. The orders must be included in the registry within 24 hours after issuance or registration.

2. The information contained in the registry is available at all times to a court, a law enforcement agency, and <u>other governmental agency</u> upon request.

COMMENTARY

This section requires a state agency to maintain a registry of all orders for protection issued or registered in the state and requires that the orders be included in the registry within 24 hours after issuance or registration. State registries of orders for protection typically are located in state criminal justice or law enforcement agencies. The advantages of charging a state's law enforcement agency with this responsibility is that the agency may be able to incorporate orders of protection in its existing system for verification of state warrants, etc., and that system is available around the clock.

Model Full Faith and Credit Statute

SECTION 1. Full faith and credit for valid foreign protection order.

Any valid protection order related to domestic or family violence, issued by a court of another state, tribe, or U.S. territory shall be accorded full faith and credit by the courts of this state and enforced as if it were issued in this state.

SECTION 2. Valid foreign protection order.

A protection order issued by a state, tribal or territorial court related to domestic or family violence shall be deemed valid if the issuing court had jurisdiction over the parties and matter under the law of the state, tribe or territory. There shall be a presumption in favor of validity where an order appears authentic on its face.

A defendant must be given reasonable notice and the opportunity to be heard before the order of the foreign state, tribe or territory was issued, provided, in the case of ex parte orders, notice and opportunity to be heard was given as soon as possible after the order was issued, consistent with due process.

Failure to provide reasonable notice and opportunity to be heard shall be an affirmative defense to any charge or process filed seeking enforcement of a foreign protection order.

SECTION 3. Exclusion from full faith and credit.

A protection order entered against both the plaintiff and defendant shall not be enforceable against the plaintiff in a foreign jurisdiction unless:

(a) the defendant filed a cross or counter petition, complaint or other written pleading was filed seeking such a protection order and

(b) the issuing court made specific findings of domestic or family violence against both the plaintiff and defendant and determined that each party was entitled to such an order.

SECTION 4. Statewide Protection Order Registry.

(1) The _____ State police (or other agency designated by the governor) shall establish a statewide registry of protection orders related to domestic or family violence and shall maintain a complete and systematic record and index of all valid temporary and final civil and criminal court orders of protection.

(2) The data fields of the statewide registry shall include, but need not be limited to, the following:

(i)   The names of the plaintiff and any protected parties.

(ii)   The name and address of the defendant.

(iii)   The date the order was entered.

(iv)   The date the order expires.

(v)   The relief granted under _____(specify relief awarded and citations related thereto, and designate which of the violations are arrestable offenses).

(vi)   The judicial district and contact information for court administration for the court in which the order was entered.

(vii)   Where furnished, the Social Security number, date of birth of and description of the defendant.

(viii) caution indicator stating whether the defendant is believed to be armed and dangerous.

(ix)   Brady record indicator stating whether the defendant is prohibited from purchasing or possessing a firearm under federal law.

(3) The clerk of the issuing court or the clerk of the court where a foreign order of protection is filed shall send, on a form prescribed by the _____ State Police (or registry agency designated by the governor), a copy of the protection order to the statewide protection order registry so that it is received within 24 hours of the entry an order issued within the state or the filing of a foreign order. The _____ State Police (or other agency designated by the governor) shall enter orders in the statewide protection order registry within eight hours of receipt.

(4) The statewide protection order registry shall be available at all times to inform courts, dispatchers and law enforcement officers of any valid protection order issued within the state or filed as a foreign order for purposes of enforcement in the state.

SECTION 5. Filing of foreign protection order.

(1) A plaintiff who obtains a valid order of protection in another state, tribe or U.S. territory may file that order by presenting a certified copy of the foreign order to a clerk of court in the judicial district where the plaintiff believes enforcement may be necessary.

(2) Filing shall be without fee or cost.

(3) A clerk of court shall forward a copy of the foreign protection order to the local police or sheriff's office and the statewide protection order registry upon application of a plaintiff seeking enforcement.

(4) The clerk shall provide the plaintiff with a copy bearing proof of filing with the court and entry into the statewide protection order registry.

(5) Filing and entry of the foreign order in the statewide protection order registry shall not be prerequisites for enforcement of the foreign protection order.

SECTION 6. Law Enforcement

A law enforcement officer may rely upon a copy of any foreign protection order which has been provided to the officer by any source and may also rely on upon the statement of any person protected by a foreign order that the order remains in effect. A law enforcement officer acting in good faith shall be immune from civil and criminal liability in any action arising in connection with a court's finding that the foreign order was not enforceable.

IN THE COURT OF COMMON PLEAS OF ALLEGHENY COUNTY, PENNSYLVANIA
FAMILY DIVISION

```
                           )
                           )
_____    )
        Plaintiff          )
                           )
        vs.                )    No._____
                           )
                           )
_____    )
        Defendant          )
```

FINAL ORDER OF COURT

NOTICE TO DEFENDANT: IF DEFENDANT VIOLATES THIS COURT ORDER, AS SET
FORTH IN PARAGRAPHS 1 THROUGH 3, DEFENDANT SHALL BE ARRESTED ON THE
CHARGE OF INDIRECT CRIMINAL CONTEMPT WHICH IS PUNISHABLE BY A FINE OF UP
TO $1,000.00 AND A JAIL SENTENCE OF UP TO SIX (6) MONTHS.

AND NOW, this_____day of_____, 19_____, upon
consideration of the Petition filed in this matter,

_____

it is ORDERED, ADJUDGED and DECREED as follows:

1. Defendant is:
   a) prohibited from having ANY CONTACT with Plaintiff and
      Plaintiff's minor children
   b) directed to refrain from abusing, harassing or stalking
      Plaintiff and Plaintiff's minor child(ren);
   c) restrained from entering the place of employment, business
      or school of the Plaintiff and of Plaintiff's minor
      child(ren).

2. Defendant is completely excluded from the residence at

_____

and from any other residence where Plaintiff may live.   Exclusive
possession of these premises is granted to Plaintiff; Defendant shall
have no right or privilege to enter or be present on the premises.
IF FOR ANY REASON DEFENDANT RETURNS TO PLAINTIFF'S RESIDENCE WITHOUT
WRITTEN PERMISSION OF THE COURT, DEFENDANT SHALL BE ARRESTED ON THE
CHARGE OF INDIRECT CRIMINAL CONTEMPT.

3. Custody of the parties' minor child(ren),_____

_____ is granted to the Plaintiff.

"Final Order-Page 1"

15

NOTICE TO LAW ENFORCEMENT OFFICIALS

The Police who have jurisdiction over the Plaintiff's residence, OR any location where a violation of the Order occurs OR where the Defendant may be located, shall enforce this Order.

If Defendant violates any of the provisions in the paragraphs set forth above, Defendant shall be arrested on the charge of Indirect Criminal Contempt. An arrest for violation of this Order may be without warrant, based solely on probable cause, whether or not the violation is committed in the presence of the police.

Subsequent to an arrest, the police officer shall seize all weapons used or threatened to have been used during the violation of the protection Order or during prior incidents of abuse. The Sheriff shall maintain possession of the weapons until further order of this Court.

When the Defendant is placed under arrest for violation of the Order, the Defendant shall be taken by the police to the presiding District Justice OR Pittsburgh City Court Magistrate in the area where the alleged violation occurred OR to the County Night Court. A "COMPLAINT FOR INDIRECT CRIMINAL CONTEMPT" shall then be completed and signed by the police officer OR the Plaintiff.

If sufficient grounds for violation of this Order are alleged, the Defendant shall be arraigned, bond set, and both parties given notice of the final hearing date.

---

    4. If there is no existing support or alimony pendente lite order the Defendant is directed to pay temporary support for:

_____ as follows:_____

This Order for Support shall remain in effect until a final support order is entered by this Court. However, this Order shall lapse automatically if the Plaintiff does not file a Complaint for Support with the Court within 15 days of the date of this Order. This paragraph shall not be construed as a finding of the Defendant's actual support obligations, which will be determined at the support hearing. Any adjustments in the final amount of support shall be credited, retroactive to this date, to the appropriate party.

"Final Order - Page 2"

16

5. All costs of filing, service and certification are waived as to the Plaintiff and are imposed on Defendant.

_____6. Defendant shall pay $_____ to Plaintiff as

compensation for the plaintiff's following losses: _____

_____

OR

_____6. Plaintiff is granted leave to present a petition, with appropriate notice to Defendant, to the prevailing Family Division Motions' Judge to request recovery of out-of-pocket losses. The Petition shall include an exhibit itemizing all claimed out-of-pocket losses, copies of all bills and estimates of repair, and an order scheduling a hearing before a Family Division arbitration panel at the convenience of the Court. The Pennsylvania Rules of Civil Procedure governing compulsory arbitration shall apply at the hearing. No filing fee shall be required by the Prothonotary's Office for the filing of the petition.

7. All provisions of this Order shall expire in one year, on

_____.

BY THE COURT:

Consented to:

_____ J.

_____

_____

_____

_____

"Final Order-Page 3"

17

HOFSTRA LAW REVIEW

Volume 21	Summer 1993

PROVIDING LEGAL PROTECTION FOR BATTERED WOMEN: AN ANALYSIS OF STATE STATUTES AND CASE LAW

Catherine F. Klein[*]
Leslye E. Orloff[**]

    [*] Associate Professor and Director, The Families and the Law Clinic, Columbus School of Law, The Catholic University of America. Director of Catholic University's clinical domestic violence program since 1981.

    [**] Founder of Clinica Legal Latina, the domestic violence program at Ayuda, Inc., a community based legal services program for immigrant and refugee women in Washington, D.C. Ms. Orloff has been representing immigrant battered women since 1983, and is currently Ayuda's Director of Program Development responsible for domestic violence policy work on both local and national levels.

    The authors wish to express their gratitude to their research assistants, Mary Ellen Droll and Jennifer Ferrante, without whose tireless efforts this Article never could have been completed, and to the staff of the *Hofstra Law Review* for their diligence in editing. All errors are, of course, our own.

C.   Conduct Sufficient to Support Issuance of a Civil Protection Order[227]

The following sections discuss the various types of acts which courts have identified as abuse sufficient to support the issuance of a protection order. In *Knuth v. Knuth*,[228] the Minnesota Court of Appeals discussed generally the broad range of acts which may warrant a civil protection order.[229] The court held that a civil protection order may issue not only for actual physical harm, but also for acts which inflict the fear of imminent bodily injury.[230] While the court must find some overt action indicating present intent to do harm or cause fear of imminent harm, the court does not need to find an overt physical act.[231] A verbal threat can be sufficient to inflict fear of imminent physical harm.[232] The cases which follow reflect this broad approach to defining domestic abuse.

Victims of domestic abuse experience a cycle of violence which escalates over time.[233] Victims of domestic violence suffer various types of abuse during the course of their relationships with batterers. The various forms of abuse that can form the basis for issuance of a civil protection order may include emotional abuse, threats, harassment, and stalking. Such abuse often escalates into attempts to harm the victim, sexual assault, and battery.[234] As the frequency of battering episodes increase, the more severe each battering incident often becomes. When battering continues over years, it becomes more and more dangerous, progressing from punches to the use of weapons.[235] Since the cycle of violence in an abusive relationship tends to escalate into more violent behavior, civil protection orders should issue based on a wide range of abuse in order to permit early intervention and prevention of more serious injuries.[236]

---

227. *See generally* MODEL CODE, *supra* note 15, at §§ 102, 201.
228. 1992 Minn. App. LEXIS 696 (Minn. Ct. App. June 19, 1992).
229. *Id.*
230. *Id.*
231. *Id.*
232. *Id.*
233. TERRIFYING LOVE, *supra* note 4, at 30.
234. TERRIFYING LOVE, *supra* note 4, at 44 (indicating that 66% of women reported battering becoming more frequent, 65% reported that physical abuse worsened, and 73% reported psychological abuse becoming more severe); BROWNE, *supra* note 171, at 68.
235. GILLESPIE, *supra* note 124, at 129 (stating that the number of women hit with an object in the most serious incident of violence was twice the number hit with an object in the first incident); *see also* TERRIFYING LOVE, *supra* note 4.
236. Domestic violence is cyclical. The violence increases in both frequency and severity

1. Criminal Acts

A wide range of criminal acts may form the basis for a civil protection order. State statutes specifically authorize protection orders based on almost any criminal act,[237] including physical abuse of the petitioner or a child,[238] criminal trespass,[239] kidnapping,[240]

---

unless there is outside intervention. Ganley, *supra* note 21, at 23. Ganley emphasizes that:

> Domestic violence consists of a wide range of behaviors, including some of the same behaviors found in stranger violence. Some acts of domestic violence are criminal (hitting, choking, kicking, assault with a weapon, shoving, scratching, biting, rape, unwanted sexual touching, forcing sex with third parties, threats of violence, harassment at work, stalking, destruction of property, attacks against pets, etc.) while other behaviors may not constitute criminal conduct (degrading comments, interrogating children or other family members, suicide threats or attempts, controlling access to the family resources: time, money, food, clothing, shelter, as well as controlling the abused party's time and activities, etc.). Whether or not there has been a finding of criminal conduct, evidence of these behaviors indicates a pattern of abusive control which has devastating effects on the family.

Id.

237. *See, e.g.*, CONN. GEN. STAT. ANN. § 46b-38a(3) (West 1992); D.C. CODE ANN. § 16-1002 (1992); LA. REV. STAT. ANN. § 46:2132 (West 1992); N.Y. FAM. CT. ACT § 812 (McKinney Supp. 1994).

238. ALA. CODE § 30-5-2 (1992); ALASKA STAT. § 25.35.060 (1992); ARIZ. REV. STAT. ANN. § 13-3601 (1992); CAL. FAM. CODE § 5500 (West 1993); COLO. REV. STAT. ANN. § 14-4-101 (1992); CONN. GEN. STAT. ANN. § 46b-15 (West 1992); DEL. CODE ANN. tit. 10, § 945 (1992); D.C. CODE ANN. § 16-100 (1992); FLA. STAT. ANN. § 741.30 (West 1992); GA. CODE ANN. § 19-13-1 (1992); HAW. REV. STAT. § 586-1 (1992); IDAHO CODE § 39-6303 (1992); 725 ILCS 40/2311 (1993); IND. CODE ANN. § 34-4-5.1-1 (1992); IOWA CODE ANN. § 236.2 (West 1992); KAN. STAT. ANN. § 60-3102 (1992); KY. REV. STAT. ANN. § 403.720 (Baldwin 1992) (issuing for threats of physical and sexual abuse as well); LA. REV. STAT. ANN. § 46:2132 (West 1992); ME. REV. STAT. ANN. tit. 19, § 26 (1992); MD. CODE ANN., FAM. LAW § 4-501 (1992); MASS. GEN. L. ANN. ch. 209A, § 1 (West 1992); MICH. COMP. LAWS ANN. § 93.21 (West 1992); MINN. STAT. ANN. § 518B.01 (West 1992); MISS. CODE ANN. § 93-21-3 (1992); MO. REV. STAT. § 455.010 (1992); MONT. CODE ANN. § 40-4-121 (1992); NEB. REV. STAT. § 42-903 (1992); NEV. REV. STAT. ANN. § 33.018 (1992); N.H. REV. STAT. ANN. § 173-B:1 (1992); N.J. STAT. ANN. § 2C: 25-19 (West 1992); N.M. STAT. ANN. § 40-13-2 (Michie 1992); N.Y. FAM. CT. ACT § 812 (McKinney Supp. 1994); N.C. GEN. STAT. § 50B-1 (1992); N.D. CENT. CODE § 14-07.1-01 (1992); OHIO REV. CODE ANN. § 3113.31 (Baldwin 1992); OKLA. STAT. ANN. tit. 43, § 322-60.1 (West 1992); OR. REV. STAT. § 107.705 (1992); 23 PA. CONS. STAT. ANN. § 6102 (1992); R.I. GEN. LAWS § 15-15-1 (1992); S.C. CODE ANN. § 20-4-20 (Law. Co-op. 1992); S.D. CODIFIED LAWS ANN. § 25-10-1 (1992); TENN. CODE ANN. § 36-3-601 (1992); TEX. FAM. CODE ANN. § 71.01 (West 1992); UTAH CODE ANN. § 30-6-1 (1992); VT. STAT. ANN. tit. 15, § 1101 (1992); VA. CODE ANN. § 16.1-233 (1992); WASH. REV. CODE ANN. § 26.50.010 (West 1992); W. VA. CODE § 48-2A-2(3) (Supp. 1993); WIS. STAT. ANN. § 813-12 (West 1992); WYO. STAT. § 35-21-122 (1992).

239. *See, e.g.*, DEL. CODE ANN. tit. 10, § 945 (1993); N.J. STAT. ANN. § 2C:25-19 (1992); N.M. STAT. ANN. § 40-13-2 (Michie 1992); WASH. REV. CODE ANN. § 10.99.020 (1992).

240. DEL. CODE ANN. tit. 10, § 945 (1993); N.J. STAT. ANN. § 2C:25-19 (West 1992); WASH. REV. CODE ANN. § 10.99.020 (West 1992).

burglary,[241] malicious mischief,[242] interference with child custody,[243] and reckless endangerment.[244]

Research data supports this approach. Of violent crimes by intimates reported by female victims, 85-88% were assaults, 10-11% were robberies, and 2-3% were rapes.[245] Approximately one-quarter of the assaults were aggravated, meaning that the offender had used a weapon or had seriously injured the victim. The remaining assaults were simple, indicating either a minor injury—bruises, black eyes, cuts, scratches, swelling, or undetermined injuries requiring less than 2 days of hospitalization—or a verbal threat of harm.[246] One-half of these incidents classified as "simple assaults" actually involve bodily injury at least as serious as the injury inflicted in 90% of all robberies and aggravated assaults.[247] If reported, one-third of all domestic violence cases would have been charged as felony rape or felony assault if they had been committed against strangers.[248] Epidemiologic surveys found that abuse ranged from being slapped, punched, kicked, or thrown bodily to being scalded, choked, smothered, or bitten.[249] Typically, assaultive episodes involve a combination of assaultive acts, verbal abuse, and threats. Over 80% of all assaults against spouses and ex-spouses result in injuries. Victims of marital violence have the highest rates of internal injuries and unconsciousness.[250] The injury rate is only 54% for victims of stranger vio-

---

241. N.J. STAT. ANN. § 2C:25-19 (West 1992); WASH. REV. CODE ANN. § 10.99.020 (West 1992).

242. N.J. STAT. ANN. § 2C:25-19; N.Y. FAM. CT. ACT § 812(1) (McKinney 1993) (defining the offense of disorderly conduct to include conduct not in a public place); WASH. REV. CODE ANN. § 10.99.020 (West 1992).

243. DEL. CODE ANN. tit. 10, § 945 (1993); *see also* Gasaway v. Gasaway, 616 N.E.2d 610 (Ind. 1993) (awarding protection order based on respondent's attempt to kidnap his child).

244. N.Y. FAM. CT. ACT § 812(1) (McKinney 1992); WASH. REV. CODE ANN. § 10.99.020 (1992).

245. HARLOW, *supra* note 3, at 2; *see also* KLAUS & RAND, *supra* note 3.

246. *Id.*

247. NIJ CPO STUDY, *supra* note 19, at 4; *see also* PATRICK A. LANGAN & CHRISTOPHER A. INNES, BUREAU OF JUSTICE STATISTICS, PREVENTING DOMESTIC VIOLENCE AGAINST WOMEN 1, 3 (1986).

248. *Women and Violence: Hearings on Legislation to Reduce the Growing Problem of Violent Crime Against Women Before the Senate Comm. on the Judiciary*, 101st Cong., 2d Sess. 72 (1990) (statement of Helen R. Newborne, Executive Director, and Sally Goldfarb, Staff Attorney, NOW Legal Defense and Education Fund on Violence Against Women).

249. Browne, *supra* note 1, at 3186. In a study of abusive men, one-third reported that their partners sustained broken bones or other substantial injuries as a result of their violence. James Ptacek, *Why Do Men Batter Their Wives?*, in FEMINIST PERSPECTIVES ON WIFE ABUSE 135 (Kersti Yllo & Michele Bogard eds., 1988).

250. Browne, *supra* note 1, at 3186. Women are three times more likely than men to re-

lence.[251]

Case law indicates that battery is the most common criminal ground for issuance of a civil protection order. Courts issue civil protection orders for striking and kicking the petitioner,[252] beating the petitioner,[253] breaking an infant's leg,[254] shoving an infant's face against a door,[255] yanking the petitioner by the hair,[256] pulling out the petitioner's hair,[257] throwing the petitioner on the floor,[258] bruising a child's back, legs, and buttocks,[259] physically restraining the petitioner,[260] twisting the petitioner's wrist,[261] pounding the petitioner's head on the floor,[262] choking the petitioner,[263] slapping

---

quire medical care for injuries sustained in family assaults. Glenda Kaufman et al., *The Drunken Bum Theory of Wife Beating*, 34 SOC. PROBS. 218 (1987).

251. Browne, *supra* note 1, at 3186.

252. *See generally* People v. Ballard, 249 Cal. Rptr. 806 (Ct. App. 1988) (affirming issuance of order where respondent grabbed and hit petitioner, held her outside of a window and made her urinate on the floor); Colorado v. Brockelman, 1993 Colo. App. LEXIS 270 (Ct. App. Oct. 21, 1993) (affirming order where defendant hit victim in face several times and choked her); Todd v. Todd, 772 S.W.2d 14 (Mo. Ct. App. 1989) (affirming order where respondent stuck and kicked his wife); Gloria C. v. William C., 476 N.Y.S.2d 991 (Fam. Ct. 1984) (granting petition where respondent hit the petitioner in the head, punched her in the stomach while pregnant, and threw her to the floor); Commonwealth v. Smith, 552 A.2d 292 (Pa. Super. Ct. 1988) (issuing order where respondent hit petitioner with his car and struck petitioner on head and neck with an open and closed fist).

253. Parkhurst v. Parkhurst, 793 S.W.2d 634 (Mo. Ct. App. 1990) (affirming grant where respondent beat petitioner on one occasion); Delisser v. Hardy, 749 P.2d 1207 (Or. Ct. App. 1988) (holding protection order properly issued on basis of defendant's forced entry into petitioner's apartment, physical abuse of petitioner and his threats to get her fired from her job).

254. Yankoskie v. Lenker, 526 A.2d 429 (Pa. Super. Ct. 1987) (holding civil protection order properly issued where the respondent broke his infant son's leg and shoved his son's face against a cellar door).

255. *Id.*

256. Pierson v. Pierson, 555 N.Y.S.2d 227 (Fam. Ct. 1990); *see also* Sielski v. Sielski, 604 A.2d 206 (N.J. Super. Ct. Ch. Div. 1990) (granting a protection order where defendant yanked petitioner from her bed by her hair, slapped her about the face and neck, attempted to push her face in the toilet, threw cold water on her, and yanked at her pubic hair).

257. *Pierson*, 555 N.Y.S.2d at 227.

258. *Id.*; *see also* Gloria C. v. William C., 476 N.Y.S.2d 991 (Fam. Ct. 1984) (granting petition where respondent hit the petitioner in the head, punched her in the stomach while pregnant, and threw her to the floor); Murray v. Murray, 623 N.E.2d 1236 (Ohio Ct. App. 1993).

259. *Pierson*, 555 N.Y.S.2d at 227. *But see* Harriman v. Harriman, No. 97826, 1990 Conn. Super. LEXIS 1200, at *1 (Conn. Super. Ct. Sept. 25, 1990) (holding that spanking a child on one occasion is insufficient to issue a civil protection order).

260. Synder v. Synder, 629 A.2d 977 (Pa. Sup. Ct. 1993).

261. Sell v. Sell, No. 00063, 1991 Pa. Super. LEXIS 1746 (Pa. Super. Ct. June 6, 1991) (holding that wife's need to seek medical treatment after husband twisted her wrist was sufficient to issue a civil protection order).

262. *Murray*, 623 N.E.2d 1236.

the petitioner on the face and neck,[264] attempting to push the petitioner's face in the toilet,[265] throwing cold water on the petitioner,[266] yanking at the petitioner's pubic hair,[267] punching a pregnant petitioner in the stomach,[268] and ordering trained dogs to attack the petitioner.[269]

Other criminal acts which are grounds to issue a civil protection order include: firing shots into the petitioner's home,[270] assaulting the petitioner's friend,[271] forcibly or unlawfully entering the petitioner's home,[272] and breaking down petitioner's door.[273]

Several courts have specifically issued civil protection orders based on criminal acts involving a motor vehicle.[274] These have included striking the petitioner with a car,[275] pursuing the petitioner in a high speed chase,[276] attempting to pull the petitioner from her car,[277] and driving away quickly while the petitioner had her hands on the car, cauing her to be thrown into a tree.[278] In *Christenson v.*

---

263. Colorado v. Brockelman, 1993 Colo. App. LEXIS 270 (Colo. Ct. App. Oct. 21, 1993); *see also Synder*, 629 A.2d 977.

264. Sielski v. Sielski, 604 A.2d 206, 207 (N.J. Sup. Ct. Ch. Div. 1990).

265. *Id.*

266. *Id.*

267. *Id.*

268. Gloria C. v. William C., 476 N.Y.S.2d 991 (Fam. Ct. 1984).

269. Jane Y. v. Joseph Y., 474 N.Y.S.2d 681, 682 (Fam. Ct. 1984).

270. Clifford v. Krueger, 297 N.Y.S.2d 990 (Sup. Ct. 1969).

271. People v. Stevens, 506 N.Y.S.2d 995, 996 (Sup. Ct. 1986) (issuing a protection order where respondent unlawfully entered wife's home and assaulted her friend).

272. *Id.; see also* People v. Williams, 300 N.Y.S.2d 89 (N.Y. 1969) (holding protection order properly granted where defendant refused to leave his grandparents' home and threatened his uncle with a knife when confronted); Delisser v. Hardy, 749 P.2d 1207, 1208 (Or. Ct. App. 1988) (affirming the grant of an order where defendant, inter alia, forced his way into petitioner's apartment); State v. Kilponen, 737 P.2d 1024 (Wash. Ct. App. 1987) (holding defendant's conviction for armed burglary was sufficient basis for issuing protection order); Johnson v. Miller, 459 N.W.2d 886 (Wis. Ct. App. 1990) (entering step-daughter's residence by force sufficient to support protection order).

273. People v. Stevens, 506 N.Y.S.2d 995, 996 (Sup. Ct. 1986).

274. *See, e.g.,* Christenson v. Christenson, 472 N.W.2d 279 (Iowa 1991); *see also* Harper v. Harper, 537 So. 2d 282 (La. Ct. App. 1988); Capps v. Capps, 715 S.W.2d 547 (Mo. Ct. App. 1986); Commonwealth v. Smith, 552 A.2d 292 (Pa. Super. Ct. 1988).

275. *Smith*, 552 A.2d at 292.

276. *Christenson*, 472 N.W.2d at 279.

277. *Harper*, 537 So. 2d at 282; *see also* Synder v. Synder, 629 A.2d 977 (Pa. Super. Ct. 1993).

278. *Capps*, 715 S.W.2d at 547. In one 1968 case, Seymour v. Seymour, 289 N.Y.S.2d 515 (Fam. Ct. 1968), the court held that a husband's attempt to force his wife's car off the road by abruptly swerving his car in front of her did not constitute a family offense because it did not constitute an assault resulting in physical pain or injury or disorderly conduct under the Penal Code. Today, many jurisdictions, including New York, would issue a civil

Christenson,[279] the court issued a protection order to the petitioner when the respondent initiated a high speed car chase, rejecting the respondent's argument that the car chase did not amount to an assault.[280] The court liberally construed the domestic violence act, noting that it served a protective, rather than punitive, function.[281] It held that the pursuit of the petitioner at high rates of speed qualified as an assault since the defendant had the ability to strike the petitioner's car during the chase, which could have led to a collision resulting in physical injury.[282]

Finally, courts will also appropriately issue a civil protection order when someone other than the petitioner is injured by violence directed toward the petitioner. In *Johnson v. Miller*,[283] the court issued a civil protection order where a step-father physically injured his step-daughter during an attempt to injure her mother.[284] The court noted that:

> [w]hether [the defendant's] anger was directed exclusively at [his step-daughter] or at both women—or neither—is beside the point. His violent conduct [during the step-daughter]'s presence in the home in which she resided—and which resulted in physical injury to her—coupled with his return and forcible entry into [her] residence, provides an adequate foundation for a determination that he "may [have] engage[d] in domestic abuse" of [her].[285]

This decision recognizes that a civil protection order should be issued even if the defendant's violence injures someone other than his intended target. By the batterer's own violent actions, he creates a dangerous environment where unintended victims may be injured. In these cases, a civil protection order should issue based on the attempt, or based on the battery via transferred intent.[286]

---

protection order in such a case based on attempts or harassment. *See, e.g.*, Hayes v. Hayes, 500 N.Y.S.2d 475, 476 (Fam. Ct. 1986).

279. 472 N.W.2d 279 (Iowa 1991).

280. *Id.* at 280-81.

281. *Id.* at 280.

282. *Id.*

283. 459 N.W.2d 886 (Wis. Ct. App. 1990).

284. *Johnson*, 459 N.W.2d at 887.

285. *Id.* at 887 (quoting WIS. STAT. ANN. § 813.12 (West 1990)).

286. The concept of transferred intent is well established in both criminal and tort law. *See, e.g.*, Jackson v. Follette, 462 F.2d 1041, 1047 n.10 (2d Cir. 1972); *see also* Yates v. Evatt, 111 S. Ct. 1884, 1886 (1991). The concept of transferred intent first appeared in criminal law and then became part of tort law. The criminal rule finds guilt in cases where a shooting, striking, throwing of an object, or poisoning results in an unexpected injury to an

Criminal domestic violence cases also illustrate criminal acts which could warrant and support issuance of a civil protection order. Successful criminal domestic violence prosecutions include where the defendant beat the victim with a breadboard,[287] stabbed the victim,[288] punched the victim in the face resulting in memory loss,[289] sodomized the victim,[290] held the victim outside of a window,[291] forced the victim to urinate on the floor,[292] assaulted the victim,[293] forced the victim into her car, drove on the wrong side of the road, and threatened to kill them both,[294] and drove the victim onto a dirt road, pulled out a knife, and ordered her to strip.[295]

2. Sexual Assault and Marital Rape

State statutes and case law in all fifty states, the District of Columbia, Puerto Rico, and all U.S. territories[296] recognize marital rape and sexual assault of a spouse or a cohabitant as domestic violence. Thirty-two states, the District of Columbia, and Puerto Rico issue civil protection orders based on sexual abuse of the petitioner.[297] In five additional states, the rape of a spouse or a cohabi-

---

unintended person. The intent to injure is transferred from the intended to the unintended victim. In tort law as well, cases hold the defendant liable for a battery to an unintended person where the intent was to commit a battery against another person. *See* WILLIAM L. PROSSER & W. PAGE KEETON, THE LAW OF TORTS 37-39 (5th ed. 1984).

287. People v. Thompson, 206 Cal. Rptr. 516, 517 (Ct. App. 1984).

288. Arizona v. Lavers, 814 P.2d 333 (Ariz.), *cert. denied*, 112 S.Ct. 343 (1991).

289. State v. Harper, 761 P.2d 570, 571 (Utah Ct. App. 1988).

290. *Thompson*, 206 Cal. Rptr. at 517.

291. People v. Ballard, 249 Cal. Rptr. 806, 807 (Ct. App. 1988).

292. *Id.*

293. People v. Singleton, 532 N.Y.S.2d 208 (Crim. Ct. 1988); *see also* Hawaii v. Ibuos, 857 P.2d 576 (Haw. 1993).

294. State v. Hobbs, 801 P.2d 1028, 1029 (Wash. Ct. App. 1990).

295. Gilbert v. Georgia, 433 S.E.2d 664 (Ga. Ct. App. 1993).

296. Sexual Abuse Act of 1986 § 87(b), 18 U.S.C. §§ 2241-45 (1993).

297. ALASKA STAT. § 25.35 (1993); ARIZ. REV. STAT. ANN. § 13-3602 (1994); ARK. CODE ANN. § 9-15-206 (Michie 1993); CAL. FAM. CODE § 55-231 (West 1993); CONN. GEN. STAT. ANN. § 46b-15 (West 1993); DEL. CODE ANN. tit. 10, §§ 945-46 (1993); D.C. CODE ANN. §§ 16-1001, 16-1004 (1993); FLA. STAT. ANN. § 741.30 (West 1993); GA. CODE ANN. §§ 19-13-1, 19-13-4 (1993); IDAHO CODE § 39-6303 (1993); 750 ILCS 60/102, 60/210 (1993); LA. REV. STAT. ANN. § 46:2132 (West 1992); ME. REV. STAT. ANN. tit. 19, § 766 (West 1992); MD. CODE ANN., FAM. LAW §§ 4-501, 4-506 (1993); MASS. GEN. L. ANN. ch. 209A, §§ 1, 3 (1992); MINN. STAT. ANN. § 518B.01 (West 1992); MO. REV. STAT. §§ 455.010, 455.020 (Vernon 1993); NEV. REV. STAT. ANN. §§ 33.018, 33.020 (Michie 1993); N.H. REV. STAT. ANN. § 173-B:1 (1992); N.J. STAT. ANN. §§ 2C:25-3, 2C:25-13 (West 1993); N.M. STAT. ANN. §§ 40-13-2, 40-13-3 (Michie 1993); N.Y. FAM. CT. ACT § 842 (McKinney Supp. 1994); OHIO REV. CODE ANN. § 3113.31 (Anderson 1992); OKLA. STAT. ANN. tit. 22, §§ 60.1, 60.2 (West Supp. 1994); OR. REV. STAT. § 107.705 (1992); 23

tant is a violation of the criminal code, and thus is a criminal act which supports the issuance of a civil protection order.[298] Only seven states define a rape or sexual assault sufficient to issue a civil

---

PA. CONS. STAT. ANN. §§ 6102(a), 6107(b) (1992); P.R. LAWS ANN. tit. 8, § 601 (1990); R.I. GEN. LAWS § 15-5-3 (1993); S.C. CODE ANN. § 20-4-40 (Law. Co-op. 1992); UTAH CODE ANN. §§ 30-6-1, 30-6-2 (1993); WASH. REV. CODE ANN. §§ 26.50.010, 25.050.030 (West 1993); W. VA. CODE §§ 48-2A-2, 48-2A-5 (1993); WIS. STAT. ANN. § 813-12 (West 1993); WYO. STAT. §§ 35-21-102, 35-21-103 (1993).

In four of these states, husbands and cohabitants can be charged with rape of their wives or girlfriends. GA. CODE ANN. § 16-6-1(a) (1993); MASS. GEN. L. ANN. ch. 265, § 22 (1992); N.J. STAT. ANN. § 2C:14-5(b) (West 1993); OR. REV. STAT. § 163.305 (1992).

Seventeen of these states' statutes authorize issuance of a civil protection order based on a definition of rape or sexual assault of a family member that is broader than that defined in the states' criminal statutes. Since civil protection order proceedings are civil and preventative in nature, states have been willing to issue civil protection orders based on broader definitions of sexual assault and rape than that required when the offender is being charged criminally with rape or sexual assault. *See, e.g.,* ARIZ. REV. STAT. ANN. § 13-1406 (1993) (charging husband with sexual assault of wife if husband used force or threat); CAL. PENAL CODE § 262 (West 1993) (charging husband with rape if force or threat was used *and* if wife reports rape within 90 days, unless wife is mentally incapacitated); CONN. GEN. STAT. ANN. § 53a-67 (West 1993) (requiring that spouse/cohabitant be charged with more than first degree rape); IDAHO CODE § 18-6107 (1993) (charging husband with rape only when he uses force, violence, threat of immediate and great bodily harm, intoxicating substance, narcotic or anesthetics, or if wife is mentally incapacitated); LA. REV. STAT. ANN. § 14.41 (West 1993) (charging husband/cohabitant with rape only if there is a court order of separation or an order prohibiting physical or sexual abuse); MINN. STAT. ANN. § 609.349 (West 1993) (charging husband with rape only if spouses are living apart or if one party has filed for legal separation); NEV. REV. STAT. ANN. § 200.373 (Michie 1993) (charging husband with rape only if force or threat was used); N.H. REV. STAT. ANN. §§ 632-A2, 632-A3, & 632-A5 (1992) (charging husband with rape of wife only if wife is mentally incapacitated or under the age of consent); N.M. STAT. ANN. § 30-9-10, 30-9-11 (Michie 1993) (charging husband with rape only if the parties are separated or legal action has been filed for divorce or separation); OHIO REV. CODE ANN. § 2907.02 (Anderson 1993) (charging husband with rape only if force or threat of force is used, unless wife is mentally incapacitated); OKLA. STAT. ANN. tit. 21, § 1111 (West Supp. 1994) (charging husband with rape only if he used force or threat of force); 18 PA. CONS. STAT. ANN. § 3103 (1993) (providing that husband/cohabitant can only be charged with lesser crime of spousal sexual assault); R.I. GEN. LAWS § 11-37-1 (1993) (providing husband cannot be charged with first degree rape unless wife is mentally incapacitated, and is chargeable only with rape in all other circumstances); S.C. CODE ANN. § 16-3-658 (Law. Co-op. 1992) (charging husband with rape only if parties are separated); UTAH CODE ANN. § 76-5-402 (1993) (providing that husband cannot be with rape); WASH. REV. CODE ANN. §§ 9A.44.010, 9A.44.040, 9A.44.050 (West 1993) (limiting rape charges against husbands to first degree and second degree rape only); W. VA. CODE § 61-8B-6 (1993) (charging husband with lesser offense of sexual assault of a spouse).

For a full discussion of marital rape, see DIANA E.H. RUSSELL, RAPE IN MARRIAGE 375-81 app. II (1990).

298. COLO. REV. STAT. ANN. § 18-3-402 (West 1993); GA. CODE ANN. § 13A-6-60 to -61 (1975); IND. CODE ANN. § 35-42-4-1(b) (West 1993); NEB. REV. STAT. § 28-319 (1992); VT. STAT. ANN. tit. 13, § 3252 (1993); *see* Merton v. State, 500 So. 2d 1301 (Ala. Crim. App. 1986).

protection order as narrowly as they do criminal rape.[299]

Twenty-nine states and the District of Columbia have statutes authorizing civil protection orders based on sexual abuse of a child.[300] Courts have also issued civil protection orders based on sexual abuse of the petitioner's child.[301] Defendants have been convicted for sexu-

---

299. HAW. REV. STAT. §§ 707-730 to 707-732 (1992) (charging husbands with first through third degree rape only, not fourth or fifth degree rape); IOWA CODE ANN. § 709.2-.4 (West 1993) (charging only husband with first or second degree rape; both husbands and cohabitants can be charged with third degree sexual abuse of a mate, which carries a lesser penalty, unless wife is mentally incapacitated); KAN. CRIM. CODE ANN. §§ 21-3501, 21-3502 (Vernon 1993) (charging husband with rape); MONT. CODE ANN. §§ 45-5-502, 45-5-503 (1993) (providing that husbands/cohabitants can be charged with rape and sexual assault); N.C. GEN. STAT. § 14-27.8 (1993) (providing that husband can be charged with rape regardless of whether the parties are separated); VA. CODE ANN. § 18.2-61 (Michie 1993) (providing that husband who rapes wife can be charged with marital sexual assault where there is physical injury if wife reports assault within 10 days); WYO. STAT. §§ 6-4-302 to -307 (1993) (providing that husband can be charged with first or second degree rape but not with third or fourth degree rape).

300. ALASKA STAT. § 25.35 (1993); ARIZ. REV. STAT. ANN. § 13-3602 (Supp. 1994); ARK. CODE ANN. § 91-15-206 (1993); CAL. FAM. CODE § 55 (West 1993); CONN. GEN. STAT. ANN. § 46b-15 (West 1993); DEL. CODE ANN. tit. 10, § 945 (1993); D.C. CODE ANN. § 16-1004 (1993); FLA. STAT. ANN. § 741.30 (West 1993); IDAHO CODE § 39-6303 (1993); 750 ILCS 60/102, 60/201 (1993); KAN. CIV. PROC. CODE ANN. § 60-3107 (Vernon 1993); LA. REV. STAT. ANN. 46:2132 (West 1992); ME. REV. STAT. ANN. tit. 19, § 766 (West 1992); MASS. GEN. L. ANN. ch. 209A, §§ 1, 3 (1992); MINN. STAT. ANN. § 518B.01 (West 1992); MISS. CODE ANN. §§ 93-21-3, 93-21-15 (1993); MO. REV. STAT. §§ 455.010, 455.020 (Vernon 1993); NEV. REV. STAT. ANN. § 33-018 (Michie 1993); N.M. STAT. ANN. § 40-13-2 (Michie 1993); OHIO REV. CODE ANN. § 3113.31 (Anderson 1992); OKLA. STAT. ANN. tit. 22, § 60.1 (West Supp. 1994); 23 PA. CONS. STAT. ANN. § 6102(a) (1993); P.R. LAWS ANN. tit. 8, § 601 (1992); R.I. GEN. LAWS § 15-5-3 (1993); S.C. CODE ANN. § 20-4-40 (Law. Co-op. 1992); UTAH CODE ANN. §§ 30-6-1, 30-6-2 (1993); VT. STAT. ANN. tit. 15, § 1104 (1993); WASH. REV. CODE ANN. §§ 26.50.010, 26.050.030 (1993); W. VA. CODE § 48-2A-2 (1993); WIS. STAT. ANN. § 813-12 (West 1993); WYO. STAT. §§ 35-21-102, 35-21-103 (1993).

301. E.g., Campbell v. Campbell, 584 So. 2d 125, 126 (Fla. 1991) (issuing a protection order where father committed sexual battery on his three year old daughter); Wright v. Wright, 583 N.E.2d 97 (Ill. App. Ct. 1991) (issuing mother a civil protection order against her husband and his son, both of whom were sexually abusing her daughters); Keneker v. Keneker, 579 So. 2d 1083, 1084 (La. Ct. App. 1991) (granting non-custodial mother a temporary protection order on behalf of her minor child based on custodial father's alleged inappropriate sexual behavior toward the child); Cooke v. Naylor, 573 A.2d 376, 377 (Me. 1990) (holding court properly issued civil protection order on behalf of minor child based on alleged sexual abuse); Lucke v. Lucke, 300 N.W.2d 231, 232 (N.D. 1980) (affirming issuance of civil protection order against father who attempted an incestuous relationship with his 18 year old daughter); Rosenberg v. Rosenberg, 504 A.2d 350, 351 (Pa. Super. Ct. 1986) (granting protection order where respondent sexually abused his 10 year old daughter); see also Tung v. Oshima, 1993 Minn. App. LEXIS 691 (Minn. Ct. App. June 29, 1993) (reversing denial of a protection order predicated on alleged sexual abuse upon finding an abuse of discretion in accepting respondent's explanation of why he was bathing with his seven year-old and four year-old).

al assault of their wives.[302] Clearly, courts may issue civil protection orders based on marital rape and sexual assault in those jurisdictions where the state may criminally prosecute a defendant on that basis.

Marital rape is an integral part of marital violence.[303] Numerous studies confirm that between 33% and 46% of battered women are raped and/or sexually assaulted by their abusive partners.[304] Between 50% and 85% of women who have experienced rape in an intimate relationship such as marriage indicate that they have been sexually assaulted at least 20 times by their partners.[305] Research indicates the most violent assaults often include sexual as well as physical attacks, and that battered women who are sexually assaulted by their partners typically experience more severe non-sexual attacks than

---

302. State v. Schackart, 737 P.2d 398 (Ariz. Ct. App. 1987) (upholding conviction where defendant ordered estranged wife to remove her clothes and sexually assaulted her); People v. Thompson, 206 Cal. Rptr. 516 (Ct. App. 1984) (affirming defendant's conviction for spousal rape where wife reported at least two incidents); State v. Ulen, 623 A.2d 70 (Conn. App. Ct. 1993) (upholding conviction for sexual assault where evidence showed defendant violated a protection order, forced wife to engage in sex at gunpoint, and inserted barrel of gun into her vagina); State v. Wendling, No. 12015, 1990 WL 197957 (Ohio Ct. App. Dec. 6, 1990) (affirming decision holding respondent in contempt of civil protection order based on marital rape); Commonwealth v. Shoemaker, 518 A.2d 591 (Pa. Super. Ct. 1986) (convicting husband who came to wife's residence while they were separated, threatened her with a knife, and forced her to have oral sex and vaginal intercourse).

303. *See* WOMEN'S ACTION COALITION, WAC STATS: THE FACTS ABOUT WOMEN 49, 55 (1993) [hereinafter WAC STATS].

304. BROWNE, *supra* note 171, at 2-5; RUSSELL, *supra* note 297; Irene H. Frieze & Angela Browne, *Violence in Marriage*, *in* FAMILY VIOLENCE: CRIME AND JUSTICE, A REVIEW OF RESEARCH 163 (Lloyd Ohlin & Michael Tonry eds., 1989). Research by the State of Kentucky found 79% of domestic violence victims had experienced forced sexual relations with a spouse and 21% with a live-in partner. The majority of victims were assaulted more than once and many indicated several different types of sexual abuse: 75% forced vaginal intercourse, 57% forced sex after being beaten, 36% forced oral-genital sex, 30% forced anal intercourse, 16% forced sex with an object, and 8% forced sex in the presence of others. FREDERICK J. COWAN, ATTORNEY GENERAL, ADULT ABUSE, NEGLECT AND EXPLOITATION: A MEDICAL PROTOCOL FOR HEALTH CARE PROVIDERS AND COMMUNITY SERVICE AGENCIES 129 (1991). Almost 80% of battered women are forced to have sex with their abuser after the battered women has said "no." Lenore E. Walker, Eliminating Sexism to End Battering Relationships, Paper Presented at the American Psychological Association (1984). Fifty-nine percent of battered women reported being repeatedly sexually abused, and an additional 13.9% reported being raped by their batterer at least once. Campbell, *supra* note 119, at 36.

305. DAVID FINKELHOR & KERSTI YLLO, LICENSE TO RAPE: SEXUAL ABUSE OF WIVES 23 (1985) (finding that 10% of women report at least one sexual assault in response to force or threat by a husband or partner and that 50 to 87% of women who experienced rape in an intimate relationship were sexually assaulted at least 20 times). Approximately 14% of wives are sexually assaulted in some manner by their husbands. OFFICE OF THE ATTORNEY GENERAL, SEXUAL ASSAULT/ABUSE: A HOSPITAL/COMMUNITY PROTOCOL FOR FORENSIC AND MEDICAL EXAMINATION 3 (1991); Frieze & Browne, *supra* note 304, at 188.

other abused women.[306] Approximately 75% of battered women who killed or tried to kill their abusers had been raped by them.[307] Clearly, both state legislatures and a growing number of courts recognize that sexual assault can often be an integral part of the cycle of violence in an abusive relationship, and protection against continued sexual assaults must be available.

3. Interference with Personal Liberty

A batterer may resort to tactics which, although not necessarily violent in and of themselves, seek to control and frighten an abuse victim. Such conduct often serves to restrict or interfere with the victim's activities and freedom. Consequently, eight states and Puerto Rico provide by statute that civil protection orders will issue based on interference with the petitioner's personal liberty.[308] Case law delineates the variety of acts which might constitute interference with personal liberty forming the basis for issuance of a civil protection order. These have included: concealing children and parental kidnapping,[309] locking the petitioner out of the marital home and threatening to physically remove her,[310] physically restraining petitioner from leaving her home or calling the police,[311] and grabbing the steering wheel of petitioner's car while she is driving, pulling the car out of gear, and attempting to pull the car to the side of the road.[312] An Illinois court criminally convicted a man for unlawful restraint of his wife, based on a violation of an existing order of protection.[313]

---

306. LEE H. BOWKER, BEATING WIFE BEATING 52-54, 56-59 (1983).

307. Campbell, *supra* note 119; *see also* EWING, *supra* note 180, at 9.

308. CONN. GEN. STAT. ANN. § 46b-15 (West 1993); DEL. CODE ANN. tit. 10, § 945 (1993); GA. CODE ANN. § 19-13-1 (1993); 725 ILCS 5/112A-3 (1993); NEV. REV. STAT. ANN. § 33.018 (Michie 1993); N.H. REV. STAT. ANN. § 173-B:1(1992); P.R. LAWS ANN. tit. 8, § 601 (1990); VT. STAT. ANN. tit. 15, § 1104 (1992); WYO. STAT. § 35-21-102 (1993).

309. Sanders v. Shepard, 541 N.E.2d 1150 (Ill. App. Ct. 1989) (enforcing a civil protection order issued based on concealment of child and parental kidnapping).

310. Wagner v. Wagner, 15 Pa. D. & C.3d 148, 151-52 (C.P. 1980) (issuing civil protection order where respondent locked the petitioner out of the marital home and threatened to physically remove her from the home).

311. *In re* Marriage of Blitstein, 569 N.E.2d 1357, 1358-59 (Ill. App. Ct. 1991) (affirming protection order issued where respondent physically restrained petitioner from calling the police or leaving her home).

312. Ickes v. Ickes, 3 Pa. D. & C.4th 166 (C.P. 1989) (issuing protection order where respondent grabbed steering wheel of petitioner's car three times while she was driving, tried to pull the car out of gear, and tried to pull the car to the side of the road).

313. People v. Williams, 582 N.E.2d 1158, 1160 (Ill. App. Ct. 1991) (upholding conviction for unlawful restraint where respondent grabbed petitioner from behind and refused to let her go).

Indeed, many states' statutes will specifically issue protection orders based on false imprisonment.[314] The courts and legislatures need to continue to identify and broaden the range of behavior which restrict a petitioner's movement and activities that may serve as grounds for issuance of a civil protection order.[315]

4. Threats

Protection orders may also issue on the basis of threats of violence or acts which place the petitioner in fear of imminent bodily harm. Threats are acts of domestic violence because they seek to intimidate and control the petitioner. Social science research reveals that threats and harassment, left unchecked, frequently escalate to greater violence.[316] Although the common stereotype of "domestic violence" tends to be that of relatively minor assaults and squabbles, 41% of battered women report being regularly threatened by their abusers,[317] and over one-third of domestic assaults involve severe actions, such as punching, kicking, choking, beating up, and threatening with or using a gun or a knife.[318] Many battered women's lives are threatened.[319] Of all women killed by their abusers, 41% to 50% previously had been threatened with death and 39% had been threatened or assaulted with a weapon.[320] Threats are often effectively

---

314. *See, e.g.*, DEL. CODE ANN. tit. 10, § 947 (Supp. 1993); ME. REV. STAT. ANN. tit. 19, § 766 (West Supp. 1992); MD. CODE ANN., FAM. LAW § 4-505 (Supp. 1993); MINN. STAT. ANN. § 518B:01 (West Supp. 1993); MO. REV. STAT. § 455.050 (Vernon Supp. 1993); NEV. REV. STAT. ANN. § 33-020 (Michie Supp. 1993); N.H. REV. STAT. ANN. § 173-B:4 (Supp. 1992); N.J. STAT. ANN. § 2C:25-19 (West 1992); 23 PA. CONS. STAT. ANN. § 6108 (1991); WASH. REV. CODE ANN. § 10.99.040 (1993); W. VA. CODE § 48-2A-5 (Supp. 1993).

315. Examples of other tactics batterers use to restrict a domestic violence victim's movement and/or ability to flee a violent relationship that could serve as a basis for issuance of a civil protection order under this theory might include threats to turn the domestic violence victim in for deportation if she flees or threats that if she leaves, she will never see her children again.

316. GILLESPIE, *supra* note 124, at 129.

317. Diane R. Follingstad et al., *The Role of Emotional Abuse in Physically Abusive Relationships*, 5 J. FAM. VIOLENCE 107, 113 (1990).

318. Angela Browne, Testimony before the U.S. Senate Committee on the Judiciary (Dec. 1990).

319. EDWARD W. GONDOLF & ELLEN R. FISHER, BATTERED WOMEN AS SURVIVORS 6 (1988) (finding 70% of battered women have their lives threatened); ILLINOIS COALITION AGAINST DOMESTIC VIOLENCE, WOMAN ABUSE: FREQUENT AND SEVERE 1991 (50% of battered women have their lives threatened).

320. Sometimes, these threats lead the battered woman to retaliate when she believes her death is imminent. *See* P.D. Chimobos, *quoted in* Leslie Henderson, *Till Death Do Us Part: Abuse by Husband Drove Woman to Murder*, KNOXVILLE J. Feb. 28, 1984, at p. A1; *see also* EWING, *supra* note 180.

used by batterers to secure the return of battered women to abusive homes.[321]

Consequently, nearly all states, the District of Columbia, and Puerto Rico issue civil protection orders based on threats of physical abuse.[322] Courts specifically recognize a wide range of behaviors which constitute threats. A threat to kill the petitioner is the most common threat for which a court will issue a civil protection order.[323] In *Pendleton v. Minichino*,[324] a Connecticut court found present and immediate danger sufficient to issue a civil protection order based on the respondent's prior history of depression and his recent remark to petitioner that "[t]his time I'm not going alone. You

---

321. Joel Dvoskin, *Legal Alternatives for Battered Women Who Kill Their Abusers*, 6 BULLETIN OF THE AAPL 335, 350 (1978).

322. ALA. CODE § 30-5-7 (1989); ALASKA STAT. § 25-35.010 (1991); ARIZ. REV. STAT. ANN. § 13-3601 (Supp. 1993); CAL. FAM. CODE § 5650 (West 1993); COLO. REV. STAT. ANN. § 14-4-102 (West Supp. 1993); CONN. GEN. STAT. ANN. § 46b-15 (West Supp. 1993); DEL. CODE ANN. tit. 10, § 947 (Supp. 1993); D.C. CODE ANN. § 16-1005 (1989); FLA. STAT. ANN. § 741.30 (West Supp. 1993); HAW. REV. STAT. § 586-5.5 (Supp. 1992); IDAHO CODE § 39-6306 (1993); 750 ILCS 5/112A-14 (1993); IND. CODE ANN. § 34-4-5.1-5 (West Supp. 1992); IOWA CODE ANN. § 236.5 (West Supp. 1993); KAN. CIV. PROC. CODE § 60-3107 (Vernon Supp. 1993); KY. REV. STAT. ANN. § 403.750 (Michie/Bobbs-Merill Supp. 1992); LA. REV. STAT. ANN. § 46:2136 (West 1982); ME. REV. STAT. ANN. tit. 19, § 766 (West Supp. 1992); MD. CODE ANN., FAM. LAW § 4-505 (Supp. 1993); MASS. GEN. L. ANN. ch. 209A, § 3 (West Supp. 1992); MICH. COMP. LAWS ANN. § 93-21 (West 1992); MINN. STAT. ANN. § 518B.01 (West Supp. 1993); MISS. CODE ANN. § 93-21-15 (Supp. 1993); MO. REV. STAT. § 455-050 (Vernon Supp. 1993); NEB. REV. STAT. § 42-924 (Supp. 1993); NEV. REV. STAT. ANN. § 33.020 (1993); N.H. REV. STAT. ANN. § 173-B:4 (Supp. 1992); N.J. STAT. ANN. § 2C:25-19 (West 1992); N.M. STAT. ANN. § 40-13-5 (Michie Supp. 1993); N.Y. FAM. CT. ACT § 841 (McKinney Supp. 1994); N.C. GEN. STAT. § 50B-3 (1989); N.D. CENT. CODE § 14-07.1-01 (Supp. 1993); OHIO REV. CODE ANN. § 3113.31 (Anderson Supp. 1992); OKLA. STAT. ANN. tit. 22, § 60.4 (West 1992); OR. REV. STAT. § 107.718 (1991); 23 PA. CONS. STAT. ANN. § 6108 (1991); P.R. LAWS ANN. tit. 8, § 621 (Supp. 1990); R.I. GEN. LAWS § 15-15-3 (Supp. 1993); S.C. CODE ANN. § 20-4-60 (Law. Co-op. 1985); S.D. CODIFIED LAWS ANN. § 25-10-5 (1984); TEX. FAM. CODE § 71.11 (West Supp. 1993); UTAH CODE ANN. § 30-6-2 (Supp. 1993); VT. STAT. ANN. tit. 15, § 1104 (1989); VA. CODE ANN. § 16.1-253.1 (Michie Supp. 1993); WASH. REV. CODE ANN. § 26.50.030 (West Supp. 1993); W. VA. CODE § 48-2A-5 (Supp. 1993); WIS. STAT. ANN. § 813.12 (West 1993); WYO. STAT. § 35-21-103 (1988).

323. *See, e.g.*, Glater v. Fabianich, 625 N.E.2d 96 (Ill. Ct. App. 1993) (finding threat where respondent said he "wanted [petitioner] erased"); Roe v. Roe, 601 A.2d 1201 (N.J. Super. Ct. App. Div. 1992) (upholding order of protection based upon husband's threats to kill his wife); Eichenberger v. Eichenberger, 1993 Ohio App. LEXIS 5282 (1993); Strollo v. Strollo, 828 P.2d 532, 534-35 (Utah Ct. App. 1992) (reversing dismissal of application for protection order based on respondent's threat to kill the petitioner if she served him with divorce papers); People v. Salvato, 285 Cal. Rptr. 837 (Ct. App. 1991); Hall v. Hall, 408 N.W.2d 626 (Minn. Ct. App. 1987) (upholding issuance of order where husband made threats to kill wife during custody proceedings).

324. 1992 Conn. Super. LEXIS 915 (Super. Ct. 1992).

better watch your back."[325] While other evidence of abuse existed, including physical assault and property damage, the court concluded that the threat alone could constitute family violence sufficient to issue a protection order.[326] Other conduct which courts have held constitutes a threat sufficient to support a civil protection order includes threats of violence,[327] threatening and following the petitioner,[328] leaving a threatening note,[329] threatening to physically remove petitioner from the home if she did not voluntarily leave,[330] threatening to burn down petitioner's home with her in it,[331] threatening to get the petitioner fired from her job,[332] and verbally and physically abusing the petitioner in front of their child.[333] Courts have also perceived intimidating threats in acts such as leaving a shredded marriage certificate[334] or, in the criminal context, tomato juice covered clothes, on the victim's doorstep.[335]

Several cases recognize a threat sufficient to issue or extend a protection order where the defendant will be or has been recently released from jail. In *Campbell v. Campbell*,[336] the Florida District Court of Appeals upheld the trial court's determination that the respondent's release from jail, in the context of past violence, sexual battery of his child, and expressed resentment against his wife, posed a threat sufficient to support the issuance of a civil protection order.[337] In *Cruz-Foster v. Foster*,[338] the District of Columbia Court

---

325. *Id.* at *4-*5.

326. *Id.* at *24-*25.

327. Glater v. Fabianich, 625 N.E.2d 96 (Ill. Ct. App. 1993) (affirming a finding of danger where respondent told petitioner "[w]e're going to have a chat and it won't be pretty"); Harper v. Harper, 537 So. 2d 282 (La. Ct. App. 1988) (upholding a protection order based on husband's constant threats); Parkhurst v. Parkhurst, 793 S.W.2d 634 (Mo. Ct. App. 1990) (finding verbal threats of violence sufficient); Synder v. Synder, 629 A.2d 977 (Pa. 1993) (finding a threat where respondent threatened to have sex with petitioner).

328. Banks v. Pelot, 460 N.W.2d 446 (Wis. Ct. App. 1990) (upholding issuance of civil protection order based on respondent following and threatening the petitioner) (unpublished decision; full text at 1990 WL 130858).

329. Boniek v. Boniek, 443 N.W.2d 196 (Minn. Ct. App. 1989) (upholding issuance of a civil protection order based on respondent leaving parties' marriage certificate cut up into little pieces with a threatening note on petitioner's doorstep, his driving around the petitioner's home, and his becoming physically aggressive toward an insurance salesman he found in the petitioner's home).

330. Wagner v. Wagner, 15 Pa. D. & C.3d 148 (C.P. 1980).

331. Ickes v. Ickes, 3 Pa. D. & C.4th 166 (C.P. 1989).

332. Delisser v. Hardy, 749 P.2d 1207 (Or. Ct. App. 1988).

333. *In re* Marriage of Ingram, 531 N.E.2d 97 (Ill. App. Ct. 1988).

334. Boniek v. Boniek, 443 N.W.2d 196 (Minn. Ct. App. 1989).

335. People v. Salvato, 285 Cal. Rptr. 837 (Ct. App. 1991).

336. 584 So. 2d 125 (Fla. Dist. Ct. App. 1991).

337. *Id.* at 126.

of Appeals vacated the trial court's decision not to extend a protection order to the petitioner where the respondent had been recently released from jail after serving a sentence for contempt of a prior civil protection order, and where the respondent came to and telephoned the petitioner's work place.[339] The appellate court held that the "entire mosaic" of past abuse is critical to a trial court's determination whether to extend a protection order.[340] The Court of Appeals vacated and remanded the trial court's decision because the judge did not consider the entire history of past events, including severe and frequent abuse, threats to kill, false imprisonment, and chronic violations of an existing protection order, which might have suggested the truly threatening nature of the defendant's behavior in lurking about the petitioner's work place and calling her.[341]

In *Maldonado v. Maldonado*,[342] the District of Columbia Court of Appeals recognized the seriousness of threats made by an incarcerated defendant.[343] The appellate court reversed the trial court's denial of an extension of a protection order where the trial court's sole basis for denying the extension was the fact that defendant was incarcerated during the duration of the civil protection order.[344] The court of appeals specifically noted that:

> with respect to the portion of the original order barring threats directed at the wife and children and the telephoning of the wife, the wife would be left open to harassment or threatening communications from the husband should he gain access to a telephone. In addition, threats can be communicated by mail or through third parties. Although threats to commit physical harm by one incarcerated may, in some instances, not rise to the level of seriousness that physical abuse does, such conduct nonetheless can have significant adverse effects upon the victim . . . . At a minimum, the wife is entitled to be free of abuse or threats by the husband whether committed by telephone or the mail.[345]

A California court has also criminally convicted a defendant for

---

338. 597 A.2d 927 (D.C. Ct. App. 1991).
339. *Id.*
340. *Id.* at 931.
341. *Id.* at 932.
342. 631 A.2d 40 (D.C. Ct. App. 1993).
343. *Id.*
344. *Id.* at 44.
345. *Id. But see* Trowell v. Meads, 618 So. 2d 351 (Fla. 1988) (refusing to issue permanent protection order where defendant threatened petitioner by telephone from prison).

acts which included making threats over the telephone to his wife.[346] Having provided the basis for a criminal prosecution, this behavior should also be sufficient to issue a civil protection order.

Batterers often make threats of suicide as a method of exerting control over their battered intimate partner. These threats are often made in an effort to convince her that she should dismiss a civil protection order petition or recant previously given testimony.[347] Unfortunately, recent threats of suicide by the respondent may not be sufficient to issue a civil protection order where there have been no concurrent acts of violence. In *Bjergum v. Bjergum*,[348] the court reversed the entry of a full civil protection order, despite the petitioner's allegations that the respondent had threatened to commit suicide as recently as a week prior to the hearing.[349]

In *Hayes v. Hayes*,[350] the court dismissed a former wife's petition for a civil protection order which had been based on her former husband's threat to shoot her and her boyfriend and burn down her house, since the statement was made to her daughter and the respondent did not authorize or understand that the daughter would relay the threat to the petitioner.[351] However, the analysis used in *Hayes* is inconsistent with other case law which holds a person criminally liable for threats to another person even where the threat is communicated only to a third party. The District of Columbia Court of Appeals, in *United States v. Baish*,[352] held that a person threatens another when he utters words which are intended to convey a desire to inflict physical injury and these words are communicated or conveyed to someone—either the object of the threat or to a third party.[353] Therefore, in the *Hayes* case, the defendant committed a criminal threat when he conveyed to his daughter as a third party his intent to physically injure his former wife. The threat is just as dangerous whether or not the third party relays the threat directly to the person threatened.

---

346. People v. Salvato, 285 Cal. Rptr. 837 (Ct. App. 1991) (upholding conviction where respondent left threatening messages on victim's telephone machine. Respondent's message stated that there would be "bad trouble" if the petitioner did not agree to his property settlement terms).

347. Ganley, *supra* note 21, at 19, 23.

348. 392 N.W.2d 604 (Minn. Ct. App. 1986).

349. *Id.* at 606.

350. 500 N.Y.S.2d 475 (Fam. Ct. 1986).

351. *Id.* at 478.

352. 460 A.2d 38 (D.C. Ct. App. 1983).

353. *Id.* at 42.

5. Attempts To Harm

Protection orders should issue based on an attempt to harm the petitioner. This is a particularly important ground for issuance of a civil protection order because of the role attempts play in controlling a victim of abuse. A court's refusal to issue a civil protection order based on an attempt to injure the petitioner may reinforce, in both parties' minds, the legitimacy of the batterer's behavior. Law enforcement officials and the courts should act against attempts to harm, as they are clear precursors to further violence, serious injury, or death.[354]

An attempt to harm a family member demonstrates that the respondent is disposed to violence not only on that occasion but on others as well.[355] Attempts are punished as crimes under criminal codes because a defendant who attempts to commit a crime "has sufficiently manifested [his] dangerousness."[356] Consequently, the legislatures of thirty-nine states, the District of Columbia, and Puerto Rico authorize courts to issue civil protection orders based on attempts to harm.[357] Case law illustrates the variety of behavior that

---

354. Domestic violence tends to escalate in both frequency and severity over time. BROWNE, *supra* note 171, at 68; Geraldine Butts Stahly, Victim Rights and Issues: Special Problems of Battered Woman as Victim/Witness in Partner Abuse Cases, Paper Presented at the Western Society of Criminology Conference, Los Vegas, Nevada (Feb. 27, 1978). The pattern of abuse has a distinct and predictable cycle. GILLESPIE, *supra* note 124, at 129. Typically episodes involve a combination of assaultive acts, verbal abuse and threats. Browne, *supra* note 1, at 3186. In a study of abusive men, one third reported that their partners sustained broken bones or other substantial injuries as a result of their violence. *See* James Ptacek, *Why Do Men Batter Their Wives?, in* FEMINIST PERSPECTIVES ON WIFE ABUSE 135 (Kersti Yllo & Michele Bogard eds. 1988).

355. WAYNE R. LaFAVE & AUSTIN W. SCOTT, JR., CRIMINAL LAW 499 (2d ed. 1986).

356. *Id.* at 495.

357. ALA. CODE § 30-5-7 (1989); ALASKA STAT. § 25-35.010 (1991); ARIZ. REV. STAT. ANN. § 13-3601 (Supp. 1993); CAL. FAM. CODE § 5650 (West 1993); CONN. GEN. STAT. ANN. § 46b-15 (West Supp. 1993); DEL. CODE ANN. tit. 10, § 947 (Supp. 1993); D.C. CODE ANN. § 16-1005 (1989); FLA. STAT. ANN. § 741.30 (West Supp. 1993); GA. CODE ANN. § 19-13-4 (Supp. 1993); IDAHO CODE § 39-6306 (1993); 725 ILCS 5/112A-14 (Supp. 1993); IND. CODE ANN. § 34-4-5.1-5 (West Supp. 1992); KAN. CIV. PROC. CODE § 60-3107 (Vernon Supp. 1993); LA. REV. STAT. ANN. § 46:2136 (West 1982); ME. REV. STAT. ANN. tit. 19, § 766 (1992); MD. CODE ANN., FAM. LAW § 4-505 (Supp. 1993); MASS. GEN. L. ANN. ch. 209A, § 3 (West Supp. 1993); MINN. STAT. ANN. § 518B.01 (West Supp. 1993); MISS. CODE ANN. § 93-21-15 (Supp. 1992); MO. REV. STAT. § 455-050 (Vernon Supp. 1993); NEV. REV. STAT. ANN. § 33.020 (Michie Supp. 1993); N.H. REV. STAT. ANN. § 173-B:4 (Supp. 1993); N.J. STAT. ANN. § 2C:25-3 (West 1992); N.M. STAT. ANN. § 40-13-5 (1989); N.Y. FAM. CT. ACT § 841 (McKinney Supp. 1994); N.C. GEN. STAT. § 50B-3 (1989); N.D. CENT. CODE § 14-07.1-02 (Supp. 1993); OHIO REV. CODE ANN. § 3113.31 (Anderson Supp. 1992); OKLA. STAT. ANN. tit. 22, § 60.4 (West 1992); OR. REV. STAT. § 107.718 (1991); 23 PA. CONS. STAT. ANN. § 6108 (1991); P.R. LAWS ANN. tit. 8, § 621

constitutes attempts to harm sufficient for issuance of a civil protection order. This behavior includes: the respondent repeatedly grabbing the steering wheel of the petitioner's car while petitioner was driving, and pulling the car out of gear and attempting force the car to the side of the road;[358] the respondent attempting to have an incestuous relationship with his eighteen-year-old daughter;[359] and the respondent attempting to assault the petitioner.[360] Courts have identified why attempts to harm are sufficient to find domestic violence. In *Ickes*,[361] the court found domestic abuse sufficient to issue a civil protection order where the respondent attempted to force the plaintiff's car off the road "[b]ecause the inquiry focuses on the fear generated in plaintiff and not on any actual injury inflicted."[362] Most courts will issue protection orders based on attempts. Those few cases in which the court failed to issue a civil protection order despite substantial evidence of an attempt to harm the petitioner have occurred in a minority of jurisdictions, where the statute authorizing civil protection orders at the time the cases were decided incorporated a higher criminal standard of proof for attempt.[363] Criminal attempt requires, 1) the intent to do an act or bring about certain circumstances proscribed by law, and 2) an act beyond mere preparation in further-

---

(Supp. 1990); R.I. GEN. LAWS § 15-15-3 (Supp. 1992); S.D. CODIFIED LAWS ANN. § 25-10-5 (1984); TENN. CODE ANN. § 36-3-605 (1991); TEX. FAM. CODE Ann. § 71.11 (West Supp. 1993); UTAH CODE ANN. § 30-6-2 (Supp. 1993); VT. STAT. ANN. tit. 15, § 1103 (1989); VA. CODE ANN. § 16.1-253.1 (Michie Supp. 1993); W. VA. CODE § 48-2A-5 (Supp. 1993); WIS. STAT. ANN. § 813.12 (West 1993); WYO. STAT. § 35-21-103 (1988).

358. Ickes v. Ickes, 3 Pa. D. & C.4th 166 (C.P. 1989); *see also* Gilbert v. Georgia, 433 S.E.2d 664 (Ga. 1993) (convicting defendant where evidence sufficient to support of finding of reasonable apprehension of fear without harm. Defendant drove wife to dirt road, pulled knife on her and forced her to strip).

359. Lucke v. Lucke, 300 N.W.2d 231 (N.D. 1980).

360. Yankoskie v. Lenker, 526 A.2d 429 (Pa. Super. Ct. 1987).

361. 3 Pa. D. & C.4th 166.

362. *Id.*

363. The court in Popeski v. Popeski, 3 Pa. D. & C.4th 200 (C.P. 1989), denied a petition for a civil protection order where respondent threw a set of keys which struck her son and threw a butcher knife across the room, because the court found insufficient evidence of intent to harm. The court in Seymour v. Seymour, 289 N.Y.S.2d 515 (Fam. Ct. 1968), dismissed a petition for a civil protection order assuming that respondent had attempted to force petitioner's car off the road, because the statute at that time required a finding that respondent's actions had resulted in physical pain or injury. In *Stanzak v. Stanzak*, the Ohio Court of Appeals reversed the grant of a civil protection order issued following an incident where the respondent backed up a car near the petitioner. 1990 Ohio App. LEXIS 3958 (Ct. App., Sept. 10, 1990). The court found insufficient evidence to support a finding that the respondent attempted or threatened to injure the petitioner.

ance of the intent.[364]

In family violence cases, state legislatures, courts, and law enforcement officials need to address attempts to harm as strong indicators of a person's propensity for more serious and deadly violence in the future. Courts should issue civil protection orders based on attempts, whether such attempts are intentional or undertaken with reckless disregard for an intimate's safety. This approach is grounded in research documenting the escalating nature of domestic violence.[365] It is also supported by legal scholars who urge that, in criminal cases, recklessness should constitute sufficient mens rea for a conviction for an attempt to commit a crime.[366]

6. Harassing Behaviors

Harassment is another powerful ground for issuing a protection order. A swift and determined official response to harassment will often stave off later, more violent behavior. Batterers use a broad variety of harassing tactics to exert continued control over their intimate partners, including emotional abuse.[367] Some women have been followed and harassed for months, even years, after leaving an abusive partner.[368] The longer that violence continues in a relationship the more serious and dangerous it becomes.[369] Moreover, batterers feel less remorseful and more justified in their violence as the abuse continues.[370] If the police and courts respond swiftly, seriously punishing harassing behavior, they may often impede the cycle of violence from continuing further by undermining the batterer's growing sense of legitimacy in his violence.

Twelve state statutes issue protection orders based on harassment of the petitioner,[371] and courts in many states have interpreted a

---

364. LaFave & Scott, *supra* note 355, at 495.

365. *See supra* note 354.

366. LaFave & Scott, *supra* note 355, at 502.

367. Follingstad et al., *supra* note 317, at 113 (discussing six different types of emotional abuse and the resulting impact on the victims).

368. Browne, *supra* note 171, at 114. Women who fled their batterers have been forced back at gunpoint, forced to return when the batterer held a gun to their child's head, and tracked across state lines to get them to return and tracked down after many years. Ewing, *supra* note 180, at 28.

369. Gillespie, *supra* note 124, at 129.

370. Angela Browne, Assault and Homicide at Home: When Battered Women Kill, Paper Presented at the National Family Violence Research Conference (Aug. 1984), *reprinted in* 3 Advances in Applied Psychology 68.

371. Del. Code Ann. tit. 10, § 945 (Supp. 1993) ("engaging in a course of alarming or distressing conduct in a manner which is likely to provoke a violent or disorderly response

wide range of behavior to constitute harassment sufficient to issue a civil protection order. Harassing behavior includes following the petitioner,[372] threatening the petitioner,[373] calling the petitioner a "bitch,"[374] preventing the petitioner from leaving a room,[375] pulling telephone cords out of the wall to prevent the petitioner from calling the police,[376] driving around the petitioner's home,[377] cutting up the parties' marriage certificate and leaving it with a threatening note on petitioner's doorstep,[378] initiating a high speed car chase,[379] interfering with petitioner's living,[380] calling the petitioner at work seventy-five times within a period of a month,[381] filing frivolous legal actions against the petitioner,[382] moving within two blocks of the petitioner's house,[383] loitering in front of the battered women's shelter where the petitioner stayed,[384] pounding nails into the petitioner's

---

or which is likely to cause humiliation, degradation, or fear in another person"); IDAHO CODE § 39-6303 (1993); 725 ILCS 5/112A-3 (Supp. 1993); MINN. STAT. ANN. § 518B.01 (West Supp. 1993); MO. REV. STAT. § 455.010 (Vernon 1993); NEV. REV. STAT. ANN. § 33.018 (Michie 1986); N.J. STAT. ANN.   § 2C:25-19 (West 1993); N.M. STAT. ANN. § 40-13-2 (Michie Supp. 1993) (including telephone contact and repeatedly driving by residence or workplace); N.Y. FAM. CT. ACT Law § 812(1) (McKinney Supp. 1994); R.I. GEN. LAWS § 15-15-1 (1988) (criminal statute); W. VA. CODE § 48-2A-2 (Supp. 1993); WIS. STAT. ANN. § 813.122 (West Supp. 1993).

372. In re The Marriage of McCoy, 1993 WL 512877 (Ill. App. Ct. Dec. 9, 1993) (issuing protection order where husband followed and approached children in violation of a protection order); Banks v. Pelot, 460 N.W.2d 446 (Wis. Ct. App. 1990) (affirming issuance of issued protection order where respondent followed and threatened the petitioner); State v. Sarlund, 407 N.W.2d 544 (Wis. 1987) (affirming that defendant's acts, in constantly writing petitioner letters, confronting her friends and dates, contacting her parents and employers, and following her to and from school, constituted harassment sufficient to support a protection order).

373. In re Marriage of Hagaman, 462 N.E.2d 1276, 1278-79 (Ill. App. Ct. 1984); Roe v. Roe, 601 A.2d 1201, 1206-07 (N.J. Super. Ct. App. Div. 1992); Kilmer v. Kilmer, 486 N.Y.S.2d 483 (N.Y. App. Div. 1985); People v. Derisi, 442 N.Y.S.2d 908 (Sup. Ct. 1981); Banks, 460 N.W.2d at 446 (Wis. Ct. App. 1990).

374. Capps v. Capps, 715 S.W.2d 547, 549 (Mo. Ct. App. 1986).

375. In re Marriage of Blitstein, 569 N.E.2d 1357 (Ill. App. Ct. 1991).

376. Id.

377. Boniek v. Boniek, 443 N.W.2d 196, 198 (Minn. Ct. App. 1989).

378. Id.

379. Christenson v. Christenson, 472 N.W.2d 279, 280 (Iowa 1991).

380. In re Marriage of Hagaman, 462 N.E.2d 1276 (Ill. App. Ct. 1984); see also Rogers v. Rogers, 556 N.Y.S.2d 114 (App. Div. 1990).

381. Johnson v. Cegielski, 393 N.W.2d 547 (Wis. Ct. App. 1986).

382. Id.

383. Knuth v. Knuth, 1992 Minn. App. LEXIS 696 (Ct. App. June 19, 1992).

384. Id.

car tires,[385] opening the petitioner's mail,[386] making unwanted telephone calls to the petitioner,[387] constantly writing the petitioner letters,[388] meeting with the petitioner's friends and dates,[389] contacting the petitioner's parents and employers,[390] repeated calls and letters implying that force would be used in an effort to visit with the parties' child,[391] entering the petitioner's car,[392] entering the petitioner's home,[393] standing outside the petitioner's apartment three or four times a day screaming curses at her,[394] sending the petitioner unwanted pizza and service calls,[395] throwing things at the petitioner,[396] and pushing the petitioner down stairs and out the door.[397]

　　　The court's decision in *Traiforos v. Mahoney*[398] illustrates the importance of issuing protection orders based on harassing behavior. In *Traiforos*, the petitioner filed for a protection order under the domestic violence statute based on harassment.[399] The trial court, applying its broad discretionary powers, converted an action for domes-

---

385. *Id.*

386. *Id.*

387. Thomas v. Maryland, 1993 Md. LEXIS 172 (Dec. 6, 1993) (holding 30 unsolicited phone calls in one month constituted harassment, despite petitioner's acceptance of collect calls); Cote v. Cote, 599 A.2d 869, 871 (Md. Ct. Spec. App. 1992); Anthony T. v. Anthony J., 510 N.Y.S.2d 810, 811 (Fam. Ct. 1986).

388. State v. Sarlund, 407 N.W.2d 544, 546 (Wis. 1987).

389. *Id.*

390. *Id.*; *see also* Delisser v. Hardy, 749 P.2d 1207, 1208 (Or. Ct. App. 1988) (affirming issuance of protection order where defendant forced his way into petitioner's apartment, physically abused her, threatened to get her fired from her job, and called her employer).

391. Tillman v. Snow, 571 N.E.2d 578, 579-580 (Ind. Ct. App. 1991) (affirming issuance of civil protection order against natural father and paternal aunts which prohibited contact with the parties' child where the natural father made repeated attempts to visit child through telephone calls and letters to mother and adoptive father stating that "I want to see my daughter and I will" and stating that the father would come to see the children and would not be stopped. These communications were held to constitute abuse and were sufficient to show mental abuse and harassment disturbing the petitioner's peace in light of the natural father's prior abuse of the mother). However, some courts have ignored real harassment of the petitioner. For example, in Grant v. Wright, 536 A.2d 319 (N.J. Super. Ct. App. Div. 1988), the court found no harassment sufficient to issue a permanent restraining order where there was no actual physical abuse but where respondent removed petitioner's belongings from their mutual residence, placed them in storage while the petitioner was away from the home and left the storage key in petitioner's car.

392. Cote v. Cote, 599 A.2d 869, 871 (Md. 1992).

393. *Id.*

394. Goldring v. Goldring, 424 N.Y.S.2d 270, 273 (App. Div. 1980).

395. Saliterman v. State, 443 N.W. 2d 841, 843 (Minn. Ct. App. 1989).

396. Holcomb v. Holcomb, 574 N.Y.S.2d 115 (App. Div. 1991).

397. *Id.*

398. 1992 Minn. App. LEXIS 633 (Ct. App. July 7, 1992).

399. *Id.*

tic abuse to one for harassment, and issued a no harassment order.[400] The appellate court, finding that the petitioner would have received a functionally similar order had she filed under the correct
statute, upheld the no-harassment order.[401]

Courts have placed some reasonable limits on the issuance of
civil protection orders based on harassment. For example, in *Didonna
v. Didonna*,[402] the court held that the husband's constant and unre-
lenting discussions with his two teenage daughters about the impending break up of his marriage did not constitute harassment for purposes of issuing a civil protection order.[403] The court found these discussions to be the unfortunate, albeit annoying, result of the marriage
break up.[404] In *Rouse v. Rouse*,[405] the Florida District Court held
that a wife's faxed letters to the husband petitioner's business place
politely requesting to schedule visitation with their children did not
constitute harassment or frustrate the petitioner's business.[406]

7. Emotional Abuse

Thirteen innovative state statutes recognize some forms of emotional abuse as bases to issue a protection order.[407] The Immigration

---

400. *Id.* (noting that under the domestic violence statute, a protection order cannot issue
based on harassment, and fashioned a response as appropriate for the situation).

401. *Id.* at *6.

402. 339 N.Y.S.2d 592 (Fam. Ct. 1972).

403. *Id.*; *see also* E.K. v. G.K., 575 A.2d 883 (N.J. Super. Ct. App. Div. 1990) (upholding refusal to issue a restraining order based on harassment when the mother disciplined child
in manner which the father disapproved, even though the child was injured accidently, since
no evidence existed that the mother acted to harass the father); Roofeh v. Roofeh, 525
N.Y.S.2d 765 (Sup. Ct. 1988) (refusing to issue a civil protection order prohibiting the respondent wife from smoking in the presence of her husband and children. However, the court
ordered the wife to limit her smoking to the sitting room not in the presence of the children.).

404. *Didonna*, 339 N.Y.S.2d at 592.

405. 595 So. 2d 1013 (Fla. Dist. Ct. App. 1992).

406. *Id.* at 1014.

407. DEL. CODE ANN. tit. 10, § 945 (Supp. 1992) (insulting, taunting other conduct likely to cause humiliation, degradation or fear); HAW. REV. STAT. § 586-1 (Supp. 1993) (emotional distress); 725 ILCS 5/112-3A(6) (1993) (intimidation, such as creating a disturbance at
petitioner's place of employment; repeatedly telephoning petitioner's place of employment,
home, or residence; repeatedly following petitioner about in a public place; repeatedly keeping
the petitioner under surveillance by remaining present outside of her home, school, place of
employment, vehicle or other place occupied by the petitioner or by peering in the
petitioner's window; repeatedly threatening to improperly remove a child of petitioner from
the jurisdiction, improperly concealing that child from petitioner or making a single such
threat following an attempted or actual improper removal or concealment; threatening physical
force, confinement or restraint on one or more occasions); ME. REV. STAT. ANN. tit. 19,

and Naturalization Act's Battered Spouse Waiver provisions recognize that emotional abuse is a form of spousal abuse.[408] Under this law and the regulations promulgated pursuant thereto, battered spouse waivers are granted upon a showing of extreme cruelty, allowing battered spouses to move from conditional to permanent residency.[409]

Case law supports recognizing both mental and physical abuse. In *Lucke v. Lucke*,[410] the court held that adult abuse was not limited to physical abuse or the threat of imminent physical harm, but also included mental abuse.[411] In *Lucke*, the court issued a civil protection order against a father when he attempted to initiate an incestuous relationship with his eighteen year old daughter.[412] In *Boniek v. Boniek*,[413] the court considered evidence of mental abuse during twenty-five years of marriage to support the issuance of a civil protection order.[414] The defendant left the parties' mutilated marriage certificate on the petitioner's doorstep, drove around her home, and physically assaulted a salesperson in her home.[415] The court concluded that "[v]iewing the evidence in its totality, and in light of [respondent's] history of abusive behavior, sufficient evidence exists

---

§ 26 (West Supp. 1992) (tormenting); MO. REV. STAT. § 455.010 (Vernon Supp. 1993) ("Harassment [is] engag[ing] in purposeful or knowing course of conduct involving more than one incident that alarms or causes distress to another person and serves no legitimate purpose. Conduct must be such as would cause a reasonable person to suffer substantial emotional distress and must actually cause substantial emotional distress to the petitioner."); NEV. REV. STAT. ANN. § 33.018(5) (Michie 1986) (knowing, purposeful or reckless course of conduct to harass); N.H. REV. STAT. ANN. § 173-B:I (1990 & Supp. 1992) (intimidation); N.J. STAT. ANN. . § 2C:25-19 (West Supp. 1993) (intimidation); N.M. STAT. ANN. § 40-13-2(c)(2) (Michie Supp. 1993) (severe emotional distress); N.Y. FAM. CT. ACT § 821-1(a) (McKinney Supp. 1994) (menacing); OHIO REV. CODE ANN. § 3113.31 (Anderson 1992); W. VA. CODE § 48-2A-2 (Michie Supp. 1993) (psychological abuse; intimidation); WIS. STAT. ANN. § 813-122 (West 1993) (intimidation).

    408. *See* Immigration and Nationality Act, 8 U.S.C. § 1186 (Supp. IV 1992).

    409. Immigration and Nationality Act, 8 U.S.C. § 1186(a) (Supp. IV 1992); 8 C.F.R. § 216.5(e)(3)(i) (1993) (defining "'was battered by or was the subject of extreme cruelty' as including, but [] not limited to, being the victim of any act or threatened act of violence, including any forceful detention, which results or threatens to result in physical or mental injury. Psychological or sexual abuse or exploitation, including rape, molestation, incest (if the victim is a minor) or forced prostitution shall be considered acts of violence").

    410. 300 N.W.2d 231 (N.D. 1980).

    411. *Id.* at 234.

    412. *Id.* at 233.

    413. 443 N.W.2d 196 (Minn. Ct. App. 1989).

    414. *Id.* at 198.

    415. *Id.* at 196.

to infer present intent to inflict fear of imminent physical harm."[416] The court further noted that the history of abuse included both physical and mental abuse. In *Melora v. Melora*,[417] the court upheld issuance of a protection order without a finding of physical abuse where a family offense had been committed by the respondent, the petitioner was in fragile health due to a heart condition, and emotional abuse led petitioner to fear the respondent.[418] In *Tillman v. Snow*,[419] the court affirmed the issuance of a civil protection order against a natural father and paternal aunts. The court prohibited contact with the parties' child where the natural father made repeated attempts to visit the child through telephone calls and letters to the mother and adoptive father stating that "I want to see my daughter and I will."[420] The aunts called and stated that the father would come to see the children and would not be stopped.[421] The court held that these communications, in light of the natural father's prior abuse of the mother, constituted mental abuse and formed the basis for a no-contact order.[422] In *Gasaway v. Gasaway*,[423] the court issued a protection order based on harassment and emotional distress where the respondent attempted to improperly remove and conceal the parties' child.[424]

As in the case of civil protection orders based on harassment, the courts do place some limits on issuing civil protection orders based on emotional abuse. In *Didonna v. Didonna*,[425] the court refused to issue a civil protection order based on a husband's constant conversations with his two teenage daughters about the impending break up of his marriage, finding that such discussions did not constitute sufficient emotional distress to issue a civil protection order.[426]

Social science research indicates that battered women often suffer extreme psychological abuse, including forced isolation from

---

416. *Id.* at 198.
417. 536 N.Y.S.2d 842 (App. Div. 1989).
418. *Id.*
419. 571 N.E.2d 578 (Ind. Ct. App. 1991).
420. *Id.* at 580.
421. *Id.*
422. *Id.*
423. 616 N.E.2d 610 (Ill. 1993).
424. *Id.*
425. 339 N.Y.S.2d 592 (Fam. Ct. 1972).
426. *Id.*; *see also* Murray v. Murray, 631 A.2d 984 (N.J. 1993) (reversing issuance of protection order, holding respondent's pre-divorce statements of an absence of sexual attraction insufficient to issue order).

friends[427] and actual confinement in their homes.[428] One survey reports that 72% of battered women indicate that the emotional abuse had a more severe impact on them than the physical abuse.[429] Escalating emotional abuse was an indicator of forthcoming physical abuse for 54% of battered women.[430] Women who suffered severe emotional abuse were more likely to believe that their batterer would carry out his threats or that his behavior or claims were somehow justified.[431] Among women who are physically abused, 98% report incidences of emotional abuse as well.[432] Further, verbal and emotional abuse often escalate into more violent behavior.[433]

Despite this evidence, some courts underestimate the seriousness of emotional abuse. In *Keith v. Keith*,[434] the court denied a protection order against a father who had previously sexually abused his minor daughters, even though his close proximity caused them stress, fear and emotional strain.[435] In dicta, a Connecticut superior court in *Pendleton v. Minichino*[436] concluded that verbal abuse or argument minus any present danger or likelihood of physical violence does not

---

427. Batterers are able to psychologically control their victims using a combination of isolating tactics and disinformation tactics. Victims are isolated from social networks and support systems. Psychological control over the victims can increase to the point where the abuser literally determines reality for his victim. This often prevents discovery of the violence while the allowing the abuser to avoid being held accountable for his behavior. Ganley, *supra* note 21, at 20.

This isolation works very effectively to the batterer's advantage. At least 43% of battered women who had been abused tell no one about the abuse. Where they do seek someone to talk to about the problem of the abuse, they most often turn to a family member (61%) or friend (49%). SCHULMAN, *supra* note 1, at 4; Angela Browne, Assault and Homicide at Home: When Battered Women Kill, Paper Presented at the National Conference for Family Violence Research (August 1984).

428. EWING, *supra* note 180, at 9-10. Nearly 50% of battered women were forbidden by their batterers to have personal friends or to have such friends in the home. Actual physical imprisonment was reported by 30%. These women reported having been locked in closets, locked in or physically confined to their homes, and tied to furniture. *Id.*

429. Follingstad et al., *supra* note 317, at 114.

430. *Id.* at 115.

431. *Id.* at 114-115. Ridicule was rated the "worst" form of emotional abuse by 45% of battered women. Ganley, *supra* note 21, at 22-23 (noting that physical and psychological abuse are closely interwoven by abusers. Their attacks are aimed at the victim's particular sensibilities and vulnerabilities. When victims learn from experience that verbal threats will be backed up with physical assaults, psychological battery becomes a very effective means to control the victim's behavior).

432. Follingstad et al., *supra* note 317, at 113.

433. TERRIFYING LOVE, *supra* note 4, at 44.

434. 28 Pa. D. & C.3d 462 (C.P. 1984).

435. *Id.* at 465.

436. 1992 Conn. Super. LEXIS 915 (Super. Ct. April 2, 1992).

constitute family violence for purposes of issuing a civil protection order.[437] These cases fail to recognize the interrelatedness of physical abuse and emotional abuse that most domestic violence victims suffer. Courts which adopt this approach ignore the preventative purpose of protection order proceedings, and opt instead to require that the victim suffer at least one actual beating.

8. Damage to Property

Batterers often damage property to terrorize, threaten, and exert control over a victim of domestic violence.[438] Consequently, nine progressive state statutes issue civil protection orders based on malicious property damage.[439] Recognizing that damage to property is a form of abuse, courts have found various kinds of property damage to be sufficient grounds to support issuance of civil protection orders. Protection orders have issued, in part, based on property damage which includes pulling telephone cords from a wall while the petitioner tried to call police,[440] destroying furniture, breaking a window and skylights, chopping holes in roof with an axe, and driving a truck through a garage wall,[441] damaging the petitioner's car,[442] and destroying jointly owned household property.[443] Other property damage which should serve as a basis for the issuance of a civil protection order includes injuring or killing a family pet,[444] damaging the

---

437. *Id.* at *21.

438. Ganley, *supra* note 21, at 23. Sentimental and personal property was damaged by 59% of batterers. Follingstad et al., *supra* note 317, at 113. Approximately 80% of batterers engage in violent behavior towards other targets, such as harming pets and destroying objects. Lenore E. Walker, Eliminating Sexism to End Battering Relationships, Paper Presented at the American Psychological Association (1984).

439. DEL. CODE ANN. tit. 10, § 945 (Supp. 1992); GA. CODE ANN. § 19-13-1 (Michie Supp. 1993); HAW. REV. STAT. § 586-1 (Supp. 1992); IND. CODE ANN. § 34-4-5.1 (West Supp. 1993); N.H. REV. STAT. ANN. § 173-B:1 (Supp. 1992); N.J. STAT. ANN. § 2C:25-19 (West 1992); N.M. STAT. ANN. § 40-13-2 (Michie Supp. 1993); TENN. CODE ANN. § 36-3-601 (1991); WASH. REV. CODE ANN. § 10.99.020 (West Supp. 1993).

440. *In re* Marriage of Blitstein, 569 N.E.2d 1357 (Ill. App. Ct. 1991).

441. Kreitz v. Kreitz, 750 S.W.2d 681 (Mo. Ct. App. 1988).

442. Pendleton v. Minichino, No. 506673, 1992 Conn. Supr. LEXIS 915 (Super. Ct. Apr. 2, 1992) (issuing an *ex parte* temporary protection order suspending visitation where respondent destroyed petitioner's car and jointly owned household property, including a shower curtain, pushed and shoved petitioner, struck petitioner and threatened that "[t]his time I'm not going alone. You better watch your back").

443. *Id.*; *see also* Iowa v. Zeien, 505 N.W.2d 498 (Iowa 1993) (holding criminal conviction for damaging contents of estranged wife's home proper even though property damaged was marital property).

444. There is a strong connection between family violence and animal abuse. In 83% to 88% of families where children are abused, animals in the home are also abused, usually by

petitioner's clothing, and destroying other items of sentimental value to the petitioner.

9. Stalking

Both state statutes and case law authorize issuance of civil protection orders based on stalking behavior intended to harass and intimidate the petitioner. States have begun to recognize stalking as a ground to issue a civil protection order.[445] Courts have issued civil protection orders on behalf of petitioners who are stalked by their intimates. Stalking includes following and threatening the petitioner,[446] cutting up the parties' marriage certificate and leaving it with a threatening note on the petitioner's doorstep,[447] driving around the petitioner's house,[448] moving within two blocks of the petitioner's house,[449] and loitering in front of the battered women's shelter where petitioner stayed.[450] Like harassing and threatening behavior, stalking often escalates into more violent conduct.[451] Courts and the police need to be authorized to address this behavior early to prevent further violence.

In recent years, forty-six states and the District of Columbia have enacted stalking statutes which criminalize stalking behavior.[452] A

---

the abusive parents. WASHINGTON HUMANE SOCIETY, CHILD ABUSE AND CRUELTY TO ANIMALS.

445. N.M. STAT. ANN. § 40-13-2 (Michie Supp. 1993); N.J. STAT. ANN. § 2C:25-19 (West Supp. 1993); OKLA. STAT. ANN. tit. 22, § 60.1 (West 1992); R.I. GEN. LAWS §§ 11-59-2 to -3 (Supp. 1993).

446. Banks v. Pelot, 460 N.W.2d 446 (Wis. 1990) (holding that a court may issue a protection order based on the respondent following and threatening the petitioner); Knuth v. Knuth, No. C1-92-482, 1992 Minn. App. LEXIS 696 (Ct. App. June 19, 1992) (upholding court extension of civil protection order based on respondent moving within two blocks of the petitioner's home, loitering around the domestic violence shelter where the petitioner had stayed, following petitioner, opening the petitioner's mail and pounding nails into her car tires).

447. Boniek v. Boniek, 443 N.W.2d 196 (Minn. Ct. App. 1989) (upholding issuance of civil protection order based on former husband leaving the parties' shredded marriage license with a threatening note on the petitioner's door step, driving around the petitioner's home, and becoming aggressive with an insurance salesman in the petitioner's home).

448. *Id.*

449. *Knuth*, 1992 Minn. App. LEXIS at *696.

450. *Id.*

451. NATIONAL CLEARINGHOUSE FOR THE DEFENSE OF BATTERED WOMEN, STATISTICS PACKET 30 (1990).

452. *See* ALA. CODE § 13A-6-90 (Supp. 1993); ALASKA STAT. § 11.41.260 to .270 (Supp. 1993); ARK. CODE ANN. §§ 5-71-229, 5-13-301, & 5-71-208 to -209 (Supp. 1993); CAL. PENAL CODE § 646.9 (West Supp. 1993); COLO. REV. STAT. ANN. § 18-9-111 (1990 & Supp. 1993); CONN. GEN. STAT. ANN. §§ 53a-181(c) & (d) (West Supp. 1993); DEL. CODE

federally funded task force on anti-stalking legislation, created by Congress in 1992, recommends that states amend their statutes to make stalking a felony.[453] The task force, operating under the auspices of the Department of Justice's Office of Justice Programs, is developing a model anti-stalking statute.[454] The task force's report notes that stalking contains an "element of escalation that raises what initially may be bothersome and annoying—but legal—behavior to the level of obsessive, dangerous and even violent acts. Stalking victims, therefore, need to be provided with appropriate means to protect themselves against potential violence before it occurs."[455] To achieve this preventive goal, the task force recommends that stalking victims receive civil protection orders.[456] The task force predicts that protection orders will provide early intervention in stalking cases and prevent later violence.[457]

The recently released National Institute of Justice Report "Project To Develop A Model Anti-Stalking Code For States" compiled by the federal task force provides a profile of the existing state stalking stat-

---

ANN. tit. 11, § 1312(A) (Supp. 1992); D.C. CODE ANN. § 22-504 (1989); FLA. STAT. ANN. § 784.048 (West Supp. 1993); GA. CODE ANN. §§ 165-90 to -91 (Supp. 1993); HAW. REV. STAT. § 711-1106.5 (Supp. 1992); IDAHO CODE § 18-7905 (Supp. 1993); 750 ILCS 5/12-7.3 to -7.4 (Supp. 1993); IND. CODE ANN. §§ 35-33-1-1, 35-45-10 (1986 & Supp. 1993); IOWA CODE ANN. § 708.11 (Supp. 1993); KY. REV. STAT. ANN. § 508.140 (Supp. 1992); LA. REV. STAT. ANN. § 14:40.2 (Supp. 1992); MASS. GEN. L. ANN. ch. 265, § 43 (Supp. 1993); MICH. COMP. LAWS ANN. § 750.411h-1 (Supp. 1993); MINN. STAT. ANN. § 609.746 (1993); MISS. CODE ANN. § 97-3-107 (1992); MO. REV. STAT. § 455.010 & 455.085 (Supp. 1993); MONT. CODE ANN. § 45-5-220 (1993); NEB. REV. STAT. § 28-311.02 to .05 (Supp. 1992); NEV. REV. STAT. ANN. § 200.575 (Supp. 1993); N.H. REV. STAT. ANN. § 173:1-7 (Supp. 1993); N.J. STAT. ANN. § 2C:12-10 (West Supp. 1993); N.M. STAT. ANN. § 30-3A-1 to -4 (Michie 1993); N.Y. PENAL LAW §§ 120.13-14 (McKinney Supp. 1994); N.C. GEN. STAT. § 14-277.3 (1993); N.D. CENT. CODE § 12.1-17 to -07.1 (Supp. 1993); OHIO REV. CODE ANN. § 2903.21 (Anderson 1992); OKLA. STAT. ANN. tit. 21, § 1173 (Supp. 1993); OR. REV. STAT. § 133.310 (Supp. 1993); 18 PA. CONS. STAT. ANN. § 2709 (1983); R.I. GEN. LAWS § 11-59-1 (Supp. 1993); S.C. CODE ANN. § 16-3-1070 (Law. Co-op. 1992); S.D. CODIFIED LAWS ANN. § 22-19A-1 (Supp. 1993); TENN. CODE ANN. § 39-17 to -315 (Supp. 1993); TEX. PENAL CODE ANN. § 42.07 (West 1989); UTAH CODE ANN. § 76-5-106.5 (Supp. 1993); VT. STAT. ANN. tit. 13, §§ 1061-63 (Supp. 1993); VA. CODE ANN. § 18.2-60.3 (Michie Supp. 1993); WASH. REV. CODE ANN. § 9a.46.020 (West Supp. 1993); W. VA. CODE § 61-2-9a (West 1993); WIS. STAT. ANN. § 947.013 (West Supp. 1993); WYO. STAT. § 1-1-126 (Supp. 1993).

453. NATIONAL INSTITUTES OF JUSTICE, PROJECT TO DEVELOP A MODEL ANTI-STALKING CODE FOR STATES (1993) [hereinafter MODEL ANTI-STALKING CODE].

454. *Id.*

455. *Id.*

456. *Id.*

457. George Lardner, Jr., *Federal Task Force Suggest States Make Stalking a Felony Offense,* WASH. POST, Sept. 12, 1993, at A19.

utes.[458] The report found that state statutes vary considerably in the
definitional elements of stalking. Most typically define stalking as
"wilful, malicious, and repeated following and harassing of another
person."[459] However, most statutes require threatening behavior and
criminal intent on the part of the defendant to find stalking. Thirty-
four jurisdictions define stalking to include behavior which would
cause a reasonable person to feel threatened even where there is not
verbal threat.[460] State stalking statutes also consistently require a
"course of conduct" which is typically defined as a series of acts over
a period of time evidencing a continuity of purpose.[461] Many state
codes also provide both misdemeanor and felony classifications for
stalking.[462] For example, a recent amendment to California's stalking
law now makes it a misdemeanor for an identified batterer to enter
the property of a battered women's shelter without consent.[463] Six
states provide for conditions for pre-trial release including no contact
with the victim.[464] Commentators on the stalking laws have also
urged the adoption by courts of a partially subjective "reasonable
battered woman" standard which recognizes that acts not normally
threatening to an average person may terrify an abuse victim.[465]

---

458. MODEL ANTI-STALKING CODE, *supra* note 453, at 13.

459. *Id.*

460. *Id.*

461. *Id.* at 21.

462. *Id.*

463. Daniel M. Weintraub, *Wilson Signs Get-Tough Bills Aimed at Stalking: Legislation: One Measure Widens Definition of Crime. Others Stiffen Criminal and Civil Penalties,* L.A. TIMES, Sept. 30, 1993, at 28.

464. MODEL ANTI-STALKING CODE, *supra* note 453, at 28.

465. Note, *Legal Responses to Domestic Violence,* 106 HARV. L. REV. 1498, 1535 (1993).

Civil Protection Orders: The Benefits and Limitations for Victims of Domestic Violence

Executive Summary

Susan L. Keilitz, Project Director
Paula L. Hannaford
Hillery S. Efkeman

This research was supported by grant number 93-IJ-CX-0035 from the National Institute of Justice. Points of view are those of the authors and do not necessarily represent the position of the U.S. Department of Justice.

49

CIVIL PROTECTION ORDERS: THE BENEFITS AND LIMITATIONS
FOR VICTIMS OF DOMESTIC VIOLENCE

Executive Summary

In 1994, the National Center for State Courts initiated a study of the
effectiveness of civil protection orders under a grant from the National Institute of
Justice.[1] At that time, civil protection orders had become available in all fifty states, but
many states still placed significant restrictions on their availability and the scope of relief
provided in them.[2] The National Center's study was designed to build on the prior
research of others who had explored the reasons why civil protection orders might be
more or less effective in providing safer environments for victims and in enhancing their
opportunities for escaping violent relationships.[3] These earlier studies had concluded
that the effectiveness of protection orders depends on the comprehensiveness of relief
provided in protection orders, the specificity of the protection order terms, and how well
and consistently the orders are enforced. The National Center's study looked at other
factors that might influence the effectiveness of protection orders, including accessibility
to the court process, linkages to public and private services and sources of support,
and the criminal record of the victim's abuser.

---

[1] This research was supported by grant number 93-IJ-CX-0035 from the National Institute of Justice.
Points of view are those of the authors and do not necessarily represent the position of the U.S.
Department of Justice. The full report is available on loan from the National Center for State Courts library
(757-253-2000) or may be purchased for the cost of copying, postage, and handling. The authors of this
summary and the full report are Susan Keilitz, Hillery Efkeman, and Paula Hannaford.
[2] "Developments in the Law: Legal Responses to Domestic Violence." (May 1993). *Harvard Law Review*
106(7)
[3] The Urban Institute. (1996). *The Violence Against Women Act of 1994*. Washington, DC; M. Chaudhuri
and K. Daly (1991). "Do Restraining Orders Help? Battered Women's Experience with Male Violence and
Legal Process." In E. Buzawa and C. Buzawa (Eds.). *Domestic Violence: The Changing Criminal Justice
Response*. Westport, CT: Greenwood Press; P. Finn and S. Colson. (March 1990). "Civil Protection
Orders: Legislation, Practice and Enforcement." *National Institute of Justice Issues and Practice*.
Washington, DC: U.S. Department of Justice, Office of Justice Programs, National Institute of Justice.

Examining Protection Orders in Three Jurisdictions

The National Center's study examined the civil protection order process and the environments in which the process takes place in three jurisdictions with different processes and service models.[4] These jurisdictions are the Family Court in Wilmington, Delaware, the County Court in Denver, Colorado, and the District of Columbia Superior Court.[5] The expectation in examining these three jurisdictions was that the different models they use would produce various results and that these variations might hold implications for improving practices in other jurisdictions. The key structural differences among the study sites relevant to the court's role in ensuring that protection orders serve their intended function are the court intake process, the level of assistance petitioners for orders receive, and access to court hearings.

The process for obtaining a protection order is more centralized in Delaware and Denver than it is in the District of Columbia. In Delaware and Denver. petitioners also are provided direct assistance when they file petitions. In Delaware, specially educated and trained court staff in a Domestic Violence Unit assist petitioners, while in Denver, help is provided by volunteers and staff of a private victim service agency (Project Safeguard). At the time of the study, petitioners in the District of Columbia received no assistance other than the attention of a court clerk in completing petition forms.

The docketing for protection order hearings varies considerably among the three courts. Denver has a consolidated docket, with a single judge who hears petitions for temporary orders and presides at hearings for permanent orders exclusively. Temporary orders are available on an ex parte calendar every afternoon and hearings for permanent orders are set every morning.

---

[4] On some factors that also might affect the effectiveness of civil protection orders the three jurisdictions are more alike than different. In each of the three jurisdictions, petitioners can obtain an ex parte order of protection during business hours Monday through Friday, but there is no weekend or after hours access to an emergency civil protection order. (In all three sites, criminal no-contact orders can be issued in cases where the perpetrator has been released from custody after an arrest.) In each site, police may arrest respondents without a warrant based on probable cause that the respondent violated the protection order. Violations can be prosecuted as a misdemeanor offense. Orders are also enforceable through contempt proceedings in the court.

[5] The District of Columbia has undergone significant change in the manner in which the court, law enforcement, and prosecution address domestic violence. The descriptions in this report reflect how the

The Family Court in Delaware holds ex parte hearings twice daily—once in the morning and again in the afternoon, but hearings for permanent orders are set only on Fridays. Three commissioners preside over ex parte and permanent order hearings. In the District of Columbia, petitioners seeking an ex parte order must wait for the judge assigned to hear emergency matters, including warrants. Hearings for permanent orders are held daily and assigned to a judge in the Family Division who sits in a monthly rotation on the protection order calendar.

Evaluating Benefits in the Context of Victims' Experiences

The study findings are based on four sources of data: (1) initial telephone interviews conducted with 285 women petitioners for protection orders in the three project sites approximately one month after they received a protection order (temporary or permanent); (2) follow-up interviews with 177 of the same group of petitioners about six months later; (3) civil case records of petitioners who participated in the study; (4) criminal history records of men named in the protection orders the study participants obtained.[6] The analysis of the data was informed by on-site interviews with judges, court managers and staff, victim services representatives, members of police domestic violence units, and prosecutors and by observations of hearings for temporary and permanent orders.

court and system operated at the time the study commenced, however. The system is still in the beginning stages of implementing an ambitious reform plan that includes a domestic violence court.
[6] The method of selecting participants for the study places some limitations on the strength of the conclusions that can be drawn from the study findings. First, the participants were not randomly selected, which limits the extent to which we can say they are representative of other women who seek protection orders in the study sites. We also do not know what proportion of the women who were asked to participate declined. However, this proportion is likely not of any appreciable size because the recruiters reported that few women did not agree to participate. The participants' self-selection for the study poses a second threat to the validity of the findings, which is that those women who were willing to participate may have some characteristics that distinguish them from the other victims who might seek a protection order. Third, all of the participants had a telephone or access to one. This sets them apart from women with fewer resources and those who do not have a place where it is safe to have a telephone conversation, including most women who were staying in a shelter or other temporary residence. (Interviewers were able to speak with some women who were in transient situations.)

Across the three project sites, 554 women agreed to participate in the study and signed a consent form (Delaware, 151; Denver, 194; District of Columbia, 209).[7] Project staff were able to complete an initial interview with 285 of the women (51 percent) who were recruited (Delaware, 90; Denver, 90; District of Columbia, 105). These women formed the study groups in each site.[8] Approximately 60 percent (177) of these women participated in the follow-up interviews.

Measuring the Effectiveness of Protection Orders

The National Center's study applied two primary measures of effectiveness: (1) improvement in the quality of the women's lives (women's reports that their lives have improved since getting the order, that they feel better about themselves, and that they feel safer), and (2) extent of problems related to the protection order (women's reports of repeated occurrences of physical or psychological abuse, calling at home or work, coming to the home, stalking, and other problems related to the order).

To quantify these measures of effectiveness, we developed an index of the variables that comprise each measure. The indexes allow more meaningful analyses of relationships among the dependent (or outcome) variables that make up the indices and the many independent variables that could be associated with the effectiveness of protection orders. Each of the variables in the indexes has a score of 1. For the Well-being Index the possible range of scores is 0 (the lowest level of effectiveness) to 3 (the highest level). For the Problems Index the possible range of the values is from 0

---

[7] In each of three sites, women who filed petitions for protection orders were recruited in person for the study. Recruitment for the study began in July 1994 at staggered times across the sites as project staff visited each site and trained individuals to recruit women. The recruiters explained the purpose of the study and what participation in it would entail. If the woman agreed to participate, the recruiters asked her to sign a consent form.

[8] Reasons for attrition among the women recruited for the study are numerous and varied, but difficulty in contacting the women by phone was a major factor. About one fifth of the women did not participate because they did not respond to phone messages asking them to return the call using a toll free number. Other communication obstacles included disconnected telephones (16 percent), inability to leave a message or get an answer at the number provided (10 percent), wrong phone numbers (4 percent), and no phone (3 percent). Other reasons why staff were unable to complete interviews included women changing their mind about participating (9 percent), repeatedly broken or postponed appointments (7 percent), not having obtained an order (6 percent), moving (4 percent), and having petitioned for an order against a family member who was not an intimate partner 5 percent).

(indicating the highest level of effectiveness) to 7 (the lowest level of effectiveness). The values of the Problems Index are the inverse of those for the Well-being Index: the greater the number of types of problems the participant experienced, the higher her score on the Problems Index.

Summary of Key Findings and Implications for Practice

- Civil protection orders are valuable for assisting victims regain a sense of well-being.

Table 1: Effectiveness Measured by Quality of Life	Initial Interview (n=285)	Follow-up Interview (n=177)
Life Improved	%	%
All Sites	72.3	85.3
Delaware	82.2	87.5
Denver	74.4	89.7
District of Columbia	61.9	79.4
Feel Better		
All Sites	72.3	92.7
Delaware	82.2	92.9
Denver	74.4	93.1
District of Columbia	61.9	92.1
Feel Safer		
All Sites	73.7	80.5*
Delaware	77.8	83.7
Denver	83.3	82.9
District of Columbia	61.9	71.4

For nearly three-quarters of the study participants, the short term effects of the protection order on the participants' well-being were positive (see Table 1). These positive effects improved over time, so that by the time of the six-month follow-up interview, the proportion of participants reporting life improvement increased to 85 percent. Over 90 percent reported feeling better about themselves, and 80 percent of those with a protection order in effect felt safer. Furthermore, in both the initial and follow-up interviews, 95 percent of the participants stated that they would seek a protection order again.

55

- **In the vast majority of cases, civil protection orders deter repeated incidents of physical and psychological abuse.**

Table 2: Effectiveness Measured by Problems with Orders: All Sites	Initial Interview (n=268)		Follow-up Interview (n=167)	
	#	%	#	%
No problems experienced	194	72.4	109	65.3
Respondent called home/work	43	16.1	29	17.4
Respondent came to home	24	9.0	14	8.4
Respondent stalked victim	11	4.1	12	7.2
Respondent physically re-abused victim	7	2.6	14	8.4
Respondent psychologically re-abused victim	12	4.4	21	12.6
Respondent caused other problems	3	1.1	1	0.6

A majority of the participants in both the initial and follow-up interviews reported having no problems (72.4 percent and 65.3 percent, respectively)(see Table 2). Repeat occurrences of physical abuse were reportedly rare, but varied greatly across the study sites, particularly in the follow-up interviews. In the initial interviews, 4.1 percent of the participants reported repeated physical abuse. At the six month follow-up, that proportion doubled to 8.4 percent. The incidence of repeated physical abuse was much higher, however, in Delaware (10.9 percent) and the District of Columbia (11.9 percent) than in Denver, where only about 2 percent of the participants reported being re-abused physically.

Psychological abuse was reported by 4.4 percent of the study participants initially, but after six months the reported incidence rose to 12.6 percent. As occurred in the reports of repeated physical abuse, there was a high level of variance across the sites on this measure. Psychological abuse was highest in Delaware (23.6 percent) and lowest in the District of Columbia (1.7 percent), with Denver falling in the middle (13.3 percent).

56

The most frequently reported problem in both the initial and follow-up interviews was calling the victim at home or work (16.1 percent and 17.4 percent, respectively). In both the initial and follow-up interviews about 9 percent of the participants reported that the respondent came to the victim's home. Stalking was relatively infrequently reported. In the initial interviews about 4 percent of the participants reported being stalked by the respondent; this figure rose to about 7 percent in the follow-up interviews.[9]

- **The study participants experienced severe abuse.**

Table 3: Nature of Abuse Before Protection Order					
All Sites (n=285)	**#**	**%**	**By Site**	**#**	**%**
Threatened or Injured with a Weapon	105	36.8	Delaware	29	32.2
			Denver	33	36.7
			District of Columbia	43	41.0
Severe Physical Abuse: Beaten or Choked	155	54.4	Delaware	55	61.1
			Denver	48	53.3
			District of Columbia	52	49.5
Mild Physical Abuse: Slapping, Grabbing, Shoving, Kicking	239	83.9	Delaware	80	88.9
			Denver	79	87.8
			District of Columbia	80	76.2
Intimidation through Threats, Stalking, Harassment	282	98.9	Delaware	90	100
			Denver	90	100
			District of Columbia	102	97.1

Over one-third of the study participants had been threatened or injured with a weapon; over half the participants had been beaten or choked, and 84 percent had

---

[9] The majority of participants with children reported that they did not experience any problems related to the children. However, in contrast to the whole group of participants, the proportion of participants with children who reported having *any* problems rose from 31 percent in the initial interviews to 42 percent in the follow-up interviews. This difference makes sense intuitively, because participants with children are more likely to be in situations where problems could occur, such as seeing the respondent upon the exchange of children for visitation. In the initial and follow-up interviews, the two most frequently reported types of problems related to children were problems at exchange of children for visitation (initial 3.9 percent, follow-up 2.1 percent) and threatening to keep the children (initial 2.1 percent, follow-up 3.5 percent). No one reported that the respondent actually kept the children. Four participants in the first interview and one in the follow-up interview reported that the respondent did not return the children at the appointed time.

suffered milder physical abuse, such as slapping, kicking, and shoving.[10] While the use of weapons to threaten or injure the participants occurred for most women only once or twice, over 40 percent of the participants experienced severe physical abuse at least every few months, and 10 percent experienced such abuse weekly. About 10 percent of the participants sought a protection order after only a week, but 15 percent of the women experienced abuse for one to two years, and nearly one quarter had endured the respondent's abusive behavior for over five years.

Most significantly, the longer the women experienced abuse, the more intense the abusive behavior became; consequently, the longer a victim stays in a relationship the more likely it is that she will be severely injured by the abuser.[11] This finding indicates that victims should be counseled at the earliest moment they come in contact with a public or private service that the likelihood of the abusive behavior abating without a specific intervention is low. Victims should receive assistance in developing a safety plan and understanding the importance of enlisting neighbors, friends, and co-workers in following the plan.

---

[10] To assess the nature of the abusive behavior experienced by the study participants, the project applied the categories of abusive behaviors used by the Urban Institute and the Association of Family and Conciliation Courts in an evaluation of the use of mediation in family mediation when domestic violence might be occurring between the parties. See. L. Newmark, A. Harrell, and P. Salem. (April 1994). *Domestic Violence and Empowerment in Custody and Visitation Cases: An Empirical Study on the Impact of Domestic Abuse.* Madison, WI: Association of Family and Conciliation Courts. These categories were distilled from the specific acts included in the Conflict Tactics Scale developed by Straus (M. Straus. (1979). "Measuring Family Conflict and Violence: The Conflict Tactics Scales." *Journal of Marriage and the Family,* XLI: 75-88.)

[11] To examine relationships between the intensity of the abuse the participants experienced and other variables, an index of abuse intensity was created through factor analysis. The duration of abuse was highly correlated with more severe abuse and more frequent abuse. The score for the rotated factor matrix for the duration of abuse variable was 0.598, resulting in a factor score coefficient of .231.

- **The majority of abusive partners have a criminal record.**

All Sites (n=244)	#	%	By Site	#	%
Table 4: Number of Respondents with a Criminal Arrest History					
All Crime Types	158	64.8	Delaware (n=90)	62	68.9
			Denver (n=60)	46	67.6
			District of Columbia (n=86)	50	58.1
Violent Crime	129	52.9	Delaware	56	62.2
			Denver	40	58.8
			District of Columbia	33	38.4
Drug and Alcohol Related Crimes	72	29.5	Delaware	25	27.8
			Denver	22	32.4
			District of Columbia	25	29.1
Other Crimes	121	49.6	Delaware	49	54.4
			Denver	31	45.6
			District of Columbia	41	47.7

Sixty-five percent of the respondents had a prior criminal arrest history.[12] These charges consisted of a variety of offenses including violent crime (domestic violence, simple assault, other violence, and weapons charges), drug and alcohol-related crimes (drug and DUI offenses) and other categories of crimes (property, traffic and miscellaneous offenses). Of the 131 respondents with any history of violent crime, 109 had prior arrests for violent crimes other than domestic violence. These findings are generally consistent with a study conducted in Quincy, Massachusetts that found that

---

[12] The sources of the criminal history records and their inclusiveness in regard to the sample of participants varied across the project sites. In Delaware, the Family Court provided statewide data on the respondents to all the orders issued to participants in the study. The Family Court could achieve this level of inclusiveness because the Family Court records include the names of the respondents. In Denver and the District of Columbia, project staff had to obtain the names of the respondents from the participants' case files. At each of these sites, project and court staff could not locate the files of all the participants and consequently also could not obtain the names of all the respondents. In Denver, the Colorado Division of Criminal Justice provides statewide criminal histories. In the District of Columbia, project staff obtained criminal records from the automated system of the Superior Court. The criminal history records are not likely to be comprehensive. Because of the close proximity that the District of Columbia and Delaware have to neighboring jurisdictions (Northern Virginia and Maryland for the District of Columbia, and Maryland, Pennsylvania and New Jersey for Delaware), the criminal records in these sites may significantly underrepresent the total amount of prior criminal activity for the respondents. In Denver, the arrest histories for respondents may be more representative of their actual prior arrest record because Denver is centrally located within a comparatively large state-wide reporting jurisdiction.

"80 percent of abusers have prior criminal histories . . . and half have prior violence records."[13]

If the woman's abuser had an arrest record for violent crime, she was significantly less likely to have been available for a second interview.[14] Furthermore, respondents with arrest histories for drug and alcohol related crimes and for violent crime tended to engage in more intense abuse of their partners than did other respondents. These findings strongly support the need for greater attention to safety planning for victims whose abusers have a record of violent crime, as well as the need for protection orders to require both substance abuse and batterer treatment for respondents with arrest records for drug and alcohol related offenses. Concomitantly, judges need to have the criminal arrest histories available for review when they are crafting protection orders. Judges and victim service providers should stress to victims the need for vigilance in taking safety precautions and using law enforcement and the court to enforce their protection orders.

- **The criminal record of the respondent is associated with improvements in well-being and in curbing abusive conduct.**

For the Well-being Index, participants are more likely to report positive outcomes when the respondent has a record of violent crime. Protection orders therefore can be particularly helpful for improving the well-being of women when their abuser has been sufficiently (and probably publicly) violent in the past to be arrested for the behavior. For the Problems Index, in the initial interviews, the participants whose abuser had a

---

[13] M. Schachere. (December 1995). "STOP Grants Training Conferences Highlight Successful Strategies." *National Bulletin on Domestic Violence Prevention* 1(6). The Quincy study focused in part on the effectiveness of a highly coordinated and accurate reporting system between the civil and criminal court systems. The comparatively high criminal arrest rates reported in the Quincy study may reflect the accuracy of that jurisdiction's reporting system rather than an abnormally higher violent crime rate relative to the sites included in this study.

[14] These findings related to the respondents criminal history suggest that the women not interviewed a second time may have had less positive feelings about themselves than did the women who were interviewed a second time. On the other hand, participants who obtained orders against respondents with an arrest record for violent crime tended to have higher scores on an index of subjective measures of effectiveness of protection orders. They also may have suffered repeated physical abuse, psychological abuse, or other violations of the protection order to a greater degree than the women participating in the follow-up interviews.

higher number of arrests tended to report a greater number of problems with the protection order.[15] In the follow-up interviews, the participants whose abuser had at least one arrest for a violent crime other than domestic violence were more likely to experience a greater number of problems with the protection order.[16]

These findings indicate that protection orders obtained against respondents with a criminal history are less likely to be effective in deterring future violence or avoiding other problems than those obtained against respondents without such a history. Because protection orders provide petitioners with less protection against respondents with a high number of arrests, and more specifically with a history of violent crime, the need for aggressive criminal prosecution policies becomes more critical. Criminal prosecution of such individuals may be required to curb their abusive behavior. Reliance on a protection as the sole intervention in these cases may not be the most effective deterrence against further abuse.

The relationships between the respondents' criminal histories and both the improved quality of life and reported problems with protection orders indicate that the dual interventions of criminal and civil process are likely to be most helpful to women whose abusers have been arrested in the past. Criminal prosecution may address the violence more effectively, while the civil protection order bolsters the victim's self-esteem and gives greater feelings of security.

- **Temporary protection orders can be useful even if the victim does not follow through to obtain a permanent order.**

The most commonly cited reason for not returning for a permanent order was that the respondent had stopped bothering the petitioner (35.5 percent), which suggests that being the subject of the court's attention can influence the abuser's behavior. Also, one-fourth of the study participants who obtained only a temporary protection order engaged in safety planning at that time. The court process thus offered an opportunity for educating victims about the actions they could take to protect themselves. This

---

[15] Analysis of Variance, $F = 1.6271$, $p = .0439$.
[16] Analysis of Variance, $F = 4.8820$, $p = .0285$.

finding indicates that courts and victim service providers should capitalize on this opportunity by spending more time in safety planning and assessing victims' needs when they petition for temporary orders.

- **The court process can influence the victim's active participation in deterring further violence in her life.**

A more centralized process and direct assistance to petitioners for protection orders may encourage women with a temporary order to return to court for a permanent order. The proportion of women who returned to court for a permanent order following a temporary order was significantly higher in Denver (60 percent) than in the District of Columbia (44 percent).[17] In addition, a higher proportion of women developed a safety plan in Denver, where each petitioner is assisted by an advocate from Project Safeguard, in comparison to Delaware and the District of Columbia. Study participants in Denver also reported far fewer repeated occurrences of physical violence compared to the participants in Delaware and Denver.

- **The full potential for comprehensive relief in protection orders has not been achieved.**

Exclusive use of the family residence is an available remedy in each of the project sites and can be critical for the both the safety and psychological stability of the victim, but the court in Denver is much more disposed than the other courts to order the respondent to vacate a common residence in both temporary and permanent orders. Also, although considerable proportions of the respondents had histories of violent crime and drug or alcohol related offenses, few of the protection orders required the respondent to participate in batterer or substance abuse. Courts should revise protection order petitions and uniform orders to include all possible forms of relief available to victims. Making the forms more user friendly and instructive as to the relief

---

[17] The return rate for participants in Delaware differs considerably from Denver and the District of Columbia, primarily because the majority of participants in Delaware were recruited for the study when they appeared for the hearing on the permanent order.

available will allow petitioners greater opportunity to consider what types of relief are likely to be helpful to them.

- **Victims do not use the contempt process to enforce orders.**

Few of the study participants filed contempt motions for violations of the protection order. In 130 cases (89.7 percent), no contempt motions were filed. Thirteen cases (9.0 percent) had one contempt motion and only two cases (1.4 percent) had more than one contempt motion. Of the cases in which contempt motions were filed, the court held a hearing on the matter in nine cases and granted the motion in five of these cases. The low use by participants of the civil contempt process to enforce protection orders indicates that the court should do more to inform victims about the availability of and the process for filing contempt motions.[18] Judges should advise victims during hearings about the avenues of enforcement, including law enforcement, the court, and courts in other states. Furthermore, the protection order should include a statement regarding the order's enforceability locally, throughout the state, and in other states. This need to provide easily accessible and understandable information about the enforcement process has become more acute in the wake of the Violence Against Women Act's full faith and credit provisions for protection orders.[19]

- **The potential for linking victims to services through the court process has not been achieved.**

Overall, more than three-fourths (77.5 percent) of the study participants received some type of service or assistance, either before or after they obtained a protection order. However, the participants' private circle of friends and relatives accounted for a large proportion of the assistance victims received. Although an array services is

---

[18] Participants in Denver also reported little use of the contempt process to enforce orders, but this is most likely because the policy of the City Attorney is to vigorously prosecute violations of protection orders. The City Attorney's domestic violence unit works closely with the police department to coordinate arrests, arraignments, and prosecution. They reportedly obtain a high proportion of guilty pleas because the prosecution efforts have been successful.

[19] *The Violence Against Women Act of 1994*, Pub.L. No. 103-322, Title IV, 108 Stat. 1902-55 §40221 (2265-2266).

63

available to victims from both governmental sources, such as police and prosecutor victim assistance units, and the community, such as victim counseling, shelters for battered women and their children, pro bono legal services, and employment and education counseling, a relatively low proportion of victims appears to be making a connection to these services. The court should ensure that petitioners for protection orders receive not only information about the services available to them but also assistance in accessing the services.

- **Law enforcement agencies can do more to assist prosecutors in developing cases for prosecution, to arrest perpetrators, and to help victims access the civil protection order process.**

Table 5: Police Procedures	Delaware		Denver		District of Columbia	
	#	%	#	%	#	%
Petitioner Called Police Following CPO Incident	58	96.7	56	93.3	80	89.9
Police Came to the Scene	46	79.3	50	89.3	75	93.8
Police Interviewed Witnesses at the Scene	25	59.5	27	55.1	27	37.5
Police Took Notes at Scene	31	72.1	28	60.9	46	64.8
Police Arrested Respondent	9	55.0	27	87.1	14	41.2
Police Informed Petitioner About CPO Availability	35	60.3	37	60.7	69	77.5
Police Informed Petitioner About CPO Procedures	33	56.9	32	53.6	63	70.8
Petitioner Believes Police Were Helpful	31	52.5	27	45.0	39	43.8

The reported use of police services varied across the sites, as did the responses of the police (see Table 5). In Delaware, for example, a higher proportion of the participants had called the police following the incident that spurred them to seek a protection order (Delaware, 97 percent, Denver, 93 percent, District of Columbia, 90 percent), but the police came to the scene of the incident in a lower proportion of the cases (Delaware, 79 percent, Denver, 89 percent, District of Columbia, 94 percent).

64

Once at the scene, however, the police in Delaware (Wilmington Police and New Castle County Police) were more likely to take notes and interview witnesses. The police arrested the respondent in Denver in a considerably higher proportion of the cases, particularly in comparison to the District of Columbia (87 percent compared with 41 percent). In each of the sites, however, the proportion of participants who reported that the police had told them how to obtain a civil protection order was too low for good practice (Delaware, 57 percent; Denver, 54 percent; District of Columbia, 71 percent).

Because law enforcement officers are on the front lines of the fight against domestic violence, they should be more aggressive in ascertaining probable cause to arrest abusers, as well as in informing victims about the civil protection order process. The role of law enforcement officers in enforcing protection orders has become even more critical since the enactment of the Violence Against Women Act. The full faith and credit provision of VAWA places greater responsibility on law enforcement officers to respond effectively to victims' calls for enforcement of protection orders issued by jurisdictions outside the local or state jurisdiction. Law enforcement training in domestic violence, arrest policies, and enforcement procedures should be an integral and mandatory component of officer preparation and continuing education, not just an isolated topic at the academy and a low priority activity for veterans.

Continued Research on Current and Future Initiatives

A significant movement has developed to implement new approaches to redressing family violence and addressing the needs of its victims.[20] Over the course of the past few years, a wave of legislative reforms in the states and at the federal level has accelerated this movement. Chief among these is the Violence Against Women Act (VAWA), enacted by Congress in 1994.

The VAWA presents a pivotal opportunity to increase the effectiveness of protection orders through several changes in current practice that will affect access to protection orders and enhance enforcement remedies. The VAWA provisions include

[20] *See* National Council of Juvenile and Family Court Judges. (1992). *Family Violence: State-of-the-Art Court Programs.* Reno, NV: National Council of Juvenile and Family Court Judges.

65

full faith and credit for protection orders, sanctions for interstate violation of protection orders, and substantial grant opportunities that are building the capacities of state and local jurisdictions to coordinate the efforts of law enforcement, prosecutors, courts, corrections, and providers of victim services, batterer treatment, and medical, mental health, and social services.

Many of the initiatives funded by VAWA include the implementation of data collection and communication systems and enhancement of coordinated community interventions. These initiatives are likely to encourage improved processes for obtaining and enforcing protection orders and for incorporating protection orders as a key component in the web of responses to domestic violence. Future research should capitalize on the data collection and community coordination systems that are evolving with VAWA and other funding. The most effective interventions can only be determined by examining the interactive dynamics of domestic violence, including the nature of abuse experienced by victims, the criminal histories of the abusers, the use of criminal history information in crafting orders and counseling victims, the actions of police and prosecutors, the enforcement and effects of specific terms (including supervised visitation and batterer and substance abuse treatment), and the application of full faith and credit for protection orders. The National Center's study demonstrates that the effectiveness of civil protection orders is inextricably linked to the quality of the system of government and community services in which protection orders operate. Issuing a protection order is only one part of the remedy.

STATE ex rel. Denise WILLIAMS,
Plaintiff,

v.

Honorable William J. MARSH, Judge,
16th Judicial Circuit, Defendant.

Denise WILLIAMS, Appellant,

v.

Edward M. WILLIAMS, Respondent.

Nos. 62765, 62762.

Supreme Court of Missouri,
En Banc.

Jan. 12, 1982.

Wife petitioned for relief under the Adult Abuse Act to restrain her husband from entering her dwelling and to obtain a temporary order of custody. The Circuit Court, Jackson County, William J. Marsh, J., dismissed the petition, and wife appealed and also brought an original proceeding for a writ of mandamus. The Supreme Court, Higgins, J., held that: (1) Adult Abuse Act did not violate constitutional requirement that bills contain no more than one subject which shall be clearly expressed in their titles by containing provisions relating to child custody and support which were not referred to in its title where provisions on child custody and support were fairly related to and served purpose of aiding victims of domestic violence and preventing future incidents of adult abuse; (2) provisions in Adult Abuse Act permitting courts to issue ex parte orders of protection to exclude respondents from home or from contact with children for 15-day period did not deprive respondent of due process where Act was necessary to secure important governmental interests in protection of victims of abuse and prevention of further abuse, only time ex parte order could be issued was when there was immediate and present danger of abuse, nothing in Act suggested that respondent could not obtain hearing earlier than 15 days, ex parte order was required to be served upon respondent, and only judge in his discretion could issue ex

parte order; and (3) provisions in Adult Abuse Act permitting trial court to include certain provisions in ex parte or full order of protection, violation of which were misdemeanors, did not violate constitutional requirements of separation and nondelegation of power where court's discretion was limited to determining whether situation warranted issuance of all or less than all of three restraining orders expressly available under the Act.

Reversed and remanded; preliminary writ of mandamus made peremptory.

Bardgett, J., concurred in part in separate concurring opinion filed.

Seiler, J., concurred in separate concurring opinion of Bardgett, J.

Welliver, J., dissented in separate dissenting opinion filed.

1. Constitutional Law ⚖=46(1)

Constitutional questions normally are decided only when necessary to disposition of case presented.

2. Parties ⚖=1

Standing is related to doctrine which prohibits advisory opinions because latter requires court to dispose of only those issues which affect rights of parties present and if party's interests are unaffected by resolution of issue he has no standing to raise it.

3. Constitutional Law ⚖=42.1(3)

Wife had standing to object to trial court's ruling that Adult Abuse Act was unconstitutional where wife derived actual and justiciable interest susceptible of protection from trial court's holding that she had unqualified right to relief available under Act. V.A.M.S. §§ 455.010–455.085.

4. Constitutional Law ⚖=45

Circuit courts have authority to declare act of legislature unconstitutional so long as question has not been determined by Supreme Court.

5. Constitutional Law ⚖=45

Determination of constitutionality of acts of legislature may be made sua sponte by circuit court judges.

6. Constitutional Law ⊸45

Trial court had authority to determine sua sponte constitutionality of Adult Abuse Act since it was making subject-matter jurisdiction determination which may be made sua sponte at any time. V.A.M.S. §§ 455.-010–455.085; V.A.M.R. 55.27(g)(3).

7. Constitutional Law ⊸46(2)

Trial court could rule on constitutionality of provision in Adult Abuse Act authorizing warrantless arrests of persons who violate orders issued under the Act even though its holding went beyond relief which was requested and constitutionality of that provision was not directly in issue where trial court held provisions of Act inseverable and, if sections at issue had been found to be constitutional, facial unconstitutionality of warrant provision would have voided entire Act. V.A.M.S. §§ 455.010–455.085.

8. Constitutional Law ⊸42.1(3)

Wife, who sought to enforce Adult Abuse Act against her husband, had standing to challenge trial court's ruling that Act was unconstitutional even though husband did not appear in case where controversy was adequately presented to Supreme Court on appeal from trial court's ruling and on wife's petition for writ of mandamus in briefs filed by by wife, trial court judge, and amicus curiae. V.A.M.S. §§ 455.010–455.085.

9. Statutes ⊸107(1)

Test to determine if title of bill violates constitutional prohibition against bills containing more than one subject is whether all provisions of statute fairly relate to same subject, have natural connection therewith or are incidents or means to accomplish its purpose. V.A.M.S.Const.Art. 3, § 23.

10. Statutes ⊸107(2)

Adult Abuse Act did not violate constitutional requirement that bills contain no more than one subject which shall be clearly expressed in their titles by containing provisions relating to child custody and support which were not referred to in its title where provisions on child custody and support were fairly related to and served purpose of aiding victims of domestic violence

and preventing future incidents of adult abuse. V.A.M.S. §§ 455.010–455.085; V.A.M.S.Const.Art. 3, § 23; Laws 1980, p. 441.

11. Constitutional Law ⊸251.3, 278(1)

Due process guarantee is intended to protect individual against arbitrary acts of government and to protect right to use and enjoy one's property without governmental interference. V.A.M.S.Const.Art. 1, § 10; U.S.C.A.Const.Amend. 14.

12. Constitutional Law ⊸252.5

Before guarantee of due process comes into play, there must be deprivation by government of constitutionally protected interest. V.A.M.S.Const.Art. 1, § 10; U.S.C.A.Const.Amend. 14.

13. Constitutional Law ⊸251.6

Notice and opportunity to be heard must be provided by state in meaningful manner prior to deprivation of protected interest. V.A.M.S.Const.Art. 1, § 10; U.S.C.A.Const.Amend. 14.

14. States ⊸24

State legislatures have broad power to enact laws to protect general health, welfare, and safety.

15. Breach of the Peace ⊸16
Constitutional Law ⊸312(1)

Provisions in Adult Abuse Act permitting courts to issue ex parte orders of protection to exclude respondents from home or from contact with children for 15 day period did not deprive respondent of due process where Act was necessary to secure important governmental interests in protection of victims of abuse and prevention of further abuse, only time ex parte order could be issued was when there was immediate and present danger of abuse, nothing in Act suggested that respondent could not obtain hearing earlier than 15 days after order was granted, ex parte order was required to be served upon respondent, and only judge in his discretion could issue ex parte order. V.A.M.S. §§ 455.085–455.045; V.A.M.S.Const.Art. 1, § 10; U.S.C.A.Const. Amend. 14.

16. Breach of the Peace ⇐16
Constitutional Law ⇐83(3)

Adult Abuse Act did not violate constitutional prohibition against imprisonment for debt where Act made violation of ex parte order of protection of which respondent has notice of violation of full order of protection criminal but set forth no punishment for violation of ancillary orders dealing with child support, maintenance, or attorney fees. V.A.M.S. §§ 455.045, 455.050, subds. 1–7, 455.075, 455.085; V.A.M.S.Const. Art. 1, § 11.

17. Constitutional Law ⇐258(2)

Vagueness, as due process violation, takes two forms: one is lack of notice given potential offender because statute is so unclear that men of common intelligence must necessarily guess at its meaning and other is that statute fails to set out explicit standards for those who must apply it, resulting in arbitrary and discriminatory application. U.S.C.A.Const.Amends. 5, 14; V.A.M.S. Const.Art. 1, § 10.

18. Breach of the Peace ⇐16

Adult Abuse Act was not void for vagueness because it failed to give adequate warning as to what conduct is proscribed where Act provided sufficient direction and guidance for judges who must apply it in that abuse was defined and protection orders under the Act were to issue only when immediate and present danger of abuse was found. V.A.M.S. §§ 455.010–455.085; U.S.C.A.Const.Amend. 14; V.A.M.S.Const.Art. 1, § 10.

19. Constitutional Law ⇐70.1(10)

Duty and power to define crime and ordain punishment is exclusively vested in legislature.

20. Breach of the Peace ⇐16
Constitutional Law ⇐62(5)

Sections of Adult Abuse Act permitting trial court to include certain provisions in ex parte or full order of protection, violation of which were misdemeanors, did not violate constitutional requirements of separation and nondelegation of power where court's discretion was limited to determin-ing whether situation warranted issuance of all or less than all of three restraining orders expressly available under the Act. V.A.M.S.Const.Art. 2, § 1; Art. 3, § 1; V.A.M.S. §§ 455.045, 455.050.

21. Arrest ⇐63.4(5), 68

Generally, warrantless arrest upon probable cause for felonies or misdemeanors may constitutionally be authorized by statute but warrantless arrest in arrestee's home is impermissible absent consent to enter or exigent circumstances.

22. Breach of the Peace ⇐16

Provision in Adult Abuse Act authorizing warrantless arrests of respondents was not unconstitutional where provision authorized warrantless arrest where probable cause existed to believe that violation of protection order had occurred and did not authorize warrantless in-home seizure of respondents. V.A.M.S. §§ 455.010 et seq., 455.085; V.A.M.S.Const.Art. 1, § 15; U.S.C. A.Const.Amends. 4, 14.

Sherrill L. Rosen and Marcia K. Welsh, Legal Aid of Western Mo., Kansas City, for relator; Phyllis Gelman, New York City, of counsel.

John E. Turner, Kansas City, for respondent.

Michael A. Wolff and Jesse A. Goldner, Nina Balsam, John Ashcroft, Atty. Gen., Simon Tonkin, Asst. Atty. Gen., St. Louis, for amicus curiae.

HIGGINS, Judge.

Denise Williams petitions this court for a writ of mandamus to compel the trial court to issue an order of protection, an order restraining her husband from entering her dwelling and a temporary order of custody as authorized by The Adult Abuse Act, §§ 455.010–.085, RSMo Supp.1980. In a separate action she appeals the trial court's dismissal of her petition filed under Chapter 455, RSMo Supp.1980. The appeal was consolidated with the mandamus action because both present the same issues concerning the trial court's determination that

Chapter 455, RSMo Supp.1980 violates a number of provisions of the Missouri and United States Constitutions. The preliminary writ is made peremptory; the judgment of dismissal is reversed, and the cause is remanded for further proceedings consistent with the writ herein issued.

After a hearing on plaintiff's petition for an *ex parte* order of protection, the trial court found: plaintiff, Denise Williams, and respondent, Edward M. Williams were married; one child was born of the marriage; the couple had been living separately for approximately five months prior to the hearing, plaintiff having custody of the child; respondent's home address was unknown although his place of employment was known [1] and his estimated wages were $1,000 per month; during the separation respondent provided no support or maintenance to plaintiff or the child with the exception of a small amount of clothing for the child; plaintiff leased or rented her residence individually; on November 13, 1980, and on numerous previous occasions, respondent (a 230 lbs., former Golden Gloves boxer) "intentionally, knowingly and wilfully beat petitioner ... causing ... serious physical injury ... requiring peti-

tioner to be hospitalized ..." for 12 days. The court concluded: respondent was a former adult household member whose actions constituted abuse; he had "purposely placed petitioner in apprehension of immediate physical injury; and thus plaintiff had "shown an unqualified right to the temporary relief available under §§ 455.035 and 455.045."

The court dismissed the petition because it held the Adult Abuse Act, in general and specifically §§ 455.035, .045 and .085, RSMo Supp.1980 unconstitutional, and thus unenforceable.

The Adult Abuse Act, S.B. 524, (codified at §§ 455.010 to 455.085, RSMo Supp.1980) was adopted by the Missouri Legislature on June 13, 1980, and became effective August 13, 1980. It was adopted by the Missouri Legislature as a result of an increased awareness nationally of the prevalence of domestic violence and of the need to protect the victims of that violence.[2] It is part of a nationwide trend to legislate in this area.[3] Existing remedies such as peace bonds, regular criminal process, and tort law have proved to be less than adequate in aiding the victims of abuse and in preventing further abuse.[4]

1. All attempts to notify respondent husband of this appeal have failed; communication by mail sent to him at his alleged place of employment has been returned.

2. *See*, e.g., Domestic Violence and Legislation with Respect to Domestic Violence: Hearings Before the Subcommittee on Child and Human Development, 95th Cong., 2d Sess. (1978) (hereinafter cited as Domestic Violence Hearings); D. Martin, Battered Wives (1976); M. Straus, R. Gelles & S. Steinmetz, Behind Closed Doors (1980); Buzawa & Buzawa, Legislative Responses to the Problem of Domestic Violence in Michigan, 25 Wayne L.Rev. 859 (1979); Freeman, Le Vice Anglais? Wife-Battering in English and American Law, 1⊮ Fam.L.Q. 199 (1977); Gayford, Wife-Battering: A Preliminary Survey of 100 Cases, 1 Brit.Med.J. 194 (1975); Gelles, Abused Wives: Why Do They Stay, 38 J. Marr. & Fam. 659 (1976); Taub, Ex Parte Proceedings in Domestic Violence Situations: Alternative Frameworks for Constitutional Scrutiny, 9 Hofstra L.Rev. 95 (1980); Comment, Spouse Abuse: A Novel Remedy for a Historic Problem, 84 Dick.L.Rev. 147 (1979); Comment, Wife Beating: Law and Society Confront the Castle Door, 15 Conz.L.Rev. 171

(1979); Note, The Battered Wife's Dilemma: To Kill or Be Killed, 32 Hastings L.J. 895 (1980).

3. *E.g.*, Alaska Stat. §§ 09.55.600–640 (Cum. Supp.1980); Haw.Rev.Stat. §§ 585–1 to –4 (Supp.1980); Ill.Ann.Stat. ch. 69, § 25 (Smith-Hurd Cum.Supp.1981–1982); Iowa § 236.1–11 (Cum.Supp.1980–1981); Mass.Ann.Laws ch. 209A, §§ 1–6 (Michie/Law Co-op 1981); Neb. Rev.Stat. §§ 42–901 to 927 (1943). The statutes vary greatly in their provisions; some are available only if a dissolution proceeding is pending, some make contempt the remedy for violation of an order, others make violation of an order a criminal offense. *See* Center for Women Policy Studies, State Legislation on Domestic Violence 415 (August/September 1980); *See, e.g.,* Cal.Penal Code § 273.6 (West Cum.Supp.1981).

4. *See* Comment, Wife Abuse: The Failure of Legal Remedies, 11 J.Mar.Prac. & Proc. 549 (1978). *See generally* articles cited note 3 *supra*. *See also State* v. *Errington*, 310 N.W.2d 681, 682 (Minn.1981); *Lucke* v. *Lucke*, 300 N.W.2d 231, 233 (N.D.1981); *Boyle* v. *Boyle*, No. M 475, slip op. at 4 (Ct.C.P.Allegheny

An adult who is abused by a present or former adult household member, may petition the circuit court for relief under the Act. Two types of relief are available: *ex parte* orders issued without notice to the respondent or a hearing, and orders issued after notice and an on record hearing. Violation of an *ex parte* order of protection of which the respondent has notice or of a full order of protection is declared to be a class C misdemeanor for which the respondent may be arrested without a warrant.

A.

[1] Jurisdiction of the mandamus action is in this Court because the validity of a Missouri statute is involved, and this is an original proceeding. Mo.Const. art. V, §§ 3, 4. Respondent husband has not filed a brief in the appeal[5] and has not participated in the mandamus action at any stage. This situation presents whether the parties are seeking an advisory opinion and, in particular, whether said parties have standing.[6] Constitutional questions normally are decided only when necessary to the disposition of the case presented. *State ex rel. Board of Mediation v. Pigg*, 362 Mo. 798, 244 S.W.2d 75 (banc 1951).

[2] Standing is related to the doctrine which prohibits advisory opinions because the latter requires the court to dispose of only those issues which affect the rights of the parties present. If a party's interests are unaffected by resolution of an issue he has no standing to raise it. *Id.* 244 S.W.2d at 79. Thus an opinion resolving an issue which the adversaries have no standing to raise is necessarily advisory.

[3] The trial court held that plaintiff had "an unqualified right to the ... relief available under the Act." This ruling confers upon the plaintiff standing to argue in support of the Act because from it she derives an actual and justiciable interest

County, Pa.), *reprinted in* 5 Fam.L.Rep. 2916, 2916–17 (1979).

5. Had the actions not been consolidated, the appeal would have been dismissed. Rule 84.08.

susceptible of protection. *In Interest of D.M.H.*, 516 S.W.2d 785, 787 (Mo.App.1974). *See In re Estate of Van Cleave*, 574 S.W.2d 375 (Mo. banc 1978).

[4–6] The question remains whether the trial court during an *ex parte* hearing may appropriately rule the Act unconstitutional *sua sponte.* Circuit Courts have the authority to declare an Act of the Legislature unconstitutional so long as the question has not been determined by this Court. *Stemme v. Siedhoff*, 427 S.W.2d 461 (Mo. 1968). In addition, this determination may be made *sua sponte.* Judges in this state are duty bound by oath to uphold the United States and Missouri Constitutions. In *Ex parte Smith*, 135 Mo. 223, 36 S.W. 628 (1896), this Court stated:

> [I]f it be true, as must be true, that an unconstitutional law *is no law*, then its constitutionality is open to attack at any stage of the proceedings and even after conviction and judgment, and this upon the ground that *no crime* is shown, and therefore the trial court had no jurisdiction because its criminal jurisdiction extends only to such matters as the *law* declares to be *criminal*; and if there is no law making such declaration, or, what is tantamount thereto, if that law is unconstitutional, then the court which tries a party for such an *assumed* offense, transcends its jurisdiction ....

Id. 36 S.W. at 630; *see, Kansas City v. Hammer*, 347 S.W.2d 865 (Mo.1961) and cases cited. To the extent that the trial court acting on its own held facially unconstitutional those sections entitling plaintiff to the relief sought, it was making a subject matter jurisdiction determination which the court may make *sua sponte* at any time. Rule 55.27(g)(3).

[7] The Court's rulings concerning § 455.085 RSMo Supp.1980, were not directly in issue and went beyond the relief which

6. Though neither party raises the issue of standing, it is within the notice of this Court because it is a jurisdictional matter antecedent to the right of relief. *See State ex rel. Schneider v. Stewart*, 575 S.W.2d 904, 909 (Mo.App. 1978).

plaintiff requested. These holdings, however, are also jurisdictional in so far as they are related to the facial unconstitutionality of the sections involved, because the entire chapter was held inseverable. Thus, if the sections specifically involved were constitutional, the facial unconstitutionality of § 455.085 RSMo Supp.1980 would void the entire Act. *See State ex rel. Board of Mediation v. Pigg*, 244 S.W.2d at 79.

[8] The absence of respondent husband in this case has not infringed upon the policies underlying the standing requirement. The briefs of plaintiff, defendant judge, and many *amicus curiae* [7] have adequately presented the controversy to the Court; and the case has not been created by parties not directly affected. *See Ryder v. County of St. Charles*, 552 S.W.2d 705, 707 (Mo. banc 1977). The Act is new and the state judiciary needs guidance because "[w]hether they do or do not enforce the statute they may be subject to a multiplicity of suits", and where public concern and interest in judicial economy are involved, this Court "may decide constitutional questions even *ex mero motu.*" *State ex rel. McMonigle v. Spears*, 358 Mo. 23, 26–27, 213 S.W.2d 210, 212 (banc 1948).

B.

This Act is presumptively constitutional:

It is a cardinal rule of statutory construction that where a statute is fairly susceptible of a construction in harmony with the Constitution, it must be given that construction by the courts and, unless that statute is clearly repugnant to the organic law, its constitutionality must be upheld.

Chamberlin v. Missouri Elections Commission, 540 S.W.2d 876, 879 (Mo. banc 1976). The United States Supreme Court in *Gregg v. Georgia*, 428 U.S. 153, 96 S.Ct. 2909, 49 L.Ed.2d 859 (1976), responding to a constitutional challenge to the Georgia death penalty statutes, stated that:

this language need not be construed in this way [in an unconstitutionally broad manner], and there is no reason to assume that the Supreme Court of Georgia will adopt such an open-ended construction.

Id. at 201, 96 S.Ct. at 2938.

The legislature is deemed to be aware of the inhibitions imposed by the constitution and therefore if statutory language is susceptible to two constructions, one constitutional and the other unconstitutional, it should be construed in a manner consistent with the provisions of the constitution.

Americans United v. Rogers, 538 S.W.2d 711, 723 (Mo. banc 1976) (Bardgett, J., concurring) *cert. denied*, 429 U.S. 1029, 97 S.Ct. 653, 50 L.Ed.2d 632 (1976). Indeed, this Court's construction of the Act becomes part of the statutory scheme as if it had been so amended by the Legislature. *See State v. Crawford*, 478 S.W.2d 314 (Mo. 1972); *cf. City of St. Joseph v. Hankinson*, 312 S.W.2d 4 (Mo.1958).

I.

[9] The trial court ruled that the Act violates Mo.Const. art. III, § 23, which provides that "[n]o bill shall contain more than one subject which shall be clearly expressed in its title ..." because it contains provisions relating to children, *i.e.*, custody and support, rather than relating exclusively to adults, and thus contains more than one subject. The title of Senate Bill 524 is "an Act relating to the abuse of adults by an adult household member, with penalty provisions." 1980 Mo. Laws 441. The test to determine if a title violates § 23 is whether "all of the provisions of the statute fairly relate to the same subject, have a natural connection therewith or are the incidents or the means to accomplish its purpose." *State ex rel. Jardon v. Industrial Development Authority*, 570 S.W.2d 666, 677 (Mo. banc 1978). The subject of the Act is adult

7. *Amicus curiae* include: The State Trial Judges Section of the Judicial Conference of Missouri; The Missouri Attorney General; Legal Services of Eastern Missouri, Inc.; The Missouri Peace Officers Association; Missouri Council of Churches; The Missouri Association for Social Welfare, et al.

abuse; the purpose of the Act is to protect household members by preventing further violence. The question is whether the child custody provisions fairly relate to the subject of adult abuse and promote the purpose of the Act.

[10] Studies have shown that the victim of adult abuse is usually a woman. *See* articles cited note 2, *supra.* In a large percentage of families, children have been present when the abuse occurred. In one study, fifty-four percent of the battered women interviewed reported that their husbands had committed acts of violence against their children as well as against them. Gayford, *supra,* note 2 at 196. Even if the child is not physically injured, he likely will suffer emotional trauma from witnessing violence between his parents. Abuse appears to be perpetuated through the generations; an individual who grows up in a home where violence occurs is more likely either to abuse others as an adult or to be a victim of abuse. *See* authorities cited note 2, *supra.* Adult abuse, therefore, is a problem affecting not only the adult members of a household but also the children. The most compelling reason for an abused woman to remain in the home subject to more abuse is her financial dependency; this is particularly true for the women with children. Gelles, *supra* note 2, at 660. The orders pertaining to child custody, support, and maintenance are all fairly related to and serve the purpose of aiding victims of domestic violence and preventing future incidents of adult abuse.

II.

The court held that §§ 455.035–.045 of the Act facially violate the due process guarantees of U.S.Const., amend. XIV and Mo.Const. art. I, § 10 by permitting a respondent to be deprived of constitutionally protected interests prior to notice or an adversary hearing. The trial court found the *ex parte* orders of protection constitutionally infirm because the Act, on its face, may be applied to exclude a respondent from his home or from contact with his children for a fifteen day period prior to notice or hearing. The trial judge concedes that the goal of the statute is legitimate and important, but nevertheless ruled it unconstitutional because of its impact on important personal rights. He reached this conclusion by finding: that the facts upon which an *ex parte* order may be issued are not easily verifiable and thus not appropriate for presentation by affidavit to the court, as required by *Mitchell v. W. T. Grant Co.,* 416 U.S. 600, 617–18, 94 S.Ct. 1895, 1905, 40 L.Ed.2d 406 (1974); and that there is no procedure by which the respondent can dissolve the *ex parte* orders. *Fuentes v. Shevin,* 407 U.S. 67, 86, 92 S.Ct. 1983, 1997, 32 L.Ed.2d 556 (1972).

Sections 455.020–.035, RSMo Supp.1980 set out the procedure for obtaining an *ex parte* order of protection. The person seeking an order of protection files a verified petition with the clerk of the circuit court or, if the court is unavailable, with "any available circuit or associate circuit judge in the city or county having jurisdiction . . . ." The judge may grant the *ex parte* orders only "for good cause shown" which is defined as "[a]n immediate and present danger of abuse to the petitioner." "Abuse" is defined as "inflicting, other than by accidental means, or attempting to inflict physical injury, on an adult or purposely placing another adult in apprehension of immediate physical injury." Section 455.-010(1), RSMo Supp.1980. Three orders may be issued *ex parte*: restraining the respondent from further acts of abuse; restraining the respondent from entering the family dwelling unit; and granting temporary custody of any minor children. The statute permits an order restraining the respondent from entering the family dwelling unit to issue in favor of a spouse who otherwise has no property interest in the home. An *ex parte* order of protection remains in effect until the hearing, which is to be held "[n]ot later than fifteen days after the filing of a petition . . . ." Sections 455.035–.045, RSMo Supp.1980.

[11, 12] The due process guarantee is intended to protect an individual against arbitrary acts of the government. *Wolff v.*

McDonnell, 418 U.S. 539, 558, 94 S.Ct. 2963, 2976, 41 L.Ed.2d 935 (1974) (citing *Dent v. West Virginia,* 129 U.S. 114, 123, 9 S.Ct. 231, 233, 32 L.Ed. 623 (1889)). Furthermore, it protects the right to use and enjoy one's property without governmental interference. *Fuentes v. Shevin,* 407 U.S. at 81,⁻ 92 S.Ct. at 1994. Before the guarantee of due process comes into play, however, there must be a deprivation by the government of a constitutionally protected interest. *Mathews v. Eldridge,* 424 U.S. 319, 332, 96 S.Ct. 893, 901, 47 L.Ed.2d 18 (1976). The interests which are subject to temporary deprivation through the issuance of an *ex parte* order constitute significant liberty and property interests falling "within the purview of the Due Process Clause." [8] *See Fuentes v. Shevin,* 407 U.S. at 90, 92 S.Ct. at 1999; *Lassiter v. Department of Social Services,* 452 U.S. 18, 101 S.Ct. 2153, 2160, 68 L.Ed.2d 640 (1981); *Little v. Streater* 452 U.S. 1, 101 S.Ct. 2202, 2209, 68 L.Ed.2d 627 (1981); *Stanley v. Illinois,* 405 U.S. 645, 651, 92 S.Ct. 1208, 1212, 31 L.Ed.2d 551 (1972). Thus the procedures available under the Act must meet the constitutional standard.

[13] Notice and an opportunity to be heard must be provided by the state in a meaningful manner prior to deprivation of a protected interest. *Fuentes v. Shevin,* 407 U.S. at 80, 92 S.Ct. at 1994; *Boddie v. Connecticut,* 401 U.S. 371, 377, 91 S.Ct. 780, 785, 28 L.Ed.2d 113 (1971). This rule is not necessarily applied when there is only a temporary taking, as is the case here. Due process is a flexible concept, *Goss v. Lopez,* 419 U.S.⸗ 565, 578, 95 S.Ct. 729, 738, 42 L.Ed.2d 725 (1975); the same procedures need not be applied in all instances. The extent and nature of procedures depends upon weighing of the private interests affected and the governmental functions involved. *Arnett v. Kennedy,* 416 U.S. 134,

167–68, 94 S.Ct. 1633, 1650–1651, 40 L.Ed.2d 15 (1974). The United States Supreme Court in *Mathews v. Eldridge, supra,* identified a third factor to be considered in the balancing formula; the risk of erroneous deprivation using the existing procedures. *See Lassiter v. Department of Social Services,* 101 S.Ct. at 2159 (Stewart, J.), 2165 (Blackmun, J., dissenting) (*Mathews v. Eldridge, supra,* balancing test used in analysis of North Carolina's termination of parental rights statute).

The first factor is the private interest affected. The respondent has two private interests at stake; a property interest in one's home and a liberty interest in custody of one's children. These interests are significant, the importance of which has been emphasized by the United States Supreme Court. *See cases, supra.*

The second factor in the balancing formula is the governmental interest. *Mathews v. Eldridge,* 424 U.S. at 347, 96 S.Ct. at 908, The Adult Abuse Act is an exercise of the state's police power. Through the procedures established to aid victims of domestic violence, the legislature promotes the general health, welfare, and safety of its citizens. The magnitude of the problem of domestic violence is evidenced by statistics compiled by the FBI in 1978 which indicate that one-fourth of all homicides in the United States occur within the family.[9] The petitioner's interests which are protected by the state in furthering its interests are the same as those of the respondent. The parties, irrespective of marital status, may own or rent the dwelling jointly, although under the Act this is not required. If it becomes unsafe for both parties to remain in the home, one may need to be excluded. The choice is reduced to the victim of the abuse leaving or the court ordering the abuser to leave. Parents may have an equal interest

---

8. Defendant contends that two interests are involved; in his home and in custody of the children. In some cases there may be a third protected interest—the liberty interest of a respondent in his reputation. *See* Taub, *supra* note 2, at 104–06. Any one of these interests

may be sufficient to warrant procedural safeguards required by the Due Process Clause.

9. Domestic Violence Hearings, *supra* note 2, at 2 (statement of Steve Y'Barra). *See generally* authorities cited in note 2, *supra.*

in maintaining custody of their children.[10] Both interests are important and have been accorded deference by the courts.

[14] The Missouri Legislature has established a mechanism whereby the state can intervene when abuse of one adult by another household member occurs or is threatened and thus prevent further violence. State legislatures have broad power to enact laws to protect the general health, welfare, and safety. *Day-Brite Lighting, Inc. v. Missouri*, 342 U.S. 421, 423–24, 72 S.Ct. 405, 407–408, 96 L.Ed. 469 (1952). States also have been given deference in adopting reasonable summary procedures when acting under their police power. *Mackey v. Montrym*, 443 U.S. 1, 17, 99 S.Ct. 2612, 2620, 61 L.Ed.2d 321 (1979).

The third factor in the test in *Mathews v. Eldridge, supra* is "the fairness and reliability of the existing pretermination procedures, and the probable value, if any, of additional procedural safeguards." *Id.* 424 U.S. at 343, 96 S.Ct. at 907. "The risk of wrongful use of the procedure must also be judged in the context of the issues which are to be determined at that proceeding." *Mitchell v. W. T. Grant Co.*, 416 U.S. at 617, 94 S.Ct. at 1905.

An *ex parte* order of protection is analogous to a temporary restraining order because both are injunctions issued prior to notice or hearing. *See* § 455.045.1, 2, RSMo Supp.1980; *Perseverance Common School District No. 90 v. Honey*, 367 S.W.2d 243, 247 (Mo.App.1963). *Ex parte* orders restraining acts of abuse or entrance into the dwelling are issued upon a showing of "an immediate and present danger of abuse to the petitioner." Section 455.035, RSMo Supp.1980. As in a proceeding to obtain any other restraining order, the petitioner must satisfy the court that grounds exist to justify granting this order.[11] This will, in most instances, require the petitioner to appear personally before the court at which time the credibility of the petitioner can be tested.[12] In addition, the judge may be able to see first hand "the evidence of violence manifested in burns, cuts, bruises, and fractures." *Boyle v. Boyle, supra* note 4, slip op. at 7. *See United States v. Freeman*, 160 F.Supp. 532, 534 (D.D.C.1957), aff'd, 254 F.2d 352 (D.C.Cir.1958); *Ockel v. Riley*, 541 S.W.2d 535, 540 (Mo. banc 1976). If the petitioner is unable to appear because of injuries, this may be alleged and proof thereof will allow the court to determine that there is "[a]n immediate and present danger of abuse."

A protection order, if granted, remains in effect until the hearing which is to be held "[n]ot later than fifteen days after the filing of a petition." Section 455.040.1, RSMo Supp. 1980. This sets a maximum period that the order could be effective without some hearing. Nothing in the statute suggests that the respondent could not obtain an earlier hearing. Concerning other restraining orders, Rule 92.02(b) provides that a party against whom a temporary restraining order has been issued may, upon two days' (or shorter time if the court so prescribes) notice to the opposing party, receive a hearing on the order. This rule is equally applicable to orders issued under the Act. The statute requires that the petition, notice of the hearing date, and any *ex parte* order of protection be served upon the respondent. Section 455.040.2, RSMo Supp. 1980. The court at the same time may include in the notice information regarding the respondent's right to request an earlier hearing and the procedure to be followed.

10. This differs from those cases where the state is attempting to remove children from the custody of the natural parent, *see, e.g., Stanley v. Illinois*, 405 U.S. 645, 92 S.Ct. 1208, 31 L.Ed.2d 551 (1972), and vest custody in the court. Here, one parent retains custody.

11. The determination made by the court in adult abuse cases is also analogous to a probable cause determination for issuance of a warrant "on oath or affirmation of the complain-

ant." Rule 21.04. *See* Rule 21.05. The forms issued by this Court for seeking relief under the Act similarly require verification and as such are affidavits of facts upon which the Court may act. Sections 455.020, 455.025, RSMo. *See also* Order, Supreme Court of Missouri, en banc, August 8, 1980.

12. Judge Marsh, in this case, conducted an *ex parte* hearing on Mrs. William's petition.

The Supreme Court in *Fuentes v. Shevin, supra,* outlined categories of cases where outright seizures have been allowed. 407 U.S. at 91, 92 S.Ct. at 2000. The first is where seizure has been directly necessary to secure an important governmental or general public interest; the second is where there has been a special need for prompt action; the third is where the state has kept strict control over its monopoly of legitimate force: there is a government official responsible for determining that seizure was necessary under standards set out in "narrowly drawn statutes." *Id.* at 91, 92 S.Ct. at 2000.

[15] The Act meets the foregoing standards. The Act is directly necessary to secure important governmental interests, *i.e.,* protection of victims of abuse and prevention of further abuse. The situation where the challenged Act is to be applied are those where prompt action is necessary, *i.e.,* when there is "[a]n immediate and present danger of abuse"—the only time the *ex parte* order may be issued. The government has kept strict control over its powers. Only a judge in his discretion, may issue the *ex parte* orders. This differs from the procedure where "[p]rivate parties, serving their own private advantage, may unilaterally invoke state power to replevy goods from another" disapproved in *Fuentes v. Shevin, supra* at 93, 92 S.Ct. at 2001. Under the Adult Abuse Act, the petitioner requests the court to act on his or her behalf. The court, not the clerk, must issue the order and the orders are not to be issued routinely but only after the petitioner has filed a verified petition showing good cause.

The burden is on the challenger to show that this exercise of the state's police power is unreasonable, *Caesar's Health Club v. St. Louis County,* 565 S.W.2d 783, 786 (Mo.App. 1978), *cert. denied,* 439 U.S. 955, 99 S.Ct. 353, 58 L.Ed.2d 346 (1978), a burden not here carried. The interests and procedures considered, these *ex parte* order provisions comply with due process requirements because they are a reasonable means to achieve the state's legitimate goal of pre-

venting domestic violence, and afford adequate procedural safeguards, prior to and after any deprivation occurs.

III.

[16] The court found that the Act is unconstitutional because it authorizes imprisonment for debt in violation of Mo. Const. art. I, § 11 by making criminal failure to pay support orders. The statute makes criminal violation of the *ex parte* order of protection, § 455.045, RSMo 1980 Supp., of which the respondent has notice, and violation of a full order of protection. Sections 455.050.1, 455.085, RSMo 1980 Supp. The statute sets forth no punishment for violation of ancillary orders dealing with child support, maintenance, or attorney's fees. Sections 455.050.2–7, 455.075, RSMo Supp.1980. Therefore, there can be no imprisonment for debt and the Act does not violate Mo.Const. art. I, § 11.

IV.

The trial court held the Act void for vagueness because it fails to give adequate warning as to what conduct is proscribed and thus violates U.S.Const. amend. XIV and Mo.Const., art. I, § 10. Defendant argues that § 455.085, RSMo Supp.1980 is impermissibly vague because "one cannot know what conduct is prohibited by reading §§ 455.045 and 455.050, RSMo Supp.1980, for they provide for the delineation of the prohibited conduct by the Judge." The trial court cites *United States v. National Dairy Product Corp.,* 872 U.S. 29, 83 S.Ct. 594, 9 L.Ed.2d 561 (1963), where the Supreme Court held that a criminal statute "must be sufficiently focused to warn of both its reach and coverage." *Id.* at 33, 83 S.Ct. at 598. The trial court also cites *Grayned v. City of Rockford,* 408 U.S. 104, 92 S.Ct. 2294, 33 L.Ed.2d 222 (1971), to assert that the Act is vague because it "impermissibly delegates basic policy matters to ... judges" *Id.* at 108, 92 S.Ct. at 2299. Defendant has improperly mixed the vagueness prohibition with his attack on the Act as an impermissible delegation of legislative power in violation of Mo.Const.

art. II, § 1 and art. III, § 1 (addressed separately below). One vice of vagueness, as a complete lack of clarity in statutory language, is that the authority charged with its enforcement may "read into" the law whatever suits its purpose resulting in arbitrary application. The converse is not true; statutory language is not vague simply because it permits an authority to make a decision.

[17] Vagueness, as a due process violation, takes two forms. One is the lack of notice given a potential offender because the statute is so unclear that "men of common intelligence must necessarily guess at its meaning." *Connally v. General Construction Co.,* 269 U.S. 385, 391, 46 S.Ct. 126, 127, 70 L.Ed.322 (1926); *see Broadrick v. Oklahoma,* 413 U.S. 601, 93 S.Ct. 2908, 37 L.Ed.2d 830 (1973). The other is that the statute fails to set out "explicit standards" for those who must apply it, resulting in arbitrary and discriminatory application. *Grayned v. City of Rockford,* 408 U.S. at 108, 92 S.Ct. at 2299.

As to the former, "[i]f terms or words used in the statute are of common usage and are understandable by persons of ordinary intelligence, they satisfy the constitutional requirements as to definiteness and certainty." *Prokopf v. Whaley,* 592 S.W.2d 819, 824 (Mo. banc 1980); *State v. Williams,* 473 S.W.2d 382 (Mo.1971).

Section 455.085.3, RSMo Supp.1980 states:

> Violation of the terms and conditions of an *ex parte* order of protection, of which the respondent has notice, shall be a class C misdemeanor. Violation of the terms and conditions of a full order of protection shall be a class C misdemeanor.

Under this section violation of an *ex parte* order is a misdemeanor only if "respondent has notice." This section provides the individual subject to an *ex parte* order an absolute right to be personally served with notice expressly stating what conduct on his or her part is criminal. *See also* § 455.-040.2, RSMo Supp.1980. A full protection order may be issued only after a hearing on record, and notice and an opportunity to be

heard is given to the respondent. Sections 455.010(5) and 455.040, subd. 2, RSMo Supp. 1980 require personal service of the full order of protection. There are only two (full protection) or three (*ex parte*) limited orders which may be issued against respondent. For example, an *ex parte* order may state that respondent (named) shall not abuse, threaten to abuse, molest, disturb the peace of the petitioner (named), enter the dwelling unit (house, apartment) of the petitioner, or interfere with petitioners custody of children (named). From the face of these sections it is clear that contravention of the specific orders which are limited in number and of which the respondent is personally informed is a violation of § 455.-085.3, RSMo Supp.1980.

It is further determined that to insure that the respondent has knowledge, the notice served upon him should expressly include a statement informing him that a violation of the order is a class C misdemeanor and stating the maximum penalty associated therewith. This is required by the clear intent expressed by the legislature in §§ 455.010(4), (5), 455.040.1, 2 and 455.085, RSMo Supp.1980, that respondent be informed by complete notification. *See again* Order, Supreme Court, August 8, 1980.

[18] The Act provides sufficient direction and guidance for the judges who must apply it. The protection orders are to issue only when an "immediate and present danger of abuse to the petitioner" is found. Section 455.035, RSMo Supp.1980. Abuse is further defined as "inflicting, other than by accidental means, or attempting to inflict physical injury, on an adult or purposely placing another adult in apprehension of immediate physical injury." Section 455.-010(1), RSMo Supp.1980. "On a challenge to a statute or ordinance as being unconstitutionally vague ... the language is to be treated by applying it to the facts at hand." *Prokopf v. Whaley,* 592 S.W.2d at 824. The trial court expressly found that the evidence was "overwhelming and abundantly clear that petitioner has shown all of the elements required by Chapter 455 that

would otherwise (if not for the constitutional issues) entitle her to the relief she seeks" and that petitioner had shown "an unqualified right to the temporary relief." This demonstrates that no arbitrary or discriminatory application is presently or potentially in issue. The trial court was fully aware of the standards for granting relief and how to apply the Act.

V.

The trial court also found the Act violates the requirements of separation and non-delegation of power under art. II, § 1 and art. III, § 1, Mo.Const. because it vests the judiciary with the legislative power to declare what conduct constitutes a crime.

Article II, § 1, Mo.Const. provides:

The powers of government shall be divided into three distinct departments—the legislative, executive, and judicial—each of which shall be confided to a separate magistracy, and no person, or collection of persons, charged with the exercise of powers properly belonging to one of those departments, shall exercise any power properly belonging to either of the others, except in the instances in this constitution expressly directed or permitted.

Article III, § 1, Mo.Const. provides:

The legislative power shall be vested in a senate and house of representatives to be styled "The General Assembly of the State of Missouri."

It is argued that although § 455.045 and § 455.050, RSMo Supp. 1980 specify certain acts which may be prohibited, the use of "may include" [13] makes the sections open-ended, thus permitting the court to include any other terms or conditions it wishes, the violation of which is criminal. This, it is asserted, permits the court to perform the legislative functions of defining what conduct constitutes a crime. If the judiciary were given the general power to randomly select and define action(s) as criminal, guided only by the "shall be to protect the petitioner" language, it would violate the

Missouri constitution. *See State v. Raccagno*, 530 S.W.2d 699, 708 (Mo.1975). For this reason, defendant's interpretation of "may" must be avoided if a constitutional interpretation is available. *Chamberlin v. Missouri Elections Commission*, 540 S.W.2d 876 (Mo. banc 1976).

In *Rhodes v. Bell*, 230 Mo. 138, 130 S.W. 465 (Mo.1910), this Court recognized that "the Legislature has confided to other branches the performance of duties which in a particular sense might be denominated legislative, which no one has ever thought or contended violated the great principle of independence between the separate departments of government." *Id.* 130 S.W. at 468. The modern tendency of the courts is toward greater liberality in permitting grants of discretion to administrative officials in order to facilitate the administration of law as the complexity of government and economic conditions increases. *Milgram Food Stores, Inc. v. Ketchum*, 384 S.W.2d 510 (Mo.1964). The statutory vesting of some regulatory discretion has been permitted where it "relates to the administration of a police regulation and is necessary to protect the public morals, health, safety and general welfare; or where personal fitness is a factor . . . ." *Id.* at 514, quoting *Ex parte Williams*, 345 Mo. 1121, 139 S.W.2d 485, 490 (1940). These principles are equally true with respect to legislative grants of authority to the judiciary, to the extent necessary for the implementation of legitimate legislative goals. This trend is not to be interpreted as exemplifying judicial indifference to these constitutional prohibitions; rather it is the recognition that the boundaries which separate the powers and functions of the governmental branches are difficult to point out and that in some areas they may overlap. *Rhodes v. Bell, supra.* This Court has found unconstitutional delegations of power: *See, e.g., State v. Raccagno*, supra; *Automobile Club of Missouri v. City of St. Louis*, 334 S.W.2d 355 (Mo.1960). It has also ruled constitutional legislation which

13. Section 455.045 and 455.050, RSMo Supp. 1980, state that the protective order "shall be to protect the petitioner from abuse and may

include:" (the section continues with a list of specific orders).

empowers courts, officials, commissions or boards to make determination or promulgate rules pursuant to general statutory directives. *See, e.g., State ex rel. Fire Dist. of Lemay v. Smith*, 353 Mo. 807, 184 S.W.2d 593 (banc 1945); *State v. Dixon*, 335 Mo. 478, 73 S.W.2d 385 (banc 1934); *Ketring v. Sturges*, 372 S.W.2d 104 (Mo.1963); *City of St. Joseph v. Hankinson*, 312 S.W.2d 4 (Mo. 1958); *State ex inf. Wallach v. Loesch*, 350 Mo. 989, 169 S.W.2d 675 (1943). *Rhodes v. Bell, supra.*

[19] The duty and power to define crimes and ordain punishment is exclusively vested in the Legislature. *State v. Raccagno*, 530 S.W.2d at 703. In *State v. Raccagno, supra*, a statute delegated to the Director of Revenue the power "to promulgate reasonable and necessary regulations and make the *violation* of a *regulation* the criminal offense." *Id.* at 702. The statute was held unconstitutional because it "delegated the power to the director of revenue to say whether or not the failure to pay the tax authorized ... would be criminally punishable." *Id.* Unlike the present case, the nonlegislative authority was there empowered to decide "whether or not a violation of any specific provision of the law would constitute a criminal offense ...." *Id.* at 703.

[20] Although under the Adult Abuse Act no misdemeanor can occur until a protection order is issued, this is not analogous to defining a crime. Under § 455.085, RSMo Supp. 1980, violation of the terms of either an *ex parte* or full order of protection is a misdemeanor. In § 455.045, RSMo Supp. 1980 three specific orders are delineated and in § 455.050, RSMo Supp.1980 there are two. In these sections the words "may include" indicate that the judge has the limited discretion to include all or less than all of the two or three restraining orders expressly available. Contrary to defendant's contention the discretion applies to the number and not the terms of an order(s). Section 455.035, RSMo Supp.1980 specifically governs when these orders may issue. Under these sections, the court makes the limited determination whether a

situation warrants issuance of any or all of the orders which the legislature previously defined as criminal.

If the legislature prescribes conditions necessary for an annexation, it may delegate to the courts the power to determine whether those conditions exist and such is a proper judicial function. *City of St. Joseph v. Hankinson*, 312 S.W.2d at 8. If drug regulation statutes specifically limit the Division of Health authority to identifying and listing of drugs, which fall within a statutory definition, the possession of which is criminal, no unconstitutional delegation occurs. *State v. Bridges*, 398 S.W.2d 1 (Mo. banc 1966). The present case is analogous. Under this Act the court is only authorized to determine whether a legislatively defined right to relief exists. The power exercised by the judiciary under the Act is judicial in nature. The power to issue a restraining order is solely judicial. *Cf.* Rule 92. The determination of whether a litigant is entitled to relief under a statute is also a judicial function. The legislative function of designating a crime was performed by the Legislature when Chapter 455 was enacted.

VI.

The trial court held that § 455.085, RSMo Supp. 1980 authorizes warrantless arrest under conditions which violate the Fourth Amendment of the United States Constitution, made applicable to the states through the Fourteenth Amendment, *Mapp v. Ohio*, 367 U.S. 643, 81 S.Ct. 1684, 6 L.Ed.2d 1081 (1961), and by art. I, § 15 of the Missouri Constitution. It is contended that this section permits an arrest in the arrestee's home without a warrant, consensual entry, or exigent circumstances, and is thus void "on its face", citing *Payton v. New York*, 445 U.S. 573, 100 S.Ct. 1371, 63 L.Ed.2d 639 (1980).

In *Sibron v. New York*, 392 U.S. 40, 88 S.Ct. 1889, 20 L.Ed.2d 917 (1968), the United States Supreme Court refused to engage in "the abstract and unproductive exercise of laying the extraordinarily elastic categories of [a statute permitting "stop and frisks"] next to the categories of the Fourth Amendment in an effort to determine whether the two are in some sense compatable, [because] [t]he constitutional validity of a warrantless search is pre-eminently the sort of question which can only be decided in the concrete factual context of the individual case. In this respect it is quite different from the question of the adequacy of the procedural safeguards written into a statute which purports to authorize the issuance of search warrants in certain circumstances. *See Berger v. New York,* 388 U.S. 41 [87 S.Ct. 1873, 18 L.Ed.2d 1040] (1967)." *Id.* at 59, 88 S.Ct. at 1901. The statute in *Sibron v. New York, supra,* is similar to § 445.085, RSMo Supp. 1980 in that both generally authorize activities which may or may not be offensive to the Fourth Amendment. With the purpose of settling questions regarding the facial validity of the Act, this contention is addressed with the admonition that official actions violate the Fourth Amendment and not general authorization statutes such as the one examined in *Sibron v. New York, supra.*

[21] Section 455.085.1, RSMo Supp. 1980 authorizes warrantless arrest where probable cause exists to believe that a violation of a protection order has occurred. Generally, warrantless arrests upon probable cause for felonies or misdemeanors may constitutionally be authorized by statute. *United States v. Watson,* 423 U.S. 411, 417, 96 S.Ct. 820, 824, 46 L.Ed.2d 598 (1976), and cases cited therein; *State v. Wiley,* 522 S.W.2d 281 (Mo. banc 1975); *State v. Vollmar,* 389 S.W.2d 20 (Mo.1965); *State v. Cantrell,* 310 S.W.2d 866 (Mo.1958); § 544.215, RSMo 1978. However, a warrantless arrest in the arrestee's home is impermissible absent consent to enter or exigent circumstances. *Payton v. New York,* 445 U.S. at 590, 100 S.Ct. at 1382. It is the warrantless in-home seizure which defendant argues is impermissibly authorized by § 455.085.1, RSMo Supp. 1980. Section 455.085.2 states:

> The same procedures, including those designed to protect constitutional rights, shall be applied to the respondent as those applied to any individual detained in police custody.

Procedurally it is required that when an in-home arrest occurs either a warrant or consent to enter the house be obtained or that exigent circumstances exist. These procedures are "designed to protect constitutional rights" and are to "be applied to the respondent", § 455.085.2, RSMo Supp. 1980.

[22] This section does not authorize unconstitutional arrests; and if such an arrest were to occur under the guise of the Act then the respondent would be entitled to the same remedy as "any individual detained in police custody." *Id.*

C.

The presumptive constitutionality of the Adult Abuse Act is not overcome by any of the attacks presented.

Accordingly, the judgment dismissing the petition in No. 62762 is reversed and the cause is remanded for further proceedings; the preliminary writ of mandamus in No. 62765 is made peremptory.

DONNELLY, C. J., and RENDLEN and MORGAN, JJ., concur.

BARDGETT, J., concurs in part in separate concurring opinion filed.

SEILER, J., concurs in separate concurring opinion of BARDGETT, J.

WELLIVER, J., dissents in separate dissenting opinion filed.

BARDGETT, Judge, concurring in part.

I concur in the result reached and in the principal opinion except for that portion upholding the constitutionality of § 455.-085.3 which makes the violation of an order of protection a crime—a class C misdemeanor.

This is not a criminal case and the question whether the misdemeanor conviction of one for violation of a protective order could be constitutionally upheld ought, in my opinion, await that kind of case. My reservations about this matter flow from the fact that the conduct of a spouse does not become a crime unless and until the judge so declares and then only with respect to that one person. This *law* does not prohibit certain conduct as criminal generally but rather leaves it to a judge to decide whether certain conduct, if engaged in in the future, will be criminal only as to a particular person. Certain acts of an abusive type are criminal by general law—assault and battery—and are a crime regardless of who commits them, but that is not the case under § 455.085.3. I have no particular difficulty with contempt proceedings which may involve incarceration for the violation of an injunctive order—an order of protection—but that is not a crime.

The statute does not make the act of entering one's home a crime. The only time that act becomes a criminal act is when, and if, a judge declares it to be criminal by prohibiting it in a protective order with respect to a particular person. Thus, § 455.085.3 delegates to a judge the power to say what conduct constitutes a crime and whether or not certain conduct, if engaged in by a particular person, will be a crime. The drug cases are not analogous. In those cases the *administrative agency* identified the drug which produced the statutorily proscribed effects and the possession of that drug was then prohibited *generally* as to all people. Neither the agency nor a judge decided that possession of the drug by a particular *person* would be a crime, but that possession of the drug by others would not be a crime.

I believe it highly questionable whether a crime can, under our Constitution, be so personalized; nevertheless, the issue of the constitutionality of § 455.085.3 is unnecessary to the adjudication of this case. I therefore reserve judgment on that matter until the case occurs in which that issue is decisive. I concur in all other aspects of the principal opinion.

WELLIVER, Judge, dissenting.

I respectfully dissent. I believe that the circuit judges, who prior to the principal

opinion have held the Adult Abuse Act to be unconstitutional, are in a far better position to perceive the invasions of personal rights flowing from the application of this act than we who sit in these halls.

When we permit child custody, support and maintenance provisions, usually found in Chapter 452, to be hidden behind the newly created term which we now denominate as "Adult Abuse", when we permit the orders contemplated by the act to be entered without notice or hearing, and, when we permit circuit judges to define the elements of crime on a case by case basis without notice or hearing, then we by judicial interpretation have rendered a nullity: (1) the long established rule of statutory construction that penal statutes must be strictly construed against the state, (2) the constituional prohibition, Mo.Const. art. III, § 23, that "[n]o bill shall contain more than one subject which shall be clearly expressed in its title . . . ," and (3) due process of law, U.S.Const.Amend. XIV, Mo.Const. art. I, § 10.

The Adult Abuse Act exhibits the fullest potential for creating nine new evils for every evil it would seek by its terms to correct.

131 Ill.App.3d 1018
87 Ill.Dec. 40

**PEOPLE of the State of Illinois,
Plaintiff-Appellee,**

v.

**Leland BLACKWOOD,
Defendant-Appellant.**

No. 3–84–0295.

Appellate Court of Illinois,
Third District.

March 15, 1985.

Rehearing Denied May 1, 1985.

Defendant was convicted in the Circuit Court, Rock Island County, Dennis DePorter, P.J., of misdemeanor violation of an order of protection issued under Domestic Violence Act, and defendant appealed. The Appellate Court, Heiple, P.J., held that: (1) defendant could raise challenge to adequacy of complaint for the first time on appeal; (2) complaint was adequate; (3) complaint was not required to allege specific mental state; and (4) Domestic Violence Act was not unconstitutionally vague or overbroad.

Affirmed.

1. Criminal Law ⇐1032(5)
Complaint which does not charge an offense can be challenged for first time on appeal.

2. Criminal Law ⇐1043(1)
Complaint could be challenged on appeal, although challenge in trial court was not in proper form, where court passed upon the merits.

3. Breach of the Peace ⇐16
Complaint alleging violation of Domestic Violence Act sufficiently informed defendant of specific acts for which conviction against him was sought by stating acts which allegedly violated protective order. S.H.A. ch. 38, ¶ 111–3(a)(3); ch. 40, ¶¶ 2302–8(c)(1), 2302–12(a).

4. Indictment and Information ⇐88
When a particular mental state is not part of definition of offense, it is possible that charging instrument need not allege specific mental state, such as when crime charged is such that it is virtually impossible for person to commit and not have guilty mind or when mental state is implicit from specific allegation of defendant's act as set forth in charging instrument. S.H.A. ch. 38, ¶ 111–3(a)(3).

5. Breach of the Peace ⇐16
Complaint was not required to allege that defendant violated protective order under Domestic Violence Act with specific mental state since terms used implied that protagonist knowingly caused victim to suffer undue distress where defendant was charged with threatening and harassing ex-wife. S.H.A. ch. 38, ¶ 111–3(a)(3); ch. 40, ¶¶ 2302–8(c)(1), 2302–12(a).

6. Criminal Law ⇐1030(2)
Challenge to statute alleging vagueness and overbreadth could be brought for the first time on appeal since specific evidence or factual inquiry would add nothing to record which would facilitate proper resolution of issues raised and dealt with by reference to judicial standards.

7. Criminal Law ⇐13.1(1)
Statute is void for vagueness when it fails to adequately give notice as to what action or conduct is proscribed; failure to give adequate notice occurs when person of reasonable intelligence must necessarily guess at meaning of statute.

8. Breach of the Peace ⇐16
Domestic Violence Act was not unconstitutionally vague, although terms employed were vague to a certain extent, where certain measure of generality must

be tolerated to give effect to intended scope of Act and "guesswork" engendered by breadth of language was not excessive. S.H.A. ch. 40, ¶ 2301–1 et seq.

9. Breach of the Peace ⚖️16
Constitutional Law ⚖️90.1(1)

Domestic Violence Act was not impermissibly overbroad, it could not be reasonably interpreted to prohibit constitutionally protected conduct, although it proscribed individual from threatening or harassing his ex-wife, as the only speech for which individual could reasonably be punished under Act was form of expression which would not be subject to constitutional protection. S.H.A. ch. 40, ¶ 2301–1 et seq.; U.S.C.A. Const.Amend. 1.

10. Constitutional Law ⚖️90(1)

Statute is unconstitutionally overbroad when reasonable interpretation might infringe upon protected expression. U.S.C.A. Const.Amend. 1.

Thomas A. Lilien, Asst. State Appellate Defender, Robert Agostinelli, Deputy State Appellate Defender, Ottawa, for defendant-appellant.

James T. Teros, State's Atty., Rock Island, Gary F. Gnidovec, John X. Breslin, State's Attorneys Appellate Service Com'n, Ottawa, for plaintiff-appellee.

HEIPLE, Presiding Justice:

Defendant, Leland Blackwood, was convicted of the Class A misdemeanor of violating an order of protection (Ill.Rev.Stat. 1983, ch. 40, par. 2302–12(a)). On appeal, defendant challenges the sufficiency of the complaint charging the offense of which he was convicted. He also challenges the constitutionality of the criminal provisions of the Domestic Violence Act (Ill.Rev.Stat. 1983, ch. 40, par. 2302–8(c)(1), 2302–12(a)). We affirm.

On June 20, 1983, the circuit court of Rock Island County entered an order of protection on behalf of Barbara Blackwood, defendant's ex-wife. The order directed defendant to refrain from "striking, threat-ening, harassing or interfering with the personal liberty in any fashion" of Barbara.

On February 10, 1984, Barbara filed a criminal complaint against defendant. The complaint alleged the entry of the order of protection and the terms thereof. The complaint further alleged that defendant had threatened and verbally harassed her.

On March 26, 1984, the cause was called for bench trial. Defendant made an oral motion to dismiss the complaint for failure to state an offense and lack of particularity to allow the defense to proceed. The court denied the motion for lack of a writing, untimeliness and because the complaint was sufficient to inform the defendant of the charge. The prosecution was then allowed to amend the complaint to add specific details for the benefit of the defense. The amended complaint set forth the time and place of the alleged violations as well as a recitation of the words constituting the threats and harassment. To wit:

"' * * * Leland Blackwood started cʰ··· ing Barbara Blackwood and yelled tʰ· Barbara Blackwood that she was a 'f...ing whore,' a dead bitch and that he had a plot waiting for her, and Leland Blackwood further stated to Barbara Blackwood that 'it's not over and he would get his chance.' '"

At trial, Barbara testified essentially in accordance with the allegations of the amended complaint. Defendant denied the occurrence of the encounter. No other witnesses were called. Defendant was then convicted as charged.

[1, 2] Defendant argues that the complaint violated section 111–3(a)(3) of the Criminal Code (Ill.Rev.Stat.1981, ch. 38, par. 111–3(a)(3)) in that no mental state was alleged. He further contends that the original complaint lacked sufficient specificity to state an offense.

Before addressing the merits of defendant's arguments, we must first dispose of the State's contention that the procedural grounds cited by the trial court for the denial of the motion to dismiss should foreclose review on the merits. It is uncontroverted that the defendant challenged the sufficiency of the complaint in the trial court. While the challenge was not proper in form, the court passed upon the merits. Moreover, a complaint which does not charge an offense can be challenged for the first time on appeal. (*People v. Pujoue* (1979), 61 Ill.2d 335, 335 N.E.2d 437.) Thus, defendant's challenge to the complaint is reviewable on the merits.

[3] At the outset we reject any contention that the charge lacked specificity or was deficient in failing to state the "means used" in violating the protective order. The motion to amend the complaint was granted. The record reveals no objection to the motion or a request for a continuance to prepare to meet the specifics alleged in the amended complaint. The purported deficiencies in the original complaint were not incurable as in cases such as *People v. Allen* (1972), 8 Ill.App.3d 176, 289 N.E.2d 467 (failure to allege a cognizable offense) or *People v. Johnson* (1979), 69 Ill.App.3d 248, 25 Ill.Dec. 732, 387 N.E.2d 388 (failure to charge that a revolver was loaded in a prosecution for unlawful use of weapons). Furthermore, the complaint as amended satisfied due process and double jeopardy considerations by informing defendant of the specific acts for which a conviction against him was sought. In so holding, we decline to reach the question of whether a complaint which merely tracks the language of the order of protection sufficiently particularizes the offense to notify the accused of the charges against him. (*People v. Grieco* (1970), 44 Ill.2d 407, 255 N.E.2d 897.) Accordingly, the only issue remaining relative to the sufficiency of the complaint is the necessity of alleging a mental state.

Except in the case of an absolute liability offense, a person is not guilty of an offense unless he acts with either intent, knowledge, recklessness or negligence (Ill.Rev. Stat.1981, ch. 38, par. 4–3(a)). From this defendant concludes that mental state is an essential element of an offense. Thus, it is argued, failure to allege a mental state in the complaint constitutes an omission of an essential element of the offense in violation of section 111–3(a)(3) of the Criminal Code (Ill.Rev.Stat.1981, ch. 38, par. 111–3(a)(3)). In support of this syllogism defendant cites cases reversing convictions for mob action where the charging instrument failed to allege a mental state. *People v. Grant* (1981), 101 Ill.App.3d 43, 56 Ill.Dec. 478, 427 N.E.2d 810; *People v. Leach* (1972), 3 Ill.App.3d 389, 279 N.E.2d 450.

[4] Section 4–3 has been construed to mean that if the statutory definition of an offense refers to a particular mental state with which the offense must be committed, then that mental state is an element of the offense which must be alleged (*People v. Mager* (1976), 35 Ill.App.3d 306, 341 N.E.2d 389). However, where a particular mental state is not a part of the definition of an offense, it is possible that the charging instrument need not allege a specific mental state. For example, where the crime charged is such that it is virtually impossible for a person to commit it and not have a guilty mind, no mental state need be alleged (*People v. Clark* (1979), 71 Ill.App.3d 381, 27 Ill.Dec. 680, 389 N.E.2d 911). Also, where the mental state of knowledge is implicit from the specific allegation of defendant's act as set forth in the charging instrument, it is beyond serious contention that defendant was sufficiently apprised of the crime charged. *People v. Shelton* (1969), 42 Ill.2d 490, 248 N.E.2d 65.

[5] In the case at bar, under either the original complaint or the complaint as amended, it cannot be seriously argued that the defendant was not informed that he was charged with a knowing violation of the order of protection. The defendant was charged with threatening and harassing his ex-wife. Even in day-to-day usage, these terms imply that the protagonist knowingly causes his victim to suffer undue distress. Add in the factor of defendant's knowledge that he was subject to an order which at the very least restrained him from unnecessarily inflicting himself upon his ex-wife and one is inexorably led to the conclusion that defendant's conduct

as charged must have been knowing and wilful. In point of fact, it is highly doubtful that this court would affirm a conviction for threats or harassment unwittingly made. Thus, we conclude that mental state was not an element which had to be alleged in the complaint.

Defendant also challenges the constitutionality of the Domestic Violence Act. The crux of the argument is that the statutory language is so vague and overbroad that the possibility of criminal penalties thereunder necessarily chills certain constitutional rights.

[6] The State contends that the defendant has waived this issue by failing to raise it in the trial court. In addition to this aspect of waiver, we also recognize that a constitutional challenge to this portion of the Act would have been appropriate upon initial entry of the order of protection. However, no appeal was taken from the original order. The defendant contends that since this is a pure question of law, we should entertain the question in spite of the failure to raise it below. We agree. Vagueness and overbreadth questions are dealt with by reference to judicial standards. Specific evidence or factual inquiry at the trial level would add nothing to the record which would facilitate proper resolution of the issues raised. Thus, we turn to the merits of the challenge.

[7] A statute is void for vagueness where it fails to adequately give notice as to what action or conduct is proscribed (*People v. Vandiver* (1971), 51 Ill.2d 525, 283 N.E.2d 681). Failure to give adequate notice occurs where a person of reasonable intelligence must necessarily guess at the meaning of the statute. *Connally v. General Construction Co.* (1925), 269 U.S. 385, 46 S.Ct. 126, 70 L.Ed. 322.

[8] There is little doubt that the terms employed in the Domestic Violence Act are vague to a certain extent. However, impossible and unrealistic standards of specificity are not required. (*People v. Dednam* (1973), 55 Ill.2d 565, 304 N.E.2d 627.) In addition to the language used, considera-

tion is given to the legislative objective and the evil the statute seeks to remedy.

Considering all of the aforestated principles, we conclude that the statute is not unconstitutionally vague. The Domestic Violence Act contemplates the protection of a potential victim from the universe of physical and psychological abuses which only someone as close as a relative can inflict. A statute which has its objective a safety net against such interferences cannot be expected to address every conceivable form of abuse. Thus, a certain measure of generality must be tolerated to give effect to the intended scope of the Act. Furthermore, "guesswork" engendered by the breadth of the language is not excessive. The subjectivity that doomed the laws challenged in *Coates v. Cincinnati* (1971), 402 U.S. 611, 91 S.Ct. 1686, 29 L.Ed.2d 214 and *People v. Klick* (1977), 66 Ill.2d 269, 5 Ill.Dec. 858, 362 N.E.2d 329 is not present there. In those cases, statutes phrased in terms of conduct calculated or intended to annoy others were held unconstitutionally vague. Obviously, an infinite variety of conduct might annoy some individuals but not others. Here, on the other hand, the statute is phrased in terms of conduct intended by one specific individual to inflict undue distress upon a specific individual or group of individuals. Thus, the scope of conduct which can be conceivably punished under the Act is greatly narrowed. In this regard, we are inclined to follow *People v. Parkins* (1979), 77 Ill.2d 253, 32 Ill.Dec. 909, 396 N.E.2d 22. There, our Supreme Court upheld "an Act * * * to prevent harassment by the use of telephone communications" (Ill.Rev.Stat.1977, ch. 134, par. 16.4–1(2)) against a vagueness challenge. As we believe the range of punishable conduct to be narrower in the Domestic Violence Act context than in the telephone harassment context, we conclude *a fortiori* that the statute here is not unconstitutionally vague.

[9, 10] The statute is also challenged for overbreadth. Defendant argues that the Act is impermissibly overbroad in that it may be reasonably interpreted to prohibit

constitutionally protected conduct (*Grayned v. City of Rockford* (1972), 408 U.S. 104, 92 S.Ct. 2294, 33 L.Ed.2d 222). Defendant submits that the proscription of threatening or harassing his ex-wife could be interpreted to chill his exercise of First Amendment rights. This argument is devoid of merit. The only speech for which defendant could be reasonably punished under the Act is that form of expression which would not be subject to constitutional protection under any circumstances. (See *e.g. People v. Holder* (1983), 92 Ill.2d 444, 71 Ill.Dec. 677, 451 N.E.2d 831 (intimidation statute is constitutional)). The argument raised in defendant's brief concerning possible applications of the Act to innocent speech is equally unavailing. A statute is unconstitutionally overbroad when a *reasonable* interpretation might infringe upon protected expression. The examples proffered by defendant involve patently unreasonable applications of the criminal provisions of the Act. Thus, there is no serious threat to First Amendment rights.

Accordingly, we affirm the judgment of the circuit court of Rock Island County.

AFFIRMED.

BARRY and SCOTT, JJ., concur.

Alvin D. BLAZEL, and Others
Similarly Situated, Plaintiffs,

v.

The Honorable Ann Walsh BRADLEY,
Judge for the Circuit Court of Mara-
thon County, Branch III, in her Official
Capacity, Defendant.

No. 87–C–179–C.

United States District Court,
W.D. Wisconsin.

Nov. 7, 1988.

Husband brought action to challenge
constitutionality of Wisconsin statute
which permits ex parte temporary restraining order in domestic abuse action. Husband moved for summary judgment. The
District Court, Crabb, Chief Judge, held
that: (1) statute did not violate due process, and (2) ex parte order violated due
process.

Motion granted in part and denied in
part.

1. Constitutional Law ⚖=44

State waived requirement, if any, to
join Attorney General as party, where assistant Attorney General was representing
defendant, had actual notice of constitutional challenge, and failed to notify court
that addition of Attorney General as party
was required.

2. Constitutional Law ⚖=274(5), 277(1)

Statute permitting issuance of ex parte
temporary restraining order in domestic
abuse action threatened deprivation of
property and liberty interests under due
process clause. W.S.A. 813.12, 813.12(3)(b);
U.S.C.A. Const.Amends. 5, 14.

3. Constitutional Law ⚖=251.6

Due process requires predeprivation
hearing unless extraordinary circumstanc-

es necessitate prompt action without hearing or unless sufficient safeguards are provided. U.S.C.A. Const.Amends. 5, 14.

4. Constitutional Law ⊜312(4)

Circumstances of domestic abuse cases are not sufficiently unusual or extraordinary to justify ex parte temporary restraining order without due process predeprivation hearing; threat of harm was less to general public then to private individuals; immediate action was not required in all cases; and deprivation was initiated by private party. W.S.A. 813.12, 813.12(3)(b); U.S.C.A. Const.Amends. 5, 14.

5. Constitutional Law ⊜312(4)

Wisconsin statute permitting ex parte temporary restraining order in domestic abuse action complied with due process, even though it did not provide for prior notice of hearing, did not require victim's personal appearance, and did not explicitly require allegation of an immediate risk of abuse; only judge of family court commissioner could issue order; postdeprivation hearing was to be provided within seven days; statute required verified petition based on personal knowledge and containing specific allegations; only victim could petition for order; and legislature intended statute to permit order upon showing of imminent danger. W.S.A. 767.23(1)(a, j), (1n), 813.12, 813.12(3)(b); Wis.St.1975, §§ 247.23, 813.025; U.S.C.A. Const. Amends. 5, 14.

6. Constitutional Law ⊜312(4)

An abuse victim's personal appearance in court was not a due process requirement for an ex parte temporary restraining order in a domestic abuse action. W.S.A. 813.12, 813.12(3)(b); U.S.C.A. Const. Amends. 5, 14.

7. Breach of the Peace ⊜17

Wisconsin statute permitting ex parte temporary restraining order in domestic abuse action required victim to make showing of imminent danger. W.S.A. 813.12, 813.12(3)(b).

8. Breach of the Peace ⊜20
Constitutional Law ⊜274(5), 312(4)

Ex parte temporary restraining order that required husband to avoid his home

and children for seven days deprived him of property and liberty without due process, where wife's petition contained no allegation of a risk of immediate harm, but only alleged that husband had assaulted her two weeks earlier and there had been previous assaults. W.S.A. 813.12(5)(b); U.S.C.A. Const.Amends. 5, 14.

James Jannetta, Wausau, Wis., for plaintiffs.

James H. McDermott, Asst. Atty. Gen., Madison, Wis., for defendant.

CRABB, Chief Judge.

This is a civil action brought pursuant to 42 U.S.C. § 1983 in which plaintiffs ask the court to declare unconstitutional Wis.Stat. § 813.12(3)(b), which permits the issuance of *ex parte* temporary restraining orders in domestic abuse actions. The case is before the court on the parties' cross-motions for summary judgment. Jurisdiction is present under 28 U.S.C. §§ 1331 and 1343.

I conclude that Wis.Stat. § 813.12 provides the essential due process protections that are required before the state may constitutionally deprive plaintiffs of the protected liberty and property interests at stake when a temporary restraining order is issued in a domestic abuse action. It is explicit in the statute that judicial participation and a verified petition containing detailed allegations are required before an *ex parte* order may issue and that a prompt post-deprivation hearing must be provided. And in light of the statute's legislative history, it is implicit that *ex parte* orders are to be issued only upon an allegation of risk of imminent and irreparable harm based on personal knowledge.

From the findings of fact proposed by the parties, I find that no genuine dispute exists as to the following material facts.

FACTS

Plaintiff Alvin Blazel is an adult resident of Wisconsin. Defendant Ann Walsh Bradley is the duly elected Circuit Court Judge of Branch III of the Marathon County Circuit Court in Wausau, Wisconsin.

On March 13, 1987, plaintiff's wife, Donna Blazel, filed a petition for a temporary restraining order and injunction in the Marathon County Circuit Court, Branch III. Pursuant to Wis.Stat. § 813.12(5)(b), she was provided with a simplified form on which to file her petition. The form states that the allegations are made "under oath" and has preprinted responses that the petitioner can check indicating the petitioner's relation to respondent, whether both are adults, and the petitioner's legal interest in his or her residence. The form provides a space for the petitioner to describe the necessity for the order. In this space the form states "The respondent engaged in or might engage in domestic abuse to me because: (The conduct must include an intentional infliction of or threat to inflict physical pain, physical injury or illness; impairment of physical condition; or sexual contact or sexual intercourse without consent, as set forth in s. 940.225(1)(2) or 3, [sic] Wis.Stats.)." The form has a space where the petitioner must describe "what happened, when, where, who did what to whom." The petition then lists the types of protection that may be ordered, including requiring respondent to avoid petitioner's residence or to avoid contacting her, and a line marked "Other." The petitioner is to mark any of the boxes which apply.

In the space provided for a description of abuse Donna Blazel alleged as follows: "2–28–87 he grabbed me by the back of my hair & tried to throw my neck out, which hurts my arthritis. Called Mara. Co. Sheriff's Dept. About Feb. 12, 1987, threw a loaf of bread at me & then hit me in the back of the head with his fist and tried to throw my neck out, called MCSD and signed an abuse complaint."

Donna Blazel marked with an "X" the lines on the pre-printed petition indicating she was requesting that the court immediately issue a temporary restraining order requiring the named respondent to avoid his residence and to avoid contacting petitioner or causing any other person to have contact with her, and directing the sheriff to place her in physical possession of her residence.

On March 13, 1987, the day Donna Blazel filed the petition, defendant issued a temporary restraining order on a pre-printed form, ordering Alvin Blazel to avoid the petitioner's residence, to avoid contacting petitioner or causing any person other than a party's attorney to contact petitioner, and to leave the children in the home. The first two requirements were preprinted and then marked by the judge. The last requirement was typed on a line marked "other." The order provided that it was in effect until the injunction hearing, which a handwritten entry indicated was scheduled for March 19, 1987.

The temporary restraining order was issued without any notice to Alvin Blazel. He first became aware of the matter on March 14, 1987, when he was served with the order.

Alvin and Donna Blazel own their residence jointly.

On March 19, 1987 Donna Blazel failed to appear at the injunction hearing and the action was dismissed. On the same day, Donna Blazel filed a second petition with the Marathon County Circuit Court, again requesting a domestic abuse restraining order. In the petition she repeated the allegations she had made in her first petition and added others about earlier incidents. She checked the boxes indicating that she wished an order requiring the respondent to avoid their residence and to avoid contacting her. In the space entitled "Other" she requested that respondent's family and friends be prevented from contacting her or the children on their property.

On March 19, 1987 Hon. Vincent Howard, Circuit Court Judge, issued an *ex parte* temporary restraining order similar to the one Judge Bradley had issued with the additional requirement that respondent's family and friends should avoid contact with petitioner and children at petitioner's residence.[1]

Donna Blazel executed a dismissal of the second action on March 24, 1987 and the court dismissed the action on March 30, 1987.

---

1. Judge Howard is not a defendant in this ac-   tion. In plaintiffs' preliminary pretrial confer-

Between March 1, 1986 and March 3, 1987, at least 29 petitions for domestic abuse restraining orders were filed with the Circuit Court for Marathon County. Most involved the issuance of a temporary restraining order. It appears that some were issued without notice to the respondent.

Gerhardt Getzin, a family law practitioner in Wausau, Wisconsin, was involved in thirteen of these cases. In each case, the court issued an *ex parte* domestic abuse restraining order based on the petition alone. In many of these cases, there was no judicial contact with the petitioner.

OPINION

[1] Plaintiffs' challenge to Wis.Stat. § 813.12(3) is directed to what they contend

ence statement, counsel stated that plaintiffs were considering changing the designation of the defendant to "Marathon County Circuit Court" in order to encompass the second order. However, they have not moved to amend the complaint to add Judge Howard as a defendant.

2. In some circumstances, persons challenging the constitutionality of a Wisconsin statute are required to add the Attorney General for the State of Wisconsin as a party. In a hearing before this court, the assistant attorney general representing the defendant in this case stated that he would advise the court promptly if this was required in this case. He has failed to do so. Because the attorney general is representing the defendant in this action and thus has actual notice of the constitutional challenge, and because the assistant attorney general in this action failed to notify this court that the addition of the attorney general as a party was required, I find that if this requirement was applicable, the state has waived it.

3. The statute defines domestic abuse as intentional infliction of physical pain, physical injury or illness, intentional impairment of physical condition, violation of § 940.225(1), (2), or (3) [sexual assault], or a threat to engage in any of the prohibited conduct by an adult family or household member against another adult family or household member. § 813.12(1)(a).

The relevant portions of § 813.12 read as follows:

(3)(a) A judge or family court commissioner shall issue a temporary restraining order ordering the respondent to avoid the petitioner's residence, [except that if petitioner and respondent are not married, the respondent owns the premises where the petitioner re-

is the statute's authorization of procedures that violate due process.[2] They argue that it is unconstitutional for judges and family court commissioners to issue temporary restraining orders without notice to the respondent, ordering the respondent to avoid petitioner's home and not to contact the petitioner simply because the petitioner alleges sufficient facts for a judge or family court commissioner to find "reasonable grounds to believe that the respondent has engaged in, or based on prior conduct of the petitioner and the respondent[,] may engage in, domestic abuse of the petitioner."[3] Plaintiffs contend that the statute is deficient on its face and as applied because it does not require notice or hearing before the order is issued and because it does not incorporate necessary safeguards that would render an *ex parte* order constitu-

sides and the petitioner has no legal interest in the premises, the judge or family court commissioner may order the respondent to avoid the premises for a reasonable time until the petitioner relocates], or any premises temporarily occupied by petitioner or both, and to avoid contacting or causing any person other than a party's attorney to contact the petitioner unless the petitioner consents in writing, if all of the following occur:

1. The petitioner submits to the judge or family court commissioner a petition alleging facts set forth under sub. (5)(a).

2. The judge or family court commissioner finds reasonable grounds to believe that the respondent has engaged in, or based on prior conduct of the petitioner and the respondent may engage in domestic abuse of the petitioner....

(b) Notice need not be given to the respondent before issuing a temporary restraining order under this subsection....

(c) The temporary restraining order is in effect until a hearing is held on the issuance of an injunction under sub. (4). A judge or family court commissioner shall hold a hearing on issuance of an injunction within 7 days after the temporary restraining order is issued....

(5)(a) The petition shall allege facts sufficient to show the following:

1. The name of the petitioner and that the petitioner is the alleged victim.

2. The name of the respondent and that the respondent is an adult.

3. That the respondent engaged in, or based on prior conduct of the petitioner and the respondent may engage in, domestic abuse of the petitioner.

tional, such as sworn statements, evidence of a pattern of abuse, allegations of imminent danger, narrowly drawn definitions, and intensive review of specific allegations.

The statute at issue is a fairly recent response to the growing public understanding of the serious problem of domestic abuse. It was preceded by an earlier version of the statute, § 813.025, enacted in 1979, and repealed and replaced with the current statute, § 813.12, in 1983. Both contain essentially similar provisions concerning *ex parte* temporary restraining orders.

Wisconsin is not alone in having this type of legislation. Every state and the District of Columbia have enacted legislation intended to respond to the problem of domestic violence. *See Ex Parte Protection Orders: Is Due Process Locked Out?*, 58 Temple Law Quarterly 841, 841 n. 1 (1985). Thirty-seven of these statutes provide *ex parte* preliminary relief. *Id.* at 848 n. 37. No federal court has yet addressed the constitutionality of any of these statutes, although the Eastern District of Wisconsin considered the constitutionality of a similar statute in the divorce context. *See Geisinger v. Voss*, 352 F.Supp. 104 (E.D.Wis. 1972). Four state courts, including the Wisconsin court of appeals, have considered due process challenges to state statutes permitting *ex parte* orders in domestic abuse cases and have upheld the statutes. *See Schramek v. Bohren*, 145 Wis.2d 695, 429 N.W.2d 501 (Ct.App.1988); *Marquette v. Marquette*, 686 P.2d 990 (Okla.App.1984); *State v. Marsh*, 626 S.W. 2d 223, 231 (Mo.1982) (en banc); *Boyle v. Boyle*, 12 D. & C.3d 767, 775 (C.P.Alleg. 1979).

1. Analysis of Wisconsin Decision

In the recent *Schramek* decision, the Wisconsin court of appeals considered claims that § 813.12 is unconstitutional on its face and as applied because of inadequate notice of hearing, denial of a hearing before issuance of a temporary restraining order, denial of the right to a jury trial, vagueness, overbreadth, and denial of equal protection. The court rejected each

of these claims. (Because the plaintiffs in this case challenge only the statute's notice and hearing provisions, I will not examine the court of appeals' discussion and rejection of Schramek's other constitutional claims.)

In *Schramek*, the plaintiff contended that the statute violated the due process clause because it failed to provide for notice of the injunction hearing and the nature of the charge so as to permit the respondent to prepare a defense and make objections. The court of appeals found that due process was satisfied by the statute's requirements that the petitioner name the petitioner and respondent, and describe the circumstances of the alleged assault, and that the petition be served on the respondent seven days before the injunction hearing.

In this case, plaintiffs' attack on the statutory notice requirements differs from that made in *Schramek*. Here plaintiffs contend that the statute violates the due process clause not because the notice of the injunction hearing is insufficient, but because there is no notice to respondents before the *ex parte* temporary restraining order is issued. On this issue, *Schramek* provides no guidance.

On another issue, however, the plaintiff in *Schramek* raised a claim identical to that raised by plaintiffs in this case: that the statute is unconstitutional because it does not provide for any hearing prior to the issuance of an *ex parte* temporary restraining order. In its brief analysis of this claim, the state court of appeals relied solely on *Lossman v. Pekarske*, 707 F.2d 288 (7th Cir.1983), a case in which county authorities had removed plaintiff's children from his custody without prior notice or hearing pursuant to Wis.Stat. § 48.19(1). That statute provides that a child may be taken into custody when authorities have reasonable grounds to believe that "the child ... is in immediate danger from his or her surroundings and removal from those surroundings is necessary...." Wis.Stat. § 48.19(1)(d)(5). The children were removed after authorities had learned that the father "was constantly drunk, beat and kicked the children brutally, threatened to kill them, kept loaded guns around the house . . ., and fed them inadequately." 707 F.2d at 289. The Court of Appeals for the Seventh Circuit found that due process was not violated because the threat to the children's safety was an emergency that justified a deprivation without notice or hearing. 707 F.2d at 291–92.

After discussing *Lossman,* the Wisconsin Court of Appeals held as follows:

Similarly, sec. 813.12, Stats., protects individuals from domestic abuse. Thomas' safety was in jeopardy. The action taken from his protection was an ex parte hearing which resulted in a TRO. The statute provides for a prompt post-deprivation hearing, which, in this case, as in *Lossman,* demonstrated the justification for initially issuing the TRO and for delaying the hearing. See *id.* at 291–92. We find no constitutional infirmity in the statutory procedure or in its present application.

Schramek, 145 Wis.2d at 707–08, 429 N.W.2d 501.

The court's analysis in *Schramek* was based on the alleged danger to the petitioner. The court found the statute constitutional only because the petitioner's "safety was in jeopardy." *Id.* Although the court did not hold explicitly that the danger must be immediate, it is reasonable to assume from its reliance on *Lossman* that the court found the danger to the petitioner to be immediate. In *Lossman* the Court of Appeals for the Seventh Circuit had found the removal of plaintiff's children to be constitutional only because there was immediate danger. The state court of appeals did not consider explicitly whether the statute required an allegation of immediate danger before an order may issue, but because the plaintiff challenged the statute on its face and as applied, and the court found the statute to be constitutional, the decision might be read as holding that § 813.12 requires such an allegation.

If the holding of the Wisconsin court of appeals is that an *ex parte* temporary restraining order may issue only when there are allegations of immediate harm, I agree

with it. To make that point explicit, I hold that the statute must be construed to require such allegations, for the reasons discussed hereafter.

The three decisions of other state courts considering the constitutionality of *ex parte* temporary restraining orders in domestic abuse cases provide little guidance when analyzing the Wisconsin statute because the provisions of the statutes considered in those cases are different from those of the Wisconsin statute. It is necessary to analyze the specific provisions of the Wisconsin statute and its legislative history in light of constitutional requirements of due process to determine whether the statute violates the due process clause.

2. Due Process Analysis

As a general rule, *ex parte* temporary restraining orders are available only rarely and only after petitioners have satisfied stringent requirements. *See, e.g., Granny Goose Foods, Inc. v. Brotherhood of Teamsters,* 415 U.S. 423, 439, 94 S.Ct. 1113, 1124, 39 L.Ed.2d 435 (1974); *American Can Co. v. Mansukhani,* 742 F.2d 314, 321 (7th Cir.1984); Fed.R.Civ.P. 65(b). "Our entire jurisprudence runs counter to the notion of court action taken before reasonable notice and an opportunity to be heard has been granted both sides of a dispute." *Granny Goose,* 415 U.S. at 439, 94 S.Ct. at 1124. Under the federal rules an applicant for an *ex parte* temporary restraining order must provide specific facts in affidavits or in a verified complaint that show immediate and irreparable injury will occur before the adverse party can appear, must certify reasons why notice should not be required, and must post a bond for payment of costs and damages that may be incurred. Fed.R.Civ.P. 65(b).

Plaintiffs take the position that any state temporary restraining order is unconstitutional if it does not comport with the same requirements as Rule 65(b). However, neither the legislative history of Rule 65(b) nor the cases interpreting it suggest that the rule codifies constitutional requirements which must be satisfied before an *ex parte* temporary restraining order may issue. It is more helpful to look to cases analyzing various types of *ex parte* temporary deprivations of liberty or property to determine whether process is due in this particular factual context and, if so, what process is due.

[2] Some process is due before a Wisconsin judge or family court commissioner may issue an *ex parte* temporary restraining order under § 813.12 because the order can cause two distinct deprivations. First, by requiring that the alleged abuser avoid the petitioner's residence, in which the respondent may well have a cognizable property interest, the statute threatens a deprivation of property which triggers due process protections. *See, e.g., North Georgia Finishing, Inc. v. DiChem, Inc.,* 419 U.S. 601, 95 S.Ct. 719, 42 L.Ed.2d 751 (1975); *Fuentes v. Shevin,* 407 U.S. 67, 92 S.Ct. 1983, 32 L.Ed.2d 556 (1972). Second, the order may implicate cognizable liberty interests if it deprives an alleged abuser of his relation with his children. The Supreme Court has found that the liberty interest protected by the Fifth and Fourteenth Amendments includes the right to establish a home and bring up children. *Board of Regents v. Roth,* 408 U.S. 564, 572, 92 S.Ct. 2701, 2706, 33 L.Ed.2d 548 (1972). Accordingly, the state may not terminate the parent-child relationship without a hearing. *Stanley v. Illinois,* 405 U.S. 645, 92 S.Ct. 1208, 31 L.Ed.2d 551 (1972); *Lassiter v. Department of Social Services,* 452 U.S. 18, 101 S.Ct. 2153, 68 L.Ed.2d 640 (1981).

It is true that when an *ex parte* temporary restraining order is issued, there is only a temporary expulsion from the home and interruption of the parent-child relationship and not a termination of rights. The short duration of the deprivation may affect the nature of the process that must be provided, but it does not eliminate the basic requirement of due process protections. *Fuentes,* 407 U.S. at 86, 92 S.Ct. at 1997.

[3] Because the Wisconsin order can deprive plaintiffs of protected liberty and property interests, it implicates due process protections. The question is the nature of

the protections that must be provided. Since notice and opportunity to be heard are the cornerstone of due process, *id.* 407 U.S. at 80, 92 S.Ct. at 1994; *Granny Goose,* 415 U.S. at 439, 94 S.Ct. at 1124, a pre-deprivation hearing is required unless extraordinary circumstances necessitate prompt action without a hearing, *Fuentes,* 407 U.S. at 82, 90, 92 S.Ct. at 1995, 1999, or unless sufficient safeguards are provided. *See, e.g., North Georgia,* 419 U.S. 601, 95 S.Ct. 719; *Mitchell v. W.T. Grant,* 416 U.S. 600, 94 S.Ct. 1895, 40 L.Ed.2d 406 (1974); *Del's Big Saver Foods v. Carpenter Cook, Inc.,* 603 F.Supp. 1071 (W.D.Wis.1985), *aff'd,* 795 F.2d 1344 (7th Cir.1986).

[4] Circumstances justifying the postponing of notice and hearing "must be truly unusual," *Fuentes,* 407 U.S. at 90, 92 S.Ct. at 1999, and must be shown to have met three criteria:

First, in each case, the seizure has been directly necessary to secure an important governmental or general public interest. Second, there has been a special need for very prompt action. Third, the State has kept strict control over its monopoly of legitimate force: the person initiating the seizure has been a government official responsible for determining, under the standards of a narrowly drawn statute, that it was necessary and justified in the particular instance.

Id. at 91, 92 S.Ct. at 2000. One could argue that the circumstances of domestic abuse restraining orders fulfill these criteria, but the fit is not perfect. First, the threat of harm is less to the general public than to a private individual. Second, there is not necessarily a need for prompt action. In some cases immediate action may be imperative, but in others it may not be. Third, the deprivation is not initiated by the government but by a private petitioner. The circumstances are not comparable to those cases in which seizure or suspension without notice or hearing based on extraordinary circumstances has been permitted. *See, e.g., North American Storage Co. v. Chicago,* 211 U.S. 306, 29 S.Ct. 101, 53 L.Ed. 195 (1908) (seizure of allegedly contaminated poultry); *Ewing v. Mytinger &*

Casselberry, Inc., 339 U.S. 594, 70 S.Ct. 870, 94 L.Ed. 1088 (1950) (seizure of mislabelled drugs); *Phillips v. Commissioner*, 283 U.S. 589, 51 S.Ct. 608, 75 L.Ed. 1289 (1931) (seizure of money due on taxes); *Federal Deposit Insurance Corp. v. Mallen*, —— U.S. ——, 108 S.Ct. 1780, 100 L.Ed.2d 265 (1988) (suspension of an indicted official of a federally insured bank); *Barry v. Barchi*, 443 U.S. 55, 99 S.Ct. 2642, 61 L.Ed.2d 365 (1979) (suspension of a horse trainer suspected of drugging race horses).

[5] As well as permitting deprivation without prior notice and hearing when extraordinary circumstances exist, the Supreme Court has found such action to be constitutional when appropriate safeguards are provided. To determine what safeguards must be provided in a particular factual situation, a court must consider three factors: the private interest that will be affected; the risk of an erroneous deprivation under existing procedures and the probable value of additional procedures; and the government's interests, including the burdens imposed by additional procedural requirements. *Mathews v. Eldridge*, 424 U.S. 319, 335, 96 S.Ct. 893, 903, 47 L.Ed.2d 18 (1976); *see also Perry v. Federal Bureau of Investigation*, 781 F.2d 1294 (7th Cir.) (en banc), *cert. denied*, 479 U.S. 814, 107 S.Ct. 67, 93 L.Ed.2d 25 (1986) (*Mathews* factors applied to deprivations of liberty interests).

Weighing the *Mathews* factors, it is apparent that substantial procedural protections are mandated by the strength of the respondent's interest in his home and family and the evident risk of erroneous deprivation when mere allegations in a verified petition may be the basis for an *ex parte* temporary restraining order. However, the strength of the petitioner's countervailing interest in her home and family, the government's interest in preventing abuse,

and the possibility that prior notice may incite domestic violence, suggest that those protections should not extend to prior notice.[1]

While helpful, this weighing of interests within the *Mathews* framework does not provide substantial guidance as to what specific procedural protections are required to ensure that the respondent's interests are protected and the interests of the petitioner and the government are not jeopardized unduly. For a clearer indication of the specific procedural safeguards that ensure the proper protection of interests here, it is necessary to turn to a line of cases decided before *Mathews v. Eldridge* but employing a similar analysis. *See Sniadach v. Family Finance Corp.*, 395 U.S. 337, 89 S.Ct. 1820, 23 L.Ed.2d 349 (1969); *Fuentes*, 407 U.S. 67, 92 S.Ct. 1983; *W.T. Grant*, 416 U.S. 600, 94 S.Ct. 1895; *North Georgia*, 419 U.S. 601, 95 S.Ct. 719 (all reviewing state statutes allowing repossession of property or garnishment without prior notice and hearing).

As with domestic abuse restraining orders, repossession and garnishment involve conflicting interests of petitioner and respondent. Debtors have a protected ownership interest in their wages and property and creditors have strong competing interests since they are owed money and can claim at least partial ownership of the property. In addition, as with domestic abuse cases, providing prior notice involves substantial risks: once notified of the proceeding, the debtor in possession could sell or hide the property. Finally, where the state statutes do not require documentary proof or specific allegations, there is substantial risk of erroneous deprivation.

Although the cases are not entirely consistent, I can conclude that in creditor repossession cases the Supreme Court has

---

4. The Wisconsin statute recognizes that when the petitioner has no legal interest in the home, it is improper to protect the petitioner by ordering the respondent away from the home for the 7 days a temporary restraining order may be in effect. Wis.Stat. § 813.12(3)(a), (am) provides that "If the respondent and the petitioner are not married, the respondent owns the premises

where petitioner resides, and the petitioner has no legal interest in the premises, in lieu of ordering the respondent's avoid petitioner's residence ... the judge or family court commissioner may order the respondent to avoid the premises for a reasonable time until the petitioner relocates...."

established that the due process clause requires either a pre-deprivation hearing or at least four minimum procedural safeguards: participation by a judicial officer; a prompt post-deprivation hearing; verified petitions or affidavits containing detailed allegations based on personal knowledge; and risk of immediate and irreparable harm. *See North Georgia,* 419 U.S. at 607, 95 S.Ct. at 722; *Mitchell,* 416 U.S. at 605–09, 94 S.Ct. at 1899–1901; *Fuentes,* 407 U.S. at 93, 92 S.Ct. at 2000; *Sniadach,* 395 U.S. at 339, 89 S.Ct. at 1821. *See also* discussion of these cases in *Del's Big Saver Foods v. Carpenter Cook, Inc.,* 603 F.Supp. 1071.

Both on its face and as it was applied to plaintiff, the Wisconsin statute satisfies three of these criteria explicitly. It allows only a judge or a family court commissioner to issue an *ex parte* temporary restraining order, Wis.Stat. § 813.12(3)[5]; it provides for a post-deprivation hearing within seven days, Wis.Stat. § 813.12(3)(c); and it requires a verified petition based on personal knowledge and containing specific allegations. The pre-printed form states that the petition is made under oath. As such it is a verified petition. *Bradburn v. McIntosh,* 159 F.2d 925, 931 (10th Cir.1947); *Herbert v. Roxana Petroleum Corp.,* 12 F.2d 81, 83 (E.D.Ill.1926). The statute requires more than a conclusory claim that petitioner is entitled to a restraining order. A petitioner must allege facts sufficient to show "that the respondent engaged in, or based on prior conduct of the petitioner and the respondent may engage in, domestic abuse of the petitioner." The petitioner must "[s]tate what happened, when, where, and who did what to whom."

In this case, both orders against plaintiff were issued by a judge, both orders provided for a post-deprivation hearing within seven days, and neither issued on the basis of merely conclusory allegations. Donna

Blazel alleged specific and detailed facts about alleged abuse: the date the alleged incidents occured and specific physical actions by the respondent.

[6] Plaintiffs argue that the statute does not satisfy the third criterion of a verified petition or affidavit containing detailed allegations based on personal knowledge because the petitioner is not required to present evidence substantiating the allegations or to appear personally before the judge or family court commissioner and because the judicial officials make no more than a "perfunctory paper review" of the petitions. Although it might be a better procedure for the presiding judge or court commissioner to require the petitioner to appear personally before the court so that the court may evaluate petitioner's credibility and perhaps see physical evidence of abuse such as bruises or scratches, *see Marquette v. Marquette,* 686 P.2d 990; *State v. Marsh,* 626 S.W.2d at 231 (en banc); *Boyle v. Boyle,* 12 D. & C.3d at 775, a personal appearance is not a constitutional requirement. In *W.T. Grant,* 416 U.S. 600, 94 S.Ct. 1895, the Supreme Court found a Louisiana sequestration statute constitutional in part because the state showed that documentary proof was generally available to the court where a creditor requests an *ex parte* sequestration based on the existence of a debt. However, the existence of documentary proof was not the only procedural protection the statute provided. In addition, no other case in this line has suggested that documentary proof or personal appearance before a judicial officer is required, and under Fed.R.Civ.P. 65(b), *ex parte* temporary restraining orders may be issued on the basis of affidavits without other documentary or physical proof.

Finally, although the statute does not require explicitly that allegations be based on personal knowledge, it can be read fair-

---

5. Family court commissioners are parajudicial appointed officers of the state court with broad authority. Wisconsin Legislative Council, Powers and Duties of Family Court Commissioners, Information Memorandum 78-8 (1978). Commissioners' duties include presiding, based on the referral of a judge, at certain types of divorce, maintenance, and child support hearings, Wis.Stat. § 767.13, and issuing temporary orders for support of spouse and children, Wis. Stat. § 767.23. Plaintiffs have not argued that family court commissioners are not judicial officials who would satisfy the due process requirement of judicial participation.

ly as requiring it. If the victim of the abuse is the only person who can petition for a temporary restraining order, the lack of a specific requirement is not troubling because it is the victim who will have personal knowledge of the alleged abuse or threats of abuse. The language of the statute suggests that only an abuse victim may be the petitioner. The court is directed to issue orders ordering respondent to avoid "petitioner's residence." Wis.Stat. § 813.12(3)(a). The court may issue a petition if, among other things, it has reason to believe that domestic abuse may occur "based on prior conduct of the petitioner and the respondent." Ordering respondent to avoid petitioner's residence and examining the conduct of petitioner and respondent make no sense unless petitioner and the abuse victim are one and the same.

The only evidence suggesting that someone other than the alleged abuse victim may petition the court is an analysis by the Legislative Research Bureau of an early version of Act 204, the act which was eventually codified as § 813.12. The earlier version contained the words "family or household member" where the final version uses "petitioner." The analysis mentions in passing that the petitioner need not be the "family or household member who is the alleged domestic abuse victim." Legislative Research Bureau, LRB–3651/1, 1983–84 Legislature. Because this interpretation is based on language different from that in the final version of the act and is inconsistent with that language, I conclude that the statute permits only the alleged abuse victim to petition for a temporary restraining order and that the allegations in the petition must be based on personal knowledge. This conclusion is borne out by the facts of this case: the petitioner was the abuse victim and had personal knowledge of her allegations.

The fourth procedural safeguard is a showing of risk of immediate and irreparable harm. It is only the risk of immediate harm that justifies the issuance of an *ex parte* temporary restraining order. Otherwise issuance of the restraining order could await notice to respondent and the holding of an adversarial hearing. Neither the

Wisconsin statute nor the pre-printed petition form requires an allegation that there is immediate risk of abuse, and Donna Blazel did not make such an allegation in her petition.

Defendant cites the three state court decisions upholding similar statutes in support of her argument that the Wisconsin statute is valid despite the omission. However, the cases cited addressed statutes different from the Wisconsin statute; all contained an explicit requirement that immediate harm be shown. *See Marquette v. Marquette*, 686 P.2d at 992 n. 3; *State v. Marsh*, 626 S.W.2d at 229; *Boyle v. Boyle*, 12 D. & C.3d at 774.

Defendant is correct, however, in asserting that state statutes bear a presumption of constitutionality and that federal courts should hesitate before striking down a state statute for a constitutional deficiency. *See, e.g., Gregg v. Georgia*, 428 U.S. 153, 201, 96 S.Ct. 2909, 2938, 49 L.Ed.2d 859 (1976); *Alaska Packers Asso. v. Industrial Accident Comm'n of California*, 294 U.S. 532, 543, 55 S.Ct. 518, 522, 79 L.Ed. 1044 (1935). It is well established that federal courts should construe state statutes in a manner that would make the statute constitutional if such a reading is reasonable in light of the statute's language and legislative history. *See, e.g., Fletcher v. Peck*, 10 U.S. (6 Cranch) 87, 128, 3 L.Ed. 162 (1810) (Marshall, C.J.); J. Hurst, *Dealing With Statutes* (1982).

[7] An examination of the legislative history of the Wisconsin statute reveals that although there is no explicit provision that petitioners must allege immediate and irreparable harm, the legislature intended that the statute permit the issuance of an *ex parte* temporary restraining order only on a showing of risk of immediate and irreparable harm. In 1979 the legislature enacted Wis.Stat. § 813.025 as part of comprehensive legislation on domestic abuse. In 1983 it enacted the current statute which plaintiffs challenge in this case, Wis. Stat. § 813.12. The *ex parte* temporary restraining order provision of the current statute is only slightly different from the

predecessor statute. It permits a temporary order to stand for seven days as opposed to the five days allowed previously; it permits family court commissioners as well as judges to issue the orders; it expands the types of violent behavior and threat of violent behavior that justify issuance of an order; and it clarifies that the petition need not be filed in conjunction with a request for a final injunction. *See,* Legislative Research Bureau, LRB-3651/1, 1983–84 Legislature; Drafter's Note, written by Jane Limprecht, Legislative Attorney, LRBa2825/1dn, Jan 30, 1984; compare Wis.Stat. § 813.025 (repealed) and Wis. Stat. § 813.13. None of the statutory features challenged in this case were modified in the 1983 statute.

The legislative history of the current statute contains no discussion of the relevant features of the *ex parte* temporary restraining order. However, legislative history of the predecessor, § 813.025, suggests that the legislature was aware of the constitutional requirement that *ex parte* orders be issued only when risk of immediate and irreparable harm exists and that it intended to require that showing.

Wis.Stat. § 813.025 was enacted after the legislature had considered a 1972 decision of the Eastern District of Wisconsin discussing the constitutionality of Wis.Stat. § 247.23(1) (repealed 1979) which permitted *ex parte* restraining orders in divorce actions.[6] *Geisinger v. Voss,* 352 F.Supp. 104. In *Geisinger,* a Wisconsin family court commissioner had ordered plaintiff away from the residence he shared with his wife pursuant to § 247.23(1), without notice or hearing. Mr. Geisinger contended that his right to due process was violated by the

court's *ex parte* order based only on Mrs. Geisinger's allegation that she "fears her legal rights will be jeopardized if [Mr. Geisinger] is allowed to live in the same household." *Id.* at 105. Because the district court judge evaluated the merits of plaintiff's claim only for the purpose of determining whether a three-judge court should be convened to consider the constitutionality of the Wisconsin statute,[7] his discussion of the constitutional defects of the statute is dicta, but its influence on the Wisconsin legislature makes it relevant to the analysis of the statute. The district court suggested that the statute would be found unconstitutional under *Fuentes v. Shevin,* 407 U.S. 67, 92 S.Ct. 1983, because it allowed a state court to issue an *ex parte* order without evaluating the need for it in the particular case, or having to find that there was risk of immediate, irreparable harm, or why the petitioner was unable to leave the home instead of the respondent. *Id.* at 110–11.

An information memorandum prepared in 1978 for the special council on domestic violence analyzed the application of § 247.23(1) and potential constitutional problems with specific reference to the *Geisinger* decision. Powers and duties of family court commissioners [relating to domestic violence] at 8–9, Information memorandum 78–8, Wisconsin Legislative Council, 1978. In a section entitled "Constitutional Issues Concerning the Requisite Showing to Secure an Order to Vacate," the authors interpreted the *Geisinger* decision as suggesting that a pre-hearing order would be constitutional only if there was a showing of imminent harm.[8] In another

---

6. The statutory language was rather vague:
    In every action affecting marriage, the court or family court commissioner may, during the pendency thereof, make such temporary orders ... as in its discretion it shall be deemed just an reasonable, ... and may prohibit either spouse from imposing any restraint on the personal liberty of the other.... Wis.Stat. 247.23(1) (repealed). However, Wisconsin courts had construed it to permit *ex parte* orders.

7. Until 1976, 28 U.S.C. § 2281 required that a three-judge panel review constitutional challenges to state statutes.

Apparently plaintiff did not pursue his claim, for although the judge determined that a three-judge panel should be convened, there is no indication of further proceedings in the case.

8. The memorandum also noted the district court's suggestion that the petitioner show she is unable temporarily to reside elsewhere. Because I find that the cases illuminating the procedural protections required by the due process clause do not suggest that a petitioner must show why he or she cannot leave his home in order to be entitled to an *ex parte* order, I will not consider this aspect of the district court opinion further.

section, the memorandum contains a review of the practice followed by different counties in granting *ex parte* orders and the finding that courts in Dane, LaCrosse, and Polk Counties required an allegation of imminent danger of physical abuse, and that apparently most other counties required a higher showing than that required by the statute. *Id.* at 7.

Wis.Stat. § 813.025 was enacted shortly after the domestic violence memorandum was published. Unlike the repealed § 247.23, § 813.025 required a specific allegation that the statute criminalizing battery and aggravated battery had been or might be violated. The discussion in the memorandum suggests that when the legislature enacted § 813.025 it was aware of the constitutional deficiencies of § 247.23, and wished to avoid them, and that it realized that an *ex parte* order would be constitutional only if it were issued upon allegations of immediate and irreparable harm.

Because the relevant provisions of the current statute are essentially identical to those of the earlier § 813.025, it is proper to infer that the legislative intent motivating the first statute is applicable to the second statute. *See Allen v. Grand Central Aircraft Co.*, 347 U.S. 535, 541–53, 74 S.Ct. 745, 748–55, 98 L.Ed. 933 (1954) (Court considered legislative intent motivating Stabilization Act of 1942 to determine meaning of similar portions of 1952 Defense Production Act); 2A N. Singer, *Sutherland Statutory Construction,* § 51.02 (4th ed. 1984).

A decision by the Wisconsin supreme court provides further support for the proposition that the legislature realized the need for allegations of immediate and irreparable harm. In *In re Marriage of Sandy v. Sandy,* 106 Wis.2d 230, 316 N.W. 2d 164 (1982), the state supreme court considered a challenge to Wis.Stat. § 767.23(1)(a), (j), and (ln), which permitted the state court to issue an order evicting one spouse from the family home without any showing of actual or threatened violence, pursuant to a divorce proceeding and after notice and hearing. In its analysis of the statute's requirements, the court com-

pared it to § 813.025, noting that the committee discussions and the reference materials prepared by the Legislative Council "suggest strongly that the reason for the requirement in sec. 813.025(2)(a), Stats., of a showing of actual or threatened physical violence was to avoid possible constitutional problems if *ex parte* orders to vacate were allowed to issue without such a showing." *Id.* 106 Wis.2d at 238, 316 N.W.2d 164. The court went on to say that "the greater showing of need after 1972 was undoubtedly due" to the suggestion in *Geisinger* that a showing of imminent physical harm was constitutionally required. *Id.* at 239, 316 N.W.2d 164. Applying this evidence of legislative intent to the question before it, the court found that the requirement of showing physical violence is applicable only to *ex parte* orders. *Id.* at 241, 316 N.W.2d 164.

Finally, in the recent decision, *Schramek v. Bohren,* 145 Wis.2d 695, 429 N.W.2d 501, the Wisconsin Court of Appeals held that the statute was constitutional. Although it did not consider whether Wis.Stat. § 813.12 requires allegations of imminent harm before an order may issue, its finding of constitutionality is entitled to considerable deference.

I conclude that when the legislature required a showing of physical violence in Wis.Stat. § 813.025, it intended that showing to be a showing of imminent danger. I base this conclusion on the evidence of the legislature's awareness of the requirement of immediate and irreparable harm, its obvious desire to avoid in § 813.025 the constitutional problems the federal district court had found with § 247.23, and its deliberate inclusion of a requirement that petitioners allege that physical violence has occurred or may occur in the future, coupled with the presumptions that courts should find a statute constitutional when its language and history lend themselves reasonable to that interpretation and that federal courts should defer to a state court's finding that its own state's statute is constitutional. Because of the lack of any significant differences between § 813.025 and the statute challenged in this case, I conclude that the legislature intended § 813.12 to include the same requirement that the complainant make a showing of imminent danger before an *ex parte* order may issue. It is unnecessary to find that the legislature also intended to require a showing that the harm be irreparable. Any allegation of bodily harm makes that showing.

Because the statute's requirement of a showing of physical violence encompasses a requirement that the violence be shown to be imminent, the statute provides all the procedural safeguards necessary to satisfy the due process clause. Accordingly, I hold that when § 813.12 is construed to require a showing of imminent harm, the statute is constitutional on its face.[9]

[8] A holding of facial validity does not necessitate a finding that the statute was applied constitutionally to Alvin Blazel or other plaintiffs in the class. Although Donna Blazel's petitions were the basis for the two orders entered against Alvin Blazel, they contain no allegation of a risk of immediate harm. In the first, she states only that Alvin Blazel has assaulted her some two weeks before. There is no allegation that she feared he would attack her again in the near future. In the second petition, she adds allegations of previous assaults, but again, there is no allegation of a risk of imminent harm. I conclude that the *ex parte* order that required Alvin Blazel to avoid his home and children for seven days deprived him of property and liberty interests without due process of law, and that plaintiff is entitled to a declaration that his constitutional rights were violated. Plaintiff has not sought money damages from defendant, and she is immune from them. *Stump v. Sparkman*, 435 U.S. 349, 98 S.Ct. 1099, 55 L.Ed.2d 331, *rehearing denied*, 436 U.S. 951, 98 S.Ct. 2862, 56 L.Ed.2d 795 (1978) (judicial immunity prevents imposition of money damages in civil suits against judicial officers for judicial actions).

Whether any of the other plaintiffs were similarly deprived is something that cannot be determined from the present record. Plaintiffs have not filed copies of the petitions which were the basis for the orders issued against the other plaintiffs in the class, from which I might determine whether those petitions contained the requisite allegations of imminent harm. However, even if these plaintiffs were to submit evidence and I were to find that the petitions did not contain the requisite allegations and that plaintiffs' due process rights had been abridged, plaintiffs would not be entitled to monetary relief because[1] the defendant is immune from damages. *See id.*

ORDER

IT IS ORDERED THAT plaintiff's motion for summary judgment is GRANTED in part and DENIED in part. It is further ORDERED that defendant's motion for summary judgment is GRANTED in part and DENIED in part. Wis.Stat. § 813.12 is constitutional on its face if construed as it should be to require that the complainant allege that the risk of physical harm is imminent. However, the statute was applied unconstitutionally to plaintiff Alvin D. Blazel.

9. To ensure that petitioners are aware that they must allege a risk of imminent harm, the state might consider revising the simplified form it provides for petitions for *ex parte* restraining orders to make it explicit that such an allegation is necessary.

Mutual Restraining Orders in Domestic Violence Civil Cases

by Mary U. O'Brien

I. Introduction

Mutual restraining orders result when a trial court imposes restraints on both parties to a domestic violence matter; they usually prohibit each from having contact with, and from committing further acts of abuse against, the other party. Depending upon the domestic abuse laws of the state in question, they can be based upon either civil or criminal complaints.

Mutual civil orders of protection may be entered under several circumstances. Both parties may have applied for an order of protection, and, after a hearing, the court may find each to have committed an act of abuse prohibited by that state's statute. In some instances, mutual civil restraining orders may issue upon consent of the parties. The most offensive mutual civil orders result when the judge presiding over a domestic violence matter grants a restraining order to the victim and also issues restraints against her, even though the respondent has not applied

for such relief.[1] The last two types of mutual restraining orders are subject to due process questions,[2] and all three types are dangerous for the victim.[3] This

Mutual restraining orders generate the impression before the court, the police, and other persons that both parties are equally abusive.

article focuses on mutual civil orders of protection since they are more common than mutual criminal orders of protection. It includes a discussion of why these orders are dangerous and some defensive strategies that counsel should consider to avoid their entry.

II. Why Mutual Restraining Orders Are Dangerous

Mutual civil restraining orders create substantial problems for victims of domestic violence.[4] First, they generate the impression before the court, the police, and other persons that both par-

Mary U. O'Brien is a staff attorney at the National Center on Women and Family Law, Inc., 275 Seventh Ave., Suite 1206, New York, NY 10001; (212) 741-9480; HN1193@ handsnet.org. She also continues to serve part-time as a staff attorney at the Legal Aid Society of Morris County in Morristown, New Jersey.

---

[1] Catherine F. Klein, *Full Faith and Credit: Interstate Enforcement of Protective Orders Under the Violence Against Women Act of 1994*, 29 A.B.A. FAMILY L.Q. 253, 266 (1995); *see also* NATIONAL COUNCIL OF JUVENILE & FAMILY COURT JUDGES, MODEL CODE ON DOMESTIC AND FAMILY VIOLENCE § 310 (1994) (hereinafter Model Code), which prohibits mutual protection orders unless proper due process considerations are observed.

[2] Klein, *supra* note 1.

[3] Joan Zorza, *Women Battering: High Costs and the State of the Law*, 28 CLEARINGHOUSE REV. 383, 392 (Special Issue 1994).

[4] *Id.* at 392–93.

ties are equally abusive. Courts entering mutual orders fail to recognize that the true victim may have acted in self-defense and that the other party is not afraid of her. In some instances, mutual orders are entered in the absence of proof that the initial complainant committed an act of abuse against her batterer. Once a mutual order is entered, however, that order usually does not state the specific type or degree of abuse each party committed, so both litigants are subsequently identified as batterers without any written distinctions characterizing the act of abuse each perpetrated.

Second, mutual restraining orders may subject both parties to subsequent criminal charges and immediate arrest, even where one party is falsely accused by the other. If children are in the household and the victim is arrested, they may be placed with the actual abuser. Or if both parents are arrested and no relative or friend is available to care for the children, they may end up in foster care. In some instances, abusers repeatedly file false criminal charges against their victims, thereby disrupting their victims' daily activities and rendering them unable to maintain custody of children or to sustain employment.

In some states, a presumption exists that custody should be awarded to the nonabusive parent and domestic violence is a factor the court must or is encouraged to consider in determining custody disputes.[5] Domestic violence victims subject to mutual orders of protection, however, lose that benefit and protection because they may be viewed by judges hearing their custody matters as being as violent as their abusers.[6] Once a victim has been labelled abusive

or potentially abusive, she is not likely to get sympathy from the court—a problem that could ultimately affect her rights to custody and support.[7] In addition, because parents who lose custody are usually required to pay child support, a domestic violence victim subject to a mutual restraining order may lose her day in court, lose access to justice, and end up in worse shape than when she started.

Mutual restraining orders that are imposed after only one party to domestic violence has filed a complaint or petition alleging abuse violate the victim's right to notice and due process.[8] Such orders are often issued against the initial petitioner without an opportunity for her to be heard, and sometimes without even an oral allegation by the respondent that he was subjected to abuse.[9] Usually the trial court makes no findings of fact that each party committed one or more acts of abuse or that the original petitioner poses a threat to the respondent or that she was not acting in self-defense.[10] Due process requirements must be met prior to imposition of any restraints against a party because of one's basic constitutional liberty interest in being unrestrained and also because of the impact mutual restraints can have upon further civil or criminal litigation between parties to these matters.[11]

Mutual restraining orders create problems for law enforcement. When police officers are called to the scene of a domestic dispute and the parties are subject to a mutual restraining order, the police will not know which party has violated the order unless one party has obvious physical injuries. Too often, in such instances, police arrest both parties, thereby further victimizing the vic-

---

[5] Nechama Masliansky, *Child Custody and Visitation Determinations When Domestic Violence Has Occurred*, in this issue; National Ctr. on Women & Family Law, State Custody Laws with Respect to Domestic Violence (July 1995) (Item No. 131); *see also* ALA. CODE § 30-1-130 to 136 (Michie Supp. 1995) (effective July 31, 1995).

[6] *See* Klein, *supra* note 1, at 267 & n.57; Zorza, *supra* note 3, at 393.

[7] *See* Zorza, *supra* note 3, at 393.

[8] *See id.* at 392.

[9] *Id.*

[10] *Id.*

[11] *See* Klein, *supra* note 1, at 267.

tim and any children in the household.[12]

In addition, mutual restraining orders perpetuate gender bias against women. Studies have documented that serious violence against women by male partners occurs much more often than violence against men by female partners and that injuries to women are more severe than to men.[13]

Mutual orders of protection fail to make abusers accept responsibility for their behavior since they permit abusers to claim that their partners were also abusive. Domestic violence experts believe abusers must accept responsibility if they are to change their behavior.[14] In addition, the victim is likely to suffer embarrassment and humiliation when family, friends, work associates, and other acquaintances learn she too has been classified as an abuser. Victims' self-esteem is usually already low, and when they are characterized as batterers it may drop even lower.[15]

For all of these reasons, it is critical that practitioners who represent domestic violence victims be aware of the pitfalls of mutual civil restraining orders and of defensive strategies to prevent their entry.

III. Due Process Objections to Mutual Restraining Orders

Individuals have a basic constitutional right to due process beginning with the right to adequate notice of charges against them and the nature of any relief sought.[16] Within this framework, one is entitled to the right to appear and be heard and to participate in the proceed-

ing in a meaningful manner.[17] Mutual restraining orders have been repeatedly criticized for their failure to comply with due process requirements, yet they continue to be issued despite their fundamental constitutional defects.[18]

Mutual restraining orders imposed in the absence of due process protections not only fail to survive constitutional review but also serve actually to punish and further victimize victims who cannot defend themselves. Indeed, because of the possible imposition of a mutual restraining order, victims must consider whether to proceed with a hearing at all since they could be labeled also as abusers and be restrained from certain activities.[19] Furthermore, victims without counsel may not be aware of the possibility of arrest and incarceration resulting from mutual restraints.[20] If given ad-

State laws concerning mutual restraining orders do not always address due process requirements.

vance notice of the hearing, the victim could make an informed decision as to whether to proceed. Alternatively she could dismiss her complaint and either wait unfortunately for a more serious domestic violence incident to occur or have weaker restraints incorporated into a matrimonial agreement if the parties are married or into a custody or support matter if the parties are unmarried.

State laws concerning mutual restraining orders vary greatly from one state to another and do not always address due process requirements. For

---

[12] See Zorza, *supra* note 3.

[13] *Id.*; *see also* National Ctr. on Women & Family Law, Resources on Gender Bias in the Courts (Aug. 1994) (Item No. 199); Russell P. Dobash et al., *The Myth of Sexual Symmetry in Marital Violence*, 39 Soc. Probs. 71–91 (1992).

[14] Zorza, *supra* note 3, at 392; *see also* Lee H. Bowker, Ending the Violence 73–74 (1986); Daniel Willbach, *Ethics and Family Therapy: The Case Management of Family Violence*, 15 J. Marital & Fam. Therapy 43, 48 (1984).

[15] See Zorza, *supra* note 3.

[16] U.S. Const. amend. XIV, § 1.

[17] Baker v. Baker, 904 P.2d 616, 619 (Okla. Ct. App. 1995) (Clearinghouse No. 50,911) (citing Bailey v. Campbell, 862 P.2d 461, 469 (Okla. 1991)).

[18] *Id.* at 617–18; *see also* Mechtel v. Mechtel, 528 N.W.2d 916 (Minn. Ct. App. 1995) (Clearinghouse No. 50,657); Moreno v. Moore, 897 S.W.2d 439 (Tex. Ct. App. 1995).

[19] See Klein, *supra* note 1.

[20] See Zorza, *supra* note 3, at 392–93.

example, Illinois law prohibits mutual orders of protection unless both parties file written pleadings, prove past abuse by the other party, and the court, after a hearing, makes findings and issues separate orders.[21] Under Maryland law, courts may issue mutual orders of protection only when both parties have filed a petition and when the court finds by clear and convincing evidence that mutual abuse has occurred and that both parties acted primarily as aggressors and not primarily in self-defense.[22] California's statute is similar to Maryland's.[23] In Utah, mutual orders of protection are prohibited except in extenuating circumstances or if the court finds such an order is necessary to protect both parties and the parties consent to the order's entry.[24] New Jersey prohibits mutual restraining orders by consent; they may be entered only when both parties have filed complaints and a finding is made or admission obtained that each has committed an act of domestic violence.[25]

Even where state laws have been enacted to ensure that due process is afforded to litigants, some trial judges disregard the statutory law as well as the relevant case law.[26]

In 1995, appellate tribunals in Oklahoma, Minnesota, and Texas handed down opinions reversing the trial courts' issuance of mutual restraining orders which had been imposed upon victims without consideration of their due process rights.[27] In each of these cases, the respondent had been awarded an order of protection against his victim, without the respondent having filed a complaint or petition alleging abuse of any sort, without advance notice to the victim that she should be prepared to defend herself, and without even an oral allegation by the respondent that he had been abused.[28] In each, mutual restraints were imposed by judicial fiat, although in *Mechtel* and *Moreno*, the victim had alleged substantial incidents of abuse.[29] Most surprisingly, in two of these cases, *Baker v. Baker* and *Mechtel v. Mechtel*, the trial courts gave no weight to earlier published opinions in each state holding that mutual restraining orders violated the petitioner's right to notice and the opportunity to prepare a defense.[30] In *Baker* and in *Moreno v. Moore*, the trial courts also overlooked state law that required that a petition alleging specific acts of abuse be filed and served in order for a litigant to obtain an order of protection.[31]

The trial court in *Baker* justified issuance of mutual restraints because it concluded that petitioner's statements to respondent had provoked him to confront her at a friend's home, grab her, and twist her arm.[32] However, finding that petitioner had not been "put on notice that at the scheduled hearing . . . she would be subjected to allegations of domestic abuse" and that "her rights" could be "affected by judicial process," the appellate court determined that peti-

---

[21] ILL. REV. STAT. ch. 750, para. 60/215 (Smith-Hurd Supp. 1996).

[22] MD. CODE ANN., FAM. LAW § 4-506(c)(2)–(3) (1995).

[23] CAL. FAM. CODE § 6305 (West Supp. 1996) (amended by 1995 Cal. Stats. 246, § 2).

[24] UTAH CODE ANN. § 30-6-4.5 (1995).

[25] N.J. STAT. ANN. § 2C:25-29(a); State of New Jersey Domestic Violence Procedures Manual 45 n.18 (1994).

[26] *See Baker,* 904 P.2d 616; *Mechtel,* 528 N.W.2d 916; *Moreno,* 897 S.W.2d 439.

[27] *Baker,* 904 P.2d 616; *Mechtel,* 528 N.W.2d 916; *Moreno,* 897 S.W.2d 439.

[28] *See Mechtel,* 528 N.W.2d at 918; *Baker,* 904 P.2d at 617–18; *Moreno,* 897 S.W.2d at 441–42; FitzGerald v. FitzGerald, 406 N.W.2d 52, 53–54 (Minn. Ct. App. 1987) (Clearinghouse No. 42,616); Gibilisco v. Gibilisco, 875 P.2d 447, 448–49 (Okla. Ct. App. 1994) (Clearinghouse No. 49,854).

[29] *Mechtel,* 528 N.W. 2d at 917; *Moreno,* 897 S.W.2d at 440–41.

[30] *FitzGerald,* 406 N.W.2d 52; *Gibilisco,* 875 P.2d 447.

[31] *Baker,* 904 P.2d at 619; *Moreno,* 897 S.W.2d at 442.

[32] *Baker,* 904 P.2d at 618.

tioner had been denied her constitutional rights.[33]

In *Moreno*, the trial court's actions were even more egregious. Texas state law prohibits mutual restraining orders unless consented to by the parties or unless separate petitions are filed by the parties and the trial court makes findings of fact following an evidentiary hearing.[34] In *Moreno*, the victim's testimony, which included her assertion that respondent had threatened her with a knife and had used Mace against her, established a substantial history of abuse by the respondent. But the trial court, without making findings of fact, refused to enter a protective order unless the order was mutual.[35] Although the published opinion is unclear as to the basis for this decision, respondent alleged that petitioner damaged some personal property, he contradicted her testimony about one incident, and he denied the use of Mace.[36] When petitioner's counsel argued that imposition of mutual restraints was prohibited by the Family Code, since respondent had not filed a complaint and the parties had not agreed to a mutual order, the court reportedly stated, "Get somebody else" to hear the case.[37]

Mechtel, *Baker*, and *Moreno* are recent examples of situations in which counsel's effective appellate advocacy served to protect their clients from the potential for continuing negative consequences arising from mutual restraining orders.[38] In addition, the appellate courts' decisions served to instruct the judiciary that its indifference toward or ignorance of a litigant's basic constitutional rights will not be tolerated.

On the federal level, the Violence Against Women Act of 1994 (VAWA) requires that full faith and credit be given by a sister state (or Indian tribe)

Mutual restraining orders entered in the absence of a complaint by both parties and without specific findings are excepted from the full-faith-and-credit requirement of the Violence Against Women Act.

to a protective order issued by another state (or Indian tribe) in certain circumstances.[39] However, mutual restraining orders entered in the absence of a complaint by both parties and without specific findings are excepted from VAWA's full-faith-and-credit requirement.[40]

Advocates representing clients who are subject to a mutual restraining order entered in another state should make several inquiries. First, the advocate should determine whether state law in the client's state of residence sets forth any specific requirements that must be met immediately or within a specific time period so as to require the state's courts and law enforcement personnel to recognize the client's foreign order of protection as valid under the VAWA, and whether the client has complied with such requirements.[41] In most cases, clients should be advised to comply with applicable state law to ensure their personal safety. Second, the advocate

---

[33] *Id.* at 619.

[34] *Moreno*, 897 S.W.2d at 441; *see also* TEX. FAM. CODE ANN. § 71.11, 71.12(a), 71.121 (Vernon Supp. 1996).

[35] *Moreno*, 897 S.W.2d at 440–41.

[36] *Id.* at 441.

[37] *Id.* at 441; *see also* Gender Bias Task Force of Texas Final Report 67–68 (Feb. 1994), which says that approximately 50 percent of attorneys responding to a survey reported that judges frequently issued mutual restraining orders even when only one party presented evidence of abuse.

[38] *See Baker*, 904 P.2d 616; *Mechtel*, 528 N.W.2d 916; *Moreno*, 897 S.W.2d 439.

[39] Violence Against Women Act of 1994 (VAWA), 18 U.S.C. § 2265.

[40] 18 U.S.C. § 2265(c); *see also* Klein, *supra* note 1.

[41] *See* Klein, *supra* note 1, at 257–66, for a discussion of existing state procedures and a model approach for enforcement of foreign protection orders under the VAWA.

105

should ascertain whether both parties to the mutual order of protection were accorded their due process rights by the trial court in the state where the order was entered. If the client's batterer was awarded an order of protection against her and she was not accorded due process, the advocate should explore alternative means of defeating that portion of the order. Useful information as to accepted local or state procedures can sometimes be obtained by informally contacting court personnel who deal with domestic abuse matters regularly, the local prosecutor who is assigned to family violence matters, other local attorneys with domestic violence expertise, and even state court administrative personnel assigned to domestic violence matters. If litigation is required to defeat that part of the order, the advocate should weigh the benefits of immediately proceeding against the risk of probably having to notify the batterer of the commencement of those proceedings in the foreign court and revealing to the abuser the client's general location. If the client believes the abuser knows her location, and other possible remedies are determined to be inappropriate or nonexistent, litigation should probably be commenced immediately, provided steps are taken to protect her from retaliatory violence and harassment.

Victims' advocates in states where domestic abuse statutes fail to address the VAWA exception to full-faith-and-credit recognition of foreign orders of protection should seek enactment of remedial legislation to ensure that mutual restraining orders are prohibited unless due process requirements are met. The VAWA is supportive of this goal since it limits funding to states that do not pass laws that comply with due process requirements.[42] In addition, state legislators need to develop uniform, specific procedures for litigants to follow to ensure that foreign orders of protection are in fact accorded full faith and credit

when a party relocates to another state; such legislation also would assist parties who seek to have declared null and void those portions of mutual orders entered without due process.

Although due process requirements represent a well-intentioned effort of legislators and courts to satisfy objections to mutual restraining orders imposed without requisite notice and a hearing, as noted above, some trial courts continue to ignore these fundamental procedures.[43] Moreover, simply meeting those due process objections falls far short of abating the severe consequences a victim may suffer once she is also labeled an abuser.

IV. Cross-Complaints: Proceed with Caution

It is not uncommon for an abuser who has been served with his victim's complaint or petition for protection to then file a cross-complaint or cross-petition against her. Occasionally, after a serious incident, the true abuser may arrive at the courthouse or local authority before his victim and be the initial complainant, especially if he has previously sought advice of counsel.

A recent New Jersey case, *Mann v. Mann*, demonstrates the disastrous results that can occur when a victim, served with a cross-complaint for a domestic violence restraining order at the final hearing on her own domestic violence complaint, failed immediately to request an adjournment to prepare a defense or to consider alternative strategies.[44] The trial court refused to find husband guilty of committing either criminal trespass or harassment, the offenses with which he had been charged, but did find by a preponderance of the evidence that wife had committed acts of domestic violence under state law (criminal mischief and harassment).[45] Consequently, wife's complaint was dismissed, and husband was granted a final restraining order that, inter alia,

---

[42] 18 U.S.C. § 2101(c)(3); *see also* Klein, *supra* note 1, at 267–68.

[43] *E.g.*, *Baker*, 904 P.2d 616; *Mechtel*, 528 N.W.2d 916; *Moreno*, 897 S.W.2d 439.

[44] Mann v. Mann, 637 A.2d 170 (N.J. Super. Ct. App. Div. 1993).

[45] *Id.* at 171.

awarded him sole possession of the marital residence and custody of their children.[46] In its opinion affirming the trial court's action, the appellate court found that husband's service of his domestic violence complaint upon his wife immediately prior to final hearing on her complaint was not prejudicial to her interests since no contemporaneous objection on that basis had been made.[47]

Mann should be fair warning of the need to stop and critically evaluate the strengths and weaknesses of a domestic violence matter before proceeding to a hearing involving cross-complaints. A common tactic among sophisticated defense counsel is to advise defendants in domestic violence matters to file a cross-complaint if even a slight possibility of success exists. This is an excellent defense strategy because if both parties are determined to be abusive, the true victim will not receive any benefit from the court's consideration of abuse in awarding custody. In other instances, the abuser may be able to intimidate the victim into dismissing her complaint by using this technique. Worse yet, an alleged abuser may even be awarded an order of protection and receive custody, as in *Mann*.

Advocates should also be cognizant of, and attempt to evaluate before the hearing, any known prejudices of the individual judge who is to hear the case and how that court views victims who are charged with abuse. Where counsel learns in advance that a particular judge may be biased toward men or holds women to a higher standard of behavior than men, counsel should try to have the case reassigned to a judge who has a reputation for fairness to all litigants.

These words of caution are not to suggest that it is impossible to prevail on behalf of the real victim where cross-complaints are pending, especially if the facts regarding the recent incident in question are favorable and there is a substantial history of abuse. In such cases, if the client wants to proceed, she should do so. For example, if the client can establish either that her abuser is lying about her conduct or that she fought back in self-defense or in defense of another person, she should be treated as a battered victim by the court.[48] Or if her abuser is quite large and she is much smaller than him, a trial judge could well believe that she could not have made her abuser fearful for his personal safety. It is especially important to prove that the client has good reason to continue to be afraid of her abuser, that she is incapable of intimidating him or seriously harming him, and that she has sustained severe

It is not uncommon for an abuser to file a cross-complaint against his victim.

injuries and/or is likely to sustain severe injuries if she is not awarded an order of protection. In short, it is imperative to demonstrate through the client's testimony, the testimony of other witnesses if available, and other evidence, such as visible signs of injury, pictures, medical or police records, torn or ripped clothing, or other destroyed property, that the client is the only victim.

V. Options to Proceeding on Mutual Complaints

In some situations, to avoid the possible entry of mutual restraints or entry of a protective order against the client and dismissal of the client's complaint, it is ultimately preferable to negotiate dismissal of cross-complaints. This may be necessary, for example, where counsel has reason to believe that the client will be a poor witness or that the court hearing the matter may perceive the client to be equally responsible for violent behavior and where there are serious problems of proof.

Victims' advocates have encountered clients who lack detailed memo-

---

[46] *Id.*

[47] *Id.* at 172.

[48] LENORE E. WALKER ET AL., DOMESTIC VIOLENCE & THE COURTROOM: UNDERSTANDING THE PROBLEM—KNOWING THE VICTIM (1995).

ries of specific incidents of abuse or who, because of the ongoing nature of the violence and indignities perpetrated upon them, cannot distinguish one incident from another or cannot tie any incident to a particular time frame. Victims who use alcohol to self-medicate themselves in an effort to dull their pain or who are intimidated into drinking by their batterers may have difficulty remembering specific incidents.[49] Some victims repress memories of abuse in order to enable them to face each new day.[50] Time and events are blurry to those victims because one day is as difficult as another. If a cross-complaint has been filed against such a client, and counsel doubts that the client will be able to testify with specificity, counsel would be wise to consider whether the client should proceed to a hearing.

Other limited options available to such a client include seeking safety in a battered women's shelter and allowing her complaint to be dismissed or trying to persuade the batterer to reach an agreement that provides at least limited protection. Such agreement can be incorporated into a matrimonial order or included in a custody or support order, with the domestic violence cross-complaints dismissed.

Where there is a strong possibility that the trial court could find that the client provoked her abuser's attack, even though the act of abuse she committed may have been much less substantial than that inflicted upon her, defensive strategies should also be considered. For example, in *Moreno*, it appeared that the

trial judge believed the victim committed an act of criminal mischief, which he viewed as provocation for her abuser to retaliate with force.[51]

Similarly, even in those cases in which the client asserts that she acted in self-defense, counsel must evaluate whether the court could find her act as threatening as that of her abuser. Since domestic violence cases are extremely fact sensitive, it may be helpful to evaluate, by carefully questioning the client as to her recent and past history of abuse, whether she was a primary aggressor or if she acted primarily in self-defense. If counsel determines that the client was not a primary aggressor and that she acted primarily in self-defense, this should be elicited through testimony in court. In those states where courts must consider, before issuing a mutual order of protection, which party was the primary aggressor and which party was primarily acting in self-defense, counsel can use such testimony to fashion a persuasive argument that a cross-complaint against the client should be dismissed.[52] Even in states that do not require consideration of these factors by the trial court, an excellent argument can be presented based upon this theory, with reference to statutory authority in other states and to the model code.[53]

Other proof problems counsel are likely to encounter include the probable lack of even one witness to corroborate all or part of a client's story. This can be crucial, especially where a judge is unsure which party to a matter is more credible. If police were called to the

---

[49] Jerry P. Flanzer, *Alcohol and Family Violence: Then to Now—Who Owns the Problem*, in AGGRESSION, FAMILY VIOLENCE & CHEMICAL DEPENDENCY 61-79 (Ronald T. Potter-Efron & Patricia S. Potter-Efron eds., 1990); Heather R. Hayes & James G. Emshoff, *Substance Abuse and Family Violence*, in FAMILY VIOLENCE PREVENTION & TREATMENT 281 (Robert L. Hampton et al. eds., 1993); conversations with domestic violence victims' advocates at Jersey Battered Women's Services (JBWS), Morris County, N.J. (1990–96); Evan Stark & Anne H. Flitcraft, *Spouse Abuse*, in VIOLENCE IN AMERICA: A PUBLIC HEALTH APPROACH 140–41 (Mark L. Rosenberg & Mary Ann Fenly eds., 1991). The latter authors indicate abused women are 16 times more likely to become alcoholics and 9 times more likely to abuse drugs than women who are not battered.

[50] Conversations with domestic violence victims' advocates at JBWS (1990–96).

[51] *Moreno*, 897 S.W.2d at 440–41.

[52] *E.g.*, MD. FAM. CODE ANN. § 4-506(C)(2), (3) (1995); CAL. FAM. CODE § 6305 (West Supp. 1996).

[53] *E.g.*, MD. FAM. CODE ANN. § 4-506(C)(2), (3) (1995); UTAH CODE ANN. § 30-6-4.5 (1995); MODEL CODE, § 310 (and commentary thereon).

Stay Current on Family Law and Family Violence

The National Center on Women and Family Law, Inc. (NCWFL), a nonprofit organization established in 1979, provides case consultation and technical assistance on issues such as custody, support, and family violence. NCWFL participates as *amicus* in cases involving cutting-edge matters, works collaboratively with numerous organizations, and conducts public-policy analyses. It also trains attorneys, paralegals, judges, and battered women's advocates.

Its extensive publications include a national newsletter, *The Women's Advocate*; handbooks and information packets for lay persons; guidebooks and manuals for attorneys and advocates; and the *New York Family Law Bulletin*.

NCWFL has over 65 publications in print, over half of which are devoted to various aspects of domestic violence. Titles include the following:

- answers to essential questions, in BATTERED WOMEN: THE FACTS (May 1996);

- GUIDE TO INTERSTATE CUSTODY: A MANUAL FOR DOMESTIC VIOLENCE ADVOCATES (2d ed. 1995) and other publications on interstate custody;

- THE EFFECT OF WOMAN ABUSE ON CHILDREN (2d ed. 1994);

- more titles on child custody and visitation in cases of spousal abuse or child sexual abuse, including state-by-state statutory surveys, articles on expert testimony, and joint-custody materials;

- NATIONAL HANDBOOK ON TEEN DATING VIOLENCE AND THE LAW (June 1996);

- two publications on tort actions resulting from domestic violence;

- three publications on helping rural and disabled battered women and battered women of color;

- state-by-state compilations, including relocation

of custodial parents, abuse in same-sex relationships, stalking, and the marital rape exemption;

- titles on mutual orders of protection, joint counseling, batterers' pathology, the military, and immigration laws;

- three titles on police and arrest policies;

- two titles on medical and health care protocols;

- a publication on protecting the safety of battered women through change of name and social security number and another on voter-address confidentiality for battered persons;

- three publications on confidentiality, including PROTECTING CONFIDENTIALITY OF VICTIM-COUNSELOR COMMUNICATIONS (1993); and

- eight publications on mediation and family law, including MEDIATION—A GUIDE FOR ADVOCATES AND ATTORNEYS REPRESENTING BATTERED WOMEN (1990); MEDIATION AND YOU (1991); MEDIATION GUIDELINES AND SCREENING GUIDES (1992); MEDIATION IN FAMILY LAW CASES (1993); and MEDIATION OF DOMESTIC VIOLENCE CASES (1994).

Additional publications cover numerous aspects of child support, including CUSTODY, VISITATION AND CHILD SUPPORT (1993) and THE "GOOD CAUSE" EXCEPTION TO THE COOPERATION REQUIREMENT FOR APPLICANTS FOR AFDC CHILD SUPPORT (1995).

Newsletter $50/yr. Call or write for NCWFL's complete publications list on battered women, child custody and visitation, child support, confidentiality, interstate custody, mediation, and other topics. Training and consultation also available.

National Center on Women and Family Law, Inc., 275 Seventh Avenue, New York, NY 10001; (212) 741-9480; fax (212) 741-6438; HN1193@handsnet.org

---

scene of the incident, or officers investigated the incident shortly after it occurred, records and other information should be available from the police and the officer subpoenaed to court. Even a friend, relative, or any other person with relevant firsthand information can greatly enhance the victim's credibility in recounting events in court. While objectively evaluating the likelihood of success in any matter can be very difficult if cross-complaints are pending, counsel clearly should recommend pro-

ceeding to hearing only when well informed of the relevant law in each case and only after thoroughly evaluating the client's own ability to tell her story credibly.

As alluded to above, in some states if parties are seriously contemplating divorce or separation, or have actually filed a matrimonial, custody, or support action, clients may be advised to enter into consent orders or agreements in that action—conditioned upon the dismissal of domestic violence cross-complaints—that will provide for mutual or individual restraints against specific conduct. Such orders can be tailored to suit the needs of the parties and to ensure that any mandatory arrest provisions of a specific state's domestic abuse act cannot be invoked.[54] However, since mutual or individual restraints incorporated into another family law order are less enforceable than those in domestic violence final restraining orders, the victim is afforded only minimal protection from abuse.[55] Consequently, nondomestic violence restraining orders should be considered only if the client's case is weak in terms of proof and she is faced with a cross-complaint.

Restraints in the matrimonial or other family law action may serve to avoid exposing the client to possible criminal and/or contempt charges for violations of a domestic violence restraining order that requires immediate arrest[56] or to possible adjudication as an abuser where such judgment could have a negative impact upon her quest for child custody.[57] If necessary, restraints in a matrimonial or other family action can be enforced by way of filing a motion for enforcement of the litigant's rights. Only in rare instances would orders obtained on such enforcement motions call for the incarceration of a party. If abuse that falls within the conduct prohibited by the state's abuse-prevention statute recurs, the client should still be able to file a new complaint and obtain a final domestic violence restraining order.[58] Where this strategy is utilized and the abuser is represented, he should be warned by his counsel to refrain from violent and abusive behavior or he will face the certainty of further domestic violence court proceedings. Where the opposing party is unrepresented, counsel may request the court to admonish both parties about this possibility.

If the client is not party to another family matter, or does not want to file a matrimonial, custody, or support action, she may choose to negotiate dismissal of mutual complaints and voluntarily separate from the abuser, rather than be subject to the punitive effects of an alleged violation of a restraining order. If a client chooses this route, she should be urged to have a safety plan, which could include staying at a battered women's shelter or with family or friends at least temporarily. In this instance, the client is likely to be very discouraged and to feel legitimately that the legal system has failed her.

Finally, even though she may have a strong case, the client may decide to dismiss her complaint voluntarily and to return to her abuser if the abuser also

---

[54] NATIONAL CTR. ON WOMEN & FAMILY LAW, MANDATORY ARREST: PROBLEMS AND POSSIBILITIES A-1 to A-28 (1994); Zorza, *supra* note 3, at 393; *see also* N.J. STAT. ANN. § 2C:25-31 (West 1995); N.Y. CRIM. PROC. L. § 140.10(4) (McKinney Supp. 1996).

[55] Such orders are not entitled to full faith and credit under 18 U.S.C. § 2265. Also, mandatory arrest statutes may apply only to orders of protection obtained under a state's domestic abuse laws. *See also* Joan Zorza, *Protecting the Children in Custody Disputes When One Parent Abuses the Other*, 29 CLEARINGHOUSE REV. 1113, 1125 n.107 (Apr. 1996); National Ctr. on Women & Family Law, Voter Address Confidentiality for Domestic Violence Advocates (1995) (Item No. 65), as to limited application of states' laws protecting the confidentiality of a victim's location.

[56] NATIONAL CTR. ON WOMEN & FAMILY LAW, *supra* note 54; Zorza, *supra* note 3, at 393; N.J. STAT. ANN. 2C:25-31 (West 1995); N.Y. CRIM. PROC. L. § 140.10(4) (McKinney Supp. 1996).

[57] *See supra* note 5 and accompanying text.

[58] This relief may not be available in every state. *See* Felton v. Felton, No. 95-646 (Ohio Ct. App. Dec. 11, 1995), *on appeal*, No. 96-0198 (Ohio Sup. Ct. filed Jan. 25, 1996). In *Felton*, the Ohio Court of Appeals affirmed the trial court's dismissal of appellant's post-divorce petition for an order of protection, in part because it found that she was adequately protected by a no-molestation provision incorporated into the parties' divorce judgment. The reviewing court indicated that there had been no need for petitioner to seek an order of protection and that in the interests of judicial economy the trial judge's order to respondent to abide by the terms of the no-molestation clause was an adequate disposition of the matter.

dismisses his complaint. While this decision is frustrating to advocates, the client must be allowed to make it for herself, even though her abuser probably filed his complaint primarily to intimidate her into returning to him. Some victims must experience repeated incidents of truly violent attacks upon themselves before they make the final decision to leave their batterers permanently.[59] Other victims are able to leave only when they realize the impact of the violence upon their children or when their children are being physically abused.[60]

VI. Representing a Victim Against Whom Restraints Have Been Entered

Advocates representing a client against whom a restraining order has been entered, or who is a party to mutual restraints, should determine whether dismissal of the complaint and dissolution of the restraint can be negotiated. Otherwise, counsel must offer the client strong words of advice. That all contact with the other party should be avoided, particularly if certain alleged violations of the restraints could result in the client's immediate arrest, should be emphatically made clear to the client. Where children must be exchanged for visitation purposes, cautionary language should be included in the order of protection to allow limited contact between the parties for that purpose only, preferably at a police station or with a third party present to facilitate the exchange and to serve as a witness if required in the future.

Despite appropriate advice to represented litigants, they, as well as litigants

who are unrepresented and uninformed of the law, sometimes are charged with violations that result in their arrest.[61]

Dual arrests are a particular problem in states where the law mandates the arrest of offenders charged with certain violations of restraining orders. In states with strong mandatory arrest statutes, and where police are mandated to arrest at the scene of a domestic violence incident if they have probable cause to believe a family offense has been committed, researchers have documented a substantial increase in arrests of *both* parties, even when mutual restraints have not been ordered.[62] According to a source in New York City, when police receive complaints of assault from both parties, most officers arrest both and let a judge decide whether one party acted in self-defense.[63] Another New York City advocate[64] reports an increase in

Dual arrests are a particular problem in states where the law mandates the arrest of offenders charged with certain violations of restraining orders.

calls from victims who have been arrested along with their abuser since the state's mandatory arrest statute applicable to family violence became effective on January 1, 1996.[65] Some women may resist seeking assistance from police at all to enforce an order of protection or when attacked because they have a justifiable concern that they may be arrested themselves.[66]

VII. Conclusion

The continuing deprivation of domestic violence victims' basic due process

---

[59] Zorza, *supra* note 55, at 1117; LENORE E. WALKER, THE BATTERED WOMAN 234–39 (1979); MARY MARECEK, BREAKING FREE FROM PARTNER ABUSE 51–64 (1993).

[60] LEE H. BOWKER, ENDING THE VIOLENCE 88–94 (1986).

[61] See NATIONAL CTR. ON WOMEN & FAMILY LAW, *supra* note 54, at 16–23.

[62] *Id.*

[63] Conversation with Maureen Geogolis, Deputy Director, Victims Services Police Programs (DVPP/DVIEP), New York, N.Y. (Apr. 29, 1996).

[64] Conversation with Katya Frischer, Esq., Urban Justice Center, New York, N.Y. (Apr. 23, 1996).

[65] N.Y. CRIM. PROC. L. § 140.10(4) (McKinney Supp. 1996).

[66] See NATIONAL CTR. ON WOMEN & FAMILY LAW, *supra* note 54, at 16–23; Zorza, *supra* note 3, at 393.

rights in civil courts can and should be addressed by continuing education of the judiciary in each jurisdiction.[67] Training should emphasize that the legislative intent underpinning each state's domestic violence laws is to protect victims of family violence and to deter further violence. Judges should also know that domestic violence is emotionally damaging to children, who may be abused as well, and that children who witness domestic violence are at a higher risk of becoming violent themselves.[68] Finally, judges should be educated about the importance of making batterers accountable for their behavior and about the dynamics of domestic violence,[69] as many (though by no means all) are appointed or elected without ever having practiced family law or have had no substantive contact with this issue prior to assuming the bench. Understanding the dynamics of domestic violence is important because judges, as well as police and other service providers, become frustrated with litigants who repeatedly obtain restraining orders, dismiss them, reconcile, and are reinjured by abusers.[70]

Advocates interested in ameliorating the unintended consequences of mandatory arrest statutes recommend more comprehensive police training as well as the adoption of legislation directing police, before effectuating dual arrests, to consider the comparative injuries of the parties, to determine who is the primary aggressor, and to investigate the history of abuse between parties as well as the potential for future injury and the issue of self-defense.[71] In addition, many recommend increasing the availability of victims' services, such as shelters and victims' advocates, so women are more able to avoid contact with their abusers and informed of the law and other resources available to them. Others recommend increasing victims' access to legal counsel and trained domestic violence court personnel, who can intervene and assist victims, as a way to limit the unfortunate consequences of dual arrests. Finally, and crucially, more meaningful prosecution of batterers should ultimately force them to accept responsibility for their conduct and should help in convincing them to modify their behavior.[72]

Until such laws are enacted and improved safeguards are put into place, victims' advocates must be alert to the need to defend their clients vigorously against the imposition of mutual restraints. Advocates should also be aware of the various options they may use to avoid abusive issuance of mutual restraint orders and the improper enforcement of sanctions for violating such orders.

---

[67] *See* WALKER ET AL., *supra* note 48; JANET CARTER ET AL., DOMESTIC VIOLENCE IN CIVIL COURT CASES—A NATIONAL MODEL FOR JUDICIAL EDUCATION (1992).

[68] WALKER ET AL., *supra* note 48; CARTER ET AL., *supra* note 67, at 2, 20–54; *see also* NATIONAL CTR. ON WOMEN & FAMILY LAW, *supra* note 54, at 23–35.

[69] *See* WALKER ET AL., *supra* note 48; JANET CARTER ET AL., *supra* note 67.

[70] WALKER ET AL., *supra* note 48; JANET CARTER ET AL., *supra* note 67; NATIONAL CTR. ON WOMEN & FAMILY LAW, *supra* note 54, at 29, 33–34.

[71] NATIONAL CTR. ON WOMEN & FAMILY LAW, *supra* note 54, at 26–34.

[72] *Id.*

Full Faith and Credit: Interstate Enforcement of Protection Orders Under the Violence Against Women Act of 1994

CATHERINE F. KLEIN*

I. Introduction

In August of 1994, Congress passed the controversial Crime Bill.[1] Amidst the controversy, however, there was one act incorporated into the Bill that received bipartisan support: the Violence Against Women Act of 1994 (VAWA).[2] The VAWA is one of the Crime Bill's largest crime-prevention programs, providing $1.6 billion to confront the national problem of gender-based violence.[3] The Violence Against Women Act attempts to make crimes committed against women considered in the same manner as those motivated by religious, racial, or political bias. "The Violence Against Women Act is intended to respond both to the underlying attitude that this violence is somehow less serious

* Associate Professor and Director, The Families and the Law Clinic, Columbus School of Law, The Catholic University of America's clinical domestic violence program. The author wishes to express her gratitude to her research assistants, Erin O'Keefe and Julie Sippel.

1. Pub. L. No. 103-322, 108 Stat. 1796. The Crime Bill provides for $30 billion for punishment and prevention programs.
2. The Violence Against Women Act of 1994, Pub. L. No. 103-322, Title IV, 108 Stat. 1902-55 (codified in scattered sections of 8 U.S.C.A., 18 U.S.C.A., & 42 U.S.C.A.) [hereinafter VAWA].
3. *See* MAJORITY STAFF OF SENATE COMM. ON THE JUDICIARY, 103D CONG., 1ST SESS., THE RESPONSES TO RAPE: DETOURS ON THE ROAD TO EQUAL JUSTICE, at 14 (Comm. Print 1993) [hereinafter EQUAL JUSTICE]. "The Violence Against Women Act recognizes that there is no place—home, street, or school—where women are spared the fear of crime. This bill seeks above all to address the vital necessity and right of women to be free from violence." *Id.*

than other crime and to the resulting failure of our criminal justice system to address such violence."[4]

The VAWA addresses the problems of gender-based violence under five titles. Title I, Safe Streets for Women, increases sentences for repeat offenders who commit crimes against women.[5] Title II, Safe Homes for Women, focuses on crimes of domestic violence.[6] Title III, Civil Rights for Women, creates the first civil rights remedy for violent gender-based discrimination.[7] Title IV, Safe Campuses, grants funds to be spent on problems faced by women on the nation's college campuses. Title V, Equal Justice for Women in the Courts, provides training for state and federal judges to combat widespread gender bias in the courts.

This article focuses on Title II, Safe Homes for Women, specifically, interstate enforcement of protection orders. Prior to the enactment of VAWA, the majority of states did not afford full faith and credit to protection orders issued in sister states.[8] This was a serious breach in

---

4. Staff of Senate Comm. on the Judiciary, The Violence Against Women Act of 1994, S. Rep. No. 138, 103d Cong., 1st Sess., at 38 (1993).

5. Title I also expands evidentiary protection for sexual assault victims, allocates moneys to states for the purpose of targeting these crimes as a top priority, takes steps to increase safety for women in public parks and transit systems, and creates a Justice Department task force on violence against women.

6. Title II provides for a national, toll-free hotline to assist victims of domestic violence, creates a federal remedy for interstate crimes of abuse, requires states to recognize protection orders issued by sister states, provides more resources to fight domestic violence, and gives states incentives to treat domestic violence as a serious crime.

7. Equal Justice, *supra* note 3. Senator Joseph Biden commenting on the new civil rights remedy in the Violence Against Women Act,

I believe that this provision is the key to changing the attitudes about violence against women. This provision recognizes that violent crimes committed because of a person's gender raise issues of equality as well as issues of safety and accountability. Long ago, we recognized that an individual who is attacked because of his race is deprived of his rights to be free and equal; we should guarantee the same protection for victims who are attacked *because* of their gender. Whether the violence is motivated by racial bias or ethnic bias, or gender bias, the laws protection should be the same.

See generally, W.H. Hallock, *The Violence Against Women Act: Civil Rights for Sexual Assault Victims*, 68 Ind. L.J. 577, 585 (1993):

Women, and almost exclusively women, of every race, economic class, and ethnic group are the targets of such crime. Since women, because of their very status as women, remain the primary target for sexual assault by men, sex crimes can be considered a form of sex discrimination.

8. Seven jurisdictions have state statutes that accord full faith and credit to foreign protection orders. See Ky. Rev. Stat. Ann. § 426.955 (Baldwin 1993); Nev. Rev. Stat. Ann. § 33.090 (1986); N.H. Rev. Stat. Ann. § 173B:11-6 (1993); N.M. Stat. Ann. § 40-13-6 (Michie Supp. 1993); Or. Rev. Stat. § 24.185 (1993); R.I. Gen. Laws § 15-15-8 (1994); W. Va. Code § 48-2A-3(e) (Supp. 1993). New Mexico affords full faith and credit to orders of tribal courts. N.M. Stat. Ann. § 40-13-6(D) (Michie 1994). Nevada accepts a foreign protection order as evidence of the facts on which it was based to issue its own civil protection order. Nev. Rev. Stat. Ann. § 33.090 (1993).

the protection afforded victims of domestic violence. Without full faith and credit statutes, a state only has the power to protect victims of domestic violence within its boundaries, limiting the protection afforded to victims if they are forced to move or flee to another state.

Prior to the VAWA, in order to receive protection in the foreign state, a victim had to petition the foreign state's court for a new protection order. Because of due process requirements, the batterer had to be served with notice regarding pending protection proceedings, thus revealing the victim's whereabouts and putting the victim in a dangerous situation. In the absence of a full faith and credit statute, jurisdictional problems could arise. A state may not have jurisdiction to issue a new protection order unless abuse takes place within its boundaries. In addition, there are other problems that arise out of the requirement of refiling for a protection order including: additional filing fees; language barriers; the difference in each state's domestic violence laws regarding availability, duration, and scope of protection; inadequate transportation; access to legal assistance; and child care facilities.

This article examines existing procedures for enforcing interstate protection orders in states that have full faith and credit statutes. It then proposes methods by which practitioners can utilize the VAWA under their state's existing systems and explores model approaches to implementing the VAWA by looking at the roles that practitioners, courts, and law enforcement officials should play. Finally, this article will address the issues of mutual protection orders and the creation of a new federal crime under the VAWA.

II. Full Faith and Credit: An Interpretation of the VAWA

The Violence Against Women Act establishes that states must grant full faith and credit to protection orders issued in foreign states or tribal courts.[9] Any protection order issued by one state or

---

9. VAWA, 18 U.S.C.A. § 2265, providing in part:

(a) FULL FAITH AND CREDIT. Any protection order issued that is consistent with subsection (b) of this section by the court of one state or Indian tribe (the issuing State or Indian tribe) shall be accorded full faith and credit by the court of another State or Indian tribe (the enforcing State or Indian tribe) and enforced as if it were the order of the enforcing State or tribe.

(b) PROTECTION ORDER. A protection order issued by a State or tribal court is consistent with this subsection if

(1) such court has jurisdiction over the parties and matter under the law of such State or Indian tribe; and

(2) reasonable notice and opportunity to be heard is given to the person against whom the order is sought sufficient to protect that person's right to due process. In the case of ex parte orders, notice and opportunity to be heard must be provided

tribe[10] shall be treated and enforced as if it were an order of the enforcing state. The Act extends to permanent, temporary, and *ex parte* protection orders. Full faith and credit is afforded during the period of time in which the order remains valid in the issuing state. Protection orders are only afforded full faith and credit under the Act, however, if the due process requirements of the issuing state were met. The Act specifies that the issuing court must have had both personal and subject matter jurisdiction, and that the respondent received reasonable notice and an opportunity to be heard. Furthermore, the full faith and credit provision applies to *ex parte* orders if notice and opportunity to be heard were provided within the issuing state's statutory requirement or within a reasonable time after the order was issued. Because the VAWA requires that due process be met before a protection order is afforded full faith and credit, it does not extend full faith and credit to mutual protection orders that do not comply with due process.[11]

The failure to satisfy due process requirements is the only exception to the full faith and credit provision. A sister state's valid order would be accorded full faith and credit, even if the victim were ineligible for a protection order in the enforcing state. For example, a victim of abuse in a same sex relationship would be able to obtain a protection order in the District of Columbia, but might not be able to obtain one under the laws of Montana.[12] Under the VAWA, however, Montana would have to afford full faith and credit to the order issued by the District of Columbia even though the victim would have been ineligible for protection in Montana.[13]

The VAWA does not require the victim to register her foreign protection order in the enforcing state. Although there are advantages to

---

within the time required by State or tribal law, and in any event within a reasonable time after the order is issued, sufficient to protect the respondent's due process rights.

10. For the purposes of this article the terms state and court shall also apply to Indian tribes and to tribal courts.

11. VAWA, 18 U.S.C.A. § 2265 (c)(1)(2). *See infra* notes 51-59 and accompanying text discussing mutual protection orders.

12. *See* MONT. CODE ANN. § 40-4-121 (1994).

13. *See* Barbara J. Hart, *State Codes on Domestic Violence Analysis, Commentary, and Recommendations*, 43 JUV. & FAM. CT. J. 43, n.4 (1992). Some variations in state domestic violence statutes include: the parties' eligibility for protection, offenses that give rise to protection, and the duration and scope of protection. Prior to the VAWA, these variations might preclude a victim's ability to seek protection in a sister state. *See also* Catherine F. Klein & Leslye E. Orloff, *Providing Legal Protection for Battered Women: An Analysis of State Statutes and Case Law*, 21 HOFSTRA L. REV. 801 (1993) (reviewing and analyzing extensively states' civil protection statutes and caselaw).

registering protection orders,[14] requiring registration could leave victims unprotected and vulnerable from the time they enter a new state until the time they become aware of and satisfy registration requirements. Under the VAWA, a victim with a valid protection order receives continuous protection until the expiration of that order, regardless of which state she has entered. Furthermore, even if a victim chooses to register a protection order in a new state, the VAWA does not require the new state to provide the respondent with additional notice. These are important considerations that provide immediate protection while ensuring confidentiality of the victim's whereabouts.

Choice of law is another consideration under the VAWA. Courts have taken several different approaches when facing choice of law problems.[15] The VAWA states that a foreign order is afforded full faith and credit and is "enforced as if it were the order of the enforcing state."[16] If, for example, a woman obtains a protection order in Maryland and later flees to Pennsylvania, which state's law would apply is a choice of law problem. Under the language of the VAWA, it seems clear that Pennsylvania law would apply because the order "shall be enforced as if it were the order of the enforcing state."[17] Thus, Pennsylvania would treat the order as if it had been issued by a court of Pennsylvania and would apply its own law.

III. Examination of Existing State Procedures for Enforcement of Foreign Protection Orders

Because the interstate enforcement provision of the VAWA is vague, states are left to their discretion as how to set up procedures to implement it effectively. Even prior to the enactment of the VAWA, there were a few state statutes that afforded foreign protection orders full faith and credit. New Hampshire, West Virginia, Kentucky, and Oregon have existing procedures to enforce their full faith and credit statutes. Section III of this article will examine the current procedures of Kentucky, West Virginia, and Oregon. This section will also discuss the New Hampshire procedures and suggest that other states use New Hampshire as a model for implementing the interstate enforcement provision of the VAWA. When examining existing state procedures

---

14. *See infra* note 41 and accompanying text discussing the advantages of registering of protection orders.

15. *See generally* Herma Hill Kay, *Theory into Practice: Choice of Law in the Courts*, 34 MERCER L. REV. 521 (1983) (identifying and evaluating the different choice of law theories used by the courts).

16. VAWA, 18 U.S.C.A. § 2265.

17. VAWA, 18 U.S.C.A. § 2265.

for enforcing the full faith and credit provision, it is important to consider that some of the states' requirements are not in compliance with the VAWA and that the VAWA is superseding.

A. *Kentucky*

The full faith and credit statute in Kentucky applies to any foreign order, not just civil protection orders.[18] The statute states that a copy of any foreign order may be filed with the Kentucky court and is to be treated as if it were an order of the Kentucky court.[19]

Prior to the VAWA, Kentucky enforced sister state protection orders under this broad full faith and credit statute by requiring the victim to file a certified copy of the foreign protection order with a Kentucky court. There is a major flaw in this procedure, however, because current Kentucky practice requires that notice of the filing be sent to the respondent. This notice requirement reveals to the batterer the new location of the victim, which may jeopardize the victim's safety.[20] Another problem under Kentucky's current full faith and credit statute is that it does not afford a victim complete protection unless she has filed her foreign order with the court. The police will not arrest someone for violation of a foreign protection order that has not been filed. By requiring the victim to file a copy of the foreign order, the state has left victims who have recently fled to Kentucky or who are not aware of the filing requirement extremely vulnerable. If law enforcement agencies will not enforce foreign orders until they are filed with the court, there is a serious gap in the protection afforded to the victims from the time they enter the state until the time they comply with the statute.

Because this broad full faith and credit statute is not designed specifically to address domestic violence orders, it fails to consider the special needs of a victims fleeing from their batterers. Some factors to consider are: victims who have fled their home states because of domestic violence may not be entering Kentucky during court hours; they may not have access to legal assistance, adequate transportation, or adequate child care; and they may fear that by going to court their batterers will be informed of their whereabouts.

---

18. KY. REV. STAT. ANN. § 426.955 (Baldwin 1993).
19. *Id.*
20. Lisa Lerman, *A Model State Act: Remedies for Domestic Abuse*, 21 HARV. J. LEGIS. 61 (Winter 1984):

> If the wife does manage to escape, her husband often stalks her like a hunted animal. He scours the neighborhood, contacts friends and relatives, goes to all the likely places where she may have sought refuge, and checks with public agencies to track her down. . . .

Id. at 79, n.64.

The Kentucky Coalition Against Domestic Violence and the Kentucky Supreme Court have been working together to finalize a process that would prevent disclosure of the victim's new location.[21] The proposed procedure would require the victim, upon arrival in Kentucky, to take the protection order to the local prosecutor. The local prosecutor would then verify that due process requirements had been met in the state that issued the order. After verification, the prosecutor would then make a motion to the court to have the foreign order entered as a Kentucky order.[22] This proposed procedure is to take effect as policy, rather than by written rule or statute. It is presumed that a victim who has fled to Kentucky will become aware of its interstate enforcement procedure by contacting local law enforcement agencies, courts, or domestic violence advocates. The proposed procedure does not address all situations or solve all problems. First, the proposed procedure involving the prosecutor seems more onerous than the prior registration requirement. Also, it is unlikely that prosecutors will make verification of foreign protection orders a priority. It is unclear exactly how a prosecutor will verify a foreign order. Second, these procedures do not cover a victim who needs protection from the batterer, but who has not taken it to a prosecutor to have it verified. It has been suggested that in such a situation, the woman should receive an emergency protection order. Emergency protection orders are available on a twenty-four-hour basis in every county of Kentucky. This alternative would not only give rise to jurisdictional problems, but due process would require that the batterer be informed of the new order and that the batterer be served before the order would be effective. This procedure is inconsistent with the VAWA because it requires a woman who already has a protection order to obtain a new one before she will be protected in Kentucky. This undermines the purpose of the full faith and credit provision in the VAWA.

B. *West Virginia*

Unlike Kentucky, the State of West Virginia has a full faith and credit statute in its Domestic Relations chapter.[23] This statute provides that any foreign order "shall be accorded full faith and credit and be

---

21. Conversation with Sharon Currens, Kentucky Domestic Violence Association. For information regarding interstate enforcement of protection orders in Kentucky, contact Ms. Currens at 502/526-2189.

22. Conversation with Susan Clary, General Counsel to the Kentucky Supreme Court. For more information on the proposed procedures to enforce foreign protection orders, contact Ms. Clary at 502/564-4176.

23. W. VA. CODE § 48-2A-3(e) (1994).

enforced as if it were an order of this state if its terms and conditions are substantially similar'' to those of West Virginia.[24] Under this article of the West Virginia Code, there is a subsection that provides for a registry of foreign orders. There is a proviso, however, that says that the registry subsection is not effective until a central automated computer system becomes available. Such a system is not yet available.[25]

Although there is an absence of an automated computer system, there are current procedures in West Virginia to enforce an out of state order. A protected party entering West Virginia can take a foreign order to a local law enforcement agency. Once filed with the police, the foreign order will be treated by law enforcement as if it were an order of West Virginia. In a situation where a victim is trying to enforce a foreign order, whether it was filed with police or not, a victim can take the order to magistrate court. The magistrate decides whether the terms and conditions of the foreign order are ''substantially similar'' to the terms and conditions necessary to obtain and order in West Virginia.[26] The VAWA does not limit full faith and credit to orders that are ''substantially similar'' to the orders issued by the enforcing state. Under the VAWA, if due process requirements were satisfied in the issuing state, all other states must accord the order full faith and credit.[27]

There are no fees either for filing an order with law enforcement agencies or seeking enforcement at magistrate court. It is important that states waive filing fees because the additional economic burden may discourage women from receiving the protection they deserve.

C. *Oregon*

Oregon also recognizes orders from sister states.[28] Upon the victim's arrival in Oregon, a foreign order is automatically afforded full faith and credit for thirty days.[29] The victim has thirty days after entering Oregon to register the order. The victim may register an order after

---

24. W. VA. CODE § 48-2A-3(e) (1994).

25. For further information regarding interstate enforcement procedures in West Virginia, contact the magistrate court in the county where seeking enforcement.

26. For more information on enforcement of a foreign protection order in West Virginia, contact the West Virginia Coalition Against Domestic Violence at 304/765-2250.

27. *See supra* notes 9-11 and accompanying text discussing due process requirements in the VAWA's full faith and credit provision.

28. For information regarding enforcement of a foreign protection order in Oregon, contact the Oregon Coalition Against Domestic and Sexual Violence at 503/223-7411.

29. OR. REV. STAT. § 24.185(1) (1993). A foreign protection order is treated like an order issued by Oregon ''immediately upon the arrival in this state by the person protected by the restraining order and shall continue to be so treated for a period of thirty days without any further action by the protected person.'' *Id.*

thirty days; however, the victim will not be protected until the order is registered. The victim may file at no charge a copy of her order with a clerk of any circuit court.[30] After the order is filed, the clerk is required to treat the foreign order in the same manner as an order of the State of Oregon.[31] If at the time of filing the woman provides written certification that the batterer was personally served in the proceeding that gave rise to the protection order, the clerk will forward a copy of the order to the county sheriff.[32] The foreign order is enforceable until it expires under its own terms, or until it is terminated by the Oregon court.[33]

An important aspect of Oregon's statute is the enforcement powers granted to law enforcement officers. A police officer may enforce a foreign protection order and make a warrantless arrest in two situations. The first situation is if there is probable cause to believe that an order was violated and the victim provides a copy of a foreign protection order and swears that she has lived in Oregon for thirty days or less. Second, the police officer may also arrest a person if there is probable cause to believe that an order was violated and the victim has filed a copy of her order with the court.[34] The legislature has provided qualified immunity for police officers acting on foreign protection orders.[35] Police officers are not subject to liability for making arrests on foreign orders as long as the police officer reasonably believes that the document presented to the officer is an accurate copy of the foreign protection order.[36]

The Oregon statute takes important steps in protecting women from domestic violence. By allowing victims thirty days to file their orders, the statute considers that they may not be able to register their orders immediately upon arrival in the state. Also, the process for registration has been made fairly easy, and with a written certification that the batterer was personally served, a victim is able to have an order forwarded to local law enforcement agencies. Also, by permitting the police to make probable cause arrests for violations of foreign protection

---

30. OR. REV. STAT. § 24.185(2) (1993).

31. OR. REV. STAT. § 24.115(1) (1993).

32. OR. REV. STAT. § 24.185(3) (1993) (law also provides that after the sheriff receives a copy of a foreign order, the sheriff shall enter the order into the Law Enforcement Data System).

33. OR. REV. STAT. § 24.185(4) (1993).

34. OR. REV. STAT. § 133.310(4)(a)(b) (1993).

35. OR. REV. STAT. § 133.315(2) (1993) (an officer is immune from civil liability if the officer has a reasonable belief that the foreign order is accurate).

36. A representative from the Oregon State Sheriffs' Association suggested that unless the document is written in "Crayola crayons," the police would err on the side of intervening and enforcing the restraining order.

orders and extending qualified immunity to the police, the legislature has taken necessary steps in ensuring that law enforcement officials can play their part in protecting victims of domestic violence.

The state full faith and credit statute does not address all the problems faced by victims of domestic violence who arrive in Oregon. While it does provide victims a thirty day opportunity to register their protection orders, it does not protect women who have been in the state for longer than thirty days and have not yet filed their order. It is important to note that although registration has many advantages, the VAWA full faith and credit provision does not require any registration.

D. *New Hampshire*

Under New Hampshire state law, a foreign protection order receives full faith and credit. The New Hampshire full faith and credit statute and the procedures used to enforce it currently provide the most extensive protection to a victim with an out of state protection order. The New Hampshire protection order statute provides that any foreign protection order "shall be given full faith and credit throughout the state."[37] The only condition is that the foreign order be similar to a protection order issued in New Hampshire.[38]

The procedures for enforcement under the statute provide that a victim may file a certified copy of any foreign order with any district court and swear under oath that the foreign order is still in effect.[39] Next, the clerk of the court must read the foreign order in its entirety to determine whether it is similar to a New Hampshire order as required by the statute. If there are questions regarding the similarity, the clerk may consult a judge. If there are questions about authenticity, however, the clerk may contact a clerk of the issuing state.

If the clerk makes the determination that the foreign order is similar, the clerk then provides the victim with an affidavit to sign, attesting to the fact that the foreign order is still in effect in the issuing state. The foreign order is then attached to the affidavit and filed with the district court.

New Hampshire has a computer generated form called the Foreign Protective Order Affidavit.[40] The form has two sections. The first section is to be completed and signed by the protected party and also is to be notarized. The second section is a checklist for court use only. The checklist serves as a record of those who have received

---

37. N.H. Rev. Stat. Ann. § 173-B:11-b (1993).
38. *Id.*
39. *Id.*
40. *See* Appendix for a copy of the Foreign Protective Order Affidavit.

copies of the foreign order and affidavit. The clerk determines which law enforcement agencies should receive copies. For example, copies may be sent to the jurisdictions where the woman lives, works, or perhaps visits family members. If the woman chooses, she may deliver copies of the order and affidavit to the appropriate law enforcement agencies directly. Although the original affidavit and attached foreign order are filed in district court, the clerk is required to carefully note in the record to whom and when copies of the order and affidavit were given or sent. This serves as a method of ensuring that the appropriate law enforcement officials received copies of the protection order.

Another important aspect of the New Hampshire procedures is that foreign orders may be enforceable without any registration. Police officers may rely upon a foreign order if the victim shows the order and makes a verbal statement that the order is still in effect. New Hampshire not only allows officers to enforce foreign orders without a registration requirement but also provides the opportunity for victim's to have their orders sent to the appropriate law enforcement officials. The New Hampshire process allows for the benefits of registration without making it a condition for protection.

IV. Model Approach to Interstate Enforcement Under the VAWA

An assessment of the current applications of state full faith and credit statutes reveals certain essential elements for the successful enforcement of foreign protection orders. None of the states surveyed had fees for a victim to file a protection order in a new state. It is necessary to eliminate additional economic burdens so that all victims will have adequate access to protection.

The VAWA's full faith and credit provision does not require registration of protection orders. Thus, states may encourage registration, but cannot make registration a condition for full faith and credit. Registration can be an important method of combatting domestic violence. There are reasons why registration should be encouraged: It is an excellent method of informing law enforcement officials of existing protection orders and it can relieve law enforcement officials of the burden of assessing the validity of foreign protection orders at the scene of a domestic incident.[41] However, registration should never be a condition

---

41. The states that currently have registries are Connecticut, Florida, Kentucky, Massachusetts, Rhode Island, South Dakota, and Oregon. *See Developments in the Law—Legal Responses to Domestic Violence: II. Traditional Mechanisms of Response to Domestic Violence,* 106 HARV. L. REV. 1505 (1993).

for enforcement of foreign protection orders. By requiring registration, the very purposes of the VAWA are undermined. A victim may not have access to or knowledge of registration procedures at the time she enters the new state. Mandatory registration leaves the victim unprotected until she is able to register her protection order. Under the VAWA, a victim with a valid foreign protection order should be protected from the moment she crosses state lines.

An important consideration in the enforcement of foreign protection orders is police liability. Police officers play a vital role in preventing domestic violence.[42] Many victims first learn about the rights and services available to them through police contact.[43] More importantly, studies show that effective police responses to domestic violence can prevent future violence. The Minneapolis Domestic Violence Experiment, conducted by the National Institute of Justice, found that "victims of domestic assault are twice as likely to be assaulted again if the police do not arrest the attackers."[44] Ineffective police responses, however, serve to exacerbate the problems of domestic violence.

Police fear liability when entering into a domestic violence situation, specifically for false arrest.[45] Because police are essential to the effective enforcement of domestic laws, they must be able to carry out their duties without threat of criminal or civil liability. Many states have explicitly provided qualified immunity for police officers acting under their state's domestic violence statute. Thirty-one states have qualified immunity statutes within their domestic violence code protecting police officers

---

In order to aid the identification of violators, Massachusetts has created a computerized registry of batterers placed under such orders and domestic abuse offenders generally. . . . The central registry is intended both to enhance effective monitoring in specific cases and to isolate and identify repeat offenders who move between jurisdictions and multiple abusive relationships.

Id. at 1512, n.41.

42. *See* Klein & Orloff, *supra* note 13, at 1006 (discussing how police act as a critical "link between the abuse victim and the legal and social service systems").

43. *See* Attorney General's Task Force on Domestic Violence, at 18 (Sept. 1984) (indicating that a law enforcement agency is usually the first and often the only agency called on to intervene in family violence incidents). *See also* Klein & Orloff, *supra* note 13, at 1007 (listing state statutes that require police to inform domestic violence victims of services available).

44. *See* Amy Eppler, *Battered Women and the Equal Protection Clause: Will the Constitution Help Them When the Police Won't?*, 95 YALE L. J. 788, 791, n.16 (1986) (study compared the effectiveness of arrest, mediation, or ordering the violent spouse to leave the home).

45. *See* Lerman, *supra* note 20, at 130 (stating that "[p]olice have expressed concern, that as a result of implementing new domestic violence laws, they will be deluged with litigation brought by irate husbands").

from liability.[46] Police officers may also assert an immunity defense to federal actions brought under 42 U.S.C. § 1983.[47]

Jurisdictions, concerned about the increased liability that may be faced by an officer's good faith effort to enforce an out of state order, should consider enacting qualified immunity statutes which would apply only to officers' good faith attempts to enforce protection orders, not to the failure to enforce valid orders. Oregon specifically immunizes police officers who make arrests for the violation of a foreign protection order if the officer reasonably believes that the foreign order is an accurate copy.[48] Moreover, immunity statutes may not be necessary to provide protection to police officers, because common law has traditionally shielded state actors from liability.[49]

Another suggested procedure for states to consider when trying to implement the full faith and credit provision of the VAWA is to make changes to court protection order forms. The court forms should clearly inform both the respondent and law enforcement officials that the order is valid and enforceable in all fifty states, the District of Columbia, and tribal lands. The standardized protection order form should clearly

---

46. *See* ALA. CODE § 30-6-12 (1994); ARIZ. REV. STAT. ANN. § 13-3601(B) (1994); ARK. CODE ANN. § 5-53-134(e) (Michie 1993); CAL. FAM. CODE § 6272(b) (Deering 1994); COLO. REV. STAT. § 18-6-803.6 (1994); CONN. GEN. STAT. ANN. § 46(b)-38b (West 1994); D.C. CODE ANN. § 16-1033 (1994); FLA. STAT. ANN. § 741.29 (5) (West 1995); HAW. REV. STAT. § 709-906(6) (1994); IDAHO CODE § 39-6314 (1994); ILL. ANN. STAT. ch. 725, para. 5/112A-31 (Smith-Hurd 1994); IOWA CODE ANN. §§ 236.11, 236.12(4) (West 1994); KAN. STAT. ANN. § 22-2308 (1993); KY. REV. STAT. ANN. § 403.755(2) (Michie/Bobbs-Merrill 1994); LA. REV. STAT. ANN. § 2142 (West 1994); MASS. GEN. LAWS ANN. ch. 209A § 6(7) (West 1994); MINN. STAT. ANN. § 518B.01 (subd. 14(b)) (West 1995); MISS. CODE ANN. § 93-21-27 (1993); MO. ANN. STAT. § 93-21-27 (1993); N.H. REV. STAT. ANN. § 173-B:11-b (1993); N.J. STAT. ANN. § 2C:25-22 (West 1994); N.M. STAT. ANN. § 40-13-7 (Michie 1994); N.C. GEN. STAT. § 50B-5(b) (1994); N.D. CENT. CODE § 14-07.1-11(2) (1993); OR. REV. STAT. § 133.315 (1994); R.I. GEN. LAWS § 12-29-3(d) (1994); UTAH CODE ANN. § 30-6-8 (1994); WASH. REV. CODE § 10.99.070 (1990); WIS. STAT. § 968.075(6m) (1993); WYO. STAT. § 7-20-106 (1994).

47. Laura S. Harper, Note, *Battered Women Suing Police for Failure to Intervene: Viable Legal Avenues After* DeShaney v. Winnebago County Dep't of Social Servs., 75 CORNELL L. REV. 1393 ("[u]nder the qualified immunity doctrine, state officers performing discretionary functions are immune from lawsuits for damages provided that their conduct does not violate clearly established statutory or constitutional rights of which a reasonable person would have known." *Id.* at 1400.).

48. OR. REV. STAT. § 133.315(2) (1993).

49. Linda B. Lengyel, *Survey of State Domestic Violence Legislation*, 10 LEGAL REFERENCE SERVICES Q. 59 (1990) ("There is substantial authority from the United States Supreme Court and state court decisions to reach the conclusion that the police officer may rely on the general application of the principles of 'good faith', or as it is often called 'qualified immunity'." *Id.* at 74.).

cite the full faith and credit provision of the VAWA as authority. Prior to having court orders changed, practitioners can put law enforcement officials and the respondent on notice by clearly stating that the order is subject to full faith and credit under the VAWA.[50] This can be achieved by handwriting or typing a statement right on the existing court protection order form that provides notice that the order is subject to full faith and credit pursuant to the VAWA.

V. Mutual Protection Orders

The VAWA addresses the types of mutual protection orders entitled to full faith and credit. A mutual protection order is an order entered against both parties, requiring both to abide by the restraints and other forms of relief in the civil protection order.[51] There are three ways in which a mutual protection order can be issued. The first situation is when the batterer counterclaims or files an independent petition for a civil protection order. Both the petitioner and the respondent must demonstrate abuse that did not occur in self-defense before the judge can issue a valid mutual protection order. The second situation is when the parties agree to a mutual protection order. A third situation can occur when a judge issues an order without a request from either party or upon the request of one party and without hearing evidence as to abuse by both parties. The last two types of mutual orders are excepted from the full faith and credit provision of the VAWA. Congress recognized the problems with mutual orders and through the VAWA put a limit on their use. Mutual orders are not afforded full faith and credit unless both parties submitted a written request for a protection order and the order was issued upon a showing of mutual abuse.[52]

---

50. A sample statement could read:

Respondent was afforded both notice and opportunity to be heard in the hearing that gave rise to this order. Pursuant to the Violence Against Women Act of 1994 (Pub. L. No. 103-322, 108 Stat. 1796, 18 U.S.C.A. § 2265), this order is valid in all fifty states, the District of Columbia, tribal lands, and United States territories.

51. Two alternatives to civil protection orders are for the woman to leave her batterer without seeking legal assistance, or for the woman to file criminal charges. For many reasons these alternatives are often less attractive to victims of domestic violence. *See* Elizabeth Topliffe, *Why Civil Protection Orders Are Effective Remedies for Domestic Violence But Mutual Protective Orders Are Not*, 67 IND. L.J. 1039, 1041-42 (1992).

52. VAWA, 18 U.S.C.A. § 2265 (c)(1)(2). The VAWA states that mutual orders are:

Not entitled to full faith and credit if

(1) no cross or counter petition, complaint, or other written pleading was filed seeking such a protection order; or

(2) a cross or counter petition has been filed and the court did not make specific findings that each party was entitled to such an order.

Although some aspects of mutual orders may seem appealing,[53] they have been criticized as "undermin[ing] the purpose and strength of domestic violence statutes, which seek to end violence and hold batterers accountable."[54] Mutual protection orders, issued absent a showing of mutual abuse, are detrimental because they ignore "due process rights and psychological well-being of the victim, problems with enforcement, and the effect of mutual orders in future judicial proceedings."[55]

Due process requirements must be met when there is a liberty or property interest at stake. Mutual protection orders seek to deny victims their liberty interest in not being restrained.[56] For a civil protection order to be issued against a batterer, due process requires that the victim show evidence of abuse or potential danger. Thus, in order for a mutual order to be issued, due process also requires the batterer to make a showing of danger or abuse by the victim. Mutual orders, issued by the court without an evidentiary hearing by both parties, deprives victims of their liberty interests in not being restrained without due process of law.

The psychological well-being of the victim is also adversely affected by the issuance of mutual orders. Mutual orders send a message from the court that somehow the actions of the victims warrant the issuance of a restraining orders against them. Furthermore, mutual orders result in problems of enforcement. Mutual orders fail to identify who is the aggressor and who is the victim which often causes confusion and leads to police arresting the victim, both parties, or no one at all.

Finally, mutual orders impact future proceedings to the disadvantage of the victim.[57] Evidence of the issuance of a mutual order can be used in future divorce proceedings, thus affecting child custody determinations. The abuser can use a mutual protection order in future civil and criminal proceedings, brought by the victim, as evidence of mutual abuse.

These concerns about the dangers of mutual protection orders are reflected in the VAWA. The VAWA specifically excepts mutual protec-

---

53. *See* Topliffe, *supra* note 51 (Stating that attorneys and judges are mistaken in their belief that mutual orders are good because the parties have agreed to it or because they are more expeditious. Victims of domestic violence only agree to mutual orders because of the dynamics of their abusive relationships and that the expeditious process may not be beneficial to victims.).

54. *See* Klein & Orloff, *supra* note 13, at 1074 (discussing how the legal system's focus in domestic violence cases should be upon identifying, restraining, and punishing the primary aggressor in the relationship, not the victims who are attempting to protect themselves).

55. *See* Topliffe, *supra* note 51 (discussing the criticisms and concerns of mutual protection orders).

56. *Id.* at 1058.

57. *Id.* at 1062.

tion orders that are granted without due process from the provision granting full faith and credit to civil protection orders.[58] Furthermore, the VAWA limits funding to states that fail to enact legislation prohibiting mutual orders without evidence of mutual abuse.[59]

VI. Creation of a New Federal Crime

Two sections of the Safe Homes for Women Act create new federal crimes for domestic violence. These sections may offer victims another avenue of protection through the U.S. Attorney's Offices and the federal courts. Section 2261 makes interstate domestic violence a federal offense.[60] It is a federal crime to cross state lines with the intent of injuring a spouse or intimate party when such action results in bodily injury. Furthermore, this section states that it is also a federal crime to force a spouse or intimate partner across state lines when an injury occurs as a result of the travel.

Section 2262 makes the interstate violation of a protection order a federal offense.[61] The Act prohibits a person from crossing state lines and engaging in conduct that violates a valid protection order. Proof

---

58. VAWA, 18 U.S.C.A. § 2265 (c)(1)(2).

59. VAWA, 18 U.S.C.A. § 2101(c)(3), states are eligible for grants if the states certify that their laws, policies, or practices prohibit issuance of mutual restraining orders or protection except in cases where both spouses file a claim, and the court makes detailed findings of fact indicating that both spouses acted primarily as aggressors and that neither spouse acted primarily in self-defense.

60. VAWA, 18 U.S.C.A. § 2261. This section provides in part:

(a) OFFENSES.

(1) CROSSING A STATE LINE. A person who travels across a state line or enters or leaves Indian country with the intent to injure, harass, or intimidate that person's spouse or intimate partner, and who, in the course of or as a result of such travel, intentionally commits a crime of violence and thereby causes bodily injury to such spouse or intimate partner. . . .

(2) CAUSING THE CROSSING OF A STATE LINE. A person who causes a spouse or intimate partner to cross a state line or to enter or leave Indian country by force, coercion, duress, or fraud and, in the course or as a result of that conduct, intentionally commits a crime of violence and thereby causes bodily injury to the person's spouse or intimate partner. . . .

61. VAWA, 18 U.S.C.A. § 2262, providing in part:

(a) OFFENSES.

(1) CROSSING A STATE LINE. A person who travels across a state line or enters or leaves Indian country with the intent to engage in conduct that

(A)(i) violates the portion of a protection order that involves protection against credible threats of violence, repeated harassment, or bodily injury to the person or persons for whom the protection order was issued; or

(ii) would violate subparagraph (A) if the conduct occurred in the jurisdiction in which the order was issued; and

(B) subsequently engages in such conduct. . . .

of specific intent is not required under the Act, rather, a showing of objective evidence is sufficient, such as a history of abuse and the timing of the travel.[62] This is important in jurisdictions that border other states and interstate travel is frequent.

There are several factors practitioners should consider when advising clients whether to ask the U.S. Attorney's Office to bring a federal action on their behalf. First, there are additional penalties for a defendant found guilty of the new federal crimes of domestic violence.[63] The federal crime creates a new penalty for crossing state lines and violating a valid protection order. Second, in a federal suit there is the advantage of federal resources in investigation and prosecution. The Senate Judiciary Committee recognized that the federal crimes were "an appropriate response to the problem of domestic violence, because of the interstate nature, transcend the abilities of state law enforcement agencies."[64] In addition, section 2264 of the VAWA mandates restitution for victims of these new domestic violence crimes.[65] Under this section, victims shall receive restitution for the full amount of losses including medical expenses; physical therapy expenses; lost income; attorney fees; and travel, child care, and temporary housing expenses.[66]

In January of 1995, the U.S. Attorney for the Southern District of West Virginia charged a man in the first federal domestic violence case. Christopher Bailey was indicted on January 4, 1995, by a grand jury for interstate domestic violence and federal kidnapping after bringing his unconscious wife to a Kentucky hospital. Bailey faces up to life imprisonment and $500,000 in fines. The FBI has been involved in the investigation and has alleged that Christopher Bailey seriously injured his wife in their home in West Virginia and then traveled through West Virginia, Kentucky, and Ohio for six days with his wife sometimes tied up in the trunk. Because the federal domestic violence law is untested, Bailey is also charged with federal kidnapping since that crime is "tried and true."[67]

VII. Conclusion

The Violence Against Women Act of 1994 makes an essential step toward providing more extensive protection for victims of domestic

---

62. S. REP. No. 138, 103d Cong., 1st Sess., at 61 (1993).

63. *Id.*

64. *Id.* at 62.

65. VAWA, 18 U.S.C.A. § 2264 ("[t]he issuance of a restitution order under this section is mandatory.").

66. VAWA, 18 U.S.C.A. § 2264.

67. Maryclaire Dale, *Man to Face Federal Charges in Wife's Beating*, THE CHARLESTON GAZETTE, Jan. 5, 1995, at P1A.

violence. The federal approach recognizes that domestic violence is a national problem that crosses state lines. First, the VAWA mandates that states recognize and enforce foreign protection orders. The existing procedures in New Hampshire for interstate enforcement most closely correspond to the intent of the VAWA. New Hampshire provides for immediate enforcement of a foreign order without requiring registration of the order. The police are authorized to enforce a foreign order when the victim presents the order and swears to its authenticity. Moreover, New Hampshire has a system in place that allows victims to register their orders and have them sent to appropriate law enforcement agencies. The registration does not require any fees, nor does it require that any notice be sent to the batterer. Furthermore, New Hampshire has a computer-generated form that the protected party signs to certify that the foreign order is presently in effect in the foreign state. The form also serves as a record of those who have received copies of the foreign order.

Second, the VAWA discourages the use of mutual protection orders. The VAWA limits full faith and credit to mutual orders that were issued upon a showing of mutual abuse. The VAWA also extends funding to states that have laws that prohibit the issuance of mutual protection orders unless both parties file a claim, and the court makes a finding that both were primary aggressors.

Finally, the VAWA's creation of federal domestic violence crimes provides a new approach to combat domestic violence. The VAWA makes it a crime to cross state lines and injure a spouse or intimate partner. It is also a federal crime to cross state lines and violate a valid protection order. These new federal crimes provide the advantages of federal resources in investigation and prosecution. Also, under the VAWA, full restitution to the victim is mandated. For these reasons the Violence Against Women Act provides important new protection for victims of domestic violence.

Appendix

THE STATE OF NEW HAMPSHIRE

Merrimack County   Suncook Court

_____ Docket No.

FOREIGN PROTECTIVE ORDER AFFIDAVIT

I, the undersigned, do hereby swear under oath that:

To the best of my knowledge and belief the attached certified copy of the Foreign Protective Order, Docket Number _____, issued in the state of _____, on _____, is presently in effect as written;

_____   _____
Date   Signature of Protected Party

Personally appeared the above named individual and made oath that the above affidavit by him/her subscribed is, in his/her belief, true.

In witness whereof I hereunto set my hand and official seal.

_____   _____
Date   Notary Public/Justice of the Peace

- -

FOR COURT USE ONLY:
Pursuant to RSA 173-B:11-b, the attached order shall be given full faith and credit throughout New Hampshire and be fully enforceable in this state as long as it is in effect in the issuing state. (Check the appropriate box(es) below).

☐ A copy of this affidavit and the referenced foreign protective order have been mailed/delivered in hand (circle one) to the protected party, to be retained by protected party. Date _____.

☐ A copy of this affidavit and the referenced foreign protective order has been mailed/delivered in hand (circle one) to _____, the appropriate enforcement agency. Date _____.

☐ Two copies of this affidavit and the referenced foreign protective order have been delivered in hand to the protected party. The protected party agrees to deliver one copy to _____, the appropriate enforcement agency. Date _____.

☐ A copy of this affidavit and the referenced foreign protective order have been mailed/delivered in hand (circle one) to _____. Date _____.

_____   _____
Date   Signature of Clerk of Court

MODEL CODE ON
DOMESTIC AND FAMILY VIOLENCE

CHAPTER 4

FAMILY AND CHILDREN

Sec. 401. Presumptions concerning custody.

In every proceeding where there is at issue a dispute as to the custody of a child, a determination by the court that domestic or family violence has occurred raises a rebuttable presumption that it is detrimental to the child and not in the best interest of the child to be placed in sole custody, joint legal custody, or joint physical custody with the perpetrator of family violence.

COMMENTARY

Support for the presumptions incorporated in this section, that domestic violence is detrimental to the child and that it is contrary to the child's best interest to be placed in sole or joint custody with the perpetrator thereof, is extensive. This section compels courts, attorneys, custody evaluators, and other professionals working with cases involving the custody of children to consider the impact of domestic and family violence on these children. This mandate is not limited to courts issuing orders for protection but includes courts hearing divorce, delinquency, and child protection cases.

Sec. 402. Factors in determining custody and visitation.

1. In addition to other factors that a court must consider in a proceeding in which the custody of a child or visitation by a parent is at issue and in which the court has made a finding of domestic or family violence:

(a) The court shall consider as primary the safety and well-being of the child and of the parent who is the victim of domestic or family violence.

(b) The court shall consider the perpetrator's history of causing physical harm, bodily injury, assault, or causing reasonable fear of physical harm, bodily injury, or assault, to another person.

2. If a parent is absent or relocates because of an act of domestic or family violence by the other parent, the absence or relocation is not a factor that weighs against the parent in determining custody or visitation.

COMMENTARY

This section was constructed to remedy the failure of many custody statutes to give courts direction related to appropriate consideration of domestic and family violence in contested custody cases. Paragraph (a) of subsection 1 elevates the safety and well-being of the child and abused parent above all other "best interest" factors in deliberations about custodial options in those disputed custody cases where there has been a finding of abuse by one parent of the other. It contemplates that no custodial or visitation award may properly issue that jeopardizes the safety and well-being of adult and child victims.

Paragraph (b) compels courts to consider the history, both the acts and patterns, of physical abuse inflicted by the abuser on other persons, including but not limited to the child and the abused parent, as well as the fear of physical harm reasonably engendered by this conduct. It recognizes that discreet acts of abuse do not accurately convey the risk of continuing violence, the likely severity of future abuse, or the magnitude of fear precipitated by the composite picture of violent conduct.

Subsection 2 recognizes that sometimes abused adults flee the family home in order to preserve or protect their lives and sometimes do not take dependent children with them because of the emergency circumstances of flight, because they lack resources to provide for the children outside the family home, or because they conclude that the abuser will hurt the children, the abused parent, or third parties if the children are removed prior to court intervention. This provision prevents the abuser from benefitting from the violent or coercive conduct precipitating the relocation of the battered parent and affords the abused parent an affirmative defense to the allegation of child abandonment.

Sec. 403. Presumption concerning residence of child.

In every proceeding where there is at issue a dispute as to the custody of a child, a determination by a court that domestic or family violence has occurred raises a rebuttable presumption that it is in the best interest of the child to reside with the parent who is not a perpetrator of domestic or family violence in the location of that parent's choice, within or outside the state.

COMMENTARY

This section articulates a rebuttable presumption that the residence of the child in the context of domestic or family violence should be with the non-perpetrating parent in the location chosen by that parent. This presumption builds on the one enumerated in section 401. It is designed to defeat any assertion by a perpetrator of domestic or family violence that custody and residence with the abused parent should only be presumptive if the abused adult remains within the jurisdiction of the marital domicile. It recognizes that the enhanced safety, personal, and social supports, and the economic opportunity available to the abused parent in another jurisdiction are not only in that parent's best interest, but are, likewise and concomitantly, in the best interest of the child.

Sec. 404. Change of circumstances.

In every proceeding in which there is at issue the modification of an order for custody or visitation of a child, the finding that domestic or family violence has occurred since the last custody determination constitutes a finding of a change of circumstances.

COMMENTARY

This section provides that in proceedings concerning modification of an order for custody or visitation of a child, a finding by the reviewing court that domestic or family violence has occurred constitutes a finding of a change of circumstances.

Sec. 405. Conditions of visitation in cases involving domestic and family violence.

1. A court may award visitation by a parent who committed domestic or family violence only if the court finds that adequate provision for the safety of the child and the parent who is a victim of domestic or family violence can be made.

2. In a visitation order, a court may:

(a) Order an exchange of a child to occur in a protected setting.

(b) Order visitation supervised by another person or agency.

(c) Order the perpetrator of domestic or family violence to attend and complete, to the satisfaction of the court, a program of intervention for perpetrators or other designated counseling as a condition of the visitation.

(d) Order the perpetrator of domestic or family violence to abstain from possession or consumption of alcohol or controlled substances during the visitation and for 24 hours preceding the visitation.

(e) Order the perpetrator of domestic or family violence to pay a fee to defray the costs of supervised visitation.

(f) Prohibit overnight visitation.

(g) Require a bond from the perpetrator of domestic or family violence for the return and safety of the child.

(h) Impose any other condition that is deemed necessary to provide for the safety of the child, the victim of domestic or family violence, or other family or household member.

3. Whether or not visitation is allowed, the court may order the address of the child and the victim to be kept confidential.

4. The court may refer but shall not order an adult who is a victim of domestic or family violence to attend counseling relating to the victim's status or behavior as a victim, individually or with the perpetrator of domestic or family violence as a condition of receiving custody of a child or as a condition of visitation.

5. If a court allows a family or household member to supervise visitation, the court shall establish conditions to be followed during visitation.

COMMENTARY

Subsection 1 permits the award of visitation to a perpetrator of domestic violence only if protective measures, including but not limited to those enumerated in subsection 2 of this section, are deemed sufficient to protect the child and the abused parent from further acts or threats of violence or other fear-engendering conduct. The Model Code posits that where protective interventions are not accessible in a community, a court should not endanger a child or adult victim of domestic violence in order to accommodate visitation by a perpetrator of domestic or family violence. The risk of domestic violence directed both towards the child and the battered parent is frequently greater after separation than during cohabitation; this elevated risk often continues after legal interventions.

Subsection 2 lists the protective conditions most routinely imposed on visitation by the perpetrator of domestic and family violence. It is not intended to be exhaustive, nor does this subsection contemplate that each provision should be imposed on every custody order.

Subsection 3 recognizes that it may be necessary to withhold the address of the adult victim and children from the perpetrator and others in order to prevent stalking and assault of adult and child victims in their undisclosed residence. Research reveals that one of the most effective methods of averting violence is denying the abuser access to the victim, which can be facilitated by preserving the confidentiality of the victim's address.

Subsection 4 prohibits a court from ordering a victim of domestic or family violence to attend counseling related to the status or behavior as a victim as a condition of receiving custody of a child or as a condition of visitation. It does not preclude the court from ordering other types of counseling, such as substance abuse counseling or educational classes.

Subsection 5 requires a court to establish conditions to be followed if the court allows a family or household member to supervise visitation. When those supervising visitation are furnished clear guidelines related to their responsibility and authority during supervision, they are better able to protect the child should the perpetrator engage in violent or intimidating conduct toward the child or adult victim in the course of visitation.

Sec. 406. Specialized visitation center for victims of domestic or family violence.

1. The insert appropriate state agency shall provide for visitation centers throughout the state for victims of domestic or family violence and their children to allow court ordered visitation in a manner that protects the safety of all family members. The state agency shall coordinate and cooperate with local governmental agencies in providing the visitation centers.

2. A visitation center must provide:

(a) A secure setting and specialized procedures for supervised visitation and the transfer of children for visitation; and

(b) Supervision by a person trained in security and the avoidance of domestic and family violence.

COMMENTARY

Supervised visitation centers are an essential component of an integrated community intervention system to eliminate abuse and protect its victims. Visitation centers may reduce the opportunity for retributive violence by batterers, prevent parental abduction, safeguard endangered family members, and offer the batterer continuing contact and relationship with their children. This section requires a state to provide for the existence of visitation centers but does not mandate that the state own or operate such centers, nor that the centers be operated at public expense. See Appendix III.

Sec. 407. Duty of mediator to screen for domestic violence during mediation referred or ordered by court.

1. A mediator who receives a referral or order from a court to conduct mediation shall screen for the occurrence of domestic or family violence between the parties.

2. A mediator shall not engage in mediation when it appears to the mediator or when either party asserts that domestic or family violence has occurred unless:

(a) Mediation is requested by the victim of the alleged domestic or family violence;

(b) Mediation is provided in a specialized manner that protects the safety of the victim by a certified mediator who is trained in domestic and family violence; and

(c) The victim is permitted to have in attendance at mediation a supporting person of his or her choice, including but not limited to an attorney or advocate.

COMMENTARY

This section requires mediators who receive referrals or orders from courts to screen for domestic or family violence between the parties. Screening must include an assessment of the danger posed by the perpetrator, recognizing that victims of domestic violence are at sharply elevated risk of as they attempt to end the relationship, and utilize the legal system to gain essential protective safeguards. Subsection 2 articulate a practice standard for the mediator who discovers that domestic or family violence has occurred. See Appendix III.

Drafters note: Drafters must look to general provisions concerning mediation in their state laws and insert exception as provided in sections 311 and 408.

The Model Code provides alternative sections concerning mediation in cases involving domestic or family violence. Both of the sections provide directives for courts hearing cases concerning the custody or visitation of children, if there is a protection order in effect and if there is an allegation of domestic or family violence. Neither of these sections prohibits the parties to such a hearing from engaging in mediation of their own volition. For the majority of jurisdictions, section 408(A) is the preferred section. For the minority of jurisdictions that have developed mandatory mediation by trained, certified mediators, and that follow special procedures to protect a victim of domestic or family violence from intimidation, section 408(B) is provided as an alternative.

Sec. 408(A). Mediation in cases involving domestic or family violence.

1. In a proceeding concerning the custody or visitation of a child, if an order for protection is in effect, the court shall not order mediation or refer either party to mediation.

2. In a proceeding concerning the custody or visitation of a child, if there is an allegation of domestic or family violence and an order for protection is not in effect, the court may order mediation or refer either party to mediation only if:

(a) Mediation is requested by the victim of the alleged domestic or family violence;

(b) Mediation is provided by a certified mediator who is trained in domestic and family violence in a specialized manner that protects the safety of the victim; and

(c) The victim is permitted to have in attendance at mediation a supporting person of his or her choice, including but not limited to an attorney or advocate.

COMMENTARY

Subsection 1 makes it explicit that referrals to mediation by a court in the context of domestic or family violence, not only mandates for participation, are impermissible. Judicial referrals are compelling and often viewed by litigants as the dispute resolution method preferred by the court. Also see commentary following section 311.

Subsection 2 authorizes courts to require mediation or refer to mediation when there is an allegation of domestic or family violence only where there is no protection order in effect and the three enumerated conditions for mediation are met. First, the court should not approve mediation unless the victim of the alleged violence requests mediation. The second requisite condition for court-approved mediation in the context of domestic violence contains two components: that mediation be provided in a specialized manner that protects the safety of the victim and that mediators be certified and trained in domestic and family violence. Guidelines have been generated by mediators, scholars, and advocates. Paragraph (c) of subsection 2 reflects the policy recommendations, promulgated by the collaborative studies of mediators, advocates, and legal scholars, that at the victim's option, he or she may have another party present during mediation. This person may be the victim's attorney, an advocate, or some other person of the victim's choosing.

Sec. 408(B). Mediation in cases involving domestic or family violence.

1. In a proceeding concerning the custody or visitation of a child, if an order for protection is in effect or if there is an allegation of domestic or family violence, the court shall not order mediation or refer either party to mediation unless the court finds that:

(a) The mediation is provided by a certified mediator who is trained in the dynamics of domestic and family violence; and

(b) The mediator or mediation service provides procedures to protect the victim from intimidation by the alleged perpetrator in accordance with subsection 2.

2. Procedures to protect the victim must include but are not limited to:

(a) Permission for the victim to have in attendance at mediation a supporting person of his or her choice, including but not limited to an attorney or advocate; and

(b) Any other procedure deemed necessary by the court to protect the victim from intimidation from the alleged perpetrator.

COMMENTARY

Subsection 1 authorizes a court to order or refer parties in a proceeding concerning custody or visitation of a child only under two conditions, that mediation is provided by a certified mediator who is trained in domestic and family violence and procedures are provided that protect the victim from intimidation.

Subsection 2 enumerates the procedures that must be followed by a mediator to protect the victim from intimidation. Paragraph (a) reflects the policy recommendations, promulgated by the collaborative studies of mediators, advocates, and legal scholars, that at the victim's option, he or she may have another party present at mediation. This person may be the victim's attorney, an advocate, or some other person of the victim's choosing. Paragraph (b) authorizes the court to impose any additional procedure deemed necessary to protect the victim from intimidation.

Sec. 409. Duties of children's protective services.

1. The state administrator of children's protective services shall develop written procedures for screening each referral for abuse or neglect of a child to assess whether abuse of another family or household member is also occurring. The assessment must include but is not limited to:

(a) Inquiry concerning the criminal record of the parents, and the alleged abusive or neglectful person and the alleged perpetrator of domestic or family violence, if not a parent of the child; and

(b) Inquiry concerning the existence of orders for protection issued to either parent.

2. If it is determined in an investigation of abuse or neglect of a child:

(a) That the child or another family or household member is in danger of domestic or family violence and that removal of one of the parties is necessary to prevent the abuse or neglect of the child, the administrator shall seek the removal of the alleged perpetrator of domestic or family violence whenever possible.

(b) That a parent of the child is a victim of domestic or family violence, services must be offered to the victimized parent and the provision of such services must not be contingent upon a finding that either parent is at fault or has failed to protect the child.

COMMENTARY

This section underscores the premise that protection of the abused child and the non-perpetrating parent should be the guiding policy of child protective services agencies. Subsection 1 requires the state's administrator of child protective services to develop both an assessment tool and investigation procedures for identification of violence directed at family or household members in addition to the child alleged to be at risk. Identification of adult domestic or family violence through careful intake screening and preliminary risk assessment, followed by thorough investigation, is essential if parents are to be afforded the life preserving assistance necessary for effective parenting and child protection.

Paragraph (a) of subsection 2 codifies the premise that when a parent or parent-surrogate has abused a child or poses a continuing risk of abuse or violence towards anyone in the family or household, and the agency concludes that safety can only be accomplished if those at risk live separate and apart from the perpetrator, the agency should either assist the non-perpetrating parent in seeking the legal exclusion of the perpetrator from the home or itself pursue removal of the perpetrator from the home. The perpetrator should be removed rather than placing the abused child or children in foster care or other placement. This provision does not require that a perpetrator be removed from the home if both the child and the victim of domestic violence can be adequately protected by other interventions. Paragraph (b) of subsection 2 requires that the agency make services available to parents of abused children under the supervision of the agency, who have been victimized by domestic or family violence. This subsection requires that services for parents victimized by domestic or family violence are to be undertaken whether or not the abused parent is found to bear any culpability for the abuse of a child under the supervision of the agency; findings of neglect, abuse, or any failure to protect by the parent victimized by domestic or family violence are not a prerequisite for service.

138

Adolescents' Exposure to Violence and Associated Symptoms of Psychological Trauma

Mark I. Singer, PhD; Trina Menden Anglin, MD, PhD; Li yu Song, PhD; Lisa Lunghofer, PhD

Objective.—To examine the extent to which adolescents are exposed to various types of violence as either victims or witnesses, and the association of such exposure with trauma symptoms; specifically, the hypotheses that exposure to violence will have a positive and significant association with depression, anger, anxiety, dissociation, posttraumatic stress, and total trauma symptoms.

Design and Setting.—The study employed a survey design using an anonymous self-report questionnaire administered to students (grades 9 through 12) in six public high schools during the 1992-1993 school year.

Participants.—Sixty-eight percent of the students attending the participating schools during the survey participated in the study (N=3735). Ages ranged from 14 to 19 years; 52% were female; and 35% were African American, 33% white, and 23% Hispanic.

Results.—All hypotheses were supported. Multiple regression analyses of the total sample revealed that violence exposure variables (and to a lesser extent, demographic variables) explained a significant portion of variance in all trauma symptom scores, including depression (R^2=.31), anger (R^2=.30), anxiety (R^2=.30), dissociation (R^2=.23), posttraumatic stress (R^2=.31), and total trauma (R^2=.37).

Conclusions.—A significant and consistent association was demonstrated linking violence exposure to trauma symptoms within a diverse sample of high school students. Our findings give evidence of the need to identify and provide trauma-related services for adolescents who have been exposed to violence.

(*JAMA.* 1995;273:477-482)

VIOLENCE HAS become an undeniable part of the lives of many adolescents living in the United States. Firearm homicide is the second-leading cause of death for all 15- to 19-year-olds.[1] Adolescent males are at particular risk: firearm injuries are the leading cause of death among both African-American and white teenage males.[2] Although the large majority of adolescents will not become the victims of homicide, many are exposed to other types of violence. In fact, the rate of violent victimization among those 12 to 19 years old is twice that of adults over the age of 25 years.[3]

Recent surveys have attempted to document the extent of adolescents' ex-

From the Mandel School of Applied Social Sciences, Case Western Reserve University, Cleveland, Ohio (Drs Singer, Song, and Lunghofer); and the Department of Pediatrics, University of Colorado School of Medicine, and Section on Adolescent Medicine, The Children's Hospital, Denver, Colo (Dr Anglin).
Reprint requests to Mandel School of Applied Social Sciences, Case Western Reserve University, 10900 Euclid Ave, Cleveland, OH 44106-7164 (Dr Singer).

posure to violence. A 1989 national survey of more than 11 000 eighth and 10th graders revealed they had both engaged in and been the victims of violence: 39% of students had been in at least one physical fight within the past year. Students also reported significant exposure to violence in their neighborhoods: 33% had been threatened with bodily harm; 15% had been robbed; and 16% had been attacked. School offered little refuge: 34% of students reported being threatened and 13% reported being attacked at school during the past year.[4] The National Crime Victimization Survey found that 9% of all secondary school students reported having been victimized by crime in or around their schools over a 6-month period, but only 2% experienced one or more violent crimes.[5]

Studies limited to urban populations paint an even more dismal picture of adolescents' exposure to violence. A 1988 Urban Institute study, which involved interviews with 387 ninth- and 10th-grade males randomly selected from inner-city

Washington, DC, schools, found high rates of victimization: 27% had been attacked, threatened, or robbed by a person with a weapon and 12% had been badly beaten by someone not a member of their household.[6] A 1992 questionnaire survey of a representative sample of all ninth- to 12th-grade students enrolled in New York City public schools yielded similar findings: during a single school year, 36% of students reported being threatened with physical harm and 25% of students were involved in a physical fight at home, at school, or in the neighborhood.[7] Rates of witnessing serious and lethal violence are also alarmingly high. In a study of 246 inner-city adolescents, 42% reported seeing someone shot or knifed and 22% reported seeing someone killed.[8] Finally, in a national study of gun-related violence in and around inner-city schools in four different states, 23% of students had been victims of gun-related violence.[9]

Despite mounting concern about youth violence and attempts to document its prevalence, little information exists regarding the effects of exposure to violence on the mental health of adolescents. Much of the research done to date has focused on the effects of exposure to war and the impact of such acute trauma as witnessing a sniper attack.[10-17] Relying primarily on clinical-descriptive methods and anecdotal evidence, these studies suggest that exposure to violence is associated with anxiety,[18] posttraumatic stress disorder symptoms,[19,20] depression,[21] and aggression.[22,23]

The mental health and behavioral effects of children's and adolescents' exposure to familial abuse have also been explored. A variety of consequences, similar to the effects on youth exposed to war and sniper attacks, have been described: posttraumatic stress disorder, difficulty controlling anger, aggressive behavior, chronic anxiety, and substance abuse.[24-29]

The few empirical studies conducted to date have focused either on children or on specific subpopulations of adolescents liv-

139

ing in high-violence neighborhoods. For example, in a study of 165 children aged 6 to 10 years, reports of being victimized and witnessing violence were significantly associated with reports of emotional distress and depression.[30] A significant relationship was also identified between exposure to violence and posttraumatic stress disorder symptoms in a nonrandom sample of 221 inner-city African-American youths (7 to 18 years old) involved in a federally funded summer program.[31] An independent study of urban youth had similar findings: the lifetime incidence of exposure to violent events was 39% among this group, and the rate of posttraumatic stress disorder among exposed youths was 24%.[32]

The documented prevalence of violence exposure among adolescents and the convergence of findings from early studies citing the adverse effects of this exposure indicate a pressing need for further empirical investigation. Understanding the mental health sequelae to violence is essential to developing treatment strategies for violence-exposed youth and may also assist in both primary and secondary violence-prevention efforts.

This study examines the extent to which adolescents are exposed to various types of violence as either victims or witnesses, and the effects of exposure to violence on their mental health. Our study tests the hypotheses that exposure to violence has a positive and significant association with depression, anger, anxiety, dissociation, and posttraumatic stress. Additionally, we hypothesize that exposure to violence will have a positive and significant relationship to overall psychological trauma status (the combination of all trauma symptoms). Therefore, in this study, psychological trauma status is defined as the degree to which adolescents report symptoms of depression, anxiety, posttraumatic stress, dissociation, and/or anger.

METHODS

The study protocol was approved by the University Review Committee for Human Studies of Case Western Reserve University, Cleveland, Ohio. The study employed a survey design using a 25-minute anonymous self-report questionnaire administered to high school students in the 1992-1993 school year during usual school hours. The questionnaire was designed to be understood at the 5th-grade reading level and was pretested on a socioeconomically diverse sample of adolescents. Students were informed that their participation was completely voluntary.

The sampling pool consisted of all students present in six public high schools, grades 9 through 12. Schools included two Cleveland city high schools, one Cleveland area suburban high school, one small-city high school in northeast Ohio, and two Denver (Colo) city high schools. Students in the Cleveland and Denver city high schools resided predominantly in neighborhoods with lower socioeconomic status. The small-city high school was located in an economically depressed area whose residents, primarily blue-collar workers, were experiencing high rates of unemployment. Students from the suburban school resided in a small upper-middle-class town.

Variables and Instrumentation

Demographic Variables.—Demographic information included age, gender, race/ethnicity, parental composition in home, and educational level of mother and father. Race was categorized into four groups: African American, Hispanic, white, and other. To measure parental composition in home, respondents were asked with whom they lived: mother only, father only, mother and father, or neither mother nor father. This question did not distinguish between biological parents and other parental figures. Respondents were also asked the educational level of their parents, separately for father and mother, on eight response categories ranging from "grade school or less" to "attended graduate or professional school." Parental education was measured by the highest educational level achieved by respondents' father or mother.

Recent Exposure to Physical Violence.—Recent exposure to violence was measured by a 22-item scale designed by the authors. This scale measured five specific acts of violence: threats, slapping/hitting/punching, beatings, knife attacks, and shootings. For the first three types, separate items were designed to capture the site where the violence occurred: at home, at school, or in the neighborhood. Reports on knife attacks and shootings were not site specific. Adolescents were asked to report separately violence they had experienced directly and personally witnessed over the past year. A six-point Likert scale ranging from "never" (a score of 0) to "almost every day" (a score of 5) was used to assess the frequency of exposure to each type of violence.

Past Exposure to Physical Violence.—A 10-item scale was designed to measure past exposure to violence. Adolescents were asked to report specific acts of violence they had experienced directly or personally witnessed while growing up, not including the past year. The same violence categories described above were employed; however, the sites (home, school, neighborhood) were excluded because of the time elapsed between the event and the requested memory recall. A four-point Likert scale ranging from "never" (a score of 0) to "very often" (a score of 3) was used to assess the frequency of each type of violence.

Sexual Abuse/Assault.—Adolescents were asked if they had been "made to do a sexual act" against their wishes (1) in the past year or (2) "while growing up," not including the past year. Similar questions asked whether they had witnessed someone else being made to perform a sexual act against his or her wishes. The items that measured being the victim or witness of sexual abuse/assault in the past year used the same Likert format as in the recent exposure to violence scale; the items that asked about sexual abuse/assault while growing up used the same Likert construction as in the past exposure to violence scale. Two variables measuring sexual abuse/assault over a subject's lifetime, one for personally experiencing and one for witnessing, were computed by combining and averaging recent and past exposure.

Trauma Symptoms.—Trauma symptoms were measured using the Trauma Symptom Checklist for Children (TSC-C),[33] developed to assess sequelae of childhood trauma/abuse and written to be understandable to children as young as 8 years. The TSC-C contains 54 items and six subscales: anxiety, depression, posttraumatic stress, dissociation, anger, and sexual concerns; it has been shown to be psychometrically reliable in a number of studies.[34-36] Reported reliability based on Cronbach's α is as follows: anxiety, .85 for nine items; depression, .89 for nine items; posttraumatic stress, .86 for 10 items; dissociation, .83 for 10 items; anger, .84 for nine items; sexual concerns, .68 for 10 items; and total TSC-C, .96 for 54 items.[37] Based on samples of sexually abused children, the TSC-C subscales have been shown to correlate significantly with the Child Behavior Checklist for Children (mean $r=.67$)[37,38] and with the Children's Depression Inventory (mean $r=.53$),[34,39] thus demonstrating concurrent validity. Each item is presented in a four-point Likert format ranging from "never" (a score of 0) to "almost all the time" (a score of 3). Scale scores are derived by summating responses to individual items. Requests by school administrators resulted in the removal of all items related to the sexual concerns subscale.

All five subscales used in this study achieved acceptable reliability for this sample, based on Cronbach's α values: anxiety, .82; depression, .86; posttraumatic stress, .87; dissociation, .83; anger, .89; and total TSC-C, .95.

Analysis Plan

Principal Component Analyses.—Before testing the relationships between violence exposure and trauma symptoms,

140

Table 1.—Students Victimized by and Witnessing Violence Within the Past Year, by Gender

| | % of Students | | | | | | | |
| | Denver (Colo) Central City (n=1265) | | Cleveland (Ohio) Central City (n=1228) | | Small Ohio City (n=862) | | Cleveland Suburb (n=379) | |
Type of Violence	Female	Male	Female	Male	Female	Male	Female	Male
Students Victimized by Violence								
Threatened at home	25.0	22.7	25.4	23.7	32.2	28.9	13.7	16.9
Threatened at school	38.6	42.4	30.5	34.8	38.9	48.3	12.1	32.3
Threatened in neighborhood	23.4	37.3	29.1	42.9	18.1	36.6	7.4	12.7
Slapped/hit/punched at home	44.1	31.9	47.4	36.1	56.2	39.8	34.2	26.5
Slapped/hit/punched at school	27.2	40.9	22.4	32.5	17.7	37.9	13.7	44.4
Slapped/hit/punched in neighborhood	9.0	24.2	17.6	31.6	11.1	23.7	2.6	12.7
Beaten at home	8.1	5.1	10.4	8.6	9.1	6.3	3.7	3.2
Beaten or mugged at school	5.2	10.4	3.6	9.1	4.0	5.6	0.5	1.1
Beaten or mugged in neighborhood	5.2	10.5	8.8	22.4	4.0	11.5	0.5	3.2
Sexually abused/assaulted	16.2	4.6	16.3	7.0	17.3	3.9	12.1	1.6
Knife attack or stabbing	7.5	14.1	9.1	16.0	3.8	14.9	0	5.8
Shot at or shot	11.9	28.3	10.1	33.4	4.0	18.8	0.5	2.6
Students Witnessing Violence								
Threatened at home	39.5	32.4	47.1	39.2	41.5	34.6	16.8	16.4
Threatened at school	82.6	84.4	79.0	81.8	87.6	89.3	63.7	70.4
Threatened in neighborhood	52.7	61.4	72.9	78.2	52.0	69.9	22.1	28.6
Slapped/hit/punched at home	44.4	33.6	57.7	47.5	52.3	39.3	25.8	20.6
Slapped/hit/punched at school	88.1	89.3	86.0	88.3	93.3	93.2	60.5	81.0
Slapped/hit/punched in neighborhood	49.8	63.4	75.9	82.3	50.6	67.0	16.3	25.4
Beaten at home	16.9	11.7	31.1	23.4	18.6	16.1	4.2	1.1
Beaten or mugged at school	72.8	76.8	74.8	74.7	82.1	81.7	23.7	32.3
Beaten or mugged in neighborhood	35.6	46.6	67.3	72.2	35.8	52.4	5.3	11.1
Sexually abused/assaulted	17.6	16.0	20.0	21.3	19.3	16.1	15.3	9.0
Knife attack or stabbing	30.4	38.1	43.7	46.3	27.9	34.9	6.8	14.3
Shot at or shot	37.1	48.8	48.8	62.2	25.3	35.5	4.7	5.3

we performed separate principal component analyses on the 22 recent exposure to violence items and the 10 past exposure to violence items using varimax rotation as a data-reduction method; that is, we wanted to use as few variable clusters (components) as possible to explain the maximum amount of variance in the violence exposure items. The correlation matrix was examined first to determine whether the data were appropriate for principal component analysis. The Kaiser-Meyer-Olkin (KMO) measure of sampling adequacy (MSA)[40] was used as the index to determine whether all items shared significant variance (MSA=.60 was used as the criterion). Additionally, the anti-image correlation matrix was examined to determine whether each item shared significant variance with other items. An item with an MSA value less than .60 was deleted from the analysis because of the small amount of shared variance with other items. After the variable clusters were established, reliability tests were performed.

Multiple Regression Analyses.—Subsequent to the above analyses, variable cluster scores were generated for use in multiple regression analyses. Hierarchical multiple regression analyses were conducted on the TSC-C to determine the

effects of students' recent and past exposures to violence on their mental health status, controlling for their demographic attributes. Separate equations were developed for the TSC-C total score and for each of the five subscales: anxiety, depression, stress, dissociation, and anger. For each analysis, seven demographic variables were treated as control variables and entered as an initial block. The demographic variables included age, living arrangement (two-parent household vs non–two-parent household), race, gender, and parental education. The eight response categories for parental education were grouped into three categories, and then two dummy variables, non–high school graduate and college graduate, were created; high school graduate was used as a reference group. Similarly, two dummy variables, Hispanic and white, were created for "race"; African American was treated as a reference group. A second block of variables, composed of scores generated from the variable clusters of the recent exposure to violence and past exposure to violence scales, lifetime victim of sexual abuse/assault score, and lifetime witness to sexual abuse/assault score, was entered into the model to examine the effects of these variables on adolescents' trauma status.

RESULTS

Description of the Sample

A final sample of 3735 students was obtained, representing 68% of the 5509 students in all the schools in the survey. The representativeness of our sample was tested by comparing completed questionnaires from each school with the school's overall distribution of students by age, gender, and race. Our sample is representative of each school, with a few exceptions. White students were underrepresented in the small-city high school in Ohio. In one of the Denver city schools, females were overrepresented and African Americans were underrepresented. In the other Denver city school, Hispanics were underrepresented. However, the above differences between our sample and the sampling population were relatively small—all within 6%.

For the total sample, the mean age was 16 years (SD, 1.2 years; range, 14 to 19 years). Female students composed 52% of the sample. The sample was 35% African American, 33% white, 23% Hispanic, and 9% other. About one in four students (28%) had at least one parent who had graduated from college. Slightly more than half the students (56%) had at least one parent who had graduated from high school but

Adolescents' Exposure to Violence—Singer et al **479**

Component	Variable	Correlation Between Component and Variable	Cronbach's α	Eigenvalue*
Recent Violence Exposure				
Witnessed in neighborhood	Slapped/hit/punched	.78		
	Beaten or mugged	.71	.87	6.26
	Threatened	.69		
Victimized or witnessed at home	Self been slapped	.70		
	Self been threatened	.68		
	Someone else been slapped/hit/punched	.67		
	Self been beaten	.64	.75	2.10
	Someone else been threatened	.62		
	Someone else been beaten	.59		
Witnessed at school	Someone else been threatened	.79		
	Someone else been slapped/hit/punched	.77	.80	1.75
	Someone else been beaten or mugged	.73		
Shooting/knife attack	Self been attacked or stabbed	.68		
	Someone else been shot at or shot	.65		
	Self been shot at or shot	.65	.70	1.39
	Someone else been attacked or stabbed	.63		
Victimized at school or in neighborhood	Slapped/hit/punched at school	.65		
	Slapped/hit/punched in neighborhood	.63		
	Beaten or mugged at school	.60		
	Beaten or mugged in neighborhood	.52	.68	1.13
	Threatened at school	.52		
	Threatened in neighborhood	.51		
Past Violence Exposure				
Witnessed	Someone else been slapped/hit/punched	.82		
	Someone else been threatened	.79	.80	3.78
	Someone else been beaten or mugged	.76		
Shooting/knife attack	Self been shot at or shot	.75		
	Someone else been shot at or shot	.70		
	Self been attacked or stabbed	.69	.71	1.41
	Someone else been attacked or stabbed	.60		
Victimized	Slapped/hit/punched	.78		
	Threatened	.74	.66	1.20
	Beaten or mugged	.68		

*Eigenvalue represents the amount of variance among a scale's variables accounted for by a specific scale component. It is the column sum of squares for a component.

not college. For 16% of students, neither parent had graduated from high school. Fifty-three percent of students were living with both their mother and father.

Univariate Analyses

Overall levels of victimization by violence within the past year were high, particularly among male adolescents in large-city high schools (Table 1). When all sites were considered, 33% to 44% of male adolescents reported being slapped/hit/punched at school, and 3% to 22% reported being beaten or mugged in their own neighborhoods. In addition, 3% to 33% of male adolescents reported being shot at or shot within the preceding year, and 6% to 16% reported being attacked or stabbed with a knife. Rates of victimization of female adolescents by violence within the previous year also varied by school site: slapped/hit/punched at home, 34% to 56%; attacked or stabbed with a knife, 0% to 9%; shot at or shot, 0.5% to 12%; and sexually abused/assaulted, 12% to 17%. With the major exceptions of physical victim-

ization at home and sexual abuse/assault, female adolescents reported lower victimization rates than male adolescents.

Rates of recent witnessing of violence were also high (Table 1). Recent witnessing of violence by male students varied by school site for selected acts: someone else sexually abused/assaulted, 9% to 21%; someone else beaten up or mugged at school, 32% to 82%; someone else beaten up or mugged in the neighborhood, 11% to 72%; someone else attacked or stabbed with a knife, 14% to 46%; and someone else shot at or shot, 5% to 62%. Recent witnessing of violence by female students also varied by school site: someone else sexually abused/assaulted, 15% to 20%; someone else beaten up or mugged at school, 24% to 82%; someone else attacked or stabbed with a knife, 7% to 44%; and someone else shot at or shot, 5% to 49%.

Principal Component Analyses

Recent Exposure to Violence.—Five variable clusters (components) were extracted, and approximately 57% of the

total variance on the 22 items was explained by these variable clusters.

The items constituting each cluster are outlined in Table 2, grouping the items by type of violence, by being a witness or victim, and by the site of violence. The five variable clusters comprised (1) three items that measured being a witness of neighborhood violence, (2) six items that measured being a witness or victim of violence at home, (3) three items that measured being a witness of violence at school, (4) four items that measured being a witness or victim of a shooting or knife attack (none of the questions in this variable cluster were site specific), and (5) three items that measured being a victim of neighborhood or school violence; all five had acceptable reliability.

Past Exposure to Violence.—Three variable clusters were extracted from the 10 items that measured past exposure to violence (Table 2). These three variable clusters explained 64% of the variance among the items. The cluster-

Adolescents' Exposure to Violence—Singer et al

142

Table 3.—Multiple Regression Analysis for Trauma Symptom Checklist for Children Total Scale and Subscale Scores

	Variance Explained (R^2), by Scale					
	Total Scale	Anxiety	Depression	Posttraumatic Stress	Dissociation	Anger
Demographic variables	.08	.10	.12	.09	.04	.03
Violence exposure variables	.29	.20	.19	.22	.20	.27
Total adjusted R^2	.37	.30	.31	.31	.23	.30

ing of items was consistent with the results from the recent exposure to violence index. The three variable clusters comprised (1) three items that measured being a witness of past violence, (2) four items that measured past exposure to very serious violence (being a witness or victim of a shooting or knife attack) and (3) three items that measured being a victim of past violence; all had an acceptable Cronbach's α values.

Computation of Variable Cluster/Component Scores.—Based on the results of the principal component analyses, eight variable cluster scores were created (three for past violence exposure and five for recent violence exposure). To avoid multicollinearity in subsequent regression analyses, correlations between pairs of variable cluster scores were examined. Only recent exposure to shooting and knife attack and past exposure to shooting and knife attack were found to be highly correlated (r=.62); therefore, an average score computed as a measure of "lifetime" exposure to shooting and knife attack was used in the following regression analyses.

Multiple Regression Analyses

Through multiple regression analyses, the relationship between violence exposure and overall trauma symptoms (measured by total TSC-C score) was assessed for students across school sites. After controlling for demographic variables, violence exposure variables explained a significant proportion of variance in the total TSC-C score and in each subscale score. The variance explained by violence exposure variables was 29% for the total TSC-C score and ranged from 19% to 27% across the symptom subscales (Table 3). Thus, violence exposure was a salient factor in predicting trauma symptoms; the greater the violence exposure, the higher the scores for total trauma symptoms and for each symptom subscale.

The relative importance of variables in predicting trauma symptom status was determined by comparing standardized regression coefficients, B weights. Because of the large sample size, relatively small B weights (β<0.10) achieved statistical significance. Since B weights of this magnitude are considered weak, only significant values (B≥0.10) will be reported.

Gender was the only significant and powerful contributor within the demographic variables block, with results indicating that female students had higher scores on the total TSC-C (B=−0.26, P<.01) and on the anxiety (B=−0.32, P<.01), depression (B=−0.31, P<.01), posttraumatic stress (B=−0.25, P<.01), dissociation (B=−0.16, P<.01), and anger (B=−0.11, P<.01) subscales. The most important violence exposure variable clusters, as judged by their standard regression coefficients across TSC-C subscales, were being a witness or victim of violence at home (B range, 0.16 to 0.23; P<.01); being threatened, slapped/hit/punched, and/or beaten or mugged in the past (B range, 0.14 to 0.18; P<.01); and being the victim of sexual abuse/assault (B range, 0.08 to 0.20; P<.01). A notable exception was the anger subscale, for which exposure (witness or victim) to a shooting or knife attack (B=0.21, P<.01) and being a witness of past violence (B=0.21, P<.01) were additional important covariates.

COMMENT

The data indicate that adolescents in this study had been exposed to considerable levels of violence. Adolescent males from large-city schools had the greatest levels of victimization and witnessing severe violence, such as stabbings and shootings; however, adolescent males from the small-city school also evidenced substantial exposure to severe violence. While suburban youths had relatively low exposure to severe violence, boys from this site had high exposure to lesser forms of violence in school. With few exceptions, exposure to violence at home was greater for female than male adolescents, and the same was true for witnessing and being the victim of sexual abuse/assault. Female gender was the strongest demographic predictor of trauma symptoms.

The data also disclosed reliable statistical associations between exposure to violence and trauma symptoms. Each of the six initial hypotheses was supported: violence exposure had a positive and significant independent association with depression, anger, anxiety, dissociation, posttraumatic stress, and total trauma symptoms.

Certain types of violence exposure were highly associated with specific categories of trauma symptoms. Having been a recent witness or victim of home violence; having been sexually abused/assaulted; and having been a past victim of threats, slaps/hits/punches, or beatings or muggings were strongly associated with total TSC-C score and with four of the five subscale scores: anxiety, dissociation, stress, and depression. Important predictors of anger included having been a recent victim or witness of home violence; having been a witness or victim of a knifing or shooting; and having been a past witness to threats, slaps/hits/punches, or beatings or muggings. It should be noted that because of school-related constraints, sexual abuse/assault was operationalized by use of a single item rather than multiple items, which would have been a more rigorous method.

In this study, we found that substantial percentages of adolescents had been exposed to violence as either victims or witnesses, and such exposure was reliably associated with psychological trauma. Numerous clinical studies and reports suggest that repeated exposure to violence during childhood can result in serious developmental and emotional sequelae.[18-20,41-43] Previous reports have linked stress, depression, and/or anxiety to school failure,[44,45] reduced interest in play,[44] and suicidal ideation.[46] Studies have also documented the negative effects of stress and anger on children's health status.[47,48] Most recently, symptoms of depression and hopelessness were found to be associated with self-reported use of violence within a sample of urban black adolescents.[49]

Given the above, physicians and other health care professionals should be trained to screen adolescents for violence exposure as part of routine health care visits. When seeing adolescents with physical injuries in acute care settings, health care professionals should also discern how the trauma occurred; in particular, they need to be sensitive to the needs of adolescents victimized by interpersonal violence. Such screening should also occur in other settings, such as school guidance offices and community mental health centers. Furthermore, basic mental health services designed to address violence-related trauma symptoms should be readily available to all adolescents who need them, as such services are integral to the well-being of our children.

While our study was limited by the

143

geographic scope from which the sample was drawn and provided correlational rather than causal inferences, it nonetheless represents one of the largest and most in-depth empirical investigations to date of the relationship between violence exposure and trauma symptoms. The results of our study support and extend the findings of previous empirical studies demonstrating a relationship between violence exposure and symptoms of psychological distress.[30-32] This relationship would be further elucidated by prospective, longitudinal studies of children and adolescents and by samples

representative of diverse locations.

As public awareness and concern over violence grow, the opportunity exists to establish a broad and diverse research agenda to gain information about youth violence. The centerpiece of such an agenda could be an ongoing national study to monitor continuously the violence exposure of our youth. A comparable effort has been conducted on an annual basis since 1975 to monitor drug use among this nation's youth[50]; it has served to disseminate valuable information used to establish drug-related policies and programs. We must consider

exposure to violence a public health epidemic worthy of our most comprehensive and well-reasoned efforts.

The research for this study was supported by grant 93.1058A from the Ohio Department of Mental Health, Columbus, and by grants from the Treu-Mart Fund, Cleveland, Ohio, and the Nord Family Foundation, Lorain, Ohio.

We thank the students, teachers, and principals of the participating schools. We thank Raymond Lorion, PhD, and William Saltzman, PhD, for their collaboration in the development of the measures of exposure to violence. We also thank Michael Walker, executive direetor of the Task Force on Violent Crime, Cleveland, Ohio, for sharing his wisdom and perceptions with the research team.

References

1. Fingerhut LA, Ingram DD, Feldman JJ. Firearm and nonfirearm homicide among persons 15 through 19 years of age: differences by level of urbanization, United States, 1979 through 1989. *JAMA.* 1992;267:3048-3053.
2. Koop CE, Lundberg GD. Violence in America: a public health emergency: time to bite the bullet back. *JAMA.* 1992;267:3075-3076. Corrections: *JAMA.* 1992;268:3074; and 1994;271:1404.
3. Bureau of Justice Statistics. *Criminal Victimization in the United States, 1992.* Washington, DC: US Dept of Justice; 1993. Publication NCJ-144776.
4. American School Health Association. *The National Adolescent Student Health Survey: A Report on the Health of America's Youth.* Oakland, Calif: Third Party Publishing Co; 1989.
5. Bureau of Justice Statistics. *School Crime: A National Crime Victimization Survey Report.* Washington, DC: US Dept of Justice; 1991. Publication NCJ 131645.
6. Brounstein PJ, Hatry HP, Altschuler DM, Blair LH. *Patterns of Substance Use and Delinquency Among Inner-city Adolescents: Report to the National Institute of Justice.* Washington, DC: The Urban Institute; 1989.
7. Center for Disease Control and Prevention. Violence-related attitudes and behaviors of high school students—New York City, 1992. *MMWR Morb Mortal Wkly Rep.* 1993;42:773-777.
8. Schubiner H, Scott R, Tzelepis A. Exposure to violence among inner-city youth. *J Adolesc Health.* 1993;14:214-219.
9. Sheley JF, McGee ZT, Wright JD. Gun-related violence in and around inner-city schools. *AJDC.* 1992;146:677-682.
10. Garbarino J. *A Note on Children and Youth in Dangerous Environments: The Palestinian Situation as a Case Study.* Chicago, Ill: Erickson Institute; 1989.
11. Baker A. The psychological impact of the Intifada on Palestinian children in the occupied West Bank and Gaza: an exploratory study. *Am J Orthopsychiatry.* 1990;60:496-505.
12. Ziv A, Kruglanski AW, Shulman S. Children's psychological reaction to wartime stress. *J Pers Soc Psychol.* 1974;30:24-30.
13. Straker G, Moosa F. Posttraumatic stress disorder: a reaction to state-supported child abuse and neglect. *Child Abuse Negl.* 1988;12:383-395.
14. Dawes A, Tredoux C, Feinstein A. Political violence in South Africa: some effects on children of the violent destruction of their community. *Int J Ment Health.* 1989;18:16-43.
15. Pynoos R, Frederick C, Nader K, et al. Life threat and posttraumatic stress in school age children. *Arch Gen Psychiatry.* 1987;44:1057-1063.
16. Malmquist CP. Children who witness parental murder: post-traumatic aspects. *J Am Acad Child Adolesc Psychiatry.* 1986;25:320-325.
17. Terr L. Psychic trauma in children and adolescents. *Psychiatr Clin North Am.* 1985;8:815-831.
18. Pynoos RS, Eth S. Children traumatized by witnessing acts of personal violence. In: Eth S,

Pynoos R, eds. *Post-traumatic Stress Disorder in Children.* Washington, DC: American Psychiatric Press; 1985:17-43.
19. Garbarino J, Dubrow N, Kostelny K, Pardo C. *Children in Danger: Coping With the Consequences of Community Violence.* San Francisco, Calif: Jossey-Bass Inc Publishers; 1992.
20. Pynoos RS, Frederick C, Nader K, et al. Life threat and posttraumatic stress in school age children. *Arch Gen Psychiatry.* 1987;44:1057-1063.
21. Freeman LN, Mokros H, Poznanski EO. Violent events reported by normal urban school-aged children: characteristics and depression correlates. *J Am Acad Child Adolesc Psychiatry.* 1993;32:419-423.
22. Bell C, Jenkins E. Traumatic stress and children. *J Health Care Poor Underserved.* 1991;2:175-185.
23. Shakoor B, Chalmers D. Co-victimization of African-American children who witness violence: effects on cognitive, emotional, and behavioral development. *J Natl Med Assoc.* 1991;83:233-238.
24. Famularo R, Fenton T, Kinscherff R. Child maltreatment and the development of posttraumatic stress disorder. *AJDC.* 1993;147:755-760.
25. Dodge KA, Bates JE, Pettit GS. Mechanisms in the cycle of violence. *Science.* 1990;250:1678-1683.
26. Hibbard RA, Ingersoll GM, Orr DP. Behavioral risk, emotional risk, and child abuse among adolescents in a nonclinical setting. *Pediatrics.* 1990; 86:896-901.
27. Browne A, Finkelhor D. Impact of child sexual abuse: a review of the research. *Psychol Bull.* 1986; 99:66-77.
28. Lewis DO. From abuse to violence: psychophysiological consequences of maltreatment. *J Am Acad Child Adolesc Psychiatry.* 1992;31:383-391.
29. Council on Scientific Affairs, American Medical Association. Adolescents as victims of family violence. *JAMA.* 1993;270:1850-1856.
30. Martinez P, Richters JE. The NIMH Community Violence Project, II: children's distress symptoms associated with violence exposure. *Psychiatry.* 1993;56:22-35.
31. Fitzpatrick KM, Boldizar JP. The prevalence and consequences of exposure to violence among African-American youth. *J Am Acad Child Adolesc Psychiatry.* 1993;32:424-430.
32. Breslau N, Davis GC, Andreski P, Peterson E. Traumatic events and posttraumatic stress disorder in an urban population of young adults. *Arch Gen Psychiatry.* 1991;48:216-222.
33. Briere J. *Professional Manual for the Trauma Symptom Checklist for Children (TSC-C).* Odessa, Fla: Psychological Assessment Resources. In press.
34. Lanktree CB, Briere J, de Jonge J. Effectiveness of therapy for sexually abused children: changes in Trauma Symptom Checklist for Children scores. Presented at the 101st annual meeting of the American Psychological Association; August 1993; Toronto, Ontario.
35. Evans JJ, Briere J, Boggiano AK, Barrett M. Reliability and validity of the Trauma Symptom Checklist for Children in a normal sample. Pre-

sented at the Conference on Child Maltreatment; January 1994; San Diego, Calif.
36. Elliot DM, Briere J. Forensic sexual abuse evaluations of older children: disclosures and symptomatology. *Behav Sci Law.* 1994;12:261-277.
37. Lanktree CB, Briere J, Hernandez RT. Further data on the Trauma Symptom Checklist for Children (TSC-C): reliability, validity and sensitivity to treatment. Presented at the 99th annual meeting of the American Psychological Association; August 1991; San Francisco, Calif.
38. Achenbach TM. *Manual for the Child Behavior Checklist/4-18.* Burlington: University of Vermont Department of Psychiatry; 1991.
39. Kovacs M, Beck AT. An empirical clinical approach toward a definition of childhood depression. In: Schultersbrandt JG, Raskin A, eds. *Depression in Childhood: Diagnosis, Treatment and Conceptual Models.* New York, NY: Raven Press; 1977: 43-57.
40. Kaiser HF. A second generation little jiffy. *Psychometrika.* 1970;35:401-415.
41. Sack WH, Aangel RH, Kinzie JD, Rath B. The psychiatric effects of massive trauma on Cambodian children, II: the family, the home, and the school. *J Am Acad Child Psychiatry.* 1986;25:377-383.
42. Wolfe DA, Wekerle C, McGee R. Developmental disparities of abused children: directions for prevention. In: Peters RD, McMahon RJ, Quinsey VL, eds. *Aggression and Violence Throughout the Lifespan.* Newbury Park, Calif: Sage Publications Inc; 1992:31-51.
43. Greene MB. Chronic exposure to violence and poverty: interventions that work for youth. *Crime Delinquency.* 1993;39:106-124.
44. Pynoos RS, Nader K. Psychological first aid and treatment approach to children exposed to community violence: research implications. *J Trauma Stress.* 1988;1:445-473.
45. Dryfoos JG. *Adolescents at Risk: Prevalence and Prevention.* New York, NY: Oxford University Press; 1990.
46. Berman AL, Jobes DA. *Adolescent Suicide Assessment and Intervention.* Washington, DC: American Psychological Association; 1991.
47. Johnson SB. Chronic illness and pain. In: Mash EJ, Tertal LG, eds. *Behavioral Assessment of Childhood Disorders.* New York, NY: Guilford Press; 1988:491-527.
48. Tal A, Miklich D. Emotionally induced decrease in pulmonary flow rates in asthmatic children. *Psychosom Med.* 1976;38:190-200.
49. DuRant DH, Cadenhead C, Pendergrast RA, Slavens G, Linder CW. Factors associated with use of violence among urban black adolescents. *Am J Public Health.* 1994;84:612-617.
50. Johnston LD, O'Malley PM, Bachman JG. *Smoking, Drinking and Illicit Drug Use Among American Secondary School Students, College Students and Young Adults: Secondary School Students.* Washington, DC: National Institute on Drug Abuse; 1992;1. Publication NIH 93-3480.

144

by Jeffrey L. Edleson, Ph.D.

Mothers and Children: Understanding the Links

By: Jeffrey L. Edleson, Ph.D., University of Minnesota. This article is primarily drawn from an earlier work: Schechter, S. & Edleson, J.L. (1994). *In the Best Interest of Women and Children: A Call for Collaboration Between Child Welfare and Domestic Violence Constituency.* Briefing paper presented at the Conference on Domestic Violence and Child Welfare: Integrating Policy and Practice for Families, Wingspread, Racine, Wisconsin, June 8-10, 1994.

Twice over the past three decades social reform movements have called public attention to problems of family violence. In the 1960's when Dr. Henry Kempe "redis-covered" the battered child a new wave of public concern took hold (Helfer & Kempe, 1968). A decade later, the resurgent women's movement rediscovered yet another hidden form of abuse: wife beating (see Schechter, 1982). In over two decades since the founding of the first American battered women's shelters, public interest in the issue of woman battering has grown dramatically, most recently expressed in the 1994 passage of the federal Violence Against Women Act.

After two decades of overlapping movements an important question concern-ing our current understandings of family violence remains unanswered: the link between woman battering and child abuse. It is surprising that after so many years of public attention it is only in recent years that a discussion of this link has begun to appear in the literature. Several studies shed light on this overlap and raise serious concerns that we are overlooking an important area of research, policy making, and intervention. At present, there is much more we need to know about the overlap between woman and child abuse.

Estimates of the number of abused children who live in homes where their mothers are also being physically abused vary. For example, child protection workers in the Massachusetts Department of Social Services (Massachusetts DSS) reported statewide that an average of 32.48 percent of their cases also involved domestic violence (Hangen, 1994). A somewhat higher estimate was obtained in Straus and Gelles' 1985 national survey of over 6,000 American families (see Straus & Gelles, 1990). They found that 50 percent of the men who frequently assaulted their wives also frequently physically abused their children. They also found that mothers who were beaten were at least twice as likely to physically abuse their children than were mothers who were not abused. Walker's (1984) study of 400 battered women also revealed that 53 percent of the fathers and 28 percent of the mothers physically abused their children.

These data appear to establish a link between woman battering and child abuse.

What we currently do not understand is if one type of violence precedes the other or if they occur as part of the same violent incidents. We don't know, for example, the degree to which child neglect might be the result of a mother reeling from the results of her own victimiza-tion. We have little information on how institutions such as the civil and criminal justice system and child welfare agencies do or do not respond differently to families where both woman battering and child abuse are occurring.

The degree to which children witness domestic violence and to what extent such witnessing influences child social development and mental health is a grow-ing concern whenever woman abuse and child abuse are identified. It is estimated that the number of children who witness violence (but are not themselves abused) is between 3.3 million (Carlson, 1984) and 10 million (Straus, 1991) children in the United States each year. These estimates appear to be computed by taking either the number of battered or of severely battered women estimated in national surveys of family violence (e.g. Straus, Gelles & Steinmetz, 1980; Straus & Gelles, 1990) and computing the expected number of children residing in those homes. The disparity in the estimates is largely a result of how different researchers define domestic and family violence. No nationally representa-tive survey has been conducted specifically of children who witness domestic violence.

A few studies have established a link between prior victimization and youth violence. In the largest study to date, Singer et al. (1995) conducted a survey of 3,735 students in six urban and suburban public high schools in two different states. They found that "being a recent victim or witness to home violence. . . was strongly associated" with total trauma symptoms and four of five trauma subscales: anxiety, depression, stress, and dissociation (p. 481).

There is no consensus on whether a child who witnesses violence in his or her home is by definition a victim of child abuse and neglect. The term "witness" is defined differently in many studies and may include viewing or hearing an actual violent event as well as seeing the aftermath (e.g. injuries to mother, police intervention) of such violence. Does witnessing violence involve "mental and emotional injury," a reportable form of child abuse in the majority of U.S. jurisdictions (Younes & Besharov, 1988)? In some jurisdictions child witnessing of woman abuse is reported to child protection agencies. Sometimes children are placed in temporary care outside of a home if the mother discloses she is a victim of domestic violence. In other localities the mother's victimization is not a determining factor in out-of-home placements, nor is a child who witnesses domestic violence often reported to authorities.

The apparent fragmentation in the delivery of

Between Woman Battering and Child Abuse

services to battered women and abused children is addressed by several demonstration projects which have integrated safety for mothers and their children. The most notable efforts include:

• Collaboration between Michigan's Families First and its Domestic Violence Prevention & Treatment Board (DVPTB);

• Integration of a domestic violence unit within the Massachusetts Department of Social Services' child protection services; and

• Advocacy for Women and Kids in Emergencies (AWAKE) at Children's Hospital in Boston (see Schechter, 1994).

Michigan's initiative, called "Finding Common Ground," began in 1993 with a dialogue between Families First and the DVPTB. Within six months a training for Families First staff was provided by the DVPTB. This is the first family preservation effort within domestic violence programs in the United States. Michigan's effort places five family preservation teams within collaborating battered women's shelter programs to work to provide joint safety to women and children referred from the shelter. (A domestic violence curriculum for family preservation practitioners was supported by this project and is discussed in an article on page 3.)

The Domestic Violence Unit of the Massachusetts DSS evolved from responses to several child fatalities in 1989 in which the murdered children's mothers were also victims of domestic violence. DSS has assigned domestic violence specialists to six regional offices to provide case consultation, training, and work for systems changes aimed at providing greater safety to mothers and children. Domestic violence working groups review system-wide practices that might be changed to be more sensitive to issues of domestic violence. In addition, DSS has established several pilot projects in which child protection workers and domestic violence specialists work closely together on teams that are handling severe cases of woman and child abuse. DSS also has supported the establishment of supervised visitation centers, a children's evaluation service, and the development of training materials. (More information on this program will appear in the next issue of *Synergy*.)

AWAKE was established in 1986 and was the first program in a pediatric setting to work with both battered women and their children. The Children's Hospital in Boston created a

program that offers support and advocacy services to battered women at the same time the hospital works with their children. Battered women and their children work with an AWAKE advocate who has personal experience with family violence. Advocates, hospital staff, and outside agencies collaborate to provide safety for both mothers and their children.

These programs are but three of a number that are being established across the country. Very little data exist on their effectiveness and efficiency. However, contrary to expectations, by including the concerns for the mother's as well as the child's safety, the length of work with the family seemed to shorten, rather than lengthen (Hangen, 1994). Funding for and evaluation of demonstration projects such as those being undertaken in Michigan and Massachusetts would help us to better understand the consequences of linking mother's and children's safety in social intervention. An ongoing forum in which programs exchange information about demonstration projects should be supported.

There is a national need to understand the link between woman battering and child abuse. By developing a national agenda addressing this link, both the public and policy makers would be informed of the problem and its extent. This effort would also provide important clues to program developers and service providers about the best practices for improving the safety of women and child victims of violence.

References.

Carlson, B.E. (1984). Children's observations of interparental violence. In A.R. Roberts (Ed.), *Battered women and their families*, (pp. 147-167), NY: Springer.

Felix, A.C. III & McCarthy, K.F. (1994). *An analysis of child fatalities 1992.* Boston: Massachusetts Department of Social Services.

Hangen, E. (1994). *D.S.S. interagency domestic violence team pilot project: program data evaluation.* Boston: Massachusetts Department of Social Services.

Helfer, R.E. & Kempe, C.H. (1968). *The battered child.* Chicago, IL: University of Chicago Press.

Pecora, P.J., Whittaker, J.K., Maluccio, A.N., Barth, R.P. & Plotnick, R.D. (1992). *The child welfare challenge: Policy, practice, and research.* New York, NY: Aldine De Gruyter.

Schechter, S. (1982). *Women and male violence: The visions and struggles of the battered women's movement.* Boston: South End.

Schechter, S. (1994). *Model initiatives linking domestic violence and child welfare.* Briefing paper presented at the conference on Domestic Violence and Child Welfare: Integrating Policy and Practice for Families, Wingspread, Racine, Wisconsin, June 8-10, 1994.

Singer, M.I., Anglin, T.M., Song, L. & Lunghofer, L. (1995). Adolescents' exposure to violence and associated symptoms of psychological trauma. *Journal of the American Medical Association,* 273, 477-482.

Straus, M.A. (1991, September). *Children as witnesses to marital violence: A risk factor for life long problems among nationally representative sample of American men and women.* A paper presented at the Ross Roundtable on "Children and Violence," Washington, D.C.

Straus, M.A. & Gelles, R.J. (1990). *Physical violence in American families.* New Brunswick, NJ: Transaction Publishers.

Straus, M.A., Gelles, R.J. & Steinmetz, S.K. (1980). *Behind closed doors: Violence in the American family.* Garden City, NY: Anchor/Doubleday.

Younes, L.A. & Besharov, D.J. (1988). State child abuse and neglect laws: A comparative analysis. In D.J. Besharov (Ed.), *Protecting children from abuse and neglect: Policy and practice* (pp. 353-490). Springfield, IL: Thomas.

5

147

Children: the secondary victims of domestic violence

Dorothy J. Thormaehlen, L.C.S.W.-C., and Eena R. Bass-Feld, M.A., A.T.R., C.P.C.

Ms. Thormaehlen is clinical director
of the Sexual Assault and Domestic
Violence Center, Inc., Baltimore,
Maryland and maintains a private
psychotherapy practice specializing
in the treatment of victim populations.
Ms. Bass-Feld is a child art therapist
at the Sexual Assault and Domestic
Violence Center and specializes
in treating children in her
private practice.

ABSTRACT: *Children who grow up in violent households can easily become the next generation of victims of violence or perpetrators of violence. Recognizing and responding to the special needs of children who witness domestic violence is essential in any effort to reduce or prevent cycles of abuse. As physicians focus on domestic violence, they are in a key position to identify children who are symptomatic from witnessing trauma and to make appropriate referrals.*

"Children learn what they live" is a well known maxim that encourages parents to consider the effects of their behavior on children. Children who witness domestic violence are no exception to learning from what they experience. They often grow up exhibiting the same violent behaviors as their parents. That patterns of violent behavior may be passed from one generation to the next has been substantiated by family violence researchers.[1] An estimated 30% of those who witness violence in their homes become perpetrators of violence. This is considerably higher than the abuse rate of 2% to 4% found for children in the general population.[1]

Children in violent homes receive the message that violence is an effective means of gaining control over others. At the same time, it traumatizes children to see the people they love most—and on whom they are most dependent—fighting and hurting each other. Children who witness violence live in constant fear of being hurt themselves because they are dependent on volatile, unpredictable adults who display violent behavior.

Estimates from a national interview sample indicate sons who witness their father's violence have a 1,000% greater rate of wife abuse than sons who do not.[2] Our clinical experience also indicates that a propensity toward family violence is, in part, a direct result of growing up witnessing violence in the home. Almost 90% of our clients who are victims of domestic violence were raised in households where they witnessed domestic violence; many were physically or sexually abused as children. Almost without exception,

Reprints: Dorothy J. Thormaehlen, LCSW-C, Sexual Assault and Domestic Violence Center, 6229 N. Charles Street, Baltimore, Maryland 21212.

149

the men in our programs for batterers (those who commit domestic violence) report being exposed to violence between their parents. The children we counsel are frightened and emotionally distressed by the violence they witness as well as the violence they experience directly as physical or sexual abuse.

While the overall problem of family violence is a societal one that must be addressed at many levels to promote change, the effects of violence are experienced individually. By assisting individual patients through outreach, support, and referral, physicians can help break the family cycles of abuse.

The experience of the child witness

As secondary victims of domestic violence, child witnesses have not received the public and professional attention that has been focused on direct victims of child abuse since the 1950s.[3] Nevertheless, it is estimated that each year in the United States, 3.3 million children ages three to seventeen are at risk of exposure to violence between their parents;[4] of these, approximately 35% directly experience victimization in some way.[5]

That so many children can in essence be "forgotten" may be attributed to the dynamics of the abusive family; an implicit rule is "keeping the secret."[6] The silence has been aided by societal denial of the problem of domestic violence in general and reluctance to challenge the privacy of the family unit.

Children experience a myriad of traumas growing up in a violent household. They may overhear the violence; they may be exposed to threats of violence; or they may witness violent acts such as the throwing of objects randomly or at someone, pushing, slapping, spitting, kicking, hitting, beating, threats with a weapon, use of a weapon, hostage holding, and sexual assault. Such violence is often intentional and repetitive; it also includes mental abuse and intimidation as integral parts of the abuse.

Over time, child witnesses may be exposed to drug abuse and alcoholism, separations and divorce, relocations, and additional perpetrators of violence. Our experience indicates such factors significantly increase the likelihood that these children will have similar tendencies later in life. A terrifying portrait of fear and chaos emerges that affects them socially, psychologically, educationally, and physically.[7]

Characteristics of child witnesses

Feelings. Many children seen in a crisis center are victims of more than one kind of abuse. Among our clients who witness domestic violence and experience child sexual assault, the carryover between populations is as much as 70%. These children generally exhibit feelings of guilt, shame, lack of trust, poor self-esteem, helplessness, and hopelessness. They may present as high-functioning children who excel in school or sports, but they have difficulty expressing their feelings. They may deny the violence, make excuses for their parents' behav-

ior, or avoid talking about it. They also may express concern about other family members' ability to deal with the stress and violence. Two of the most difficult issues for the child witness are the ambivalence and conflict felt towards the perpetrator; the child both loves the person and hates his or her behavior.

Behavior. Domestic violence as behavior is seen many times when an older child is abusive toward a younger sibling, patterning behavior after that of perpetrators. Such children have learned poor problem solving skills and are unable to control their anger and impulses. When frustrated and challenged, they resort to violence. They seem unable to communicate feelings and thoughts in a healthy way. Their sense of personal boundaries is poor and they lack respect for others' privacy or belongings. Siblings may play out among themselves what occurs in the parental relationship.

Gender differences. Girls may be protective of the mother and identify with her. Many deny stress and trauma and/or learn a response of passivity. Boys tend to identify with the father/aggressor, bullying and/or inflicting violence on their peers or siblings. As boys enter puberty, they may express anger at the mother in the form of lost esteem because of her inability to change her situation. They may blame her as well.

Roles. Child witnesses of domestic violence often assume certain characteristic roles. Perfectionist children use all their strength to cope and to attempt to control a chaotic home environment. Scapegoated children act out in an effort to divert the parents' feuding. Clown-like children allow themselves to be patronized or laughed at to diffuse family anxiety.

Growth and development. The unpredictable, volatile home environment is extremely stressful to normal child growth and development. Some children fail to reach normal developmental landmarks or even regress (e.g., bed-wetting or soiling after having been toilet trained).

Table 1 lists behaviors according to age that may further help physicians identify domestic violence witnesses. These behaviors may continue into the next developmental stage.

Case histories

The following clinical presentations illustrate behaviors and symptoms that physicians may see in children who witness domestic violence.

Young child. Mrs. F. sought treatment for her two sons, ages four and a half and two, who had witnessed violence since birth. She said her estranged husband continued to harass her. The court had awarded joint custody of the children. Mrs F. said the children were more violent with each other and more emotionally withdrawn from her after visiting their father. She occasionally noted bruises and cigarette burns on her sons' bodies, but neither the father nor the boys provided an explanation.

Both boys tore their teddy bears apart. The older boy's primary exhibited behavior was aggression toward his brother

Table 1. Behaviors associated with domestic violence witnesses*			
Infants	**Toddlers**	**School-age children**	**Teenagers**
Injury to the body	Injury to the body	Injury to the body	Injury to the body
Poor health	Frequent illness	Frequent illness	Loss of childhood
Fretful sleep pattern	Shyness, withdrawn behavior	Psychosomatic complaints	"Perfect" child or "caretaker"
Lethargy	Low self-esteem	Hitting, stealing, lying	Helplessness
Physical neglect (diaper rash, sores)	Reluctance to be touched	Nightmares	Anger at the abused parent (loss of respect)
Vaginal or rectal discharge (often associated with sexual abuse)	Difficulty in preschool or daycare (e.g., aggressiveness, biting, hitting, difficulty sharing)	Eating disorders	Identification with aggressor
Excessive crying	Poor speech development	Repetitive self abuse	Isolation (fearful of bringing friends home)
	Separation difficulties (clinging, yelling, hiding, shaking)	Nervous disorder (e.g., stuttering, tics)	Delinquent behavior (e.g., running away)
	Excessive fantasy in play	Lack of motivation	Difficulty with siblings
		Poor grades	Heightened suicide risk (thoughts of doing away with self or parents)
		Depression	
		Need to be perfect	
		Withdrawal	Drug/alcohol abuse
		Attention-seeking	Sexual acting out
		Sophisticated knowledge of sex	
		Drug/alcohol abuse	
		Regression (e.g. thumb-sucking, bed-wetting)	
		Protective of mother	
		Assuming parental role with younger siblings	
		Difficulty with siblings (displaced anger)	
		Identification with aggressor	

Developed by SADVC, Inc., Baltimore County

and the family dog. He was unable to stay in preschool because he bit and pinched other children. He was described as lethargic and still in need of an afternoon nap because he had frequent nightmares. The teacher said he was a "sad little boy" who showed no excitement or interest in playing with the toys or other children. He recently had begun to wet his pants during the day. His mother said he had stopped dressing himself.

The younger boy was asthmatic. He suffered from continual diaper rash following his regression to wetting. He had minimal speech and refused to communicate with anyone but his mother. He cried and had tantrums at any frustration.

During the interview and initial sessions, the children refused to separate from their mother. They were so fearful that she had to stay in the room and play with the toys with them.

Diagnostic indicators in this case were

- reported aggression;
- physical injuries;
- poor health;
- regressions;
- separation difficulties;
- poor speech development;

- lethargy; and
- tantrums.

Latency-aged child. Larry was an obese ten-year-old whose parents had been in a violent relationship since his birth. He was suspicious and hypervigilant in all new situations. He had repeated second grade and was now doing below average work in fourth grade. He also had a speech impediment. Among his few friends he was usually the target of taunts. The object of Larry's anger was his five-year-old sibling.

Larry assumed the protector role toward his mother. He wanted to be "the man in the family." Feeling it was his responsibility to shield his mother from violence, he often put himself in the middle of his parents' fights. At other times, wanting his mother to care for him, he curled up in bed with her at night.

During the course of therapy, Larry was encouraged to identify and express his feelings. This was difficult because he denied any emotions, positive or negative. He initially refused to admit his parents ever disagreed. He was adept at using mature verbalizations to defend himself against showing emotion. Drawing helped him express and talk about some of his

151

frightened, angry feelings. When therapy terminated, Larry was beginning to make some positive changes. He felt better about his capabilities, had lost some weight, and was involved in an organized boys group. His parents realized they also needed therapy and had joined domestic violence support groups. Larry was referred for long-term individual therapy. It was hoped that eventually Larry and his parents would be involved in family therapy.

Diagnostic indicators in this case were

- regression;
- weight problem;
- poor academic record;
- speech difficulty;
- aggression;
- poor peer relationships; and
- confused family roles.

Adolescent. Soni, a 16-year-old who excelled artistically, was the middle child of recovering alcoholics. Her father had stopped physically abusing her mother, but continued to abuse her verbally and emotionally. Soni had taken on a protector role in the family. She was disturbed by her mother's sadness and her decision to stay in the marriage. She expressed concern about her eight-year-old sibling's constant crying and inability to maintain friends.

Two years earlier, Soni had been hospitalized after attempting suicide with an overdose of antidepressants prescribed for her sleep difficulties, lack of appetite, inability to concentrate, and poor school achievement. At the time of admission, she had a black eye that she said her boyfriend had caused. During the hospitalization, she was treated for marijuana and alcohol abuse.

Soni was articulate and spoke of the family violence and chaos in a very adult manner. She took responsibility for her father's violent outbursts by saying, "If only I had put away my clothes...." When asked to talk about her feelings, however, she cried and withdrew. She did share her feelings of isolation when she reported being afraid to bring her friends home because of her father's unpredictability.

Diagnostic indicators in this case were

- suicide attempt;
- familial history of alcoholism;
- drug abuse;
- physical injury;
- isolation;
- depression;
- difficulty dealing with feelings;
- adult demeanor;
- protective role; and
- sense of assumed responsibility.

Treatment

Children. Witnesses to domestic violence can be helped by counseling that includes educational, supportive, and emo-

tional approaches. The child ideally is offered individual sessions to establish a trusting alliance with the therapist. Then the child enters into group therapy to encourage interpersonal skills development and help break through feelings of shame, isolation, and denial. Children respond well to art, play, and verbal therapies.

The goal of counseling is to help children understand that they are not responsible for the domestic violence and chaos at home, that they cannot change it, and that they cannot control it. Children are informed that the first and foremost concern must be for their safety and that of their siblings. They are taught to identify feelings and to express them in a healthy manner. They are taught to deal with intense feelings of anger by using coping mechanisms such as punching a pillow, going out for a run, or talking it out. Therapists also work on building the child's self-esteem and sense of personal worth.

Parents. Parents willing to participate in counseling are taught alternative, nonviolent methods of discipline and communication. They learn to modify their behavior and establish logical consequences—rather than emotional or physical responses—to negative behaviors. They learn to give their children rules and limits so that there is a sense of control and order in their lives, which otherwise are disordered and unstructured. Parents also are encouraged to attend parenting classes and affiliate with groups such as Parents Anonymous for additional support with their children.

The role of the physician

Because domestic violence is associated with shame and secrecy, it is often difficult to convince victims (abused parents, usually the mother) to make changes for themselves. They may be motivated, however, when they are made aware that staying in an abusive situation is detrimental to the physical and emotional well-being of the children. Before a child's behavior can improve, the child must be in a safe environment. Parents more readily accept referrals to shelters, support and counseling agencies, police, and the legal system when approached in this manner.

In Maryland, physicians are required by law to report suspected cases of child abuse or neglect to the local department of social services or the police. They can refer a suspected adult victim of domestic violence to the police, local domestic violence program, or an emergency room as appropriate. Physicians can broach the subject of domestic violence and let victims know that, as informed doctors, they are a resource for both the victim and the children. It is vital that physicians approach such patients in a supportive and reassuring manner to avoid making them feel they are being judged negatively as a parent, which only increases shame and secrecy.

As the medical community becomes more aware of this problem in our society—a problem that persists generation after generation—we can try to meet the needs of battered parents and child witnesses. In doing so, we may be able to help end the cyclic problem of domestic violence.

References

1. Gelles RJ, Conte, JR. Domestic violence and sexual abuse of children: A review of research in the eighties. *Journal of Marriage and the Family.* 1990; 52:1045–58.
2. Straus MA, Gelles RJ, Steinmetz SK. *Behind Closed Doors: Violence in the American Family.* Garden City, NY: Anchor. 1980.
3. Peled E, Davis D. *Groupwork with Child Witnesses of Domestic Violence: A Practitioner's Manual.* Minneapolis: The Domestic Abuse Project. 1992; 1–13.
4. Carlson BE. Children's observations of interparental violence. In: Roberts AR (ed). *Battered Women and Their Families.* New York: Springer. 1984; 147–67.
5. Davis D. *Working with Children From Violent Homes.* Santa Cruz, California: Network Publications. 1986.
6. Gruszski RJ, Brink JC, Edelson JL. Support and education groups for children of battered women. *Child Welfare* 1988; 67:435.
7. Jaffe PG, Wolfe DA, Wilson, KA. *Children of Battered Women.* Newbury Park, California: Sage. 1990; 31.

The Sexual Assault and Domestic Violence Center, Inc., is a private, nonprofit, comprehensive treatment center for victims of sexual assault and domestic violence in Baltimore County. The office number is (410) 377-8111. The 24-hour hotline is (410) 828-6390. The location and phone numbers of other county programs throughout the State of Maryland can be obtained through the Maryland Network Against Domestic Violence, 1-800-MD-HELPS. ■

Results of a Curriculum Intervention with Seventh Graders Regarding Violence in Relationships

Sandra S. Krajewski,[1] Mary Fran Rybarik,[2] Margaret F. Dosch,[3] and Gary D. Gilmore[3]

This research measured the effects of a violence prevention curriculum on the knowledge and attitudes of seventh grade health education students (N = 239) about woman abuse using a valid and reliable inventory. Pretests, post-tests, and post-post-tests were administered to experimental and comparison groups. The experimental group received the curriculum intervention, Skills for Violence-Free Relationships. *Significant differences were found between the experimental and comparison groups from pretest to post-test on both the knowledge (p = .0027) and attitude (p = .0089) sections of the inventory. This impact did not remain stable at post post-test. These results confirm those found in other studies and reinforce recommendations of the battered women's movement to integrate violence-free principles into school curricula. Within the experimental group, significant gender differences were found only on the attitude section from post-test to post post-test (p = .0335); females showed greater change over time. Such limited change was not unexpected in a middle school population given the reported formative nature of the subjects' gender acquisition as contrasted with those at an older age.*

KEY WORDS: curriculum intervention; prevention; middle school; violence in relationships; valid and reliable inventory; woman abuse.

[1]University of Wisconsin-La Crosse, Women's Studies Department, 1725 State Street, La Crosse, Wisconsin 54601.
[2]Lutheran Hospital-La Crosse, 1910 South Avenue, La Crosse, Wisconsin 54601.
[3]University of Wisconsin-La Crosse, Health Education Department, La Crosse, Wisconsin 54601.

93

0885-7482/96/0600-0093$09.50/0 © 1996 Plenum Publishing Corporation

INTRODUCTION

The acknowledgement of violence as an important American public health concern is a recent phenomenon which has impacted how we view violence prevention. In addition, violence prevention has been re-focused in light of epidemiological data that support the hypothesis that violence occurs most often between acquaintances or family members rather than between strangers (Stark and Flitcraft, 1988; Wilson-Brewer and Jacklin, 1991).

Current research (American Medical Association, 1992) suggests that one in three women will be assaulted by a domestic partner in her lifetime. This translates into two to four million women a year (Berrios and Grady, 1991; U.S. Department of Health and Human Services, 1990; Van Hasselt *et al.*, 1988; Wilson-Brewer and Jacklin, 1991).

The gendered nature of domestic violence contributes to its invisibility. As Senator Biden (1993) so eloquently states,

> If the leading newspapers were to announce tomorrow a new disease that, over the past year, had afflicted from 3 to 4 million citizens, few would fail to appreciate the seriousness of the illness. Yet, when it comes to the 3 to 4 million women who are victimized by violence each year, the alarm rings softly. (p. 1079)

Hopefully, increased public awareness created by the highly publicized cases in the media in the mid 1990s will heighten the priority of woman abuse prevention in our society.

In the past few years, children from homes where woman abuse occurs have begun to receive more attention (Geffner *et al.*, 1988; Kashani *et al.*, 1992; Peled, 1993). Each year at least 3.3 million children witness this abuse (Sonkin and Durphy, 1989).

Accurate statistics are often difficult to obtain because domestic violence is considered a private, family matter. Collection of accurate statistics is further complicated by use of inconsistent categories by law enforcement agencies or missed diagnoses by health care professionals (Berrios and Grady, 1991; Finkelhor *et al.*, 1988). Additionally due to inconsistent use of the terms "domestic violence" and "abuse" from study to study, it is difficult to make comparisons.

DEFINITION OF TERMS

Because of these inherent problems with definitions in the field of domestic violence, the terms used in this article are defined primarily by the curriculum that was used for the intervention described in the present study (Levy, 1984). *Skills for Violence-Free Relationships*—a curriculum for young people ages 13–18 developed by the Southern California Coalition on Battered Women (Levy, 1984) and used nationally (Jaffe *et al.*, 1990; Jones, 1987, 1991; Levy, 1984). The goals of the curriculum are:

Participants will be able to define the terms *abuse, domestic violence,* and *battered woman.* Participants will know facts that dispel the most common myths about battered women.

Participants will know why battering in intimate relationships happens. Participants will have skills and knowledge that will reduce the likelihood that they will be abused or abuse their partners. (Levy, 1984, p. 10).

Abuse or Battering—"the use of physical, verbal, and emotional force and attack to control and maintain power by frightening and intimidating someone over a period of time" (Levy, 1984, p. 23). " . . .Battering is not a gender-neutral experience . . .it is a pattern of coercive control over women" (Schechter, 1988, p. 300).

Domestic Violence—"is abuse in a family or household including woman or spouse abuse, child abuse, incest, sibling abuse, elder abuse" (Levy, 1984, p. 23).

Battered Woman—"a victim of repeated physical and emotional abuse by a husband, ex-husband, boyfriend or lover who is jealous and controlling and who uses threats and verbal abuse as well as beatings" (Levy, 1984, p. 23).

Woman Abuse—a type of domestic violence which Stark and Flitcraft (1988) defined as synonymous with battering. The term *woman abuse* is used throughout this study.

PURPOSE OF THE STUDY

The purpose of the present study was to measure the effects of a violence prevention curriculum on the knowledge and attitudes of seventh grade health education students about woman abuse. Although school-based educational interventions had been developed by battered women's advocates, none has been evaluated with a valid and reliable instrument (Edington and Last, 1991; Family Crisis Shelter, 1987; Jaffe *et al.*, 1992; Jones, 1987, 1991; Kelly, 1988; Levy, 1984, 1991; Peterson and Gamache, 1988). Unlike previous studies, this study was conducted using a valid and reliable instrument developed for this curriculum (Rybarik *et al.*, 1995). While the overall research completed by the present authors assessed curricular impact more broadly, this present report focuses specifically on the impact of the curriculum on the knowledge and attitudes of the students.

EFFECTS OF WOMAN ABUSE ON CHILDREN

Woman abuse affects child witnesses directly through exposure to aggressive role models (Davis, 1988; Humphreys, 1991; Jaffe *et al.*, 1990; Wildin *et al.*, 1991), and indirectly through the stress created for their mothers (Jaffe *et al.*, 1990). Practitioners in the field describe how witnessing a loved one's abuse reinforces a child's powerlessness and their tendency to blame themselves for their mother's abuse (Loar, 1994). In addition, as woman abuse becomes more severe and more frequent in the home, children experience a 300% increase in physical violence by the male abuser (Straus and Gelles, 1990). "Children's responses to witnessing their mother being assaulted by their fathers will vary according to their age, sex, stage of development, and role in the family" (Jaffe *et al.*, 1990, p. 27).

Since woman abuse is not a gender neutral term, the variable gender was a focus of this study. The literature reveals that a gendered response to woman abuse varies with the amount of violence witnessed. At low levels of violence, boys become more aggressive while girls become more passive (Jaffe *et al.*, 1986; Wolfe *et al.*, 1988). At higher levels of violence, boys become more passive while girls become more aggressive. Jaffe *et al.* (1990) hypothesize that with increased exposure, children try more unusual or dramatic coping responses.

Gender also appears to impact the delayed effects of children witnessing woman abuse. Johnston (1988) studied abusive men's self-esteem, their attitudes toward women, and their experience or observation of violence as a child. It was found that men who observed or experienced violence in their homes as children were more likely to abuse their partners. Bennett (1991) discussed a delayed impact on girls manifested by a sense of loss that may extend resolution into the adult years, thus leaving females vulnerable to depression or developmental difficulties far beyond childhood.

The mechanisms through which violence may be transmitted from one generation to the next and the magnitude of violence which may be transmitted from generation to generation are complex processes not agreed upon by experts in the field (Belsky, 1993). Research is made more difficult by the fact that painful events are often hidden unconsciously from memory (Bowlby, 1980; Main *et al.*, 1985). Furthermore, research findings are often difficult to compare because of the lack of distinction between abuse and neglect, in addition to the interaction between the two (Belsky, 1993). Because of these difficulties with intergenerational research findings, considerable controversy exists (Belsky, 1993).

While intergenerational violence transmission has been theoretically linked with child and adult social adjustment problems (Bandura, 1973, 1977), it alone cannot account for the high rate of woman abuse in this country (Belsky, 1993; Dobash and Dobash, 1992; Pence and Shepard, 1988; Schechter, 1992). In fact, Emery (1989) found that "the majority of those who experience abuse in their families of origin are not abusive in their families of procreation" (p. 323). A study utilizing multiple regression techniques failed to find a causal link between witnessing parental abuse and child adjustment problems (Wolfe *et al.*, 1988).

Clearly, as research indicates, intervention in the violent family alone will not put an end to woman abuse. The general population, not just children from violent families, needs to be educated about the prevention of woman abuse (Family Crisis Shelter, 1987; Jaffe *et al.*, 1992; Jones, 1987, 1991; Kelly, 1988; Levy, 1984, 1991; Peterson and Gamache, 1988).

PREVENTION

Primary prevention programs must address attitudes about sex roles and issues about the use of power and control in intimate relationships (Jaffe *et al.*, 1992). The most effective age to intervene is not agreed upon by experts in the field. Violence researchers such as Finkelhor *et al.* (1988) feel that adolescence is the age to reach youth. Adolescence is a stage of physical and moral development in which humans establish individual identities and intimate relationships (Jaffe *et al.*, 1990).

Hancock (1989), however, felt that stereotypes take over by adolescence. For example, a boy's experience of adolescence is one of increased power; a girl's is one of increased risk. Brown and Gilligan's (1993) work with girls aged 9-16 demonstrates that for girls, at least, this feeling of increased risk is already present prior to adolescence.

Other experts think primary prevention programs aimed at early and pre-adolescents in middle school are ideal for several reasons: (1) adolescents have been exposed to role models at home, in schools, in the community, and in the media that promote violence in intimate relationships; (2) adolescence is the time of first developing intimate relationships outside of family; (3) adolescents may be better able to cope with violence within a family than younger children because of support from school and peers; (4) adolescents can be positive partners in changing behaviors and attitudes, as evidenced by successful educational programs dealing with smoking, drugs, diet, and exercise; and (5) there is the possibility of reaching adolescents who have been witnesses to their mother's abuse without singling them out (Jaffe *et al.*, 1990; Randall, 1992; Smith and Williams, 1992).

Middle schools are strategic places to identify and positively affect a large number of early- and pre-adolescents who are beginning to develop their own intimate relationships and who may be at risk for becoming victims or abusers (Elias and Branden-Muller, 1994; Jaffe *et al.*, 1990). Intervention with adolescents through their school curricula would increase awareness of woman abuse and of the attitudes which promote tolerance of woman abuse in our society. As Wilson-Brewer and Jacklin (1991) have observed, "If violence is almost always the result of behavioral choices, then it can be prevented through the use of educational interventions designed to change young people's knowledge, attitudes, and behavior patterns that could lead to violence" (p. 271).

RESEARCH HYPOTHESES

The effects of the curriculum *Skills for Violence-Free Relationships (SVFR)* on the knowledge and attitudes of female and male seventh grade health education students in a small Midwestern city was tested using the following six major null hypotheses:

1. There will be no statistically significant difference between the experimental and the comparison groups on change score values from pretest to post-test on the knowledge section about woman abuse.

2. There will be no statistically significant difference between the experimental and the comparison groups on change score values from post-test to post-post-test on the knowledge section about woman abuse.

3. There will be no statistically significant difference between the experimental and the comparison groups on change score values from pretest to post post-test on the knowledge section about woman abuse.

4. There will be no statistically significant difference between the experimental and the comparison groups on change score values from pretest to post-test on the attitude section about woman abuse.

5. There will be no statistically significant difference between the experimental and the comparison groups on change score values from post-test to post post-test on the attitude section about woman abuse.

6. There will be no statistically significant difference between the experimental and the comparison groups on change score values from pretest to post post-test on the attitude section about woman abuse.

METHODS

Pretests, post-tests and post post-tests were administered to both the experimental and comparison groups to measure the impact of the curriculum on changes in the students' knowledge of and attitudes toward woman abuse. Identifying codes were used in order to maintain anonymity and allow for matching of pretests, post-tests, and post post-tests for individual students. A cover letter gave written instructions for completing the code and inventory. In addition, oral instructions were read to each class by one researcher before each testing session.

Demographic questions relating to the student's gender, age, ethnic/racial origin, and socioeconomic status helped in describing and comparing the groups and in matching pretests, post-tests, and post post-tests. The post-test and post post-test also asked the subjects open-ended questions about developing a safety plan for themselves or for helping another person who was involved in an abusive relationship. Since these safety plan data were qualitative in nature and not directly related to the knowledge and/or attitudes sections of the inventory, the data were not analyzed for the present report. Given the formative nature of gender acquisition during middle school years, additional analyses were conducted on the data in order to detect any gender distinctions in the observations within the experimental and comparison groups over time.

Instrumentation

The inventory developed and tested for validity and reliability was intended for use with *Skills for Violence-Free Relationships (SVFR)*, which is a curriculum developed for use with 13- to 18-year-olds (Levy, 1984). *SVFR* challenges sex role stereotypes, offers alternative conflict resolution strategies, and assumes that violence is related to power and control (Jaffe *et al.*, 1990; Jaffe *et al.*, 1992).

Statements on the inventory were criterion-referenced to the goals of the curriculum and corresponded to its chapter divisions. The statements were divided into four sections: demographics, knowledge, attitudes, and safety plans. These sections followed the format of Jones' (1987) evaluation, which was developed for use with junior and senior high school students in a statewide education program in Minnesota.

The knowledge section consisted of 18 statements requiring true-false responses. The attitude section consisted of 12 statements followed by a five point Likert type scale ranging from strongly agree to strongly disagree. A copy of the complete inventory is included in Appendix A.

The inventory was tested for content validity utilizing national jurors with expertise in domestic violence, child abuse, or child development. It was tested for reliability using test-retest methods. Validity, reliability, and readability procedures are explained in detail in a previous article (Rybarik *et al.*, 1995).

Subject Selection

Since the curriculum was geared to adolescents and the literature indicated early adolescence to be an ideal time to offer primary educational prevention programs, a middle school setting was chosen to administer the curriculum. *Healthy People 2000* (U.S. Department of Health and Human Services, 1990) identified school health education as a preferred setting to teach nonviolent conflict resolution skills.

The study was conducted with predominately European-American (78.8%) seventh grade health education students in middle schools in a Midwestern city with a population base of 50,000. Seventh grade was chosen in this particular school district because Health Education is offered only in seventh grade in middle school and eleventh grade in the high school.

Permission to do the research was obtained from the Research and Design Committee of the School District. Parents/guardians of the students were notified of the research project by the teachers 1 week prior to the initial testing date. Only two students were excluded from the study due to lack of parent/guardian consent. Completion of the inventory represented the students' consent to participate in the study ($N = 239$).

Because seventh grade health education classes were used and assignment to groups could not be randomized, the research design was a quasi-experimental nonequivalent control group design (Campbell and Stanley, 1963). To control for crossover of information between groups, all seventh grade health classes at one school for the first semester were the experimental group, and all seventh grade health classes at another school for the first semester were the comparison group. Since the regular school health education curriculum may have included information on some aspects of communication skills, assertiveness, or conflict resolution skills, content in the comparison group could not be completely controlled.

The schools were chosen by consensus of the school district administration and health education teachers from two middle schools in the district, based on the following information:

1. School A had four health education classes per semester, each class averaging 30 students. All four classes were taught by the same teacher.

2. School B had four health education classes the first semester, with an average of 23 students per class. The classes were taught by two health education teachers (two classes each).

Because School A had one teacher who could consistently teach all four health education classes, School A subjects comprised the experimental group and received the intervention. Subjects at School B made up the comparison group and did not receive the intervention. Subjects at both

School A and School B were pretested, post-tested and post post-tested by one researcher within the same week of each other.

Within 1 week of pretesting, subjects in the experimental group were team-taught the *SVFR* curriculum for ten consecutive health education class meetings (two weeks) by their health education teacher and a counselor from the local battered women's shelter. Both the teacher and the counselor were oriented to the curriculum during a day-long training session offered by the director of the shelter. The counselor was also available to provide support for children who identified personal experiences with abuse issues while the curriculum was being taught. Post-testing was done with both groups within 1 week after the intervention with the experimental group. Post post-testing was done with both groups five months after the post-tests.

Statistical Treatment

Initial data analyses included descriptive analyses comparing demographics and pretest scores for the experimental and comparison groups. This was done to determine if the groups were similar and could be compared. Descriptive analyses included measures of central tendency, variability, and frequencies for age, gender, and ethnic/racial backgrounds. Socioeconomic status was compared based on the number of students receiving free lunch per school. The groups were found to be appropriately similar.

For both the knowledge section (Hypotheses 1, 2, and 3) and the attitude section (Hypotheses 4, 5, and 6), change score values were compared between the experimental and comparison groups using the Mann-Whitney U test. Calculated Mann-Whitney U values were incorporated into z score calculations given sample sizes which exceeded 20 (Siegel, 1956). In order to measure change within the experimental and comparison groups based on gender, Wilcoxon matched-pairs-signed-ranks values were incorporated into z score calculations given sample sizes which exceeded 25 (Siegel, 1956). The level of significance (p) was set at .05 for all statistical calculation in this study.

RESULTS

Null hypotheses 2, 3, 5, and 6 failed to be rejected. Null Hypotheses 1 and 4 were rejected because significant differences were found between the experimental and comparison groups from pretest to post-test on both the knowledge section and the attitude section. The results of the statistical analyses are summarized in Table I.

Gender differences were also tested for significance. Within the experimental group, significant gender differences were found ($p = .0335$) on the attitude section from post to post post-test, where females scored higher than males. Other testing failed to reveal significant gender differences in either the experimental or comparison groups. The results of the statistical analyses for gender are summarized in Table II.

Negative z scores were recorded in both knowledge and attitude sections from post to post post-test and from pretest to post post-test. These results are summarized in Tables I and II.

DISCUSSION

Clearly, the intervention had a significant impact on both knowledge and attitude results. However, the difference did not stay stable over time. This is not uncommon with one time educational interventions (Green and

Table I. Change Score Values Between Experimental and Comparison Groups

Tests	Knowledge change scores	Attitude change scores
Pretest to Post-test	$z = 2.99\ p = .0027^a$	$z = 2.61\ p = .0089^a$
Post-test to Post Post-test	$z = -1.39^b\ p = .1656$	$z = -0.74^b\ p = .4583$
Pretest to Post Post-test	$z = -0.03^b\ p = .9790$	$z = -0.08^b\ p = .9350$

[a]Statistically significant.
[b]Negative z scores indicate comparison group scored higher than the experimental group.

Table II. Gender Differences in Knowledge and Attitude Change Scores Within Experimental and Comparison Groups

Tests	Knowledge change scores	Attitude change scores
Pretest to Post-test (comparison)	$z = -0.87^b\ p = 0.3832$	$z = -1.60^b\ p = 0.1090$
Pretest to Post-test (experimental)	$z = -0.23^b\ p = 0.8115$	$z = 0.49\ p = 0.6186$
Post-test to Post Post-test (comparison)	$z = 1.30\ p = 0.1924$	$z = 0.52\ p = 0.5989$
Post-test to Post Post-test (experimental)	$z = 0.33\ p = 0.7376$	$z = 2.12\ p = 0.0335^a$
Pretest to Post Post-test (comparison)	$z = 0.84\ p = 0.4015$	$z = 1.93\ p = 0.0535$
Pretest to Post Post-test (experimental)	$z = 0.25\ p = 0.7999$	$z = 1.48\ p = 0.1379$

[a]Statistically significant.
[b]Negative z scores indicate that males scored higher than females within experimental and comparison groups.

Kreuter, 1991). Longitudinal studies indicate that the impact of violence prevention education weakens in as little as two years (Vooijs and van der Voort, 1993). These unstable results confirm recommendations made by the battered women's movement to school districts to effect change: schools must not rely on one time interventions to change knowledge and attitudes about violence; rather, schools need to educate their teachers to integrate the violence-free principles and materials directly into their curricular process (Family Crisis Shelter, 1987; Jaffe et al., 1992; Jones, 1987, 1991; Kelly, 1988; Levy, 1984, 1991; Peterson and Gamache, 1988).

In light of recent findings which illustrate that witnessing woman abuse impacts girls and boys differently (Jaffe et al., 1986, 1990; Kashani et al., 1992; Peled, 1993; Wolfe et al., 1988), this report examined gender differences in curricular impact. Females in the experimental group were found to have significantly higher attitude changes from post-test to post post-test. No other significant gender differences were found. This was expected in view of the age of the sample.

The acquisition of gender is a process which allows greater flexibility in roles at younger ages (Brown and Gilligan, 1993; Stern, 1991). For example, "tom-boys" are more acceptable at age 10 than at age 16. The more rigid enforcement of gender in teen years could be a contributing factor to marked differences found in studies of high school students. (Family Crisis Shelter, 1987; Jaffe et al., 1992; Jones, 1987, 1991; Levy, 1984). The subjects of the present study had a mean age of 12.3, and may be in the process of acquiring the less flexible gender roles related to becoming women and men. This process may result in the subjects giving less differentiated answers. However, this period of time may represent one of the better opportunities for prevention-oriented education. Further research focusing on gender differences using samples in various age categories would clarify differences due to gender or to age.

The quantitative nature of the data collected in the knowledge and attitude sections of the inventory may not be sensitive to the nuances of gender differentiation with a middle school sample, Additional qualitative data collected simultaneous with these data will be examined in the future for gender differences. Continuing longitudinal research on these participants also will use gender as an important variable to study.

The negative z scores (Tables I and II) are of interest because, although they were not statistically significant, they did signify differences in a direction unexpected by the researchers. In Table I, negative z scores in both the knowledge and the attitude change scores from post-test to post post-test and from pretest to post post-test signify that the comparison groups' change score means were higher than the experimental groups'. In Table II, the negative z scores from pretest to post-test within the experimental group signify that males had higher change score means than females in the knowledge section. This was also true within the control group for both the knowledge and attitude sections. Higher scores do not necessarily mean that the change was in the preferred direction of knowledge or attitude, however. Further research will need to be conducted to clarify the reasons for these findings.

CONCLUSIONS AND RECOMMENDATIONS

Positive effects on knowledge and attitudes of seventh grade health education students were recorded from pretest to post-test. The change in knowledge and attitudes, although short-term, indicates that the curriculum can affect knowledge and attitudes. Central to the significance of this study is the fact that this is the first time a change in knowledge and attitudes has been measured with a valid and reliable instrument. The lack of significant change recorded at post post-test further supports the position of the battered women's movement that intervention must not be a one-time event, but must be an ongoing process to be effective. Further research with these participants would contribute to a better understanding of the long-term impact of this intervention.

The present research, with its valid and reliable instrument, also should be helpful to community and school activists seeking integration of violence prevention principles into their school curricula. This research information should allow presenters to offer data to support recommendations for the *SVFR* curriculum. These results are limited to *SVFR* and seventh grade subjects who are predominantly European-American. Generalizability may be restricted by the limited cultural variation within the sample. Further testing of the inventory and the curriculum with larger and more diverse samples would strengthen supportive data.

The next phase of the project will involve analyzing qualitative data from the pretest, post-test and post post-tests. The researchers hypothesize that this data will further support the effectiveness of the intervention.

The *SVFR* curriculum represents a valuable initial effort in violence prevention programs. However, because American culture not only sanctions violence but also teaches how to be violent, we believe, a one time prevention program is not sufficient. The curriculum identifies certain prevention skills that can be integrated into an entire school environment in order to incorporate the value of nonviolence. Nonviolence, we believe, must be modeled for all to see in the actions and behaviors of all school personnel—administrators, teachers, coaches, classified staff, and students. This would be one proactive and wholistic approach to address the problem of violence in American culture.

APPENDIX A: INVENTORY

Dear Student,

People treat each other in many different ways. Sometimes, relationships between people become abusive or violent. I am interested in what you know or think about relationships. I am asking you to answer some questions.

Your answers are very important to us. They will help us in developing ways to help students have relationships without abuse or violence.

This semester, all seventh grade health students in this school are being asked to take these surveys. If there is a question that you are unable to answer, skip it and go on to the next question.

Do not put your name on these papers. No one will know who answered each questionnaire. You will be given a code number to use. If you have questions as you take the survey, feel free to come up and ask me quietly.

Thank you very much.

M. Fran Rybarik
Master of Public Health/Community
Health Education Program
University of Wisconsin, La Crosse

DO NOT PUT YOUR NAME ON THESE PAPERS

Write the last four digits of your phone number on the following lines:

_____   _____   _____   _____

Please take your time and think about each statement before you answer. The following questions are background information.
1. How old were you on November 1, 1992?   _____ years
2. Are you a boy or a girl? Check one: _____Boy   _____ Girl
3. What is your ethnic/racial background? Check one:
    _____Native American (American Indian)
    _____Asian American
    _____African American (Black)
    _____Hispanic American
    _____European American (White)
    _____Other (Write it in) _____

4. Which television shows do you watch regularly?
   List three _____

5. What is your most favorite television show?
   List one _____

6. Do you watch violent shows on TV?
   Check the best answer:
   ___Never/Rarely
   ___Sometimes
   ___Often
   ___Almost Always/Always

The next questions are true or false statements.
Please circle the T if you think the statement is true; circle the F if you think the statement is false; Circle only one answer for each statement

1. When people abuse their partner, they are trying to control them.   T   F
2. People are not really being abusive as long as they don't physically harm another person.   T   F
3. Most adult victims of abuse are women.   T   F
4. A person can be a victim of emotional abuse as well as physical abuse.   T   F
5. People of color are more likely to be in abusive relationships than white people.   T   F
6. Violence is more likely to occur in relationships when one partner has more power and control than the other.   T   F
7. Popular and successful people are not likely to have violent relationships.   T   F
8. Some males believe that they have the right to be violent in relationships with females.   T   F
9. Once a pattern of abuse is present in a relationship, it tends to get worse as time passes.   T   F
10. Abuse is more common in poor families than in families that have more money.   T   F
11. If a female is abused, she has done something to cause it or ask for it.   T   F
12. Under our legal system, women and children have been thought of as the property of husbands and fathers.   T   F
13. Violence in a dating relationship will usually stop after marriage.   T   F
14. It is easy for females to leave abusive relationships when they decide to leave.   T   F
15. If someone feels scared, threatened, or controlled by what another person says or does, they are in an abusive relationship.   T   F
16. People with less education are more likely to be violent in

relationships.   T   F
17. Some people make you so mad you can't help but hit them.   T   F
18. When a woman is hurt or killed due to abuse, both the
abuser and society are responsible.   T   F

The next section asks your opinion about each statement.

There are five sets of words listed after each statement. Please read each statement carefully, then circle the set of words that best describes your opinion about that statement.

1. Except for self defense, there is never a good reason for one person to slap another person.

Strongly Agree   Agree   Not Sure   Disagree   Strongly Disagree

2. Females should be responsible for raising children and doing the housework.

Strongly Agree   Agree   Not Sure   Disagree   Strongly Disagree

3. A person who abuses someone while using alcohol or other drugs is responsible for that violent behavior.

Strongly Agree   Agree   Not Sure   Disagree   Strongly Disagree

4. Males who hit, slap, kick, punch, pinch or shove are acting violently.

Strongly Agree   Agree   Not Sure   Disagree   Strongly Disagree

5. If someone is jealous, it shows how much that person cares for their partner.

Strongly Agree   Agree   Not Sure   Disagree   Strongly Disagree

6. Sometimes, teenagers get so angry they cannot help hitting somebody.

Strongly Agree   Agree   Not Sure   Disagree   Strongly Disagree

7. It is no one else's business if a husband hits his wife.

Strongly Agree   Agree   Not Sure   Disagree   Strongly Disagree

8. Females who hit, slap, kick, punch, pinch, or shove are acting violently.

Strongly Agree   Agree   Not Sure   Disagree   Strongly Disagree

169

9. If there is violence between dating partners, it is likely that violence will get worse when they get married.

Strongly Agree   Agree   Not Sure   Disagree   Strongly Disagree

10. Males should take control in relationships and be the head of the house.

Strongly Agree   Agree   Not Sure   Disagree   Strongly Disagree

11. When a husband and wife share equal power in a marriage, it is bound to cause some violent fights.

Strongly Agree   Agree   Not Sure   Disagree   Strongly Disagree

12. If a male hits a female he loves because he is jealous, it's okay.

Strongly Agree   Agree   Not Sure   Disagree   Strongly Disagree

The next questions are "fill in the blank."

For the next questions, please write your answers on the lines provided. Write down as many answers as you can think of for each question.

1. Your friend asks to borrow your tape player. You have decided not to let anyone borrow it. Write down how you would tell your friend in an assertive way that he/she cannot use your tape player.

_____

_____

_____

2. If someone close to you was being abused, what could you do?

_____

_____

_____

3. If someone close to you was being abused, where could you send them to get help?

_____

_____

_____

4. If you were involved in a violent friendship or dating relationship, who would you tell about it?

Check all that you would tell:

_____Brother	_____Friend
_____Church leader	_____Mother
_____Counselor	_____Sister
_____Father	_____Teacher
_____No one	_____Other (Who would it be?)

_____

5. If you were involved in a violent friendship or dating relationship, what could you do about it? Write as many things as you can.

_____

_____

_____

6. If you were being abusive to someone in a relationship, what could you do?

_____

_____

_____

7. If you were being abusive to someone in a relationship, where could you go to get help?

_____

_____

_____

8. If someone you know beat up his wife or girlfriend, what could you do?

_____

_____

_____

THE END

THANK YOU VERY MUCH FOR YOUR HELP!!!

Answer Key

True/False Section
Expected answers:

Multiple Choice Section
Expected direction of answers:

1.	T
2.	F
3.	T
4.	T
5.	F
6.	T
7.	F
8.	T
9.	T
10.	F
11.	F
12.	T
13.	F
14.	F
15.	T
16.	F
17.	F
18.	T

1. Agree
2. Disagree
3. Agree
4. Agree
5. Disagree
6. Disagree
7. Disagree
8. Agree
9. Agree
10. Disagree
11. Disagree
12. Disagree

REFERENCES

American Medical Association (1992). *Diagnostic and treatment guidelines on domestic violence* (Pamphlet No. AA 22-92-406 20M). Chicago, IL: Author.

Bandura (1973). *Aggression: A Social Learning Analysis,* Prentice Hall, Englewood Cliffs, NJ.

Bandura (1977). *Social Learning Theory,* Prentice Hall, Englewood Cliffs, NJ.

Belsky, J. (1993). Etiology of child maltreatment: A developmental-ecological analysis. *Psychological Bull.* 114: 413-431.

Bennett, L. (1991). Adolescent girls' experiences of witnessing marital violence: A phenomenological study. *J. Advan. Nurs.* 16: 431-438.

Berrios, D. C., and Grady, D. (1991). Domestic violence: Risk factors and outcomes. *West. J. Med.* 155: 133-135.

Biden, J. (1993). Violence against women: The congressional response. *Am. Psychologist* 48: 1077-1087.

Bowlby, J. (1980). Attachment and loss. 3. *Loss, Sadness, and Depression,* Basic Books, New York.

Brown, L., and Gilligan, C., (1993). *Meeting at the Crossroads,* Harvard University Press, Cambridge.

Campbell, D. T., and Stanley, J. C. (1963). *Experimental and Quasi-experimental Designs for Research,* Rand McNally, Chicago.

Davis, K. E. (1988). Interparental violence: The children as victims. *Issues Comp. Pediatr. Nurs.* 11: 291-302.

Dobash, R. E., and Dobash R. P. (1992). *Woman, Violence, and Social Change*, Routledge, New York.

Edington, L. E., and Last, E. G. (eds.). (1991). *Violence in Families*, Department of Human Services, Indianapolis, IN, Available from Domestic Violence Schools Training Project, C/o Women's Studies Outreach 623 Lowell Hall, 610 Langdon Street, Madison, WI 53703.

Elias, M. J., and Branden-Muller, L. R. (1994). Social and life skills development during the middle school years: An emerging perspective. *Middle School J.* 25(3): 3-7.

Emery, R. E. (1989). Family violence. *Am. Psychologist* 44: 321-328.

Family Crisis Shelter. (1987). *When love really hurts: Dating violence curriculum*, Wiliston, ND: Author. (ERIC Document Reproduction Service No. ED 286 120).

Finkelhor, D., Hotaling, G. T., and Yllo, K. (1988). *Stopping Family Violence: Research Priorities for the Coming Decade*, Sage, Beverly Hills, CA.

Geffner, R., Rosenbaum, A., and Hughes, H. (1988). Research issues concerning family violence. In Van Hasselt, V. B., Morrison, R. L., Bellack, A. S., and Hersen, M. (eds.), *Handbook of Family Violence*, Plenum, New York, pp. 457-481.

Green, L. W., and Kreuter, M. (1991). *Health Promotion Planning: An Educational and Environmental Approach* (second edition), Mayfield, Mountain View, CA.

Hancock, E. (1989). *The Girl Within*, Dutton, New York.

Humphreys, J. (1991). Children of battered women: Worries about their mothers. *Pediatr. Nurs.* 17: 342-345.

Jaccard, J., and Becker, M. A. (1990). *Statistics for the Behavioral Sciences* (second edition), Wadsworth, Belmont, CA.

Jaffe, P. G., Sudermann, M., Reitzel, D., and Killip, S. M. (1992). An evaluation of a secondary school primary prevention program on violence in intimate relationships. *Viol. Vict.* 7: 129-146.

Jaffe, P., Wolfe, D. A., Wilson, S., and Zak, L. (1986). Family violence and child adjustment: A comparative analysis of girls' and boys' behavioral symptoms. *Am. J. Psychiatry* 143: 74-77.

Jaffe, P. G., Wolfe, D. A., and Wilson, S. K. (1990). *Children of Battered Women*, Sage, Newbury Park, CA.

Johnston, M. (1988). Correlates of early violence experience among men who are abusive toward female mates. In Hotaling, G. T., Finkelhor, D., Kirkpatrick, J. T., and Straus, M. A. (eds.), *Family Abuse and Its Consequences*, Newbury Park, CA, Sage, pp. 192-202.

Jones, L. E. (1987). [Minnesota coalition for battered women: School curriculum project evaluation report.] Unpublished raw data, personal communication. May 15, 1992.

Jones, L. E. (1991). The Minnesota school curriculum project: A statewide domestic violence prevention project in secondary schools. In Levy, B. (ed.), *Dating Violence: Young Women in Danger*, Seal, Seattle.

Kashani, J. H., Daniel, A. E., Dandoy, A. C., and Holcomb, W. R. (1992). Family violence: Impact on children. *J. Am. Acad. Child Adol. Psychiatry* 31: 181-189.

Kelly, L. (1988). *Surviving Sexual Abuse*, University of Minnesota Press, Minneapolis.

Levy, B. (1984). *Skills for Violence-Free Relationships*, Southern California Coalition on Battered Women, Los Angeles. Available from Minesota Coalition for Battered Women, 570 Asbury Street Suite 201, St. Paul, MN 55104.

Levy, B. (ed.) (1991). *Dating Violence: Young Women in Danger*, Seal, Seattle.

Loar, L. (1994, April). *The tangled web: animal cruelty and family violence*, Paper presented at The Tangled Web: The Intersections of Child Abuse and Animal Abuse Conference, La Crosse, Wisconsin.

Main, M., Kaplan, N., and Cassidy, J. (1985). Security in infancy, childhood and adulthood: A move to level representation. In Bretherton, I., and Waters (eds.), Growing points in attachment theory & research. *Monogr. Soc. Res. Child Devel.* 50(1-2, Serial No. 207).

Peled, E. (1993). Children who witness women battering: Concerns and dilemmas in the construction of a social problem. *Child. Youth Serv. Rev.* 15: 43-52.

Pence, E., and Shepard, M. (1988). Integrating feminist theory and practice: The challenge of the battered women's movement. In Yllo, K., and Bograd, M. (eds.), *Feminist Perspectives on Wife Abuse*, Sage, Newbury Park, pp. 282-298.

Petersen, K. S., and Gamache, D. (1988). *My Family and Me: Violence Free,* Minnesota Coalition for Battered Women, St. Paul.

Randall, T. (1992). Adolescents may experience home, school abuse. *J. Am. Med. Assoc.* 267: 3127-3129.

Rybarik, M. F., Dosch, M. F., Gilmore, G. D., and Krajewski, S. S. (1995). Violence in relationships: A seventh grade inventory. *J. Fam. Viol.* 10: 223-251.

Schechter, S. (1988). Building bridges between activists, professionals, and researchers. In Yllo, K., and Bograd, M. (eds.), *Feminist Perspectives on Wife Abuse,* Sage, Newbury Park, CA, pp. 299-312.

Schechter, S. (1992, October). *Reframing the issues: Effective interventions with battered women,* Paper presented at the Domestic Violence Training Project for Health Workers, Madison, WI.

Schlotzhauer, S. D., and Littell, R. C. (1987). *SAS System for Elementary Statistical Analysis,* SAS Institute, Cary, NC.

Siegel, S. (1956). *Nonparametric Statistics for the Behavioral Sciences,* McGraw-Hill, New York.

Smith, J. P., and Williams, J. G. (1992). From abusive household to dating violence. *J. Fam. Viol.* 7: 153-165.

Sonkin, D. J., and Durphy, M. (1989). *Learning to Live Without Violence: A Handbook for Men,* Volcano Press, Volcano, CA.

Stark, E., and Flitcraft, A. (1988). Violence among intimates: An epidemiological review. In Van Hasselt, V. B., Morrison, R. L., Bellack, A. S., and Hersen, M. (eds.), *Handbook of Family Violence,* Sage, Newbury Park, CA, pp. 293-317.

Stern, L. (1991). Disavowing the self in female adolescence. In Gilligan, C., Rogers, A., and Tolmen, D. (eds.), *Women, Girls and Psychotherapy,* Haworth Press, New York.

Straus, M., and Gelles, R. (1990). *Physical Violence in Families,* Transaction, New Brunswick.

U.S. Department of Health and Human Services. (1990). *Healthy People 2000: National Health Promotion and Disease Prevention Objectives,* U.S. Government Printing Office, Washington, DC.

Van Hasselt, V. B., Morrison, R. L., Bellack, A. S., and Hersen, M. (eds.) (1988). *Handbook of Family Violence,* Plenum, New York.

Vooijs, M. W., and van der Voort, T. H. A. (1993). Learning about television violence: The impact of a critical viewing curriculum on children's attitudinal judgments of crime series. *J. Res. Devel. Ed.* 26(3): 133-142.

Wildin, S. R., Williamson, W. D., and Wilson, G. S. (1991). Children of battered women: Developmental and learning profiles. *Clin. Pediatr. Phil.* 30: 299-304.

Wilson-Brewer, R., and Jacklin, B. (1991). Violence prevention strategies targeted at the general population of minority youth. *Publ. Health Rep.* 106: 270-271.

Wolfe, D. A., Jaffe, P., Wilson, S. K., and Zak, L. (1988). A multivariate investigation of children's adjustment to family violence. In Hotaling, G. T., Finkelhor, D., Kirkpatrick, J. T., and Straus, M. A. (eds.), *Family Abuse and Its Consequences,* Sage, Newbury Park, CA, pp. 228-241.

U.S. Department of Justice
Office of Justice Programs
Office of Juvenile Justice and Delinquency Prevention

OJJDP — Office of Juvenile Justice and Delinquency Prevention

Shay Bilchik, Administrator

FACT SHEET # 21 December 1994

Violent Families and Youth Violence

Terence P. Thornberry

Violent Families and Youth Violence

Compared to other industrialized nations, America's rates of criminal violence are unacceptably high. Pervasive violence adversely affects our streets, schools, work places, and even our homes.

While we have come to recognize the extent of family violence, we know much less about its consequences, particularly its effects on children growing up in violent families. This fact sheet examines this issue for one outcome, involvement in violent behavior during adolescence. It addresses two questions.

First, are children who are victims of maltreatment and abuse during childhood more apt to be violent when they are adolescents? And second, are children who are exposed to multiple forms of family violence—not just maltreatment—more likely to be violent?

Methods

Data from the Rochester Youth Development Study are used in this analysis. This ongoing study of delinquency and drug use began with 1,000 7th and 8th grade students attending the public schools of Rochester, New York in 1988. Youngsters at high risk for serious delinquency were oversampled, but the data presented here are weighted to represent the cohort of all 7th and 8th graders. The youths and their primary caretaker were interviewed every six months until the adolescents were in the 11th and 12th grades. Students who left the Rochester schools were also contacted. The overall retention rate was 88 percent. In addition to personal interviews, the project collected data from schools, police, social services, and related agencies.[1]

Delinquency is measured by self-reports of violent behavior. Every six months the interviewed youths indicated their involvement in six forms of violent behavior, ranging from simple assault to armed robbery and aggravated assault. The measure used in this analysis is the cumulative prevalence of such behavior over the course of the interviews.

Child Maltreatment and Delinquency

Practitioners and researchers have long been interested in whether early childhood victimization is a significant risk factor for later involvement in violence. To examine this issue, information was collected on maltreatment from the Child Protective Service files of the Monroe County, New York, Department of Social Services for all study subjects. Maltreatment includes substantiated cases of physical or sexual abuse or neglect. To examine prior victimization as a risk factor for later violence, we have considered only those instances of maltreatment that occurred before age 12.

Sixty-nine percent of the youths who had been maltreated as children reported involvement in violence as compared to 56 percent of those who had not been maltreated (Figure 1).[2] In other words, a history of maltreatment increases the chances of youth violence by 24 percent.

Figure 1 - Self-Reported Violence by History of Childhood Maltreatment

Other analyses of these data indicate that maltreatment is also a significant risk factor for official delinquency and other forms of self-reported delinquency; for the prevalence and frequency of delinquency; and for all these indicators when gender, race/ethnicity, family structure, and social class are held constant.[3]

Multiple Family Violence

If direct childhood victimization increases the likelihood of later youth violence, does more general exposure to family violence also increase the risk? To address this question, three different indicators of family violence were examined: partner violence, family climate of hostility, and child maltreatment.

Partner violence was measured by the Violence Subscale of the Conflict Tactics Scale (Straus, 1988). It was based on parent interview data and indicates the level of violence between the subject's parent and his or her spouse.[4] The family climate of hostility scale — also taken from the parent interview — measures the extent to which there was a) generalized conflict in the family, and b) family members physically fought with one another. The child maltreatment measure is similar to the one used earlier, but now includes cases of maltreatment in which any children in the subject's family are victimized, not just the study participant.

Figures 2 through 4 demonstrate that, for each type of family violence, adolescents who live in violent families have higher rates of self-reported violence than do youngsters from non-violent families. The results for partner violence illustrate this finding. Seventy percent of the adolescents who grew up in families where the parents fought with one another self-reported violent delinquency as compared to 49 percent of the adolescents who grew up in families without this type of conflict. Similar patterns can be seen for the other two indicators of family violence.

Figure 2 - Self-Reported Violence
by Partner Violence

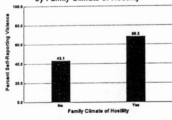

Figure 3 - Self-Reported Violence
by Family Climate of Hostility

Figure 4 - Self-Reported Violence
by Child Maltreatment in the Family

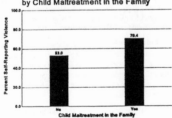

The final issue we examined was the consequences of growing up in families experiencing multiple forms of violence (Figure 5). While thirty-eight percent of the youngsters from non-violent families reported involvement in violent delinquency, this rate increased to 60 percent for youngsters whose family engaged in one of these forms of violence, to 73 percent for those exposed to two forms of family violence, and further increased to 78 percent for adolescents exposed to all three forms of family violence. Exposure to multiple forms of family violence, therefore, doubles the risk of self-reported youth violence.

Figure 5 - Self-Reported Violence
by Number of Types of Family Violence

Summary

This analysis examined the relationship between family violence and youth violence. Adolescents who had been direct victims of child maltreatment are more likely to report involvement in youth violence than non-maltreated subjects. Similarly, adolescents growing up in homes exhibiting partner violence, generalized hostility, or child maltreatment also have higher rates of self-reported violence. The highest rates were reported by youngsters from multiple violent families. In these families, over three-quarters of the adolescents self-reported violent behavior. In other words, children exposed to multiple forms of family violence report more than twice the rate of youth violence as those from nonviolent families.

References

1 See David Huizinga, Rolf Loeber, and Terence Thornberry, *Urban Delinquency and Substance Abuse*. Washington, DC: U.S. Department of Justice, Office of Juvenile Justice and Delinquency Prevention, 1993. A technical report is also available that provides a detailed discussion of sampling, attrition, and data collection procedures.

2 This relationship is significant at the .01 level. All other relationships reported in this paper are significant at the .001 level.

3 Carolyn Smith and Terence P. Thornberry, *The Relationship Between Childhood Maltreatment and Adolescent Involvement in Delinquency and Drug Use*. Working Paper No. 17 . Criminal Justice Center. State University of New York at Albany.

4 If the subject's parent did not have a spouse or other partner, Partner Violence equals zero since the adolescent was not exposed to this type of family violence, at least during the course of our study.

This Fact Sheet was prepared by Dr. Terence P.Thornberry, Professor, School of Criminal Justice, State University of New York at Albany. He is also Director of the Rochester Youth Development Study. The work was supported by OJJDP grant #86-JN-CX-0007. The Rochester Youth Development Study is one of three coordinated research projects carried out under OJJDP's Program of Research on Causes and Correlates of Delinquency.

FS-9421

Child Abuse and Domestic Violence: Legal Connections and Controversies

HOWARD A. DAVIDSON*

I. Introduction

The complex web connecting child maltreatment and adult domestic violence was noted in an American Bar Association publication over fifteen years ago.[1] Since then, a national study of family violence has found a strong substantive correlation between adult partner abuse and child abuse. Both partners were found to be more likely to be abusive toward their children in homes where mothers were victims of domestic violence,[2] but the literature also indicates that children are three times more likely to be abused by their fathers or father-substitutes.[3] When spouse abuse was severe, one study found 77 percent of the children in those homes had also been abused.[4] A survey of battered women's shelters found that approximately 70 percent of the children who came to those shelters had been abused or neglected.[5] In one review of medica

* Howard Davidson, J.D., is Director of the ABA Center on Children and the Law.

1. Howard Davidson, *Domestic Violence: Its Relation to Child Abuse*, 1 LEGAL RESPONSE: CHILD ADVOC. & PROTECTION 1 (1979). This article cites Lenore Walker's findings reported in her book, THE BATTERED WOMAN, that "as many as one third of all adult males who beat their spouses also abuse their children" and cites studies that child abuse is 129% more likely in families with domestic violence.

2. MURRAY A. STRAUS & RICHARD J. GELLES, PHYSICAL VIOLENCE IN AMERICAN FAMILIES: RISK FACTORS AND ADAPTATIONS TO VIOLENCE IN 8,145 FAMILIES (1990)

3. Mary McKernan. McKay, *The Link Between Domestic Violence and Child Abuse: Assessment and Treatment Considerations*, 73 CHILD WELFARE 29, 30 (1994)

4. MURRAY A. STRAUS ET AL., BEHIND CLOSED DOORS: VIOLENCE IN THE AMERICAN FAMILY (1980).

5. J. Layzer et al., *Children in Shelters*, 15 CHILDREN TODAY 5-11 (1986).

records, battered women were found six times more likely than nonbattered women to have their children reported for child abuse.[6]

The relationship between child abuse and domestic violence can be divided into four law-related topics. I will address each in this article and explore the implications for attorneys, judges, and lawmakers. Finally, based on my work on these issues,[7] I will propose ten public policy reforms to help assure a more sensitive approach toward the children affected by domestic violence.

The first, and clearest, link between child abuse and domestic violence is that women battered by their adult male partners[8] frequently report their batterers have also committed child physical and/or sexual abuse within their homes. Abusers often have been brutal in their treatment toward everyone in the family. Sometimes, children have been abused inadvertently—injured by blows or weapons meant to harm an adult in the home—or they have been hurt when intervening to protect a battered parent. Some children have even been killed in the "crossfire" of adult domestic violence. While domestic violence and child abuse are commonly found in the same households, however, legal interventions for the two offenses have been quite distinct—and often at odds with each other.

Secondly, some battered women have been either unable or unwilling to shield their children from a batterer's child maltreatment, and they may find themselves charged with violating laws governing failure to protect children from abuse. Therefore, a victim of domestic violence whose children also have been abused may find herself involved in multiple court proceedings, possibly at different courthouses, in which

---

6. Evan Stark & Anne H. Flitcraft, *Women and Children at Risk: A Feminist Perspective on Child Abuse*, 18 INT. J. HEALTH SERV. 97-119 (1988). In the cases of child abuse identified within this study, approximately 50% of the children were abused by the father or father-figure in the home, 35% were abused by the battered women, and the remainder were abused by others or by both father and mother.

7. I have expanded my understanding about the connections between child maltreatment and domestic violence by developing an *Annotated Bibliography Concerning the Correlation Between Child Abuse and Wife Battery* for the ABA Center on Children and the Law in 1991; by participating in the American Medical Association's March 1994 National Conference on Family Violence: Health and Justice; attending an invitational conclave titled "Domestic Violence and Child Welfare: Integrating Policy and Practice for Families," held in June 1994, at the Wingspread Conference Center in Racine, Wisconsin; and researching and writing a report for then ABA President, William Ide, titled *The Impact of Domestic Violence on Children*.

8. The overwhelming majority of adult domestic violence is committed upon women by men. Of spousal violence incidents reported in the National Crime Survey, 91% were victimizations of women committed by husbands or ex-husbands. PATSY A. KLAUS & MICHAEL R. RAND, FAMILY VIOLENCE: BUREAU OF JUSTICE STATISTICS SPECIAL REPORT (1984).

she is alleged to be both an assault victim and civilly,[9] as well as criminally,[10] responsible for her children's abuse. The state may be seeking to remove the children from her care, place legal limitations on the care and custody of her children, terminate her parental rights, and hold her criminally liable or even imprison her as an accessory to her children's abuse.

A third connection between child abuse and domestic violence is that, unfortunately, some parents who are the victims of violence are also the perpetrators of abuse upon their children. These abusive parents may face civil child protective judicial intervention, such as removal of their children by the state and/or termination of parental rights, and criminal child abuse prosecution while, at the same time, they are involved in the courts in protecting themselves from domestic violence.

Fourthly, merely witnessing repeated adult domestic violence, even in the absence of abuse directed against the children themselves, might appropriately lead to some exercise of authority to assure that such children receive therapy to help them overcome the trauma of having lived in a chronically violent home. Permitting children to be exposed to a perpetually brutal environment may itself be an act of psychological or emotional child abuse/neglect that alone, in extraordinary circumstances, could justify the intervention of child protection agencies and the courts. Thankfully, researchers have begun to pay special attention to the suffering of children who have lived in violent homes.[11] Attorneys, judges, and lawmakers must do the same.

Until recently, most social workers, law enforcement personnel, physicians, lawyers, and judges working in the field of child abuse have not devoted attention to the family connections between child maltreatment and domestic violence. Many still do not. Too often, government and private sector resources focused on prevention, intervention, and treatment specifically respond to either child abuse/neglect or domestic violence but not to situations where the two may be found in tandem.

States and communities typically have dual, separate systems charged with the protection of children and adult domestic violence victims. There has been little regard for addressing the family system in which

---

9. *See* Jill A. Phillips, *Re-Victimized Battered Women: Termination of Parental Rights for Failure to Protect Children From Child Abuse*, 38 WAYNE L. REV. 1549 (1992).

10. William W. Blue, State v. Williquette: *Protecting Children From Abuse Through the Imposition of a Legal Duty*, 12 AM. J. TRIAL ADVOC. 171 (1988).

11. *See, e.g.*, PETER G. JAFFE ET AL., CHILDREN OF BATTERED WOMEN (1990); ENDING THE CYCLE OF VIOLENCE: COMMUNITY RESPONSES TO CHILDREN OF BATTERED WOMEN (Einat Peled et al. eds., 1995).

violence may be pervasive. Formal protocols for coordination and joint training among those working in each arena (including foster care providers) are essential, but such protocols are still rare. Without adequate cross-system training and appropriate supportive services, there is justifiable fear among experts that simply increasing understanding of the links between domestic violence and child abuse may lead to higher levels of inappropriate and harmful intervention.

Generally, government social service agencies and courts are structured and organized in ways that treat child abuse and domestic violence as separate, categorical issues. State or local "protective service" agencies that combine authority and competency to address both child abuse and domestic violence are even more rare than "family courts" that have all-encompassing jurisdiction over civil and criminal aspects of child abuse and domestic violence, and related child custody, visitation, and support issues.[12] Federal, state, or local financing for intervention and treatment that addresses child maltreatment and adult domestic violence has almost always been provided for separate, rather than integrated, funding streams. The separation of these issues also affects legal professionals because, generally, lawyers who specialize in domestic violence cases are an entirely different group from those attorneys whose work focuses on child abuse. They have seldom been trained together.

II. When Batterers Abuse Both Adult Partners and Their Children

When a batterer abuses an adult partner, as well as physically, sexually, or emotionally abuses children, there should be one system capable of effectively responding to both sets of acts. Fragmentation of responses can lead to disjointed actions and harmful results for both children and the parents who are trying to protect them from abuse. For this reason, the 1994 ABA report, *The Impact of Domestic Violence on Children*, urged states to pass and enforce laws that require police and the courts to protect children during the domestic violence intervention process.

Proposed intervention reforms include training law enforcement officers who respond to domestic violence calls to see and speak with the children in the home to better address the immediate safety, shelter, and medical assistance needs of those children. It is also important that

---

12. In August 1994, the ABA House of Delegates passed a resolution reaffirming the Association's support for the creation of well-staffed and supported Unified Children and Family Courts.

relationships between police and state and local child protective services (CPS) agencies be improved so CPS can quickly be brought into a case, when appropriate, to protect the child and non-abusive parent as one unit. CPS investigators should be required by law to inquire about violent behavior of all those living in the households of reported victims of child maltreatment. The stereotypical, and erroneous, view that mothers alone are to be held accountable for their children's abuse (a position unfortunately reinforced by the sole focus of most child protective court proceedings being on the mother) must be replaced by holistic, household violence assessments and safety-oriented response plans.

Where intervention is deemed necessary to protect children from imminent harm due to abuse, the ABA report on *The Impact of Domestic Violence on Children* calls for actions that do not precipitously separate adult domestic violence victims from their children. Laws should be focused on keeping domestic violence victims with their children, unless doing so would subject those children to imminent risk of serious harm. The most common statutes relevant to this issue, which have emerged only in the past decade or so, grant juvenile court judges clear authority to order the removal of violent adults from a home and no longer rely on the more traditional "protection" available through foster care placement of abused children. Therefore, because state laws generally require that "reasonable efforts" be made to allow maltreated children to remain in their own homes so long as there is no imminent risk to their health and safety, such efforts, when taken by government CPS agencies and judges, should include removing perpetrators of violence from the home by the police and with a court order, where necessary.

The ABA report suggests that adult victims of domestic violence be given legal authority to seek court orders of protection that apply to both themselves and their children, as well as to receive information from police about how to access such court assistance. CPS case workers should be assisting domestic violence victims in obtaining that judicial help, and CPS agencies, in accord with the *Model Code on Domestic and Family Violence (Model Code),*[13] should be statutorily empowered to seek court-ordered removal of domestic violence perpetrators and the issuance of other protective orders. All such orders must be promptly carried out with the assistance of the police. For these protections to be effective, CPS case workers, supervisors, and their legal support personnel must become familiar with the applicable laws and court procedures for obtaining protective or restraining orders.

---

13. NATIONAL COUNCIL OF JUVENILE AND FAMILY COURT JUDGES, MODEL CODE ON DOMESTIC AND FAMILY VIOLENCE § 409 (1994).

In light of the link between adult and child battering, *The Impact of Domestic Violence on Children* states that courts hearing both criminal and civil child protection matters pertaining to child physical and sexual abuse and child neglect should always seek information about the existence of domestic violence in that family—and any court actions that have been taken in response to such violence. The report also calls for establishment of courthouse security measures to protect abused children and their protective parents from domestic violence perpetrators because when batterers realize, often in court, that they are losing power and control over their victims, they may react in a violent rage directed at their victims, families, and court personnel.

When courts and CPS agencies are considering removal and reunification of abused children, their deliberations also must address the need to promote the safety of the child's non-abusive parent. Agency and court actions should always be supportive of the goal of violence-free families and a parent should never be required to remain with an abusive partner as a condition of the child being returned home from foster care. Where case settlements are used to avoid child maltreatment adjudications, these settlements also should never compel parents to remain with, or return to, their batterers.

When making child placement and family re-integration decisions, CPS agencies and courts should use carefully constructed and thoroughly evaluated risk assessment instruments. These instruments should include an appraisal of the family's domestic violence history as well as the present ability of non-abusive parents to keep violence from erupting in the home. In accord with section 409 of the *Model Code*, CPS workers should have, and meticulously follow, protocols for determining whether abuse of adult household members has occurred and is likely to recur. This determination process should include the opportunity for direct worker access to criminal records, court protective orders, and offender probation information.

Even where batterers do not abuse their children, the nature of their domestic violence may be deemed sufficient to justify the termination of their parental rights. For example, courts have terminated a batterer's parental rights where his acts of domestic violence included stabbing the mother to death in front of the children[14] and where a batterer had repeatedly abused the children's mother during the marriage, ultimately pleading guilty to her murder.[15] In a nonhomicide spousal abuse case, the rights of both parents were terminated after the court found that

---

14. *In re* Sean H., 586 A.2d 1171 (Conn. App. 1991).
15. Nancy Viola R. v. Randolph W., 356 S.E.2d 464 (W.Va. 1987). *See also* Kenneth B. v. Elmer Jimmy S., 399 S.E.2d 192 (W.Va. 1990).

both had continually engaged in mutual domestic violence in front of the children for many years.[16]

III. Parental Failure to Protect Children from Abuse

Some CPS interventions against non-abusive parents begin when, for example, a mother refuses to allow a case worker investigating a report of child abuse or child neglect into her home. Such noncooperation may occur because the mother is afraid that if the worker sees the child, and the adult batterer in the home hears about it, she will be beaten up, possibly severely, and the abuser may also further retaliate by harming the child. Actions by CPS against a non-abusive parent may also begin because a case worker perceives that a mother was irresponsible toward her child in not leaving the abuser (or not leaving quickly enough). Those conclusions often disregard the fact that many batterers threaten to kill their partners, their children, or their partner's children if their partners leave the relationship. Some batterers have carried out such threats.

One advocate for domestic violence victims, in explaining why battered women remain with their abusive partners, has stated:

I want to highlight children as one of the most common reasons that many of us stay. We can better protect our children if we are there and can see the abuser than if we're on the run, and he has the opportunity and advantage of being able to track us down.[17]

If victims leave, batterers also threaten their victims with harm if they do not return home. Some carry out those threats. Many non-abusive domestic violence victims thus face a "catch-22" that would immobilize most parents without considerable financial resources to flee to a faraway destination and live independently, safely, and well.

Fortunately, there have been efforts to alter the attitudes that result in CPS "blame the victim" responses. In Massachusetts, Project Protect was a pioneering effort by the state's Department of Social Services to identify domestic violence as a risk factor for child abuse and to improve CPS coordination with police in the area of domestic violence. One adverse consequence of this program, however, was that some involuntary intervention took place in families where only domestic violence and, possibly, some child neglect were found but where previously there would not have been any CPS involvement.

---

16. *In re* Theresa "CC," 576 N.Y.S.2d 937 (App. Div. 1991).
17. Sarah Buel, *The Dynamics of Family Violence*, CONFERENCE HIGHLIGHTS, COURTS AND COMMUNITIES: CONFRONTING VIOLENCE IN THE FAMILY 11 (1993).

The concern about CPS over-intervention led Massachusetts to institute three alternative CPS practices to Project Protect that should be widely replicated:

1. Use of CPS consultants and special staff for assistance in child maltreatment cases where domestic violence has occurred;
2. Use by CPS of a special multidisciplinary team to help integrate child abuse and domestic violence interventions; and
3. Creation by CPS of a Domestic Violence and Child Protection Advisory Board (Michigan has a similar body) that reviews proposed CPS training and policy initiatives for their impact on domestic violence victims. An alternative recommendation is to have CPS agencies create adult domestic violence victim panels to help better inform their work.

Section 409 of the *Model Code* rightfully suggests that a battered woman with children should not have to formally enter the CPS "system" and face a CPS agency or court finding that she is "at fault" for her child's abuse or has failed to protect the child from abuse in order to receive protective assistance from CPS, or elsewhere, for themselves and their children. Referrals for family support services should be available through domestic violence shelters, as has been promoted by Michigan's Families First Program. The shelters in Michigan now have access to flexible program dollars for clients whose immediate financial needs include emergency rental payments/security deposits, child care, transportation, etc.

On the other hand, the question of how the law should address the "passive partners" to child abuse has perplexed many child advocates. State laws specifically authorize children to be adjudicated as abused or neglected due to parents' omissions (i.e., failures to act or carry out parental duties, or permitting children to be endangered) as well as for the deliberate commission of unlawful acts themselves. Yet, one attorney reported what is clearly a reality throughout the country: In sixteen years of working in the courts, she had never seen a father even charged with "failure to protect" when the child abuser was the mother.[18] In a classic example of legally sanctioned gender bias, it is mothers, not fathers, who find themselves facing such charges. Fathers who abandon their children rarely face criminal responsibility. As long as fathers do not live with their children's mothers, laws generally excuse them from any legal responsibility, other than for payment of child support, even when their failure to care for their children has been quite harmful.

Only a few state statutes provide affirmative defenses, such as duress or inability to act caused by fear of the abuser's reprisals, to a charge

---

18. *Id.* at 13.

of failure to protect children. One law, in Minnesota, provides a defense where ". . . at the time of the neglect there was a reasonable apprehension in the mind of the defendant that acting to stop or prevent the neglect would result in substantial bodily harm to the defendant or the child in retaliation."[19]

In an article analyzing state codes on domestic violence, Barbara Hart recommended that, in raising a defense to a charge of failure to protect children, non-abusive parents be permitted to introduce evidence about the following factors: (1) domestic violence; (2) its impact on the parent's beliefs, perceptions, coping strategies, and behavior related to the "failure to protect" allegation; and (3) the reasonableness of the parent's apprehension (based on expert testimony) that acting to stop or prevent the abuse would be ineffective, or that such action would further endanger the targeted child or the non-abusive parent.[20] Another approach to remedy inappropriate failure to protect charges would be to permit battered mothers so accused to introduce expert testimony on "battered women's syndrome" that would aid judges and juries in understanding what limited her ability to insulate her children from the abuse.

In 1982 the ABA Center on Children and the Law published a series of *Recommendations for Improving Legal Intervention in Intrafamily Child Sexual Abuse Cases.*[21] Section 2.1 calls for consideration of all the following factors by CPS agencies, prosecutors, and the courts in deciding whether to make parents who have not sexually abused their children parties to civil child protective proceedings, such as actions to place children in foster care, to compel parents to participate in treatment, or to terminate parental rights:

- Whether parents knew, or had reasonable cause to believe, their children had been abused and failed to take reasonable steps to prevent it;
- The actions parents took to protect, support, and care for their children following disclosure of the abuse; and
- Whether parents voluntarily agreed to participate in specialized counseling or treatment programs, and to accept other protective services.

These three factors are meant to serve as an alternative to the widespread state statutory provisions that allow parents to be civilly adjudi-

---

19. MINN. STAT. ANN. § 609.378 (Supp. 1995).

20. Barbara J. Hart, *State Codes on Domestic Violence: Analysis, Commentary and Recommendations,* 43 JUV. & FAM. CT. J. No. 4, 80 (1992).

21. It should be noted that these are not formal ABA policies but were a product of the Center designed to help policymakers consider legislative reform in the area of intrafamilial sexual abuse of children.

cated for abuse or neglect of their children solely because they "allow" or "permit" their children's abuse at the hands of another adult. The commentary to the *Recommendations* additionally states that there should not be judicial intervention against any parent when children can be fully protected by that parent.

It has always been a controversial suggestion that some mothers may condone, consciously or unconsciously, their children's sexual abuse for fear of dissolution of the family unit if the abuse is disclosed. The commentary notes that non-abusive parents are often vulnerable to scapegoating and displaced anger from their abusers. In addition, some children are enlisted by their abusers in elaborate patterns to deceive non-abusive parents, or worse, children are threatened that disclosures will split up their families and lead to further violence.

Section 3.5 of the *Recommendations*, in accordance with the laws and court decisions of most states, suggests that parents not be held criminally responsible for abuse inflicted by another unless they either participated in committing that abuse or had actual knowledge of the abuse and intentionally failed to take reasonable steps to prevent it. Key to this element, as it relates to domestic violence victims, is how "reasonable steps" are defined within the context of a violent home environment. Generally, there are three types of cases in which mothers are held criminally liable for failing to protect their children from the abuse of another:

1. The mother was present when the abuse took place but did nothing to prevent it from happening;
2. The mother left the child alone with the abuser, knowing that he had in the past abused the child; and
3. The mother discovered her child's abuse but failed to seek medical attention for the child.

In one criminal case that addressed the failure to protect issue, an appellate court found no statute or common law principle to impose a legal duty on a parent for failing to prevent a child's father from abusing her.[22] A Wisconsin case, however, ruled to the contrary in upholding a parent's conviction related to the physical abuse of children by another, based on a failure to protect charge, even in the absence of a statute specifically imposing such a parental duty. The court held there was a special relationship, under common law, between parent and child that imposed an affirmative obligation to prevent child abuse by another.[23]

Historically, civil child protective court actions have outnumbered criminal prosecutions of parents for child abuse. Appellate decisions

---

22. Knox v. Commonwealth, 735 S.W.2d 711 (Ky. 1987).
23. State v. Williquette, 385 N.W.2d 145 (Wis. 1986).

imposing civil sanctions, such as the termination of parental rights, against parents who fail to protect their children from abuse also out-number cases holding non-abusive parents criminally responsible for their children's abuse. However, in recent years child homicide prose-cutions against parent (or parent-substitute) perpetrators have in-creased, and as a consequence the charging of non-abusive parents as accessories to these crimes, or under failure to protect principles, is becoming more common.

One civil decision affirmed termination of a non-abusive mother's parental rights based on her failure to take proper measures to protect her children from her husband's abuse even though there was evidence that the mother had been abused by, and was fearful of, her husband and despite her claim that this abuse and fear prevented her from pro-tecting the children or leaving the home with them.[24] The court noted that the mother had returned to the abusive environment of her own volition, and that, after the serious abuse of her children, the mother stated she would not leave her husband because she loved him.

Two additional appellate decisions on termination of a mother's pa-rental rights approached the domestic violence issue quite differently. In a Michigan case the court affirmed a trial court's termination action based on the mother's failure to prevent her husband from physically and sexually abusing the children and on the risk that she would be unable to protect them in the future.[25] One judge, in dissent, objected to the trial court's conclusion that the mother would be at risk of entering into another abusive relationship—the view that "once a battered woman, always a battered woman." That dissenting judge also cited a publication illustrating the "catch-22" situation that domestic violence victims too often find themselves in:

> If the [battered] woman fears that she will be blamed for failure to protect her children from the abuser, she may be reluctant to cooperate, fearing the [CPS] agency will take her children away from her. If the agency's personnel is untrained in domestic violence, its personnel may indeed blame the mother for failure to leave her children's abuser.[26]

On the other hand, a West Virginia court reversed the termination of the mother's parental rights where the decree had been based on the mother knowingly allowing her husband to sexually abuse the chil-dren even though the mother's delay in reporting the abuse had centered

---

24. State v. G.P., 453 N.W.2d 477 (Neb. 1990).

25. *In re* Farley, 469 N.W.2d 295 (Mich. 1991).

26. *Id.* at 301 (citing National Council of Juvenile and Family Court Judges, *Spousal Assault: A Probation/Parole Protocol For Supervision of Offenders*, at 16 (1989)).

on her inability to get away from the abusive spouse.[27] The trial court erroneously assumed that the mother would reconcile with her husband, thereby exposing her children to further abuse by him, and she was not given a chance to show that she could safely provide for her children.

Appellate decisions also have addressed the issue of whether formerly battered spouses are, for purposes of child custody, unfit parents. A Texas court held that evidence of a parent's spousal abuse victimization, by itself, cannot be considered relevant to the issue of whether awarding custody to that parent would significantly impair the child.[28] The court concluded that to hold otherwise would deter battered spouses from reporting their own abuse out of concern that they might then lose their children. The court, noting the state's child custody statute, indicated that previous spousal abuse could, in custody proceedings, be heavily weighted against the batterer.

IV. When Domestic Violence Victims Also Abuse Their Children

Government child protective services agencies must always try to determine whether abuse of children is a manifestation of a parent's coping with her own violent environment and whether domestic violence is a causal factor in a parent's neglect. Some mothers, for example, may be frozen by fear or focusing their energy on their batterer's demands. Others may use excessive corporal punishment in efforts to control children's behavior in order to appease a volatile mate and to prevent any disturbances that might cause the violent partner's wrath and abusive behavior to escalate. Other parents may withdraw from their family, and their children, in a single-minded effort to protect themselves. Of course, there are abusive parents whose maltreatment of their children has no justification whatsoever.

CPS agencies must have policies to ensure that all their cases are adequately screened for the presence of domestic violence in the child's family home, foster home, or kinship care placement. Those personnel assigned to reporting hotlines, and those sections of CPS that conduct intake assessments of reports, should be required to inquire about the existence of domestic violence in the homes of children reported for abuse or neglect. CPS policies should also provide for a prompt, effective, and sensitive response when CPS learns, through referrals from the courts, police, shelters, or other sources, that a family experiencing domestic violence has also been suspected of child abuse.

---

27. *In re* Betty J.W., 371 S.E.2d 326 (W. Va. 1988).
28. Lewelling v. Lewelling, 796 S.W.2d 164 (Tex. 1990).

Supportive services to rehabilitate parents who have abused their children must include a focus on *all* the violence that has been part of those parents' home environments. Abusive parents who have themselves been battered in adult intimate relationships require special therapeutic attention. Courts involved in those parents' lives should work closely with treatment providers to gauge, as best as possible, when an abusive parent is ready to resume full, unmonitored protective care of their children in a home devoid of any violent interactions.

V. Meeting the Needs of Children Who Have Been Exposed to Domestic Violence

Estimates are that between 3.3 million and 10 million children annually observe domestic violence within their homes.[29] An estimated 87 percent of children in homes with domestic violence witness that abuse.[30] Children who are victims of child abuse, as well as those who are only exposed to the abuse of others, tend to be more aggressive and punitive toward their own children or to be violent and demonstrate a general disregard for the rights and welfare of others.[31] Boys who witness parental violence during their childhoods are at a much higher risk of becoming physically aggressive in later dating and marital relationships. Also, some children may have been living in a home where actual physical battering of a parent was rare but where they constantly felt fearful and threatened due to the possible flare-up, at any moment, of interparental violence.

Addressing the needs of children who have lived in a violent household, whether they were abused or not and whether severe physical violence between their parents was frequent or not, is a critical factor in reducing future violence. The literature clearly shows that children who witness domestic violence exhibit symptoms similar to those of abused children generally, including the perpetuation of violence. Since state laws do not explicitly define children exposed to domestic violence as children in need of legal protection, those who work within the legal process must exercise responsibility to see to it that such children receive the help they need in order to avoid perpetuating the cycle of violence so harmful to families and society as a whole.

---

29. Bonnie E. Carlson, *Children's Observations of Interpersonal Violence*, BATTERED WOMEN AND THEIR FAMILIES 160 (1984); Murray A. Straus, Children as Witnesses to Marital Violence: A Risk Factor for Life-Long Problems Among a Nationally Representative Sample of American Men and Women (unpublished paper, 1991).
30. LENORE E. WALKER, THE BATTERED WOMAN SYNDROME 59 (1984).
31. Brandt F. Steele, *The Psychology of Child Abuse*, 17 FAM. ADVOC. 21 (1995).

Lawyers involved with violent families must be vigilant to help assure that custody, visitation, and other parenting arrangements do not add to such a child's sense of endangerment.[32] Child protection and securing therapeutic assistance for children who have been emotionally affected by domestic violence must be predominant concerns of judges hearing cases involving such children, of the attorneys who represent their parents' interests, and of children's court-appointed guardians *ad litem*. To help assure children's interests are fully considered in adult battering cases that warrant special concerns about their safety, courts and child advocacy programs should consider appointment of specially trained guardians *ad litem* in civil and criminal domestic violence proceedings.

There is also much that government can do to promote accessibility of therapeutic help for children exposed to violence in their homes. The following is a proposed ten-point policy agenda for assuring a more child-centered response to family violence cases generally:

1. Congress and state legislatures should require that all government-supported family violence programs have a significant amount of funds earmarked for enhanced public and private agency responses to the children of domestic violence victims, including services for children who are living with their parents in shelters.

2. Legislation should specify, and provide adequate funding for, child protective services, law enforcement, prosecution, and judicial training and technical assistance on how to address the needs of children and their protective parents as part of the law's response to child abuse and domestic violence cases.

3. To provide funding for the first two items, lawmakers should consider earmarking crime victim funding (or other penalty assessments imposed in criminal proceedings) for use by programs providing services to children of domestic violence victims and for education programs for social services personnel, police, prosecutors, and judges that are focused on such children's needs.

4. Government human services and justice personnel should be prodded by legislatures to focus on methods (such as coordinating councils) by which they can improve coordination between, and services provided by, social workers, police, and the courts that will help better address the needs of children of domestic violence victims.

---

32. *See* Naomi R. Cahn, *Civil Images of Battered Women: The Impact of Domestic Violence on Child Custody Decisions*, 44 VAND. L. REV. 1041 (1991).

5. Where courts deem it necessary for children's protection, they should order abusive parents to stay away from their children (and the places their children frequent) as part of custody decrees or restraining orders, and the law should permit mandatory arrest by the police, without the necessity of a warrant, of parents who violate such provisions.

6. Legislators should fund the development of supervised visitation centers, programs that can be used to safely facilitate parent-child contact where there is concern about a parent's violent or other abusive behavior, or where there is risk of a parental abduction of the child.

7. Government support for child protective services and domestic violence programs should include a mandate for the development of inter-agency protocols, action plans, research, and program evaluations that address how children in violent homes can be better served.

8. Public aid to community mental health programs should be conditioned on state and local studies of how the mental health needs of children exposed to violence within their homes, including situations where children have experienced *both* domestic violence and child abuse, can be better addressed.[33]

9. Elected prosecutors should be encouraged to organize family violence units, rather than separate child abuse and adult domestic abuse units, so as to promote an integrated and coordinated response to families experiencing multiple forms of violence.

10. Funding should be provided for studying the ways in which the legal system and the courts respond to battered women whose children also have been abused.

VI. ABA Report

The 1994 ABA report, *The Impact of Domestic Violence on Children*, carefully titled the section addressing the connections between child maltreatment and domestic violence as "Explore the Child Abuse Nexus," which reflects the anxiety among many who work in the domestic violence arena that harmful policies may be initiated without an appropriate study of their anticipated impact. Advocates for battered women have appropriately expressed great concern about cases where

---

33. An excellent overview of the research on the therapeutic needs of children exposed to domestic violence can be found in B.B.R. Rossman, *Children in Violent Families: Current Diagnostic and Treatment Considerations*, 10 FAM. VIOLENCE & SEXUAL ASSAULT BULL. 29 (1994).

mothers finally get up the courage, and secure the means, to flee with their children from a violent mate, only to find themselves charged with child neglect for either remaining in that violent home too long, or in replacing that home (as many women must) with a temporary shelter-type residence that is not conducive to the health and welfare of their children.

The response to abused mothers by child protective services agencies and the courts has, too often, been inherently punitive. It has been too common for those intervening in the lives of such women and their children to only be apprised of, and to act on the basis of, part of the family's overall problems.

The 1994 ABA report urged extreme care "so that . . . interventions do not become unintentional bludgeons used against children and their battered parents" and that responses "not pit battered parents and children against each other."[34] It promoted legal action—judicial promotion of a safety plan—that would exclude abusers from the households of children where necessary to secure a safe sanctuary for children and their nonabusive parents. It suggested that parents not be labelled or punished simply for having lived with an abuser.

To put these concepts into practice will require a very different approach to community "protective services" work, and possibly new laws as well. Attorneys and judges, as well as human services personnel, will need to be trained in a more holistic approach to family violence intervention. There should be no requirement of "substantiated" CPS agency findings of child abuse or neglect, or court adjudications that fault parents for their behavior, as a precondition to delivery of services to children and families that have experienced domestic violence.

As this article was nearing publication, the U.S. Advisory Board on Child Abuse and Neglect issued its fifth report, entitled *A Nation's Shame: Fatal Child Abuse and Neglect in the United States*. The report noted[35] that:

- Domestic violence is the "*single major precursor* to child abuse and neglect fatalities in the United States";
- Many battered women are deterred from reporting their abuse, and their children's maltreatment, by fears of losing custody; and
- Many child abuse prevention programs direct their attention to mothers, failing entirely to focus on the men who batter.

---

34. *The Impact of Domestic Violence on Children, supra* note 7, at 17.
35. U.S. Advisory Board on Child Abuse and Neglect, A Nation's Shame: Fatal Child Abuse and Neglect in the United States (Apr. 1995), at 124.

This report recommended,[36] and this author concurs, that state and local agencies design (with use of federal Family Preservation and Support funds, as well as other public and private monies) child abuse and neglect prevention programs *specifically for men*. It also urged, and I endorse, the *integration of services and training* on child abuse and domestic violence.

VII. Conclusion

Violence in American homes is a fundamental societal ill, one that is linked with the much larger problems of crime and violence generally. We must, as attorneys, judges, and others who have influence in changing government policies related to violence and in altering the legal system's response to violence, better recognize and address the inherent links between child abuse, domestic violence, dating violence, juvenile delinquency, and violent crime in general. Assuring that we improve our understanding of and reactions to violence in the home must become one of our top priorities.

---

36. *Id.* at 142.

Family Violence in Child Custody Statutes: An Analysis of State Codes and Legal Practice

THE FAMILY VIOLENCE PROJECT*
OF THE NATIONAL COUNCIL OF JUVENILE
AND FAMILY COURT JUDGES

I. Historical Perspective

Removal of fault from divorce codes in the 1970s shifted the focus of family law from economic protection of the dependent spouse to equitable distribution of property. Also during this period, state legislatures amended custody codes to encourage joint custody and participation by fathers in parenting of children. Consequently, many family law attorneys moved their aggressive advocacy on behalf of battered spouses and their children away from divorce and custody proceedings and into civil protection order proceedings. But in the past twenty years, we have learned that domestic violence is a pervasive, complex, and frequently lethal problem that challenges all family law attorneys whether they represent a victim, a perpetrator, or a child from a violent

* The following staff members and consultants of the Family Violence Project are responsible for researching and writing this article: Merry Hofford, M.A., Director; Christine Bailey, M.A., J.D., Project Attorney; Jill Davis, J.D., Legal Associate; and Barbara Hart, M.S.W., J.D., consultant to the Family Violence Project and Legal Director for the Pennsylvania Coalition Against Domestic Violence. In addition, our thanks to Linda McGuire, Visiting Professor at the University of Iowa, College of Law, who assisted in the research.

Support for the research and development of this article has been provided by the Conrad N. Hilton Foundation through the Model Code Implementation Project and by the U.S. Department of Health and Human Services through the Resource Center on Domestic Violence: Child Protection and Custody, Grant Award # 90-EV-0014.

family.[1] We now know that family violence does not end when the battered spouse leaves, and the time of separation and divorce is dangerous not only for the family members but for the attorneys involved.[2] Social scientists[3] and legal researchers[4] have documented the detrimental impact of family violence not only on the children who are victims of physical abuse in violent homes but also on children who witness violence that occurs between their parents.

The good news is that an examination of current state statutes reveals a dramatic increase in legislation concerning child custody in cases

1. *See generally* Mary Ann Dutton & Catherine L. Waltz, *Understanding Domestic Violence*, 17 FAM. ADVOC. 14 (1995); Catherine F. Klein & Leslye E. Orloff, *Representing a Victim of Domestic Violence*, 17 FAM. ADVOC. 24 (1995); Barbara Salomon, *Guilty Until Proven Innocent: Representing the Alleged Abuser*, 17 FAM. ADVOC. 30 (1995); Marvin R. Ventrell, *The Child's Attorney*, 17 FAM. ADVOC. 72 (1995).

2. Salomon, *supra* note 1, at 30; Joan M. Cheever & Joanne Naiman, *The Deadly Practice of Divorce*, NAT'L L. J., Oct. 12, 1992, at 1, 28-29; Martha R. Mahoney, *Legal Images of Battered Women: Redefining the Issue of Separation*, 90 MICH. L. REV. 2 (1991).

3. *See generally* Maura O'Keefe, *Predictors of Child Abuse in Maritally Violent Families*, 10 J. OF INTERPERSONAL VIOLENCE 1, 3 (1995) (compared to normative samples, children who are exposed to marital violence are at an increased risk for both internalizing and externalizing behavioral problems, and children who both witness marital violence and who are victims of abuse are at an even higher risk for behavior problems); Mildred Daley Pagelow, *Justice for Victims of Spouse Abuse in Divorce and Child Custody Cases*, 8 VIOLENCE AND VICTIMS 1, 69 (1993) (the research shows that children who live in households where their fathers beat their mothers are victims of domestic violence whether the abuse is direct or indirect); Daniel G. Saunders, *Child Custody Decisions in Families Experiencing Woman Abuse*, 39 SOCIAL WORK 1, 51 (1994) (subjecting children to the victimization of their mothers is a severe form of psychological maltreatment, even a single episode of violence can produce post-traumatic stress disorder in children); and Susan Schechter et al., *Domestic Violence and Children: What Should the Courts Consider?*, 1 JUV. & FAM. JUST. TODAY 4, 10 (1993) (recent research suggests a continuum regarding the association between violence and mental health problems for children, with those children who witnessed violence standing in between those from nonviolent homes and those who were abused).

4. Naomi R. Cahn, *Civil Images of Battered Women: The Impact of Domestic Violence on Child Custody Decisions*, 44 VAND. L. REV. 4, 1041, 1055-58 (1991) (children who witness family violence showed more aggression, impaired cognitive and motor abilities, and delayed verbal development compared to a control group); HOWARD A. DAVIDSON, A REPORT TO THE PRESIDENT OF THE AMERICAN BAR ASSOCIATION, THE IMPACT OF DOMESTIC VIOLENCE ON CHILDREN 1 (1994) (there is no doubt that children are harmed in more than one way—cognitively, psychologically, and in their social development—merely by observing or hearing the domestic terrorism of brutality against a parent at home); Catherine F. Klein & Leslye E. Orloff, *Providing Legal Protection for Battered Women: An Analysis of State Statutes and Case Law*, 21 HOFSTRA L. REV. 801, 964 (1993) (citing cases where courts considered evidence of spousal abuse in custody determinations even where abuse was not directed against the children).

involving family violence. Currently, forty-four states and the District of Columbia have enacted custody statutes which contain some provisions concerning domestic violence to guide judges who determine child custody and visitation.[5] Five years ago less than sixteen states had such statutes.[6]

The bad news is that the rapid pace of state legislative reform in the area of child custody and family violence makes it difficult for attorneys to keep up with statutory amendments. Gender bias reports have criticized lawyers and judges for ignoring or minimizing the issue of domestic violence, or disbelieving parties' reports concerning family violence in custody disputes.[7] Some legal scholars and advocates have recently censured some family law attorneys for their lack of education on the dynamics of family violence and for such inappropriate practices as failing to present evidence of abuse at trial, entering into mediated agreements that may be dangerous to victims of family violence, encouraging clients to trade protection for money, or making other inappropriate settlements.[8]

This article analyzes state custody statutes that refer to domestic violence in the context of separation and divorce; addresses the dynamics of family violence as it relates to legal practice in child custody disputes; and reviews various evidentiary considerations, safety provisions, and unique statutory provisions. To heighten awareness of the custody laws and the considerations required of courts in deciding child custody, the article provides a critical examination of legal practice in states with statutory presumptions involving family violence. The article concludes with a call to action for family law attorneys to return to aggressive advocacy for battered spouses and children in divorce and child custody cases.

II. Statutory Analysis

A. *Best Interest of the Child*

In thirty-five states, the law mandates that courts consider domestic violence when determining the best interest of a child.[9] In two other

---

5. See the chart of state statutes at 225-27 for an analysis of provisions concerning domestic violence in state custody statutes.

6. Barbara J. Hart, *State Codes on Domestic Violence: Analysis, Commentary and Recommendations*, 43 Juv. & Fam. Ct. J. 3, 29 (1992).

7. Karen Czapanskiy, *Domestic Violence, the Family, and the Lawyering Process: Lessons from Studies on Gender Bias in the Courts*, 27 Fam. L. Q. 247, 255-57 (1993).

8. Klein & Orloff, *supra* note 4, at 814, 958.

9. See column 1 of the chart at 225-27.

custody codes, judicial consideration of domestic violence as a "best interest" factor exists as a grant of authority rather than as a requirement.[10]

Although including domestic violence as a factor to be considered under a best interest standard is not the simple solution to a complex problem,[11] it is a sound statutory basis for aggressive legal argument in custody cases involving family violence. Some national organizations advocate amending state statutes to require courts to consider spousal abuse as a significant factor when determining custody awards.[12] Section 402 of the Model Code on Domestic and Family Violence was constructed to elevate the safety and well-being of the child and abused parent above all other best interest factors when there has been a finding of abuse by one parent of the other.[13]

B. *Joint Custody*

While joint custody theoretically may enhance gender equity and fathers' involvement with their children, in cases involving family violence, researchers have found that children living under joint custody orders in high conflict families are more emotionally troubled and behaviorally disturbed than those in sole custody.[14] Moreover, legal and psychological researchers do not recommend an award of joint custody in families where there is an inability to agree on child rearing, family disorganization, imbalances of power, financial inequities, coercion, and intimidation—all characteristics found in violent families.[15]

Eleven state statutes reflect this cautionary note by mandating that a court either consider domestic violence as contrary to the best interest of a child or to a stated preference for joint custody or expressly prohibit an award of joint custody when a court makes a finding of the existence

---

10. Or. Rev. Stat. § 107.137 (1993) and Minn. Stat. Ann. §§ 257.025, 518.17 (West 1995).

11. Cahn, *supra* note 4, at 1070-1071.

12. Stephen B. Herrell & Meredith Hofford, Nat'l. Council of Juv. & Fam. Ct. Judges, Family Violence: Improving Court Practice (1990).

13. Nat'l Council of Juv. & Fam. Ct. Judges, Model Code on Domestic and Family Violence § 402, at 33 (1994) [hereinafter Model Code].

14. Janet R. Johnston et al., *Ongoing Post Divorce Conflict: Effects on Children of Joint Custody and Frequent Access,* 59 Amer. J. Orthopsychiatry 576 (1989); Judith S. Wallerstein & Janet R. Johnston, *Children of Divorce: Recent Findings Regarding Long-Term Effects and Recent Studies of Joint and Sole Custody,* 11 Pediatrics in Rev. 197 (1990).

15. Adele Harrell, *A Guide to Research on Family Violence, published for Courts and Communities: Confronting Violence in the Family* (Mar. 1993).

of domestic violence.[16] For example, a finding by a Montana court that one parent physically abused the other parent, or the child, is a sufficient basis for finding that joint custody is not in the best interest of the child.[17] Although the New Hampshire statutes contain a presumption that joint legal custody is in the best interest of minor children, the statute also requires a court to consider family abuse as harmful to children and as evidence in determining whether joint legal custody is appropriate.[18] The Arizona statute prohibits joint custody if a court finds the existence of significant domestic violence or if the court finds by a preponderance of the evidence that there has been a significant history of domestic violence.[19]

Whether a statute prohibits joint custody when a court makes a finding of family violence or directs the court to consider family violence with the authority to deny joint custody, the trend is to recognize the complexity of domestic violence cases. The legislatures are granting broader authority to courts so that they may make appropriate custody orders.

C. *Parental Rights and Responsibilities*

1. FRIENDLY PARENT PROVISIONS

Ten state child custody statutes include a public policy statement concerning a parent's abilities to allow an open, loving, and frequent relationship between the child and the other parent.[20] Eighteen states include such provisions in their list of factors that a court is required to consider when determining the best interest of the child.[21] Battered women's advo-

---

16. ARIZ. REV. STAT. ANN. § 25-332 (1994); COLO. REV. STAT. ANN. § 14-10-124 (West 1994); FLA. STAT. ANN. § 61.13 (West 1995); IDAHO CODE § 32-717 (1994); ILL. ANN. STAT. ch. 750, para. 5/602 (Smith-Hurd 1994); MONT. CODE ANN. §§ 40-4-212, -222, -224 (1993); N.H. REV. STAT. ANN. § 458:17 (1993); N.D. CENT. CODE § 14-09-06.2 (1993); R.I. GEN. LAWS § 15-5-16 (1994); TEX. FAM. CODE ANN. § 14.021 (West 1994); WYO. STAT. §§ 20-2-112, -113 (1994).
17. MONT. CODE ANN. § 40-4-224 (1993).
18. N.H. REV. STAT. ANN. § 458:17 (1993).
19. ARIZ. REV. STAT. ANN. § 25-332 (1994).
20. CAL. FAM. CODE § 3020 (West 1995); COLO. REV. STAT. ANN. § 14-10-124 (West 1994); FLA. STAT. ANN. § 61.13 (West 1995); GA. CODE ANN. § 19-9-3 (1994); IOWA CODE ANN. § 598.41 (West 1994); MO. ANN. STAT. § 452.375 (Vernon 1994); MONT. CODE ANN. § 40-4-222 (1993); NEV. REV. STAT. § 125.460 (1993); N.J. STAT. ANN. § 9:2-4 (West 1995); and TEX. FAM. CODE ANN. § 14.021 (West 1994).
21. ALASKA STAT. §§ 25.20.090, 25.24.150 (1994); ARIZ. REV. STAT. ANN. § 25-332 (1994); COLO. REV. STAT. ANN. § 14-10-124 (West 1994); FLA. STAT. ANN. § 61.13 (West 1995); ILL. ANN. STAT. ch. 750, para. 5/602 (Smith-Hurd 1994); IOWA CODE ANN. § 598.41 (West 1994); KAN. STAT. ANN. § 60-1610 (1994); ME. REV. STAT. ANN. tit. 19, §§ 214, 581, 752 (West 1994); MICH. COMP. LAWS ANN. § 722.23 (West 1994); MINN. STAT. ANN. § 518.17 (West 1995); MO. ANN. STAT. § 452.375 (Vernon 1994); OHIO REV. CODE ANN. § 3109.04 (Anderson 1994); OKLA.

cates vehemently oppose such "friendly parent" provisions in cases involving family violence believing that the justice system frequently punishes the victims of violence for their seeming lack of cooperation.[22] Their concerns include the use of children to control the abused spouse, the continued danger and threat to the victim and children, and gender bias issues.[23] Recently, the ABA's Center on Children and the Law stated that friendly parent provisions are inappropriate in domestic violence cases and proposed that state legislatures amend such laws.[24]

When a statute lists a friendly parent provision as a factor for the court to consider when determining the best interest of a child, there usually are other statutory provisions that an attorney can use in a case involving domestic violence. For example, the Minnesota custody statute has a lengthy list of factors that a court must consider when determining the best interest of a child including each parent's disposition to encourage and permit frequent and continuing contact by the other parent with the child. But the statute also provides an exception for cases in which there is a finding of domestic violence. In addition, the statute directs the court to consider the effect the actions of an abuser will have on a child if domestic abuse has occurred between the parents.[25]

Although Arizona statutes require a court to consider which parent is more likely to allow the child frequent and meaningful continuing contact with the other parent, the court must also consider the nature and extent of coercion or duress used by a parent in obtaining an agreement regarding custody.[26] When the statute requires a court to consider all the factors listed, the attorney can use a finding of domestic violence or coercion by one parent against the other to balance the "friendly parent" provision, thereby allowing the court to award custody as best protects the child and the adult victim of family violence.

2. Parental Responsibilities

All the state statutes that refer to a parent's right to frequent and continuing contact also have in the same provision a reference either to parental responsibilities or mitigating language.[27] Statutory language

---

Stat. Ann. tit. 43, § 112 (West 1995); Tex. Fam. Code Ann. § 14.012 (West 1994); Utah Code Ann. § 30-3-10.2 (1994); Vt. Stat. Ann. tit. 15, § 665 (1993); Va. Code Ann. § 20-124.3 (Michie 1994); and Wis. Stat. Ann. § 767.24 (West 1994).
    22. Joan Zorza, *"Friendly Parent" Provisions in Custody Determinations*, 1992 Clearinghouse Rev. 921.
    23. *Id.* at 923-24.
    24. Davidson, *supra* note 4, at 15.
    25. Minn. Stat. Ann. § 518.17 (West 1995).
    26. Ariz. Rev. Stat. Ann. § 25-332 (1994).
    27. *See* statutes cited *supra* note 20.

referring to parental responsibilities ensures that a court consider each parent's ability to be responsible for the child's health, safety, and welfare. For instance, a Missouri statute declares that the public policy of the state is to ensure that a child has frequent and meaningful contact with both parents after the parents have separated or dissolved their marriage and to encourage parents to share decision-making rights and responsibilities of child rearing.[28] The section also requires a court to determine the custody arrangement that will best assure both parents share such decision-making responsibility and authority and such frequent and meaningful contact between the child and each parent as is indicated in the best interest of the child under all relevant circumstances.

The statutes in Maine refer to awards of allocated, shared, or sole parental rights and responsibilities.[29] In addition to the capacity of each parent to allow and encourage frequent and continuing contact between the child and the other parent, the statutes require a court to consider the motivation of the parties involved and their capacities to give the child love, affection, and guidance; and the capacity of each parent to cooperate or to learn to cooperate in child care.

3. CHILD-FOCUSED PROVISIONS

There is a growing movement in both the legal sphere and human services sector to advocate for children's rights and interests within their family independently of parental rights.[30] Some state legislatures have drafted statutory provisions with the child as the focus.[31] For example, the Iowa code requires a court, insofar as is reasonable and in the best interest of the child, to award custody which will assure the child the opportunity for the maximum continuing physical and emotional contact with both parents unless direct physical harm or significant emotional harm to the child, other children, or a parent is likely to result from such contact with one parent.[32] The statute also requires a court that is determining the best interest of the child to consider whether each parent can support the other parent's relationship with the child. Other factors which the court must consider include

---

28. Mo. ANN. STAT. § 452.375 (Vernon 1994).

29. ME. REV. STAT. ANN. tit. 19, §§ 581, 752 (West 1994).

30. Carla Garrity & Mitchell A. Baris, *Custody and Visitation: Is It Safe?*, 17 FAM. ADVOC. 40 (1995); Ventrell, *supra* note 1, at 73. *See Domestic Violence Bibliography*, 17 FAM. ADVOC. 84 (1995).

31. *See* IOWA CODE ANN. § 598.41 (West 1994); TEX. FAM. CODE ANN. § 14.012 (West 1994); UTAH CODE ANN. § 30-3-10.2 (1994); and VT. STAT. ANN. tit. 15, § 650 (1993).

32. IOWA CODE ANN. § 598.41 (West 1994).

whether the parents can communicate with each other regarding the child's needs; whether both parents have actively cared for the child before separation; whether a parent is opposed to joint custody; and whether the safety of the child, other children, or the other parent will be jeopardized by an award of joint custody or by unsupervised or unrestricted visitation.

Instead of the typical phrase concerning the parents' rights to have frequent contact with the child, the Family Code of Texas provides a policy statement with the children's rights as its focus.[33] The section is drafted to assure that *children* (emphasis added) will have frequent and continuing contact with parents who have shown the ability to act in the best interest of the child. Also, the section requires courts to provide a stable environment for the child to encourage parents to share in the rights and responsibilities of raising their children after the parents have separated or dissolved their marriage. Finally, the section prohibits a court from appointing joint conservators if credible evidence is presented of a history or pattern of past or present child neglect, or physical or sexual abuse by one parent directed against the other parent, a spouse, or any child.

Child-centered provisions focus first on what is best for the child rather than on what is best for the parents. Such progressive legislation truly promotes the "best interest" of the child principle that a majority of states embrace.

D. *Safety and Other Unique Provisions*

While the general public, judges, attorneys, and other justice system personnel are frequently impatient with battered spouses for not leaving the abuser, often assuming that the victim and children will be safer after separation, data reveal that leave-taking is fraught with danger. In fact, the abuse may escalate at the time of separation and often continues after legal interventions.[34] Nationally, the Model Code on Domestic and Family Violence provides a statutory scheme based on the protection and safety of all victims of family violence and the prevention of future violence in families.[35]

---

33. TEX. FAM. CODE ANN. § 14.021 (West 1994).

34. Hart, *supra* note 6, at 33; Mahoney, *supra* note 2, at 63.

35. MODEL CODE, *supra* note 13, at 1.

Section 101. The Model Code on Domestic and Family Violence must be construed to promote:
1. The protection and safety of all victims of domestic or family violence in a fair, prompt, and effective manner; and
2. The prevention of future violence in all families.

Several state custody statutes include innovative provisions that address safety concerns of family members in domestic violence cases. Currently, twenty-eight states have provisions related to safe custody or visitation arrangements, absence or abandonment of the family residence by a victim of family violence, and confidentiality of records and the address of victims of family violence.[36]

1. SAFETY OF CUSTODY OR VISITATION ARRANGEMENT

Based on the statutory preference for joint custody of children and frequent and continuing contact with both parents, many family law attorneys engage their clients in divorce planning that maximizes the child's time with both parents. Researchers now emphasize that a parent's right to visitation cannot take precedence over a child's exposure to danger or the threat of harm. In addition, researchers stress that attorneys must balance a child's need for protection from psychological and physical harm with the child's need to maintain a positive, supportive relationship with both parents.[37]

The most prevalent statutory provision concerning the safety of family members mandates a court to make awards of custody or grants of visitation, or both, that best protect the child and the abused spouse from harm. For example, the state laws of Michigan include a section that provides guidance for a court determining the frequency, duration, and type of visitation.[38] The factors the court must consider include the reasonable likelihood of abuse of the child or a parent resulting from the exercise of visitation, and the threatened or actual detention of a child with the intent to retain or conceal the child from the other parent. Arizona state law provides that the person who has committed an act of domestic violence has the burden of proving that visitation will not endanger the child or significantly impair the child's emotional development.[39]

Other state statutes broaden a court's authority to address the safety of other family members.[40] The purpose of such "safety" legislation is to limit the parent's and child's exposure to potential domestic conflict or violence and to ensure the safety of *all* family members.[41]

---

36. *See* column 6 of the chart at 225-27.

37. Garrity & Baris, *supra* note 30, at 40.

38. MICH. COMP. LAWS ANN. § 722.27a (West 1994).

39. ARIZ. REV. STAT. ANN. § 25-332 (1994).

40. *See, e.g.*, HAW. REV. STAT. § 571-46 (1994); N.H. REV. STAT. ANN. § 458: 17 (1993); R.I. GEN. LAWS § 15-5-16 (1994); and WYO. STAT. §§ 20-2-112 to -113 (1994).

41. CAL. FAM. CODE § 3100 (West 1995). *See generally* IOWA CODE ANN. § 598.41 (West 1994); and MO. ANN. STAT. § 452.375 (Vernon 1994).

2. ABANDONMENT OR ABSENCE FROM RESIDENCE

Some state statutes recognize that the time of separation is difficult and dangerous for a battered spouse, and that courts should not punish the victim of abuse for any self-protective measures taken.[42] For instance, Kentucky law provides that the court must not consider abandonment of the family residence by a custodial party if the party was physically harmed or was seriously threatened with physical harm by his or her spouse.[43]

Similarly, Michigan provides that courts shall not construe a custodial parent's temporary residence with the child in a domestic violence shelter as evidence of the custodial parent's intent to retain or conceal the child from the other parent.[44] These provisions are in accord with the national perspective that attempts by victims to flee an abuser and time spent at a shelter should not create any presumption of parental negligence.[45]

3. CONFIDENTIALITY OF RECORDS/ADDRESS

Experts recognize that disclosure to the abuser of certain records and the address of a child and parent leaving a violent home can endanger the victim, the child, and the people sheltering them. As a result, the ABA's Center on Children and the Law recently called for amendments to the Uniform Child Custody Jurisdiction Act's affidavit requirement that discloses past and current addresses of the child.[46] Some states have incorporated provisions concerning confidentiality of certain information.[47] For example, if a party is staying in a shelter for victims of domestic violence or other confidential location, the Family Code of California requires a court to design custody and visitation orders that prevent disclosure of the location of the shelter or other confidential

---

42. *See generally* COLO. REV. STAT. ANN. § 14-10-124 (West 1994) (absence of a spouse or leaving home by a spouse because of spouse abuse is not a factor in determining the best interest of the child.); ME. REV. STAT. ANN. tit. 15, §§ 214, 581, 752 (West 1994) (abandonment of the family residence shall not be considered as a factor in determining parental rights and responsibilities when the abandoning parent has left the residence at the request or insistence of the other parent).

43. KY. REV. STAT. ANN. § 403.270 (Michie/Bobbs-Merrill 1994).

44. MICH. COMP. LAWS ANN. § 722.27a (West 1994).

45. DAVIDSON, *supra* note 4, at 14, and MODEL CODE, *supra* note 13, § 402, at 33.

46. DAVIDSON, *supra* note 4, at 14.

47. *See generally* ME. REV. STAT. ANN. tit. 15, §§ 214, 581, 752 (West 1994) (court may deny access to records and information if the access is not in the best interest of the child or access is sought for the purpose of causing detriment to the other parent); MASS. GEN. LAWS ANN. ch. 208, § 31 (West 1994) (a court may prohibit disclosure of the address of a child or a party if it is necessary to ensure the health, safety, or welfare of the child or party).

location.[48] Missouri authorizes a court to delete the address of the custodial parent or the child from any reports and records made available to the noncustodial parent if the court has granted the noncustodial parent restricted or supervised visitation because he or she has abused the custodial parent or the child.[49] Provisions concerning confidentiality allow a court to award custody in cases involving family violence without unduly jeopardizing the safety and well-being of the parent, child, and others involved.

4. OTHER PROVISIONS

The growing concern of the justice system for the safety, autonomy, and protection of victims of family violence is reflected by several other statutory provisions. The Arizona statute contains a provision which requires a court to consider the nature and extent of coercion or duress used by a parent in obtaining an agreement regarding custody.[50] Similarly, the Vermont statute requires a court to reject an agreement between parents concerning child custody if the court finds that the agreement is not in the best interest of a child or the parents did not reach the agreement voluntarily.[51] The Family Code of California allows spouses to meet investigators and mediators separately if there is a history of domestic violence or a protective order is in effect between the parties.[52]

Pennsylvania law requires a court when making an award of custody, partial custody, or visitation to a parent convicted of certain crimes to appoint a qualified professional to provide counseling to the offending parent and to take testimony from the professional before issuing any order of custody or visitation.[53] The counseling must include a program of treatment or individual therapy designed to rehabilitate the parent, and the therapy must address but is not limited to issues regarding physical and sexual abuse, domestic violence, the psychology of the offender, and the effects of abuse on the victim. The court is given

48. CAL. FAM. CODE § 3031 (West 1995).
49. MO. ANN. STAT. § 452.375 (Vernon 1994).
50. ARIZ. REV. STAT. ANN. § 25-332 (1994).
51. VT. STAT. ANN. tit. 15, § 666 (1993).
52. CAL. FAM. CODE §§ 3113, 3181 (West 1995). For statutory provisions concerning mediation of cases involving family violence, *see* N.M. STAT. ANN. § 40-4-8 (Michie 1994) and N.C. GEN. STAT. § 50-13.1 (1994). For guidelines for mediators, see ACADEMY OF FAMILY MEDIATORS, MEDIATION OF FAMILY DISPUTES INVOLVING DOMESTIC VIOLENCE, REPORT OF THE AFM TASK FORCE ON SPOUSAL AND CHILD ABUSE (1995). A brief review of debate over mediation of cases involving domestic violence may be found in LISA NEWMARK ET AL., DOMESTIC VIOLENCE AND EMPOWERMENT IN CUSTODY AND VISITATION CASES (1994).
53. 23 PA. CON. STAT. ANN. § 5303 (1994).

broad authority by the statute to require subsequent counseling and reports and to schedule hearings for modification of any order to protect the well-being of the child.

As state legislatures add provisions in their custody codes that authorize courts to address the protection and safety of all victims of family violence and the prevention of future violence, it is imperative that judges and family law attorneys become cognizant of the complexity and subtlety of each case involving family violence so that the they can craft the most appropriate custody award under the circumstances.

E. *Presumptions Related to Domestic Violence*

Custody codes in eight states establish rebuttable presumptions related to domestic violence.[54] The codes in four states create rebuttable presumptions against the award of sole or joint custody of children to perpetrators of domestic violence.[55] The codes in the other four states incorporate presumptions related to joint custody by providing a rebuttable presumption against joint custody if a court determines that a parent is a perpetrator of domestic violence.[56] Also, the codes in three states articulate a presumption against unsupervised visitation when a court finds that the noncustodial parent has perpetrated domestic violence.[57] Finally, two statutes include an additional presumption that a child not reside with a perpetrator of domestic violence.[58]

A provision in the Louisiana code stating the court cannot deny the abused parent custody based on the adverse effects experienced because

---

54. DEL. CODE ANN. tit. 13, § 705A (1994); FLA. STAT. ANN. § 61.13(2)(b)(2) (West 1995); IDAHO CODE § 32-717B(5) (1994); LA. REV. STAT. ANN. § 9:364(A) (West 1994); MINN. STAT. ANN. § 518.17 subd. (2)(d) (West 1995); N.D. CENT. CODE § 14-05-22.3 (1993); OKLA. STAT. ANN. tit. 10, § 21.1(D) (West 1995); WIS. STAT. ANN. § 767.24(2)(b)2.c (West 1994). *See also* MODEL CODE, *supra* note 13, §§ 401, 403, at 33-34.

55. DEL. CODE ANN. tit. 13, § 705A (1994); LA. REV. STAT. ANN. § 9:364(A) (West 1994); OKLA. STAT. ANN. tit. 10, § 21.1(D) (West 1995); N.D. CENT. CODE § 14-05-22.3 (1993).

56. FLA. STAT ANN. § 61.13(2)(b)(2) (West 1995); IDAHO CODE § 32-7178(5) (1994); MINN. STAT. ANN. § 518.17 subd. (2)(d) (West 1995); WIS. STAT. ANN. § 767.24(2)(b)2.c (West 1994).

57. LA. REV. STAT. ANN. § 9:364 (West 1994); OKLA. STAT. ANN. tit. 10, § 21.1(D) (West 1995); N.D. CENT. CODE § 14-05-22.3 (1993).

58. DEL. CODE ANN. tit. 13, § 705A(b) (1994); FLA. STAT. ANN. § 61.13(2)(b)(2) (West 1995). MODEL CODE, *supra* note 13, § 403, at 34 is similar and provides that:

> In every proceeding where there is at issue a dispute as to the custody of a child, a determination by a court that domestic . . . violence has occurred raises a rebuttable presumption that it is in the best interest of the child to reside with the parent who is not a perpetrator of domestic . . . violence.

of domestic violence is in effect a presumption.[59] The Louisiana code also specifies that the presumption fails when the court finds that both parents have committed domestic violence, and directs the court to award sole custody to the parent "who is less likely to continue to perpetrate family violence."[60]

Only Oklahoma's statute requires that domestic violence be established by clear and convincing evidence before the presumption is operative.[61] Other codes trigger the presumption only upon conviction of serious crimes.[62] The Wisconsin statute requires only evidence of a crime of interspousal battery or abuse, as defined in the civil protection order statute, to activate the presumption.[63] North Dakota requires credible evidence of domestic violence.[64] The remaining codes merely specify that if a court determines there has been domestic violence, the

59. LA. REV. STAT. ANN. § 9:364(A) (West 1994). The statute suggests that the adverse effects of domestic violence on the abused parent may be a basis for an award to the perpetrator only if the battering parent has successfully completed a specialized batterer treatment program, refrained from the abuse of illegal drugs or alcohol, demonstrated the absence or incapacity of the abused parent and proved that an award to the perpetrator would be in the best interests of the child.

Other state codes create preclusions. For example, the Texas Family Code precludes an award of joint custody in the context of domestic violence. TEX. FAM. CODE ANN. § 14.021(h) (West 1994). The Pennsylvania statutes requires that a parent who has been convicted of designated crimes of domestic violence or child abuse may not be awarded either custody or visitation until a qualified professional offers the court testimony that the perpetrator has participated in specialized counseling and does not pose a risk of harm to the child. 23 PA. CONS. STAT. ANN. § 5303 (1994). The Washington code directs that if limitations on access will not adequately protect a child from harm or abuse, the court must deny access. WASH. REV. CODE ANN. § 26.09.191 (2)(d)(I) (West 1995).

60. LA. REV. STAT. ANN. § 9:364(B) (West 1994). The Delaware code provides that when a court determines there has been domestic abuse by both parents against each other, prior to deciding custody and the residence of the child, the court must refer the case to the child protective services agency for investigation. DEL. CODE ANN. tit. 13, § 705A(d) (1994).

61. OKLA. STAT. ANN. tit. 10, § 21.1(D) (West 1995).

62. The presumptions are narrowly crafted in Delaware, Florida, and Idaho. For example, in Delaware, the presumption against a joint or sole custody award to a batterer applies only to those parents who have been criminally convicted of crimes, any felony and serious misdemeanors, involving domestic violence or criminal contempt of a civil protective order; in Florida, the presumption is applicable only where a parent has been convicted of a felony of the second degree or higher involving domestic violence; in Idaho, the presumption applies only when the batterer is "a habitual perpetrator." Statutes were drafted in this fashion to account for the possibility that abused parents who use violence in self-defense or to protect children might face and have to overcome the rebuttable presumption. The line was thus drawn so that only parents who inflict serious violence would be burdened with the adverse presumption.

63. WIS. STAT. ANN. § 767.24(2)(b)2.c. (West 1994). Bertram v. Killian, 394 N.W.2d 773 (Wis. Ct. App. 1986).

64. N.D. CENT. CODE § 14-05-22.3 (1993) and N.D. R. OF EVID. 301 (a).

presumption arises.[65] Furthermore, while there is little case law interpreting the "domestic violence presumption" codes, recently published and unpublished cases have tended to limit the circumstances in which the presumption is activated.[66] Finally, some codes delineate the standard of proof[67] or the type of evidence that must be adduced[68] to overcome the presumption or to obtain modification of an order entered pursuant to the presumption.

III. Analysis of Practice

A. *Evidentiary Considerations*

An emerging trend in a minority of state statutes is for the state legislature to draft a list of relevant evidence for a court to consider when making determinations of child custody in cases involving family violence.[69] Such lists serve as valuable guidelines for a family law attorney who suspects his or her client may be a victim or perpetrator of family violence.

---

65. LA. REV. STAT. ANN. § 9:364(A) (West 1994); MINN. STAT. ANN. § 518.17 subd. (2)(d) (West 1995).

66. Brown v. Brown, 867 P.2d 477 (Okla. Ct. App. 1993); Schestler v. Schestler, 486 N.W.2d 509 (N.D. 1992).

67. North Dakota provides that the presumption may be rebutted by "clear and convincing" evidence. N.D. CENT. CODE § 14-05-22.3 (1993). Louisiana sets the standard by a preponderance of the evidence. LA. REV. STAT. ANN. § 9:364(A) (West 1994).

68. The Delaware code specifies that the presumptions may be overcome where there are no further acts of domestic violence and the perpetrator has completed a specialized batterer treatment program, any drug or alcohol program deemed necessary by the court, and the award to the perpetrator of custody or visitation would be in the best interest of the child. A perpetrator may also overcome the presumption by demonstrating extraordinary circumstances that show there is no significant risk of continuing violence against any family or household member. DEL. CODE ANN. tit. 13, § 705A (1994). Similarly, the Louisiana statute provides that the perpetrating parent may overcome the presumption by successful completion of a batterer treatment program, by refraining from the abuse of illegal drugs or alcohol, or by demonstrating the absence or incapacity of the abused parent and that an award to the perpetrator would be in the best interests of the child. LA. REV. STAT. ANN. § 9:364(A) (West 1994). The North Dakota code permits the perpetrator unsupervised visitation if he can show that unsupervised visitation will not endanger the child's physical or emotional health. N.D. CENT. CODE § 14-05-22.3 (1993). The Wisconsin statutes provides that the perpetrating parent may overcome the presumption against joint custody by adducing "clear and convincing evidence that the abuse will not interfere with the parties' ability to cooperate in . . . future decision making [related to shared custody]." WIS. STAT. ANN. § 767.24(2)(b)2.c (West 1994).

69. ARIZ. REV. STAT. ANN. § 25-332 (1994); CAL. CODE § 3011 (West 1995); and HAW. REV. STAT. § 571-46 (1994).

For instance, the Arizona statute requires courts to consider all relevant factors in determining the existence of domestic violence, including, but not limited to, a finding from another court of competent jurisdiction, police reports, medical records, child protective services records, domestic violence shelter records, school records, and witness testimony. The Family Code of California allows courts to require substantial independent corroboration of abuse by one parent against another, including, but not limited to, written reports by law enforcement agencies, child protective services or other social welfare agencies, courts, medical facilities, or other public agencies or private non-profit organizations providing services to victims of sexual assault or domestic violence.

The Hawaii statute broadens the general mandate, and a court must consider evidence of family violence in determining the best interest of a child when establishing custody and visitation rights. The court must consider evidence of spousal abuse, determine who was the primary aggressor, and the frequency and degree of family violence. The issues of primary aggressor and frequency and degree of violence in the family are important evidentiary considerations in child custody cases involving family violence, especially if both parties claim to have been victims of spousal assault. Reports from law enforcement agencies and medical facilities are crucial evidence when determining primary aggressor and frequency and degree of violence.

B. *Practice Under Presumption Statutes*

States have enacted the presumption statutes outlined above within the last five years. In order to assess the impact of these provisions on custody practice and to evaluate whether they have remedied the failure of prior custody laws, a preliminary investigation of the current practice in "domestic violence presumption states" was undertaken.[70] The investigation evaluated whether "domestic violence presumption" provisions have remedied the failure of prior custody laws[71] to adequately address domestic violence and safeguard adult victims and children from continuing or escalating violence. Several themes emerged.

---

70. Linda A. McGuire and Barbara J. Hart interviewed a limited number of judges, attorneys, advocates, court administrators, court services personnel, and law professors in the eight "presumption" states. The report on practice in these jurisdictions is thus preliminary, at best. Further investigation and discussion is warranted.

71. Thirty-four states and the District of Columbia have enacted custody statutes which require courts to consider domestic violence when fashioning custody and visitation awards. Only eight include rebuttable presumptions related to domestic violence. *See* Hart, *supra* note 6, at 29. *See also* chart at 225-27.

1. THE PRIVATE BAR IS REMARKABLY UNINFORMED ABOUT DOMESTIC
   VIOLENCE, AND THE QUALITY OF REPRESENTATION AFFORDED VICTIMS
   BY THE BAR IS UNEVEN.

A number of those interviewed suggested that removing fault from the divorce codes in the 1970s shifted the focus of family law from remediation of marital misconduct and protection of the dependent spouse against future economic peril to equitable, but fault-free, distribution of marital property and allocation of alimony awards with little, if any, consideration of the economic losses occasioned by domestic violence or other marital conduct. Since fault became largely irrelevant, many family law attorneys stopped inquiring about intimate violence and eliminated marital misconduct from claims for economic relief.

Concurrently, states modified custody codes to facilitate post-divorce participation by fathers in the parenting of children. As a result, the controlling legal principle in custody litigation, "the best interest of the child," expanded to incorporate "friendly parent" and "frequent and continuing contact with both parents" provisions. Joint legal and physical custody became the preferred custodial award in many states. Mediation gained popularity as the method of dispute resolution which would best facilitate post-separation cooperation between parents and paternal access to the children. Courts offered mediation as a way to reduce animosity between parents and to assist them in constructing parenting plans for the future without dwelling on the past.

As a consequence of the changes in attitudes and laws, some attorneys do not consider domestic violence germane to the issues they must address in divorce or custody proceedings. Rather, many family lawyers see the civil protection or restraining order proceeding as the appropriate, and exclusive, venue for dealing with violence by one adult partner against another. This legal attitude creates strong impediments to aggressive advocacy on behalf of battered women and children.

Participants in the inquiry believe that many in the private bar are not aware that domestic violence is a pervasive social problem that affects the well-being of battered parents and children;[72] that members of the private bar do not identify those among its clients who are victims of abuse; that they do not fully comprehend the violence inflicted by

---

72. Klein & Orloff, *supra* note 4, at 958-59; Saunders, *supra* note 3, at 51-59; ENDING THE CYCLE OF VIOLENCE: COMMUNITY RESPONSES TO CHILDREN OF BATTERED WOMEN (Einat Peled et al. eds., 1995); DAVIDSON, *supra* note 4, at 21.   *Cf.* *Taking Domestic Violence Seriously*, FLA. B.J., Oct. 1994, at 68. The Florida Bar Association has distinguished itself in dedicating a special issue to domestic violence.

the perpetrator or the risk of continuing abuse;[73] that they do not understand the nexus between domestic violence and child maltreatment;[74] that they do not adduce evidence at trial to fully inform the court about the danger and detriment posed by the perpetrator's violence both to the other parent and the child;[75] and that they do not craft custodial recommendations that adequately safeguard the child and the abused parent from future violence.[76]

---

73. Hart, *supra* note 6, at 23.

[Those] crafting the statutes were clear that domestic violence was intentional, instrumental behavior dedicated to control of the family. [D]omestic violence is not impulsive, abnormal, anger-driven bursts of violence that dissipate with a short period of "cooling off." [It does not] disappear if wives accommodate husbands' demands perfectly. [B]attered women may be at the most acute risk of lethal retaliation from the moment they decide to separate from the perpetrator until the time that the abuser decides not to further retaliate against the battered woman for leaving the relationship or the abuser concludes that he no longer is interested in a relationship with or control over the battered woman.

CAROLINE W. HARLOW, U.S. DEP'T OF JUST., FEMALE VICTIMS OF VIOLENT CRIME 13 (1991) (Separated and divorced women are fourteen times more likely than married women to report having been a victim of violence by a spouse or ex-spouse, and although separated or divorced women comprised 10% of all women in the study, they reported 75% of the domestic violence.).

74. Susan Schechter & Jeffrey L. Edleson, In the Best Interest of Women and Children: A Call for Collaboration Between Child Welfare and Domestic Violence Constituencies (June 8-10, 1994) (briefing paper presented at the conference on Domestic Violence and Child Welfare: Integrating Policy and Practice for Families, Wingspread, Racine, Wisconsin); Evan Stark & Anne Flitcraft, *Women and Children at Risk: A Feminist Perspective on Child Abuse*, 18 INT'L J. OF HEALTH SERVICES 97-118 (1988) (Since abuse by husbands and fathers is instrumental, directed at subjugating, controlling, and isolating, when a woman has separated from her batterer and is seeking to establish autonomy and independence from him, his struggle to dominate her may increase, and he may turn to abuse and subjugation of the children as a tactic of control of their mother.).

75. Hart, *supra* note 6, at 33. "Abuse of children by batterers may be more likely when the marriage is dissolving, the couple has separated, and the husband and father is highly committed to continued dominance and control of the mother and children." HARLOW, *supra* note 73. Spousal abuse in metropolitan Toronto: Research report on the response of the criminal justice system, Solicitor General of Canada Rep. No. 1989-02 (1989) (One quarter of the women in the study reported threats against their lives during custody visitation.).

76. Saunders, *supra* note 3. One participant reported that she has developed a standard list of the responsibilities of custody supervisors which she asks that the judge incorporate in orders. Items often included in supervision directives are: The supervisor shall at all times be able to see and hear the child. The supervisor shall accompany the parent during transportation. The supervisor shall interact respectfully with the custodial parent. The supervisor shall advise the custodial parent or counsel for the custodial parent of any violations of the visitation provisions. Should the supervisor conclude that the visiting parent plans to abduct the child or commit a violent criminal act, the supervisor shall immediately inform law enforcement.

Participants also noted that attorneys too often fail to introduce relevant evidence on domestic violence in custody cases. Moreover, participants complained that attorneys do not thoroughly identify and preserve for trial documentary evidence, including, but not limited to, protection orders, both civil and criminal; 911 tapes; voice mail tapes; police reports; medical records; criminal histories; conviction records; letters written by the perpetrator; journals kept by the victim or children; and pictures of the abused woman and children. Similarly, participants disapprovingly believe that attorneys do not interview or depose witnesses early enough in the case to properly preserve evidence and enhance negotiations. Attorneys also fail to call in experts in cases that require highly knowledgeable testimony.

Furthermore, there are disincentives related to domestic violence practice. Some participants noted that battering husbands are highly litigious.[77] Courts often protract domestic violence custody cases, which can exhaust the resources of attorneys in solo practice or in small firms. The emotional drain of representing battered women may also be high, especially when courts are unresponsive to the risks posed by domestic violence.[78] On the other hand, exposure to malpractice is increasing for attorneys who fail to address issues of domestic violence in custody and divorce representation.[79]

Study participants also noted that law schools and continuing legal education programs often do not incorporate domestic violence in the curricula on custody dispute resolution.[80] Core courses on custody infrequently address domestic violence. Those which do often employ faculty who are not expert on the subject and who offer perspectives that undercut the protective mandates of the codes.

---

77. *See* Marsha B. Liss & Geraldine Butts Stahly, *Domestic Violence and Child Custody, in* BATTERING AND FAMILY THERAPY: A FEMINIST PERSPECTIVE 175, at 181 (Marsali Hansen & Michele Harway eds., 1993).

78. One participant noted that five children of the abused women she represents have been killed by batterers in the last month. State law makes it a crime to relocate with the children even prior to the entry of a custody order. Few judges are receptive to requests for removal, even when independent risk assessment is presented which suggests the children or mother are in danger of lethal assault.

79. LEONARD KARP & CHERYL L. KARP, DOMESTIC TORTS: FAMILY VIOLENCE, CONFLICT AND SEXUAL ABUSE § 1.28A (1993).

80. This conclusion of the participants in this preliminary investigation is supported by legal commentary and other studies of legal practice. Klein & Orloff, *supra* note 4. However, law schools around the country have begun to incorporate domestic violence into their curricula, both in core courses and clinics. *See* Mithra Merryman, *A Survey of Domestic Violence Programs in Legal Education,* 28 NEW ENG. L. REV. 383 (1994); Joan S. Meier, *Notes from the Underground: Integrating Psychological and Legal Perspectives on Domestic Violence in Theory and Practice,* 21 HOFSTRA L. REV. 1295 (1993).

2. LEGAL SERVICES ATTORNEYS ARE RELATIVELY WELL-INFORMED ABOUT DOMESTIC VIOLENCE.

Because legal services attorneys in many jurisdictions are knowledgeable about domestic violence, the quality of representation afforded low-income victims is better than that offered by the private bar. Numbers of legal services programs have developed specialized practice for custody cases in the context of domestic violence.

While the funding for legal services programs has sharply diminished in the last decade, slashing the numbers of poor clients that can be served, a significant number of legal services programs in "domestic violence presumption" states have prioritized domestic violence cases, including both protection order and custody matters.[81] These offices have facilitated the development of pro bono pools to supplement family law representation.[82] Several offer continuing legal education courses on custody in the context of domestic violence. Training is free to those who commit to taking one contested domestic violence custody or divorce case a year. Legal services staff provide supportive services to pro bono counsel, including mentoring and service as co-counsel in complex cases. Finally, many legal services programs work closely with local domestic violence programs.[83]

3. FEW JURISDICTIONS HAVE COURT SYSTEMS THAT ARE "USER-FRIENDLY" TO PRO SE CUSTODY LITIGANTS.

Increasingly, abused women are proceeding pro se in custody matters.[84] They seem to fare best in judicial districts that have adopted

---

81. Legal Services in Oklahoma has prioritized family law, and Legal Services of Eastern Oklahoma estimates that as many as 95% of the divorce cases they handle involve domestic violence. *See also* legal services in Florida and Minnesota. However, in Idaho, cuts in legal services funding for civil litigation was terminated custody representation and pro bono services are very limited.

82. *See* Legal Aid programs in Miami and Jacksonville, Florida, and throughout Oklahoma. The availability of representation in family law matters in Oklahoma is particularly important because battered parents are not able to achieve temporary custody orders under the civil protection order statute. Specialized pro bono pools are being developed on domestic violence family law matters and enhanced supportive services will be offered. Plans are in the offing to institute custody and divorce clinics to inform pro se litigants and to assist in pleadings development.

83. For example, in Tulsa the legal services program does intake at the shelter once a week. Priority is given to emergencies referred by the domestic violence program.

84. This is not universally true throughout the "presumption" states, and the practice is less apparent in jurisdictions with accessible options for quality representation. Participants identified three reasons for this trend: waiting periods for legal services or pro bono representation are too long, the women are above the legal services income guidelines but financially not able to retain counsel, or the women cannot find counsel informed about domestic violence and willing to advocate for critical protections.

special programs to assist with preparation of the pleadings, risk assessment, safety planning and development of an access plan.[85]

Divorce kits have been crafted in several of the "presumption" states. While these facilitate access for battered women, most participants noted that unrepresented battered women confront enormous difficulties in custody litigation.[86]

4. THE JUDICIARY IS LARGELY UNINFORMED ABOUT DOMESTIC VIOLENCE AND JUDICIAL PRACTICE IS INCONSISTENT.

Judges, like lawyers, have strong biases that conflict with the protective intent underlying "presumption" codes. Many judges are reluctant to impose limitations on visitation awards to batterers. Participants advise that practice varies from judge to judge, and variance within a single judicial district may be as wide as variance between districts. Few judges impose protective limitations on visitation in the context of domestic violence, and fewer limit access to supervised visitation. Protective conditions incorporated into custody orders are often boilerplate provisions that are not crafted to the particular circumstances of the parties.[87] Furthermore, judges almost never deny abusive parents access to their children. The paucity of case law related to these relatively new statutes and the inexperience of many custody judges must surely account for the variances in protective provisions.[88]

---

85. Such programs are available in Broward and Dade counties in Florida. One is court-based and the other is in the legal aid office. The office of the family court psychologist for the state of Delaware assists pro se litigants in completing forms and seeking fee waivers, but does not offer legal advice or education to applicants.

86. In Florida, the bar developed divorce kits to facilitate pro se practice. Participants noted that divorce lawyers are beyond the financial reach of many battered women and too many middle income parents are not able to pay counsel once retained. The kits were crafted to assure access to the courts without imposing a financial liability on the bar.

87. MODEL CODE, *supra* note 13, § 405, at 34. Participants most often complained that the lack of supervised visitation facilities eliminated any real capacity to protect children and abused parents during visitation. However, even where specialized batterer education or treatment services are offered in a judicial district, only a handful of judges mandate participation by batterers. This appeared ironic to participants since in an increasing number of jurisdictions both parents in all divorce cases with custody components are being mandated to participate in parenting courses.

88. For example, in Oklahoma, the custody judges are specially appointed and sit at the will of the trial courts. Many have been recently appointed and have no judicial experience. The custody judiciary falls at the low end of the hierarchy of judicial prestige. External incentives for upgrading practice are few. Caseloads are heavy. Opportunities for expanding critical knowledge are limited.

Judges are no less captives of the dominant discourse on appropriate custodial arrangements than are attorneys. The "friendly parent," "frequent and continuing contact," and "joint custody preference" provisions in custody law and the social science literature about the post-separation needs of children have shaped judicial beliefs, as well as practice, for the past two decades. These stand in sharp contrast to the statutes and social science literature on domestic violence and the post-separation well-being of children and abused parents.[89] Although a learning curve problem is apparent,[90] bias also operates.[91]

---

89. Hart, *supra* note 6, at 34.

[R]esearch confirms that the post-separation adjustment of children is not facilitated by joint custody or frequent visitation arrangements when there is chronic conflict and violence between the divorced parents. The more frequent the access arrangement between children and the noncustodial parent, the greater the level of physical and emotional abuse and conflict between the parents. The more severe the parental conflict, the greater the child's distress and dysfunctional behavior.

90. *Id.* Participants reported that a substantial number of judges conclude that violence directed toward the mother, even in the presence of the children, does not adversely effect children to a degree that limitations on access should be imposed. Nor do many judges apprehend the risks posed to the children during custodial access. An even greater number believe that the risks posed to the abused mother during visitation are not sufficient cause for imposing limitations or supervised visitation.

One participant reported that judges in her district deemed battered mothers "unfit" because they removed the children from the violent home and took them to shelter for protection. Another stated that attorneys in the jurisdiction advise clients against introducing the issue of domestic violence in the custody proceeding because the judges are inflamed by allegations of abuse, believing them to be specious and raised only for strategic advantage. Another participant said that judges will not admit evidence of domestic violence in divorce and custody proceedings if they have not been litigated elsewhere previously.

91. Participants reported that while judges now admit evidence on domestic violence, they often consider it of marginal import even when the rebuttable presumption is operative. Courts offer spontaneous commentary on the importance of children having a strong relationship with their fathers or assert fathers have equal rights to children, implying that the preservation of relationship and the securing of fatherhood are social mandates that supersede the rights of the children and abused parent to safety and well-being. Gender bias studies reveal that as many as half of the sitting judiciary are resistant to consider domestic violence as a factor in custody adjudications. Klein & Orloff, *supra* note 4, at 958.

An exploratory study of women who utilized domestic violence services in California found that when a court was cognizant of allegations that a father physically or sexually abused his children, the court was more likely to award the father full custody than when such allegations were not made. Liss & STAHLY, *supra* note 77. However, the bias of judges is not singular; it mirrors bias in the culture. One participant reported that a state representative in leadership in the judiciary committee considering the "presumption" code queried, "You mean if I shoot my wife in the head and kill her, you'd call me a bad father?" In another state the private bar initially lobbied hard against the reform, firmly convinced that violence by perpetrators was marginal and that, in balance, contact with a battering father was better for children than no paternal relationship.

Judicial education on domestic violence and its implications for crafting custody and visitation awards is uneven.[92] In most jurisdictions, it is optional and the quality of the courses offered is variable.[93]

Participants reported that family courts have not developed administrative rules, bench guides, or practice protocols on domestic violence custody cases.[94] However, in states that have instituted unified family courts, judges are better able to manage domestic violence cases and are more conscientious about protecting abused parents and children.[95]

5. SPECIALIZED COURT SERVICES RELATED TO DOMESTIC VIOLENCE CUSTODY CASES ARE SORELY WANTING.

Unfortunately, few jurisdictions have instituted specialized court services for domestic violence custody cases. The exceptions are notable and worthy of replication.[96] Court services staff members are not avail-

---

92. In Delaware and Florida, judicial education was offered to the bench immediately after passage of the "presumption" provision. In Florida there is mandatory judicial training on domestic violence every two years. A core curriculum and supplementary courses are offered.

Participants advise that much of the judicial education on domestic violence and its nexus to custody awards is undertaken by domestic violence programs and legal services organizations rather than by the administrative offices of the courts. Participants felt that the amount of time and the content of judicial training provided by community agencies is more appropriate to the task of abbreviating the learning curve than that offered by the courts.

93. One problem identified about course development on domestic violence is that experts in the field are not well utilized. Instead, courses are sometimes crafted by those skeptical about code reforms or unaware of the dangers posed by battering parents to children and to abused parents after separation.

94. *Cf.* Superior Court, State of California, County of Santa Clara, *Santa Clara County Family Court Services Policy and Procedure Regarding Domestic Violence Issues* (1993).

95. In many jurisdictions in Florida, the movement to a unified family court has reduced forum shopping and resulted in fewer conflicting orders (i.e., previously entered custody awards in civil protection orders, custody orders, neglect and dependency orders involving the parties are readily available to the judiciary who are both informed and persuaded, if not bound, by previously issued awards).

96. In Broward County, Florida, the office of family court services provides comprehensive support to the courts related to domestic violence cases. There is no income guideline for the services. The program employs investigators and court psychologists. In cases where the parties make cross-allegations of domestic violence the court will order a custody evaluation and psychological screens. The children are also interviewed and evaluated. Although it is not an advocacy program, case managers do accompany battered women to custody court. All staff are trained on domestic violence and most receive upwards of four days of training each year. Internal office protocols give direction to the work. These support services make the court user-friendly and significantly inform judicial deliberations.

The London Family Court Clinic in London, Ontario, has provided advocacy for children and abused parents involved in the justice system. This includes assessment, counseling, and prevention services, as well as training for the bar, bench, and community.

able in most jurisdictions to undertake risk assessment related to abduction or recurring violence toward the abused parent or child during visitation.[97] Thus, courts are usually not able to make informed judgments based on independent risk assessment.

6. DOMESTIC VIOLENCE CUSTODY CASES ARE NOT MANDATED TO MEDIATION IN MOST "PRESUMPTION" STATES.

Whether by statute, court rule or practice guidelines, when a custody case is identified as one involving domestic violence, courts in "presumption" states do not mandate battered adults attend mediation.[98] However, the methods of identifying domestic violence cases are flawed. Most identification is attained by pleadings. While some identification is by screening performed by court staff or mediators, the screening techniques appear unsophisticated. Most jurisdictions allow battered adults who affirmatively elect mediation to use mediation services. Yet few court-annexed mediators are specially trained on domestic violence, and specialized practice procedures and facilities are not yet available.[99]

Study participants noted that there is no data available to the bar or the advocacy community on the outcomes of mediated custody cases. They fear that the further custody cases are removed from judicial proceedings and public scrutiny, the less likely the rule of law will apply, the more battered adults will have to compromise their legal rights for safety, and the greater the risk posed to children in the context of domestic violence.

---

97. In New Jersey, pursuant to implementation of the civil protection order statute, the Administrative Office of the Supreme Court and the Attorney General promulgated a procedures manual. It contains a "Visitation Risk Assessment Interview Sheet," which is utilized by court services staff before any award of visitation is made, but only in those cases where the custodial parent requests such assessment. DOMESTIC VIOLENCE PROCEDURES MANUAL, App. 10 (N.J. 1994).

98. Ada County, Idaho, is an exception to this trend. With legal services not providing civil representation and with only a small pro bono program, mediation is the primary method for resolution of contested custody cases. Screening is employed; informal standards for practice have been implemented; a protocol for practice is in process; and parties are referred to trained, specialized mediators when deemed appropriate for mediation despite the violence.

But when a custody case is "waived out of mediation" because of domestic violence in Wisconsin, the same mediator is often assigned to do a custody evaluation. The waiver may not occur until well after mediation has begun. Abused women are not advised that they are entitled to an independent custody evaluator. There is no required training on domestic violence for mediators or evaluators.

99. In Illinois, not a "presumption" state, the custody mediation program in Cook County utilizes specialized procedures. Mediators are required to participate in domestic violence training. The Administrative Office of the Courts has undertaken extensive education of mediators about domestic violence.

217

7. Evaluators and Guardians ad Litem Utilized by the Courts
   Have Minimal Specialized Training on Domestic Violence.

Participants noted that custody evaluators and guardians ad litem were the professionals least trained about domestic violence of any actors in the civil justice system.[100] While guardians ad litem are not used routinely in most "presumption" states, many judicial districts employ custody evaluators. Evaluators and guardians are heavily influenced by the social and legal policies that facilitate contact with the noncustodial parent without regard to the risks attendant upon contact or relationship. They, like mediators, are not guided as much by law as by their training and predilections about appropriate post-separation custodial arrangements. Many appear to marginalize domestic violence as a factor with significant import for abused adults and children in custodial outcomes.

Finally, participants noted that the greater the role of custody evaluators and mediators, the less courts take responsibility for decision-making in custody cases. Consequently, they assert that decision-making deferred to nonjudicial personnel works to the detriment of battered women and children.

8. The Award of a Protection Order to an Abused Parent in
   Most "Presumption" States Is Not Dispositive of the Claim of
   Domestic Violence in Custody Proceedings.

Courts enter many protection orders by agreement of the parties; as a result, the court does not make findings of fact about the abuse. Thus, the fact that a court has entered a protection order carries little weight in many custody proceedings. But if there has been a violation and a conviction or plea, the order is deemed dispositive of the claim of domestic violence. Criminal convictions on domestic violence typically compel the same conclusion. Moreover, since custody courts have independent jurisdiction over custody claims, the custody adjudicator may set aside the custody awards in protection orders. However, many judges view custody awards in protection orders with significant deference when the parties have independently reached an agreement on the

---

100. Minnesota may be the exception to this trend. Guardians are offered a formal course of training, which includes specific instruction on domestic violence. A protocol for guardian practice, containing guidelines on domestic violence, is now in process. Court services custody evaluators are also trained on domestic violence. The domestic violence community has not participated in the planning or development of the training curricula and question the efficacy thereof. In Florida, a domestic violence manual has been devised for guardians and training has begun in several circuits. Governor's Task Force on Domestic Violence, The First Report of the Governor's Task Force on Domestic Violence (1994).

custody provisions in the protection order or when the court has found that the perpetrator abused the children.

9. THE LACK OF SECURE SUPERVISED VISITATION FACILITIES JEOPARDIZES THE PROTECTIVE MANDATES IN STATE CODES.

Participants reported that there is a dearth of secure supervised visitation facilities. As a result, the judiciary must ration these scarce resources carefully. In some communities, courts are able to employ the services of the child protective services agency. Participants reported, however, that child protective service agencies typically offer supervision only when a child is abused and the subject of a juvenile proceeding is related to that abuse.

As a consequence, if supervised visitation is ordered, the court places the responsibility for identifying a supervisor, arranging the visitation and sometimes underwriting the costs on the battered woman. If she is unable to produce a plan for supervision, the chances increase that the court will approve an unsupervised visitation or authorize a member of the perpetrator's family to provide supervision. Participants in this investigation concluded this default arrangement neither protects the child nor the abused parent.

10. IT IS NOT YET CLEAR THAT THE "DOMESTIC VIOLENCE PRESUMPTIONS" HAVE EFFECTED AMELIORATIVE AND PROTECTIVE OUTCOMES FOR CHILDREN AND ABUSED PARENTS.

Evidence of domestic violence is more often adduced and more readily admitted in custody proceedings now than before statutory reform made domestic violence relevant. The impression of participants is that, where courts are persuaded that domestic violence has occurred and the risk is continuing or escalating, the courts often award abused women sole physical custody. Yet courts do not routinely place protective conditions to safeguard women and children.

Furthermore, participants noted that an adverse presumption now confronts abused parents who have used violence in self-defense or to protect children. The numbers of abused parents required to overcome the presumption, however, are few because most codes require a showing of ongoing or serious violence before the presumption is activated. For instance, the Louisiana code contains an explicit exception for self-defense or protection of the child.[101]

In some judicial districts and states there has been specialized training of the bar, court services employees, legal services attorneys and advocates for battered women on domestic violence and the changes in

---

101. LA. REV. STAT. ANN. § 9:362(2) (West 1994).

custody laws thereon. Participants reported that in those judicial districts and states where there has been specialized training of the bar, the "presumption" has shaped judicial decision-making and has produced custody awards designed to safeguard children and abused parents. In fact, the anticipated changes in practice have been most noticeable in those jurisdictions where the courts and legal services programs developed specialized programs.

Participants gave mixed answers on the question of whether "presumption" codes better protect abused parents and children than "best interest of the child" codes that contain domestic violence as a factor courts must address in custody deliberations. Participants do believe that attorneys have litigated the issue of domestic violence more since the enactment of "presumption" codes. There is consensus among the legal community that the reformed codes that contain domestic violence as a "best interest" factor better protect abused parents and children than previous codes that did not contain such language. But it is unclear whether the reformed codes protect the victims in "presumption" states better than reformed codes protect victims in "best interest" states. The success of the battered parent in custody proceedings is a function of informed and vigorous advocacy; therefore, abused women and children fare as well under codes with a "domestic violence best interest" factor provision as under "presumption" codes. In the future, the legal community should make more assessments of both types of codes.

IV. Call to Action

Legal doctrine regarding parents' rights and responsibilities within a family has evolved as psychological and sociological theories concerning family structure that were popular ten years ago have given way to new knowledge. Consequently, laws concerning child custody in cases involving family violence are changing rapidly. Only an informed attorney can argue the various innovative provisions in child custody laws concerning family violence. Likewise, only an informed attorney can see the relevance of family violence to the issue of child custody and can articulate it well to the court. Because of the general lack of mandated, formal training for attorneys in the area of family violence, individual practitioners must seek out continuing education in this area. Local and state bar associations must take the lead in drafting protocols and training manuals for their members.[102]

102. MODEL CODE, *supra* note 13, § 512, at 48. Such courses must be prepared and presented by multidisciplinary groups including public and private agencies that provide programs for victims of family violence and programs of intervention for perpetrators, advocates for victims, and statewide coalitions. The courses must include

Custody and visitation cases that involve family violence increasingly
call for the following: (1) complex hearings and findings of fact where
abuse is alleged; (2) use of child witnesses and expert testimony;
(3) considerations of the fitness of a parent who abuses his or her
spouse as well as the impact of family violence on the battered spouse's
capacity to parent; (4) presumptions against joint custody; and (5)
more thorough consideration of the best interest of the child. But, in
a majority of divorce and contested custody cases, the abused spouse
is a pro se litigant. The ABA Center on Children and the Law has
called for attorneys to make the assistance of legal counsel more readily
available and affordable to victims of domestic violence and their children.[103] Attorneys must seek a variety of solutions to provide for the
unmet legal needs of such litigants.

Increased emphasis on court personnel, custody evaluators, child
protective service workers, and guardians ad litem in cases involving
family violence has led to less reliance on attorneys and also has been
problematic for battered women with children.[104] National standards
and recommended practices are available for courts and court-related
agencies such as court administrators, probation officers, advocates,
children's protective services workers, custody evaluators, mediators,
and other treatment providers who work with cases involving family
violence.[105] The Model Code on Domestic and Family Violence calls for
continuing education for judges, lawyers, probation officers, workers in
children's protective services, social workers, court appointed special
advocates, mediators, and custody evaluators.[106] In order to ensure a
high quality of legal education and training in family violence, family
law attorneys should collaborate with judges and various court-related
agencies in continuing education programs.

Domestic violence is a pervasive problem that devastates all family
members and challenges society at every level. It violates our communities' safety, health, welfare, and economy by draining billions annually
in social costs such as medical expenses, psychological problems, lost
productivity, and intergenerational violence. Therefore, leadership,

---

the nature, extent, and causes of family violence, practices designed to promote safety
of the victim and other family and household members, available resources for victims
and perpetrators, sensitivity to gender bias and cultural, racial, and sexual issues, and
the lethality of family violence.

The Florida Bar Association is preparing a Manual for Attorneys for Domestic
Violence Cases. The manual will be ready for distribution in June 1995.

103. DAVIDSON, *supra* note 4, at 9.
104. Mahoney, *supra* note 2, at 74.
105. DAVIDSON, *supra* note 4, at 21; HERRELL & HOFFORD, *supra* note 12, at 33.
106. MODEL CODE, *supra* note 13, § 511, at 47.

communication, and coordination are critical among legislators, law enforcement officers, social service agency personnel, judges, attorneys, health-care personnel, advocates, and educators. Attorneys should encourage the development of and should participate in a coordinated community response to family violence such as family violence councils.[107]

Data indicate that women and children are at elevated risk for violence during the process of and after separation. National judicial and bar organizations have recently emphasized safety in their efforts for victims of family violence and their children.[108] Some communities are providing programs to carry out court-ordered supervised visitation in a safe and responsible manner.[109] Attorneys should be leaders in their communities and encourage the development of resources such as supervised visitation centers which promote the safety of parents and their children and provide appropriate access and interaction between parents and children.

In conclusion, when there is domestic violence in a divorce or custody case, family law attorneys are in a pivotal position to ensure a safer future for their clients and thereby a safer community. The highest caliber counsel the family bar can offer must fill the vacuum of representation and advocacy for victims and children of domestic violence.

107. *See* MODEL CODE, *supra* note 13, ch. 5, at 39; DAVIDSON, *supra* note 4, at 21.

108. MODEL CODE, *supra* note 13, Introduction, at v, and § 406, at 35; DAVIDSON, *supra* note 4, at 4, 21.

109. *See* Brockton Family and Community Resources, Massachusetts; Family Connection Center of the Visiting Nurses Association, Marion County, Indiana; Ethical Culture Society, New York, New York; Creative Visitation YWCA, San Diego, California; Innovations, Women's Resource and Crisis Center, Amsterdam, New York. Contact the National Center on Women and Family Law for information concerning how to contact the programs listed above.

Appendix

An Analysis of Provisions Concerning
Domestic Violence in State Custody Statutes

Column Number and Explanation

1. The statute *requires* courts to consider evidence of domestic violence or abuse of a spouse when making child custody or visitation determinations.
2. The statute contains a declaration of public policy concerning frequent contact with both parents and encouraging shared parental responsibilities, or a statutory preference or presumption for joint or shared custody, or both.
3. The statute provides that domestic violence is contrary to the best interests of a child or to a stated preference for joint or shared custody, or the statute prohibits an award of joint custody if there is evidence of domestic violence.
4. The statute contains "friendly parent" provisions requiring courts to consider which parent is more likely to encourage frequent and continuing contact with the other parent.
5. The statute contains one or more presumptions concerning family violence; for example, a presumption that joint custody is not in the best interest of the child if there is evidence of family violence or a rebuttable presumption that no perpetrator of domestic violence shall be awarded custody.
6. The statute contains a provision that addresses safety concerns of family members, for example, placing the burden of proof on the person who has committed an act of domestic violence to prove that visitation will not endanger the child.

States	Section	#1	#2	#3	#4	#5	#6
Alabama	ALA. CODE § 30-3-2 (1994)						✔
Alaska	ALASKA STAT. § 25.24.150 (1994)	✔			✔		
	ALASKA STAT. § 25.20.090 (1994)	✔			✔		
Arizona	ARIZ. REV. STAT. ANN. § 25-332 (1994)	✔		✔	✔		✔
California	CAL. FAMILY CODE §§ 3000-3399 (West 1995)	✔	✔				✔
Colorado	COLO. REV. STAT. ANN. § 14-10-124 (West 1994)	✔	✔	✔	✔		✔
	COLO. REV. STAT. ANN. § 14-10-129 (West 1994)						✔
Connecticut	CONN. GENN. STAT. § 46b-56a (West 1994)		✔				
Delaware	DEL. CODE ANN. tit. 13, § 705A (1994)					✔	
	DEL. CODE ANN. tit. 13, § 706A (1994)	✔					

States	Section	#1	#2	#3	#4	#5	#6
District of Columbia	D.C. CODE ANN. §16-914 (1994)	✓					✓
Florida	FLA. STAT. ANN. § 61.13 (West 1995)	✓	✓	✓	✓	✓	✓
Georgia	GA. CODE ANN. §§ 19-9-1 to 19-9-5			✓			
Hawaii	HAW. REV. STAT. § 571-46 (1994)	✓					✓
Idaho	IDAHO CODE § 32-717 (1994)	✓					
	IDAHO CODE § 32-717B (1994)		✓	✓		✓	
Illinois	ILL. ANN. STAT. ch. 750, para. 5/602 (Smith-Hurd 1994)	✓		✓	✓		
Iowa	IOWA CODE ANN. § 598.41 (West 1994)	✓			✓		✓
Kansas	KAN. STAT. ANN. § 60-1610 (1994)	✓	✓		✓		
Kentucky	KY. REV. STAT. ANN. § 403.270 (Michie/Bobbs-Merrill 1994)	✓					✓
Louisiana	LA. REV. STAT. ANN. § 364 (West 1994)	✓				✓	✓
Maine	ME. REV. STAT. ANN. tit. 19, §§ 214, 281 & 752 (West 1994)	✓			✓		✓
Massachusetts	MASS. GEN. LAWS ANN. ch. 208, § 31 (West 1994)	✓					✓
Michigan	MICH. COMP. LAWS ANN. §§ 722.23, 722.26a & 722.27a (West 1994)	✓			✓		✓
Minnesota	MINN. STAT. ANN. § 518.17 (West 1995)	✓	✓	✓	✓	✓	
	MINN. STAT. ANN. § 257.025 (West 1995)	✓					
Mississippi	MISS. CODE ANN. § 9305-24 (1993)		✓				
Missouri	MO. ANN. STAT. § 452.375 (Vernon 1994)	✓	✓		✓		✓
	MO. ANN. STAT. § 452.400 (Vernon 1994)						✓
Montana	MONT. CODE ANN. § 40-4-212, 40-4-222 & 40-224 (1993)	✓	✓	✓			
Nebraska	NEB. REV. STAT. § 42-364 (1995)	✓					
Nevada	NEV. REV. STAT. §§ 125.460, 125.480 & 125.490 (1993)	✓	✓				
New Hampshire	N.H. REV. STAT. ANN. § 458:17 (1993)	✓	✓	✓			✓
New Jersey	N.J. STAT. ANN. tit. 9, § 9:2-4 (West 1995)	✓	✓		✓		✓
New Mexico	N.M. STAT. ANN. § 40-4-8 (Michie 1994)						✓

States	Section	# 1	# 2	# 3	# 4	# 5	# 6
New York	N.Y. Dom. Rel. Law § 240 (McKinney 1995)						✔
North Carolina	N.C. Gen. Stat. § 50-13.1 (1994)						✔
North Dakota	N.D. Cent. Code § 14-09-06.2 (1993)	✔		✔		✔	✔
	N.D. Cent. Code § 14-09-06.2 (1993)						✔
Ohio	Ohio Rev. Code Ann. § 3109.04 (Anderson 1994)	✔		✔			
	Ohio Rev. Code Ann. § 3109.051 (Anderson 1994)						✔
Oklahoma	Okla. Stat. Ann. tit. 10, § 21.1 (West 1995)	✔	✔			✔	✔
	Okla. Stat. Ann. tit. 43, §§ 112 & 112.2 (West 1995)				✔	✔	
Pennsylvania	23 Pa. Cons. Stat. Ann. § 5303 (1994)	✔			✔		✔
Rhode Island	R.I. Gen. Laws § 15-5-16 (1994)	✔		✔			✔
Texas	Tex. Fam. Code Ann. §§ 14.021, 14.07 & 14.081 (West 1994)	✔	✔	✔	✔		
Utah	Utah Code Ann. §§ 30-3-10 & 30-3-10.2 (1994)				✔		
	Utah Code Ann. §§ 30-3-34 (1994)						✔
Vermont	Vt. Stat. Ann. tit. 15, §§ 650, 665 & 666 (1993)		✔		✔		✔
Virginia	Va. Code § 20-124.3 (Michie 1994)	✔			✔		
	Va. Code § 20-124.4 (Michie 1994)						
Washington	Wash. Rev. Code Ann. § 26.09.191 (West 1995)	✔					✔
	Wash Rev. Code Ann. § 26.10.160 (West 1995)	✔					✔
West Virginia	W. Va. Code §48-2-15 (1994)						✔
Wisconsin	Wis. Stat. Ann. § 767.24 (West 1994)	✔			✔	✔	✔
Wyoming	Wyo. Stat. § 20-2-112 (1994)	✔		✔			✔
	Wyo. Stat. § 20-2-113 (1994)	✔		✔			✔

Oct. 25, 1990
[H. Con. Res. 172]

SPOUSE ABUSE—STATUTORY PRESUMPTION IN CHILD CUSTODY LITIGATION

Whereas State courts have often failed to recognize the detrimental effects of having as a custodial parent an individual who physically abuses his or her spouse, insofar as the courts do not hear or weigh evidence of domestic violence in child custody litigation;

Whereas there is an alarming bias against battered spouses in contemporary child custody trends such as joint custody and mandatory mediation;

Whereas joint custody guarantees the batterer continued access and control over the battered spouse's life through their children;

Whereas joint custody forced upon hostile parents can create a dangerous psychological environment for a child;

Whereas a batterer's violence toward an estranged spouse often escalates during or after a divorce, placing both the abused spouse and children at risk through shared custody arrangements and unsupervised visitation;

Whereas physical abuse of a spouse is relevant to child abuse in child custody disputes;

Whereas the effects of physical abuse of a spouse on children include actual and potential emotional and physical harm, the negative effects of exposure to an inappropriate role model, and the potential for future harm where contact with the batterer continues;

Whereas children are emotionally traumatized by witnessing physical abuse of a parent;

Whereas children often become targets of physical abuse themselves or are injured when they attempt to intervene on behalf of a parent;

Whereas even children who do not directly witness spousal abuse are affected by the climate of violence in their homes and experience shock, fear, guilt, long lasting impairment of self-esteem, and impairment of developmental and socialization skills;

Whereas research into the intergenerational aspects of domestic

226

violence reveals that violent tendencies may be passed on from one generation to the next;

Whereas witnessing an aggressive parent as a role model may communicate to children that violence is an acceptable tool for resolving marital conflict; and

Whereas few States have recognized the interrelated nature of child custody and battering and have enacted legislation that allows or requires courts to consider evidence of physical abuse of a spouse in child custody cases: Now, therefore, be it

Resolved by the House of Representatives (the Senate concurring),

SECTION 1. It is the sense of the Congress that, for purposes of determining child custody, credible evidence of physical abuse of a spouse should create a statutory presumption that it is detrimental to the child to be placed in the custody of the abusive spouse.

SEC. 2. This resolution is not intended to encourage States to prohibit supervised visitation.

Agreed to October 25, 1990.

In the Matter of: Barbara BAKER,
Petitioner, Appellant,

v.

James BAKER, Respondent.

No. C0–91–1967.

Supreme Court of Minnesota.

Dec. 31, 1992.

Ex parte temporary protection order
awarding custody of parties' child to wife
was entered by the District Court, Blue
Earth County, James D. Mason, J., and
husband appealed. The Court of Appeals,
481 N.W.2d 871, reversed and remanded.
Wife appealed. The Supreme Court, Gardebring, J., held that: (1) ex parte procedures of Domestic Abuse Act comply with
applicable rules as well as to process; (2)
temporary custody determinations made as
part of ex parte order for protection need
not include findings of "immediate danger
of physical harm"; and (3) "best interests"
findings are not required when making
temporary custody determinations under
Domestic Abuse Act.

Reversed.

1. Breach of the Peace ⬥20
   Constitutional Law ⬥312(4)
   Petition for ex parte relief from domestic violence which asserts fear of further acts of domestic violence, accompanied
by supporting affidavit under oath, meets
requirements of rule which provides that
notice for temporary restraining orders
may be granted unless it is clear that immediate and irreparable injury, loss or damage will result, requirements of rule which
requires trial court to recite reasons supporting ex parte relief, and requirements of
due process and Domestic Abuse Act. 48
M.S.A., Rules Civ.Proc., Rule 65.01; 51
M.S.A., General Rules of Practice, Rules
3.01, 303.04; U.S.C.A. Const.Amend. 14;
M.S.A. § 518B.01.

2. Constitutional Law ⬥251.1, 251.5
   Requirements of due process are flexible and call for such procedural protections

as particular situation demands; main factors to consider are private interests to be
affected by official action, risk of erroneous deprivation of these interests and probable value of additional safeguards, and
government interests involved. U.S.C.A.
Const.Amend. 14.

3. Breach of the Peace ⬥20
   Constitutional Law ⬥312(4)
   There is no due process violation in
granting of ex parte relief pursuant to
Domestic Abuse Act. M.S.A. § 518B.01;
U.S.C.A. Const.Amend. 14.

4. Breach of the Peace ⬥20
   Temporary custody determination entered as part of order for protection under
Domestic Abuse Act need not conform to
requirements of ex parte temporary custody orders entered as part of dissolution
proceeding; rather, determinations of custody and visitation made at time of issuance of ex parte order for protection are
governed by section of Domestic Abuse Act
giving primary consideration to safety of
victim and children. M.S.A. §§ 518.131.
subd. 3(b), 518B.01, subd. 6(a)(3).

5. Breach of the Peace ⬥20
   No "best interests" analysis was required with respect to temporary custody
determinations under Domestic Abuse Act.
M.S.A. §§ 257.025(a), 518B.01, subd. 6(b).

Syllabus by the Court

1. The procedures of the Domestic
Abuse Act, Minn.Stat. § 518B.01 (1990),
comply with Minn.R.Civ.P. 65.01 and Minn.
Gen.R.Prac. 3.01 and 303.04, as well as the
requirements of due process.

2. Temporary custody determinations
made as part of an *ex parte* order for
protection may be made on the basis of the
standards contained in Minn.Stat.
§ 518B.01, subd. 6, and need not include a
finding of "immediate danger of physical
harm," as required by the marriage dissolution statute, Minn.Stat. § 518.131, subd.
3(b) (1990).

3. Compliance with the Minn.Stat.
§ 257.025(a) (1990) requirements for particularized "best interests" findings is not

required when making temporary custody determinations under the Domestic Abuse Act.

———————

M. Sue Wilson, Christine N. Howard, Minneapolis, for appellant.

James H. Manahan, Manahan, Bluth, Green, Friedrichs & Marsh Law Office, Mankato, for respondent.

Lorraie S. Clugg, Chairperson, Family Law Section, William E. Haugh, Jr., Chairperson, Amicus Curiae Committee and Mary Lauhead, St. Paul, amicus curiae Family Law Section of Mn. State Bar Assn.

Heard, considered, and decided by the court en banc.

GARDEBRING, Justice.

This case arises from appellant Barbara Baker's application in district court for an order for protection under the Domestic Abuse Act, Minn.Stat. § 518B.01 (1990), against her estranged husband, James Baker. Based upon her affidavit and motion, the trial court issued an *ex parte* temporary restraining order that excluded James Baker from Barbara Baker's residence and restrained him from harassing her at work. The court also granted temporary custody of the couple's infant to the mother, with provisions for visitation by the father. James Baker was notified pursuant to the statute, and at the subsequent full hearing, the court found that each party was entitled to an order for protection. The court then ordered that temporary custody of the infant remain with Barbara Baker, and extensive unsupervised visitation with James Baker was scheduled.

Consequently, James Baker filed a notice of appeal. The court of appeals reversed the trial court's *ex parte* order for protection and remanded the temporary child custody determination for particularized find-

ings which reflect the dissolution standards of best interests of the child. *Baker v. Baker*, 481 N.W.2d 871 (Minn.Ct.App.1992). Barbara Baker appeals from the decision of the court of appeals. We reverse.[1]

Barbara Baker was 18 years old when she married 19-year-old James Baker in 1991. The couple's only child was born on May 19, 1991. Both parents worked at part-time jobs during the summer of 1991; when one parent was working, the other cared for the baby and when both were working, the baby was cared for by others. During the school year, both parents attended school and worked part time. Throughout the summer of 1991, tension escalated between the couple to the point that on one occasion, James threatened to kill Barbara, and punched her while she was holding the baby.

On August 30, 1991, Barbara moved out of the marital home with the baby and moved in with her aunt. After working that day, Barbara and James both separately went to the child care provider's home, where an argument began. Barbara left with the baby and went to her aunt's home. James followed and forced his way into the home and later, kicked and pushed Barbara. Barbara called the police, who arrived and removed James. James was issued a citation for fifth degree assault. James returned to Barbara's home after being released by the police, but was denied entry.

On September 3, 1991, James went to Barbara's new home and attempted to take the baby from the aunt. Barbara arrived home and an argument began. After Barbara removed her car keys from James' key ring and while she was putting them on her own key ring, James grabbed her, dragged her from the house, threw her to the ground and swung at her. James denied knocking Barbara down and claimed instead that she jumped on him and tore his

———————

1. On September 10, 1992, respondent filed a motion seeking dismissal of this appeal, on the theory that the issues have been rendered moot. It is true that since the inception of this action, the Bakers have legally divorced. While this decision, therefore, may have no impact upon these parties, the question is not moot. The

issues presented are capable of repetition, yet evade review because restraining orders are short term and temporary, and custody is at issue in countless domestic abuse proceedings. *In re Schmidt*, 443 N.W.2d 824, 826 (Minn. 1989).

shirt. The police were called again, but James had fled. James drove by afterwards and threw the keys at Barbara as she sat on the front steps. Barbara was treated at the hospital for an injury to her hand.

On September 5, 1991, Barbara filed a motion for an *ex parte* order for protection, along with an affidavit setting forth the described incidents of abuse. A temporary order for protection was issued, granting temporary custody of the couple's infant to Barbara, with supervised visitation to James. A full hearing was set for September 12, 1991.

James secured the services of an attorney, and filed a counter motion requesting an order for protection against Barbara and temporary custody of the child. At the September 12 hearing, the court took testimony on the issue of custody, and then reaffirmed its previous grant of custody of the child to Barbara, with visitation authorized for James.

The full hearing on the motions for protective orders was continued until September 20. At that time the court received additional evidence regarding both custody and the alleged abuse, and then restrained both parties from contact with the other and excluded each from the other's residence. The trial court ordered that temporary custody of the infant remain with Barbara for up to one year, unless amended before then by further court order. James was granted extensive, unsupervised visitation rights.

James Baker, through his attorney, appealed the *ex parte* order and grant of temporary custody. Barbara Baker remained unrepresented by any counsel and did not file a respondent's brief in the court of appeals. The court of appeals considered the appellant's brief alone, without the benefit of oral argument.

The court of appeals held that domestic abuse proceedings are governed by Minn. R.Civ.P. 65.01, which requires notice before temporary restraining orders may be granted unless it is clear that immediate and irreparable injury, loss or damage will result, and the applicant's attorney gives

written notice to the court of the efforts that have been made to give notice, or the reasons for not giving notice. The court noted that the printed petition and temporary order for protection forms in use in Blue Earth County both recite the existence of an emergency but called its presence "inconclusive on the topic of cause to withhold notice." *Baker v. Baker*, 481 N.W.2d at 873, n. 3. The court reversed the *ex parte* order for failure to give notice or state the reasons why notice was not required.

The court of appeals also concluded that certain statutory provisions relating to restraining orders in the context of marriage dissolution proceedings, Minn.Stat. § 518.- 131 (1990), are in *pari materia* with the provisions of the Domestic Abuse Act. Accordingly, the court held that custody and visitation determinations in an *ex parte* order for protection are governed by Minn. Stat. § 518.131, subd. 3(b), which requires a finding by the court of "immediate danger of physical harm to the minor [child]." Since the trial court had made no such finding, the court of appeals reversed the trial court's *ex parte* temporary custody award.

Finally, the court of appeals determined that the temporary custody determination made in the subsequent order for protection required particularized findings based upon the best interests of the child, citing Minn.Stat. § 257.025(a) (1990) and *In re Marriage of Schmidt*, 436 N.W.2d 99 (1989). Since the temporary award of custody of the Baker child did not contain these findings, the court of appeals remanded the custody dispute for further trial court consideration.

This case presents three distinct issues: 1) Must a proceeding for temporary relief under the Domestic Abuse Act, Minn.Stat. § 518B.01, conform to notice requirements contained in Minn.Gen.R.Prac. 303.04 and Minn.R.Civ.P. 65.01 before an *ex parte* order may issue?

2) Is a finding of "immediate danger to the [child]," pursuant to Minn.Stat. § 518.- 131, subd. 3(b), necessary before a tempo-

rary custody determination can be made within an order for protection?

3) How particularized must the findings be to support such temporary custody determinations?

The law governing the legal relationships between men and women, and their children, is complex, reflecting the potentially conflicting policy objectives of preserving families and protecting children, of allowing divorce and ensuring support, of protecting victims and assuring due process. Furthermore, its development has been incremental, reflecting that social attitudes on all of these difficult issues have been rapidly changing in the last several decades.

At issue in this case is the interplay between three of the statutes which govern related, but distinct problems: the Domestic Abuse Act, Minn.Stat. ch. 518B, which outlines a mechanism for the court to provide protection for individuals who are threatened by their family or household members; the statute governing marriage dissolution, Minn.Stat. ch. 518; and Minn. Stat. ch. 257, which relates to the welfare of children. The court of appeals has inexplicably chosen to interweave the requirements of these statutory provisions even though they were adopted by the legislature at different times, manifest different objectives and deal with different subject matters.

We begin first with the Domestic Abuse Act. In 1978, it was estimated there were 26,900 assaults upon women by their partners. Minn. Dep't of Corrections, *Minnesota Program for Battered Women,* Biennial Report 1986–87, p. 12. Shelters housed 613 women plus 726 children. *Id.* Another 2,136 requests for shelter could not be accommodated. *Id.*[2]

The Domestic Abuse Act, Minn.Stat. § 518B.01, was enacted in 1979 as one way to protect victims of domestic assault. It is a substantive statute which is complete in itself, carefully drafted to provide limited types of relief to persons at risk of further abuse by other "family or household members," whether married or not. It neither establishes nor terminates a legal relationship; it requires a demonstration of physical harm, or fear, or sexual misconduct, and the relief it provides is of limited duration. In one sense, it may be thought of as a "band-aid," designed to curtail the harm one household member may be doing to the other in the short term, until a more permanent dispute resolution can be put in place. Nothing within the plain wording of the statute suggests that reference to any other statute is necessary.

In contrast, the marital dissolution statute, Minn.Stat. ch. 518, is a complex scheme designed to detail the procedures for termination of a particular kind of legal relationship, marriage between a man and woman. Its sixty-five sections cover, among other topics, the grounds for divorce, the process for division of property, and the nature of the on-going obligations of one party to the other, including those related to financial support. It is broader than the Domestic Abuse Act, in that it covers virtually all legal aspects of the end of a relationship and is intended to provide for closure of the issues at hand, except in circumstances it carefully spells out. It is narrower in that it only covers marriage, and not the many other kinds of human relationships which may be covered by the Domestic Abuse Act. While the reach of the two statutes may incidentally overlap as to some married persons in some situations, each serves a distinct and separate public policy. Each serves different purposes and may be appropriate for different persons.

Similarly, Minn.Stat. ch. 257 relates primarily to the welfare of children, in contexts other than domestic abuse. It includes such matters as surrender of parental rights, foster home placement, declaration of parentage, and certain custody and

2. By 1985, 17 shelters statewide housed 2700 women plus 3500 children. However an additional 5700 requests for shelter went unmet. Minn. Dep't of Corrections, *Minnesota Program for Battered Women,* Biennial Report 1986–87,

p. 5. From June 1986 through July 1, 1988, 16,000 requests for safe shelter were met, while close to 9,000 were not. Minn. Dep't of Corrections, *Program for Battered Women, Data Summary* (July 1, 1986 through June 30, 1988).

visitation determinations which may involve married or unmarried partners, extended family, or unrelated persons.

Nothing in the language of these three statutes suggests that they are related to one another, nor do they contain any explicit mandate to construe them together. On the contrary, the domestic abuse proceeding "shall be in **addition** to other civil or criminal remedies." Minn.Stat. § 518B.01, subd. 16, (emphasis added).

The danger of muddling together these three distinct and targeted statutory schemes is perfectly illustrated in this case: the availability of extraordinary relief intended by the passage of the Domestic Abuse Act is utterly negated by tying to it unnecessary external procedural requirements. It is in this context then that we examine the specific issues before us.

I.

[1] Court procedural rules such as Minn.R.Civ.P. 65.01 and Minn.Gen.R.Prac. 3.01 and 303.04 provide a framework to guide the bench in the majority of cases. However, some statutory remedies incorporate alternative procedures as part of the substantive relief made available. The Domestic Abuse Act provides such a scheme:

an *ex parte* restraining order is central to the substantive relief provided for under the Act. If notice, or extensive justification for the lack thereof, were required, the order would not provide the kind of immediate remedy that the Domestic Abuse Act, as a whole, contemplates.[3]

Furthermore, prior notice to the respondent could be counter-productive to the purposes of the statute. As noted by the U.S. District Court for the Western District of Wisconsin in interpreting a similar statute, such notice might, in fact, incite further domestic violence. *Blazel v. Bradley*, 698 F.Supp. 756, 763 (W.D.Wisc.1988).[4]

It can also be argued that, even if the several rules cited by the court of appeals are controlling, the procedures spelled out in the Domestic Abuse Act comply with those rules. The more stringent of these rules, Minn.R.Civ.P. 65.01, allows *ex parte* relief if two conditions are met: (1) a clear demonstration from specific facts show that immediate and irreparable injury will result before the adverse party can be heard, and (2) a written statement by petitioner's attorney of the reasons why notice should not be given.

While there is usually no attorney involved in a petition for an order for protec-

---

3. The 1992 legislature has amended the Act to make it clear that prior notice to the alleged abuser is not required.

    A finding by the court that there is a basis for issuing an *ex parte* temporary order for protection constitutes a finding that sufficient reasons exist not to require notice under applicable court rules governing applications for *ex parte* temporary relief.

    Minn.Stat. § 518B.01, subd. 7(a) (1992).

    This amendment was effective April 30, 1992 and, therefore, does not apply in this case.

4. At least one state statute specifically notes this danger in its statute for an Emergency Order of Protection.

    An emergency order of protection shall issue if petitioner * * * establish[es] that * * * [t]here is good cause to grant the remedy, regardless of prior service of process or of notice upon the respondent, because * * * the harm which that remedy is intended to prevent would be likely to occur if the respondent were given any prior notice, or greater notice than was actually given, of the petitioner's efforts to obtain judicial relief * * *.

    Ill.Ann.Stat. ch. 40, ¶ 2312–17, § 217(a)(3)(i) (Smith–Hurd 1992).

Extensive research on domestic abuse supports the assertion that the risk of danger increases once the victim makes the choice or attempts to leave the abusive relationship. *See*, Lerman, *A Model State Act: Remedies for Domestic Violence*, 21 Harv.J. on Legis. 61, 91 (1984) ("[I]f the victim of abuse tells the abuser that she might seek help, he may respond by threatening more serious violence.") (citing D. Martin, *Battered Wives*, 77–81 (1976)); Comment Quinn, *Ex Parte Protection Orders: Is Due Process Locked Out?*, 58 Temp.L.Q. 843, 870 (1985) ("The defendant might react to the news of a victim's action with anger or increased violence.") (citations omitted); *See also*, Buda and Butler, *The Battered Wife Syndrome: A Backdoor Assault on Domestic Violence*, 23 J.Fam.I.. 359, 365 (1985) ("The misdemeanor status of wife-beating often serves to compound the problem * * * [by] incit[ing] anger and greater violence."); Comment Kieviet, *The Battered Wife Syndrome: A Potential Defense to a Homicide Charge*, 6 Pepp. L.Rev. 213, 218 (1978) ("[T]he husband may be incited to further abuse his wife throughout the entire process preceeding [sic] the issuance of a contempt citation or restraining order.").

tion, the Domestic Abuse Act requires that an *ex parte* order may issue only when the petition alleges "an immediate and present danger of domestic abuse," Minn.Stat. § 518B.01, subd. 7(a), and the petition must be "accompanied by an affidavit made under oath stating the specific facts and circumstances from which relief is sought." *Id.* at subd. 4(b). The pre-printed petition itself recites that "[a]n emergency exists and [that] the petitioner fear[s] immediate and present danger of further acts of domestic violence." These requirements appear to meet the provisions of the rule, especially where it is undisputed that notice to the opposing party could exacerbate the risk of abuse, thus rendering moot the request for relief.[5]

We believe it is irrelevant whether the statute provides for separate, explicit procedures tailored for the domestic abuse setting or whether the statutory procedures fully comply with the requirements of the rules. In either case, the policy behind the requirements is implemented: in extraordinary circumstances, where risk of injury is plain, relief may be granted without notice. We hold that a petition which asserts a fear of further acts of domestic violence, accompanied by a supporting affidavit under oath, meets the requirements of Minn. R.Civ.P. 65.01 and Minn.Gen.R.Prac. 3.01 and 303.04, as well as the requirements of the Domestic Abuse Act.

[2] Even though statutes and rules may permit *ex parte* restraining orders, the respondent has due process rights which must not be violated. The requirements of due process are flexible and call for such procedural protections as the particular situation demands. The main factors to consider are: (1) the private interests to be affected by the official action; (2) the risk of erroneous deprivation of these interests and the probable value of additional safeguards; and (3) the government interests involved. *Mathews v. Eldridge*, 424 U.S. 319, 335, 96 S.Ct. 893, 903, 47 L.Ed.2d 18 (1976).

[3] There are two potentially protected "private interests" at issue here:[6] (1) the exclusion from a shared dwelling; (2) the liberty interest of a parent in custody of his or her children. In addition to restraining the respondent from committing acts of domestic abuse, the temporary order may exclude the respondent from a shared dwelling, or from the residence or place of employment of the petitioner. Minn.Stat. § 518B.01, subd. 7(a).[7]

The *ex parte* order in this case also granted temporary custody of the infant to the petitioner, with visitation to the respondent. While both parents have strong interests in the custody and enjoyment of their child, a parent's love and affection must yield to considerations of the child's welfare.[8] *State v. Whaley*, 246 Minn. 535,

---

5. The 1992 legislature has amended the Domestic Abuse Act regarding forms by adding subdivision 21.

> The state court administrator, in consultation with the advisory council on battered women, city and county attorneys, and legal advocates who work with victims, shall develop a uniform order for protection form that will facilitate the consistent enforcement of orders for protection throughout the state.

Domestic Abuse Act, ch. 571, art. 6, sec. 9, 1992 Minn.Laws 2032.

6. The party has no right to commit acts of domestic abuse, of course. The petitioner has a protected liberty interest in personal security. *Ingraham v. Wright*, 430 U.S. 651, 673, 97 S.Ct. 1401, 1413, 51 L.Ed.2d 711 (1977).

7. In this case, the petitioner had moved from the shared dwelling and the respondent was merely restrained from entering the petitioner's

new residence, a right the respondent never possessed.

8. Even in cases such as this one where no physical abuse of the child has been alleged, the child suffers emotional distress at seeing a parent abused by another. Quinn, *Ex Parte Protection Orders: Is Due Process Locked Out*, 58 Temp. L.Q. 843, 844 (1985). In addition, children exposed to violence "may reproduce their parents' behavior as adults." Taub, *Ex Parte Proceedings in Domestic Violence Situations: Alternative Frameworks for Constitutional Scrutiny*, 9 Hofstra L.Rev. 95, 96 (1980).

One study estimated that up to 50% of those involved in domestic violence grew up in violent homes. Quinn, *Ex Parte Protection Orders: Is Due Process Locked Out*, 58 Temp.L.Q. 843, 844 n. 4. *See also*, United Nations, *Violence Against Women in the Family*, 24 (1989) (citing a 30 year longitudinal study that showed ongoing parental conflict and violence as "significantly predictive

75 N.W.2d 786, 791 (1956). As we will discuss in Section II of this opinion, the Domestic Abuse Act recognizes the preeminence of the child's welfare by allowing an award of temporary custody only "on a basis which gives primary consideration to the safety of the victim or the children." Minn.Stat. § 518B.01, subd. 6(a)(3).

The second *Mathews* factor goes to the risk of erroneous deprivation of the private interests and the probable value of additional safeguards. *Mathews*, 424 U.S. at 335, 96 S.Ct. at 903. We conclude that the Domestic Abuse Act provides extensive procedural safeguards which guard against such error. The *ex parte* order must be based upon an application for an order for protection supported by a sworn affidavit alleging specific facts and circumstances of past abuse. Minn.Stat. § 518B.01, subd. 4(b). Only judges or referees may issue such orders. *Id.* at subd. 3. The *ex parte* order is very short term, *id.* at subd. 7(b) and the respondent must be given notice of the full hearing. *Id.* at subd. 5(a). The only additional procedural safeguard possible would be a requirement of notice to the respondent before an order was granted. This would result in unnecessary and possibly dangerous time delays.

Finally, we must consider the third *Mathews* factor, the government interests involved. While at first blush, it may seem that the interest at issue here is a purely private one, that is, individual freedom from further domestic assault, it is also true that the general public has an extraordinary interest in a society free from violence, especially where vulnerable persons are at risk. This is the reason that crimi-

nal prosecutions are brought in the name of the state, for example.

In another key case, *Fuentes v. Shevin*, 407 U.S. 67, 92 S.Ct. 1983, 32 L.Ed.2d 556 (1972), the Supreme Court discussed the characteristics of the "extraordinary situations" which justify postponing notice and opportunity for hearing. First, the deprivation of the property interest must be "directly necessary to secure an important governmental or general public interest." *Id.* at 91, 92 S.Ct. at 2000. Second, there must be "a special need for very prompt action." *Id.* Third, the state must keep strict control over the process by limiting its authorization to a government official acting under "the standards of a narrowly drawn statute." *Id.*

We believe that the domestic abuse situation shares these characteristics with other situations where *ex parte* relief has been allowed. First, it is not necessary to recite again the state's strong interest in preventing violence in a domestic setting. Second, inasmuch as the statute requires an allegation of an "immediate and present danger of domestic abuse," Minn.Stat. § 518B.01, subd. 7(a), there can be no argument that a special need for prompt action is shown. Finally, the statute is very narrowly drawn and, of course, compliance with its terms must be determined by a district court judge or other judicial officer before *ex parte* relief is available.

After reviewing the application of both the general *Mathews* factors and the more specific *Fuentes* factors to these facts, we conclude that there is no due process violation in the granting of *ex parte* relief pursuant to the Domestic Abuse Act.[9]

of serious adult personal crimes (*e.g.*, assault, attempted rape, rape, attempted murder, kidnapping and murder)"). In a study involving families that experienced domestic violence, 87% of the women reported that their children were aware of the violence. Note, Keenan, *Domestic Violence and Custody Litigation: The Need for Statutory Reform*, 13 Hofstra L.Rev. 407, 418 n. 80 (1985).

9. Various other courts have considered and rejected due process violations in *ex parte* orders. *See, Schramek v. Bohren*, 145 Wis.2d 695, 429 N.W.2d 501, 505-06 (App.1988) (court finding of reasonable basis for the legislature's creation of

special procedures in situations of abuse by family or household members); *Sanders v. Shephard*, 185 Ill.App.3d 719, 133 Ill.Dec. 712, 717, 541 N.E.2d 1150, 1155 (1989) (no procedural due process defect when an *ex parte* order issued upon supportive affidavits demonstrating exigent circumstances); *Grant v. Wright*, 222 N.J.Super. 191, 536 A.2d 319, 323 (App.Div. 1988), *cert. denied*, 111 N.J. 562, 546 A.2d 493 (1988) (legislature was careful to balance the rights of the defendants and the victims); *Marquette v. Marquette*, 686 P.2d 990, 996 (Okla.Ct. App.1984) (noting the need to protect victims from domestic assault and the emotional distress placed upon children witnesses, along with

II.

[4] We next turn to the question of whether a temporary custody determination entered as part of an order for protection under the Domestic Abuse Act must conform to the requirements of *ex parte* temporary custody orders entered as a part of a dissolution proceeding.

As the court of appeals correctly noted, excluding one party from the other's residence, one of the expressly included forms of temporary relief under subdivision 7(a), functionally requires control of physical custody of the children for the duration of the order.

Baker v. Baker, 481 N.W.2d at 874.

However, the court of appeals went on to conclude that statutory provisions which govern the issuance of temporary restraining orders in dissolution proceedings also control in the domestic abuse setting. Specifically, the court applied the stringent requirements of Minn.Stat. § 518.131, subd. 3(b) to the temporary custody provisions of the order for protection entered in this case. That section provides that no *ex parte* order may grant custody of minor children to "either party except upon a finding by the court of immediate danger of physical harm" to the children.

While the provisions of the Domestic Abuse Act that allow *ex parte* orders do not specifically address custody (or visitation), Minn.Stat. § 518B.01, subd. 7(a) does authorize "relief as the court deems proper." There is an obvious practical need to deal with custody issues when one parent is excluded from the home.

Moreover, other sections of the Domestic Abuse Act do contain adequate guidance for the court in determining custody and visitation issues. In the section authorizing relief after notice and opportunity for hearing, the court is directed to

award temporary custody or establish temporary visitation with regard to minor children of the parties on a basis which gives *primary consideration to the safety of the victim and children.*

Minn.Stat. § 518B.01, subd. 6(a)(3) (emphasis added). Nothing in the statute or its history suggests that this same standard should not apply to the custody determinations at the *ex parte* stage, nor that the standard of the dissolution statute should apply. Indeed, the court of appeals has apparently overlooked the 1985 amendments to the Domestic Abuse Act which specifically repealed the reference to the dissolution statute's custody standards.[10]

Accordingly, we hold that determinations of custody and visitation made at the time of the issuance of an *ex parte* order for protection are governed by Minn.Stat. § 518B.01, subd. 6(a)(3), giving primary consideration to the safety of the victim and the children.

III.

[5] Finally, we turn to the question of whether the court of appeals erred in remanding the subsequent order for protection to the trial court for findings on custody consistent with Minn.Stat. § 257.025(a), requiring a detailed "best interests" analysis. This is perhaps the most troubling issue in this case.[11]

While the Domestic Abuse Act does provide a standard for making custody and visitation determinations, it is essentially silent on the level of findings necessary. However, it is a significant leap to con-

---

the possibility of children repeating those patterns); *State ex rel. Williams v. Marsh*, 626 S.W.2d 223, 232 (Mo.1982) (finding the means reasonable, the goal legitimate, and safeguards adequate, along with the need for prompt action); *Blazel v. Bradley*, 698 F.Supp. 756, 768 (W.D.Wisc.1988) (finding statute constitutional that allowed *ex parte* temporary restraining order to issue); *but see Deacon v. Landers*, 68 Ohio App.3d 26, 587 N.E.2d 395 (1990) (The petitioner's due process rights were violated when a mutual order for protection was issued at the end of the hearing scheduled, upon oral

494 N W 2d 8

request of the respondent, without any testimony presented in support).

10. *See* Domestic Abuse Act, ch. 195, sec. 2, 1985 Minn.Laws 608.

11. We note that the 1992 legislature amended Minn.Stat. § 518B.01, subd. 6(a)(3) to provide that:

Except for cases in which custody is contested, findings under Minn.Stat. sec. 257.025, 518.17 or 518.175 are not required.

clude, as the court of appeals has done, that Minn.Stat. § 257.025(a) controls. First, as appellant argues, that provision is directed to custody determinations in contexts other than domestic abuse. Requiring conformity to its provisions would, in the guise of a discussion on findings, substitute the "best interests" standard in lieu of the "safety of the victim and child" standard of the Domestic Abuse Act. Custody orders in this setting are intended to be temporary and generally either expire or are reviewed by the court one year from their issuance. Minn.Stat. § 518B.01, subd. 6(b).

Furthermore, the hearing at which such custody determinations are to be made must be held no later than seven days from the issuance of any *ex parte* order, except in limited circumstances. Minn.Stat. § 518B.01, subd. 7(b). This is a wholly inadequate time for the parties to prepare testimony and other evidence in support of a best interests analysis, or for county personnel to conduct custody evaluations to assist the court. Thus, the effect of the court of appeals ruling is to force trial courts into making findings on a completely inadequate record, to delay order for protection hearings beyond statutory deadlines or to confound the practical need to make custody determinations. We do not believe this could be the legislature's intent.

The statute itself provides guidance in this regard. The final sentence of Minn. Stat. § 518B.01, subd. 6(a)(3) reads:

The court's deliberations under this subdivision shall in no way delay the issuance of an order for protection granting other reliefs * * *.

We believe that manifests the legislature's concern that the proper workings of the Domestic Abuse Act not be inappropriately delayed. We are directed to presume that the legislature does not intend a result that is impossible of execution. Minn.Stat. § 645.17(1) (1990). Because the application of a § 257.025(a) "best interests" analysis is impossible to execute in the context of a hearing on a domestic abuse order for protection, we hold that it does not apply here.

This conclusion is bolstered by our most recent consideration of related issues in *Vogt v. Vogt,* 455 N.W.2d 471 (Minn.1990). There we said:

The law is expected to provide immediate temporary relief, yet time for courts to decide a case fairly and thoughtfully is often in short supply. * * * The trial court has wide discretion in dealing with these matters. Ordinarily, consideration of any affidavits and some brief questioning of parties will suffice for issuance of an order for temporary relief; the order is of course subject to revision if more information subsequently comes to light. Or Court Services can conduct an abbreviated preliminary investigation, at least interviewing the parties, sorting out their respective positions and making recommendations to aid the court in arriving at its decision.

Vogt, at 475. Obviously, this "abbreviated," "brief" and "preliminary" approach will not suffice if the detailed findings of the "best interests" analysis are required.

Therefore, we hold that oral findings consistent with the "safety" standard of Minn.Stat. § 518B.01, subd. 6(a)(3) will support a custody determination pursuant to that provision.

Reversed.

The Impact of Domestic Violence on Children

A Report to the President of the American Bar Association

August 1994
Second (Revised) Printing, October 1994

The ABA Steering Committee on the Unmet Legal Needs of Children
The ABA Young Lawyers Division, Children and the Law Committee
The ABA Section of Family Law, Domestic Violence Committee
The ABA National Conference of Special Court Judges, Domestic Violence Committee
The ABA Litigation Section Task Force on Children
The ABA Criminal Justice Section, Victims Committee

Reporter: Howard Davidson, Director
ABA Center on Children and the Law
A Program of the Young Lawyers Division

Part I
Assure the Safety of Children

I am Scared
when they fight.
I am Scared
when they
fight

Domestic Violence Laws Must Require Police and Courts to Adequately Protect Children

Too often, law enforcement and judicial actions fail to meet the needs of children. When police respond to a 911 call regarding a domestic dispute, the responding officers will likely speak with the adults involved and focus on the protection of the abuse victim and, hopefully, the removal of the abusive adult. However, the officers may fail to ask if they can see and speak with the children in the home.

Police may also fail to ask adult victims of domestic violence whether they are fearful for the safety of their children or how the children themselves feel about, and have responded to, the violence. They may further fail to ask victims about shelter options that can help them and their children stay, safely, together. Finally, they may fail to inform victims of the available protections for their children (e.g., the ability to obtain restricted custody and visitation orders to restrict the abuser from inappropriate access to the children, as well as support orders to make it more economically feasible for abused parents and children, as a unit, to find an alternative safe residence).

Unfortunately, in many cases where there has been a history of domestic violence, abusers disregard court orders of protection restricting contact with their children. In such cases, police often treat 911 calls from abused parents about violation of such court orders, or reports of threats by abusers to retaliate against children, as less important than other types of domestic violence reports. Police may see themselves having less authority to arrest abusers when victim parents report that *their children are at-risk* because of the abuser's behavior. Mothers who have been abused may be afraid to tell authorities that they cannot protect their children.

Courts that hear domestic violence or child abuse/neglect cases may have more limited authority than general domestic relations courts to grant a full range of custody, visitation, child support, and other protective orders to help assure the safety and security of children from homes affected by domestic violence. In addition, judges often lack any mechanism for retrieving information on all other judicial proceedings affecting the children and their parents as well as the current status of those cases. Finally, family members who have been violent in the home may extend that violence to the courthouse, jeopardizing the safety of litigants, their children, court personnel, and the public.

The efforts of national organizations and domestic violence victim support groups to assure a more

238

thorough, comprehensive response to the problem of domestic violence are to be applauded. Drawing on their work, the following steps are important to promote the safety of children in domestic violence cases.

(a) All law enforcement officers responding to domestic calls should be trained to address the immediate safety, shelter, and medical assistance needs of the *parental victim's children*, as well as the victim herself (with assistance rendered in a fashion that does not precipitously separate victims from their children, but rather attempts to keep them together). Law enforcement training should also help assure that victims of domestic violence are informed by police officers of their legal rights.

(b) Where it has not already done so, the law should give victims of domestic violence the right to seek and obtain a protection order on their own *and their children's* behalf. These orders should encompass, where necessary: (1) *removal of the abuser from the home*; (2) *child custody*; (3) *possession of their residence*; (4) *child support*; and (5) *appropriate safe visitation* (including, where appropriate, orders denying abusers visitation or requiring appropriately supervised visitation).

(c) Law enforcement officers should provide domestic violence victims with referrals to agencies that can help victims obtain necessary court assistance on their own and their children's behalf.

(d) In some states, the law supports mandatory arrest where there is probable cause to believe that an abuser has violated an order of protection (or a condition of probation or parole). Mandatory arrest should also be considered for violations of court orders or conditions of release that have required abusers to *stay away from their children, children's school, day care center, baby sitter, or any other places their children frequent*. Mandatory arrest also should be available where abusers violate custody or visitation orders, and the effects of such mandatory arrests carefully evaluated in terms of the safety of all parties.

(e) Every party to a domestic violence judicial proceeding should be required to inform the court of all other actions *related to the family's children*, whether criminal (e.g., child abuse, child endangerment, assault), juvenile, domestic relations, child custody, adoption, child support, paternity, or other family-related court cases or dispute resolution processes, past and present. Courts should have an intra- and inter-court tracking system for all child-related cases, as well as a registry (accessible by both judges and law enforcement) of previously issued orders of protection.

(f) Courts should design their facilities and procedures to maximize courthouse security and the safety of parties, the children, and court personnel in all arenas in which domestic violence perpetrators are engaged in any legal process or court-based dispute resolution process relating to their spouses or ex-spouses and children.

RECOMMENDATION:

Appropriate law enforcement, shelter, health care, and judicial system resources should be provided to promote the safety of parents victimized by domestic violence, and their children, and to safeguard children during the course of judicial and other proceedings, including the period that court orders are in effect.

CHAPTER 726

PROTECTION OF THE FAMILY AND DEPENDENT PERSONS

726.6. Child endangerment

1. A person who is the parent, guardian, or person having custody or control over a child or a minor under the age of eighteen with a mental or physical disability, commits child endangerment when the person does any of the following:

a. Knowingly acts in a manner that creates a substantial risk to a child or minor's physical, mental or emotional health or safety.

b. By an intentional act or series of intentional acts, uses unreasonable force, torture or cruelty that results in physical injury, or that is intended to cause serious injury.

c. By an intentional act or series of intentional acts, evidences unreasonable force, torture or cruelty which causes substantial mental or emotional harm to a child or minor.

d. Willfully deprives a child or minor of necessary food, clothing, shelter, health care or supervision appropriate to the child or minor's age, when the person is reasonably able to make the necessary provisions and which deprivation substantially harms the child or minor's physical, mental or emotional health. For purposes of this paragraph, the failure to provide specific medical treatment shall not for that reason alone be considered willful deprivation of health care if the person can show that such treatment would conflict with the tenets and practice of a recognized religious denomination of which the person is an adherent or member. This exception does not in any manner restrict the right of an interested party to petition the court on behalf of the best interest of the child or minor.

e. Knowingly permits the continuing physical or sexual abuse of a child or minor. However, it is an affirmative defense to this subsection if the person had a reasonable apprehension that any action to stop the continuing abuse would result in substantial bodily harm to the person or the child or minor.

f. Abandons the child or minor to fend for the child or minor's self, knowing that the child or minor is unable to do so.

2. A person who commits child endangerment resulting in serious injury to a child or minor is guilty of a class "C" felony.

3. A person who commits child endangerment not resulting in serious injury to a child or minor is guilty of an aggravated misdemeanor.

Amended by Acts 1996 (76 G.A.) ch. 1129, § 109.

Historical and Statutory Notes

1996 Legislation

The 1996 amendment, in unnum. par. 1 of subsec. 1, substituted "mentally or physically handi-capped minor under the age of eighteen" for "minor under the age of eighteen with a mental or physical disability".

All That Glitters Is Not Gold: Mediation in Domestic Abuse Cases

by Mary Pat Treuthart

I. Introduction

For more than a decade, the use of mediation in cases where one disputant has abused the other has been consistently denounced by battered women's advocates.[1] However, much like a monster in a grade B horror film who reappears just when the protagonists have been lulled into a false sense of security, discussion of mediation in domestic abuse cases has resurfaced.

Mediation as a viable alternative in cases where domestic abuse is an issue has resurged for a variety of reasons, such as the frustration with shrinking advocacy resources for battered women, particularly those who are indigent,[2] the apparent willingness of lawyers and judges to withdraw from complex, emotionally charged matters incapable of quick resolution,[3] and reports of mediation's benefits, even in domestic abuse

---

[1] Feminists and battered women's advocates disparage the use of mediation in cases when *any* domestic abuse has been perpetrated by one disputant on the other disputant. *See generally* Andree G. Gagnon, *Ending Mandatory Divorce Mediation for Battered Women*, 15 HARV. WOMEN'S L.J. 272 (1992); Trino Grillo, *The Mediation Alternative: Process Dangers for Women*, 100 YALE L.J. 1545 (1991); Charlotte Germane et al., *Mandatory Custody Mediation and Joint Custody Orders in California: The Danger for Victims of Domestic Violence*, 1 BERKELEY WOMEN'S L.J. 175 (1985); Barbara Hart, *Gentle Jeopardy: The Further Endangerment of Battered Women and Children in Custody Mediation*, 7 MEDIATION Q. 317 (1990); Carol Lefcourt, *Women, Mediation and Family Law*, 18 CLEARINGHOUSE REV. 266 (July 1984); Lisa Lerman, *Mediation of Wife Abuse Cases: The Adverse Impact of Informal Dispute Resolution on Women*, 7 HARV. WOMEN'S L.J. 57 (1984); Mary Pat Treuthart, *In Harm's Way? Family Mediation and the Role of the Attorney Advocate*, 23 GOLDEN GATE L. REV. 717 (1993); Laurie Woods, *Mediation: A Backlash to Women's Progress on Family Law Issues*, 19 CLEARINGHOUSE REV. 431 (Special Issue Summer 1985).

[2] *See* AMERICAN BAR ASS'N CONSORTIUM ON LEGAL SERVS. AND THE PUB., REPORT ON THE LEGAL NEEDS OF THE LOW AND MODERATE INCOME PUBLIC (1994) (detailing unmet legal needs of the poor).

[3] Coping with the psychological aspects of divorce cases may be difficult for lawyers. Bruce W. Kallner, *Boundaries of the Divorce Lawyer's Role*, 10 FAM. L.Q. 389 (1977). Justice Phyllis Gangel-Jacob of the Supreme Court of the State of New York acknowledges that "judges turn their backs on these [matrimonial] cases; they wince and convey their distaste to administrators." Phyllis Gangel-Jacob, *Some Words of Caution About Divorce Mediation*, 23 HOFSTRA L. REV. 825, 826 (1995). In determining the reason why "the matrimonial case is an anathema to the bench," she speculates that it may be "because the issues are complicated, the considerations great, the decisions long-lasting, the possibility of recurring motions for modification and enforcement haunting, and finally, since there is no jury to share in the process and render a quick decision, the judge must actually listen carefully, take copious notes, and ultimately write lengthy decisions which set forth findings of fact, conclusion, and judgment." *Id.* at 827, citing Thomas E. Carbonneau, *A Consideration of Alternatives to Divorce Litigation*, 1986 U. ILL. L. REV. 1119, 1133.

Mary Pat Treuthart teaches at Gonzaga University School of Law, Box 3528, Spokane, WA 99220-3528; (509) 328-4220 ext. 3756. She is a former legal services staff attorney and program director and consultant to the National Center on Women and Family Law.

cases.[4] The purpose of this article is threefold: (1) to reiterate that mediation is never appropriate at the domestic abuse protection order stage and is similarly problematic in subsequent proceedings when the parties have a history of violence; (2) to emphasize that advocacy and attorney-assisted negotiation are the

Mediation as a viable alternative in cases where domestic abuse is an issue has resurged for a variety of reasons.

preferred means to handle cases involving domestic abuse; and (3) to explore ways in which available resources may best be used to protect the safety and interests of battered women.

II. The Mediation Process

Mediation can be characterized in different ways. Proponents describe mediation as a voluntary process in which a neutral third person assists participants in reaching a consensual agreement on disputed issues after considering available options and alternatives.[5] From a more skeptical perspective, mediation is viewed as a "private, nonappealable,

and unenforceable approach" to dispute resolution that has no consistency in its application or outcome.[6]

General agreement exists, even among mediation enthusiasts, that no matter—regardless of the specific issues involved—should be mediated when domestic abuse of a serious nature has occurred between disputants.[7] Many mediators do recognize that the use of mediation when domestic abuse is involved does not serve either their profession or the public.[8] However, other mediators are rethinking the connection between domestic abuse and mediation, perhaps because of the higher incidence of domestic abuse between intimate partners than previously suspected.[9] Taking a strict stance on the domestic abuse issue reduces the available number of suitable cases for referral to mediation.

The mediation literature purports to value voluntariness and equal bargaining power in the mediation process. Voluntary participation in the process, as well as voluntary agreement to specific terms, may be difficult to assess when battered women are involved. A victim may be too intimidated to give an informed voluntary consent to mediation.

---

[4] *See generally* David B. Chandler, *Violence, Fear, and Communication: The Variable Impact of Domestic Violence on Mediation,* 7 MEDIATION Q. 331 (1990); Kathleen O'Connell Corcoran & James C. Melamed, *From Coercion to Empowerment: Spousal Abuse and Mediation,* 7 MEDIATION Q. 303 (1990); Stephen K. Erickson & Marilyn McKnight, *Mediating Spousal Abuse Divorces,* 7 MEDIATION Q. 377 (1990); and Alison E. Gerencser, *Family Mediation: Screening for Domestic Abuse,* 23 FLA. ST. U.L. REV. 43 (1995).

[5] JAY FOLBERG & ALISON TAYLOR, MEDIATION—A COMPREHENSIVE GUIDE TO RESOLVING CONFLICTS WITHOUT LITIGATION 7 (1983).

[6] Woods, *supra* note 1, at 435.

[7] Charles A. Bethel & Linda R. Singer, *Mediation: A New Remedy for Cases of Domestic Violence,* 7 VT. L. REV. 15, 16 (1982); Patricia A. Winks, *Divorce Mediation: A Nonadversary Procedure for the No-Fault Divorce,* 19 J. FAM. L. 615, 643–44 (1980–81). There is no actual consensus about activity which constitutes "abuse of a serious nature" or the methodology to be used to determine its occurrence.

[8] In 1984, responding to these concerns, the Conference of Concerned Mediators and Concerned Advocates on Mediation of Family Law Issues resolved:

There should be no mediation where past or present domestic violence is the presenting problem. . . . Any legal rights including property or custody or protection of the victim should not be mediated if it is known at the outset or discovered during mediation that there is or has been domestic violence.

Conference of Concerned Mediators and Concerned Advocates on Mediation of Family Law Issues, Conference Minutes 13 (Nov. 10, 1984).

[9] Erickson & McKnight, *supra* note 4, at 377, state that "approximately half of all cases submitted for mediation involve some history of spousal abuse; the question therefore becomes not whether to mediate but what special steps must be taken when abuse is suspected or known."

Domestic abuse reduces the abused woman's freedom to make many choices for herself, including her freedom to choose mediation.[10] Even when the victim has "consented to" mediation, she may seem willing only because of her belief that she really has no other viable option.[11] Her abuser may have threatened her or may have convinced her that the legal system will be much more sympathetic to him (e.g., that she will lose her children or lose all financial support). Neither victim participation in the mediation process nor any agreements achieved through such an unbalanced "mediation" are truly voluntary.

Research indicates that participants sometimes feel coerced into reaching settlements in mediation.[12] Women who have experienced domestic abuse are more likely than other women to have established a pattern of deferring to their abusers in disagreements.[13] Therefore, it should be assumed that a battered woman cannot voluntarily consent to participate in mediation or to the terms of a final agreement reached through mediation.

The importance of equal bargaining power is acknowledged by mediators.[14] Mediators have exhibited limited focus, however, on identifying and attempting to remedy power imbalances.[15] Many mediators, aware that a perfect power

No *matter—regardless of the specific issues involved—should be mediated when domestic abuse of a serious nature has occurred between disputants.*

balance between two parties in a relationship can never be achieved, believe that sufficient skill and sensitivity can tip the balance of power to produce a fair outcome.[16] Mediators need to understand that no amount of skill or training can make up for the control

---

[10] Hart, *supra* note 1, at 321.

[11] The apparent voluntary participation of a battered woman who believes mediation will be less expensive and more efficient than litigation is "akin to a contract of adhesion." Karla Fisher et al., *The Culture of Battering and the Role of Mediation in Domestic Violence Cases*, 46 SMU L. Rev. 2117, 2166–67 (1993).

[12] Jessica Pearson & Nancy Thoennes, *Divorce Mediation: Strengths and Weaknesses Over Time*, in ALTERNATIVE MEANS OF DISPUTE RESOLUTION 456 (H. Dowison et al. eds., 1982). In the Pearson-Thoennes study, 23 percent of the California participants, 20 percent of the Minnesota participants, and 12 percent of the Connecticut participants agreed with the statement: "The mediator pressured me or my (ex) spouse into an agreement." *Id.*

[13] In one study, 73 percent of the victims reported that the abuser "always" or "usually" prevailed in major disagreements, compared to just 16 percent of the control sample of nonabused women. Only 9 percent of the victims said that they prevailed in major disputes about half the time, compared to 59 percent of the nonabused women. LENORE E. WALKER, THE BATTERED WOMAN 174 (1979).

[14] FOLBERG & TAYLOR, *supra* note 5, at 184–86. *But see* Penelope Bryan, *Killing Us Softly: Divorce Mediation and the Politics of Power*, 40 BUFF. L. REV. 441, 499 (1992), in which the author observes, upon closer scrutiny, "the literature proves insensitive to power issues." In support of this assessment, she refers to a recent book about divorce mediation that devotes only 16 pages out of more than 400 to the issue of power imbalances and "[i]n those sixteen pages the authors deny the existence of power imbalances or suggest that if they do exist they do not affect mediation." *Id.*, citing LENARD MARLOW & S. RICHARD SAUBER, THE HANDBOOK OF DIVORCE MEDIATION 103–19 (1990).

[15] *But see* Isolina Ricci, *Mediator's Notebook: Reflections on Promoting Equal Empowerment and Entitlement for Women*, J. DIVORCE, Nos. 3–4, 1985, at 49, 55–57 (providing intervention strategies for mediators attempting to balance power), and Joan B. Kelly, *Power Imbalance in Divorce and Interpersonal Mediation*, 13 MEDIATION Q. 85, 96 (1995) (presenting eight different potential sources of power imbalances in mediation and providing examples of mediator interventions to use and suggesting that mediators may need to recommend termination if the parties' needs are not met despite the use of empowering techniques).

[16] *See, e.g.*, Ann Milne, *Mediation—A Promising Alternative for Family Courts*, 1991 JUV. & FAM. CTS. J. 61.

MARTHA TABOR

that an abuser exerts over his victim and that negotiations between these parties cannot, in good conscience, be called "mediation."

The mere presence of the abuser may be frightening and intimidating to a battered woman, to say nothing of the prospect of attempting to negotiate with him.[17] The coercive effect of domestic abuse automatically skews the equality of bargaining power completely to the advantage of the abuser. It should be presumed that equality of bargaining

power never exists when one disputant has abused another disputant and therefore principled mediation cannot take place.

Mediation emphasizes the privacy and autonomy of the family.[18] The mediation process focuses on the relationship between the parties without assessing blame for inappropriate, asocial, or criminal behavior. The batterer is not required in mediation to admit responsibility for his abusive behavior.[19]

In our society, the battered woman is often blamed and made to feel responsible in some way for the violence perpetrated against her.[20] The notion that the victim provoked her abuser is used to justify and support male dominance and control and to reduce the societal censure for the abuser's use of physical force against the victim.[21] Since the mediation process is not designed to deter violent behavior or to protect victims, its use is particularly perilous for battered women.[22] Protection of one's safety should be considered too important to entrust to any other but the legal system, which has the power to remove the batterer from the home, to arrest when necessary, and to enforce the terms of a decree if a new assault occurs.[23]

---

[17] Martha Shaffer, *Divorce Mediation: A Feminist Perspective*, U. TORONTO FAC. L. REV. 162. 182 (1988). For a more recent analysis of the inherent power imbalance between men and women in society and in the mediation process, see generally Bryan, *supra* note 14.

[18] Bennett Wolff, *The Best Interest of the Divorcing Family—Mediation Not Litigation*, 29 LOY. L. REV. 55, 69 (1983).

[19] Woods, *supra* note 1, at 433.

[20] Proponents of mediation may believe that family violence is the result of "family dysfunction; stress reaction; inadequate coping responses due to health or mental health problems; lack of anger or frustration control; situationally precipitated crisis such as unemployment; substance or alcohol abuse. . . . Many men experience each or some of the above and do not batter their women." Barbara Hart, Mediation for Women: Same Song, Second Verse—A Little Bit Louder and A Little Bit Worse (unpublished manuscript, 1984) (available through the National Center on Women and Family Law).

[21] U.S. COMM'N ON CIVIL RIGHTS, UNDER THE RULE OF THUMB: BATTERED WOMEN AND THE ADMINISTRATION OF JUSTICE 62 (1982).

[22] Arrest may be the most effective deterrent to domestic abuse. N.Y. TIMES, Apr. 5, 1983, at C1. Many abusers go on to abuse other partners. In one study, 57 percent of victims reported their partners had been violent with former wives. MILDRED DALEY PAGELOW, FAMILY VIOLENCE 62 (1984). In another sample, a Los Angeles abusers' counselor confirmed to the researcher that all of the 150 abusers he had treated acknowledged they had abused other partners. *Id.* at 106. Only 17 percent of the victims reported involvement in other abusive relationships. *Id.* at 59.

[23] Woods, *supra* note 1, at 435–36.

III. The Domestic Abuse Protection Order Process

In the mid 1970s, as part of a larger reform movement in the area of domestic abuse, the issuance of temporary protection orders (TPOs) for emergency relief replaced the cumbersome and time-consuming order-to-show-cause process, thus permitting access to the courts in an efficient and timely fashion.[24] The current statutory schemes in most jurisdictions are designed to allow battered women to file these applications pro se or with the assistance of a lay advocate, court liaison, or volunteer from a local domestic abuse shelter or services program.[25]

A. Uncontested Cases

While some courts schedule particular days and times for the domestic violence docket, other courts hear applications for extension of TPOs on an as-needed basis. At the hearing, the judge or the clerk calls the docket to determine who is present. Due to the dynamics of the battering relationship, several no-shows on the petitioner and the respondent sides are not uncommon. These cases are often summarily dismissed without prejudice.[26] In uncontested cases where the respondent fails to appear and there is proof of service, the court normally extends the

Woefully, mediation is being employed in some jurisdictions to resolve issues of custody, visitation, child support, spousal maintenance, and property settlement at the protection order stage.

TPO order automatically or after taking additional brief testimony from the petitioner. The battered woman then can proceed on her own or with the support of a friend or family member. Sometimes lay advocates are available to aid women during this stage.[27] Occasionally, respondents appear and have no objection to the allegations of domestic violence or the relief ordered. The court generally extends the order in those situations, again after taking brief testimony or obtaining the respondent's assent on the record.

B. Contested Cases

The contested cases that remain on the docket are of two basic types: those in which the respondent denies the

---

[24] A comprehensive survey about legal remedies for battered women in the United States is the exhaustively researched (almost 400 pages in length) but very readable article by Catherine Klein & Leslye Orloff, *Providing Legal Protection for Battered Women: An Analysis of State Statutes and Case Law*, 21 HOFSTRA L. REV. 801 (1993). This work could be rightly viewed as a domestic violence handbook for scholars as well as practitioners; however, it is referred to here because the authors focus on the protection order phase of the process. The authors also mention their comprehensive training manual, which includes almost 300 pages of direct examination questions and sample pleadings, for attorneys representing battered women in the protection order process. *Id.* at 813 n.26. Klein is an associate professor and director of the Families and the Law Clinic, Columbus School of Law, Catholic University of America, Washington, D.C.; Orloff founded the Clinica Legal Latina at Ayuda, Inc., also in Washington, D.C.

[25] *Id.* at 844. *See also* Barbara J. Hart, *State Codes on Domestic Violence: Analysis, Commentary, and Recommendations*, 43 JUV. & FAM. CT. J., No. 4, 1, 11 (1992) (identifying states which provide for lay advocacy and court accompaniment by statute).

[26] Dismissing a civil protection order due to the petitioner's failure to appear may be unwise; the court should order a continuance and communicate with the petitioner. Klein & Orloff, *supra* note 24, at 1065–66 (the authors cite PETER FINN & SARAH COLSON, NATIONAL INST. OF JUSTICE, CIVIL PROTECTION ORDERS: LEGISLATION, CURRENT COURT PRACTICE, AND ENFORCEMENT 29 (1990), for the various reasons, such as physical injury, threats of additional violence, or uncertainty about the process, that might prevent the petitioner from attending the hearing).

[27] Klein & Orloff, *supra* note 24, at 1060–61; Kin Kinports & Karla Fischer, *Orders of Protection in Domestic Violence Cases: An Empirical Assessment of the Impact of the Reform Statutes*, 2 TEX. WOMEN'S L.J. 163, 182–85 (1993) (urging the expansion of the role of lay advocates in the protection order process).

alleged acts of domestic violence and those in which the respondent admits the violent acts but disputes the temporary relief granted to the petitioner. That mediation will be used to determine whether domestic abuse occurred is unlikely, although there have been rare reports of its use in similar ways.[28] If the court is satisfied that domestic abuse has occurred, then it is timely for the court to grant appropriate relief.

Woefully, mediation *is* being employed in some jurisdictions to resolve issues of custody, visitation, child support, spousal maintenance, and property settlement at the protection order stage.[29] Mediation should never be used at this stage of the process, when the most recent incident of abuse may have occurred only a few days earlier. That an ethical mediator would even attempt to reach a settlement of these issues by conducting a joint mediation session, that is, with the parties sitting in the same room together, is virtually inconceivable. Voluntariness and equality of bargaining power, which form the cornerstone of mediation's effectiveness, would be virtually nonexistent. Domestic abuse intimidates the victim and reduces her ability to represent, or even identify, her own interests. The victim may not even recognize that she is acceding to her abuser's wishes for fear of abuse and that this pattern is detrimental to her.[30] These concerns would apply even if an individual caucus or shuttle mediation format were used.[31] Nevertheless, mediation is sometimes offered to unrepresented parties as a viable shortcut to resolve these issues.

A mechanism should be in place to offer counsel for battered women at protection order hearings. If the respondent denies that domestic violence occurred, a hearing must be conducted to determine whether the statutory requirements for domestic violence are met. If not, the court has no authority to enter a protection order or to grant other relief. Even when the process is less formal, for example, where the rules of evidence are relaxed, an attorney advocate may be key to ensuring that the petitioner's case is presented fully on direct and cross-examination.

Planning for the contested case at the protection order phase presents a real strategic problem.[32] Often, there is no way to know in advance whether the respondent will appear at all, whether he will come alone, or whether an attorney will be present with him. A few courts request that counsel notify the clerk if they intend to make an appearance on behalf of the respondent. As a practical matter, this is difficult to control. Unlike small claims court, where attorneys are sometimes excluded completely by statute or court rule, attorneys who appear on behalf of either petitioners or respondents are rarely denied the opportunity to participate in the protection order hearing. The court may grant a continuance to allow an unrepresented party on either side to obtain representation. When the respondent makes such a request, the court is likely to grant it while leaving the TPO's protections in place. However, when the petitioner asks for a delay to obtain counsel, she may be required to proceed without an attorney since she is the moving party. To pit an unrepresented, battered woman against her abuser and his attorney in a contested hearing is obviously undesirable. To avoid this problem, the court should liberally grant continuances

---

[28] There have been instances of the use of mediation in criminal assault and battery cases involving intimate partners. Bethel & Singer, *supra* note 7, at 23.

[29] The concerns about mediation in specific subject areas that may arise in protection order hearings as well as in divorce or custody cases are discussed *infra*.

[30] RICHARD GELLES & MURRAY STRAUS, INTIMATE VIOLENCE 150 (1988).

[31] In this type of mediation, the disputants are in separate locations, thus preventing direct communication, and the mediator moves back and forth between them. CHRISTOPHER MOORE, THE MEDIATION PROCESS: PRACTICAL STRATEGIES FOR RESOLVING CONFLICT 263 (1986).

[32] These observations are based on my experience as a legal services lawyer representing battered women in New Jersey and Nevada and supervising students in a domestic violence mini-clinic in Washington State.

for brief periods to allow victims to obtain counsel.

When the focus is on fashioning appropriate relief, an attorney's assistance, either by negotiating with opposing counsel or by presenting arguments for court-ordered relief, is vital. Statutory schemes vary greatly in the relief that may be granted. Most statutes provide for the inclusion of no-contact provisions and awards of temporary custody with visitation.[33] A few states' statutes allow for monetary transfers for the purpose of spousal maintenance, and a greater number provide for child support.[34] At least 38 states "explicitly grant judges the latitude to grant any constitutionally defensible relief that is warranted."[35]

Many judges are reluctant without encouragement to assert their authority to order necessary financial relief.[36] This is unfortunate because economic pressure is a primary reason for battered women to reconcile with their abusive partners. Unless a temporary financial award is entered at the earliest possible point, the likelihood that a battered woman will return to her abusive partner is increased, perhaps with disastrous consequences for her and her children.[37]

The temptation may be great to allow battered women to proceed pro se through the protection order process. However, with representation at this juncture, the short-term payoff for a minimal amount of attorney labor can be high. Under either the detailed relief or the catchall statutory scheme, representation by counsel allows the greatest opportunity for battered women to obtain appropriate relief because attorneys are more likely to induce the court to exercise the full range of available options.[38] If the court is not amenable to awarding prompt and effective relief at the protection order phase, an attorney is in the best position to appeal an unfavorable decision, to continue representation in a superior court domestic relations proceeding, to advise the petitioner about other courses of action such as filing a criminal complaint, or to make a referral for other legal representation.

IV. Formal Domestic Relations Proceedings: Custody and Divorce Actions

Although the protection order process may be a temporary relief for the battered woman to get back on her feet, the issues of divorce or custody require the filing of formal pleadings at some point. Prior to the filing stage, clients may need legal advice, a unique function that may

---

[33] Klein & Orloff, *supra* note 24, at 925, 954.

[34] *Id.* at 997–98.

[35] Family Violence Project, *Family Violence: Improving Court Practice, Recommendations from the National Council of Juvenile and Family Court Judges*, 41 Juv. & Fam. Ct. J. 1, 7-18 (1990). This is sometimes referred to as a "catchall" provision. Klein & Orloff, *supra* note 24, at 912.

[36] "Judges may be uncomfortable issuing ex parte orders that evict the offender from the family home, require the payment of spousal or child support, or award custody of the children to the petitioner." Klein & Orloff, *supra* note 24, at 18. The National Council, recognizing that the victim will not be adequately protected, recommends that judges take this action. Family Violence Project, *supra* note 35, at 18. Even in New Jersey, which may have the most comprehensive statutory scheme for providing relief to victims of domestic violence, judges are not "awarding the full range of remedies afforded to victims under the statute." Lisa Memoli & Gina Plotino, *Enforcement or Pretense: The Courts and the Domestic Violence Act*, 15 Women's Rts. L. Rep. 39, 48 (1993). Judicial masters, court commissioners, and attorneys serving in judicial capacities on a pro tem basis may be even more reluctant to award necessary relief.

[37] Family Violence Project, *supra* note 35, at 18. Incidents of abuse often increase in severity and frequency over time. Lenore E. Walker, The Battered Woman Syndrome 24 (1984).

[38] Attorney representation currently may be low. In one New Jersey county where a court watch program was implemented, plaintiffs were represented in only 15 percent of cases, defendants in 21 percent. Memoli & Plotino, *supra* note 36, at 57, citing Bergen County (N.J.) Commission on the Status of Women, Community Court Watch Project (May 1993). This chilling statistic indicates that victims in some cases proceeded pro se against an abuser who was represented by counsel.

be performed only by attorneys. The essential elements of legal advice include applying the law to a specific set of facts, suggesting a particular course of action for the client, and predicting the outcome of a case or controversy.

An examination of the critical role played by an attorney in most matrimonial cases demonstrates some of the

An examination of the critical role played by an attorney in most matrimonial cases demonstrates some of the potential shortcomings of mediation, particularly where battered women are involved.

potential shortcomings of mediation, particularly where battered women are involved.[39]

A. Child Custody

Historically, child custody, whether standing alone or as part of a divorce case, was the initial legal issue referred to mediation for resolution. Attorneys and judges seemed eager to abdicate responsibility for decision making in the complex and emotionally charged area of custody. In the legal process, greater reliance is placed on input from psychologists and social workers, while "bright-line" rules have given way to vaguer standards in custody determinations and "joint custody" preferences.

The use of mediation "reduces the

likelihood that a battered woman will receive custody."[40] Women generally have a greater commitment to child rearing and may be fearful about the possibility of losing custody.[41] Fathers may be less "risk averse" and request custody to gain leverage on other issues.[42] Discussions about discrete legal issues such as custody can raise related concerns, many of them financial. Certainly, custody arrangements may affect child support and domicile in the marital residence. If custody is mediated without consideration of other issues, the mother has no other bargaining chips and only the mother has rights to forgo.[43]

"Joint custody" seems to represent the mediation ideal since the goal of the process is agreement and promotion of "win-win" results rather than a determination of the "best interest" of the children. However, true joint custody in the sense of shared decision making and caretaking is rare.[44] In practice, the typical joint custody arrangement is similar to the traditional single custodian with noncustodial visitation arrangement, with one crucial difference—in joint custody the noncustodial parent has an important veto right over the parent who provides daily care and guidance.[45] What has changed only is the authority of mothers to make decisions, and this may be dangerous for battered women compelled to deal continually with their batterers on issues concerning the children.

Mediation literature avoids discussion of the "primary caretaker" standard for

---

[39] Justice Gangel-Jacob, in expressing caution about divorce mediation as a panacea, observes that "[t]here is a lack of appreciation for the complexities of a matrimonial case; able counsel, familiar with the most recent decisions in a quickly developing field, with expertise not only in matrimonial law but in landlord tenant law, real estate law, tax law, and consumer rights law, should be on hand from the beginning and through every stage of the advanced negotiation and, if necessary, the trial." Gangel-Jacob, *supra* note 3, at 828.

[40] *Developments—Domestic Violence*, 106 HARV. L. REV. 1498, 1602 (1993).

[41] Nancy Polikoff, *Gender and Child Custody Determinations: Exploding the Myth* in FAMILIES, POLITICS, AND PUBLIC POLICY: A FEMINIST DIALOGUE ON WOMEN AND THE STATE 195 (I. Diamond ed., 1983).

[42] *Viewpoint: The Politics of Child Custody*, GUILD NOTES, May Aug. 1982, at 18.

[43] Lefcourt, *supra* note 1, at 269.

[44] *Id.*

[45] Margaret J. Nichols, Issues to Consider Regarding Mediation of Custody Disputes 4 (unpublished manuscript, 1984) (available through the National Center on Women and Family Law).

custody.[46] A higher rate of joint custody agreements result from mediation than from other prevalent means of dispute resolution, including adjudication and attorney-assisted negotiation. Most "functional plans" developed in mediation leave most of the mundane responsibilities of child rearing with the parent who has usually fulfilled them—the mother.[47]

The well-being of the children is a consistent theme promoted by mediation advocates.[48] The use of a particular dispute resolution process, however, has no impact on the children's ability to cope with the aftermath of divorce.[49] Despite the lack of evidence linking

mediation with postdivorce adjustment or "best interests" of the children, which is the standard used in most jurisdictions for custody decision making, "mediation is often the primary vehicle for resolution of custody disputes" by statute, local rule, or jurisdictional practice.[50]

However, demonstrable evidence exists that children are direct or secondary victims when domestic abuse has been perpetrated by one parent on the other.[51] Such evidence militates against joint custody arrangements. In three-fourths of the states, courts are required or permitted to consider domestic abuse as a factor in custody deci-

---

[46] Joanne Shulman & Nancy Polikoff, *Child Custody* in WOMEN AND THE LAW 6.33–.39 (Carol Lefcourt ed., 1984) (1988 Supp.) [hereinafter WOMEN AND THE LAW].

[47] Carol Bohmer & Marilyn L. Ray, *Effects of Different Dispute Resolution Methods on Women and Children After Divorce*, 28 FAM. L.Q. 223 (1994). In a New York study, mediator-negotiated agreements resulted in a substantially greater number of joint custody awards, with proportionally less actual equal sharing of child caretaking responsibilities within three to nine months after divorce. *Id.* at 232. The study was replicated in Georgia and with results similar to those reached in New York, particularly regarding caretaking responsibilities. *Id.* at 236.

[48] Shaffer, *supra* note 17, at 189. *See generally* DAVID SAPOSNEK, MEDIATING CHILD CUSTODY DISPUTES (1983); JOAN BLADES, FAMILY MEDIATION: COOPERATIVE DIVORCE SETTLEMENT 27–31 (1985). It is not clear whether mediators have any independent, rather than derivative, obligation to third parties, including children who are not present. Some mediators encourage the participation of children in custody decisions, provided they are old enough to comprehend the process. O.J. COOGLER, STRUCTURED MEDIATION DIVORCE SETTLEMENT 27–31 (1978).

[49] Pearson & Thoennes, *supra* note 12, at 62, at 474–76. Based on the results of objective tests administered to children, researchers found no consistent or significant differences in postdivorce adjustment according to exposure to mediation versus more traditional adjudicatory processes. *Id.*

[50] Hart, *supra* note 25, at 37, citing Susan Myers et al., *Divorce Mediation in the States: Institutionalization, Use and Assessment*, 12 STATE CT. J. 17 (Fall 1988).

[51] Germane et al., *supra* note 1, at 21; *see generally* Mildred Daley Pagelow, *Effects of Domestic Violence on Children and Their Consequences for Custody and Visitation Agreements*, 7 MEDIATION Q. 347 (1990).

sion making.[52] In the mediation process, battered women may lose this statutory custodial advantage.

B. Child Support

The absence of specific, codified standards in the child support area may have fueled the mediation industry.[53] However, federal law and regulations now require each state to have one set of guidelines for establishing and modifying child support orders.[54] Accordingly, the need for alternative dispute resolution in this area has been virtually eliminated.[55] This is good news for battered women for whom greater financial security overall, and for their children in particular, is a critical issue.

It is questionable whether child support should be mediated at all outside the presence of a third party who represents the child's economic interests.[56] Earlier research results indicate that joint custody mediated agreements provide for the support of children less often than either attorney-negotiated or judicially assisted settlements.[57]

If disparities in earning power exist, payment of child support by the parent who is better situated financially is appropriate even in split custody or joint physical custody arrangements.[58] If

It is questionable whether child support should be mediated at all outside the presence of a third party who represents the child's economic interests.

mediation is employed, it is imperative that neither mediators nor the process "exploits or feeds into the culturally induced tendency of women to be conciliatory and to trade away substantive benefits in return for affective and symbolic 'benefits,' especially those that are unlikely to be reaped."[59]

C. Spousal Maintenance

The extent to which spousal maintenance is addressed in mediation is not clear.[60] Before1988, spousal maintenance might have been "traded off" for higher child support payments.

In many marriages, the greatest asset is the supporting spouse's earning

---

[52] Joan Zorza, *Women Battering: High Costs and the State of the Law*, 28 CLEARINGHOUSE REV. 383, 393 (Special Issue 1994).

[53] Judith Cassetty, Mediation and Child Support (unpublished manuscript, 1984) (available through the National Center on Women and Family Law).

[54] Nancy S. Erickson, *Child Support Guidelines: A Primer*, 27 CLEARINGHOUSE REV. 734, 735 (Nov. 1993).

[55] At a family mediation training I recently attended, the trainers gave participants a copy of state child support tables and suggested this was no longer an issue for consideration in the mediation context. Family/Divorce Mediation Training sponsored by the Spokane County Dispute Resolution Center, Spokane, Washington, April 19–21, 1996.

[56] Cassetty, *supra* note 53, at 3.

[57] Bohmer & Ray, *supra* note 47, at 228. The mediated samples in three selected heterogeneous counties in New York provided for child support proportionally less frequently than the other mechanisms in all custody arrangements. *Id.* at 232. Results from a study in Georgia after passage of the Family Support Act of 1988 indicate that divorce agreement from all dispute resolution processes contained child support provisions at least 90 percent of the time. *Id.* at 237–38.

[58] Carol Lefcourt & Judith M. Reichler, *Child Support* in WOMEN AND THE LAW, *supra* note 46, at 5.09. Statutory child support guidelines may not provide for nontraditional custody or visitation arrangements. However, alternative arrangements alone should not "cause the court to vary from the guidelines unless it has been determined that there is sharing of physical custody to the extent that the primary custodial parent's expenses are substantially reduced as a result." *Id.*

[59] Cassetty, *supra* note 53, at 6, gives the example of a mother who thinks the father may be more willing to pay for children's college education if he does not have to pay "too much" child support while they are young.

[60] The structured mediation model sets forth specific guidelines for identifying the dependent spouse and determining the proper amount of support. COOGLER, *supra* note 48, at 16–17.

power, which includes the homemaker's contribution: "[T]he only possible distribution of this asset is via alimony-maintenance."[61] The economic consequences of divorce on men and women and the disparities in potential earning power based on gender are receiving growing recognition. The formal legal system may be better equipped to evaluate a homemaker's contribution and to translate it into a maintenance award.

D. Property Division

Mediation should be a reasonable method to resolve property issues between equally empowered disputants operating in good faith.[62] But certain pitfalls may affect battered women's abilities to use mediation to a greater extent than other disputants. Mediators recognize the need for outside assistance when the financial picture presented by the parties is complex.[63] The financially dominant partner, usually the husband, may urge mediation with strict instructions to avoid consulting legal counsel. One means of control typically exercised by abusers is command over financial matters in the household. As a result, many battered women have little or no information about their family income, assets, or expenditures.

Honesty and openness are essential elements of mediation; however, the withholding of information may be endemic in matrimonial matters. The

mediator has no means to compel financial disclosure. Full revelation of assets including separate property is a critical prerequisite to division of marital property. Although, even in adjudication, there is no absolute guarantee of full disclosure, the legal system offers "various, albeit imperfect, means of obtaining disclosure, including depositions, subpoenaing of records, and coercive sanctions for noncompliance or false representations."[64] When husbands control the assets, women may be vulnerable if mechanisms are not available to force disclosure.[65]

An interrelated issue is the identification and valuation of property for inclusion in the "marital pot," a complicated question in both equitable-distribution and community-property states. Financial experts may be needed to appraise and value assets.[66] Recent decisions and legislation have expanded the definition of marital property to include vested pensions; professional licenses, degrees, and practices; life insurance; and deferred employment benefits.[67] Homemakers' nonpaid contributions to the acquisition of marital assets are explicitly recognized in some states.[68]

In addition, functions routinely performed by attorneys for matrimonial clients may be lost in the mediation process. For example, if a pension is divided, the pension fund manager and the employer should be notified in writ-

---

[61] New York Task Force on Women in the Court Public Hearing 54 (Nov. 19, 1984), cited in *The Report of the New York Task Force on Women in the Courts*, 15 Ford. Urb. L.J. 3, 74 (1986–87).

[62] In a Georgia study there was no significant difference in the value of property women received in settlement from different dispute resolution mechanisms. Bohmer & Ray, *supra* note 47, at 244.

[63] Coogler, *supra* note 48, at 45.

[64] Lefcourt, *supra* note 1, at 268. *See also* Jessica Pearson, *The Equity of Mediated Divorce Agreements*, 9 Mediation Q. 179, 194–95 (1990), in which the author reports, after conducting structured telephone interviews with 302 former divorce-mediated participants, that sizable proportions of women believe their ex-spouse was dishonest about his financial situation and withheld information during mediation.

[65] Judith Avner, Mediation of Property Issues 2 (unpublished manuscript, 1984) (available through the National Center on Women and Family Law).

[66] Pearson discovered that only 8 percent and 13 percent of public and private sector mediation programs, respectively, reported using independent appraisers for marital property valuations. Pearson, *supra* note 64, at 194.

[67] Amy Pellman, *Married Women's Property Rights* in Women and the Law (1987 Supp.), *supra* note 46, at 3A-5.

[68] Judith Avner, *Equitable Distribution* in Women and the Law, *supra* note 46, at 4-4.

---

ing of the nonemployee spouse's interest in the funds, especially if distribution is deferred. Since the law in this area is in flux, diligence is required, even for legally trained persons, in order to be familiar with the most recent developments.

In most jurisdictions, injunctive relief is available to prevent dissipation of assets. Mediation offers no such safeguard. Through the use of formal discovery mechanisms, information may be obtained regarding sale, exchange, barter, or destruction of property that occurred before and after the separation of the parties. The spouse without domination or control over disposed assets may be allowed a "credit" when other property is divided. Since mediation is a "future-oriented" process, mediators may tend to exclude previously dissipated assets from consideration in the distribution of property.

In many divorce matters, allocation of property is less significant than the determination of responsibility for outstanding obligations to creditors. Mediators may be inclined to divide equally the debts or to assess responsibility for payment to the party who retains possession of a particular item, such as a motor vehicle. This approach ignores certain realties such as disparity in income of the parties or the actual ability to make payments. Mediated agreements may not have "indemnification and hold harmless" provisions, which may be necessary as a basis for a cross-claim if the former spouses are sued by a third party.

It may be more difficult to draft an agreement that provides protection in the event a bankruptcy action is initiated by one party. Mediation increases the likelihood that an innocent female spouse, who may be struggling to establish a good credit rating in her own name, will be compelled to try to satisfy joint obligations arising out of the marriage in order to protect her future financial position. In most situations, the protection of a carefully drafted property settlement agreement with advice of counsel is needed.

In order to address property issues effectively, mediators and advocates must understand the tax ramifications of the sale or exchange of property.[69] The impact of certain intraspouse transfers on eligibility for public entitlement programs (i.e., Aid to Families with Dependent Children and supplemental security income) must be considered as well. Mediators may be particularly unfamiliar with the effects of property division on poor persons since the administrative policies and regulations are complex and subject to change.[70]

If one spouse has abused the other, the victim may have a claim through a tort action to recover damages.[71] In some jurisdictions, such a claim must be pleaded as a part of the divorce petition.[72] The impact of inclusion of such claims in a mediated agreement is unclear. The inclusion of the claim only in the mediated agreement may not be sufficient to reduce the matter to judgment for enforcement purposes or to collect from a victim's compensation fund where the batterer is judgment proof.

E. Other Issues

Other complications may exist in a domestic relations case. Immigrant spouses who have been in the United States for less than two years may have

---

[69] Articles about tax consequences of certain property transfers are beginning to appear in the mediation literature. *See, e.g.,* Landis Olesker, *Qualified Domestic Relations Orders: Qualification Is Not the Problem,* 12 MEDIATION Q. 313 (1995). Despite the attempt to give information even to nonattorney mediators in a straightforward manner, some of the conceptual nuances are not easy to grasp.

[70] For more information about public entitlement issues, *see* CENTER FOR LAW & SOCIAL POLICY, PUBLIC BENEFITS ISSUES IN DIVORCE CASES: A MANUAL FOR MEDIATORS (1988).

[71] *See* Laurie Woods & Myra Sun, *Remedies for Battered Women,* in WOMEN AND THE LAW (1988 Supp.), *supra* note 46, at 9.1.

[72] Tort remedies available to victims of domestic abuse, including some various pleading requirements, can be found in Douglas D. Scherer, *Tort Remedies for Victims of Domestic Abuse,* 43 S.C. L. REV. 543 (1992).

only "conditional" status under federal immigration laws, and this becomes an underlying concern no matter what is at issue.[73] Low-income parents who receive public assistance may become ineligible for various types of benefits if they agree to certain types of joint physical custody.[74] In biracial or bicultural families, parents who disagree about custody may be concerned with preserving cultural or religious values through given custody arrangements.[75]

The participants may have emotional or mental health problems that block resolution of clearly identified legal issues. Depending on their levels of sophistication, participants and media-

Although mediation may seem well suited to postdispositional issues, the passage of time alone may not remedy balance-of-power issues.

tors may be able to identify none, some, or all of these issues. Mediators who are mental health professionals should be most sensitive to those matters. Gaps, however, remain.[76]

Even relatively simple matters could conceivably fall through the cracks in the mediation process. For example, a wife who assumed her husband's surname at the time of the marriage may have to request resumption of the use of her birth name. Failure to do so at the time of divorce might require her to institute a separate name change action, causing unnecessary expense and delay.

V. Subsequent Proceedings: Enforcement of Litigants' Rights and Motions for Modification

As domestic relations attorneys recognize, family law matters are not necessarily resolved permanently with the entry of a final judgment of divorce. Custody and visitation arrangements may be altered upon a showing of a substantial change of circumstances. A variety of occurrences may affect financial transactions such as child support and spousal maintenance.

Mediation may seem well suited to address some of these postdispositional issues.[77] Any risk to battered women would seem to be minimized at this later stage. In actuality, the danger is exacerbated.[78] The passage of time alone may not remedy balance-of-power issues.[79] The existence of domestic abuse may permanently skew the ability of parties

---

[73] Deeana L. Jang, *Caught in a Web: Immigrant Women and Domestic Violence*, 28 CLEARINGHOUSE REV. 397, 401 (Special Issue 1994); Charles Wheeler, *New Protections for Immigrant Women and Children Who Are Victims of Domestic Violence*, in this issue.

[74] *See generally* CENTER FOR LAW & SOCIAL POLICY, *supra* note 70.

[75] *See* Palmore v. Sidoti 466 U.S. 429 (1985) (Court reverses a Florida District Court of Appeals decision divesting mother of the custody of her infant child because of her remarriage to a person of a different race).

[76] *See* Suzanne M. Retzinger, *Mental Illness and Labeling in Mediation*, 8 MEDIATION Q 151 (1990).

[77] *But see* Douglas D. Knowlton & Tara Lea Muhlhauser, *Mediation in the Presence of Domestic Violence: Is It the Light at the End of the Tunnel or Is It a Train on the Track?*, 70 N.D. L. REV. 254, 265 (1994) (suggesting that the mediation process may not fully apprehend the danger to women and children in the postdispositional phase).

[78] Women who are separated or divorced are more frequently and seriously battered by former partners. Zorza, *supra* note 52, at 386. Statistical data indicate that separated and divorced women account for 75 percent of all battered women and "are 14 times more likely to be battered than women still cohabiting." *Id.*, citing CAROLINE W. HARLOW, BUREAU OF JUSTICE STATISTICS, FEMALE VICTIMS OF VIOLENT CRIME 5 (1991). *See also* Desmond Ellis, *Post Separation Woman Abuse: The Contribution of Lawyers as "Barracudas," "Advocates," and "Counsellors,"* 10 INT'L J.L. & PSYCHIATRY 403, 408 (1987).

[79] As one mediation critic has noted, "For many battered women, the period of healing and empowerment after separation from a batterer can last several years. Even if a victim no longer suffers the diminishment imposed by the battering in the relationship, she is still not free to deal with the batterer 'at arm's length,' voluntarily until he has stopped violent and coercive tactics for a substantial period of time." Hart, *supra* note 1, at 322.

to bargain effectively.[80] In addition, the very need for a modification procedure suggests that some element of the previous arrangement was unsatisfactory.

Recognition that "battering is power and control marked by violence and coercion" helps explain why the post-separation period may be particularly dangerous for the abused woman.[81] In many abusive relationships, the loss of control may enrage the batterer. Causing disruption in the battered woman's life may be a way of maintaining continued domination. Withholding child support or sums for spousal maintenance may be a control issue.

If the battered woman is alleging a change of circumstances for a custody modification (e.g., because of her desire to relocate), the batterer may be aggravated that she has moved on with her life. Remarriage or the presence of a new partner could enrage the batterer. Certainly the well-publicized events of the past few years involving high-profile disputants underscore the need for continued attorney vigilance in postdivorce proceedings.

VI. Ensuring the Availability of Advocates at Various Stages of the Process

Acknowledgment of the importance of attorney involvement on behalf of battered women throughout the entire legal process is critical. But who should provide this representation?

A. Legal Services Attorneys

Ideally, representation of battered women at the protection order stage should be provided by experienced, sensitive attorney advocates who are committed to working in this emotionally charged area. Legal services attorneys seem to be the logical choice to fulfill this role. Familiarity with the issues,

awareness of the particular needs of victims of domestic violence, and the ability to mount effective advocacy on short notice are all desirable characteristics that legal services attorneys could bring to the process. Designation of one identifiable and established group of persons to function as counsel at the protection order stage would allow for consistency and the opportunity to effectuate positive results in individual cases as well as systemically. In addition, representation of battered women at the protection order phase "is a preventative step that may ultimately reduce the need for other legal services."[82]

Constraints, most notably financial ones, exist. Work with battered women is labor intensive and can cause burnout. However, the more significant constraint may be attitudinal. Advocacy on behalf of battered women has not continued to be a high priority in many legal services programs, a phenomenon that developed during the funding crisis in the early 1980s.[83] This is true despite the express needs of the client community in many locales suggesting that domestic violence work should be a higher priority[84] and despite this work not being politically controversial for the most part to government grantors and thus attractive to private funding sources.

B. Private Attorneys

Viewed strictly as a resources issue, others in the legal community could provide competent representation, particularly in formal divorce and custody proceedings. Unlike complicated public entitlement cases, long the province of specialized public interest lawyers, the family law bar could be tapped to provide representation in domestic abuse cases. This solution may be good in theory but a little rough in practice.

Some volunteer attorneys are un-

---

[80] Knowlton & Muhlhauser, *supra* note 77, at 267 (Muhlhauser's conclusion in section titled "'Con' Position on Mediation in Domestic Violence Situation").

[81] Martha R. Mahoney, *Legal Images of Battered Women: Redefining the Issue of Separation*, 90 MICH. L. REV. 1, 93 (1991).

[82] Klein & Orloff, *supra* note 24, at 1062.

[83] See Laurie Woods, *The Challenge Facing Legal Services in the 80's*, 16 CLEARINGHOUSE REV. 26 (May 1982); Klein & Orloff, *supra* note 24, at 1062–63.

[84] Klein & Orloff, *supra* note 24, at 1062–63.

willing to accept domestic abuse cases and prefer to handle routine divorce cases that may be, in reality, more suited to resolution through mediation. The logistics involved in assigning private attorneys to represent battered women on short notice at the protection order stage may tax even the most organized volunteer lawyer programs. Despite these barriers, volunteer lawyers should remain a feasible resource. For protection orders, the most effective approach may be to establish a group of volunteers who agree to cover a particular court docket for a preestablished time period.[85] If representation is limited to the protection order phase, the client must be informed of this arrangement and a referral system must be in place to ensure continuity of representation for any subsequent proceedings.

Volunteer attorneys certainly should be considered a primary resource for custody and divorce representation. Those who are willing to take on cases involving domestic abuse could be given some sort of special recognition. Calculation of any pro bono contribution could focus more on hours of service provided rather than on numbers of cases handled.

Volunteer attorneys should be urged to represent former clients in modification and enforcement of litigant's rights proceedings. This is a difficult task because attorneys may be reluctant to volunteer initially if they sense that they could be acquiring a particular client for life. If a per-case assessment is used to gauge the extent of the volunteer attorney's contribution, then the modification proceeding should be viewed as a separate case. It certainly makes more sense for an attorney who is already knowledgeable about a particular matter to follow through rather than to assign the case to another volunteer attorney who may need a considerable amount of time to become familiar with the case's specifics. A reminder that "your name could be next on the list" to handle a modification in an unfamiliar case might encourage the volunteer attorney to represent a former client in modification and enforcement proceedings.

C. Law Students

Another potential resource for representation of battered women would be clinical programs. Unfortunately, law school clinical programs may be operating under financial constraints similar to those experienced by legal services programs. In addition, this resource is obviously dependent on geographic proximity to a law school. Legal services programs are in the best position to forge relationships with law school students interested in working with battered women. Despite limitations, law students at clinic programs may be particularly well suited to represent clients at protection order hearings since they relish the opportunity to get courtroom experience.

Law school externship programs might place students in legal services offices for the specific purpose of representing battered women. Some law schools encourage or require students to perform pro bono work before graduating.[86] Service-learning courses might require students to perform community volunteer work.[87] Student groups such as the women's law caucus could have an interest in taking on a semester- or year-long project to assist battered women. Outright volunteers may come from the student population since paid clerking positions with law firms are diminishing. Training and adequate supervision are necessary for students to represent battered women effectively;

---

[85] Perhaps a larger law firm might be persuaded to sponsor a program to represent victims of domestic violence. Apparently this approach has been used in the Washington, D.C., area where several large law firms have developed pro bono programs to assist victims of domestic abuse. *Id.* at 1064.

[86] *See* Caroline Durham, *Law Schools Making a Difference: An Examination of Public Service Requirements*, 13 LAW & INEQ. J. 39 (1994).

[87] Mary Pat Treuthart, *"Service Learning" Brings Real World into Class*, LAW TCHR., Spring 1996, at 12.

however, the enthusiasm students bring to even the most mundane tasks is generally beneficial to clients.

D. Pro Se Representation

The protection order process was designed in most states to allow battered women to file for an order pro se.[88] This approach permits greater efficiency in obtaining ex parte orders. It is effective as well, provided battered women have assistance in completing the necessary paperwork.[89]

A scheme, statutory or otherwise, that encourages battered women to attend the protection order hearing pro se is decidedly more problematic. The hearing may present the first opportunity for the victim and her abuser to come into contact with each other since the most recent battering episode. Understandably, the battered woman may be petrified, not knowing what to expect from the abuser or the process. Al-though the presence of a lay advocate may be helpful, an attorney can provide support *and* legal expertise at this critical stage of the process.

Nevertheless, many, if not most, battered women are compelled to go through the protection order hearing without legal representation. At a minimum, greater focus should be placed on preparation and dissemination of educational materials, including pamphlets and videos that realistically explain the process.[90] Private and public interest family lawyers, along with battered women's advocates, can also informally monitor the process by asking clients who have secured protection orders whether they experienced any difficulties in the process.[91]

An increasing number of litigants are filing for divorce and custody actions without counsel.[92] Self-representation may be appropriate in simple or uncontested matrimonial cases. Domestic

---

[88] Hart, *supra* note 25, at 7.

[89] New Jersey and Florida offer the most extensive, statutorily mandated assistance by court staff. *Id.* at 9.

[90] While many battered women's programs supply such materials, much of the information reflects what should *ideally* occur in court. To the best of my knowledge, no videos portray judges curtailing women's speech, expressing incredulity at a victim's testimony, refusing to grant essential relief, issuing "in-house" restraining orders, or conducting group hearings as though the parties were errant schoolchildren called en masse into the principal's office. All of these—and worse—have happened in actual hearings. As a result of the gender-bias studies conducted nationwide, legitimate concerns about judicial handling of domestic violence cases are well documented. Karen Czapanskiy, *Domestic Violence, the Family, and the Lawyering Process: Lessons from Studies on Gender Bias in the Courts*, 28 FAM. L.J. 247, 249 (1993). Increased judicial education and the gender-bias provisions in the 1990 Code of Judicial Conduct may have helped alleviate some of the previously reported problems; however, a battered woman should be given information about requesting a continuance to obtain counsel, asking to be permitted to put her side of the story on the record, and appealing an unfavorable ruling. At the same time, injecting too much realism into the information given may discourage the battered woman from proceeding at all. The above examples of courtroom proceedings gone awry underscore the need for attorney assistance. Mediation supporters might suggest that the these examples serve to demonstrate that the mediation environment is more hospitable than the courtroom setting. However, bias and inappropriate conduct are much more difficult to detect in the privatized alternative dispute resolution setting, and mediators may be less accountable for their actions. *Id.* at 273.

[91] The tragic homicide of a battered woman who failed to obtain needed relief in the protection order process prompted the establishment of a more formal court watch project in Bergen County, New Jersey, modeled after a program in Cook County, Illinois. Memoli & Plotino, *supra* note 36, at 47, citing COOK COUNTY COURT WATCHERS, INC., HOW TO START A COURT WATCHING PROJECT (ii) (1984).

[92] In one study of divorce cases conducted in Maricopa County (Phoenix), Arizona, researchers found that in 1990 "approximately 90 percent of the cases involved at least one litigant who self-represented, while in 52 percent of the cases both parties self-represented." Bruce D. Sales et al., *Is Self-representation a Reasonable Alternative to Attorney Representation in Divorce Cases?*, 37 ST. LOUIS U. L.J. 553, 594 (1992).

abuse cases do not fall into the simple category, and determining at the outset whether *any* case will be uncontested may be nearly impossible. Therefore, self-representation by battered women in the divorce or custody process should not be considered a viable option. Postdispositional proceedings may allow for some form of self-initiation such as child support enforcement where an advocate may actually handle some aspects of the case. Attorney assistance is necessary in any subsequent proceedings that would require the battered woman, if unrepresented, to deal or negotiate directly with her abuser.

VII. Conclusion

Public recognition of the problem of domestic abuse has increased steadily in the past two decades. During this same period, greater attention has been focused on mediation as a means to resolve family law disputes. These two "reform" movements have converged in part due to miscategorization of domestic abuse under the general heading of family law. Domestic abuse, simply put, is violence that involves intimate partners. While acknowledging that traditional family law issues must be decided with respect to the victim and the abuser, it is critical to remain focused on the distinction, not on the apparent overlap, when choosing a suitable dispute resolution mechanism in cases involving domestic abuse. Attorney advocacy and attorney-assisted negotiation are the most appropriate ways to handle matters where one disputant has abused the other. A renewed commitment to attorney representation is needed by public interest lawyers and by the private bar in order to protect the interests of battered women and to send a clear message that domestic abuse will not be tolerated.

THOMPSON *v.* THOMPSON.

ERROR TO THE COURT OF APPEALS OF THE DISTRICT OF COLUMBIA.

No. 17.   Argued October 27, 1910.—Decided December 12, 1910.

At common law husband and wife were regarded as one, the legal existence of the latter during coverture being merged in that of the former.

Statutes passed in pursuance of a more liberal and general policy of emancipation of the wife from the husband's control differ in terms and each must be construed with a view to effectuate the legislative intent leading to its enactment.

In construing a statute the courts must have in mind the old law and the change intended to be effected by the passage of the new.

While by § 1155 and other sections of the Code of the District of Columbia the common law was changed by conferring additional rights on married women and the right to sue separately for redress of wrongs concerning the same, it was not the intention of Congress to revolutionize the law governing the relation of husband and wife between themselves.

Under the existing statutes, a wife cannot maintain an action in the District of Columbia against the husband to recover damages for an assault and battery by him upon her person.

While the wife may resort to the Chancery Court to protect her separate property rights, *quære*, and not decided, whether she alone may bring an action against the husband to protect such rights.

31 App. D. C. 557, affirmed.

THE facts, which involve the right of a wife to maintain an action in the District of Columbia against her husband to recover damages for an assault and battery, are stated in the opinion.

Mr. Wm. M. Lewin for plaintiff in error:

Prior to the enactment of the Code it was a tort for a man to assault his wife. The provisions of the Code remove a common-law obstacle to the remedy. *Stewart* v. *Railroad Co.*, 168 U. S. 445.

These provisions will be liberally construed, for it is the duty of every State to provide, in the administration of justice, for the redress of private wrongs; if there be a civil right there must be a legal remedy. *Railway Co.* v. *Humes*, 115 U. S. 512, 521; *Bank* v. *Owens*, 2 Pet. 527, 539. And protection against tort is as necessary as the enforcement of contract. *Wills* v. *Jones*, 13 App. D. C. 482, 497.

As redress cannot be obtained in equity, because of the essential character of the case, the rule is settled that the remedy must be by a suit at law. *Van Norden* v. *Morton*, 99 U. S. 378, 380. The reasoning of the New York case upon which the Court of Appeals relies has long since been repudiated. *Freethy* v. *Freethy*, 42 Barb. (N. Y.) 641; see *Bronson* v. *Bradey*, 28 App. D. C. 250, 262; *Stickney* v. *Stickney*, 131 U. S. 227, 237.

A statute will not be so construed that remote inferences withdraw a case from its general provisions which is clearly within its words and perfectly consistent with its intent. *Railroad Co.* v. *Church*, 19 Wall. 62, 65; *Bryan* v. *Kennett*, 113 U. S. 179, 196; *Market Co.* v. *Hoffman*, 101 U. S. 112, 115, 116.

As to the wife's general right to convey, see *Luhrs* v. *Hancock*, 181 U. S. 567, 571. Construction broadens with legislation and as to broadening rights of a married woman, see 16 Stat. 45; Rev. Stat. Dist. of Col., §§ 727, 729; *Seitz* v. *Mitchell*, 94 U. S. 580, 584.

By the Code not only are her earnings her own property absolutely, §§ 1151, 1154, but she is permitted to hold them as fully as if she were unmarried, and, § 1155, to sue for their recovery, security, or protection, but, § 1155, she is also empowered to sue for torts committed against her as fully and freely as if she were unmarried.

A change in phraseology creates a presumption of a change in intent, and no word of the change should be held insignificant. *Crawford* v. *Burke*, 195 U. S. 176, 190; *Market Co.* v. *Hoffman*, 101 U. S. 115, 116.

Even under the act of 1869 a wife could contract with her husband. *Sykes* v. *Chadwick*, 18 Wall. 141, 143, 148.

And now she may sue him, even in tort, for that construction will be followed which commends itself to the judgment of the court. *May* v. *May*, 9 Nebraska, 16, 25; *Rice* v. *Sally*, 176 Missouri, 107, 130, 131; *Covlam* v. *Doull*, 133 U. S. 216, 233.

The right to her earnings necessarily implies the right to maintain her capacity to earn. The right to sue anyone, the husband not excepted, for impairment of that capacity is incidental thereto. *Traer* v. *Clews*, 115 U. S. 528, 540; *Seybert* v. *Pittsburg*, 1 Wall. 272.

This would follow from the construction of § 1151 in *pari materia* with § 1155. *Tel. Co.* v. *Lipscomb*, 22 App. D. C. 104, 113, 114; *Asphalt Co.* v. *Mackey*, 15 App. D. C. 410, 417; *Stickney* v. *Stickney*, 131 U. S. 227, 237.

Her capacity to earn is her own, and for its impairment she may recover. Evidence of such impairment is admissible under the declaration in this case. She is therefore entitled to a trial upon the merits. *Railway Co.* v. *Humble*, 181 U. S. 57, 63; *Hamilton* v. *Railroad Co.*, 17 Montana, 334, 352; *Railway Co.* v. *Harris*, 122 U. S. 597, 608; *Harmon* v. *Railroad Co.*, 165 Massachusetts, 100, 104; *Pomerene* v. *White*, 70 Nebraska, 171, 176; *Railroad Co.* v. *Kremple*, 103 Ill. App. 1; *Brooks* v. *Schwerin*, 54 N. Y. 343, 349; *Wade* v. *Leroy*, 20 How. 34, 44; *Railroad Co.* v. *Dick*, 78 S. W. Rep. (Ky.) 914; *Samuels* v. *Railway Co.*, 124 California, 294; *Railroad Co.* v. *Hecht*, 115 Indiana, 443, 446.

The Court of Appeals bases its conclusion upon the proposition that the parties are one in law. The court had previously said that that was the feudal notion and not the Christian notion. *Carroll* v. *Reidy*, 5 App. D. C. 59, 62; and see also *Bronson* v. *Brady*, 28 App. D. C. 250, 263.

Mr. A. E. I. Leckie, Mr. Creed M. Fulton, Mr. Joseph W. Cox and *Mr. John A. Kratz*, submitted for defendants in error and cited: 21 Cyc. 1517, 1518; § 450, N. Y. Code of Civ. Pro.; § 3, N. Y. Stat. of 1862; *Alward v. Alward*, 2 N. Y. Supp. 42; *Smith v. Gorman*, 41 Maine, 405, 408; *Small v. Small*, 129 Pa. St. 366; *Larison v. Larison*, 9 Ill. App. 27, 31; *Jones v. Jones*, 19 Iowa, 236; *Greer v. Greer*, 24 Kansas, 101; *Manning v. Manning*, 79 N. Car. 293; Iowa Code, 1873, §§ 2204, 2211; *Peters v. Peters*, 42 Iowa, 182; *Heacock v. Heacock*, 108 Iowa, 540; *Decker v. Kedley*, 148 Fed. Rep. 681; *Main v. Main*, 46 Ill. App. 106; *Libbey v. Berry*, 74 Maine, 286; *Abbott v. Abbott*, 67 Maine, 304; *Freethy v. Freethy*, 42 Barb. (N. Y.) 641; *Abbe v. Abbe*, 22 App. Div. 483; *Strom v. Strom*, 98 Minnesota, 427.

MR. JUSTICE DAY delivered the opinion of the court.

This case presents a single question, which is involved in the construction of the statutes governing the District of Columbia. That question is, Under those statutes may a wife bring an action to recover damages for an assault and battery upon her person by the husband?

The declaration of the plaintiff is in the ordinary form, and in seven counts charges divers assaults upon her person by her husband, the defendant, for which the wife seeks to recover damages in the sum of $70,000. An issue of law being made by demurrer to the defendant's pleas, the Supreme Court of the District of Columbia held that such action would not lie under the statute. Upon writ of error to the Court of Appeals of the District of Columbia the judgment of the Supreme Court was affirmed. 31 App. D. C. 557.

At the common law the husband and wife were regarded as one. The legal existence of the wife during coverture was merged in that of the husband, and, generally speaking, the wife was incapable of making contracts, of acquiring property or disposing of the same without her husband's consent. They could not enter into contracts with each other, nor were they liable for torts committed by one against the other. In pursuance of a more liberal policy in favor of the wife, statutes have been passed in many of the States looking to the relief of a married woman from the disabilities imposed upon her as a femme covert by the common law. Under these laws she has been empowered to control and dispose of her own property free from the constraint of the husband, in many instances to carry on trade and business, and to deal with third persons as though she were a single woman. The wife has further been enabled by the passage of such statutes to sue for trespass upon her rights in property and to protect the security of her person against the wrongs and assaults of others.

It is unnecessary to review these statutes in detail. Their obvious purpose is, in some respects, to treat the wife as a femme sole, and to a large extent to alter the common law theory of the unity of husband and wife. These statutes, passed in pursuance of the general policy of emancipation of the wife from the husband's control, differ in terms and are to be construed with a view to effectuate the legislative purpose which led to their enactment.

It is insisted that the Code of the District of Columbia has gone so far in the direction of modifying the common law relation of husband and wife as to give to her an action against him for torts committed by him upon her person or property. The answer to this contention depends upon a construction of § 1155 of the District of Columbia Code, 31 Stat. 1189, 1374, March 3, 1901. That section provides:

"SEC. 1155. Power of Wife to Trade and Sue and be Sued.—Married women shall have power to engage in any business, and to contract, whether engaged in business or not, and to sue separately upon their contracts, and also to sue separately for the recovery, security, or protection of their property, and for torts committed against them, as fully and freely as if they were unmarried; contracts may also be made with them, and they may also be sued separately upon their contracts, whether made before or during marriage, and for wrongs independent of contract committed by them before or during their marriage, as fully as if they were unmarried, and upon judgments recovered against them execution may be issued as if they were unmarried; nor shall any husband be liable upon any contract made by his wife in her own name and upon her own responsibility, nor for any tort committed separately by her out of his presence without his participation or sanction: Provided, That no married woman shall have power to make any contract as surety or guarantor, or as accommodation drawer, acceptor, maker, or indorser."

In construing a statute the courts are to have in mind the old law and the change intended to be effected by the passage of the new. Reading this section, it is apparent that its purposes, among others, were to enable a married woman to engage in business and to make contracts free from the intervention or control of the husband, and to maintain actions separately for the recovery, security and protection of her property. At the common law, with certain exceptions not necessary to notice in this connection, the wife could not maintain an action at law except she be joined by her husband. *Barber* v. *Barber*, 21 How. 582, 589. For injuries suffered by the wife in her person or property, such as would give rise to a cause of action in favor of a femme sole, a suit could be instituted only in the joint name of herself and husband. 1 Cooley on Torts, 3d edition, 472, and cases cited in the note.

By this District of Columbia statute the common law was changed, and, in view of the additional rights conferred upon married women in § 1155 and other sections of the Code, she is given the right to sue *separately* for redress of wrongs concerning the same. That this was the purpose of the statute,.when attention is given to the very question under consideration, is apparent from the consideration of its terms. Married women are authorized to sue separately for "the recovery, security or protection of their property, and for torts committed against her as fully and freely as if she were unmarried." That is, the limitation upon her right of action imposed in the requirement of the common law that the husband should join her was removed by the statute, and she was permitted to recover separately for such torts, as freely as if she were still unmarried. The statute was not intended to give a right of action as against the husband, but to allow the wife, in her own name, to maintain actions of tort which at common law must be brought in the joint names of herself and husband.

This construction we think is obvious from a reading of the statute in the light of the purpose sought to be accomplished. It gives a reasonable effect to the terms used, and accomplishes, as we believe, the legislative intent, which is the primary object of all construction of statutes.

It is suggested that the liberal construction insisted for in behalf of the defendant in error in this case might well be given, in view of the legislative intent to provide remedies for grievous wrongs to the wife; and an instance is suggested in the wrong to a wife rendered unable to follow the avocation of a seamstress by a cruel assault which might destroy the use of hand or arm; and the justice is suggested of giving a remedy to an artist who might be maimed and suffer great pecuniary damages as the result of injuries inflicted by a brutal husband.

Apart from the consideration that the perpetration of such atrocious wrongs affords adequate grounds for relief under the statutes of divorce and alimony, this construction would at the same time open the doors of the courts to accusations of all sorts of one spouse against the other,

and bring into public notice complaints for assault, slander
and libel, and alleged injuries to property of the one or
the other, by husband against wife or wife against husband.
Whether the exercise of such jurisdiction would be pro-
motive of the public welfare and domestic harmony is at
least a debatable question. The possible evils of such legislation might well make the lawmaking power hesitate to
enact it. But these and kindred considerations are addressed to the legislative, not the judicial branch of the
Government. In cases like the present, interpretation of
the law is the only function of the courts.

An examination of this class of legislation will show that
it has gone much further in the direction of giving rights
to the wife in the management and control of her separate
property than it has in giving rights of action directly
against the husband. In no act called to our attention
has the right of the wife been carried to the extent of opening the courts to complaints of the character of the one
here involved.

It must be presumed that the legislators who enacted
this statute were familiar with the long-established policy
of the common law, and were not unmindful of the radical
changes in the policy of centuries which such legislation
as is here suggested would bring about. Conceding it to
be within the power of the legislature to make this altera-
tion in the law, if it saw fit to do so, nevertheless such
radical and far-reaching changes should only be wrought
by language so clear and plain as to be unmistakable evidence of the legislative intention. Had it been the legislative purpose not only to permit the wife to bring suits
free from her husband's participation and control, but
to bring actions against him also for injuries to person or
property as though they were strangers, thus emphasizing
and publishing differences which otherwise might not be
serious, it would have been easy to have expressed that
intent in terms of irresistible clearness.

We can but regard this case as another of many attempts which have failed, to obtain by construction radical and far-reaching changes in the policy of the common law not declared in the terms of the legislation under consideration.

Some of the cases of that character are: *Bandfield* v. *Bandfield,* 117 Michigan, 80; *Abbott* v. *Abbott,* 67 Maine, 304; *Schultz* v. *Schultz,* 89 N. Y. 644; *Freethy* v. *Freethy,* 42 Barbour, 641; *Peters* v. *Peters,* 42 Iowa, 182.

Nor is the wife left without remedy for such wrongs. She may resort to the criminal courts, which, it is to be presumed, will inflict punishment commensurate with the offense committed. She may sue for divorce or separation and for alimony. The court in protecting her rights and awarding relief in such cases may consider, and, so far as possible, redress her wrongs and protect her rights.

She may resort to the chancery court for the protection of her separate property rights. 21 How. 582, 590. Whether the wife alone may now bring actions against the husband to protect her separate property, such as are cognizable in a suit in equity when brought through the medium of a next friend (21 How., *supra*), is a question not made or decided in this case.

We do not believe it was the intention of Congress, in the enactment of the District of Columbia Code, to revolutionize the law governing the relation of husband and wife as between themselves. We think the construction we have given the statute is in harmony with its language and is the only one consistent with its purpose.

The judgment of the Court of Appeals of the District of Columbia will be

Affirmed.

MR. JUSTICE HARLAN, with whom concur MR. JUSTICE HOLMES and MR. JUSTICE HUGHES, dissenting.

This is an action by a wife against her husband to recover damages for assault and battery. The declaration

contains seven counts. The first, second and third charge
assault by the husband upon the wife on three several
days. The remaining counts charge assaults by him upon
her on different days named—she being at the time pregnant, as the husband then well knew.

The defendant filed two pleas—the first that he was
not guilty, the second that, at the time of the causes of
action mentioned, the plaintiff and defendant were husband and wife and living together as such.

The plaintiff demurred to the second plea, and the
demurrer was overruled. She stood by the demurrer, and
the action was dismissed.

The action is based upon §§ 1151 and 1155 of the Code
of the District, which are as follows:

"SEC. 1151. All the property, real, personal, and mixed,
belonging to a woman at the time of her marriage, and all
such property which she may acquire or receive after
her marriage from any person whomsoever, by purchase,
gift, grant, devise, bequest, descent, in the course of distribution, by her own skill, labor, or personal exertions,
or as proceeds of a judgment at law or decree in equity,
or in any other manner, shall be *her own property as absolutely as if she were unmarried*, and shall be protected
from the debts of the husband and shall not in any way
be liable for the payment thereof: *Provided*, That no
acquisition of property passing to the wife from the
husband after coverture shall be valid if the same has
been made or granted to her in prejudice of the rights
of his subsisting creditors.

"SEC. 1155. Married women shall have power to engage in *any* business, and to contract, whether engaged
in business or not, and to sue separately upon their contracts, and *also* to sue separately for the recovery, security
or protection of their property, *and* for torts committed
against them, *as fully and freely as if they were unmarried;*
contracts may also be made with them, and they may

also be sued separately upon their contracts, whether
made before or during marriage, and for wrongs independent of contract committed by them before or during
their marriage, as fully as if they were unmarried, and
upon judgments recovered against them execution may
be issued as if they were unmarried; nor shall any husband
be liable upon any contract made by his wife in her own
name and upon her own responsibility, nor for any tort
committed separately by her out of his presence without
his participation or sanction: *Provided,* That no married
woman shall have power to make any contract as surety
or as guarantor, or as accommodation drawer, acceptor,
maker or indorser."

The court below held that these provisions did not
authorize an action for *tort* committed by the husband
against the wife.

In my opinion these statutory provisions, properly construed, embrace such a case as the present one. If the
words used by Congress lead to such a result, and if, as
suggested, that result be undesirable on grounds of public policy, it is not within the functions of the court
to ward off the dangers feared or the evils threatened
simply by a judicial construction that will defeat the
plainly-expressed will of the legislative department. With
the mere policy, expediency or justice of legislation the
courts, in our system of government, have no rightful
concern. Their duty is only to declare what the law is,
not what, in their judgment, it ought to be—leaving the
responsibility for legislation where it exclusively belongs,
that is, with the legislative department, so long as it keeps
within constitutional limits. Now, there is not here, as I
think, any room whatever for mere construction—so explicit are the words of Congress. Let us follow the clauses
of the statute in their order. The statute enables the
married woman to take, as her own, property of any kind,
no matter how acquired by her, as well as the avails of

her skill, labor or personal exertions, "as absolutely *as if she were unmarried.*" It then confers upon married women the power to engage in any business, no matter what, and to enter into contracts, whether engaged in business or not, and to sue separately upon those contracts. If the statute stopped here, there would be ground for holding that it did not authorize this suit. But the statute goes much farther. It proceeds to authorize married women "also" to sue separately for the recovery, security or protection of their property; still more, they may sue, separately, "for *torts* committed against *them,* as fully and freely *as if they were unmarried.*" No discrimination is made, in either case, between the persons charged with committing the tort. No exception is made in reference to the husband, if he happens to be the party charged with transgressing the rights conferred upon the wife by the statute. In other words, Congress, by these statutory provisions, destroys the unity of the marriage association as it had previously existed. It makes a radical change in the relations of man and wife as those relations were at common law in this District. In respect of business and property the married woman is given absolute control; in respect of the recovery, security and protection of her property, she may sue, separately, in *tort,* as if she was unmarried; and in respect of herself, that is, of her person, she may sue, separately, as fully and freely, as if she were unmarried, "for *torts* committed *against her.*" So the statute expressly reads. But my brethren think that notwithstanding the destruction by the statute of the unity of the married relation, it could not have been intended to open the doors of the courts to accusations of all sorts by husband and wife against each other; and, therefore, they are moved to add, by construction, to the provision that married women may "sue separately . . . for torts committed against them as fully and freely as if they were unmarried" these words: "Provided, however, that the wife shall *not* be entitled, in any case, to sue her husband separately for a tort committed *against her person*." If the husband violently takes possession of his wife's property and withholds it from her she may, *under the statute*, sue him, separately, for its recovery. But such a civil action will be one in tort. If he injures or destroys her property she may, *under the statute*, sue him, separately, for damages. That action would also be one in tort. If these propositions are disputed, what becomes of the words in the statute to the effect that she may "sue separately for the recovery, security and protection" of her property? But if they are conceded—as I think they must be—then Congress, under the construction now placed by the court on the statute, is put in the anomalous position of allowing a married woman to sue her husband separately, in tort, for the recovery of her property, but denying her the right or privilege to sue him separately, in tort, for damages arising from his brutal assaults upon her person. I will not assume that Congress intended to bring about any such result. I cannot believe that it intended to permit the wife to sue the husband separately, in tort, for the recovery, including damages for the detention, of her property, and at the same time deny her the right to sue him, separately, for a tort committed against her person.

I repeat that with the policy, wisdom or justice of the legislation in question this court can have no rightful concern. It must take the law as it has been established by competent legislative authority. It cannot, in any legal sense, make law, but only declare what the law is, as established by competent authority.

My brethren feel constrained to say that the present case illustrates the attempt, often made, to effect radical changes in the common law by mere construction. On the contrary, the judgment just rendered will have, as I think, the effect to defeat the clearly expressed will of the legislature by a construction of its words that cannot be reconciled with their ordinary meaning.

I dissent from the opinion and judgment of the court, and am authorized to say that MR. JUSTICE HOLMES and MR. JUSTICE HUGHES concur in this dissent.

TORT REMEDIES FOR VICTIMS OF DOMESTIC ABUSE

Douglas D. Scherer*

More than three million American women suffer severe beatings from their husbands each year.[1] Verbal threats and harassment accompany physical harm or occur without physical harm. Evidence of intentionally inflicted harm is readily available in serious cases through police reports, medical records, witnesses, and admissions by perpetrators who genuinely believe that they are justified in their abusive conduct. If the victim brings a civil action for damages based upon conduct that resulted in a criminal conviction, the perpetrator may be precluded from contesting the underlying facts in the civil action.[2] This resolves the issues of causation and liability and leaves only damages in dispute in the civil action.

In light of this, why have trial lawyers not been more active in bringing civil actions for money damages based upon domestic violence? Why have they not furthered the public interest by combatting this morally repugnant conduct? The assumption of the author is that trial lawyers simply are unaware of the potential for significant monetary damages in these actions. They mistakenly assume that such actions are barred by the interspousal immunity doctrine, even though this doctrine does not bar the great majority of potential actions. They also do not realize that nearly all jurisdictions permit litigation of matrimonial torts independent of divorce proceedings. Actions for battery and assault are available in all American jurisdictions. The suitability of these actions in domestic abuse cases that involve physical injury or

---

* Professor of Law, Touro College, Jacob D. Fuchsberg Law Center. B.A. 1962, Case Western Reserve University; J.D. 1969, Suffolk University Law School; LL.M. 1978, Harvard Law School. The author is grateful for the assistance generously provided by Professor Eileen Kaufman of the Touro College, Jacob D. Fuchsberg Law Center, Professor Beverly Birns of the State University of New York at Stony Brook, and attorneys Karen Miller and Susan Menu.

1. HANDBOOK OF FAMILY VIOLENCE 3 (Vincent B. Van Hasselt et al. eds., 1988).

2. *See* RESTATEMENT (SECOND) OF JUDGMENTS § 85(2)(a) (1982) ("A judgment in favor of the prosecuting authority is preclusive in favor of a third person in a later civil action against the defendant in the criminal prosecution."); *see also* King v. Prudential Property & Casualty Ins. Co., 684 F. Supp. 347, 349 (D.N.H. 1988) (applying New Hampshire law); Zeidwig v. Ward, 548 So. 2d 209, 214-15 (Fla. 1989); Hanover Ins. Co. v. Hayward, 464 A.2d 156, 160 (Me. 1983); Knoblauch v. Kenyon, 415 N.W.2d 286, 292 (Mich. Ct. App. 1987); Hopps v. Utica Mut. Ins. Co., 506 A.2d 294, 297 (N.H. 1985).

threat of physical injury is readily apparent. Nearly all American jurisdictions recognize the tort of intentional infliction of emotional distress, an action that is especially appropriate for a continuing pattern
of domestic abuse.

This Article discusses the use of intentional tort actions by victims
of domestic abuse who seek monetary damages. Part I discusses the
phenomenon of domestic abuse, with emphasis on physical and emotional harm and factors that justify punitive and compensatory damage
awards. Part II discusses the torts of battery, assault, and intentional
infliction of emotional distress, and the appropriateness of these actions in domestic abuse cases. Part III discusses the interspousal immunity doctrine and demonstrates the limited extent to which the doctrine bars domestic abuse tort actions. Finally, Part IV discusses
judicial acceptance of tort actions in domestic abuse cases. An Appendix, which lists reported cases, follows this Article.

I. CHARACTERISTICS OF DOMESTIC ABUSE

For purposes of this Article domestic abuse is harm intentionally
inflicted by one adult upon another during the course of or after the
termination of a domestic relationship. The phrase domestic relationship includes marital relationships and nonmarital relationships with
varying degrees of intimacy or prior intimacy.[3] Although child abuse
often occurs in tandem with abuse directed at an adult, the Article's
focus is upon adult-to-adult conduct.[4] Abuse of elders also is excluded
from consideration.[5]

---

3. An excellent 1981 article provides statistical data concerning women who
sought assistance at La Casa De Las Madres, a shelter for victims of domestic abuse in
San Francisco. One hundred and forty-six women were residents at the shelter between
March and September of 1977. Thirty-six percent were victims of abuse by men to whom
they were *not* married (the categories were: married—53%, single—20%, separated—12%, cohabiting—12%, and divorced—4%). Constance F. Fain, *Conjugal Violence: Legal and Psychosociological Remedies*, 32 SYRACUSE L. REV. 497, 565 n.349 (1981)
(citing Marta S. Ashley, *Shelters: Short Term Needs, in* BATTERED WOMEN: ISSUES OF
PUBLIC POLICY 371, 380-81 (1978)).

4. Approximately one-third of the male spouse batterers in the sample used for a
1975-78 study also beat their children. LENORE E. WALKER, THE BATTERED WOMAN 27
(1979). A 1975 study of 100 battered wives demonstrated that 54% of the wife batterers
abused their children. Suzanne K. Steinmetz, *The Violent Family, in* VIOLENCE IN THE
HOME: INTERDISCIPLINARY PERSPECTIVES 51, 62 (Mary Lystad ed., 1986). An illustrative
case is Caron v. Caron, 577 A.2d 1178 (Me. 1990), in which a man subjected his wife and
stepson to physical and emotional abuse. The court upheld an award for punitive damages of $75,000 to the woman and $35,000 to her son. *Id.* at 1181.

5. Public focus on abusive conduct among family members began with child
abuse, expanded to spousal abuse, and now extends to physical and emotional abuse of
elderly persons by younger family members. Dr. Marion Goldstein, a specialist in geriat-

Domestic abuse typically occurs in a home setting, even if the perpetrator no longer resides in the home. However, tortious conduct may occur in other settings such as the victim's place of employment. Most domestic abuse involves male perpetrators and female victims. "[P]sychiatric disorders that predispose[] individuals to violence or submission to violence"[6] is a purported cause of domestic abuse. One commentator, Mary Russell, explained the phenomenon in a "family systems theory,"[7] which treats spousal abuse as "a mutual problem rather than the fault of one partner."[8] Experts sometimes utilize a "social learning theory,"[9] which "conceptualizes violence as a learned behavior rather than psychopathology or character deficit."[10] Feminist theory also regards hostility and aggression by males against females as a "socially learned phenomenon."[11]

Russell discussed sociological theories that focus on "cultural

---

ric psychiatry, concluded that an abuser of an elderly person most often is a caregiver who "is a middle-aged woman . . . whose caregiving and self-sacrificing have brought her to exhaustion." Marion Z. Goldstein, *Elder Neglect, Abuse, and Exploitation, in* FAMILY VIOLENCE: EMERGING ISSUES OF A NATIONAL CRISIS 99, 103 (Leah J. Dickstein & Carol C. Nadelson eds., 1989). Another author, in contrast, referred to "[s]everal studies [which] found that the abuser is more likely to be a male caretaker." ROBERT T. SIGLER, DOMESTIC VIOLENCE IN CONTEXT: AN ASSESSMENT OF COMMUNITY ATTITUDES 58 (1989).

6. Mary Russell, *Wife Assault Theory, Research and Treatment: A Literature Review*, 3 J. FAM. VIOLENCE 193, 194 (1988).

7. *Id.* at 195.

8. *Id.* An example of a perverse application of this mutual problem approach is Desmond v. Desmond, 509 N.Y.S.2d 979 (Fam. Ct. 1986). A woman fled to Virginia with her children to escape abuse from her former husband. The abuse consisted of "repeated acts of physical terror and forced sex over a number of years, commingled with emotional abuse (much of which was seen or heard by the children)," *id.* at 983, and "repeated acts of assault and battery upon her face, back, and buttocks with her husband's fists and feet," *id.* at 983-84. The abuser petitioned for custody on the theory that his former wife acted improperly when she removed the children from New York. The judge permitted the woman to retain custody and continue to live in Virginia, but directed "that both parents undergo psychological counseling separately" and that they provide counseling "by a licensed mental health professional" for the children. *Id.* at 984.

9. Russell, *supra* note 6, at 195.

10. *Id.* Russell discussed "modeling," noting that a "high incidence of batterers . . . witnessed family violence as children." *Id.* Focusing on victims she wrote: "Learned helplessness . . . has been used to explain assaulted women's seeming passivity in the face of repeated violence." *Id.* Research findings "support the now widely held belief that wife abuse is learned behavior transmitted from generation to generation. Apparently some women learn to accept violent behavior and some men learn to be abusive from many factors including early childhood experiences with abuse." Bonnie Y. Lewis, *Psychosocial Factors Related to Wife Abuse*, 2 J. FAM. VIOLENCE 1, 9 (1987).

11. James V.P. Check, *Hostility Toward Women: Some Theoretical Considerations, in* VIOLENCE IN INTIMATE RELATIONSHIPS 29, 34 (Gordon W. Russell ed., 1988). Check separately analyzed the interconnected phenomena of hostility toward women and the use of aggression to express hostility. *Id.*

norms that permit such behavior and social organization that fosters its occurrence."[12] Under this approach the family "is viewed as reinforcing social inequalities based on gender and economics that increase the likelihood of abuse."[13] Russell described a 1980 national survey which "revealed that 24% of males and 22% of females viewed minor violence against their spouses as normal."[14]

Similarly, Walker evaluated the effect of religious and social customs combined with inadequate protection provided to women by the criminal justice system.[15] She concluded that religious and social customs lead a man to believe that "his rights invariably supersede" those of his wife.[16] According to Walker, "America's social, legal, and religious institutions perpetuate the myth that a woman is to blame for being battered."[17]

Clinical studies have evaluated the causes of spousal abuse and the frequency of its occurrence.[18] Domestic abuse is not confined to lower economic and social levels. Professional and white collar workers perpetrate acts of domestic abuse along with laborers, blue collar workers,

---

12. Russell, *supra* note 6, at 198.

13. *Id.*

14. *Id.*

15. LENORE E. WALKER, TERRIFYING LOVE: WHY BATTERED WOMEN KILL AND HOW SOCIETY RESPONDS 236-38 (1989).

16. *Id.* at 236.

17. *Id.* at 235. Walker wrote:

In light of all this, it is no mystery that batterers believe they have the right to "discipline" a woman. Furthermore, they believe that others, including legal authorities, have no right to interfere. And many battered women have been socialized to believe not only that their men have the right to beat them but that, if they are beaten, they must somehow deserve to be beaten. Even though many women understand that battering is the man's problem, they feel guilty nevertheless; despite what they know, they feel that somehow, some way, they could have done something "better" to help him stop himself.

Id. at 237.

18. For an excellent and comprehensive discussion of causative factors of domestic abuse, see Fain, *supra* note 3, at 510-17; *see also* Evan Stark & Anne Flitcraft, *Violence Among Intimates—An Epidemiological Review*, in HANDBOOK OF FAMILY VIOLENCE, 293, 294 (Vincent B. Van Hassett et al. eds., 1988). The authors wrote:

Feminists argue that male violence against women and children is different than other forms of domestic violence because it converges with broader patterns of discrimination. This combination of assault and discrimination against women leads to entrapment and is manifested in a distinct clinical profile—"the battering syndrome"—which evokes a range of psychosocial problems alongside injury. However, the majority of nonfeminist clinicians and researchers approach various forms of domestic violence—including wife-husband assault and elder abuse—as symptomatic of distinct family dynamics, psychopathology, and stress.

Id.

and unemployed persons. Walker's studies confirmed this fact.

> Most battered women are from middle-class and higher-income homes
> . . . . Although some battered women are jobless, many more are
> highly competent workers and successful career women. They include
> doctors, lawyers, corporation executives, nurses, secretaries, full-time
> homemakers, and others. Battered women are found in all age groups,
> races, ethnic and religious groups, educational levels, and socioeco-
> nomic groups.[19]

Walker explained the myth that "[m]iddle-class women do not get
battered as frequently or as violently as do poorer women"[20] as follows:

> Most previously recorded statistics of battering have come from
> lower-class families. However, lower-class women are more likely to
> come in contact with community agencies and so their problems are
> more visible. Middle- and upper-class women do not want to make
> their batterings public. They fear social embarrassment and harming
> their husbands' careers. Many also believe the respect in which their
> husbands are held in the community will cast doubt upon the credibil-
> ity of their battering stories.[21]

A recent comparative study of women who are "at-risk" for wife
assault noted that women of higher socioeconomic status reported being verbally assaulted and subjected to "minor physical violence" as
often as women of lower socioeconomic status.[22] However, "lower socio-

---

19. WALKER, *supra* note 4, at 18-19.

20. *Id.* at 21.

21. *Id.* at 21-22. Fain discussed this myth as follows:

Contrary to the myth that battering occurs more frequently among lower
income groups, spouse abuse may occur in any home. Extensive research has
revealed that the practice of wife abuse permeates all racial, cultural, educational, and economic classes, and occurs in both urban and rural communities.
One reason for the myth that marital abuse is a problem that exists primarily
among low income groups is the failure of medical doctors, psychologists, ministers, marriage counselors, and family members to report incidents of abuse to
the police. Thus, cases involving middle income persons may not come to the
attention of the legal community and social agencies. Although statistics are
available from police records, they are inadequate because these offenses often
are unrecorded or are classified as assaults or homicides with no indication
that they are marital abuse cases. Furthermore, police records are inadequate
indicators of the magnitude of the problem. They contain little information
about the socioeconomic level of offenders and victims. Poor persons usually
resort to the police for protection, whereas middle and upper income persons
procure the services of medical doctors, ministers, marriage counselors, and
other professionals.
Fain, *supra* note 3, at 502-03 (footnote omitted).

22. Gerald T. Hotaling & David B. Sugarman, *A Risk Marker Analysis of Assaulted Wives*, 5 J. FAM. VIOLENCE 1, 10 (1990).

economic women were more likely to be severely assaulted."[23] Reports are unclear about whether higher socioeconomic status women experience fewer serious assaults than lower socioeconomic women or whether they simply report it less. Nonetheless, research clearly shows that verbal abuse, minor physical abuse, and severe physical assault occur at all socioeconomic levels.

Low self-esteem is a common characteristic of battered women. Commentators have suggested that this characteristic is caused by domestic abuse and is not a pre-existing characteristic that leads to a relationship with an abusive partner.[24] Other research indicates that "low self-esteem and negative self-images" are characteristics that are shared by abusers and their victims, regardless of how the victims perceived themselves prior to entering into the abusive relationships.[25]

Myths and stereotypes permeate uninformed discussion of domestic abuse. Walker debunked the "myth of the masochistic woman" who "experiences some pleasure, often akin to sexual pleasure, through being beaten by the man she loves."[26] Walker's studies refute the myths that "[b]atterers are violent in all their relationships"[27] and that "[b]atterers are unsuccessful and lack resources to cope with the world."[28] Walker also identified as a myth the commonly held belief that batterers cannot change.[29] At the same time she rejected the likelihood that a "[l]ong-standing battering relationship can change for the

---

23. *Id.*

24. *Id.* at 9.

25. LEWIS OKUN, WOMAN ABUSE: FACTS REPLACING MYTHS 66 (1986).

26. WALKER, *supra* note 4, at 20. Russell cited a 1985 survey which found that "25% of college males and 14% of college females agree that assaulted wives enjoyed being hit." Russell, *supra* note 6, at 199. Abandonment of abusive conduct by a batterer may require rejection of "an entrenched system of shared socio-cultural sexist attitudes and role expectations." Jerry L. Jennings, *Preventing Relapse Versus "Stopping" Domestic Violence: Do We Expect Too Much Too Soon from Battering Men?*, 5 J. FAM. VIOLENCE 43, 48 (1990) (emphasis omitted).

27. WALKER, *supra* note 4, at 24. Walker wrote: "Based on the women in my study, I estimate that only about 20 percent of battered women live with men who are violent not only to them but also to anyone else who gets in their way. . . . Most men who batter their wives are generally not violent in other aspects of their lives." *Id.*

28. *Id.* Walker referred to findings from a study in England that "physicians, service professionals, and police had the highest incidence of wife beating." *Id.* She also noted that "batterers in this sample would be indistinguishable from any other group of men in terms of capability." *Id.* at 25.

29. "If the psychosocial-learning theory of violent behavior is accurate, then batterers can be taught to relearn their aggressive responses. Assertion rather than aggression, negotiation rather than coercion, is the goal." *Id.* at 28. Change by batterers is not easy and extends beyond abandonment of abusive conduct to rejection of "an entrenched system of shared socio-cultural sexist attitudes and role expectations." Jennings, *supra* note 26, at 48 (emphasis omitted).

better."[30]

Walker's studies revealed that family violence follows "a definite battering cycle" consisting of "the tension building phase; the explosive or acute battering incident; and the calm, loving respite."[31] Women commonly are trapped by economic considerations,[32] responsibilities to children, an emotional need to maintain a relationship that hopefully will improve, a belief that escape is impossible, and a recognition that available remedies are controlled by others.[33] They often hold a realistic belief that an abuser will threaten or beat them if they attempt to escape.[34] Escape may be impossible simply because there is no place else to go.[35]

Peterson-Lewis and her associates identified the factors that lead a woman to terminate an abusive relationship.[36] They concluded that a female victim of spousal abuse tends to stay in an abusive relationship if she perceives that factors outside her personal relationship with the

---

30. WALKER, *supra* note 4, at 28. Walker's research led her to the following conclusion:

> Relationships that have been maintained by the man having power over the woman are stubbornly resistant to an equal power-sharing arrangement. Thus, even with the best help available, these relationships do not become battering free. At best, the violent assaults are reduced in frequency and severity. Unassisted, they simply escalate to homicidal and suicidal proportions. The best hope for such couples is to terminate the relationship. There is a better chance that with another partner they can reorder the power structure and as equals can live in a nonviolent relationship.

Id. at 29.

31. *Id.* at 55.

32. Straus, Gelles, and Steinmetz noted, "Women are bound by many economic and social constraints, and they often have no alternative to putting up with beatings by their husbands." MURRAY A. STRAUS ET AL., BEHIND CLOSED DOORS: VIOLENCE IN THE AMERICAN FAMILY 44 (1981).

33. Okun discussed why victims of abuse return to their abusers after temporary escape. OKUN, *supra* note 25, at 55-56.

34. Lenore E. Walker et al., *Beyond the Juror's Ken: Battered Women*, 7 VT. L. REV. 1, 10 (1982). Fear also prevents victims from seeking help. Okun wrote:

> The fear of retribution from the batterer for seeking help or for revealing the abusive situation is another major force obstructing the woman from seeking outside intervention. These fears are justified for the most part. Many of the most severe conjugal assaults and murders are in response to battered women's attempts to seek help or to leave.

OKUN, *supra* note 25, at 72 (footnote omitted).

35. Jill Winter, Executive Director of the Huntington Coalition for the Homeless in New York, provides emergency shelter and transitional living units for homeless women and their children. Most of these women are domestic violence victims. When asked why they stayed as long as they did with abusive partners, nearly all said that they had no place else to go. Interview with Jill Winter, in New York, N.Y., May 13, 1992.

36. Sonja Peterson-Lewis et al., *Attribution Processes in Repeatedly Abused Women, in* VIOLENCE IN INTIMATE RELATIONSHIPS 107 (Gordon W. Russell ed., 1988).

abuser have caused the abuse.[37] On the other hand, a victim tends to leave if she perceives that factors within the relationship, such as the "negative attitude [of the abuser] toward her," have caused the abuse.[38] A victim who "blame[s] the harmdoer," rather than outside causes, "is likely to believe that she might be harmed again in the future" and is likely to feel anger and a desire to retaliate against the harmdoer.[39]

Research revealed common patterns in battering relationships. These include exposure of male perpetrators to abuse when they were children,[40] forcible rape of abuse victims by male perpetrators,[41] and social isolation of the couple.[42] Negative characteristics of male batterers include a "tendency to minimize and deny their violent behavior."[43] They "often see the woman as the cause of their violence."[44] They "are usually very dependent on their partners as the sole source of love, support, intimacy, and problem solving."[45] Furthermore, they demonstrate "jealousy [and] extreme suspiciousness,"[46] have "low self-esteem,"[47] and "tend to be angry and depressed."[48] Pregnancy increases the frequency of physical violence, with the focus of attack shifting from the head and face to the abdomen.[49] Abusers appear to be more violent in nonmarital relationships than in marital relationships.[50] For those who have been married, a significant portion of violence occurs during separation or after divorce.[51] Sonkin, Martin, and Walker drew

---

37. *Id.*
38. *Id.* at 108.
39. *Id.* at 113.
40. DANIEL J. SONKIN ET AL., THE MALE BATTERER: A TREATMENT APPROACH 449 (1985).
41. *Id.* at 17.
42. *Id.* at 43.
43. *Id.* at 42.
44. *Id.*
45. *Id.* at 43.
46. *Id.*
47. *Id.* at 44.
48. *Id.* at 45. The personal characteristics of male batterers, including their emotional dependence on victims, jealousy, unpredictability, and placement of blame for abuse on victims, are discussed further in OKUN, *supra* note 25, at 66-70. Research by Hamberger and Hastings revealed a high incidence of personality disorders among male batterers. L. Kevin Hamberger & James E. Hastings, *Personality Correlates of Men Who Abuse Their Partners: A Cross-Validation Study*, 1 J. FAM. VIOLENCE 323 (1986). For a profile of men subject to criminal prosecutions for domestic abuse, see Albert R. Roberts, *Psychosocial Characteristics of Batterers: A Study of 234 Men Charged with Domestic Violence Offenses*, 2 J. FAM. VIOLENCE 81 (1987).
49. OKUN, *supra* note 25, at 50.
50. *Id.* at 43.
51. Okun cited national crime statistics demonstrating that "26% of perpetrators of spouse assaults . . . were either legally separated spouses or divorced ex-spouses." *Id.*

a parallel between men who rape and men who batter. Rapists "express power and anger"[52] in their conduct. Similarly, men who batter express dominance and anger against women and obtain sexual excitement engendered by seeing a victim suffer.[53]

During the last fifteen years there has been a dramatic increase in public focus on domestic abuse. All fifty states and the District of Columbia have enacted remedial legislation.[54] The preference for nonintervention has given way to varying degrees of responsiveness by police officers[55] and judges.[56] At the same time the criminal justice system in general, and criminal court judges in particular, lack enthusiasm for domestic violence cases.[57] As Judge June Galvin described:

> The cycle of filing and dismissing charges against a family member committing an act of domestic violence is too familiar to municipal court judges, prosecutors and police officers. In retrospect, the victim of domestic violence generally wanted only one result: to have the perpetrator leave the residence, which was more or less a legally enforced "cooling off" period.[58]

---

at 49.

52. SONKIN, *supra* note 40, at 18.

53. *Id.*

54. Patricia L. Micklow, *Domestic Abuse—The Pariah of the Legal System, in* HANDBOOK OF FAMILY VIOLENCE 407, 411 (Vincent B. Van Hasselt et al. eds., 1988) (citations omitted). By contrast, "no domestic abuse statutes were in effect in the United States prior to 1975." *Id.* at 407.

55. Mandatory arrest requirements have modified the conduct of police officers. *See* Sarah M. Buel, Recent Development, *Mandatory Arrest for Domestic Violence*, 11 HARV. WOMEN'S L.J. 213, 215 (1988) (discussing the deterrent effect of arrest compared with mediation or ordering the batterer to leave the premises for eight hours); *see also* Lisa G. Lerman, *A Model State Act: Remedies for Domestic Abuse*, 21 HARV. J. ON LEGIS. 61 (1984) (presenting a comprehensive model act on domestic abuse that emphasizes victim protection). For a comprehensive Canadian study of the factors that influence police responses to spousal abuse complaints in Quebec City, see F. Lavoie et al., *Police Attitudes in Assigning Responsibility for Wife Abuse*, 4 J. FAM. VIOLENCE 369 (1989). The authors reported that police react differently to situations in which a husband "resorts to physical violence" than to situations "involving threats." *Id.* at 385. In the latter situation police "adopt a neutral position toward the abused wife. In fact, they maintain this neutral position even if the threats are repeated." *Id.*

56. Protective orders are readily available and are enforced through misdemeanor prosecutions or contempt proceedings. Many cases discuss the use of protective orders. *See* Harper v. Harper, 537 So. 2d 282 (La. Ct. App. 1988); Hall v. Hall, 408 N.W.2d 626 (Minn. Ct. App. 1987); Kass v. Kass, 355 N.W.2d 335 (Minn. Ct. App. 1984); Marquette v. Marquette, 686 P.2d 990 (Okla. Ct. App. 1984); Melvin v. Melvin, 580 A.2d 811 (Pa. Super. Ct. 1990); Yankoskie v. Lenker, 526 A.2d 429 (Pa. Super. Ct. 1987); Eichenlaub v. Eichenlaub, 490 A.2d 918 (Pa. Super. Ct. 1985).

57. WALKER, *supra* note 15, at 241 ("It is a fact that *batterers often suffer no legal consequences whatsoever for their behavior.*").

58. June R. Galvin, *Ohio's New Civil Remedies for Victims of Domestic Violence*, 8 OHIO N.U. L. REV. 248, 248 (1981); *see* Micklow, *supra* note 54, at 407-08.

Historically, concern for family privacy has shielded domestic abuse from external control despite "the social costs of exploitation and violence in unregulated family relations."[59]

There have been improvements during recent years in the criminal law response to domestic violence,[60] and civil protective orders are in general use.[61] This reflects a growing recognition of the need for intervention and effective remedies.[62] The remedies that recently have become available are aimed, however, almost exclusively at violence prevention. They do not redress physical injury and emotional harm, even for long-suffering victims. The physical injuries suffered by female victims of domestic abuse can be shocking and permanent in their disabling impact. Emotional injury likewise is extreme and comparable to injury that supports large emotional pain and suffering awards in tort litigation. Okun noted that "[v]erbal abuse from the assailant is virtually always present in battering relationships. This includes threats of murder against 20% to 40% of victims. Threats of beatings are also common and appear to be a strictly male behavior."[63] Victims feel "worthlessness, humiliation, powerlessness, helplessness, self-blame, and shame."[64]

Fear, paralyzing terror, and anxiety seem to be the most ubiqui-

---

59. Franklin E. Zimring, *Legal Perspectives on Family Violence*, 75 CAL. L. REV. 521, 533-39 (1987).

60. Lowell F. Schechter, *Introduction: Coping with Family Violence Strategies and Tactics for the 1980's*, 6 VT. L. REV. 325, 328-30 (1981).

61. *See supra* note 56.

62. Further statistics demonstrate that domestic violence has reached epidemic proportions in this society . . . . A study conducted by the National Institute of Mental Health revealed that 1.8 million women are *severely assaulted* by their husbands each year, and child abuse is considered to occur in half of these homes. Additionally, marital abuse has been a contributing factor in one fourth of all divorces in this country . . . .

Female victims often suffer severe physical injuries, sometimes resulting in death. Many non-fatal injuries require emergency medical attention. The fact that these women were beaten by their spouses, however, often is omitted from their medical files. The results of one study of hospital emergency room services indicated that of the 1,400 women treated in a given period, almost half had injuries inflicted by their spouses. Hence, the incidence of physical abuse was approximately ten times more frequent than medical files indicated.

In brief, the conjugal violence problem in this country is a national tragedy that is approaching epidemic dimensions. Family violence has been described as a systematic form of torture, a physically or emotionally destructive act, and a generic disease transmitted from one generation to the next. Statistics and studies confirm the prevalence of the problem and the extent and nature of the injuries resulting therefrom.

Fain, *supra* note 3, at 504 (footnotes omitted).

63. OKUN, *supra* note 25, at 50 (footnotes omitted).

64. *Id.* at 71.

tous emotional experiences among battered women. Victims of woman abuse are often immobilized by their fear of the batterer and his violence. This fear can literally petrify the woman so that she is unable to resist an attack or retaliate. . . . The battered woman's fear includes anticipation of further conjugal attacks and is magnified by the unpredictable nature of the assaults . . . .

   . . . .

In terms of psychiatric symptomology, battered women resemble cases of agitated depression. As a result of prolonged stress, they often manifest psychosomatic symptoms such as backaches, headaches, and digestive problems. The battered woman may appear to have aged prematurely. Often there will be fatigue, restlessness, insomnia, or loss of appetite. Great amounts of anxiety, guilt, and depression or dysphoria are typical.[65]

Follingstad and others evaluated the interrelationship between physical and emotional abuse through interviews with 234 abused women. They identified different types of emotional abuse and analyzed the frequency of occurrence and impact on the victim.[66] They discussed the forms of emotional abuse identified by other researchers, including "ridicule, verbal harassment, and name-calling"[67]; "isolation (either social or financial)"[68]; "jealousy/possessiveness"[69]; "verbal threats of abuse, harm, or torture"[70]; "threats to divorce or abandon . . . or to have an affair"[71]; and "damage to or destruction of the personal property of the woman."[72] The Follingstad study revealed that 229 of the 234 abused women (98%) had "experienced at least one in-

---

65. *Id.* at 72-73 (footnotes omitted).

66. The authors, citing earlier works by Walker and Ferraro, wrote:

[S]ome battered women described psychological degradation, fear, and humiliation as constituting the most painful abuse they experienced. This type of emotional abuse is seen as having long-term debilitating effects on a woman's self-esteem, which in turn diminishes her ability to cope with the abuse. The effects of psychological abuse therefore are seen as contributing to the cycle of violence in which the battered woman is trapped.

Diane R. Follingstad et al., *The Role of Emotional Abuse in Physically Abusive Relationships*, 5 J. Fam. Violence 107, 108 (1990) (citations omitted).

Nadelson and Sauzier noted that victims of abuse frequently report "somatic symptoms . . . such as headaches, asthma, gastrointestinal symptoms, and chronic pain. More than half of these women had prior psychiatric histories. Depression was the most frequent diagnosis." Carol Nadelson & Maria Sauzier, *Intervention Programs for Individual Victims and Their Families, in* Violence in the Home: Interdisciplinary Perspective 153, 156 (Mary Lystad ed., 1986).

67. Follingstad, *supra* note 66, at 108.

68. *Id.* at 109.

69. *Id.*

70. *Id.*

71. *Id.*

72. *Id.*

cident of emotional abuse"[73] and that "[t]he vast majority of the
women (72%) reported experiencing four or more types of emotional
abuse."[74] The following table sets forth the number of women who experienced each of the six types of emotional abuse identified by Follingstad, and the percentage of women who regarded this type as being
the most damaging to them[75]:

Form of Abuse	Number Who Experienced This Form of Emotional Abuse	Percentage Who Regarded This as the Most Damaging Form of Emotional Abuse
Ridicule	211	45.7
Threats of Abuse	174	14.9
Jealousy	170	12.2
Restriction	184	10.4
Threats to Change Marriage	113	5.9
Damage to Property	137	4.5

Follingstad noted that the women "who felt emotional abuse was
worse than physical abuse experienced significantly more ridicule than
women who thought that physical abuse was worse."[76] Ridicule "attacks the women's sense of self-esteem and destroys their ability to feel
good about themselves."[77]

According to Sonkin, Martin, and Walker, "[p]erception of loss of
control, which is inherent in battering relationships, is one of the critical factors causing psychological injury to the battered woman."[78] This
combines with feelings of betrayal,[79] fear of another beating,[80] lack of
justice,[81] and "fear that men will make good their threats to take away
their children"[82] and creates a condition of "learned helplessness."[83] In
many women psychological injury "forms a constellation of symptoms

73. *Id.* at 113.
74. *Id.*
75. *Id.* Sonkin, Martin, and Walker discussed six subcategories of psychological violence, which consisted of explicit threats of violence, implicit threats of violence, extreme controlling type of behavior, pathological jealousy, mental degradation, and isolating behavior. SONKIN, *supra* note 40, at 38-39.
76. Follingstad, *supra* note 66, at 117.
77. *Id.*
78. SONKIN, *supra* note 40, at 152.
79. *Id.* at 153.
80. *Id.* at 154.
81. *Id.*
82. *Id.* at 155.
83. *Id.* at 158.

named Battered Women's Syndrome."[84] Symptoms "include anxiety,
fear, depression, shock, anger, compassion, guilt, humiliation, confused
thinking, intrusive memories, uncontrolled reexperiencing of traumatic
events, rigidity, lack of trust, suspiciousness, hypervigilence, and increased startle response to cues of possible violence."[85]

The physical and emotional harm suffered by victims of domestic
abuse is shocking. Yet, the existence of a domestic relationship, with or
without marriage, causes lawyers to ignore possible tort actions that
seek money damages. It is as if the lawyers assume that these victims
of tortious conduct are barred in some way from obtaining a remedy
that would be available if the parties had been strangers.

Lawyers who counsel victims of domestic abuse need to employ
sensitive interview techniques to determine the amount of physical and
emotional harm suffered and to assess the likelihood of success in possible tort actions. A lawyer usually encounters a domestic abuse victim
when she seeks a divorce or civil protective order and has taken steps
to gain control over her life. A tort action may be an important additional way for her to gain control.[86]

II. CIVIL ACTIONS FOR BATTERY, ASSAULT, AND INTENTIONAL INFLICTION OF EMOTIONAL DISTRESS

The tort actions most useful for domestic abuse cases are those for
battery, assault, and intentional infliction of emotional distress. The
Restatement (Second) of Torts discusses the common-law origins of

---

84. *Id.* at 160-61. Some courts have recognized battered women's syndrome as a
defense or sentencing factor in criminal cases in which a woman has killed or assaulted a
man who physically abused her. The Louisiana First Circuit Court of Appeals upheld a
jury's finding that a woman had suffered from battered woman's syndrome because of
continuing abuse by a boyfriend. *See* Laughlin v. Breaux, 515 So. 2d 480 (La. Ct. App.
1987). Similarly, the Supreme Judicial Court of Maine accepted the trial court's finding
that a victim of domestic abuse suffered from post-traumatic stress syndrome. Caron v.
Caron, 577 A.2d 1178 (Me. 1990).

In addition, women have sought relief through the executive branch. On December
22, 1990, Governor Richard Celeste of Ohio granted clemency to 25 women who had been
denied an opportunity to advance a battered woman syndrome defense and were convicted of murder or assault upon physically abusive men. Isabel Wilkerson, *Clemency
Granted to 25 Women Convicted for Assault or Murder*, N.Y. TIMES, Dec. 22, 1990, § 1,
at 1.

85. SONKIN, *supra* note 40, at 161.

86. Elba Lopez, a highly respected advocate for battered women, reported that
very few of the women that she assists would have the emotional capacity to bring a civil
action for damages. However, Ms. Lopez intervenes at a very early stage, when her physical presence, and that of police officers, is necessary to shield a woman from violence
that may be life-threatenting. Interview with Elba Lopez, in New York, N.Y. (Feb. 23,
1991).

the torts of battery and assault.[87] Sections 13 and 18 provide for liability for battery if an actor intends "to cause a harmful or offensive contact [with another] or an imminent apprehension of such a contact,"[88] and a harmful[89] or offensive[90] contact results. Section 21 provides for liability for assault if an actor "acts intending to cause a harmful or offensive contact [with another] or an imminent apprehension of such a contact, and . . . the other is thereby put in such imminent apprehension."[91]

A battery may be committed by indirect force, such as placing in motion a force or object that makes harmful or offensive contact with the victim, and contact may be "with anything so connected with the body as to be customarily regarded as part of the other's person and therefore as partaking of its inviolability."[92] The plaintiff need not be aware of the contact at the time the actor inflicted it,[93] and contact is deemed to be harmful if there is "any physical impairment of the condition of another's body, or physical pain or illness."[94] "[C]ontact is offensive if it offends a reasonable sense of personal dignity."[95]

Unlike battery, the tort of assault requires awareness.[96] The requisite apprehension occurs when the victim "believe[s] that the act may result in imminent contact unless prevented from so resulting by the [victim's] self-defensive action or by his flight or by the intervention of some outside force."[97] The victim must apprehend imminent contact, but need not be placed in fear.[98]

That one who is aware that she is about to suffer a battery will have suffered an assault demonstrates the complementary nature of the two torts. Damages caused by a battery consist of physical injury and emotional pain and suffering. Damages caused by an assault consist of "mental disturbance, including fright, humiliation and the like, as well as any physical illness which may result from them."[99] Punitive damages are available for both torts under appropriate

---

87. RESTATEMENT (SECOND) OF TORTS §§ 13 cmt. a, 18 cmt. a (1977); see W. PAGE KEETON ET AL., PROSSER AND KEETON ON THE LAW OF TORTS §§ 9-10, at 39-46 (5th ed. 1984 & Supp. 1988) [hereinafter PROSSER & KEETON].
88. RESTATEMENT (SECOND) OF TORTS § 13(a) (1977).
89. Id.
90. Id. § 18(1)(b).
91. Id. § 21(1)(a)-(b).
92. Id. § 18 cmt. c.
93. Id. cmt. d.
94. Id. § 15.
95. Id. § 19.
96. Id. § 22.
97. Id. § 24.
98. Id. cmt. b.
99. PROSSER & KEETON, supra note 87, § 10, at 43 (footnote omitted).

circumstances.[100]

Domestic abuse often involves physical harm that will support a battery action and awareness of imminent physical harm that will support an assault action. In addition, it typically involves purposeful infliction of severe emotional harm and presents a prototype setting for use of the tort action of intentional infliction of emotional distress. This tort received recognition as an actionable form of conduct in section 46 of the Restatement (Second) of Torts.[101] A comprehensive revision of this section appeared in the 1965 Restatement (Second) of Torts, which requires intentional or reckless conduct, extreme and outrageous in nature, that results in severe emotional distress.[102] Normally, a plaintiff must prove that the defendant had an intent to inflict severe emotional distress; however, courts occasionally rely on a recklessness standard rather than an actual intent standard. Although courts require proof of severe emotional distress, juries may consider the character of the defendant's conduct to determine whether the plaintiff suffered emotional harm.[103] Therefore, evidence of physical or

---

100. *Id.* § 9, at 40-41 (citations omitted); *id.* § 10, at 43.

101. A prior version of the Restatement, RESTATEMENT (SECOND) OF TORTS § 46 (1948), provided: "One who, without a privilege to do so, intentionally causes severe emotional distress to another is liable (a) for such emotional distress, and (b) for bodily harm resulting from it." *Id.* This provision reversed the earlier approach, RESTATEMENT OF TORTS § 46 (1934), which *denied* recovery for "conduct which is intended or which though not so intended is likely to cause only a mental or emotional disturbance to another." *Id.*

102. RESTATEMENT (SECOND) OF TORTS § 46(1) (1965). The section reads in its entirety as follows:

Section 46. Outrageous Conduct Causing Severe Emotional Distress

(1) One who by extreme and outrageous conduct intentionally or recklessly causes severe emotional distress to another is subject to liability for such emotional distress, and if bodily harm to the other results from it, for such bodily harm.

(2) Where such conduct is directed at a third person, the actor is subject to liability if he intentionally or recklessly causes severe emotional distress (a) to a member of such person's immediate family who is present at the time, whether or not such distress results in bodily harm, or (b) to any other person who is present at the time, if such distress results in bodily harm.

Id. § 46.

For a discussion of the early development of the tort action and the Restatement response, see Daniel Givelber, *The Right to Minimum Social Decency and the Limits of Evenhandedness: Intentional Infliction of Emotional Distress by Outrageous Conduct,* 82 COLUM. L. REV. 42 (1982); P.R. Handford, *Intentional Infliction of Mental Distress: Analysis of the Growth of a Tort,* 8 ANGLO-AM. L. REV. 1 (1979); Willard H. Pedrick, *Intentional Infliction: Should Section 46 Be Revised?,* 13 PEPP. L. REV. 1 (1985); William L. Prosser, *Intentional Infliction of Mental Suffering: A New Tort,* 37 MICH. L. REV. 874 (1939).

103. RESTATEMENT (SECOND) OF TORTS § 46 cmt. j (1977) ("Severe distress must be proved; but in many cases the extreme and outrageous character of the defendant's con-

objective manifestations of emotional distress is not technically required, but it has significant probative value.[104] Despite the arguably vague phrase "extreme and outrageous conduct," courts and juries in different jurisdictions have acted with substantial uniformity in distinguishing between actionable conduct and "mere insults, indignities, threats, annoyances, petty oppressions, or other trivialities."[105] Comment d to section 46 supports this position.

> Liability has been found only where the conduct has been so outrageous in character, and so extreme in degree, as to go beyond all possible bounds of decency, and to be regarded as atrocious, and utterly intolerable in a civilized community. Generally, the case is one in which the recitation of the facts to an average member of the community would arouse his resentment against the actor, and lead him to exclaim, "Outrageous!"[106]

Applying this extreme and outrageous conduct standard, courts and juries have uniformly denied recovery for emotional distress when the claim is based on wrongful discharge of an employee,[107] failure by an insurance company to pay claims,[108] false arrest by police officers,[109] and financial, commercial, and real estate disputes.[110] Recovery is

---

duct is in itself important evidence that the distress has existed.") Comment j further states, "The distress must be reasonable and justified under the circumstances, and there is no liability where the plaintiff has suffered exaggerated and unreasonable emotional distress, unless it results from a peculiar susceptibility to such distress of which the actor has knowledge." *Id.* (citing *id.* cmt. f).

104. *See id.* cmt. k.

105. *Id.* cmt. d.

106. *Id.*

107. *E.g.*, Webb v. HCA Health Servs. of Midwest, Inc., 780 S.W.2d 571 (Ark. 1989); Sterling v. Upjohn Healthcare Servs., Inc., 772 S.W.2d 329 (Ark. 1989); Harris v. Arkansas Book Co., 700 S.W.2d 41 (Ark. 1985); Northrup v. Farmland Indus., Inc., 372 N.W.2d 193 (Iowa 1985) (en banc); Staples v. Bangor Hydro-Elec. Co., 561 A.2d 499 (Me. 1989); Madani v. Kendall Ford, Inc., 818 P.2d 930 (Or. 1991) (en banc); Sheets v. Knight, 779 P.2d 1000 (Or. 1989); Gearhart v. Employment Div. of Dep't of Human Resources, 783 P.2d 536 (Or. Ct. App. 1989) (en banc), *review denied*, 792 P.2d 104 (Or. 1990); Sperber v. Galigher Ash Co., 747 P.2d 1025 (Utah 1987); Dicomes v. State, 782 P.2d 1002 (Wash. 1989) (en banc). *But see* Cagle v. Burns & Roe, Inc., 726 P.2d 434 (Wash. 1986) (en banc) (holding that wrongful termination in violation of public policy is compensable intentional tort).

108. *See* D'Ambrosio v. Pennsylvania Nat'l Mut. Casualty Ins. Co., 431 A.2d 966 (Pa. 1981); Demag v. American Ins. Cos., 508 A.2d 697 (Vt. 1986).

109. *E.g.*, State v. Bolt, 689 P.2d 519 (Ariz. 1984) (en banc); Nelson v. City of Las Vegas, 665 P.2d 1141 (Nev. 1983) (per curiam).

110. *E.g.*, McGrath v. Fahey, 533 N.E.2d 806 (Ill. 1988); Steckelberg v. Randolph, 448 N.W.2d 458 (Iowa 1989); Tomash v. John Deere Indus. Equip. Co., 399 N.W.2d 387 (Iowa 1987); Butler v. Poulin, 500 A.2d 257 (Me. 1985); Buckley v. Trenton Sav. Fund Soc'y, 544 A.2d 857 (N.J. 1988); Groseth Int'l, Inc. v. Tenneco, Inc., 440 N.W.2d 276 (S.D. 1989).

likely, however, in cases that involve sexual abuse of children,[111] sexual
assault against adults,[112] sexual harassment of employees,[113] threats
against a person's life,[114] serious interference with visitation or custody
rights of parents,[115] extreme forms of harassment by debt collectors,[116]
interference with funeral services,[117] forcible and illegal eviction of te-
nants,[118] transmission of genital herpes,[119] extortion,[120] repeated ob-
scene phone calls,[121] continuous and highly insulting or threatening behavior,[122] beatings,[123] and threats of future beatings.[124]

Subsection 46(2) of the Restatement addresses liability for harm
to one person because of conduct directed at another person.[125] This
derivative liability is limited by the requirement that the plaintiff must
actually suffer severe emotional distress. Most of the cases that have
permitted recovery derived from harm to a third party have involved
sexual abuse of a child[126] or sexual assault upon a spouse.[127] Finally,
comment e to section 46 notes that "[t]he extreme and outrageous
character of the conduct may arise from an abuse by the actor of a
position, or relation with the other, which gives him actual or apparent

---

111. Croft v. Wicker, 737 P.2d 789 (Alaska 1987) (finding that parents of abused
child stated claim for intentional infliction of emotional distress); Reagan v. Rider, 521
A.2d 1246 (Md. Ct. Spec. App. 1987) (affirming award for intentional infliction of emotional distress against stepfather for long-term sexual abuse of stepdaughter); Nancy P.
v. D'Amato, 517 N.E.2d 824 (Mass. 1988) (affirming judgment for intentional infliction of
emotional distress for abused child and denial of recovery on same claim by mother and
brother of child).

112. McCalla v. Ellis, 341 N.W.2d 525 (Mich. Ct. App. 1983); Mindt v. Shavers, 337
N.W.2d 97 (Neb. 1983).

113. Bowersox v. P.H. Glatfelter Co., 677 F. Supp. 307 (M.D. Pa. 1988); Chamberlin
v. 101 Realty, Inc., 626 F. Supp. 865 (D.N.H. 1985); Shaffer v. National Can Corp., 565 F.
Supp. 909 (E.D. Pa. 1983) (mem.); Ford v. Revlon, Inc., 734 P.2d 580 (Ariz. 1987) (en
banc); O'Connell v. Chasdi, 511 N.E.2d 349 (Mass. 1987); Hogan v. Forsyth Country
Club Co., 340 S.E.2d 116 (N.C. Ct. App.), review denied, 346 S.E.2d 140 (N.C.), and
review denied, 346 S.E.2d 141 (N.C. 1986).

114. E.g., Teamsters Local 959 v. Wells, 749 P.2d 349 (Alaska 1988).

115. E.g., Sheltra v. Smith, 392 A.2d 431 (Vt. 1978).

116. E.g., Turman v. Central Billing Bureau, Inc., 568 P.2d 1382 (Or. 1977).

117. E.g., Cates v. Taylor, 428 So. 2d 637 (Ala. 1983); Meyer v. Nottger, 241 N.W.2d
911 (Iowa 1976).

118. E.g., Brewer v. Erwin, 600 P.2d 398 (Or. 1979); Pentecost v. Harward, 699 P.2d
696 (Utah 1985); Birkenhead v. Coombs, 465 A.2d 244 (Vt. 1983).

119. B.N. v. K.K., 538 A.2d 1175 (Md. 1988).

120. E.g., Chandler v. Denton, 741 P.2d 855 (Okla. 1987).

121. E.g., Ruple v. Brooks, 352 N.W.2d 652 (S.D. 1984).

122. E.g., Ford v. Hutson, 276 S.E.2d 776 (S.C. 1981).

123. See, e.g., Chandler v. Denton, 741 P.2d 855 (Okla. 1987).

124. E.g., Dickens v. Puryear, 276 S.E.2d 325 (N.C. 1981).

125. For the text of subsection 46(2), see supra note 102.

126. See supra note 111.

127. See supra note 112.

authority over the other, or power to affect his interests."[128]

The approach of the 1965 revision has been remarkably infectious. As of 1964 the highest courts of eight states had recognized the tort.[129] From 1965 through 1991 the highest courts of an additional thirty-seven states and the District of Columbia recognized the tort.[130] The highest courts of two states, Michigan and Montana, have not formally recognized the tort, but have used section 46 principles in ways that suggest that the tort action will receive formal approval in the near future.[131] The Texas Supreme Court has neither expressly recognized nor rejected the tort. However, lower court opinions in Texas reflect a general recognition of the tort.[132] Mississippi has not formally recog-

---

128. RESTATEMENT (SECOND) OF TORTS § 46 cmt. e (1977).

129. Dunn v. Western Union Tel. Co., 59 S.E. 189 (Ga. Ct. App. 1907); State Rubbish Collectors Ass'n v. Siliznoff, 240 P.2d 282 (Cal. 1952) (en banc); Fraser v. Morrison, 39 Haw. 370 (1952); Savage v. Boies, 272 P.2d 349 (Ariz. 1954); Browning v. Slenderella Sys., 341 P.2d 859 (Wash. 1959) (en banc); Knierim v. Izzo, 174 N.E.2d 157 (Ill. 1961); Samms v. Eccles, 358 P.2d 344 (Utah 1961); Alsteen v. Gehl, 124 N.W.2d 312 (Wis. 1963).

130. Medlin v. Allied Inv. Co., 398 S.W.2d 270 (Tenn. 1966); Weicker v. Weicker, 237 N.E.2d 876 (N.Y. 1968) (per curiam); Pakos v. Clark, 453 P.2d 682 (Or. 1969); First Nat'l Bank v. Bragdon, 167 N.W.2d 381 (S.D. 1969); Rugg v. McCarty, 476 P.2d 753 (Colo. 1970) (en banc); George v. Jordan Marsh Co., 268 N.E.2d 915 (Mass. 1971); Amsden v. Grinnell Mut. Reinsurance Co., 203 N.W.2d 252 (Iowa 1972); Hiers v. Cohen, 329 A.2d 609 (Conn. Super. Ct. 1973); Womack v. Eldridge, 210 S.E.2d 145 (Va. 1974); Dawson v. Associates Fin. Servs. Co., 529 P.2d 104 (Kan. 1974); Paasch v. Brown, 227 N.W.2d 402 (Neb. 1975); Eakman v. Robb, 237 N.W.2d 423 (N.D. 1975); Dean v. Chapman, 556 P.2d 257 (Okla. 1976); Harris v. Jones, 380 A.2d 611 (Md. 1977); Sheltra v. Smith, 392 A.2d 431 (Vt. 1978); Vicnire v. Ford Motor Credit Co., 401 A.2d 148 (Me. 1979); Stanback v. Stanback, 254 S.E.2d 611 (N.C. 1979); Hatfield v. Max Rouse & Sons Northwest, 606 P.2d 944 (Idaho 1980); M.B.M. Co. v. Counce, 596 S.W.2d 681 (Ark. 1980); Waldon v. Covington, 415 A.2d 1070 (D.C. 1980); Peterson v. Sorlien, 299 N.W.2d 123 (Minn. 1980), cert. denied, 450 U.S. 1031 (1981); American Road Serv. Co. v. Inmon, 394 So. 2d 361 (Ala. 1980); Hume v. Bayer, 428 A.2d 966 (N.J. Super. Ct. Law Div. 1981); Star v. Rabello, 625 P.2d 90 (Nev. 1981); Ford v. Hutson, 276 S.E.2d 776 (S.C. 1981); Dominiquez v. Stone, 638 P.2d 423 (N.M. Ct. App. 1981); Harless v. First Nat'l Bank, 289 S.E.2d 692 (W. Va. 1982); Bass v. Nooney Co., 646 S.W.2d 765 (Mo. 1983); Yeager v. Local Union 20, 453 N.E.2d 666 (Ohio 1983); Craft v. Rice, 671 S.W.2d 247 (Ky. 1984); Champlin v. Washington Trust Co., 478 A.2d 985 (R.I. 1984); Metropolitan Life Ins. Co. v. McCarson, 467 So. 2d 277 (Fla. 1985); Richardson v. Fairbanks N. Star Borough, 705 P.2d 454 (Alaska 1985); Leithead v. American Colloid Co., 721 P.2d 1059 (Wyo. 1986); McKnight v. Voshell, 513 A.2d 1319 (Del. 1986) (text in Westlaw); Kazatsky v. King David Memorial Park, 527 A.2d 988 (Pa. 1987); Morancy v. Morancy, 593 A.2d 1158 (N.H. 1991); White v. Monsanto Co., 585 So. 2d 1205 (La. 1991).

131. See Fulghum v. United Parcel Serv., Inc., 378 N.W.2d 472 (Mich. 1985); Roberts v. Auto-Owners Ins. Co., 374 N.W.2d 905 (Mich. 1985); Day v. Montana Power Co., 789 P.2d 1224 (Mont. 1990).

132. See Holloway v. Browning, 626 S.W.2d 485 (Tex. 1981) (per curiam); Stevenson v. Koutzarov, 795 S.W.2d 313, 318 (Tex. Ct. App. 1990); Bushell v. Dean, 781 S.W.2d 652, 657-58 (Tex. Ct. App. 1989), rev'd on other grounds, 803 S.W.2d 711 (Tex. 1991).

nized the tort, but references to the tort in recent cases indicate that the tort is available.[133] Indiana is the only state that has expressly rejected the tort.[134]

Therefore, it appears that the tort is available in the District of Columbia and all states except Indiana. Among the jurisdictions in which the tort is available, all but five apply section 46 principles without modification. Delaware, Rhode Island, and Wisconsin modify one of the elements of section 46.[135] Georgia and Hawaii use approaches that are based upon early state decisions that recognize the tort.[136]

The four interchangeable names used to describe the tort are intentional infliction of emotional distress, intentional infliction of mental distress, tort of outrage, and tort of outrageous conduct. The name intentional infliction of emotional distress predominates, especially in recent cases. Regardless of the name used by the state courts, however, the elements of the tort remain the same.

III.   INTERSPOUSAL IMMUNITY DOCTRINE

The early common law barred tort actions between married persons in both England and the United States.[137] Originally, the immunity of one spouse from a tort action by the other was based upon "the common law doctrine of the legal identity of husband and wife."[138] A husband owned his wife's causes of action.[139] Therefore, if a husband

---

133. *See* Benjamin v. Hooper Elec. Supply Co., 568 So. 2d 1182 (Miss. 1990); Cumberland v. Cumberland, 564 So. 2d 839, 842-43 (Miss. 1990); City of Mound Bayou v. Johnson, 562 So. 2d 1212, 1217-18 (Miss. 1990); Life & Casualty Ins. Co. v. Bristow, 529 So. 2d 620, 624 (Miss. 1988) (en banc).

134. *See* Elza v. Liberty Loan Corp., 426 N.E.2d 1302 (Ind. 1981) (Hunter, J., dissenting).

135. *See* McNight v. Voshell, 513 A.2d 1319 (Del. 1986) (text in Westlaw) (holding that "bodily harm [must] result"); Curtis v. Department for Children & Their Families, 522 A.2d 203, 208 (R.I. 1987) (holding that "physical ills" must accompany the "mental anguish"); Alsteen v. Gehl, 124 N.W.2d 312, 318 (Wis. 1963) (requiring an "extreme disabling emotional response to the defendant's conduct").

136. In East River Savings Bank v. Steele, 311 S.E.2d 189 (Ga. Ct. App. 1983), *cert. denied*, 311 S.E.2d 189 (Ga. 1984), the court wrote that " 'defendant's actions [must be] so terrifying or insulting as naturally to humiliate, embarrass or frighten the plaintiff.' " *Id.* at 190-91 (quoting Georgia Power Co. v. Johnson, 274 S.E.2d 17, 18 (Ga. Ct. App. 1980)). Hawaii requires that the acts of defendants be "intentional" and "unreasonable" and that the defendants "should have recognized their conduct as likely to result in illness." Chedester v. Stecker, 643 P.2d 532, 535 (Haw. 1982). However, the word "unreasonable" has been interpreted as meaning the same thing as the § 46 word "outrageous." *See id.*

137. *See* RESTATEMENT (SECOND) OF TORTS § 895F cmt. a (1977).

138. *Id.* cmt. b.

139. *Id.*

committed a tort against his wife, he would actually own the cause of action against himself. Similarly, he was liable for torts committed by his wife. Therefore, if she committed a tort against him, he would be personally liable for the tort against himself. The immunity doctrine avoided these unreasonable results.[140]

Married women gained separate legal identity and rights to own property as a result of married women's acts, enacted in all jurisdictions beginning in the middle of the nineteenth century.[141] As a result the courts permitted actions between spouses that related to property interests. However, interspousal immunity from suit was retained for actions involving invasion of personal rights.[142] Courts justified the retention of the doctrine for negligence actions and intentional torts such as battery, assault, and intentional infliction of emotional distress on the questionable ground that "personal tort actions between husband and wife would disrupt and destroy the peace and harmony of the home."[143] Courts also were concerned about the "possibility of trivial actions for petty annoyances"[144] and collusion between spouses that would lead to "fictitious or fraudulent claims."[145]

Thirty-nine states and the District of Columbia have eliminated interspousal immunity.[146] Among the eleven states that have retained interspousal immunity, only four[147] bar all forms of action. Two states[148] have abolished interspousal immunity for negligence actions, but have retained it for intentional torts. Three states[149] have abolished interspousal immunity for negligence actions arising out of automobile accidents, but have retained it for other negligence actions and intentional torts. One state[150] has abolished interspousal immunity for intentional torts, but has retained it for negligence actions. Finally, one state[151] has abolished interspousal immunity for the tort of battery, but has retained it for other intentional torts and for negligence actions.

Thus, the interspousal immunity doctrine bars tort actions for battery, assault, and intentional infliction of emotional distress in domes-

---

140. *Id.*
141. *Id.* cmt. c.
142. *See id.*
143. *Id.* cmt. d.
144. *Id.*
145. *Id.*
146. *See infra* note 154.
147. These states are Delaware, Georgia, Hawaii, and Louisiana. *See id.*
148. These states are Alaska and Massachusetts. *See id.*
149. These states are Nevada, Rhode Island, and Vermont. *See id.*
150. Utah. *See id.*
151. Florida. *See id.*

tic abuse cases in nine states.[152] However, such actions generally are permissible in these states after dissolution of a marriage, based upon tortious conduct that occurred during the marriage.[153] Therefore, in these states tort actions by married victims of domestic abuse are barred during marriage, but the interspousal immunity doctrine has no effect upon civil actions for domestic abuse between unmarried or formerly married persons.[154]

---

152. Alaska, Delaware, Georgia, Hawaii, Louisiana, Massachusetts, Nevada, Rhode Island, and Vermont. *See id.* In Utah only battery actions are permitted.

153. *E.g.*, Duplechin v. Toce, 497 So. 2d 763 (La. Ct. App. 1986), *writ denied*, 499 So. 2d 86 (La. 1987); Nogueira v. Nogueira, 444 N.E.2d 940 (Mass. 1983). *Contra* Stanfield v. Stanfield, 371 S.E.2d 265 (Ga. Ct. App. 1988); Counts v. Counts, 266 S.E.2d 895 (Va. 1980).

154. The following is the current status of the interspousal immunity doctrine in the United States:

District of Columbia: Abolished. D.C. CODE ANN. § 30-201 (1988) (effective in 1976); *see* Turner v. Taylor, 471 A.2d 1010, 1012, n.2 (D.C. 1984). *Alabama*: Abolished. Johnson v. Johnson, 77 So. 335 (Ala. 1917); *see* Coleman v. Coleman, 566 So. 2d 482 (Ala. 1990) (per curiam). *Alaska*: Abolished with respect to negligence actions. Cramer v. Cramer, 379 P.2d 95 (Alaska 1963). *Arizona*: Abolished. Fernandez v. Romo, 646 P.2d 878, 883 (Ariz. 1982) (en banc). *Arkansas*: Abolished. Leach v. Leach, 300 S.W.2d 15 (Ark. 1957). *California*: Abolished with respect to negligence actions, Klein v. Klein, 376 P.2d 70 (Cal. 1962) (en banc), and with respect to intentional torts, Self v. Self, 376 P.2d 65 (Cal. 1962) (en banc).

Colorado: Abolished with respect to negligence actions, Rains v. Rains, 46 P.2d 740, 743 (Colo. 1935), and with respect to intentional torts, Simmons v. Simmons, 773 P.2d 602, 603-04 (Colo. Ct. App. 1988), *cert. denied*, 773 P.2d 602 (Colo. 1989). *Connecticut*: Abolished with respect to intentional torts, Brown v. Brown, 89 A. 889 (Conn. 1914), and with respect to negligence actions, Bushnell v. Bushnell, 131 A. 432, 433 (Conn. 1925). *Delaware*: Reaffirmed. Alfree v. Alfree, 410 A.2d 161 (Del. 1979) (per curiam), *appeal dismissed*, 446 U.S. 931 (1980). *Florida*: Abolished with respect to battery. FLA. STAT. ANN. ch. 741.235 (Harrison Supp. 1989). Retained for other torts. *See* Sturiano v. Brooks, 523 So. 2d 1126, 1128 (Fla. 1988) (citing Snowten v. United States Fidelity & Guar. Co., 475 So. 2d 1211 (Fla. 1985)); Raisen v. Raisen, 379 So. 2d 352 (Fla. 1979), *cert. denied*, 449 U.S. 886 (1980). *Georgia*: Retained generally. *See* Robeson v. International Indem. Co., 282 S.E.2d 896, 898 (Ga. 1981).

Hawaii: Retained. HAW. REV. STAT. ANN. § 572-28 (Michie 1988); *see* Campo v. Taboada, 720 P.2d 181 (Haw. 1986) (citing former code section); Peters v. Peters, 634 P.2d 586 (Haw. 1981) (upholding statute's constitutionality). *Idaho*: Abolished. Lorang v. Hays, 209 P.2d 733, 737 (Idaho 1949) (community property case); *see* Rogers v. Yellowstone Park Co., 539 P.2d 566, 569 (Idaho 1975). *Illinois*: Abolished. ILL. ANN. STAT. ch. 40, para. 1001 (Smith-Hurd Supp. 1991) (effective 1986). *Indiana*: Abolished. Brooks v. Robinson, 284 N.E.2d 794, 798 (Ind. 1972). *Iowa*: Abolished. Shook v. Crabb, 281 N.W.2d 616 (Iowa 1979) (en banc); *see* McIntosh v. Barr, 397 N.W.2d 516, 517 (Iowa 1986).

Kansas: Abolished. Flagg v. Loy, 734 P.2d 1183 (Kan. 1987). *Kentucky*: Abolished. Brown v. Gosser, 262 S.W.2d 480 (Ky. 1953). *Louisiana*: Retained. LA. REV. STAT. ANN. § 9:291 (West 1991). *Maine*: Abolished. MacDonald v. MacDonald, 412 A.2d 71 (Me. 1980). *Maryland*: Abolished with respect to negligence actions, Boblitz v. Boblitz, 462 A.2d 506, 515 (Md. Ct. App. 1983), and with respect to "outrageous intentional torts," Lusby v. Lusby, 390 A.2d 77, 88 (Md. Ct. App. 1978). The dissenting opinion in Walther

IV. JUDICIAL ACCEPTANCE OF TORT ACTIONS IN DOMESTIC ABUSE CASES

Civil actions for battery, assault, and intentional infliction of emo-

---

v. Allstate Insurance Co., 575 A.2d 339 (Md. Ct. Spec. App. 1989), *cert. denied*, 580 A.2d 219 (Md. 1990), referred to interspousal immunity as "fully abrogated." *Id.* at 344 n.2 (Bell, J., dissenting).

Massachusetts: Abolished for motor vehicle accidents. Lewis v. Lewis, 351 N.E.2d 526 (Mass. 1976). This abrogation was applied retroactively in Pevoski v. Pevoski, 358 N.E.2d 416, 418 (Mass. 1976), and was extended to other negligence actions in Brown v. Brown, 409 N.E.2d 717, 719 (Mass. 1980). *Michigan*: Abolished. Hosko v. Hosko, 187 N.W.2d 236 (Mich. 1971) (per curiam). *Minnesota*: Abolished. Beaudette v. Frana, 173 N.W.2d 416 (Minn. 1969). *Mississippi*: Abolished. Burns v. Burns, 518 So. 2d 1205, 1211 (Miss. 1988) (en banc); *see* Cain v. McKinnon, 552 So. 2d 91, 93 (Miss. 1989) (stating that the *Burns* rule is applied prospectively). *Missouri*: Abolished with respect to intentional torts, Townsend v. Townsend, 708 S.W.2d 646 (Mo. 1986) (en banc), and with respect to negligence actions, S.A.V. v. K.G.V., 708 S.W.2d 651 (Mo. 1986) (en banc).

Montana: Abolished. Miller v. Fallon County, 721 P.2d 342, 345 (Mont. 1986); *see* Noone v. Fink, 721 P.2d 1275, 1276 (Mont. 1986). *Nebraska*: Abolished. Imig v. March, 279 N.W.2d 382 (Neb. 1979). *Nevada*: Abolished only in motor vehicle accident tort claims. Rupert v. Stienne, 528 P.2d 1013, 1017 (Nev. 1974). *New Hampshire*: Abolished. Gilman v. Gilman, 95 A. 657 (N.H. 1915). *New Jersey*: Abolished. Merenoff v. Merenoff, 388 A.2d 951, 962 (N.J. 1978); *see* Tevis v. Tevis, 400 A.2d 1189 (N.J. 1979).

New Mexico: Abolished with respect to negligence actions, Maestas v. Overton, 531 P.2d 947 (N.M. 1975), and with respect to intentional torts, Flores v. Flores, 506 P.2d 345, 346 (N.M. Ct. App.), *cert. denied*, 506 P.2d 336 (N.M. 1973). *New York*: Abolished. *See* N.Y. GEN. OBLIG. LAW § 3-313.2 (McKinney 1989).

North Carolina: Abolished. N.C. GEN. STAT. § 52-5 (1991). *North Dakota*: Abolished. Fitzmaurice v. Fitzmaurice, 242 N.W. 526 (N.D. 1932). *Ohio*: Abolished. Shearer v. Shearer, 480 N.E.2d 388, 394 (Ohio 1985).

Oklahoma: Abolished. Courtney v. Courtney, 87 P.2d 660 (Okla. 1938); *see* White v. White, 618 P.2d 921, 924 (Okla. 1980); Fiedeer v. Fiedeer, 140 P. 1022 (Okla. 1914). *Oregon*: Abolished with respect to negligence actions, Heino v. Harper, 759 P.2d 253 (Or. 1988), as applied retroactively, Antonnaci v. Davis, 816 P.2d 1202 (Or. Ct. App. 1991), and with respect to intentional torts, Apitz v. Dames, 287 P.2d 585 (Or. 1955). *Pennsylvania*: Abolished. Hack v. Hack, 433 A.2d 859 (Pa. 1981). *But see* Dercoli v. Pennsylvania Nat'l Mut. Ins. Co., 554 A.2d 906, 907 (Pa. 1989) (suggesting that *Hack* is limited to negligence actions). *Rhode Island*: Abolished only with respect to motor vehicle accident tort claims. Digby v. Digby, 388 A.2d 1, 4 (R.I. 1978); *see* Asplin v. Amica Mut. Ins. Co., 394 A.2d 1353, 1355 (R.I. 1978) (holding that defense of interspousal immunity not available if one of spouses has died). *South Carolina*: Abolished with respect to negligence actions, Pardue v. Pardue, 166 S.E. 101 (1932), and with respect to intentional torts, Prosser v. Prosser, 102 S.E. 787 (S.C. 1920).

South Dakota: Abolished. Pickering v. Pickering, 434 N.W.2d 758, 763 (S.D. 1989) (citing Aus v. Carper, 151 N.W.2d 611 (S.D. 1967); Scotvold v. Scotvold, 298 N.W. 266 (S.D. 1941)). *Tennessee*: Abolished. Davis v. Davis, 657 S.W.2d 753 (Tenn. 1983). *Texas*: Abolished. Price v. Price, 732 S.W.2d 316, 319 (Tex. 1987). *Utah*: Abolished with respect to intentional torts. Stoker v. Stoker, 616 P.2d 590 (Utah 1980); *see also* Noble v. Noble, 761 P.2d 1369, 1375 n.7 (Utah 1988) (reaffirming that *Stoker* did not address negligence actions). *Vermont*: Abolished only with respect to motor vehicle accident tort claims.

tional distress are effective, victim-controlled means for obtaining remedy and discouraging future abusive conduct, especially if there is no existing marital relationship. Research for this Article revealed, however, an astonishing underutilization of these civil causes of action. Among approximately 2600 reported state cases of battery, assault, or both, from 1981 through 1990,[155] only fifty-three involved adult parties in domestic relationships.[156] Similarly, during the same time frame, only four reported federal cases involved a claim or counterclaim between adult parties in a domestic relationship.[157] From 1958 through 1990 slightly more than 6000 intentional infliction of emotional distress cases were reported from all state and federal courts.[158] Evaluation of these cases revealed a total of eighteen[159] in which courts have applied the tort action to a domestic abuse fact pattern. The infrequent use of tort actions reflects surprising reluctance by lawyers to use civil actions for damages in domestic abuse cases, even though the judicial response to such cases has been overwhelmingly favorable.[160]

Richard v. Richard, 300 A.2d 637, 641 (Vt. 1973).

Virginia: Abolished. *See* VA. CODE ANN. § 8.01-220.1 (Michie 1984) (effective July 1, 1981). *Washington*: Abolished. Freehe v. Freehe, 500 P.2d 771 (Wash. 1972) (en banc), *overruled on other grounds by* Brown v. Brown 675 P.2d 1207 (Wash. 1984). *West Virginia*: Abolished. Coffindaffer v. Coffindaffer, 244 S.E.2d 338, 343-44 (W. Va. 1978). *Wisconsin*: Abolished. *See* WIS. STAT. ANN. § 766.075 (West 1981) (effective in 1947). *Wyoming*: Abolished. Tader v. Tader, 737 P.2d 1065 (Wyo. 1987).

155. These results were obtained from the West Publishing Company's Westlaw computer-assisted research service.

156. *See infra* Appendix.

157. These four cases are listed under "Federal Courts" in the Appendix to this Article. The scarcity of domestic abuse cases in federal courts should not be surprising. In such cases federal court jurisdiction almost certainly would be based upon diversity jurisdiction under 28 U.S.C. § 1332.

158. The terms "intentional infliction of emotional distress," "intentional infliction of mental distress," "tort of outrage," and "tort of outrageous conduct" were used for the computer-assisted search that created this result.

159. *See* Lewis v. Lennox, 567 So. 2d 264 (Ala. 1990); Simmons v. Simmons, 773 P.2d 602 (Colo. Ct. App. 1988), *cert. denied*, 773 P.2d 602 (Colo. 1989); Kukla v. Kukla, 540 N.E.2d 510 (Ill. App. Ct. 1989); Whittington v. Whittington, 766 S.W.2d 73 (Ky. Ct. App. 1989); Caron v. Caron, 577 A.2d 1178 (Me. 1990); McCoy v. Cooke, 419 N.W.2d 44 (Mich. Ct. App. 1988); Hudson v. DeLonjay, 732 S.W.2d 922 (Mo. Ct. App. 1987); Hassing v. Wortman, 333 N.W.2d 765 (Neb. 1983); Murphy v. Murphy, 486 N.Y.S.2d 457 (App. Div. 1985); Baron v. Jeffer, 469 N.Y.S.2d 815 (App. Div. 1983) (mem.); Halio v. Lurie, 222 N.Y.S.2d 759 (App. Div. 1961); Floyd v. Dodson, 692 P.2d 77 (Okla. Ct. App. 1984); Twyman v. Twyman, 790 S.W.2d 819 (Tex. Ct. App. 1990); Chiles v. Chiles, 779 S.W.2d 127 (Tex. Ct. App. 1989); Noble v. Noble, 761 P.2d 1369 (Utah 1988); Criss v. Criss, 356 S.E.2d 620 (W. Va. 1987); Slawek v. Stroh, 215 N.W.2d 9 (Wis. 1974); Stuart v. Stuart, 410 N.W.2d 632 (Wis. Ct. App. 1987), *affirmed*, 421 N.W.2d 505 (Wis. 1988). These cases are discussed in more detail in the Appendix to this Article.

160. California case law from 1981 through 1990 demonstrates the underutilization of tort actions in domestic abuse cases. During this ten-year period California courts

---

A complication arises if a tort action relates to domestic abuse among married persons, especially if there is a pending matrimonial action. New York apparently limits availability of the tort of intentional infliction of emotional distress, but not other torts, in domestic abuse cases involving married persons. In the 1968 case of *Weicker v. Weicker*[161] the New York Court of Appeals rejected an intentional infliction of emotional distress claim by a woman who sought a declaratory judgment that the Mexican divorce obtained by her husband, Senator Lowell Weicker, was invalid and sought an injunction prohibiting him and his new wife from holding themselves out in public as husband and wife. The court stated:

> Assuming that New York law now permits "recovery for the intentional infliction of mental distress without proof of the breach of any duty other than the duty to refrain from inflicting it" strong policy considerations militate against judicially applying these recent developments in this area of the law to the factual context of a dispute arising out of matrimonial differences.[162]

The Appellate Division of the New York Supreme Court applied the *Weicker* holding in an assault and intentional infliction of emotional distress case that involved live-in lovers.[163] The court dismissed the assault claim because the one-year statute of limitations had expired. The court also dismissed the intentional infliction of emotional distress claim because "it would be contrary to public policy to recognize the existence of this type of tort in the context of disputes, as here, arising out of the differences which occur between persons who, although not married, have been living together as husband and wife."[164]

---

heard one battery and assault case involving domestic abuse between adults. *See* Alderson v. Alderson, 225 Cal. Rptr. 610 (Ct. App.), *review denied*, 225 Cal. Rptr. 610 (1986). During the same period the courts heard six sexual assault cases that related to child sexual abuse by a father, stepfather, foster father, or step-grandfather. *In re* Venus B., 272 Cal. Rptr. 115 (Ct. App. 1990) (stepfather); Evans v. Eckelman, 265 Cal. Rptr. 605 (Ct. App. 1990) (foster father); Mary D. v. John D., 264 Cal. Rptr. 633 (Ct. App. 1989) (father), *review granted*, 788 P.2d 1155 (Cal.), *and review dismissed*, 800 P.2d 858 (Cal. 1990); Colleen L. v. Howard M., 257 Cal. Rptr. 263 (Ct. App. 1989) (stepfather); Pease v. Pease, 246 Cal. Rptr. 762 (Ct. App. 1988) (grandfather); DeRose v. Carswell, 242 Cal. Rptr. 368 (Ct. App. 1987) (step-grandfather), *review denied*, 242 Cal. Rptr. 368 (Cal. 1988). Because spousal abuse or abuse among adults in a domestic relationship occurs more frequently than sexual abuse of children by family members, the scarcity of spousal abuse cases compared with child sexual abuse cases illustrates the underutilization of torts actions in spousal abuse cases.

161. 237 N.E.2d 876 (N.Y. 1968) (per curiam).
162. *Id.* at 876-77 (citations omitted).
163. Baron v. Jeffer, 469 N.Y.S.2d 815 (App. Div. 1983).
164. *Id.* at 817. In Eller v. Eller, 524 N.Y.S.2d 93 (App. Div. 1988) (mem.), the Ap-

New Jersey permits tort actions based upon domestic abuse among married persons, but requires joinder of tort claims in pending divorce actions. In *Tevis v. Tevis*[165] the New Jersey Supreme Court concluded in dicta that a woman who allegedly had suffered a serious beating by her former husband should have raised any tort claim she had in her divorce proceedings. Because the tort action and its potential for monetary damages were relevant to the divorce proceeding, the claim "should, under the 'single controversy' doctrine, have been presented in conjunction with [the divorce action] as part of the overall dispute between the parties in order to lay at rest all their legal differences in one proceeding and avoid the prolongation and fractionalization of litigation."[166]

By contrast, a more recent decision by a New Jersey lower court in *Brown v. Brown*[167] concluded that the entire controversy doctrine did not bar a wife's tort action against her husband for a battery that occurred during the pendency of their divorce action. The court stated that although joinder would have been required if the tort had oc-

---

pellate Division of the New York Supreme Court relied upon Weicker in dismissing the former wife's counterclaim for intentional infliction of emotional distress in an action by the former husband against her for absconding with the children, of whom the husband had custody. The court stated, "Strong policy considerations have been held to militate against allowing recovery for the intentional infliction of emotional distress in matters arising out of the interpersonal relationships in a matrimonial context." *Id.* at 94. By contrast, the court in Murphy v. Murphy, 486 N.Y.S.2d 457 (App. Div. 1985), awarded damages in the amount of $45,000 to a woman for intentional infliction of emotional distress by a man with whom she had lived. The court referred to the defendant's "threats, use of force, assaults upon and general abusive conduct toward plaintiff," *id.* at 458-59, and his "deliberate and malicious campaign of harassment," *id.* at 459. The court allowed the claim because the acts of the defendant that caused the plaintiff's emotional distress occurred after the termination of the live-in relationship. The approach in *Murphy* is consistent with the two earliest lower court cases that recognized the tort of intentional infliction of emotional distress in New York. In Mitran v. Williamson, 197 N.Y.S.2d 689 (Sup. Ct. 1960), the defendant solicited illicit sex with the plaintiff and sent photos of his private parts to her. The trial court held that "[a] jury under all of the circumstances in this case could find defendant's conduct so shocking that plaintiff, as alleged, suffered severe emotional disturbance and resulting physical injuries for which defendant would be liable." *Id.* at 690. In Halio v. Lurie, 222 N.Y.S.2d 759 (App. Div. 1961), the plaintiff and the defendant had dated for two years, with plans of marriage. He married another woman, concealed the marriage from the plaintiff while continuing to see her, wrote a sarcastic letter to the plaintiff ridiculing her, and caused her emotional harm. The appellate division concluded that a cause of action exists in New York for "the intentional infliction of serious mental distress without physical impact." *Id.* at 762. In this case it was "for the trier of the facts to determine whether such injuries were actually suffered, and whether the conduct of the defendant was such that it may be said that it went beyond all reasonable bounds of decency." *Id.* at 764 (citations omitted).

165. 400 A.2d 1189 (N.J. 1979).

166. *Id.* at 1196 (citations omitted).

167. 506 A.2d 29 (N.J. Super. Ct. App. Div. 1986).

curred prior to commencement of the divorce action, the entire controversy doctrine did not require joinder because "this tort claim is sufficiently distinct and independent from the cause of action for divorce
and equitable distribution to permit separate adjudication."[168]

Other jurisdictions have rejected the approach of New Jersey and
have approved the use of tort actions for domestic abuse independent
of divorce proceedings. In *McCoy v. Cooke*[169] a woman sued her former
husband for acts of physical assault and intentional infliction of emotional distress that occurred while they were married. The trial court
in the divorce proceeding found that the defendant had repeatedly
battered the plaintiff.[170] The Michigan Court of Appeals held that res
judicata did not bar the plaintiff from pursuing her tort action separately from the divorce.[171] However, collateral estoppel prevented the
defendant from denying that the batteries occurred, although he could
"raise as an affirmative defense the issue whether and to what extent
the divorce judgment compensated plaintiff for any injuries she suffered as a result of the batteries."[172]

Similarly, in *Stuart v. Stuart*[173] the Wisconsin Supreme Court
concluded that a woman could sue her former husband three months
after the parties received a divorce for assault, battery, and intentional
infliction of emotional distress that allegedly occurred during the marriage. The court agreed with the lower court that "although joinder of
an interspousal tort action and a divorce action is permissible, it is
contrary to public policy to require such a joinder."[174]

---

168. *Id.* at 35. Interestingly, the court added the following statement: "Indeed, there
is apparently some uncertainty as to how a marital tort claim joined with a traditional
divorce action should be tried." *Id.* (citation omitted).
169. 419 N.W.2d 44 (Mich. Ct. App. 1988).
170. *Id.* at 46.
171. *Id.*
172. *Id.*
173. 421 N.W.2d 505 (Wis. 1988).
174. *Id.* at 508. The Wisconsin Supreme Court quoted with approval the following
excerpt from the court of appeals opinion:
"If an abused spouse cannot commence a tort action subsequent to a divorce, the spouse will be forced to elect between three equally unacceptable
alternatives: (1) Commence a tort action during the marriage and possibly endure additional abuse; (2) join a tort claim in a divorce action and waive the
right to a jury trial on the tort claim; or (3) commence an action to terminate
the marriage, forego the tort claim, and surrender the right to recover damages
arising from spousal abuse. To enforce such an election would require an
abused spouse to surrender both the constitutional right to a jury trial and
valuable property rights to preserve his or her well-being. This the law will not
do.
Although joinder is permissible, the administration of justice is better
served by keeping tort and divorce actions separate. . . . Divorce actions will

The Colorado Court of Appeals in *Simmons v. Simmons*[175] considered the assault, battery, and intentional infliction of emotional distress claims of a woman who alleged that her former husband threw coffee on her and "kicked, slapped, and hit her, and tore her ear."[176] The court held that public policy precludes joinder of interspousal tort claims with dissolution of marriage proceedings.[177] Similarly, in *Chiles v. Chiles*[178] the Texas Court of Appeals reversed a $500,000 judgment for intentional infliction of emotional distress. There was a jury finding that the plaintiff's former husband subjected her to " 'physical and verbal abuse, harassment, threats and generally provocative conduct' " that caused severe emotional distress.[179] The plaintiff obtained the tort claim judgment as part of a divorce action, and the Texas Court of Appeals concluded that the tort claim "should not be recognized in a divorce action."[180] The court reasoned that "in the unique and special setting of a lawsuit for divorce, [an action for intentional infliction of emotional distress without proof of physical injury] would tend to obfuscate the issues of custody, support and division of community property."[181]

In *Coleman v. Coleman*[182] the Alabama Supreme Court found that

---

become unduly complicated if tort claims must be litigated in the same action.
. . . [R]equiring joinder of tort claims in a divorce action could unduly lengthen the period of time before a spouse could obtain a divorce and result in such adverse consequences as delayed child custody and support determinations."
Id. (quoting Stuart v. Stuart, 410 N.W.2d 632, 637-38 (Wis. Ct. App. 1987), *affirmed*, 421 N.W.2d 505 (Wis. 1988)).
175. 773 P.2d 602 (Colo. Ct. App. 1988), *cert. denied*, 773 P.2d 602 (Colo. 1989).
176. *Id.* at 603.
177. *Id.* at 605.
[T]he efficient administration of dissolution cases requires their insulation from the peculiarities of matters at law. The joinder of marriage dissolution actions with claims sounding in tort or, for instance, contract would require our trial courts to address many extraneous issues, including trial by jury, and the difference between the "amicable settlement of disputes that have arisen between parties to a marriage," and the adversarial nature of other types of civil cases. Moreover, such would create tension between the acceptance of contingent fees in tort claims and our strong and longstanding public policy against contingent fees in domestic cases. We conclude that sound policy considerations preclude either permissive or compulsory joinder of interspousal tort claims, or non-related contract claims, with dissolution of marriage proceedings.
Id. at 604-05 (citations omitted).
178. 779 S.W.2d 127 (Tex. Ct. App. 1989).
179. *Id.* at 131.
180. *Id.*
181. *Id.* at 132.
182. 566 So. 2d 482 (Ala. 1990) (per curiam).

the settlement agreement executed by the parties in the divorce action barred the wife from bringing a subsequent tort action against the husband for transmission of a venereal disease during the marriage because the wife knew of her infection prior to her release of all claims in the settlement agreement. The court described the ways in which a spouse could preserve a tort claim.

> First, if the spouse does not intend a release of all known claims, he or she could expressly reserve a tort claim from the settlement and then subsequently sue in tort. Second, the divorce defendant could counterclaim with a demand for damages based upon any tort claims or the spouse plaintiff could also include a tort claim in the divorce case. Because trial by jury is not provided for in divorce actions in Alabama, the trial court could sever the claim for damages and set the severed case for a jury trial.[183]

Coleman was similar to an earlier Alabama case, *Smith v. Smith*.[184] The wife brought an independent action for assault and battery against her husband. She alleged that one of the beatings ruptured a disc, requiring surgical fusion. The court barred the independent tort action because "the parties entered into extensive settlement negotiations and . . . central to those negotiations was the fact that Mrs. Smith had injuries resulting from the marriage and had need to be compensated in some way for those injuries."[185]

Courts have permitted, or required, independent tort and matrimonial actions, but have barred recovery in tort actions if recovery for tortious conduct was obtained in matrimonial actions. In *Kemp v. Kemp*[186] the court barred an independent tort action by a woman whose husband shattered her nose when he struck her with his fist. She previously had raised the tort claim in her divorce proceeding and received damages for her injuries. Thus, res judicata barred the action because she was attempting to litigate the same cause of action a second time.[187] In *Nash v. Overholser*[188] the plaintiff could have litigated her assault and battery claims as part of her divorce proceedings, but the court did not require her to do so. The court recognized that "[d]ivorce proceedings should be handled expeditiously and with a

---

183. *Id.* at 485-86 (footnote omitted).

184. 530 So. 2d 1389 (Ala. 1988).

185. *Id.* at 1391; *cf.* Abbott v. Williams, 888 F.2d 1550 (11th Cir. 1989) (concluding that Alabama law does not require joinder of marital tort and divorce proceedings if the issues involved are distinct).

186. 723 S.W.2d 138 (Tenn. Ct. App. 1986), *appeal denied*, 723 S.W.2d 138 (Tenn. 1987).

187. *Id.* at 140.

188. 757 P.2d 1180 (Idaho 1988), *rejected on other grounds by* State v. Guzman, No. 17716, 1990 WL 178602 (Idaho Nov. 19, 1990) (unpublished opinion).

view toward minimizing emotional trauma; such proceedings certainly should not serve as a catalyst for additional spousal abuse."[189] The court noted that the wife did not plead the tort allegations in her divorce complaint, and the divorce court did not address them.[190]

The Supreme Judicial Court of Massachusetts, in *Heacock v. Heacock*,[191] concluded that a divorce decree did not bar a subsequent tort action for a battery that occurred during the marriage, even though the plaintiff presented evidence concerning the battery as part of the divorce proceedings.[192] In *Heacock* the defendant allegedly went to the residence of the plaintiff, broke a glass panel in the door when she refused to open the door, grabbed her by the arm, and "violently pulled her, causing her repeatedly to strike her head against the door frame."[193] The plaintiff sought money damages for physical injuries, including spells of dizziness, blackouts, and traumatic epilepsy.[194] The court expressed its reasoning as follows:

> A tort action is not based on the same underlying claim as an action for divorce. The purpose of a tort action is to redress a legal wrong in damages; that of a divorce action is to sever the marital relationship between the parties, and, where appropriate, to fix the parties' respective rights and obligations with regard to alimony and support, and to divide the marital estate. Although a judge in awarding alimony and dividing marital property must consider, among other things, the conduct of the parties during the marriage, the purposes for which these awards are made do not include compensating a party in damages for injuries suffered. . . . The plaintiff could not have recovered damages for the tort in the divorce action, as the Probate Court does not have jurisdiction to hear tort actions and award damages.[195]

The Indiana Court of Appeals recognized the independence of tort and matrimonial actions in *McNevin v. McNevin*.[196] The plaintiff sued her husband in a battery action because he allegedly struck and injured her during their separation. The court permitted the plaintiff's subsequent tort action because even though the plaintiff entered into a settlement agreement that divided marital assets without mentioning her plan to bring a postdivorce tort action, "an inchoate, unliquidated tort claim could not be considered by the trial court in the dissolution

---

189. *Id.* at 1181.
190. *Id.* at 1182.
191. 520 N.E.2d 151 (Mass. 1988).
192. *Id.* at 153.
193. *Id.* at 152.
194. *Id.*
195. *Id.* at 153 (citations omitted).
196. 447 N.E.2d 611 (Ind. Ct. App. 1983).

proceedings (division of property)."[197] The tort claim had "no present ascertainable value,"[198] and the trial court could not have considered it in approving the settlement had it known of the claim. Therefore, the plaintiff's "failure to disclose the claim [did] not preclude an independent action."[199]

Similarly, in *Aubert v. Aubert*[200] the Supreme Court of New Hampshire permitted a man to bring an intentional tort action against his former wife who shot him in the face with a .38 calibre revolver. He suffered permanent injury and disfigurement, and the court upheld an award for $343,000 in compensatory damages. The court held that the prior divorce decree did not bar the tort action because "a civil action in tort is fundamentally different from a divorce proceeding, and . . . the respective issues involved are entirely distinct."[201] Additionally, "the divorce court [was] without jurisdiction to award damages for personal injuries."[202]

In *Walther v. Walther*[203] the Supreme Court of Utah held that a court may not try a tort claim as part of a divorce action.[204] The court quoted from an earlier Utah case in which the court expressed concern that " 'divorce actions will become unduly complicated in their trial and disposition if torts can be or must be litigated in the same action.' "[205] Three years later the court in *Noble v. Noble*[206] reaffirmed that a divorce decree does not bar an interspousal tort claim, even if the divorce court considered the facts relating to the tort action.[207]

---

197. *Id.* at 618.

198. *Id.*

199. *Id.*

200. 529 A.2d 909 (N.H. 1987).

201. *Id.* at 911.

202. *Id.* at 912. The court also held that the criminal conviction of the wife for attempted murder collaterally estopped her from litigating the issues of causation and liability in the subsequent tort action. *Id.* at 912-13; *see supra* note 2 and accompanying text.

203. 709 P.2d 387 (Utah 1985).

204. *Id.* at 388.

205. *Id.* (quoting Lord v. Shaw, 665 P.2d 1288, 1291 (Utah 1983)). In *Shaw* the plaintiff alleged that the defendant at different times during their marriage "choked her into semi-consciousness, then pushed her out the door and off the porch[,]" "struck her and pushed her into a wall[,]" "struck and beat her[,]. . . struck their minor child who attempted to intervene," and "beat her, tore her clothes from her body, and forced her to submit to sexual intercourse against her will." *Id.* at 1289. The court wrote: "A divorce action is highly equitable in nature, whereas the trial of a tort claim is at law and may well involve, as in this case, a request for trial by jury. The administration of justice will be better served by keeping the two proceedings separate." *Id.* at 1291. The court in *Shaw* dismissed the separate tort action because the statute of limitations had run.

206. 761 P.2d 1369 (Utah 1988).

207. *Id.* at 1374.

Glen Noble, age sixty-one, shot his wife Elaine in the head at close range with a .22 calibre rifle while she lay in bed. Ms. Noble was thirty-seven at the time and became totally and permanently disabled as a result.[208] The divorce court considered Ms. Noble's needs, disabilities, and expenses that resulted from her injuries in resolving alimony and property division issues.[209] However, the state supreme court permitted Ms. Noble to proceed with her subsequent tort action, subject to a bar against "duplicate compensation."[210] The court noted that, as a general rule, interspousal tort claims likely to affect a divorce action should be resolved prior to divorce proceedings.[211]

This survey of cases demonstrates that state courts generally are receptive to battery, assault, and intentional infliction of emotional distress claims based upon domestic abuse. If the domestic abuse occurs between married persons, joinder of tort actions in pending matrimonial actions generally is not required and may be prohibited.

V. CONCLUSION

Public policy favors a vigorous response by the legal system to the widespread problem of domestic abuse. Interspousal tort immunity does not bar the great majority of potential actions. Moreover, most jurisdictions prefer independent litigation of tort and divorce actions. Tort actions for battery and assault, based upon physical injury and threats of imminent physical injury, are as appropriate in domestic abuse cases as they would be in a nondomestic setting. The tort of intentional infliction of emotional distress permits recovery for nonimminent threats and verbal abuse intended to cause severe emotional distress.

Criminal-law and civil-law approaches have had success, but more is needed. Successful actions for battery, assault, and intentional infliction of emotional distress can serve as vehicles for remedy for victims and as a reflection of societal disapproval of this particularly repugnant form of tortious conduct.

Lawyers can make an important contribution to the national effort to combat domestic abuse by bringing civil actions that seek money damages for victims of domestic abuse. Divorce lawyers play a particularly useful role in determining the appropriateness of tort actions on behalf of marital dissolution clients who also are victims of domestic abuse. These attorneys must properly coordinate tort actions and dis-

---

208. *Id.* at 1372.
209. *Id.* at 1370.
210. *Id.* at 1373.
211. *Id.* at 1371 & n.4.

solution proceedings and must pay particular attention to applicable tort statutes of limitations.[212]

---

212. The tort actions will be subject to the normal statutes of limitations for battery, assault, and intentional infliction of emotional distress actions.

APPENDIX

This Appendix discusses the domestic abuse cases that involve assault and battery claims reported from 1981 through 1990, four miscellaneous assault and battery cases prior to 1981, and domestic abuse cases that involve intentional infliction of emotional distress claims reported from 1958 through 1990.

District of Columbia: Granville v. Hunt, 566 A.2d 65 (D.C. 1989) (dismissing an assault action by a woman against her former boyfriend after a seven-year delay because of her failure to prosecute).

Alabama: Lewis v. Lennox, 567 So. 2d 264 (Ala. 1990) (awarding a woman compensatory and punitive damages in action against her former husband for assault, battery, and intentional infliction of emotional distress); Smith v. Smith, 530 So. 2d 1389 (Ala. 1988) (awarding damages for injuries in the divorce settlement agreement to a woman who raised battery claims against her former husband during divorce proceedings); Jackson v. Hall, 460 So. 2d 1290 (Ala. 1984) (barring a woman's independent battery action against her former husband because the tort claim was covered by her divorce settlement); Harrington v. Harrington, 450 So. 2d 99 (Ala. 1984) (permitting a woman who was paralyzed from the waist down because of a shooting by her husband to proceed in a battery action that was independent of her divorce action); Underwood v. Hall, 572 So. 2d 490 (Ala. Civ. App. 1990) (upholding an award of $10,000 compensatory and punitive damages for a woman's injuries to face and body, including a broken wrist, caused by abuse from the man with whom she had lived); Taylor v. Taylor, 560 So. 2d 768 (Ala. Civ. App. 1990) (awarding a woman monetary damages on part of divorce proceedings for assault and battery claims).

Arkansas: Takeya v. Didion, 745 S.W.2d 614 (Ark. 1988) (ordering a new trial because punitive damages were awarded without compensatory damages in a case that involved a single woman who dated a married man who beat her, threatened to kill her, and tried to suffocate her when she attempted to end the affair); Bruns v. Bruns, 719 S.W.2d 691 (Ark. 1986) (ordering a new trial because of erroneous jury instructions in a case that involved a battery claim by a woman who was struck from behind and pushed down her front steps by her former husband).

California: Alderson v. Alderson, 225 Cal. Rptr. 610 (Ct. App.) (awarding a woman in a complicated child support and property division dispute between an unmarried couple who lived together for twelve years $15,000 in compensatory and $4,000 in punitive damages for her assault and battery claim based upon an incident in which the defendant broke her arm), *review denied*, 225 Cal. Rptr. 610 (1986).

Colorado: Simmons v. Simmons, 773 P.2d 602 (Colo. Ct. App. 1988) (awarding a woman $15,000 in compensatory and $100,000 in punitive damages for assault, battery, and intentional infliction of emotional distress claims against her former husband who kicked, slapped, and hit her, and tore her ear), *cert. denied*, 773 P.2d 602 (Colo. 1989).

Connecticut: Braun v. Edelstein, 554 A.2d 1102 (Conn. App. Ct.) (awarding a woman $25,000 for physical and emotional injuries when the man with whom she shared a nonmarital domestic relationship became angry and assaulted her with his fists), *cert. denied*, 559 A.2d 1138 (Conn. 1989).

Delaware: Hudson v. Hudson, 532 A.2d 620 (Del. Super. Ct.) (holding that the interspousal immunity doctrine does not bar a battery action by a woman whose husband drove his car into a railroad sign to injure or kill her), *appeal refused*, 527 A.2d 281 (Del. 1987), *and appeal refused*, 540 A.2d 113 (Del. 1988).

Georgia: Catlett v. Catlett, 388 S.E.2d 14 (Ga. Ct. App.) (awarding a woman $10,000 in compensatory and $20,000 in punitive damages in an assault, battery, and false imprisonment action against her former husband who struck her, prevented her from leaving his apartment, confined her in his car, and dragged her down a stairway by her feet), *cert. denied*, 388 S.E.2d 14 (Ga. 1989).

Idaho: Nash v. Overholser, 757 P.2d 1180 (Idaho 1988) (holding that a divorce judgment does not bar an assault and battery action by a woman who alleged that her former husband physically attacked her on five occasions, including one in which the husband threw her against the corner of a shower, causing permanent injury to her arm).

Illinois: Kukla v. Kukla, 540 N.E.2d 510 (Ill. App. Ct. 1989) (requiring a woman to raise her husband's violation of a restraining order as a part of her divorce proceedings, and not as an independent tort action for intentional infliction of emotional distress, because conduct underlying the tort action had been regulated by a previous order of the domestic relations court); Palmer v. Palmer, 523 N.E.2d 1316 (Ill. App. Ct. 1988) (awarding a woman $150,000 compensatory and $5,000 punitive damages in her battery action after her husband drove his car into a bridge abutment to injure her and then beat her, which caused severe injuries including a broken neck).

Indiana: McNevin v. McNevin, 447 N.E.2d 611 (Ind. Ct. App. 1983) (holding that a woman was not required to join her tort claim based upon having been struck and injured by her husband in her divorce action).

Kansas: Ebert v. Ebert, 656 P.2d 766 (Kan. 1983) (holding that the interspousal tort immunity does not bar a woman's tort action against her husband based upon multiple incidents of alleged physical abuse, which caused a broken toe, broken ribs, facial lacerations, and other injuries).

Kentucky: Whittington v. Whittington, 766 S.W.2d 73 (Ky. Ct. App. 1989) (holding that allegations that a husband committed adultery and endorsed checks with his wife's name on them did not allege conduct that would constitute intentional infliction of emotional distress).

Louisiana: Laughlin v. Breaux, 515 So. 2d 480 (La. Ct. App. 1987) (awarding a woman $57,297 in damages following proof that she suffered from battered woman's syndrome caused by a pattern of domestic abuse by her former boyfriend that included verbal harassment, beatings, and rapes); Duplechin v. Toce, 497 So. 2d 763 (La. Ct. App. 1986) (awarding a woman $52,000 in special and general damages based upon an incident in which her husband threatened and tortured her), *writ denied*, 499 So. 2d 86 (La. 1987).

Maine: Caron v. Caron, 577 A.2d 1178 (Me. 1990) (awarding a woman $119,000 in compensatory and $75,000 in punitive damages and awarding her young son, the stepson of the defendant, $20,000 in compensatory and $35,000 in punitive damages in an assault, battery, and intentional infliction of emotional distress action against the husband/stepfather).

Maryland: Lusby v. Lusby, 390 A.2d 77 (Md. 1978) (permitting a woman to bring an intentional tort action against her husband who allegedly forced her car off the road, battered and raped her, and assisted two other men in their attempt to rape her).

Massachusetts: Heacock v. Heacock, 520 N.E.2d 151 (Mass. 1988) (holding that a woman was not required to join her tort claims in her divorce action based upon her allegation that her former husband broke a glass panel in a door, grabbed her by the arm, and violently pulled her, causing her repeatedly to strike her head against the door frame); Terrio v. McDonough, 450 N.E.2d 190 (Mass. App. Ct.) (awarding a woman $15,000 in damages following proof that she was raped and pushed down a flight of stairs by her former boyfriend), *review denied*, 450 N.E.2d 190 (Mass.), *and review denied*, 453 N.E. 1231 (Mass. 1983).

Michigan: McCoy v. Cooke, 419 N.W.2d 44 (Mich. Ct. App. 1988) (allowing recovery to a woman for battery and intentional infliction of emotional distress subject to reduction based upon a recovery that she already had received in her divorce action for her husband's assaultive conduct); Goldman v. Wexler, 333 N.W.2d 121 (Mich. Ct. App. 1983) (holding that a woman's tort claim against her former husband was not barred by her divorce decree but that the husband could raise the issue of double recovery as an affirmative defense).

Minnesota: Plath v. Plath, 428 N.W.2d 392 (Minn. 1988) (holding that a two-year statute of limitations barred a battery action by a wife based upon an allegation that her husband pushed her back, causing her to fall and break her hip); Montgomery v. Day, No. C1-87-1911, 1988 WL 24844 (Minn. Ct. App. Mar. 22, 1988) (unpublished opinion) (allowing a woman to recover damages from a former boyfriend who fractured her arm), *review denied*, 1988 WL 24844 (Minn. Apr. 28, 1988).

Mississippi: Cain v. McKinnon, 552 So. 2d 91 (Miss. 1989) (holding that the interspousal immunity doctrine does not bar an intentional tort action by a woman against her former husband based upon allegations that he savagely and brutally assaulted and beat her); Burns v. Burns, 518 So. 2d 1205 (Miss. 1988) (abolishing the interspousal immunity judicially and permitting a woman to proceed with a tort action based upon her allegation that her husband assaulted and battered her).

Missouri: Townsend v. Townsend, 708 S.W.2d 646 (Mo. 1986) (en banc) (holding that the interspousal immunity does not bar a battery action by a woman against her husband who shot her in the back); Hudson v. DeLonjay, 732 S.W.2d 922 (Mo. Ct. App. 1987) (allowing a female cohabitant to raise assault and intentional infliction of emotional distress counterclaims in property dispute).

Nebraska: Hassing v. Wortman, 333 N.W.2d 765 (Neb. 1983) (disallowing a woman's action against her former husband for intentional infliction of emotional distress because his conduct of revealing her premarital pregnancy to relatives already aware of it, revealing information to her employer that did not jeopardize her job, and engaging in other inappropriate conduct did not cause emotional distress so severe that no reasonable person could have been expected to endure it).

New Hampshire: Brown v. Brown, 577 A.2d 1227 (N.H. 1990) (excluding evidence of an annulled criminal conviction for assault in a civil battery action by a wife).

New Jersey: Tevis v. Tevis, 400 A.2d 1189 (N.J. 1979) (holding that the "entire controversy" rule required a woman to bring her tort action, based upon a beating by her husband, as a part of her divorce action); Brown v. Brown, 506 A.2d 29 (N.J. Super. Ct. App. Div. 1986) (holding that a woman was not required by the "entire controversy" rule to join her tort action with her divorce action because the divorce action already was pending when the husband allegedly battered and assaulted her).

New York: Murphy v. Murphy, 486 N.Y.S.2d 457 (App. Div. 1985) (reducing a woman's award from $90,000 to $45,000 for intentional infliction of emotional distress by a man with whom she lived for four years who killed her pet goose and subjected her to threats, assaults, and general abusive conduct); Baron v. Jeffer, 469 N.Y.S.2d 815 (App. Div. 1983) (dismissing an assault claim in a woman's action against the man with whom she had lived because of statute of limitations); Gross v. Gross, 462 N.Y.S.2d 1015 (App. Div. 1983) (awarding a woman $25,000 in damages, reduced to $15,000 on appeal, for an assault upon her by her former husband); Halio v. Lurie, 222 N.Y.S.2d 759 (App. Div. 1961) (recognizing the tort of intentional infliction of emotional distress in a case that involved a man who humiliated his former girlfriend by dating her after marrying another woman and by writing a sarcastic letter to her).

North Carolina: Gay v. Gay, 302 S.E.2d 495 (N.C. Ct. App. 1983) (awarding a woman $13,620 in compensatory and $10,000 in punitive damages following proof that her husband committed numerous assaults and batteries upon her that caused a fracture of the left leg and ankle and other injuries).

Ohio: Casalinova v. Solaro, No. 14052, 1989 WL 111942 (Ohio Ct. App. Sept. 27, 1989) (unpublished opinion) (affirming a default judgment and $100,000 damage award for a woman who suffered physical and mental abuse, with attendant injuries, on four separate occasions in nonmarital relationship), *dismissed*, 549 N.E.2d 1190 (Ohio), *cert. denied*, 110 S. Ct. 3215 (1990); Grooms v. Grooms, No. 84AP-773, 1985 WL 9879 (Ohio Ct. App. Feb. 26, 1985) (unpublished opinion) (barring a wife by the applicable statute of limitations in her assault and battery action against her husband based upon his striking her in the face, breaking her nose, and injuring her mouth and teeth); Gabriel v. DePrisco, No. L-84-063, 1984 WL 14343 (Ohio Ct. App. July 27, 1984) (unpublished opinion) (barring a woman's assault and battery action against her former husband by applicable statute of limitations); Woyczynski v. Wolf, 464 N.E.2d 612 (Ohio Ct. App. 1983) (husband sued his wife and his wife's attorney for malicious prosecution relating to domestic violence charges and she filed a counterclaim for assault which she subsequently agreed to dismiss), *overruled on other grounds by* Trussell v. General Motors Corp., 559 N.E.2d 732 (Ohio 1990); Gravill v. Gravill, No. 45542, 1983 WL 4631 (Ohio Ct. App. Aug. 25, 1983) (unpublished opinion) (civil action by a woman alleging that she suffered an assault and battery by her husband); Lanter v. Lanter, No. C-820860, 1983 WL 5124 (Ohio Ct. App. July 13, 1983) (per curiam) (unpublished opinion) (holding that a woman's action for assault by her husband barred by the interspousal immunity); Owens v. Owens, No. C-810878, 1982 WL 8622 (Ohio Ct. App. July 14, 1982) (per curiam) (unpublished opinion) (holding that the applicable statute of limitations barred a woman's assault and battery action against her husband who allegedly drove his car away when she was partially out of the car, dragging her several feet and causing a rear tire to pass over her right arm); Green v. Green, 446 N.E.2d 837 (Ohio Ct. App. 1982) (holding that a woman's assault and battery action against her husband was barred by the applicable one-year statute of limitations); Lee v. Lee, No. 339, 1981 WL 5121 (Ohio Ct. App. May 20, 1981) (unpublished opinion) (holding that an assault and battery action by woman against former husband that was filed after the marriage ended was not barred by interspousal immunity).

Oklahoma: Floyd v. Dotson, 692 P.2d 77 (Okla. Ct. App. 1984) (holding that the trial court erred when the jury awarded $10,000 in damages for intentional infliction of emotional distress for conduct of the defendant that involved a threat to use nude photos of plaintiff and a cassette recording of their love-making because jury instruction required the conduct to be unreasonable rather than extreme and outrageous).

Oregon: Apitz v. Damages, 287 P.2d 585 (Ore. 1955) (allowing the executor of a woman's estate to sue the estate of the woman's husband who had murdered her and committed suicide).

Tennessee: Whatley v. Whatley, No. 15, 1988 WL 42971 (Tenn. Ct. App. May 4, 1988) (allowing a woman to receive a jury award of $22,473 compensatory and $45,000 punitive damages, reduced by the trial judge to $14,700 compensatory and $20,000 punitive damages, in an action against her former husband that was based upon an incident in which he beat her); Kemp v. Kemp, 723 S.W.2d 138 (Tenn. Ct. App. 1986) (barring a woman from proceeding with her battery action because the tort cause of action had been considered during the divorce proceedings and the woman already had been awarded damages for her injuries).

Texas: Twyman v. Twyman, 790 S.W.2d 819 (Tex. Ct. App. 1990) (awarding $15,000 for a "negligent" infliction of emotional distress action brought against a husband who pressured his wife to engage in bondage and other sexual conduct offensive to her); Chiles v. Chiles, 779 S.W.2d 127 (Tex. Ct. App. 1989) (holding that the trial court had erred in awarding the plaintiff $500,000 for intentional infliction of emotional distress as a separate cause of action in her divorce action, despite a jury finding that there was physical and verbal abuse, harassment, threats and generally provocative conduct); Armstrong v. Armstrong, 750 S.W.2d 45 (Tex. Ct. App. 1988) (holding that a woman is not permitted to bring an independent tort action because she sought, as part of her prior divorce proceedings, a disproportionate share of the marital property because of her husband's assault upon her); Misleh v. Misleh, No. 01-86-0366-CV, 1987 WL 13524 (Tex. Ct. App. July 9, 1987) (unpublished opinion) (upholding a jury award of $7,000 in actual and $45,000 in punitive damages for assault and false imprisonment claims by a woman who was beaten by her husband); Ulrich v. Ulrich, 652 S.W.2d 503 (Tex. Ct. App. 1983) (awarding a woman $15,000 in damages as part of divorce proceedings for physical abuse by her husband that included a twisting of her ankle until it broke and a twisting of her wrist until it broke).

Utah: Noble v. Noble, 761 P.2d 1369 (Utah 1988) (permitting a woman to proceed with an independent tort action based on having been shot in the head by her husband while she lay in bed with consequent total and permanent disability even though the shooting incident was considered in her divorce proceeding, but with the provision that double recovery was not to be received); Walther v. Walther, 709 P.2d 387 (Utah 1985) (requiring a woman to litigate a battery claim that was based upon physical abuse by her husband in a tort action separate from her divorce action); Lord v. Shaw, 665 P.2d 1288 (Utah 1983) (holding that actionable torts between married persons should not be litigated in a divorce proceeding and dismissing a woman's assault and battery action because of the applicable statute of limitations).

Vermont: Ward v. Ward, 583 A.2d 577 (Vt. 1990) (holding that a woman was barred from joining her assault and battery claims against her husband in her divorce action).

West Virginia: Criss v. Criss, 356 S.E.2d 620 (W. Va. 1987) (holding that a claim of intentional infliction of emotional distress was duplicitous of assault and battery claims based upon an incident in which estranged husband of plaintiff allegedly threatened her with a hunting knife, forced her to undress, and sexually assaulted her); Coffindaffer v. Coffindaffer, 244 S.E.2d 338 (W. Va. 1978) (holding that interspousal immunity does not bar an action by a woman against her husband in which she alleged that he negligently struck her with an automobile and then intentionally assaulted her causing her further injuries).

Wisconsin: Stuart v. Stuart, 421 N.W.2d 505 (Wis. 1988) (permitting a woman to proceed with her assault, battery, and intentional infliction of emotional distress action against her former husband despite a prior divorce decree because it is contrary to public policy to require joinder even though joinder of the divorce action and interspousal tort action would be permissible); Slawek v. Stroh, 215 N.W.2d 9 (Wis. 1974) (father of an illegitimate child sought judicial determination of paternity and the mother counterclaimed with claims of assault, battery, intentional infliction of emotional distress, and seduction).

Federal Courts: Abbott v. Williams, 888 F.2d 1550 (11th Cir. 1989) (applying Alabama law in a battery and intentional infliction of emotional distress action by a woman against her former husband and concluding that prior divorce decree did not bar subsequent tort action unless the settlement agreement settled all claims, including the tort claims); Moran v. Beyer, 734 F.2d 1245 (7th Cir. 1984) (holding that the Illinois interspousal tort immunity statute was unconstitutional in an action by a woman whose husband beat her on numerous occasions and claimed that he was justified on grounds of provocation and self-defense); Reitmeier v. Kalinoski, 631 F. Supp. 565 (D.N.J. 1986) (during the course of a real property dispute between prior cohabitants a man sought partition and the woman counterclaimed based upon fifteen alleged instances of assault and battery); Abady v. Macaluso, 90 F.R.D. 690 (E.D. Pa. 1981) (man brought a complicated tort and contract action against former girlfriend and her mother; former girlfriend counterclaimed for assault, battery, intentional infliction of emotional distress, false imprisonment, and other torts).

Taking Abusers to Court

Civil Remedies for Domestic Violence Victims

Linda K. Meier and Brian K. Zoeller

T he most dangerous place for a woman in the United States has become her own home. For at least the last four years, domestic violence has posed the single largest threat of injury to women in this country—surpassing injury from heart attacks, cancer, strokes, car crashes, muggings, and rapes combined.[1]

The following is a list of startling statistics:[2]

• Every day, an average of four to five women die in the United States due to domestic violence.

• Nearly 1,400 women were killed in 1993 by their male partners.

• An estimated 2 million wives are beaten by their husbands each year, an average of 1 every 16 seconds.

• A March of Dimes study cites battering during the prenatal period as the leading cause of birth defects and infant mortality.

• Battery is listed as a contributing factor in a fourth of all suicide attempts by women and in half of all attempts by African American women.

Linda K. Meier is a partner in the law firm of Sargent & Meier in Greenwood, Indiana. Brian K. Zoeller is a third-year student at the Indiana University School of Law in Indianapolis.

• At least half of homeless women and children are in flight from domestic violence.

• In 1992, the U.S. Surgeon General ranked abuse by husbands and partners as the leading cause of injury or death to women and classified domestic violence as having reached epidemic proportions in the nation.

Domestic violence is violence committed against one person by another in the same household. The most common form is physical abuse by a spouse. Domestic violence includes pushing, shoving, pulling hair, slapping, punching, confining, abusing psychologically, and molesting sexually.

In the past, much domestic violence went unpunished or uncompensated due to interspousal immunity derived from common law. Interspousal immunity, among other things, banned actions between spouses that resulted from personal injuries inflicted by one spouse on the other.

The erosion of this rule began with the Married Women's Property Act in the middle of the 19th century.[3] The act gave wives their own legal identity, separate ownership and control of their property, and the capacity to sue and be sued without joining their husbands as a party. However, the act was not origi-

nally interpreted to allow a wife an action against her husband in tort.[4]

Eventually, many states began to carve exceptions to the interspousal immunity rule. Today, only Hawaii still recognizes the rule without exceptions. At least 39 states have abolished the rule, and partial abrogation in the other 10 states has opened the door for victims of spousal abuse to seek redress.[5]

Causes of Action

Tort law in the area of domestic violence continues to evolve. Claims may include

• assault

• battery

• defamation

• false imprisonment

• intentional and/or reckless infliction of emotional distress (most states require physical injury as an underlying tort)

• negligent infliction of emotional distress

• intentional interference with child custody, visitation, and/or a parent-child relationship

• third-party negligence

• tortious infliction of a venereal disease

• wrongful death

This article will focus on assault and

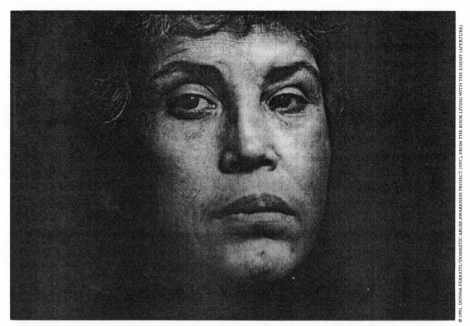

Hedda Nussbaum showed the nation the shocking nature of domestic violence. Her civil suit is pending against her abuser, Joel Steinberg, who was convicted of beating to death their illegally adopted daughter, Lisa.

battery, infliction of emotional distress, and tortious infliction of a venereal disease. The first two claims are discussed because they make up the majority of domestic violence torts. Tortious infliction of a venereal disease is discussed because in the age of AIDS, the potential damages recoverable for this tort are significant.

Assault and battery. An assault is defined as an "act by one person that creates a reasonable fear of imminent peril in the mind of another person when the actor has the apparent ability to cause bodily injury to the other person."[6] A battery is any intentional, offensive, nonconsensual touching ranging from a brutal beating to a shove or a tap in a rude, insolent, or angry manner.[7]

Most attorneys approached with a tort case involving domestic violence will be dealing with an assault or battery. A note of caution: Many victims never prosecute or follow through with a tort action. Attorneys should ask potential clients in these cases tough questions to ensure as much as possible that the victims will follow through and will not be swayed by any remaining feelings they may have for their abusers.

For example, counsel should ask the client whether she sympathizes with the abuser or makes excuses for his behavior.[8] A client who does this may well waver in her resolve to sue. If the couple has children, the attorney should also ask about the client's view of the family's stability without the abuser. Again, the client may waver if she thinks she may not be able to provide for the family without the abuser. Attorneys who fail to ask tough questions like these may end up wasting their time or the client's money.

Assault and battery case law includes situations ranging from relatively minor incidents to the near killing of the victim. In *DeLeon v. Hernandez*, for example, a Texas appellate court reversed a trial court's summary judgment against a woman who sued for assault and battery after her husband punched her in the face and body.[9] In *Waite v. Waite*, a much more serious battery was at issue. A Florida appellate court reversed summary judgment for the husband after he had severely injured his wife with a machete.[10]

DeLeon typifies assault and battery suits. As unfortunate as that scenario is, however, cases like *Waite* illustrate the unthinkable brutality that is involved much too often.[11]

Infliction of emotional distress. Although the most common domestic violence tort is assault and battery, the tort most litigated at the appellate and supreme court levels is infliction of emotional distress. In an assault and battery case, the court must decide only whether the act occurred and whether spousal immunity has been abolished in the jurisdiction. But infliction of emotional distress involves difficult public policy and legal issues that the courts have not decided uniformly.

This tort usually accompanies a claim of bodily injury that is so traumatic for the victim that it results in emotional and psychological damages needing treatment. In cases of negligent infliction of emotional distress, many jurisdictions require physical manifestations of the emotional distress as a safeguard against frivolous suits.[12] Most jurisdictions do not require physical manifestations in cases alleging reckless or intentional infliction of emotional distress.

Courts across the country, in varying degrees, require the abuser's conduct to be "extreme and outrageous." Courts use this criterion, like the physical manifestation requirement, to deter lawsuits without merit. For example, a woman might bring suit for infliction of emotional distress against her husband of five years who hit her once while they argued—clearly a battery and a terrible act, but not sufficiently outrageous to cause severe emotional distress.

Hakkila v. Hakkila offers a good example of the high threshold for outrageous conduct that many courts require. In this New Mexico case, the husband's conduct toward his wife included assault and battery, demeaning remarks, screaming, refusal to have sex, and other actions. At the time of trial, the wife was described as being temporarily emotionally disabled. The court, however, expressing concerns about "opening the door too wide" to these types of claims, ruled that the husband's actions were not sufficiently outrageous to warrant damages for emotional distress.[13]

However, in *Henriksen v. Cameron*, the court found the husband's physical and verbal abuse—which included assaulting and raping his wife and accusing her of sleeping with his brother—sufficiently outrageous to state a claim.[14] In *Twyman v. Twyman*, the court upheld a lower court award of damages for emotional distress resulting from the husband's attempt to engage his wife in "deviate sexual acts."[15]

Because courts in different jurisdictions have set different standards for this tort, attorneys considering filing these suits should carefully analyze the case law in their jurisdictions.

Tortious infliction of a venereal disease. Although most reported cases in this category involve transmitted herpes, in this age, AIDS may soon become the most significant domestic tort. All states recognize that one sexual partner may be liable to the other for transmitting a venereal disease.

Liability is based on theories of battery, tortious fraud, and negligence. Under the battery theory, even though the spouse consented to intercourse, the consent was based on a mistaken belief. The plaintiff would not have consented if he or she had known the partner had the disease, so the act amounted to a nonconsensual touching.[16]

In cases involving the theory of tortious fraud, the plaintiff alleges that the marriage relationship imposes a duty to inform the other spouse about the disease. The failure to disclose is itself the

basis for claims of constructive fraud or misrepresentation.[17]

Cases involving negligence theories also focus on a duty to warn. Courts have held that a person with a dangerous contagious disease has a duty to warn another of a risk of infection.[18] However, most courts require the infected person to have actual or constructive knowledge of the disease. The knowledge requirement is the key issue when pursuing a case of tortious infliction of a venereal disease.

For example, in *Meany v. Meany*, the wife had recovered a judgment from the trial court against the husband for the

---

Assault and battery case law includes situations ranging from relatively minor incidents to the near killing of the victim.

---

negligent infliction of a venereal disease. The appellate court reversed, stating that the husband did not have actual or constructive knowledge that he was carrying the disease.[19]

The court noted that there was no evidence the husband had ever been infected with a venereal disease. He had been treated for a "drippage," but the record did not indicate that this was a symptom of genital herpes. Nor did the record reflect anything that would prove the husband had actual or constructive knowledge of a venereal disease.

The state supreme court overruled this decision, finding sufficient evidence for the jury to conclude that the husband was negligent. The court said a drippage, coupled with the fact that the husband had had sexual relations with five different women, was sufficient for the jury to impute knowledge of the disease to the husband.[20]

Both courts agreed that constructive knowledge could include the onset of the symptoms of a venereal disease, such as warts, even if the person did not know that the warts were an actual symptom of the disease.

Actual or constructive knowledge is not difficult to prove if the infected person has sought treatment for the disease. Problems arise when the infected person's disease has not manifested itself at the time of sexual contact with the person bringing the suit.

Some jurisdictions impose greater burdens on plaintiffs for proving constructive knowledge than others, so it is important to look at local case law whenever there is no evidence of actual knowledge. When bringing a suit, the attorney must make certain that evidence can be presented that the alleged perpetrator had actual or constructive knowledge that he or she was carrying a venereal disease.

Third-Party Claims

Victims of domestic violence can also bring federal equal protection claims against third parties like police departments based on 42 U.S.C. §1983. These cases allege that domestic violence victims are not granted the same protection that other crime victims are afforded.

The Third, Ninth, and Tenth circuits have upheld the validity of these claims.[21] Previously, these actions were barred by governmental immunity.

In an equal protection claim, if a city's police department treats domestic disputes or complaints less seriously or differently than it does other disputes or complaints, the attorney can argue that the plaintiff's constitutional right to equal protection of the laws was violated. The "color of law" requirement of §1983 is met if the plaintiff proves the government exercised a "policy or custom" of treating domestic disputes less seriously than other complaints.[22]

It is helpful to determine whether aggravated conduct existed. One example would be the failure of police to respond adequately after the victim made repeated calls to report an injury. During trial, it is important to impress on the jury that the public relies on law enforcement officials for protection from violence, whether it is perpetrated by family members or strangers.

Gender Bias Claims

The crime bill enacted last year creates a federal civil rights action for gender-motivated violence that is serious enough to be a felony. It does not require that the defendant first be charged with a crime.[23]

The law appears to cover rapes and attempted rapes, including marital and date rapes. It also applies to nonsexual physical abuse, sexual abuse of children, stalking, sexual assaults and battery by boyfriends, gay-bashing attacks, violence to a woman's home or property, and transmission of sexual diseases.

A plaintiff must prove that the defendant's violence was motivated by gender.

It may be helpful to show that the defendant had a history of physically or verbally abusing other women.

Claims After Divorce

Many domestic tort cases arise in conjunction with a divorce or after a divorce. If a victim makes a claim after the marriage has been dissolved, the alleged abuser is likely to raise the doctrines of res judicata, collateral estoppel, or waiver as a defense. It is important to determine whether these doctrines will bar a tort action between former spouses after a divorce proceeding.

Res judicata and collateral estoppel preclude the relitigation of matters that were actually litigated in a previous action. Waiver involves the surrender of a legal right. Generally, courts that have addressed the issue have rejected the argument that these doctrines bar a subsequent claim against a prior spouse.[24] Some reasons for allowing a post-dissolution suit include the following:

• A tort claim is not based on the same underlying issues or claims involved in the dissolution action.[25]

• Current permissive and noncompulsory joinder rules allow a party to choose when to file a claim.

• Evidence and procedure rules to prove a tort are different from those in a dissolution proceeding.

• A plaintiff's right to a trial by jury is preserved.

• Divorce actions would become too complex with the addition of tort claims. As a result, divorces would take too long, delaying the resolution of custody and support issues.[26]

An attorney pursuing a post-dissolution tort in a jurisdiction that has not considered this issue—or even in a jurisdiction that bars post-dissolution suits —should probably agree to take the case. The modern trend is to allow post-dissolution tort suits, and arguments in favor of allowing them are persuasive.

The attorney should take care in drafting findings of fact in a divorce that would inadvertently release one spouse from any future claims that the other spouse may have. Also, if a potential subsequent tort action exists, counsel should avoid language where one spouse agrees to hold harmless the other from future claims or liabilities.

A note of caution regarding the collectability of damages should be issued to anyone pursuing a domestic tort action. Most insurance policies do not cover intentional torts, so a victim of an abuser who does not have sufficient resources to satisfy a judgment may go unrecompensed.

In some circumstances, however, the injured party is more concerned with having her day in court and being vindicated than she is with securing monetary damages. Having the justice system condemn a person for their heinous acts can help some injury victims put their lives back together. If this is the case, the attorney may want to proceed with the case as long as the client has been told about the problems with collecting on any damages awarded.

No Cure-All

The O.J. Simpson case and the incredible number of other domestic violence cases have brought this problem to the forefront of our national consciousness. With awareness, there may come progress in finding solutions to this epidemic. However, the court system cannot provide the solution to every societal problem, and domestic violence seems to be one area where the courts have been especially ineffective for a number of reasons.

First, domestic violence victims often do not wish to prosecute their abusers or bring civil actions against them because of feelings they may have for the abusers or because of the effect legal action might have on their children. Second, courts must take special care in dealing with the family and privacy issues inherent in domestic tort cases. Third, there is no consensus as to what conduct is sufficient to state a cause of action—a problem illustrated by the different standards for "outrageous" conduct in emotional distress cases.

Therefore, while the legal system is making progress in this area, attorneys who pursue domestic tort suits should not expect miracle cures for the problem of domestic violence. That is not to say that the courts and law enforcement bodies are to blame. It is the nature of the crime that makes progress difficult. For now, it appears that the court system is better equipped to compensate victims of abuse than it is to prevent the abuse from occurring in the first place. □

Notes

[1] See Antonia C. Novello, *From the Surgeon General, U.S. Public Health Service*, 267 JAMA 3132 (1992).

[2] These statistics were combined from information from the following sources: *Id. See* FEDERAL BUREAU OF INVESTIGATION, U.S. DEP'T OF JUSTICE, UNIFORM

CRIME REPORTS FOR THE UNITED
STATES, 1991 (1991); Harris Meyer, *The Bil-
lion-Dollar Epidemic*, AM. MED. NEWS, Jan.
6, 1992, at 7; *see also* Nancy Kathleen Sugg &
Thomas Inui, *Primary Care Physicians' Response to Domestic Violence: Opening Pandora's
Box*, 267 JAMA 3157 (1992).

3 LEONARD KARP & CHERYL L. KARP,
DOMESTIC TORTS: FAMILY VIOLENCE,
CONFLICT AND SEXUAL ABUSE (1989).

4 *See* William E. McCurdy, *Torts Between Persons
in Domestic Relation*, 43 HARV. L. REV. 1030,
1035-36 (1930).

5 Interspousal immunity is fully abrogated in Alabama, Alaska, Arizona, Arkansas, California,
Colorado, Connecticut, Delaware, Illinois, Indiana, Kansas, Kentucky, Maine, Maryland,
Michigan, Minnesota, Mississippi, Missouri,
Montana, Nebraska, New Hampshire, New
Jersey, New Mexico, New York, North Carolina, North Dakota, Ohio, Oklahoma, Oregon, Pennsylvania, South Carolina, South
Dakota, Tennessee, Texas, Virginia, Washington, West Virginia, Wisconsin, and Wyoming.

6 Indiana Pattern Jury Instruction No. 3101
(1989). Many other states use similar language.

7 McGlone v. Hauger, 104 N.E. 116 (Ind. App.
Ct. 1914).

8 We refer to the victims in this article as "she"
and "her" because well over 90 percent of domestic violence victims are women.

9 814 S.W.2d 531 (Tex. Ct. App. 1991).

10 593 So. 2d 222 (Fla. Dist. Ct. App. 1991);
aff'd, 618 So. 2d 1360 (Fla. 1993).

11 *See also* Simmons v. Simmons, 773 P.2d 602
(Colo. Ct. App. 1988); Catlett v. Catlett, 388
S.E.2d 14 (Ga. Ct. App. 1989), *cert. denied*,
193 Ga. App. 399 (1989); Heacock v. Hea-
cock, 520 N.E.2d 151 (Mass. 1988), *later pro-
ceeding*, 568 N.E.2d 621 (Mass. App. Ct.), *re-
view denied*, 573 N.E.2d 984 (Mass. 1991);
McCoy v. Cooke, 419 N.W.2d 44 (Mich. Ct.
App.), *appeal denied*, 430 Mich. 897 (1988);
Burns v. Burns, 518 So. 2d 1205 (Miss. 1988);
Aubert v. Aubert, 529 A.2d 909 (N.H. 1987).

12 *See, e.g.*, Twigg v. Hosp. Dist., 731 F. Supp.
469 (M.D. Fla. 1990).

13 812 P.2d 1320, 1327 (N.M. Ct. App. 1991).

14 622 A.2d 1135 (Me. 1993).

15 855 S.W.2d 619 (Tex. 1993).

16 *See* Barbara A. v. John G., 193 Cal. Rptr. 422
(Ct. App. 1983).

17 R.A.P. v. B.J.P., 428 N.W.2d 103, 106 (Minn.
Ct. App. 1988); G.L. v. M.L., 550 A.2d 525,
528 (N.J. Super. Ct. Ch. Div. 1988); Maharam
v. Maharam, 510 N.Y.S.2d 104 (App. Div.
1986), *later proceeding*, 575 N.Y.S.2d 846
(App. Div. 1991).

18 Kathleen K. v. Robert B., 198 Cal. Rptr. 273
(Ct. App. 1984).

19 631 So. 2d 14 (La. Ct. App. 1993), *cert. granted*, 635 So. 2d 238 (La. 1994), *and rev'd*, 639
So. 2d 229 (La. 1994).

20 639 So. 2d 229 (La. 1994).

21 Hynson v. City of Chester Legal Dep't, 864
F.2d 1026 (3d Cir. 1988); Balistreri v. Pacifica
Police Dep't, 855 F.2d 1421 (9th Cir. 1988);
Watson v. Kansas City, 857 F.2d 690 (10th Cir.
1988).

22 *Id.*

23 42 U.S.C.S. §1988 (1994).

24 States allowing post-dissolution tort suits are
Alaska, Arizona, Idaho, Indiana, Massachusetts,
Michigan, New Hampshire, New Jersey, Washington, and Wisconsin. States barring these suits
are Alabama, Arkansas, and Tennessee.

25 *Heacock*, 520 N.E.2d 151.

26 Stuart v. Stuart, 421 N.W.2d 505, 508 (Wis.
1988) (citation omitted).

284 N.J.Super. 3

⌊₃Christina GIOVINE, Plaintiff–Appellant,

v.

Peter J. GIOVINE, Defendant–
Respondent.

Superior Court of New Jersey,
Appellate Division.

Argued May 10, 1995.
Decided Aug. 11, 1995.

Wife brought action against husband alleging grounds for dissolution of marriage
and claims of tortious conduct by husband.
The Superior Court, Chancery Division,
Family Part, Atlantic County, struck tort
claims based on statute of limitations and
determined that wife did not have right to
jury trial. On grant of wife's motion for
leave to appeal, the Superior Court, Appellate Division, Kleiner, J.A.D., held that: (1)
wife could pursue tort claims based on alleged physical and emotional injuries sustained by continuous acts of battering during
course of marriage; (2) statute of limitations
for tort claims could be tolled based on
⌊₄evidence of battered woman's syndrome;
(3) evidence of batteries for which damages
were time barred was relevant to d······ mina-
tion of whether wife establishec ⟶tered

woman's syndrome; (4) wife was entitled to jury on claims of tortious conduct if wife could show that injury was serious and significant, resulting in permanent physical or psychological injury; and (5) wife was not entitled to jury trial on property-related claims.

Affirmed in part and reversed in part.

Skillman, J.A.D., filed opinion concurring in part and dissenting in part.

1. Husband and Wife ⚖➡205(2)

Suit of one spouse against another for injuries sustained by that spouse due to tortious conduct of other spouse is not barred by interspousal tort immunity.

2. Action ⚖➡53(1)

If circumstances surrounding domestic tort and claim for monetary damages are relevant to divorce proceeding, domestic tort must be joined with divorce proceeding under "single controversy doctrine," in order to avoid protracted, repetitive and fractionalized litigation.

See publication Words and Phrases for other judicial constructions and definitions.

3. Husband and Wife ⚖➡205(2), 232.3

Wife diagnosed with battered woman's syndrome should be permitted to sue her spouse in tort for physical and emotional injuries sustained by continuous acts of battering during course of marriage, provided there is medical, psychiatric, or psychological expert testimony establishing that wife was caused to have inability to take any action to improve or alter situation unilaterally.

4. Limitation of Actions ⚖➡55(6), 74(1)

In tort action by wife for physical and emotional injuries sustained by continuous acts of battering during course of marriage, if there is no expert proof that wife was caused to have inability to take any action to improve or alter situation unilaterally, wife cannot be deemed to be suffering from "battered woman's syndrome" and each act of abuse during marriage would constitute separate and distinct cause of action in tort,

subject to statute of limitations. N.J.S.A. 2A:14-2.

See publication Words and Phrases for other judicial constructions and definitions.

5. Limitation of Actions ⚖➡55(6), 74(1)

"Battered woman's syndrome" is not, itself, continuous tort, but is medical condition resulting from continued acts of physical or psychological misconduct; tortious conduct giving rise to medical condition must be considered continuous tort to overcome statute of limitations, because resulting psychological state, composed of varied but identifiable characteristics, is product of at least two separate and discrete physical or psychological acts occurring at different times.

6. Divorce ⚖➡145

Limitation of Actions ⚖➡74(1)

In divorce action in which spouse alleges tort claim arising from injuries sustained due to conduct of other spouse, statute of limitations for tort claim may be tolled if plaintiff establishes before trial, by medical, psychiatric or psychological evidence, that plaintiff suffers from battered woman's syndrome, which caused inability to take any action to improve or alter circumstances in marriage unilaterally; if plaintiff is proceeding without jury, court need not conduct pretrial hearing and testimony may be presented during divorce proceeding, but court must determine whether statute should be tolled before rendering decision on merits and awarding damages. N.J.S.A. 2A:14-2.

7. Limitation of Actions ⚖➡55(6)

Plaintiff spouse seeking divorce and damages for tortious conduct of defendant spouse could not recover damages for alleged tortious battery which occurred outside limitations period, as initial battering does not constitute "battered woman's syndrome" and plaintiff was able to take action as to initial battering and did not take such action in earlier complaint for divorce. N.J.S.A. 2A:14-2.

8. Husband and Wife ⚖➡232.2

Limitation of Actions ⚖➡166

Evidence of husband's alleged battering of wife was relevant in wife's action for divorce and for damages based on husband's tortious conduct, even if damages for batteries themselves were time barred, as evidence tended to establish wife's allegations of battered woman's syndrome underlying tort claims of infliction of emotional distress and negligence.

9. Divorce ⊜116

In action for divorce predicated on extreme cruelty, prior acts of extreme cruelty are always evidential to establish that last act of cruelty complained of was of such character as to make it unreasonable to expect that plaintiff would continue to cohabit with defendant. N.J.S.A. 2A:34-2, subd. c.

10. Jury ⊜11(5)

Seventh Amendment of Federal Constitution, which provides right to trial by jury in civil case, is not enforceable against states. U.S.C.A. Const.Amend. 7.

11. Jury ⊜31.2(2)

Concurrent jurisdiction of Law Division and Chancery Division does not deny party right to jury trial under State Constitution. N.J.S.A. Const. Art. 1, par. 9.

12. Jury ⊜14.5(2.1)

Wife was entitled to trial by jury on claim of interspousal tort by husband, even though claim was pursued in wife's action for divorce, if wife could establish, by written expert opinion, that wife would show, at trial, that injury was serious and significant, resulting in permanent physical or psychological injury; abrogating—*Davis v. Davis*, 182 N.J.Super. 397, 442 A.2d 208.

⌊₇⌋**13. Jury ⊜19.10(1)**

Every spouse should be entitled to demand jury trial in first pleading filed asserting interspousal tort claim in dissolution proceeding, but to qualify for jury trial, spouse must establish by written expert opinion that proofs will be introduced at trial demonstrating that injury is serious and significant, resulting in permanent physical or psychological injury; alternatively, plaintiff spouse must establish that nature of injury, whether physical or psychological, requires complex medical evidence, and spouse will be required to meet this threshold in response to motion to strike jury trial demand after all discovery

has been completed and pending matter is deemed ready for trial by court.

14. Divorce ⊜237, 253(1)

Any tort liability of first spouse to second spouse found upon tort claim alleged in dissolution proceeding must be considered upon equitable division of property and in plaintiff spouse's demand for alimony. N.J.S.A. 2A:34-23.1.

15. Jury ⊜19.10(1)

Wife had no right to jury trial on claim that premarital real property titled solely in husband's name should be included in marital estate for equitable distribution purposes, by virtue of concepts of transmutation of property, constructive/resulting trusts, implied contract, unjust enrichment, and quasi-contract, as such concepts were clearly equitable in nature, and thus should be presented solely to court as trier of fact.

James P. Yudes, Springfield, for appellant (James P. Yudes, P.C., attorneys; Charles F. Vuotto, Jr., Springfield, of counsel; Elizabeth E. Bedell, Long Branch, of counsel and on the brief).

Lee M. Hymerling, Haddonfield, for respondent (Archer & Greiner, attorneys; Mr. Hymerling, of counsel and on the brief).

Before Judges SKILLMAN, WALLACE and KLEINER.

The opinion of the court was delivered by

⌊₈⌋KLEINER, J.A.D.

On July 1, 1994, plaintiff Christina Giovine filed an eleven count complaint against defendant Peter J. Giovine denominated: "Complaint for divorce, domestic torts, equitable claims and jury trial demand." Plaintiff's complaint alleged habitual drunkenness, *N.J.S.A.* 2A:34-2(e) (count one) and extreme cruelty, *N.J.S.A.* 2A:34-2(c) (count two) as alternative grounds for the dissolution of the marriage. In counts three through six, plaintiff asserted claims for compensatory and punitive damages based upon an assault and battery which allegedly occurred in March 1972 (count three); intentional infliction of emotional injury/distress commencing in March 1972 (count four); "continuous wrong" between March 1972 and May 1993, resulting in "severe emotional and physical damage" (count five); and negligence (count six).

Counts seven through eleven of plaintiff's complaint alleged equitable claims respecting real property acquired by defendant in February 1969 prior to the marriage and titled solely in defendant's name, predicated upon the concepts of transmutation (count seven); constructive/resulting trust (count eight); implied contract (count nine); unjust enrichment (count ten); and quasi-contract (count eleven).

Plaintiff demanded a jury trial on counts three through eleven.

I—MARITAL HISTORY

Plaintiff and defendant were married on May 1, 1971. Three children were born of this marriage on August 17, 1975, July 5, 1979, and July 7, 1983.

On approximately December 31, 1978, defendant separated from plaintiff. In May 1980, he filed a complaint seeking to establish visitation rights with the two children of the marriage. On August 1, 1980, defendant filed a complaint for divorce, asserting a cause of action for dissolution of marriage predicated upon eighteen consecutive months of separation. Plaintiff filed an answer and counterclaim for divorce, alleging habitual drunkenness and extreme₉ cruelty as alternative grounds for divorce. Additionally, that counterclaim contained three counts for damages predicated upon the following torts: a specific act of assault and battery in March 1972 and a final act of assault and battery on December 28, 1978; infliction of emotional distress based upon the same acts of assault and battery; and "a continuous and unbroken wrong commencing on or about March 1972 and continuing down until December 28, 1978."

Defendant filed an answer to the counterclaim and amended his complaint for divorce, adding a cause of action for divorce based upon acts of extreme cruelty.

In July 1982, while their matrimonial action was pending, the parties reconciled and resumed living together. On July 26, 1982, both parties directed their respective attorneys to discontinue the litigation. The proceedings were dismissed by a stipulation of dismissal with prejudice dated October 25, 1982. The couple separated again in September 1993. As noted, plaintiff filed her present complaint on July 1, 1994. Defendant filed an answer and counterclaim asserting a cause of action for divorce based upon extreme cruelty.

II—PRESENT LITIGATION

On August 8, 1994, defendant filed a motion to strike certain causes of action contained within plaintiff's complaint and to strike plaintiff's demand for a jury trial on counts three through eleven. On September 20, 1994, the motion judge granted defendant's motion, striking all tortious claims occurring prior to June 30, 1992 based upon the applicable statute of limitations, *N.J.S.A.* 2A:14–2, and limiting plaintiff's proofs on her claims for emotional distress or negligence to those acts alleged to have occurred after June 30, 1992. The motion judge also determined that plaintiff did not have a constitutional right to a jury trial. We granted plaintiff's motion seeking leave to appeal those rulings, which were memorialized in an order dated November 14, 1994. We now affirm in part and reverse in part.

└₁₀III

[1, 2] Interspousal tort immunity no longer exists to bar the suit of one spouse against another for injuries sustained by one spouse due to the tortious conduct of the other. *Merenoff v. Merenoff,* 76 *N.J.* 535, 557, 388 *A.*2d 951 (1978).

[T]he abolition of the doctrine pertained to tortious conduct generally encompassing not only conventional negligence but also intentional acts, as well as other forms of excessive behavior such as gross negligence, recklessness, wantonness, and the like. The only kind of marital conduct excepted from the abolition was that involving marital or nuptial privileges, consensual acts and simple, common domestic negligence, to be defined and developed on a case-by-case approach.

[*Tevis v. Tevis,* 79 *N.J.* 422, 426–27, 400 A.2d 1189 (1979) (citation omitted).]

If the circumstances surrounding a domestic tort and a claim for monetary damages are relevant to a divorce proceeding, the domestic tort must be joined with the divorce proceeding under the "single controversy doctrine" in order to avoid protracted, repetitious and fractionalized litigation. *Id.* at 434, 400 A.2d 1189.

On appeal, plaintiff contends that the motion judge erred in refusing to follow the decision in *Cusseaux v. Pickett,* 279 *N.J.Super.* 335, 652 A.2d 789 (Law Div.1994), which concluded that "battered-woman's syndrome is the result of a continuing pattern of abuse and violent behavior that causes continuing damage." *Id.* at 345, 652 A.2d 789. As such, "it must be treated in the same way as a continuing tort." *Ibid.* Battered woman's syndrome would therefore be an exception to *N.J.S.A.* 2A:14–2, that "[e]very action at law for an injury to the person caused by the wrongful act, neglect or default of any person within this state shall be commenced within 2 years next after the cause of any such action shall have occurred." *Ibid.* The decision in *Cusseaux* substantially relied upon *State v. Kelly,* 97 *N.J.* 178, 478 A.2d 364 (1984).

In *Kelly,* the Supreme Court, relying in part on the research of Lenore E. Walker, *The Battered Woman* (1979), noted that battered woman's syndrome is a recognized medical condition. By definition, a battered woman is one who is repeatedly physically or emotionally abused by a man in an attempt to force her to do his bidding without regard for her rights. *State v. Kelly, supra,* 97 ₍₁₁₎*N.J.* at 193, 478 A.2d 364. According to experts, in order to be a battered woman, the woman and her abuser must go through the "battering cycle" at least twice. *Ibid.*

The battering cycle consists of three stages. *Ibid.* Stage one, the "tension-building stage," involves some minor physical and verbal abuse while the woman tries to prevent an escalation of the abuse by assuaging

the abuser with her passivity. *Ibid.* (citation omitted). Stage two, the "acute battering incident," is characterized by more severe battering due to either a triggering event in the abuser's life or the woman's inability to control the anger and fear she experienced during stage one. *Ibid.* (citation omitted). During stage three, the abuser pleads for forgiveness and promises that he will not abuse again. *Id.* at 193–94, 478 A.2d 364 (citation omitted). This period of relative calm and normalcy eventually ends when the cycle begins anew. *Id.* at 194, 478 A.2d 364 (citation omitted).[1]

"The cyclical nature of battering behavior helps explain why more women simply do not leave their abusers." *Ibid.* The caring and attentive behavior of the abuser during stage three fuels the victim's hope that her partner has reformed and keeps her tied to the relationship. *Ibid.* In addition, some women who grew up in violent families do not leave abusive relationships because they perceive their situations as normal. *Ibid.* Others cannot face the reality of their situations. *Ibid.* Some victims "become so demoralized and degraded by the fact that they cannot predict or control the violence that they sink into a state of psychological paralysis and become unable to take any action at all to improve or alter the situation." *Ibid.* Victims are often afraid to seek help out of shame, fear that no one will believe them, or fear of retaliation by their abusers. *Id.* at 195, 478 A.2d 364. "They literally become trapped by their own fear." *Ibid.*

₍₁₂₎In *Kelly,* the Supreme Court held that expert testimony on battered woman's syndrome was admissible to show that a woman on trial for murder who was repeatedly beaten during her marriage honestly believed that she was in imminent danger of death when she stabbed her husband, and therefore, she acted in self-defense. *Id.* at 187, 202–04, 478 A.2d 364.

In *State v. Ellis,* 280 *N.J.Super.* 533, 543, 656 A.2d 25 (App.Div.1995) (citing *State v. Kelly, supra*), we concluded that evidence of

---

1. *See* Lenore E. Walker, Roberta K. Thyfault and Angela Browne, *Beyond the Juror's Ken: Battered*   *Women,* 7 *Vt.L.Rev.* 1 (1982).

battered woman's syndrome can be introduced in a criminal proceeding as evidence to explain why a victim of a kidnapping neither attempted to escape a kidnapper nor immediately reported the kidnapping. In *Ellis*, the victim was the defendant's girlfriend.

Cusseaux v. Pickett, supra, recognized for the first time in this state, that a woman who suffers from the medically diagnosable condition of battered woman's syndrome is entitled to seek compensation for the physical and emotional injuries attributable to the abusive conduct during the course of the relationship. The trial judge found that:

> Because the battered-woman's syndrome is the result of a continuing pattern of abuse and violent behavior that causes continuing damage, it must be treated in the same way as a continuing tort. It would be contrary to the public policy of this State, not to mention cruel, to limit recovery to only those individual incidents of assault and battery for which the applicable statute of limitations has not yet run. The mate who is responsible for creating the condition suffered by the battered victim must be made to account for his actions—*all* of his actions. Failure to allow affirmative recovery under these circumstances would be tantamount to the courts condoning the continued abusive treatment of women in the domestic sphere. This the courts cannot and will never do.

> [*Cusseaux v. Pickett, supra*, 279 N.J.Super. at 345, 652 A.2d 789.]

Cusseaux established a four-part test to state a cause of action for battered woman's syndrome:

> 1) involvement in a marital or marital-like intimate relationship; and 2) physical or psychological abuse perpetrated by the dominant partner to the relationship over an extended period of time; and 3) the aforestated abuse has caused recurring physical or psychological injury over the course of the relationship; and 4) a past or present inability to take any action to improve or alter the situation unilaterally.

> [*Id.* at 344, 652 A.2d 789 (footnotes omitted).]

⌊₁₃[3, 4] We agree with the premise espoused in *Cusseaux* and conclude that a wife diagnosed with battered woman's syndrome should be permitted to sue her spouse in tort for the physical and emotional injuries sustained by continuous acts of battering during the course of the marriage, *provided* there is medical, psychiatric, or psychological expert testimony establishing that the wife was caused to have an "inability to take any action to improve or alter the situation unilaterally." *Ibid.* In the absence of expert proof, the wife cannot be deemed to be suffering from battered woman's syndrome, and each act of abuse during the marriage would constitute a separate and distinct cause of action in tort, subject to the statute of limitations, N.J.S.A. 2A:14–2. *Laughlin v. Breaux*, 515 So.2d 480, 482–83 (La.Ct.App. 1987).

Our disagreement with *Cusseaux* is predicated upon semantics. *Cusseaux* classifies battered woman's syndrome as a continuous tort.[2] The concept of "continuous tort" has been recognized in this state. *Morey v. Essex County*, 94 N.J.L. 427, 430, 110 A. 905 (E. & A. 1920) (unremitting trespass is a continuous tort); *Russo Farms, Inc. v. Vineland Bd. of Educ.*, 280 N.J.Super. 320, 327–28, 655 A.2d 447 (App.Div.1995) (claim of inverse condemnation continued to accrue as long as defendant's conduct caused plaintiff's property to be subject to continual flooding due to negligent construction of an adjoining building); *Aykan v. Goldzweig*, 238 N.J.Super. 389, 392, 569 A.2d 905 (Law Div.1989) (continuous negligent representation by an attorney is a continuous tort which tolls the statute of limitations until the representation is terminated or the client discovered or should have discovered the injury). This concept was also discussed, although not applied, in *Tortorello v. Reinfeld*, 6 N.J. 58, 66, 77 A.2d 240 (1950), in reference to a claim that a continuing course of negligent treatment by a physician should be considered a continuous tort, and not an isolated incident of negligent treatment.

---

2. A similar analysis of the continuous tort theory is discussed in *Twyman v. Twyman*, 855 S.W.2d 619 (Tex.1993), reversing *Twyman v. Twyman*, 790 S.W.2d 819 (Tex.Ct.App.1990).

₁₁₄[5] We do not adopt the conclusion in *Cusseaux* that battered woman's syndrome is itself a continuous tort. Battered woman's syndrome is more correctly the medical condition resulting from continued acts of physical or psychological misconduct. Because the resulting psychological state, composed of varied but identifiable characteristics, is the product of at least two separate and discrete physical or psychological acts occurring at different times, to overcome the statute of limitations, it is imperative that the tortious conduct giving rise to the medical condition be considered a continuous tort. As noted in *Kelly:*

> The combination of all of these symptoms—resulting from sustained psychological and physical trauma compounded by aggravating social and economic factors—constitutes the battered-woman's syndrome. Only by understanding these unique pressures that force battered women to remain with their mates, despite their long-standing and reasonable fear of severe bodily harm and the isolation that being a battered woman creates, can a battered woman's state of mind be accurately and fairly understood.
>
> [*State v. Kelly, supra,* 97 N.J. at 196, 478 A.2d 364.]

The Supreme Court in *Kelly* and the Law Division in *Cusseaux* placed substantial weight on the legislative findings which led to the enactment of the Prevention of Domestic Violence Act, N.J.S.A. 2C:25–1 to –16.[3] Those findings deserve repeating:

> The Legislature finds and declares that domestic violence is a serious crime against society; that there are thousands of persons in this State who are regularly beaten, tortured and in some cases even killed by their spouses or cohabitants; that a significant number of women who are assaulted are pregnant; that victims of domestic violence come from all social and economic backgrounds and ethnic groups; that there is a positive correlation between spousal abuse and child abuse; and that children, even when they are not themselves physically assaulted, suffer deep and

lasting emotional effects from exposure to domestic violence. It is therefore, the intent of the Legislature to assure the victims of domestic violence the maximum protection from abuse the law can provide.

> .... Further, it is the responsibility of the courts to protect victims of violence that occurs in a family or family-like setting by providing access to both emergent and long-term civil and criminal remedies and sanctions, and by ordering those remedies and sanctions that are available to assure the safety of the victims and ₁₁₅the public. To that end, the Legislature encourages ... the broad application of the remedies available under this act in the civil and criminal courts of this State.

> [N.J.S.A. 2C:25–18.]

Cusseaux had no cause to discuss the statute of limitations, N.J.S.A. 2A:14–2, as it might affect a cause of action for the medical condition of battered woman's syndrome.

[6] In *Kyle v. Green Acres at Verona, Inc.,* 44 N.J. 100, 207 A.2d 513 (1965), the Supreme Court held that N.J.S.A. 2A:14–21 "foreclose[d] a tolling of the running of [the limitations period] unless plaintiff was [insane] at the time the cause of action accrued...." *Id.* at 106–07, 207 A.2d 513. The Court carved out an equitable exception, however, where defendant's "negligent act brings about [a] plaintiff's insanity." *Id.* at 111, 207 A.2d 513. Applying equitable considerations, the Court concluded:

> [I]f plaintiff's insanity was caused by defendant's wrongful act, it may be said that such act was responsible for plaintiff's failure or inability to institute her action prior to the running of the statute of limitations. We feel that justice here requires us to carve out an equitable exception to the general principle that there is no time out for the period of time covered by the disability if the disability accrued at or after the cause of action accrued. Thus, a defendant whose negligent act brings about plaintiff's insanity should not be permitted to cloak himself with the protective garb of the statute of limitations.

3. In 1991, N.J.S.A. 2C:25–1 to –16 were repealed, and N.J.S.A. 2C:25–17 to –33 were enacted in

their place. N.J.S.A. 2C:25–18 contains the same language that was contained in N.J.S.A. 2C:25–2.

[Ibid. (footnote omitted).]

The Court added:

The equitable approach should mandate the following: A trial court shall itself without a jury hear and determine (1) whether insanity developed on or subsequent to the date of the alleged act of defendant and within the period of limitation and if so, whether that insanity resulted from the defendant's acts; and (2) whether plaintiff's suit was started within a reasonable time after restoration of sanity....

[*Id.* at 112, 207 A.2d 513.]

"Insane," as used in *N.J.S.A.* 2A:14–21, means "such a condition of mental derangement as actually prevents the sufferer from understanding his [or her] legal rights or instituting legal action." *Ibid.*

In *Jones v. Jones,* 242 *N.J.Super.* 195, 576 A.2d 316 (App.Div.), *certif. denied,* 122 *N.J.* 418, 585 A.2d 412 (1990), we applied equitable considerations to abrogate the running of the statute of limitations against an incest victim. We noted the victim's emotional condition as a justification for tolling the statute of limitations,[16] as well as the fact that the victim plaintiff was placed under physical and psychological duress by the defendant. Plaintiff's expert psychologist opined that "individuals subjected to childhood sexual abuse often find it impossible to communicate and describe such misconduct." *Id.* at 201, 576 A.2d 316. *Jones* likened plaintiff's condition to the condition of insanity, which tolls the statute of limitations in *N.J.S.A.* 2A:14–21 and provides in part:

If any person entitled to any of the actions or proceedings specified in sections 2A:14–1 to 2A:14–8 or sections 2A:14–16 to 2A:14–20 ... is or shall be, at the time of any such cause of action or right or title accruing, under the age of 21 years, or *insane,* such person may commence such action ... after his coming to or being of full age or of *sane* mind.

[*Ibid.* (emphasis added).]

We are able to draw an analogy between the status of the plaintiff in *Jones* to the status of a victim of repeated violence within the marital setting, who may "sink into a state of psychological paralysis and become unable to take any action at all to improve or alter the situation." *Kelly, supra,* 97 *N.J.* at 194–95, 478 A.2d 364 (citations omitted); *Cusseaux, supra,* 279 *N.J.Super.* at 341, 652 A.2d 789.

Jones also determined that duress may toll the statute of limitations when "it is either an element of or inherent in the underlying cause of action." *Jones, supra,* 242 *N.J.Super.* at 208, 576 A.2d 316 (citations omitted). We prefaced that conclusion with this admonition:

We do not suggest that the decisions we have cited should be applied uncritically whenever a plaintiff claims that his or her failure to initiate suit in a timely fashion was caused by a defendant's wrongful act. We are, nevertheless, of the view that, within certain limits, a prospective defendant's coercive acts and threats may rise to such a level of duress as to deprive the plaintiff of his freedom of will and thereby toll the statute of limitations.

[*Ibid.*]

As noted in *Tevis v. Tevis, supra,* 79 *N.J.* at 431, 400 A.2d 1189, the Legislature has not specified when a cause of action shall be deemed to have "accrued" for the purposes of the statute of limitations for tortious injury to property or persons. The accrual of a cause of action has been left entirely as a matter of judicial determination, interpretation and administration. *Ibid.* (citing *Rosenau v. City of New Brunswick,* 51 *N.J.* 130, 137, 238 A.2d 169 (1968)).

The role of the court in interpreting legislative intent respecting the statute of limitations is illustrated in *Jones, supra:*

Unswerving, mechanistic application of statutes of limitations would at times "inflict obvious and unnecessary harm upon individual plaintiffs" without materially advancing the objectives they are designed to serve. The legislative and judicial response to such inequities has been to provide certain statutory exceptions....

[*Jones, supra,* 242 *N.J.Super.* at 203, 576 A.2d 316 (citation omitted).]

Similarly, the Supreme Court in *Galligan v. Westfield Centre Service, Inc.*, 82 *N.J.* 188, 412 *A.*2d 122 (1980) held:

A "just accommodation" of individual justice and public policy requires that "in each case the equitable claims of opposing parties must be identified, evaluated and weighed." Whenever dismissal would not further the Legislature's objectives in prescribing the limitation, the plaintiff should be given an opportunity to assert his claim.
[*Id.* at 193, 412 *A.*2d 122 (citations omitted).]

We recognize that this same reasoning was implicated in *Lopez v. Swyer*, 62 *N.J.* 267, 300 *A.*2d 563 (1973), which concluded that a cause of action will be held not to accrue until an injured party discovers, or by an exercise of reasonable diligence and intelligence should have discovered that he may have a basis for an actionable claim, thus resulting in a tolling of the statute of limitations on equitable grounds.

We also note that in *Lopez*, the Supreme Court specifically directed that the determination whether to toll the statute of limitations is a legal question "within the province of the court." *Id.* at 274, 300 *A.*2d 563.

Likewise, in *Kyle v. Green Acres at Verona, Inc.*, *supra*, 44 *N.J.* at 112, 207 *A.*2d 513, the Supreme Court directed:

A trial court shall itself without a jury hear and determine (1) whether insanity developed on or subsequent to the date of the alleged act of defendant and within the period of limitation and if so, whether that insanity resulted from the defendant's acts; and (2) whether plaintiff's suit was started within a reasonable time after restoration of sanity....
[*Ibid.*]

That same mandate will be applicable in the trial of this matter. It will be incumbent upon plaintiff to establish pretrial, by medical, psychiatric or psychological evidence, that she suffers from battered woman's syn-

drome, which caused an inability to take any action to improve or alter the circumstances in her marriage unilaterally, so as to warrant a conclusion by the trial judge that the statute of limitations should be tolled.[4]

We construe the clear legislative statement in the preamble to *N.J.S.A.* 2C:25–18 as justification for the decision we reach: "the Legislature encourages ... the broad application of the remedies available under this act in the civil and criminal courts of this State." *Ibid.* The motion judge, in refusing to be guided by *Cusseaux*, applied *N.J.S.A.* 2A:14–2 mechanistically and totally ignored the invitation of the Legislature. We recognize that the motion judge was not bound to follow *Cusseaux*, as that opinion was rendered by a court of concurrent jurisdiction. However, as we now subscribe to the concept articulated in *Cusseaux*, we reverse the motion judge's decision and direct that plaintiff shall be entitled to present proof that she has the medically diagnosed condition of battered woman's syndrome. Plaintiff shall be entitled to sue her husband for damages attributable to his continuous tortious conduct resulting in her present psychological condition, provided she has medical, psychiatric, or psychological expert proof to establish that she was caused to have an inability "to take any action at all to improve or alter the situation." *Cusseaux*, *supra*, 279 *N.J.Super.* at 341, 652 *A.*2d 789.

Our dissenting colleague properly notes that plaintiff has failed to present any medical, physical or psychological evidence to support her claim that she suffers from the medical condition labeled battered woman's syndrome. However, the trial court dismissed count five of plaintiff's complaint alleging "continuous wrong" not because plaintiff failed to present proof of her medical condition in response to defendant's motion, but because the decision in *Cusseaux* was not binding upon a court of concurrent jurisdiction. Yet, the trial court established a discovery schedule which encompassed the *future* filing of plaintiff's expert reports. Ac-

4. Were plaintiff proceeding without a jury, the court would not be required to conduct a pretrial hearing. The testimony can be presented during the entire divorce proceeding; however, the court must determine whether the statute of limi-

tations should be tolled before rendering a decision on the merits of the cause of action and awarding damages. *Lopez v. Swyer*, *supra*, 62 *N.J.* at 275 n. 3, 300 *A.*2d 563.

cordingly, the motion judge's decision to bar all claims for injuries both psychological and physical suffered prior to June 30, 1992 was too broad and was prematurely granted. The motion to dismiss plaintiff's claim should have been decided after plaintiff was compelled to file her expert medical reports, and not prior to the completion of discovery.

IV

Although plaintiff should not have been foreclosed from attempting to prove a claim of battered woman's syndrome, the decision of the trial court dismissing certain aspects of plaintiff's complaint was correct.

[7] In the third count of plaintiff's complaint for divorce, plaintiff specifically refers to a battery which occurred in March 1972, which caused plaintiff to suffer a perforated eardrum resulting in surgery and a two-week hospitalization. Plaintiff contends she suffered a permanent loss in hearing as a result of that attack. In that count, plaintiff also contends: "The defendant has continually since March of 1972, attacked the plaintiff causing her on numerous occasions great physical and bodily injury. The last such beating having occurred in or about June of 1993."[5]

∟₂₀It is clear that the statute of limitations bars any claim asserted in count three for damages attributable to an assault and battery which allegedly occurred in March 1972. The motion judge properly dismissed that claim.

In count five of plaintiff's complaint, plaintiff repeats, by reference, the allegations of count three and then asserts:

The defendant's conduct against the plaintiff has been a continuous and unbroken wrong commencing in or about March of 1972 and continuing down until May of

1993. Said continuous course of conduct by the defendant has caused the plaintiff severe emotional damage and physical damage.

Although plaintiff does not specifically refer to battered woman's syndrome, it is clear that count five is designed to encompass that claim.

We conclude that regardless of any expert medical opinion which may hereafter be filed, all psychological or physical injury associated with the alleged March 1972 incident is barred by the statute of limitations.

As noted, the medical condition of battered woman's syndrome does not occur until a woman is battered at least twice. *Kelly, supra,* 97 *N.J.* at 193, 478 *A.2d* 364 (citations omitted). The physical and emotional injuries suffered as a result of an initial striking may give rise to a tort claim against a spouse, but such a claim must be asserted within two years of the date of injury. *N.J.S.A.* 2A:14–2. Battered woman's syndrome does not develop, if at all, until a spouse is abused a second time. One common characteristic of battered woman's syndrome is "psychological paralysis," the inability of the victim "to take any action at all to improve or alter the situation." *Kelly, supra,* 97 *N.J.* at 194–95, 478 *A.2d* 364. Here, plaintiff was able to take action. In 1980, plaintiff filed a counterclaim for divorce which alleged acts of extreme cruelty, including a battery committed in March 1972 and a final battery, committed December 28, 1978. She also alleged psychological damage attributable to those beatings. Clearly, the ∟₂₁statute of limitations, *N.J.S.A.* 2A:14–2, must bar any present cause of action predicated upon those alleged marital torts.[6]

[8] Our conclusion that plaintiff's damage claim is barred does not, however, prevent

---

5. In 1980, plaintiff's counterclaim for divorce was predicated upon the physical assault in March 1972, and on a separate assault which allegedly occurred in December 1978. Plaintiff's present complaint for divorce refers to the assault in March 1972, but it does not specifically mention the alleged assault in December 1978.

6. The parties separated December 31, 1978. They reconciled in July 1982. If the tortious act of December 28, 1978 proximately caused bat-

tered woman's syndrome, the filing of a counterclaim for divorce predicated in part upon that beating demonstrated that plaintiff as of the date of filing in September 1980 had the ability to take action to "improve or alter" her martial difficulties. *Cusseaux, supra,* 279 *N.J.Super.* at 344, 652 *A.2d* 789. We also note that plaintiff's complaint fails to specifically allege the act of assault on December 28, 1978.

the introduction of proof of those incidents (March 1972 and December 1978) in the forthcoming trial of this matrimonial action. The component of the motion judge's ruling which barred all proofs on plaintiff's claims for emotional distress or negligence to acts occurring after June 30, 1992 was error.

Obviously, in order to prove the medical condition of battered woman's syndrome, plaintiff must be permitted to prove all acts of physical or psychological misconduct. This proof will also encompass the first beating in March 1972. The medical condition is attributable to more than one act of battering. Although plaintiff may be barred from recovering damages for certain marital torts (here, the act allegedly committed in March 1972, which was pled, and on December 28, 1978, which was not specifically pled), those acts and others may be relevant in plaintiff's proofs presented to establish plaintiff's claim of emotional distress. "Relevant evidence" is defined as "evidence having a tendency in reason to prove or disprove any fact of consequence to the determination of the action." *N.J.R.E.* 401. It was error for the court to bar all evidence of abuse occurring prior to June 30, 1992. Some or all evidence of pre-1992 events may be relevant to proving plaintiff's causes of action framed in terms of infliction of emotional distress or negligence. Rulings which exclude proffered evidence are best made at trial, where the court is best able to evaluate "the logical connection between the proffered evidence and a fact in issue." |₂₂*State v. Hutchins*, 241 *N.J.Super.* 353, 358, 575 A.2d 35 (App.Div.1990).

[9] Additionally, prior acts of extreme cruelty are always evidential to establish that the last act of cruelty complained of was of such character as to make it unreasonable to expect that plaintiff would continue to cohabit with defendant. That is the basic underpinning of a cause of action for divorce predicated on extreme cruelty. *N.J.S.A.* 2A:34–2(c) defines "extreme cruelty" as:

any physical or mental cruelty which endangers the safety or health of the plaintiff or makes it improper or unreasonable to expect the plaintiff to continue to cohabit with the defendant.

[*Ibid.*]

As noted in *Scalingi v. Scalingi*, 65 *N.J.* 180, 320 A.2d 475 (1974):

Prior to the 1971 amendment, extreme cruelty was considered to be that degree of cruelty, either actually inflicted or reasonably inferred, which endangered the life or health of the aggrieved party, or rendered his or her life one of such extreme discomfort and wretchedness as to incapacitate him or her physically or mentally from discharging the marital duties.

The 1971 amendment not only embraces the foregoing, but also includes physical or mental cruelty which makes it improper or unreasonable to expect the plaintiff to continue to cohabit with the defendant. *N.J.S.A.* 2A:34–2(c). This latter provision substantially broadens the concept of extreme cruelty as it existed under the earlier statute.

[*Id.* at 183, 320 A.2d 475 (citations omitted).]

In *Scalingi*, plaintiff presented proof of prior acts of physical and mental cruelty preceding the last act of cruelty committed within three months prior to the filing of plaintiff's complaint. *Ibid.*

It is therefore clear that plaintiff must be permitted to present proofs of all acts of cruelty which occurred during the course of her marriage to defendant. Those prior acts may be offered to prove plaintiff's cause of action for divorce predicated on the grounds of extreme cruelty, or they may be offered as relevant evidence in conjunction with plaintiff's claim for damages attributable to battered woman's syndrome, intentional infliction of emotional distress and negligence.

|₂₃V

As we noted preliminarily, plaintiff's complaint demanded a trial by jury on counts three through six of her complaint alleging "domestic torts" and on counts seven through eleven alleging "equitable claims." On defendant's motion to strike plaintiff's jury trial demand, the motion judge, relying on *Boardwalk Properties, Inc. v. BPHC Acquisition, Inc.*, 253 *N.J.Super.* 515, 526–27, 602 A.2d 733 (App.Div.1991), determined that plaintiff had no constitutional right to a trial by jury and granted defendant's motion to strike.

Plaintiff contends that she has a constitutional right to a jury trial on her tort claims pursuant to *N.J. Const.* art I, ¶ 9. In support of that argument, plaintiff cites *Tweedley v. Tweedley,* 277 *N.J.Super.* 246, 649 *A.2d* 630 (Ch.Div.1994). Defendant contends that the motion judge's ruling should be affirmed, citing *Davis v. Davis,* 182 *N.J.Super.* 397, 442 *A.2d* 208 (Ch.Div.1981).

[10] The Seventh Amendment of the Federal Constitution, which provides the right to a trial by jury in a civil case, is not enforceable against the states.

By article I, paragraph 9, of the Constitution of 1947, "The right of a trial by jury shall remain inviolate." This provision means exactly what it says. Where the right to a trial by jury existed under the Constitution of 1844, the right continues unimpaired under the new Constitution. [*Steiner v. Stein,* 2 *N.J.* 367, 378–79, 66 *A.2d* 719 (1949); *See also Boardwalk Properties, Inc. v. BPHC Acquisition, Inc., supra,* 253 *N.J.Super.* at 527, 602 *A.2d* 733.]

[11] At common law, prior to 1947, cases sounding in tort carried with them a right to a jury trial. *Kenney v. Scientific, Inc.,* 213 *N.J.Super.* 372, 374–75, 517 *A.2d* 484 (App. Div.1986). The concurrent jurisdiction of the Law Division and Chancery Division does not deny a party the right to a jury trial under the State Constitution. *Fisch v. Manger,* 24 *N.J.* 66, 75, 130 *A.2d* 815 (1957); *O'Neill v. Vreeland,* 6 *N.J.* 158, 167, 77 *A.2d* 899 (1951).

[12] Nevertheless, "[i]f a court of equity, prior to 1947, would have considered the legal issue 'ancillary' or 'incidental' to the ₂₄cognizable equitable claim, then the issue was [and still is] triable without a jury." *Boardwalk Properties, Inc. v. BPHC Acquisition, Inc., supra,* 253 *N.J.Super.* at 527, 602 *A.2d* 733; *See also Fleischer v. James Drug Stores,* 1 *N.J.* 138, 150, 62 *A.2d* 383 (1948). There is no right to a jury trial if the legal issues are "germane to or grow out of the subject-matter of the equitable jurisdiction." *Fleischer v. James Drug Stores, ibid.* "However, it is incorrect to assume that all claims

arising out of the same controversy are 'germane to or grow out of the subject matter of the equitable jurisdiction.' Indeed, legal claims may grow out of a controversy that are independent of the equitable action." *Boardwalk Properties, Inc. v. BPHC Acquisition, Inc., supra,* 253 *N.J.Super.* at 528, 602 *A.2d* 733.

For example, in *Chiacchio v. Chiacchio,* 198 *N.J.Super.* 1, 7, 486 *A.2d* 335 (App.Div. 1984), the court held that a third-party complaint against Allstate Insurance Company and Allstate's counterclaim for declaratory relief, which involved legal issues relating to Allstate's liability for domestic torts allegedly committed by defendant against plaintiff under an insurance policy issued by Allstate, did not arise out of the marital relationship that gave rise to plaintiff's divorce and tort action against defendant.

In contrast, in *Apollo v. Kim Anh Pham,* 192 *N.J.Super.* 427, 430, 432, 470 *A.2d* 934 (Ch.Div.1983), *aff'd,* 224 *N.J.Super.* 89, 539 *A.2d* 1222 (App.Div.1987), the court concluded that the legal demand for damages presented by defendant in her counterclaim, based on an alleged contract wherein plaintiff promised to support defendant and her children in exchange for her cohabiting with plaintiff in Vietnam and subsequently maintaining a home for him in the United States, were ancillary to plaintiff's equitable claims for specific performance, arising out of the same facts based on theories of quantum meruit and quasi-contract.

The Chancery Division has twice considered the issue at hand. In *Davis v. Davis, supra,* 182 *N.J.Super* at 398–99, 442 *A.2d* 208, the court denied a wife's request for a jury trial on her domestic tort claim based largely on a report by the subcommittee of the ₂₅Supreme Court Committee on Matrimonial Litigation, to the effect that: "As a matter of judicial administration, no jury trial for a marital tort should be provided in an action for divorce...." Supreme Court Committee on Matrimonial Litigation, Phase Two Final Report, June 10, 1981, at 78–79. The subcommittee concluded that a domestic tort claim is closely related to equitable distribution and therefore, is incidental and ancillary to the underlying divorce action. *Id.* at 399, 442 A.2d 208. Hence, the subcommittee recommended that courts should not allow a jury trial of a domestic tort in conjunction with an action for divorce. *Ibid.* The court noted that the report had not been implemented and did not have the force of law. *Ibid.* We note that the subcommittee report did not indicate that a tort claimant does not have a right to a jury trial. The recommendation was primarily predicated upon the dictates of judicial administration, focusing upon the difficulty in accommodating a jury trial within the framework of an equitable proceeding.

The Chancery Division came to the opposite conclusion in *Tweedley v. Tweedley, supra*, 277 *N.J.Super.* at 247, 649 *A.2d* 630. First, the *Tweedley* court noted that its case was distinguishable from *Davis* because defendant amended her counterclaim for divorce from extreme cruelty to no-fault, and plaintiff's allegations of cruelty were few. *Id.* at 252, 649 A.2d 630. Therefore, the *Tweedley* court stated that it could not conclude that the tort claim was closely related to the divorce action. *Ibid.*

Tweedley also relied on *Merenoff v. Merenoff, supra.* The Supreme Court, in discussing the scope of interspousal tort liability, declared:

There is a range of activity arising in the course of a marriage relationship beyond the reach of the law of torts. Special matters of privacy and familiarity may be encompassed by a marital or nuptial privilege and fall outside the bounds of a definable and enforceable duty of care. Certain conduct may also be regarded as "consensual", involving the "give-and-take" and subtle ebb and flow of married life. In these areas courts and *juries* cannot be expected to grasp sensibly and consistently the acceptable norm of married living or chart the parameters of reasonable marital behavior as a predicate for affixing liability in tort.

⌊₂₆[*Merenoff v. Merenoff, supra*, 76 *N.J.* at 555, 388 A.2d 951 (citations omitted) (emphasis added).]

Furthermore, the Court commented:

Similarly, certain kinds of claimed injuries between married persons will be based

on simple domestic carelessness arising from activities which partake of the everyday exigencies of regular household existence and, for that reason, may not readily be controlled or influenced by the law of torts through the judicial imposition of a duty of care and the corresponding obligation to respond in damages for its breach. Thus, absent the immunity bar, the fear that trivial, exaggerated or unrealistic claims for personal injury will be brought by married persons is counterpoised by the realization that such claims for the most part will not be cognizable by courts or *rewarded by juries.*

[*Id.* at 555–56, 388 *A.2d* 951 (citation omitted) (emphasis added).]

We recognize that *Merenoff* was a consolidation of two appeals: *Merenoff v. Merenoff*, a wife's claim against her husband for the traumatic amputation of her left index finger, resulting from his alleged negligent use of a hedge trimmer; and *Mercado v. Mercado*, a wife's claim for serious burns resulting from her husband's use of a flammable substance near a stove. Neither case involved an intentional tort allegedly committed by one spouse against the other. Nonetheless, the Court concluded that interspousal immunity in all tort actions would thereafter be abolished. *Id.* at 556, 388 *A.2d* 951. In its historical analysis leading to its ultimate conclusion, *Merenoff* cited *Tevis v. Tevis*, 155 *N.J.Super.* 273, 382 A.2d 697 (1978), *rev'd on other grounds*, 79 *N.J.* 422, 400 A.2d 1189 (1979), in which the Appellate Division recognized a spouse's right to sue for interspousal intentional torts. *Tevis* involved an appeal of a jury verdict awarding compensatory and punitive damages to a former wife for injuries sustained as a result of assault and battery committed by her former husband at a time when the parties were still married. The Supreme Court stated:

Divorce or separation provide escape from tortious abuse but can hardly be equated with a civil right to redress and compensation for personal injuries. Equally arcane and unworthy is the notion that a wronged spouse, who has been injured at the hands of her or his mate, can and should resort to an arsenal of "private sanctions". Regardless of the ways a person can "get back" at one's spouse, they do not add up to an enforceable civil right of recovery for damages.

[*Merenoff v. Merenoff, supra,* 76 *N.J.* at 556–57, 388 *A.*2d 951 (citations omitted).]

┌27 We find nothing in the language of the Supreme Court to prohibit the right to a jury trial.

The Supreme Court has not had occasion to address the specific right of trial by jury to recover damages for interspousal torts since its decision in *Merenoff.* The Court did not discuss trial by jury when it later decided *Tevis v. Tevis,* 79 *N.J.* 422, 400 *A.*2d 1189 (1979) and concluded a marital tort claim must be presented in conjunction with pending matrimonial litigation by virtue of the entire controversy rule. *Id.* at 434, 400 *A.*2d 1189.

Tweedley did not merely distinguish *Davis,* but pointed out that in New Jersey, fault is not one of the criteria a court should consider in resolving the issues of support and equitable distribution. *Tweedley v. Tweedley, supra,* 277 *N.J.Super.* at 253, 649 *A.*2d 630. In addition, the court explained that it is substantively and procedurally feasible for the family court judge to hear the divorce action while permitting a jury to determine the issues of damages and fault, which are central to a domestic tort claim. *Ibid.* The court suggested that the family court judge can then allocate the damages and/or modify the support following the jury verdict. *Ibid.* Finally, the court stated that divorce actions are already complicated and subject to delay because *Tevis* requires the joinder of domestic tort claims with the underlying divorce action. *Ibid.* Therefore, the court opined that allowing a jury trial on the domestic tort claim will not increase the delay or complicate the issues. *Ibid.*

The *Davis* court provided no analysis in its decision, other than citing the report of the subcommittee of the Supreme Court Committee on Matrimonial Litigation. The *Tweedley* court, however, thoroughly explained why a jury trial on the domestic tort claim would not further complicate the divorce action or cause any more delay than

what *Tevis* already caused. In addition, the *Tweedley* court explained that the domestic tort is not ancillary to the divorce action because fault, the major issue posed by a domestic tort, is not an issue in the determination of support or equitable distribution.

┌28 We find the analysis in *Tweedley* more persuasive than that in *Davis.* In addition to the reasons expressed in *Tweedley,* we note that presently a married person may sue a spouse for damages attributable to tortious conduct. If the injured spouse chooses not to sue for divorce, the tort claimant will be entitled to a jury trial in the Law Division. However, if the injured spouse also seeks a divorce, that spouse would be deprived of a jury trial. We can find no logical reason to maintain that dichotomy.

We are mindful that since *Davis,* decided in 1981, there has not been an onslaught of matrimonial litigants challenging the deprivation of a right to a jury trial on damage claims arising from domestic torts. We infer that our courts of equity have been able to adjudicate tort claims asserted in matrimonial litigation and to ascribe damages as a component of a divorce judgment within the ambit of the expectations of the tort claimant. We envision that tort claims encompassing complex medical issues or substantial claims of permanent disability, whether physical or psychological, may warrant a jury trial. Just as *Merenoff* created an exception from the abolition of interspousal torts, claims based on "marital or nuptial privileges, consensual acts and simple, common domestic negligence, to be defined and developed on a case-by-case approach," *Tevis v. Tevis, supra,* 79 *N.J.* at 427, 400 *A.*2d 1189, we also conclude that tort claims which are not the permanent cause of serious and significant psychological or physical injuries should not give rise to a jury trial.

[13] Every tort claimant should be entitled to demand a jury trial in the first pleading filed asserting such a claim in a matrimonial dissolution proceeding. However, in order to qualify for a jury trial, the claimant must establish by written expert opinion that proofs will be introduced at trial demonstrating that the injury is serious and significant,

resulting in permanent physical or psychological injury, to be defined and developed on a case-by-case approach. Alternatively, a plaintiff must establish that the nature of the injury, whether physical or psychological, requires complex medical evidence. A tort claimant will be required to |₂₉meet this threshold in response to a motion to strike the jury trial demand after all discovery has been completed and the pending matter is deemed ready for trial by the court.

We are constrained to reverse the decision of the motion judge in this case. Plaintiff shall have the right to present her claims for compensatory and punitive damages to a jury as part of the entire dissolution of marriage proceeding, provided that plaintiff can establish that she has sustained serious or significant permanent physical or psychological damage, or that her injuries require complex medical proof.

[14] In the presentation of plaintiff's claim for damages to the jury, plaintiff obviously will present proof of her age, her physical and emotional health, and possibly claims that her occupational capacity is limited by her physical or emotional health, proximately resulting from defendant's tortious conduct. If plaintiff recovers a favorable jury verdict predicated upon those proofs, then the court thereafter shall be particularly mindful of that judgment in equitably dividing the marital property. N.J.S.A. 2A:34–23.1 directs that a court shall consider fifteen factors in equitably dividing property, including "[t]he age and physical and emotional health of the parties;" "[t]he income and earning capacity of each party;" and "[t]he debts and liabilities of the parties." Ibid.

Clearly, plaintiff's age, physical and emotional health and occupational limitations, if any, attributable to defendant's tortious conduct, may not again be considered in evaluating the equitable division of property issues. Likewise, defendant's actual liability in tort resulting in judgment must be considered in the court's decision respecting the division of property. The judgment debt owed plaintiff must also be considered in evaluating plaintiff's demand for alimony and particularly defendant's ability to pay alimony. There

may not be a double recovery from defendant.

VI

Part V of this opinion focuses solely on the right to a jury trial on counts three through six of plaintiff's complaint. Plaintiff's |₃₀jury trial demand also encompassed counts seven through eleven of her complaint, denominated "equitable claims."

Although plaintiff's notice of appeal encompassed an appeal from the decision striking her jury trial demand, plaintiff's brief on appeal focused solely upon the right to a jury trial for marital tort claims. Plaintiff's brief fails to assert any claim of error attributable to the motion judge's decision pertinent to her "equitable claims." Defendant's brief is also silent on that issue.

[15] It is quite clear that plaintiff has no right to a jury trial on her claim that premarital real property titled solely in defendant's name should be included in the marital estate for equitable distribution purposes, by virtue of the concepts of transmutation of property, constructive/resulting trusts, implied contract, unjust enrichment, and quasi-contract. Those concepts are clearly equitable in nature, and as such, they should be presented solely to the court as the trier of fact. Boardwalk Properties, Inc. v. BPHC Acquisition, Inc., supra, 253 N.J.Super. at 527, 602 A.2d 733.

VII—SUMMARY

The component of the order striking plaintiff's demand for a jury trial on counts seven through eleven is affirmed. However, the portion of the order striking plaintiff's demand for a jury trial on counts three through six is reversed. A jury trial will be permitted on these claims, provided plaintiff's proofs satisfy the threshold requirements outlined in Part V of this opinion.

The component of the order striking all tortious claims occurring prior to June 30, 1992, based upon N.J.S.A. 2A:14–2, is modified. Plaintiff is barred from pursuing a claim for damages for assault and battery on any battery occurring prior to June 30, 1992, but she is permitted to assert a claim for battered woman's syndrome attributable to acts occurring after October 25, 1982, when plaintiff's prior counterclaim for divorce was dismissed with prejudice. Our modification of the motion judge's order is without prejudice to defendant's right to again move to strike plaintiff's ╷₃₂claim of continuous tort resulting in battered woman's syndrome, should plaintiff fail to amend her complaint to allege specifically the acts of continuous violence occurring after October 25, 1982, which she contends resulted in the condition described as battered woman's syndrome.

The component of the order limiting plaintiff's proofs on her claims for emotional distress, count four, and negligence, count six, to acts occurring after June 30, 1992 is modified. Plaintiff may produce proof of facts occurring prior to June 30, 1992, if deemed relevant to proving acts occurring after June 30, 1992. Plaintiff may not recover damages for any acts of emotional distress or negligence occurring prior to June 30, 1992.

SKILLMAN, J.A.D., concurring and dissenting.

I see no need for the creation of a new tort cause of action for "battered woman's syndrome." In addition, I would conclude that plaintiff failed to present any evidence that could justify postponing the accrual of her other tort causes of action. I agree with the trial court's conclusion that plaintiff is not entitled to a jury trial with respect to her remaining tort claims because those claims are ancillary and incidental to her divorce complaint. Therefore, I would affirm the challenged portions of the trial court's order in all respects.

I

To place the majority's sweeping pronouncements in proper perspective, it is appropriate at the outset to set forth the factual allegations that the majority has found sufficient to justify recognition of a new tort action for "battered woman's syndrome" and

the postponement of accrual of plaintiff's tort claims. Those claims are set forth in four brief counts of plaintiff's complaint. The complaint's only allegation of a specific act of violence is the alleged assault and battery which occurred in March of 1972. The assault and battery count of the complaint also contains a broad conclusionary allegation that:

╷₃₂The defendant has continually since March of 1972, attacked the plaintiff causing her on numerous occasions great physical and bodily injury. The last such beating having occurred in or about June of 1993.[1]

In addition, plaintiff alleges in the counts of her complaint seeking a divorce on the grounds of habitual drunkenness and extreme cruelty that defendant would frequently come home intoxicated in the middle of the night, and on those occasions would awaken plaintiff and act abusively towards her. This count also alleges that defendant was "threatening the plaintiff" and "throwing various objects around the house" when he became intoxicated one time in 1984. The fifth count of plaintiff's complaint, which the majority construes as plaintiff's "battered woman's syndrome" claim, simply incorporates the factual allegations of the prior counts of the complaint by reference and then broadly asserts:

The defendant's conduct against the plaintiff has been a continuous and unbroken wrong commencing in or about March of 1972 and continuing down until May of 1993. Said continuous course of conduct by the defendant has caused the plaintiff severe emotional and physical damage.

Defendant filed a motion seeking various relief, including the dismissal of all of plaintiff's tort claims, except for assault and battery, and the striking of "those causes of action ... which assert tortious acts which occurred on or before June 30, 1992 based upon the applicable statute of limitations." Although the parties filed voluminous briefs

---

1. When plaintiff was deposed, she indicated that she had no recollection of any specific incident of physical abuse by defendant at any time from January 1993 until the parties separated in October 1993. Although plaintiff was not deposed

until after entry of the order that is the subject of this appeal, we granted defendant's motion to expand the record to include the transcript of this deposition.

and certifications relating to this motion, plaintiff's certifications contained no factual allegations that could support a claim that she suffers from "battered woman's syndrome." In addition to reasserting the occurrence of the March 1972 assault and battery, plaintiff alleged:

(b) Throughout the marriage, on approximately two (2) occasions per month, on Friday nights, or early Saturday, the defendant would return home after drinking excessively. He would attempt to initiate sexual intercourse. He would try to wake me up by turning on the lights, banging doors, pulling the sheets off the bed and by striking me with the flat of his hand.[2] He would pull my hair. He would throw things around the room. I experienced this, on average, at least twice a month for our entire marriage. He was out drinking with his friends every single Friday night.

(c) During these Friday night incidences he would call me "bitch" "C-nt," "whore," "f-ing son-of-a-bitch" and other vile names.

(d) These incidences would often cause me to flee the home to protect myself or avoid our children from hearing and trying to come to my rescue.

Although such allegations, if proven at trial, could support a divorce on the ground of extreme cruelty, *N.J.S.A.* 2A:34–2(c), they fall far short of what would be required to establish a case of battered woman's syndrome as described in *State v. Kelly*, 97 *N.J.* 178, 190–196, 478 *A.*2d 364 (1984). Plaintiff's certifications, which were not accompanied by any supporting medical evidence, also do not contain any allegation that might provide a foundation for a finding that she suffered from "insanity" during the marriage, as would be required to toll the period of limitations under *N.J.S.A.* 2A:14–21.

Therefore, even if it were appropriate for this court to create a new cause of action in tort for battered woman's syndrome, and to allow the tolling of the statute of limitations based on the existence of that condition, plaintiff's factual allegations fail to lay a factual foundation for a finding that she suf-

fered from such a syndrome. Accordingly, I would dismiss the appeal on the ground that leave to appeal was improvidently granted. However, since the majority has used this appeal as a vehicle to endorse novel legal theories with potentially far-reaching consequences, I consider it necessary to reach the merits and to discuss those theories.

II

"It is inadvisable to create new causes of action in tort in advance of any necessity for doing so in order to achieve a just result." *Neelthak Dev. Corp. v. Township of Gloucester*, 272 *N.J.Super.* 319, 325, 639 *A.*2d 1141 (App.Div.1994). Consequently, this court should consider whether existing tort causes of action provide an adequate remedy for conduct that may result in battered woman's syndrome before undertaking to create any new cause of action.

Any person who is a victim of violence, or the threat of violence, may recover money damages for assault and/or battery. A person may be liable for battery if "he acts intending to cause a harmful or offensive contact . . . or an imminent apprehension of such contact" and a "harmful" or "offensive" contact "directly or indirectly results." 1 *Restatement (Second) of Torts* §§ 13, 18 (1965). A person who acts with the same intent may be liable for assault even if no contact actually results if the victim is placed in "imminent apprehension" of a harmful or offensive contact. *Id.* at § 21. Consequently, any woman who is the victim of an act of battering, or a threat of battering, can bring a tort action against her assailant for each of those acts. Moreover, a battered woman would be entitled to recover not only for any economic losses resulting from those acts, such as medical expenses and lost wages, but also for pain and suffering and disability, *see Schroeder v. Perkel*, 87 *N.J.* 53, 66, 432 *A.*2d 834 (1981), which would include the psychological sequelae of any act of battering. *Wilson v. Parisi*, 268 *N.J.Super.* 213, 219–20, 633 *A.*2d 113 (App.Div.1993).

---

2. When plaintiff was deposed with respect to the period after June 30, 1992, she did not identify

any incident in which defendant struck her or inflicted any form of physical injury upon her.

The trial court's opinion in *Cusseaux v. Pickett*, 279 *N.J.Super.* 335, 343, 652 *A.*2d 789 (Law Div.1994), upon which the majority relies, simply asserts, without any supporting explanation, that "the civil laws of assault and battery [are] insufficient to redress the harms suffered as a result of domestic violence." Although the majority's opinion likewise fails to explain why the law of assault and battery fails to provide adequate means of redress for the victims of domestic violence, it suggests that the creation of an independent tort of battered woman's syndrome would allow recovery in tort for "all acts of cruelty which occurred during the course of [the] marriage," (majority op. at 22, 663 *A.*2d at 119), ¦₃₅even if those acts do not involve any battering. Under this view, plaintiff could seek money damages for the alleged emotional distress and psychological harm resulting from the alleged occasions when defendant came home late at night in an intoxicated condition and verbally abused her.

However, the creation of a cause of action that allowed recovery for incidents of verbal abuse would extend marital tort liability to conduct that would not give rise to legal liability in other contexts. Mere verbal abuse or insult is not generally a basis for the imposition of tort liability. 2 Fowler V. Harper, et al., *The Law of Torts* § 9.2 (1986); *Prosser on Torts* § 12 at 59–60 (5th ed. 1984). As observed in a comment to the Restatement of Torts, "some safety valve must be left through which irascible tempers may blow off relatively harmless steam." 1 *Restatement (Second) of Torts* § 46 comment d (1965); *cf. Ward v. Zelikovsky*, 136 *N.J.* 516, 529, 643 *A.*2d 972 (1994) (quoting Rodney A. Smolla, *Law of Defamation* § 6.12[9], at 6–54) ("[N]ame calling, epithets, and abusive language, no matter how vulgar or offensive, are not actionable" under the law of defamation). Moreover, even assuming that verbal abuse could be sufficiently outrageous and harmful to the target to give rise to a cause of action for intentional infliction of emotional distress, see *Price v. State Farm Mut. Auto. Ins. Co.*, 878 *F.Supp.* 1567 (S.D.Ga.1995); Jean C. Love, Discriminatory Speech and the Tort of Intentional Infliction of Emotional Distress, 47 *Wash & Lee L.Rev.*

123 (1990), our courts have established rigorous prerequisites for proving this cause of action:

Generally speaking, to establish a claim for intentional infliction of emotional distress, the plaintiff must establish intentional and outrageous conduct by the defendant, proximate cause, and distress that is severe. Initially, the plaintiff must prove that the defendant acted intentionally or recklessly. . . .

Second, the defendant's conduct must be extreme and outrageous. The conduct must be "so outrageous in character, and so extreme in degree, as to go beyond all possible bounds of decency, and to be regarded as atrocious, and utterly intolerable in a civilized community." Third, the defendant's actions must have been the proximate cause of the plaintiff's emotional distress. Fourth, the emotional distress suffered by the plaintiff must be "so severe that no reasonable man could be expected to endure it." By circumscribing the cause of action with an elevated ¦₃₆threshold for liability and damages, courts have authorized legitimate claims while eliminating those that should not be compensable.

[*Buckley v. Trenton Saving Fund Soc'y*, 111 *N.J.* 355, 366–67, 544 *A.*2d 857 (1988) (citations omitted).]

The kind of verbal abuse that defendant allegedly directed at plaintiff, although certainly offensive, was not "so outrageous in character, and so extreme in degree, as to go beyond all possible bounds of decency, and to be regarded as atrocious, and utterly intolerable in a civilized community." *Id.* at 366, 544 *A.*2d 857; *see Price v. State Farm Mut. Auto. Ins. Co.*, *supra*; *cf. Ruprecht v. Ruprecht*, 252 *N.J.Super.* 230, 238, 599 *A.*2d 604 (Ch.Div.1991) (holding that wife's eleven year secret adulterous affair with her employer failed "to reach the level of outrageousness necessary for liability under this tort."). In fact, serious verbal abuse, often reciprocal in nature, is a common feature of deteriorating marriages. Consequently, the verbal abuse that plaintiff ascribes to defendant could not provide the basis for a claim of intentional infliction of emotional distress.[3]

It is clear to me that we should not create a cause of action that would result in potential tort liability between domestic partners in a broader range of circumstances than apply in other contexts. Although close family relationships, such as those between a husband and wife or a parent and child, serve as primary sources of love, affection and support, the emotional significance of such relationships and the constant contact that occurs among family members who live together also produce various forms of tension, discord and verbal abuse. Verbal abuse between spouses is likely to be most frequent, and most nasty, when a marital relationship is deteriorating. As we noted in *Peranio v. Peranio*, 280 *N.J.Super.* 47, 56, 654 *A.2d* 495 (App.Div.1995):

> [T]he dissolution of a marriage is rarely a happy event. All parties suffer and even the most rational are hard pressed to avoid any emotional encounters.

[37]In my view, such emotional encounters within a marriage should not form a basis for the imposition of tort liability unless one of the parties engages in conduct that could support a claim for assault, battery or intentional infliction of emotional distress. *See Merenoff v. Merenoff*, 76 *N.J.* 535, 555, 388 *A.2d* 951 (1978) ("There is a range of activity arising in the course of a marriage relationship beyond the reach of the law of torts."). In fact, the creation of an overly expansive concept of tort liability in the marital setting would conflict with current statutory provisions that have reduced the significance of fault in matrimonial litigation, *see Kazin v. Kazin*, 81 *N.J.* 85, 92, 405 *A.2d* 360 (1979), and would unnecessarily complicate such litigation. Therefore, I would reject plaintiff's effort to gain recognition of a new tort action for battered woman's syndrome.

III

The majority opinion suggests that a primary objective of creating a new tort cause of action for battered woman's syndrome is to avoid the normal application of the statute

of limitations to bar marital tort claims. If that is the underlying reason for the creation of this new tort, it is a classic case of the tail being allowed to wag the dog. If defendant's alleged marital misconduct could be properly characterized as "continuous" or if plaintiff's mental state could be shown to constitute "insanity," the running of the statute of limitations could be tolled regardless of whether plaintiff's cause of action were labeled assault and battery, intentional infliction of emotional distress, or the amorphous new tort of battered woman's syndrome. *See Jones v. Jones*, 242 *N.J.Super.* 195, 576 *A.2d* 316 (App.Div.), *certif. denied*, 122 *N.J.* 418, 585 *A.2d* 412 (1990); *Twyman v. Twyman*, 790 *S.W.2d* 819, 820–21 (Tex.Ct.App.1990), *rev'd on other grounds*, 855 *S.W.2d* 619 (Tex.1993). To state the point another way, it seems to me that the elements that a plaintiff must prove to establish a cause of action should be analyzed separately from the question whether the plaintiff has made the kind of showing required to toll the statute of limitations.

[38]Since I have already set forth my reasons for concluding that marital tort claims should be subject to the same substantive principles of tort liability as claims arising outside the marital setting, I turn to the question whether plaintiff has shown any basis for tolling the statute of limitations. Preliminarily, I note that we are not writing on a clean slate in applying the statute of limitations to marital torts. In holding that the statute of limitations barred a wife's recovery for a severe beating administered by her husband, the Court stated in *Tevis v. Tevis*, 79 *N.J.* 422, 431–33, 400 *A.2d* 1189 (1979):

> In certain circumstances, the court has attempted to mitigate the sometimes harsh results arising from the inflexible application of [the statute of limitations] by invoking the "discovery" rule. . . .
>
> This rule is of no aid to plaintiff in the present case. She knew of her injuries and was simultaneously aware of their cause in the person of her husband at the moment of the assault and battery. . . . Plaintiff's cause of action accrued when she was battered. . . .

---

3. If plaintiff can show any act of battering or threat of battering, she would of course be entitled to recover under the law of assault and battery.

The question remains as to whether other equitable considerations may relieve plaintiff of the onus of the statute of limitations. . . .

Plaintiff apparently suffered substantial injuries but she was not incapacitated or prevented by her physical or mental trauma from pursuing her legal rights. . . . Even though defendant's conduct was grotesque and inexcusable, there is no claim that he defrauded plaintiff or that she relied upon any misleading or deceitful misrepresentation of his in forestalling civil redress.

Although *Tevis* did not consider the specific arguments plaintiff now advances for tolling the statute of limitations, I believe that *Tevis* should lead us to proceed with caution in considering any argument for postponement of the accrual of a marital tort.

A party who seeks to avoid the bar of a statute of limitations by invocation of the discovery rule or other comparable doctrine has the burden of proof. *Lopez v. Swyer*, 62 *N.J.* 267, 276, 300 A.2d 563 (1973). Consequently, such a party may not simply rely upon the allegations of the complaint in opposing a motion to dismiss but must instead present evidence in the form of affidavits, depositions, or exhibits to establish a *prima facie* basis for postponing accrual of the cause of action. *See* 4 N 27, 300 A.2d 563. It is only when the plaintiff has met this threshold burden that the court should conduct an evidentiary hearing to resolve contested factual allegations material to the issue of accrual. *Ibid.*

The majority acknowledges that "plaintiff has failed to present any medical, physical or psychological evidence to support her claim that she suffers from the medical condition labeled battered woman's syndrome" (majority op. at 18–19, 663 A.2d at 117). But the majority takes the position that plaintiff should be given an additional opportunity to present medical evidence that may justify postponement of the accrual of her cause of action, because "the trial court dismissed count five of plaintiff's complaint alleging 'continuous wrong' not because plaintiff failed to present proof of her medical condition in response to defendant's motion, but because

the decision in *Cusseaux* was not binding upon a court of concurrent jurisdiction" (majority op. at 19, 663 A.2d at 117). However, the majority's description of the trial court's rationale for dismissing all of plaintiff's pre-June 30, 1992 marital tort claims is incomplete. In fact, the trial court not only declined to recognize a new cause of action for battered woman's syndrome, but also squarely held that all marital tort claims for injuries that occurred more than two years before the filing of plaintiff's complaint were barred by the applicable two-year statute of limitations:

In my mind the issue that's raised here is the question of when does a statute of limitations bar tort claims arising out of a marital-type relationship? . . . [M]y most basic conclusion is that the defendant's motion, based on the statute of limitations, should be granted and the plaintiff should be barred from pursuing claims for damages arising out of personal injuries that may have occurred prior to . . . June 30, 1992. . . . The statute that we're dealing with makes it clear that a cause of action for damages arising out of personal injuries runs after two years. The case law makes it clear that the statute begins to run generally when the assault or the injury occurs. From that basic rule it's clear that two years after someone has been physically injured he or she is barred from proceeding with that cause of action.

The trial court then considered various exceptions to the normal operation of the statute of limitations, including not only "the concept of continuous wrong" but also "equitable tolling" and the "discovery rule." Although the trial court did not consider plaintiff's medical condition as a possible basis for tolling the limitations period, this was only because plaintiff failed to present any medical evidence that would have required consideration of such a theory. Therefore, the trial court did not act prematurely in ruling that plaintiff's pre-June 30, 1992 claims are barred by the statute of limitations.

The majority's discussion of the question whether battered woman's syndrome is a continuous tort is confusing and contradictory. On the one hand, the majority states that "[w]e do not adopt the conclusion in *Cusseaux* that battered woman's syndrome is itself a continuous tort" (majority op. at 14, 663 *A.*2d at 114). On the other hand, the majority asserts that "to overcome the statute of limitations, it is imperative that the tortious conduct giving rise to the medical condition be considered a continuous tort" (majority op. at 14, 663 *A.*2d at 114). The majority never undertakes to explain how these seemingly inconsistent statements can be reconciled. Moreover, the majority later states that "[p]laintiff shall be entitled to sue her husband for damages attributable to his continuous tortious conduct resulting in her present psychological condition, provided she has medical, psychiatric, or psychological expert proof to establish that she was caused to have an inability 'to take any action at all to improve or alter the situation.' *Cusseaux, supra,* 279 *N.J.Super.* at 341 [652 *A.*2d 789]" (majority op. at 18, 663 *A.*2d at 117). Therefore, it appears that despite its prior contrary statements, the majority views the newly created tort of "battered woman's syndrome" as a "continuous tort" for which there is no operative statute of limitations.

In support of this theory, the majority relies primarily upon two cases that involved the application of *N.J.S.A.* 2A:14–21, which provides that a cause of action shall not accrue if the aggrieved party is "insane." In *Kyle v. Green Acres at Verona, Inc.,* 44 *N.J.* 100, 207 *A.*2d 513 (1965), the Court held that even though *N.J.S.A.* 2A:14–21 does not literally apply where an injured party becomes insane subsequent to the accident that is the subject of his complaint, a defendant may be foreclosed on equitable grounds ⌊₁₄⌋from invoking the statute of limitations if the defendant's wrongful acts were the cause of plaintiff's insanity. The Court also indicated that insanity "means such a condition of mental derangement as actually prevents the sufferer from understanding his legal rights or instituting legal action." *Id.* at 113, 207 *A.*2d 513. It was undisputed that the plaintiff in *Kyle,* who was "officially committed as 'insane'" for a period of five years, *id.* at 102, 207 *A.*2d 513, qualified under this definition as insane.

In *Jones v. Jones, supra,* we held that the mental trauma resulting from a pattern of incestuous sexual abuse may constitute insanity under *N.J.S.A.* 2A:14–21, so as to toll the statute of limitations, if a plaintiff can demonstrate that she lacks "the ability and capacity, due to mental affliction allegedly caused by defendants' conduct, to assert her lawful rights." 242 *N.J.Super.* at 205, 576 *A.*2d 316. We concluded that the plaintiff's submission in opposition to the defendant's motion to dismiss, which included the treatment notes of her psychologist and the affidavit of another psychologist, *id.* at 201, 576 *A.*2d 316, raised genuine issues of material fact as to whether she suffered from such incapacity.

In contrast, plaintiff presented absolutely no evidence that she now suffers or has suffered in the past from the kind of mental affliction that could be found to constitute insanity. Plaintiff not only failed, as discussed in section II of this opinion, to allege acts of battering that could provide a factual foundation for a finding that she suffers from battered woman's syndrome, but also failed to submit any doctor's certification or report or any other medical evidence that she suffered from a "mental derangement" that was so disabling it would have prevented her "from understanding [her] legal rights or instituting legal action." *Kyle v. Green Acres at Verona, Inc., supra,* 44 *N.J.* at 113, 207 *A.*2d 513. Therefore, even assuming that under appropriate circumstances the condition of battered woman's syndrome could justify postponement of the accrual of a cause of action for assault, battery, or intentional infliction of emotional distress, plaintiff failed to present a *prima facie* case for postponing the accrual of her marital tort claims. ⌊₁₅⌋*Cf. Davis v. Bostick,* 282 *Or.* 667, 580 *P.*2d 544, 548 (1978) ("Designating a series of discrete acts, even if connected in design or intent, a 'continuing tort' ought not to be a rationale by which the statute of limitations policy can be avoided.").

IV

I turn finally to the majority's conclusion that a party asserting a marital tort claim may be entitled to a trial by jury even though his or her claim is joined in a complaint for divorce. Where a claim is cognizable in equity, the court may adjudicate "ancillary and incidental" legal claims. *Fleischer v. James Drug Stores,* 1 N.J. 138, 150, 62 A.2d 383 (1948). Consequently, "an issue which is normally triable to a jury may be ancillary and incidental to the subject matter of the equitable jurisdiction, thus allowing the issue to be determined by the court without a jury." *Apollo v. Kim Anh Pham,* 192 *N.J.Super.* 427, 431, 470 A.2d 934 (Ch. Div.1983), *aff'd o.b.,* 224 *N.J.Super.* 89, 539 A.2d 1222 (App.Div.1987); *accord Boardwalk Properties, Inc. v. BPHC Acquisition, Inc.,* 253 *N.J.Super.* 515, 527, 602 A.2d 733 (App. Div.1991). This inherent authority of a court of equity to adjudicate ancillary and incidental legal matters extends to tort claims for money damages. *Apollo v. Kim Anh Pham, supra,* 192 *N.J.Super.* at 431, 470 A.2d 934.

The trial court correctly concluded that plaintiff's tort claims are ancillary and incidental to the counts of her complaint seeking dissolution of the marriage, equitable distribution and support. The counts of plaintiff's complaint in which she asserts tort claims incorporate by reference and rely upon the same factual allegations as the divorce counts of her complaint. Indeed, the only specific factual allegations set forth in the tort counts of plaintiff's complaint that are not also set forth in the divorce counts relate to the alleged March 1972 assault and battery. Therefore, plaintiff's tort claims are "germane to [and] grow out of the subject-matter" of her equitable complaint for divorce. *Fleischer v. James Drug Stores, supra,* 1 N.J. at 150, 62 A.2d 383. Moreover, there is no indication that plaintiff "has sustained serious or significant permanent[4,3] physical or psychological damage" as a result of defendant's alleged post-June 30, 1992 marital torts or that "her injuries require complex medical proof" (majority op. at 28, 663 A.2d at 123);[4] *cf. Zahorian v. Russell Fitt Real Estate Agency,* 62 N.J. 399, 413, 301 A.2d 754 (1973). I see no need in deciding this appeal to express any opinion as to whether some marital tort claims joined in a complaint for divorce may be sufficiently independent of

the allegations of the complaint for divorce that they should not be viewed as "ancillary and incidental," thereby preserving a plaintiff's right to a trial by jury.

For the foregoing reasons, I would affirm paragraphs one and six of the November 14, 1994 order in all respects.

---

4. As previously noted, plaintiff has already been   deposed.

Charlene KUNZA, f/k/a Charlene
Pantze, Appellant,

v.

Curtis PANTZE, Respondent,

Deltauer, Inc., d/b/a The King
of Clubs Bar, Respondent.

No. C3–94–1802.

Court of Appeals of Minnesota.

Feb. 21, 1995.

Passenger injured when she exited vehicle to escape allegedly abusive driver brought action under Dram Shop Act against bar at which passenger and driver had been patrons. The District Court of Hennepin County, Myron S. Greenberg, J., entered summary judgment in favor of bar, and passenger appealed. The Court of Appeals, Harten, J., held that driver's intoxication could have been a proximate cause of passenger's injuries, and bar was not entitled to judgment as matter of law.

Reversed and remanded.

1. Appeal and Error ⚯863

On appeal from summary judgment, appellate court must determine whether there are any genuine issues of material fact and whether district court erred in its application of law.

2. Appeal and Error ⚯934(1)

On appeal from summary judgment, appellate court must view evidence in light most favorable to party against whom judgment was granted.

3. Intoxicating Liquors ⚯286, 291

To establish liability under Dram Shop Act, plaintiff must establish: (1) that sale of alcohol was in violation of statute; (2) that violation was substantially related to purpose sought to be achieved by Dram Shop Act; (3) that illegal sale was cause of intoxication; and (4) that intoxication was cause of plaintiff's injuries. M.S.A. § 340A.801, subd. 1.

4. Intoxicating Liquors ⊙291

For purposes of passenger's claim against bar under Dram Shop Act, driver's intoxication could have been a proximate cause of passenger's injuries even though passenger admitted that she opened vehicle door, apparently when vehicle was still moving, and bar was not entitled to judgment as a matter of law; passenger claimed that driver was intoxicated and physically abusing her, and that she opened door to exit vehicle, in belief that driver would stop at traffic light. M.S.A. § 340A.801, subd. 1.

5. Negligence ⊙56(1.9)

Conduct may be proximate cause of injury if conduct is substantial factor in bringing about injury.

6. Negligence ⊙56(1)

Determination of proximate cause depends on application of common sense to facts of case.

7. Negligence ⊙62(1)

Wrongful conduct may be proximate cause of injuries resulting from plaintiff's efforts to avoid direct consequences of wrongful conduct, even if plaintiff acted unreasonably in choosing means of avoidance.

Syllabus by the Court

In a dram shop action under Minn.Stat. § 340A.801, summary judgment in favor of the bar alleged to have illegally sold alcohol to a van driver is precluded where the driver's intoxication may have been a proximate cause of injuries to a passenger who fell or jumped from the van.

———

Randall J. Fuller, Gary T. LaFleur, Babcock, Locher, Neilson & Mannella, Anoka, for appellant.

Marianne Settano, Roseville, Steven E. Tomsche, Foster, Waldeck, Lind & Gries, Ltd., Minneapolis, for respondents.

Considered and decided by HUSPENI, P.J., and HARTEN and MINENKO,* JJ.

---

* Retired judge of the district court, serving as judge of the Minnesota Court of Appeals by ap-

OPINION

HARTEN, Judge.

Appellant challenges summary judgment in favor of respondent bar in her dram shop action, contending that the district court erred in ruling that her former husband's intoxication could not have been a proximate cause of appellant's injuries as a matter of law.

FACTS

This case arises from an incident occurring on November 22, 1991, in which appellant Charlene Kunza jumped or fell from a van driven by Curtis Pantze. Prior to the occurrence, the two had been drinking at the King of Clubs Bar. After leaving the bar, appellant and Pantze, who were then married, began to argue. At some point appellant opened the passenger door.

Pantze testified in his deposition that appellant threatened to jump out of the van, that he grabbed her by her hair and jacket to prevent her from doing so, but that appellant eventually succeeded in jumping out. Appellant testified in her deposition that she knew that Pantze was intoxicated and that, as they were driving, Pantze began to abuse her physically by pulling her hair and hitting her in the face. Appellant further testified that as they approached a traffic light, expecting Pantze to stop, she opened the door, but that instead of stopping, Pantze accelerated. Appellant did not remember how she left the van.

Appellant sued Pantze in negligence to recover for various injuries, including the loss of her senses of taste and smell, a collapsed lung, the "degloving" of her scalp, and the loss of some peripheral vision. Appellant and Pantze eventually settled this claim.

Appellant also sued respondent Deltauer, Inc., d/b/a King of Clubs Bar, under the dram shop act, alleging that the bar's illegal sale of alcoholic beverages to Pantze caused Pantze's intoxication and that the intoxication

pointment pursuant to Minn. Const. art. VI, § 10.

caused appellant's injuries. The district court granted Deltauer summary judgment, ruling as a matter of law that the intoxication did not cause the injuries. This appeal results.

ISSUE

Did the district court err in ruling as a matter of law that Pantze's intoxication was not a proximate cause of appellant's injuries?

ANALYSIS

[1, 2] Appellant challenges the summary judgment in favor of Deltauer. On appeal from summary judgment, this court must determine whether there are any genuine issues of material fact and whether the district court erred in its application of the law. *State ex rel. Cooper v. French*, 460 N.W.2d 2, 4 (Minn.1990). On appeal, we must view the evidence in the light most favorable to the party against whom summary judgment was granted. *Fabio v. Bellomo*, 504 N.W.2d 758, 761 (Minn.1993).

[3, 4] Appellant's cause of action against Deltauer arose under the following provision of the dram shop act:

A spouse, child, parent, guardian, employer, or other person injured in person, property, or means of support, or who incurs other pecuniary loss by an intoxicated person or by the intoxication of another person, has a right of action in the person's own name for all damages sustained against a person who caused the intoxication of that person by illegally selling alcoholic beverages.

Minn.Stat. § 340A.801, subd. 1 (1990). To establish liability under the dram shop act, a plaintiff must establish

1. That the sale of alcohol was in violation of a provision of Minn.Stat. ch. 340A;

2. That the violation was substantially related to the purposes sought to be achieved by the [dram shop act];

3. That the illegal sale was a cause of the intoxication; and

4. That the intoxication was a cause of the plaintiff's injuries.

Rambaum v. Swisher, 435 N.W.2d 19, 21 (Minn.1989). The supreme court has confirmed that the necessary causal relationship in the latter two elements is one of *proximate cause*. *Kryzer v. Champlin Am. Legion No. 600*, 494 N.W.2d 35, 36–37 (Minn. 1992). For purposes of its summary judgment motion, Deltauer conceded the first three elements; therefore, the only issue here is whether Pantze's intoxication could have been a proximate cause of appellant's injuries.

In granting Deltauer summary judgment, the district court found that there were no disputed issues of material fact. Pantze alleged that appellant jumped out of the van. Appellant alleged that she did not remember how she left the van, but she admitted opening the van door. The district court ruled that, even when the evidence is viewed in a light most favorable to appellant, Pantze's intoxication could not have proximately caused appellant's injuries because appellant voluntarily opened the van door, thereby severing the causal chain.

Appellant argues that Pantze's intoxication directly caused her injuries. Appellant testified that Pantze had been physically abusing her before she left the van, and that she knew that Pantze became violent and abusive when, and only when, he was intoxicated. Appellant suggests that her only alternatives at the time of the accident were to endure further abuse or to exit the van. In appellant's view, Pantze's intoxication caused him to be abusive; therefore, it also caused appellant to open the van door, which resulted in her injuries. Finally, appellant argues that the voluntariness or involuntariness of her departure from the van is irrelevant to the question whether the intoxication was a proximate cause of her injuries.

[5, 6] We believe that Pantze's intoxication *could* be a proximate cause of appellant's injuries and that the question should therefore be considered by a jury. Conduct may be the proximate cause of an injury if the conduct is a substantial factor in bringing about the injury. *Fiedler v. Adams*, 466 N.W.2d 39, 43 (Minn.App.1991), *pet. for rev. denied* (Minn. Apr. 29, 1991). A determination of proximate cause depends on an appli-

cation of common sense to the facts of the case. *Johnson v. Chicago Great W. Ry.*, 242 Minn. 130, 134, 64 N.W.2d 372, 376 (1954).

Deltauer argues that the voluntariness of appellant's conduct severs the causal chain from the intoxication to the injuries. Appellant contends that her actions were necessary to escape physical abuse that can be directly linked to Pantze's intoxication.

[7] Common law proximate cause cases support appellant's contention. For instance, a person's negligence in driving a motor vehicle may be the proximate cause of injuries immediately caused by a second driver's attempt to avoid a collision with the negligent driver. In *Smith v. Carlson*, 209 Minn. 268, 296 N.W. 132 (1941), a motorist sustained injuries when she lost control after swerving to avoid a collision with a wagon. *Id.* at 269–70, 296 N.W. at 133. The supreme court reversed a directed verdict in favor of the owner of the wagon, holding that the owner's negligence may have been the proximate cause of the injuries, even though there was no collision or physical contact between the automobile and the wagon. *Id.* at 272, 296 N.W. at 134. The court stated that the question of proximate cause was one of fact for the jury and that it

> should be determined by them in the exercise of practical common sense rather than by the application of abstract principles.

Id. at 274–75, 296 N.W. at 135 (citation omitted).

The court in *Smith* relied in part on the Restatement, holding that

> [a]n act done in normal response to the stimulus of the situation created by the actor's negligence is a substantial factor in bringing about the injury and not an independent intervening cause.

Id. at 272, 296 N.W. at 134 (citing Restatement (First) of Torts § 443 cmt. a (1934)). Restatement section 443 now states:

> The intervention of a force which is a normal consequence of a situation created by the actor's negligent conduct is not a superseding cause of harm which such conduct has been a substantial factor in bringing about.

Restatement (Second) of Torts § 443 (1965). A comment explains that the section applies to an act committed by the person injured and that the injured person's act need not be "reasonable" (though an unreasonable act may amount to contributory negligence). *Id.* cmt. a. In this case, appellant's act may have been a normal response to the situation created by the intoxication (i.e., the physical abuse); therefore, appellant's act may not have severed the chain of causation from Pantze's intoxication to appellant's injuries.

The court in *Smith* also relied on *Wilson v. Northern Pac. R.R.*, 26 Minn. 278, 3 N.W. 333 (1879), in which the supreme court applied this general principle to hold a railroad liable for injuries sustained by a passenger who jumped from a train to extricate himself from imminent peril. *Smith*, 209 Minn. at 272, 296 N.W. at 134 (citing *Wilson*, 26 Minn. at 284, 3 N.W. at 337). As the *Smith* court noted, the injury in *Wilson*

> was caused not by any force applied by defendant to the plaintiff, but solely by the latter's act in the emergency of jumping to avoid injury.

Id.

More recently, this court has held that a driver's negligence may be the proximate cause of injuries resulting from a collision between two other automobiles. *See Maanum v. Aust*, 364 N.W.2d 827 (Minn.App. 1985), *pet. for rev. denied* (Minn. June 14, 1985). In *Maanum*, the plaintiffs were injured in a head-on collision with a truck; the truck had been following the appellant's vehicle, which was towing a fish house without taillights. *Id.* at 829–30. The truck driver eventually lost sight of the appellant's vehicle in the snow and crossed the center line. *Id.* at 830. The court held that the act of the truck driver was "a normal response to the stimulus of a situation created by" appellant's original negligence in driving without taillights; therefore, appellant's wrongful act could have proximately caused the plaintiffs' injuries. *Id.* at 831 (citation omitted). The court noted that a driver

> may be held liable for an accident occurring through the negligent operation of his machine, although the immediate cause of

the accident was the negligent act of a third party.

Id. (quoting *Eichten v. Central Minn. Coop. Power Ass'n,* 224 Minn. 180, 190, 28 N.W.2d 862, 869 (1947)).

The cases indicate, then, that wrongful conduct may be the proximate cause of injuries resulting from the plaintiff's efforts to avoid the direct consequences of the wrongful conduct, even if the plaintiff acted unreasonably in choosing a means of avoidance. We therefore hold that Pantze's intoxication could have been a proximate cause of appellant's injuries, even though appellant's own actions may have been the immediate cause of those injuries.

This view does not conflict with prior cases involving dram shop actions. In *Kryzer,* the intoxication of the appellant's wife had caused her removal from the bar by an employee of the bar, and the wife was then injured while being removed. *Kryzer,* 494 N.W.2d at 36. The appellant in that case argued that the injuries would not have occurred but for the intoxication. *Id.* The supreme court, however, rejected such a "but for" analysis as a test of causation. *Id.* at 37. The court distinguished between the *occasion* and the *cause* of an injury and held that, while the wife's intoxication may have occasioned her ejection from the bar, it did not cause her injury. *Id.* Consequently, the court upheld the trial court dismissal of the claim against the bar. *Id.* at 36.

Deltauer also cites our recent opinion in *Weber v. Au,* 512 N.W.2d 348 (Minn.App. 1994). In *Weber,* a police officer who injured his knee while chasing and apprehending a minor who had been involved in fight, sued the bar that had sold drinks to the minor. *Id.* at 349. This court upheld a summary judgment in favor of the bar. *Id.* We stated that the officer's position amounted to an argument that the officer would not have had a duty to chase the minor "but for" the minor's intoxication, and noted that the supreme court had rejected such an analysis in *Kryzer. Id.* at 350. We held that there was no evidence that the intoxication had either caused the minor to flee the officer or caused them to fall when the officer grabbed the minor. *Id.*

In Deltauer's view, appellant is arguing that the necessary causal link exists in this case because she would not have been injured "but for" Pantze's intoxication. Deltauer contends that Pantze's intoxication is only the occasion for appellant's injuries, not the cause, and that appellant's position, which relies on a "but for" analysis, must therefore be rejected under *Kryzer.* We disagree. The causal relationship argued by appellant is much more direct and immediate and much less attenuated than the causal links deemed too remote in *Kryzer* and *Weber.* We believe that the evidence, when viewed in appellant's favor under the summary judgment review standard, indicates that Pantze's intoxication was the cause of appellant's injuries, and not merely the occasion for them.

Deltauer argues that the supreme court's decision in *Lewellin v. Huber,* 465 N.W.2d 62 (Minn.1991), compels a different result. In *Lewellin,* a driver lost control of her car when she was distracted by the playful actions of a dog riding in the car; the car then left the road and hit the plaintiff. *Id.* at 63. The plaintiff sued the owner of the dog under the state's dog owner liability statute, which holds owners strictly liable for injuries caused by their dogs. *Id.* The supreme court held that the chain of events was too attenuated to constitute legal causation in that case. *Id.* at 66. The court stated that

[i]n applying our dog owner's liability statute, public policy and legislative intent are best served by limiting proximate cause to direct and immediate results of the dog's actions.

Id. at 65–66.

Like *Lewellin,* the instant case involves a strict liability cause of action created by statute. *See Dahl v. Northwestern Nat'l Bank,* 265 Minn. 216, 220, 121 N.W.2d 321, 324 (1963) (dram shop act imposes liability without regard to fault). Nevertheless, here we decline to limit proximate cause (substantial factor in bringing about injury) by equating it with immediate cause of the injury. The supreme court has not indicated that anything other than a traditional common-law analysis should govern questions of proximate cause under the dram shop act.

We reverse the summary judgment and remand the case to the district court for trial.

DECISION

The district court erred in granting Deltauer's motion for summary judgment in appellant's dram shop action because Pantze's intoxication could have been a proximate cause of appellant's injuries.

Reversed and remanded.

345

Insurance Discrimination Against Victims of Domestic Violence

◆ ◆ ◆ ◆ ◆ ◆

Prepared by the Women's Law Project and
the Pennsylvania Coalition Against Domestic Violence
Revised - September, 1996

Insurance Discrimination Against Victims of Domestic Violence

? **How are insurance companies discriminating against victims of domestic violence?**

Many insurance companies are denying victims of domestic violence access to all kinds of insurance by using domestic violence as an underwriting criterion, i.e., a basis for determining who to cover, how much to cover and how much to charge.

? **How do insurers learn that someone is a victim of domestic violence?**

When applying for insurance, individuals often sign a release to permit the insurer to obtain medical records. Usually, it is those medical records which reveal the information. This is becoming more common because physicians have been encouraged to follow protocols to identify and document abuse for the purpose of providing help and referrals.

There are also companies, such as the Medical Information Bureau (MIB) and Equifax, that maintain databases on risk factors, including medical and non-medical factors. Insurance companies who become members of these databases are required to report client risk factors and are entitled to request risk-related information on an applicant or insured. Information relating to domestic violence can be reported and disclosed through these databases.

Insurers can also get information from other records, such as public court documents and credit reports, which are becoming popular underwriting tools and often contain information about court orders, including protection from abuse orders.

? **How does insurance discrimination hurt victims of domestic violence?**

Insurance discrimination puts victims at risk both by denying the benefits that insurance provides and by discouraging them from seeking help that may result in loss of insurance.

Without insurance, victims are unable to obtain health care for themselves and their families or provide for their families in case of death or disability. If unable to obtain health and other insurance, victims may feel they have no alternative but to stay in an abusive situation.

Victims will stop seeking appropriate and necessary medical treatment, counseling, legal intervention and other forms of assistance, as they learn that insurers use information in client records to deny them insurance. Victims will also refrain from identifying the cause of their injury. Furthermore, doctors, health care workers and other service providers who have started identifying and documenting abuse may stop if continuing to do so will put their patients at risk of losing their insurance. The enormous efforts made over the past 20 years to create new sources of assistance and avenues of relief for victims of domestic violence will be for naught.

？ Does insurance discrimination against victims of domestic violence occur frequently?

Yes. An informal survey by the staff of the Subcommittee on Crime and Criminal Justice of the United States House Judiciary Committee in 1994 revealed that eight of the 16 largest insurers in the country were using domestic violence as a factor when deciding whether to issue and how much to charge for insurance.

In May 1995, the Insurance Commissioner of Pennsylvania reported the results of a formal survey of accident, health and life insurers regarding their underwriting practices relating to domestic violence. Overall 24% of the responding insurers reported that they took domestic violence into account in determining whether to issue and to renew insurance policies. Broken down by line of insurance, domestic violence was reported to be a criterion in deciding new applications by 74% of the responding life insurers, 65% of the responding health insurers and 47% of the accident insurers.

In December 1995, the Insurance Commissioner of Kansas reported the results of a similar study of accident, health and life insurers regarding their underwriting practices relating to domestic violence. Consistent with the results of the Pennsylvania survey, 24% of the responding companies reported using domestic violence as an underwriting criterion in the issuance and renewal of insurance. Broken down by line of insurance, domestic violence was reported to be a criterion in deciding new applications by 65% of the responding life insurers, 56% of the responding health insurers and 45% of the responding accident insurers. Both the Pennsylvania and the Kansas surveys found that, of those insurers who reported using domestic violence as an underwriting criterion, few had changed their practices well over a year after these practices had gained unfavorable public attention.

A review of health insurer underwriting guidelines by the Texas Office of Public Insurance Counsel in 1995 revealed a variety of ways in which health insurers use domestic violence as an underwriting guideline. Some treat victims of domestic violence as persons with mental illness and instruct those evaluating applications to look for particular symptoms and treatment to identify victims of domestic violence and to reject as an unacceptable risk an applicant who is in current treatment or recovered zero to twelve months. Some insurers consider domestic violence as a symptom of unreported or undiagnosed alcoholism and require consideration of family stability. Some correlate domestic violence with lower socio-economic class and sub-standard living conditions and require evaluation of environmental factors and family and occupational stability as relevant to likelihood of violence.

❓ How many people are affected by these practices?

We know that many insurance companies discriminate against victims of domestic violence and that many people are victimized. (A July 1994 study by The Commonwealth Fund reported that almost four million American women were physically abused by boyfriends and husbands in 1993.)

It is difficult to say just how many people are affected by these practices. Insurers are not required to tell applicants the reasons for rejections or other adverse actions and victims may not know that domestic violence was a consideration. Those who know that domestic violence is the reason for action taken against them by an insurance company have very good reasons for not reporting discriminatory insurance practices — fear of further violence to themselves and their children from the batterer, as well as social stigma and embarrassment. Finally, insurers are not required to file the criteria they use in deciding who to insure with state insurance departments or disclose that information to the public.

349

? What are some examples of insurance company discrimination against victims of domestic violence?

Health Insurance

• A Santa Cruz, California, woman was repeatedly turned down for health insurance following review of medical records which detailed beatings by her husband.

• A California hospital reports denial of payment by HMO's for repeated treatment for injuries caused by domestic violence.

• A woman from rural Minnesota was beaten severely by her ex-husband. After she remarried, she applied for health insurance and was told that she would not be covered for treatment relating to the abuse-related pre-existing conditions of depression and neck injury.

• Three insurance companies denied health insurance to a Minnesota women's shelter because, "as a battered women's program we were high risk."

• A women's shelter in Rochester, Minnesota, was told that it was considered uninsurable because its employees are almost all battered women.

• A woman sought the services of Women House in St. Cloud, Minnesota, because the abuse during her 12-year marriage had escalated in severity. She was hospitalized for a broken jaw and spent 2 weeks in a mental health unit in a hospital. Subsequently, she was denied health insurance by two companies, including one that stated it would not cover any medical or psychiatric problems that could be related to the past abuse.

• A Washington state child was twice denied health insurance because he had been sexually abused in a day care facility.

• A Washington man who was physically attacked by his wife was denied over $1,500 worth of health coverage for injuries he sustained. He was told that his wife, who owned the company which purchased the group coverage, instructed the insurer not to cooperate with him. Following divorce, he obtained an individual policy with exclusions for pre-existing conditions relating to domestic violence.

• A York County, Pennsylvania, employer provides health insurance through a self-insured plan which excludes expenses for medical treatment arising from or related to a domestic dispute.

• A Lancaster County, Pennsylvania, woman has been unable to obtain reimbursement for emergency room treatment for injuries resulting from domestic violence under her employer's self-insured health plan. She has been billed for over $5,000.

350

Life Insurance

- In October 1993, a resident of Cumberland County, Pennsylvania, was denied life, health and mortgage disability insurance by State Farm Insurance Company and life insurance by First Colony Life Insurance Company because of information in medical records revealing a single incident of domestic violence. State Farm has since changed its policy and no longer considers domestic violence in the issuance of any line of life, health or disability insurance.

- In August 1994, Nationwide Insurance Company denied an application for life insurance in Delaware based on medical records "indicating an unstable family environment" because they included documentation of three assaults by the husband against the wife as well as marital counseling.

- Prudential Insurance Company denied an Iowa woman a life insurance policy in November 1993, because the woman had a history of multiple assaults from her boyfriend.

Disability Insurance

- An Iowa woman was sexually abused as a child and received some counseling. Despite a clear record of good health since then, when she applied for disability insurance, she was turned down on the basis of earlier treatment.

- A Washington woman was twice denied insurance due to treatment received for physical, emotional and sexual abuse inflicted on her by her family during her childhood and by her spouse during marriage. In the late 1980's her employer's disability insurance carrier denied her disability coverage because of a nervous condition related to abuse. In 1993, Cigna denied her application for an increase in life insurance coverage provided through her employer based on a diagnosis of a dissociative disorder related to counseling for abuse. Although she suffers from obesity, Type II diabetes and a seizure disorder, the abuse-related counseling is the only reason given by the insurers for denial. She has divorced her abuser, has no further contact with her family of origin and is not on any medications.

Property and Casualty Insurance

- In 1994, Allstate Insurance Company canceled the fire insurance policy of an Oregon woman after her former spouse broke in and set multiple fires around the victim's home. The woman had been abused by the former spouse throughout the marriage and left the marriage in 1992. Two weeks prior to setting the fires, the former spouse had burgled the home, breaking five windows. Initially, Allstate refused to pay the claim on the basis of the former marital relationship, even though the arsonist was not on the policy. After Allstate canceled her policy, the woman sought other coverage and was repeatedly denied because of arson, although the arsonist was convicted and in jail.

351

She was also referred to the Oregon Fair Plan, but was quoted a price for insurance that was eight times what she had previously been paying.

- The homeowner's policy of a Washington state woman was canceled by Safeco Insurance Companies in May 1993 by a letter reciting five claims filed over the 12-year life of the policy and noting concern that the most recent three occurred over a span of four months, but more importantly, the most recent one "involved a domestic violence situation of individuals that are living with" the insured. The angry ex-wife of the woman's boyfriend's brother damaged her door.

- A Washington state landlord's policy was canceled because the insurer learned that the landlord intended to rent a home to a women's shelter.

- In September 1995, Farmer's Insurance Companies denied a property claim to a Washington state woman whose former boyfriend and abuser broke into her home and stole over $5,000 worth of personal property. The woman was subjected to two years of abuse, which included physical assault, stalking and property damage. During the course of investigating the claim, the insurer disclosed to the abuser the fact that he was suspected of stealing property. He retaliated by breaking into the woman's home and beating her, shoving her head-first into the fireplace, rendering her unconscious and threatening her life if she pressed charges. The woman fled the state with her children.

- The Women Helping Battered Women shelter in Burlington, Vermont had been insured by a company for two or three years, when the insurer sent a letter to the shelter's broker stating that it would not renew the shelter's policy. The letter stated "this is a [sic] undesirable risk due to life safety issues, this class is on our prohibited list and security of location is a concern." The shelter had no history of abuse-related claims. After being rejected by at least 3 insurers, the shelter obtained coverage from a non-profit insurer the day before its coverage ran out.

- A community advocacy program serving victims of abuse in rural Minnesota purchased an automobile in order to provide transportation to its office for people in need of its services. The car was purchased in response to the transportation problems frequently encountered by women needing the program's services. When the program contacted its insurance agent to request insurance for the car, the agent told the program that the car could not be added to the program's liability policy due to the risk of increased claims created by the use of the car to transport victims of abuse who were potentially being chased by abusers.

- The property coverage of a domestic violence advocacy program in Hardwick, Vermont, which provides information, referral and other supportive services to victims of domestic violence was canceled in 1995 due to the nature of the work it did. No claims had been made under the policy. The program is still without coverage, its agent having been told by a number of insurers that they do not provide this type of coverage.

• Women's Supportive Services in Claremont, New Hampshire, had great difficulty obtaining coverage when it added a shelter in the mid-80's. Insurers contacted informed the agency that they would not cover a shelter.

? What reasons do insurers give for using domestic violence as an underwriting criterion, and why are they invalid?

1. *Some insurers say that a victim of domestic violence makes a voluntary lifestyle choice, such as skydiving or riding a motorcycle, and liken battering to a career choice, such as washing skyscraper windows, for which an insurance company should not be responsible.*

Domestic violence is a crime — not a career, a lifestyle or a choice. No one chooses to be battered and no one chooses to remain in a violent situation. Leaving a violent domestic situation is a difficult process, complicated by concerns for safety and economics.

Victims realistically fear that their batterer will pursue and harm them and/or their children if they leave. Studies show that violence does not stop and may increase after leaving.

Without money, it is impossible for a victim to get away, establish a new home and feed children. Housing is a problem: shelters offer only temporary housing, often for 30 days or less, a very difficult time frame in which to create a new life.

2. *Others argue that domestic violence is a risk factor that needs to be considered by insurers and that limiting their ability to take domestic violence into account will impair their ability to offer affordable insurance products.*

Domestic violence is a crime and a person's likelihood of being a victim of a crime should not be used as a basis for underwriting insurance.

Furthermore, insurers have produced no actuarial studies showing that domestic violence is a particular risk that changes the overall cost of insurance. We know that there are many insurers who do not use domestic violence as an underwriting criterion and they are able to stay in business and provide affordable products.

Even those companies with policies requiring denial of coverage to victims of domestic violence cover victims and resulting injuries, when as is often the case, the abuse remains unidentified. Domestic violence is therefore already factored into the pricing of insurance products without impairing the market.

In addition, insurers do not, in a scientific and consistent manner, take into account all so-called risk factors when underwriting and rating insurance. To the contrary, although there are numerous risk factors insurers can choose to use, they do not use all of them and their selection is not based solely on risk. Some classifications are not chosen because it is more cost-effective to pay the claims than to identify and segregate the information needed to use them as underwriting criteria. Others may not be used because their use would negatively impact on marketing. Even where risk is the driving force behind the selection of criteria, the determination of risk is often based on assumptions and stereotypes, rather than any scientific assessment of risk.

Nor are insurers completely free from regulation. They are subject to extensive state regulation and are restricted by law from using particular classifications for underwriting and rating, including race, age, ethnic origin, residence, sex, and some physical and mental disabilities. Despite potential or actual statistical correlation to various health claims and morbidity or mortality, these classifications have been legally decreed to be unacceptable criteria for discriminating among insurance risks.

Many laws prohibit redlining — the practice of refusing to insure or raising the cost of home-owners' insurance in high crime areas — even though one could expect more crime or damage to homes in those areas. Yet, with respect to domestic violence, insurers are essentially redlining particular homes.

By virtue of government and private initiatives, we as a society have made a decision that domestic violence cannot be tolerated and that protection must be offered to victims. Allowing insurers to deny insurance based on records created when someone takes steps to obtain assistance will deter victims from seeking help and undo all our efforts.

3. *Life insurers argue that insuring the life of a victim gives the batterer an incentive to kill and collect on the policy and, if the insured is killed, the insurer could be sued for issuing a policy with knowledge of a history of domestic violence.*

Insurers have failed to provide any evidence that insurance acts as an incentive to further domestic violence or that denying insurance deters domestic violence. Domestic violence experts find that batterers abuse for power and control, not profit. Any hypothetical danger posed by providing coverage is outweighed by the known cost of denying insurance to victims of domestic violence: the inability of the victim to care for herself and her family, the perpetuation of violence and the increased health care costs imposed on society.

Insurers are already fully protected from suit by contract and law. Insurance policy provisions typically prohibit beneficiaries from recovering when the death or injury is a result of intentional misconduct. Furthermore, state laws regulate and limit the rights of a slayer from inheriting real and personal property and receiving benefits from insurance policies arising out of or as a result of the death of the person slain.

Insurers should be fully protected from suit as long as they issue policies only with the consent of the insured and follow all applicable laws and procedures. Insurers have not identified any situation in which they have paid on a policy or been successfully sued for a homicide which resulted from the issuance of a policy with knowledge of a domestic violence situation.

? Isn't insurance discrimination against victims of domestic violence already illegal? If not, is something being done to make it illegal?

Until very recently, there have been no laws making such discrimination illegal. In 1994, insurance officials and state legislatures started considering legislation to stop insurance discrimination against victims of domestic violence. In 1995 and 1996, federal proposals were introduced. As noted below, not all legislative initiatives cover all lines of insurance. As discrimination against victims of abuse occurs in all lines, it is recommended that legislation prohibit discrimination in all lines.

State Legislative Activity

Since 1994, 15 states have taken action to prohibit insurance discrimination against victims of abuse: 14 by legislative action, 1 by regulation. Those that have enacted laws include Arizona[1], California[2], Connecticut[3], Delaware[4], Florida[5], Indiana[6], Iowa[7], Maine[8], Massachusetts[9], Minnesota[10], New Hampshire[11], New York[12], Pennsylvania[13], and Tennessee[14]. The laws of Iowa, Massachusetts, New York and Pennsylvania apply to all lines of insurance. Delaware addresses life, health, disability, home-owners and private passenger auto insurance. The laws of the other states limit their application to life and/or health and/or disability insurance. The New Jersey Commissioner of Insurance has issued a ruling prohibiting group health insurers from excluding coverage for abuse-related conditions or inquiring about abuse.[15]

Legislation is pending in Alaska, California, Georgia, Illinois, Kansas, Maryland, Michigan, West Virginia, Wisconsin, and Wyoming[16] and legislators in additional states are considering introducing legislation.

In addition, the National Association of Insurance Commissioners (NAIC), an association of all state insurance regulators, is developing model state legislation to address discrimination against victims of domestic violence. A working group of the NAIC has completed its work on four separate models addressing discrimination in all lines of insurance. The model addressing health insurance, entitled *Unfair Discrimination Against Subjects of Abuse in Health Benefit Plans Model Act*, was approved in June,

1996. The models applicable to life, disability and property and casualty insurance are being finalized and are expected to be approved by the end of 1996.

[1] 1996 Ariz. Legis. Serv. Ch. 219 (West) (to be codified at Ariz. Rev. Stat. Ann., § 20-448F (1996)).
[2] CAL. HEALTH & SAFETY CODE, §1374.75; CAL. INS. CODE § 10144.2 (Supp. 1996).
[3] CONN. GEN. STAT. § 38a-816 (Supp. 1996).
[4] 18 DEL. CODE ANN. tit. 18, §§ 2302 (5), 2304 (24) (Supp. 1996) (life, health and disability insurance); An Act to Amend Chapter 23, Title 18 of the Delaware Code Relating to Unfair Insurance Practices of Discrimination By Insurance Companies Based on an Individual's Status as a Victim of Domestic Violence (to be codified at DEL. CODE. ANN. tit. 18 § 2304 (25) (home-owners and private passenger auto insurance)).
[5] FLA. STAT. ANN. § 626.9541 (g) (3) (Supp. 1996).
[6] An Act to Amend the Indiana Code Concerning Insurance, Effective July 1, 1996 (to be codified at Ind. Code Ann.§ 27-8-24.3).
[7] IOWA CODE, § 507B.4 (7) (c) (Supp. 1996).
[8] 1996 Me. Legis. Serv. Ch. 553 (West) (to be codified at Me. Rev. Stat. Ann. tit. 24-A, §215-B (West, 1996)).
[9] MASS. GEN. L. ch. 175, §§ 95B, 108G, 120 D, ch. 176A, § 3A, ch. 176B, § 5A, ch. 176 G, § 19 (Supp. 1996).
[10] 1996 Minn. Sess. Law Serv. Ch. 278 (West) (to be codified at Minn. Stat. § 72A.20 (1996)).
[11] An Act Prohibiting the Denial of Insurance Coverage Based on the Perception or Possibility That the Prospective Insured Is a Victim of Domestic Abuse or Violence, Effective January 1, 1997, (to be codified at N.H. Rev. Stat. Ann. § 417:4(f)(1996)).
[12] 1996 N.Y. Laws Ch. 174 (A.2769E) (McKinney's) (to be codified at N.Y. Insurance Law § 2612 (McKinney 1996)).
[13] An Act Amending the Act of July 27, 1974, (to be codified at 40 P.S. § 1171.5(14)(1996)).
[14] An Act to Prohibit Unfair Denial of Health Benefit Coverage to Victims of Abuse and To Amend Tenn. Code Ann., Title 56 (to be codified at Tenn. Code Ann., Title 56 (1996)).
[15] 28 N.J.R.§ 2003, at 2005, April 15, 1996, (to be codified at N.J. Admin. Code § 11: 4-42.5).

Federal Legislative Activity

Several bills are being considered in the U.S. Congress as well. Legislation at the federal level will provide protection for victims of abuse whose health insurance plans are not governed by state insurance laws. (ERISA, the federal law regulating pensions and other employee benefit plans, preempts state insurance laws from governing certain employer-sponsored health plans.) To the extent that states are slow to pass legislation, federal legislation has the potential to offer a speedier and more comprehensive approach, assuring victims of abuse that they will receive the same protection from insurance discrimination wherever they reside.

Between March and June of 1995, Senator Wellstone[17] (MN) and Representatives Schumer[18] (NY), Wyden[19] (OR), and Molinari[20] (NY) introduced legislation directed at discriminatory acts in health insurance only. After Wyden moved to the Senate, Representatives Morella (MD) and Schumer (NY) reintroduced the Wyden bill in the House[21], as part of the Women's Health Equity Act. In the fall of 1995, Representative Sanders (VT) introduced legislation which prohibits insurance discrimination against victims of abuse in all lines of insurance, including health.[22] That bill was introduced in the Senate by Senators Wellstone and Wyden on March 20, 1996.[23] In June 1996, Representative Pomeroy (ND) introduced a similar bill in the House.[24]

The existence of these bills provided the impetus for further consideration of domestic violence in the context of health reform. On July 28, 1995 Senator Kassebaum (KS), who introduced with Senator Kennedy (MA), The Health Insurance Reform Act of 1995[25] presided over a hearing before the Senate Committee on Labor and Human Resources on the issue of insurance discrimination against victims of abuse.[26] The Committee reported favorably on the Health Insurance Reform Act of 1995, after amending it to clarify that pre-existing condition exclusions, which the bill permits but restricts, could not be used to deny or limit coverage to victims of abuse.[27] The final health reform bill, enacted as the *Health Insurance Portability and Accountability Act of 1996*, was further amended to include specific language prohibiting discrimination on the basis of domestic violence in access to group health plan coverage and to individual coverage for individuals with prior group coverage.[28]

---

[16] H.B. 395, S.B. 197, 19th Leg., 2nd Sess. (1996) (Alaska); A.B. 115, 1995-96 Reg. Sess. (CAL); H.B. 1457, S.B. 679, 143rd Gen. Ass., 1995-96 Reg. Sess. (GA); H.B. 2566, 89th Gen. Ass., 1995-96 Reg. Sess. (ILL); S.B. 444, 76th Leg., 1996 Reg. Sess. (KAN); H.B. 39, 1996 Reg. Sess. (MD); H.B. 4634; 88th Leg., 1995 Reg. Sess. (MI); H.B. 4316, 1996 Reg. Sess. (W.VA); A.B. 292, S.B. 138, 92nd Leg. Sess. (WI); H.B. 43, 53rd Leg., 1996 Reg. Sess. (WY).

[17] S. 524, 104th Cong., 1st Sess. (1995).

[18] H.R. 1191, 104th Cong., 1st Sess. (1995).

[19] H.R. 1201, 104th Cong., 1st Sess. (1995).

[20] H.R. 1920, 104th Cong., 1st Sess. (1995).

[21] H.R. 3145, 104th Cong., 2d Sess. (1996).

[22] H.R. 2654, 104th Cong., 1st Sess. (1995).

[23] S. 1630, 104th Cong., 2d Sess. (1996).

[24] H.R. 3590, 104th Cong., 2d Sess. (1996).

[25] S. 1028, 104th Cong., 1st Sess. (1995).

[26] *Health Insurance and Domestic Violence, 1995: Hearing Examining Proposal to Prohibit Insurers From Denying Health Insurance Coverage, Benefits, or Varying Premiums Based on the Status of an Individual as a Victim of Domestic Violence, Including Related Provisions of S. 524, S. 1028, and H.R. 1201 Before the Senate Committee on Labor and Human Resources, 104th Cong., 1st Sess. (1995).*

[27] H.R. Rep. No. 156, 104th Cong., 1st Sess. (1995).

[28] H.R. 3103, 104th Cong., 2d Sess. (1996).

？ What do the new laws and legislative proposals do?

Most prohibit insurers from using domestic violence as a basis for underwriting or rating insurance, meaning that they prohibit an insurer from refusing to insure someone or charging them a higher premium because they are, have been or might become a victim of domestic violence. They may also prohibit insurers from writing policies that exclude coverage for injuries resulting from domestic violence.

Some also include important provisions requiring that abuse-related information be kept confidential and that insurers develop protocols for employees, agents and contractors to make sure their interactions with victims do not either endanger the safety of the victim or result in disclosure of confidential information. They also include definitions of necessary terms and enforcement mechanisms and remedies to assure that a person complaining of insurance discrimination can obtain appropriate relief.

？ How are insurance companies reacting to legislative proposals to prohibit discrimination against victims of domestic violence?

Some insurers have changed their practices voluntarily. Some say they will only deny in the most egregious cases. All health, life and disability insurers say they must continue to look at medical condition regardless of cause. Insurers oppose the application of non-discrimination legislation to property and casualty insurance.

Some insurers voice support for legislation protecting domestic violence victims, but with limitations, urging a number of amendments and provisos to pending legislation. These include language that would allow insurers to underwrite and rate on the basis of mental and physical history regardless of the underlying cause, protect an insurer from liability for any injury resulting from compliance with the legislation, and allow insurers to deny life insurance to abusers.

Others simply oppose any limitation on their ability to consider abuse in underwriting and rating, stating that insurers should have leeway in considering this type of material information.

? What is wrong with allowing insurers to underwrite on the basis of medical conditions caused by abuse?

The purpose of the protective legislation will be undermined if it allows insurers to underwrite on the basis of medical conditions caused by abuse. Such an exception would allow an insurer to deny insurance to a victim based on medical records documenting bruises or broken bones resulting from the abuse and have the same effect as allowing an insurer to deny insurance based on the domestic violence itself. Consideration of the medical records in any way will deter victims from seeking help and leaving. The only way to end the cycle of violence is to make sure that battered individuals are able to freely seek assistance for abuse.

Permitting underwriting on the basis of abuse-related medical conditions will also enable insurers to discriminate indirectly against victims of domestic violence. Insurers will be able to deny an applicant and refuse to renew an insured based on a medical condition that is frequently associated with abuse. They will also be able to apply particular medical criteria selectively to victims of abuse, for example, determining only victims of abuse ineligible for insurance because of treatment for bruises and black eyes. Because insurers are subject to little regulation in their selection and use of medical underwriting criteria, no one will know or stop them from selecting and applying medical underwriting criteria with the express intent of weeding out abuse victims.

Furthermore, allowing insurers to consider the health status of victims of domestic violence is inconsistent with the trend toward limiting the insurer's consideration of health status in both issuance and rating of health insurance through "community rating" and "guaranteed issuance."

At the very least, any legislation permitting insurers to underwrite on the basis of abuse-related medical conditions must contain safeguards. We recommend the following language:

An insurer taking action that adversely affects a victim of abuse on the basis of a medical condition, claim or other underwriting information that the insurer knows or has reason to know is abuse-related, shall explain the reason for its action to the applicant or insured in writing and shall be able to demonstrate that the action taken and any applicable policy provision:

(A) Is otherwise permissible by law and is applied in the same manner and to the same extent to all applicants and insureds with similar medical conditions, claims or claims history without regard to whether the medical condition or claims are abuse-related.

(B) Does not have the purpose or effect of avoiding the intent and prohibitions of this Act or any other provision of law and is not based upon any actual or perceived correlation between a medical condition, type of claim or other underwriting information and abuse.

(C) Does not have the purpose or effect of treating abuse status as a medical condition or underwriting criterion.

(D) Is based on a determination, made in conformance with sound actuarial principles and supported by reasonable statistical evidence, that there is a correlation between the medical condition, claim or other underwriting information and a material increase in insurance risk.

This language attempts to prevent discriminatory use of underwriting standards. It also requires notice to the applicant or insured of the reason for any adverse insurance action and, should that insurance action be challenged, properly places the burden of proof on the party who has the information, the insurer. Similar language has been included in the NAIC model laws to prohibit insurance discrimination. Several of the state statutes contain variations of some of these safeguards. See, for example, the statutes from Arizona, California, Delaware, Indiana and Tennessee.

? **If legislation prohibits insurers from considering medical conditions caused by abuse, doesn't it create a special class of individuals who get special treatment?**

No. Prohibiting discrimination on the basis of domestic violence will assure that these victims are treated like all other applicants. It is insurers who have created the special class, singling out domestic violence as a special classification of uninsurability.

Protection for victims of domestic violence will not make inequitable an otherwise equitable system of underwriting. Insurance industry practices are not premised on either fundamental fairness or uniformity. Insurance companies already treat people differently regardless of how compelling their circumstances may be.

For example, timing and pre-existing condition clauses may result in one pregnant woman being covered while another is not. A violent neighborhood will not be taken into account, but a violent household will be in determining whether to issue insurance. Some companies cover some conditions, while others do not. In this context, it is disingenuous to argue unfairness with respect to legislation that is necessary to end domestic violence.

New Protections for Immigrant Women and Children Who Are Victims of Domestic Violence

by *Charles Wheeler*

I. Introduction

For years United States immigration laws have overlooked the plight of women and children who are victims of domestic violence. In fact, some might argue that these laws have fostered a system that has tolerated, if not abetted, physical violence and psychological abuse committed by U.S. citizen spouses or parents on immigrant spouses or children. Much-needed reform in this area finally occurred in 1994 with the passage of a law that added important protections for immigrant spouses and children.[1] However, most of those statutory provisions were implemented only when the Immigration and Naturalization Service (INS) promulgated interim regulations in March 1996.[2]

Under the Violence Against Women Act (VAWA), non-U.S.-citizen spouses and children who are victims of domestic violence may apply on their own behalf for an immigrant visa without the assistance or consent of the U.S. citizen or lawful permanent resident (LPR) abuser. Alternatively, the VAWA allows

abused spouses or children to assert an important defense against deportation.[3]

Under prior law, only the U.S. citizen or LPR spouse or parent could petition for the alien spouse's or child's immigration.[4] This process was initiated by the U.S. citizen or LPR filing an I-130 petitionthe alien spouse or child had no way of obtaining a family-based immigrant visa unless the petitioner filed this petition. U.S. citizen and LPR spouses and parents therefore controlled whether the alien spouse or child could reside or work legally in the United States. Many took advantage of this power by threatening to report the alien spouse or child to INS if either complained about physical or psychological abuse.

Therefore, under prior immigration law, the abused spouse and child were presented with a Hobson's choice: either divorce the abuser and abandon any legal right to remain in the United States or remain in the abusive relationship in the hope that such perseverance would eventually result in obtaining lawful immigration status. The situation

Charles Wheeler, formerly the executive director of the National Immigration Law Center, 1102 Crenshaw Blvd., Los Angeles, CA 90019 ((213) 938-6452), recently became senior attorney at the Catholic Legal Immigration Network in San Francisco.

---

[1] The Violence Against Women Act (VAWA) is contained in Title IV of the Violent Crime and Law Enforcement Act of 1994, Pub. L. No. 103-322, 108 Stat. 1796 (1994). The provisions that amend immigration law are codified at 8 U.S.C. §§ 1151, 1154, 1186, 1186a note, 1254, and 2245.

[2] 61 Fed. Reg. 13061 (Mar. 26, 1996).

[3] Violent Crime and Law Enforcement Act of 1994, Pub. L. No. 103-322, §§ 40701–3, 108 Stat. 1953–55.

[4] Immigration and Nationality Act § 204(a)(1).

was exacerbated further for abused immigrant spouses with U.S. citizen children since child custody and visitation decisions could be affected by whether the abused spouse was subject to deportation.

Studies and reports indicate that domestic violence within mixed households—those containing immigrant and U.S. citizen family members—is far from rare. For example, one study of mixed households in California revealed that 25 percent of Filipino and 35 percent of Latino women had been victims of domestic violence committed by their U.S. citizen or LPR spouses.[5]

The VAWA's purpose was to weaken the control of abusing parties and to create a mechanism for abused spouses or children to free themselves from such relationships without losing their ability to immigrate.[6] Under the new law, the latter can either self-petition for lawful permanent resident status based on their relationship to the U.S. citizen or LPR, or, if INS has already commenced proceedings to remove them from the country, they can apply for suspension of deportation. The new law also mandates the evidentiary standard INS must use in evaluating applications for a "battered spouse waiver." It requires INS and judges to consider "any credible evidence" relevant to petition or application.[7]

INS's interim, proposed regulations implementing the "self-petition" provisions provide detailed information on who may qualify for relief under the statute, how to file the self-petition, what documentary evidence should accompany the petition, the effect of legal termination of a marriage, and eligibility for employment authorization.[8]

Advocates had been anxiously awaiting promulgation of these regulations before deciding whether their clients were eligible for relief. As of the end of March 1996, approximately 300 to 400 applications had been filed; INS had held those applications in abeyance but will now begin adjudicating them.

Under prior immigration law, the abused spouse and child were presented with a Hobson's choice.

The Executive Office for Immigration Review has already implemented the statutory provisions that add a new form of suspension of deportation for abused spouses and children. These provisions went into effect on September 13, 1994, when President Clinton signed the legislation.

II. Self-Petition

A. Who May Apply

The VAWA amended section 204(a)(1) of the Immigration and Nationality Act to allow certain abused spouses and children to self-petition for permanent residency.[9] Persons eligible for self-petitioning include (1) abused spouses and children of U.S. citizens or LPRs; (2) nonabused spouses who are parents of abused children of U.S. citizens or LPRs; and (3) abused spouses of U.S. citizens or LPRs and their nonabused children, even if the children are not related to the U.S. citizen or LPR abuser.

B. Basic Requirements

According to the statutory provisions, to be eligible for the self-petition form of relief, the alien spouse of a U.S.

---

[5] C. Hogeland & K. Rosen, Dreams Lost, Dreams Found: Undocumented Women in the Land of Opportunity 15 (1990). *See also* J. Calvo and M. Davis, *Congress Nears Approval of Legislation to Protect Abused Aliens,* 70 Interpreter Releases 1665 (Dec. 20, 1993).

[6] H.R. Rep. No. 395, 103d Cong., 1st Sess., at 37.

[7] Immigration and Nationality Act §§ 204(a)(1)(H), 244(g), 8 U.S.C. §§ 1154(a)(1)(H), 1254(g).

[8] 61 Fed. Reg. 13061 (Mar. 26, 1996).

[9] Violent Crime and Law Enforcement Act of 1994, Pub. L. No. 103-322, § 40701, 108 Stat. 1953 (adding Immigration and Nationality Act § 204(a)(1)(A)(iii)–(iv), 204(a)(1)(B)(ii)–(iii), 8 U.S.C. § 1154(a)(1)(A)(iii)–(iv), 1154(a)(1)(B)(ii)–(iii)).

citizen or LPR must demonstrate the following: (1) that the alien spouse is of good moral character; (2) that the marriage was entered into in good faith; (3) that the alien spouse resided in the

The law does not require the self-petitioner to be currently residing with the abuser.

United States with the U.S. citizen or LPR spouse and is currently residing in the U.S.; (4) that during the marriage the alien spouse or his or her child was battered by or was the subject of extreme cruelty committed by the U.S. citizen or LPR spouse; and (5) that deportation would result in extreme hardship to the alien spouse or his or her child.[10]

Similarly, the alien child of a U.S. citizen or LPR must establish the following: (1) that the alien child is of good moral character; (2) that the alien child resided in the United States with the U.S. citizen or LPR parent and is currently residing in the United States; (3) that during that residence the alien child was battered by or was the subject of extreme cruelty committed by the U.S. citizen or LPR parent; and (4) that deportation would result in extreme hardship to the alien child.[11]

The interim regulations provide the details on how the self-petition provisions are to be implemented.

Residence. The self-petitioner must be residing in the United States and must have resided in the United States with the abuser at the time the abuse occurred. However, the law does not require the self-petitioner to have resided in the United States with the abuser for any specific period of time. Most important, the law does not require that the self-petitioner be currently residing with the abuser.[12]

Marital relationship. The self-petitioning spouse must be legally married to the abusing spouse at the time the self-petition is filed. But legal termination of the relationship through divorce, annulment, or death of the abuser while the self-petition is pending with INS will not affect the agency's decision. Nor will legal termination after approval of the self-petition affect an approved petition. However, a self-petition will be denied or approval revoked if the abused spouse remarries before obtaining LPR status.[13]

Good-faith marriage. The self-petitioning spouse must establish by a preponderance of the evidence (unless he or she married while in deportation or exclusion proceedings, in which case the standard is by clear and convincing evidence) that the marriage was entered into in good faith. The most important factor in establishing a good-faith marriage is whether the couple intended to establish a life together at the time of the marriage. Conduct after a couple is married even separation shortly thereafter is relevant only to establish intent at the time the marriage was entered into.[14]

Parent-child relationship. The self-petitioning child must be unmarried and under 21 years of age. He or she must also be the child of the abusive U.S. citizen or LPR parent but need not be the child of a self-petitioning spouse. The self-petitioning child does not have to be in the abuser's legal custody, nor do changes in parental rights or legal custody affect the status of the child's self-petition.[15]

Status of abuser. The abusing spouse or parent must be a U.S. citizen or LPR at the time the self-petition is filed. But subsequent changes in the abuser's citizenship or immigration status will not affect an approved self-petition.[16]

---

[10] Immigration and Nationality Act § 204(a)(1)(A)(iii), 204(a)(1)(B)(ii), 8 U.S.C. § 1154(a)(1)(A)(iii), 1154(a)(1)(B)(ii).

[11] *Id.* § 204(a)(1)(A)(iv), 204(a)(1)(B)(iii), 8 U.S.C. § 1154(a)(1)(A)(iv), 1154(a)(1)(B)(iii).

[12] 8 C.F.R. § 204.2(c)(1)(v), 204.2(e)(1)(v).

[13] *Id.* §§ 204.2(c)(1)(ii), 205.1(a)(3)(i)(E).

[14] *Id.* § 204.2(c)(1)(ix).

[15] *Id.* § 204.2(e)(1)(ii).

[16] *Id.* § 204.2(c)(1)(iii), 204.2(e)(1)(iii).

Definition of "abuse." To qualify as abuse under the statute, the spouse or child must show that he or she "has been battered or has been the subject of extreme cruelty" perpetrated by the alien's spouse or parent.[17] This phrase is identical to the one used in a section of the law that waives the joint petition requirement for conditional resident aliens who must petition to remove the condition after two years.[18] The regulation implementing the self-petition provisions uses the same definition of battery or extreme cruelty that governs the battered spouse waiver to the joint petition requirement.[19] Thus, abuse is "any act or threatened act of violence, including any forceful detention, which results or threatens to result in physical or mental injury." It includes psychological abuse, rape, incest, and forced prostitution.[20]

Good moral character. Although the statute does not specify any definite period during which good moral character must be established, the regulation requires three years of good moral character preceding the filing of the self-petition. Children under age 14 are presumed to be of good moral character.[21] Legal bars to establishing good moral character are set forth in the Immigration and Nationality Act.[22]

Extreme hardship. Self-petitioning spouses must show that their deportation would result in extreme hardship to themselves or their children. Self-petitioning children must show that their deportation would result in extreme hardship to themselves. The phrase "extreme hardship" has acquired a settled judicial and administrative meaning since it is also used as an eligibility requirement for suspension of deportation.[23] The same factors that are considered by immigration judges in determin-

JAN ALEXANDER

ing extreme hardship for suspension of deportation will be considered by INS when adjudicating self-petitions. These include the alien's age; the alien's ties to family in the United States and abroad; how long the alien has resided in the United States; the alien's health and availability of medical facilities in the home country; the alien's work skills and ability to obtain adequate employment in the home country; the alien's immigration history; the alien's position in the community; potential disruption of edu-

---

[17] Immigration and Nationality Act § 204(a)(1)(A)(iii)(I), (iv)(I), 8 U.S.C. § 1154(a)(1)(A)(iii)(I), (iv)(I).

[18] *Id.* § 216(c)(4)(C), 8 U.S.C. § 1186a(c)(4)(C).

[19] *Compare* 8 C.F.R. § 204.2(c)(1)(vi), 204.2(e)(1)(vi), *with* § 216.5(e)(3)(i).

[20] *Id.* § 204.2(c)(1)(vi), 204.2(e)(1)(vi).

[21] *Id.* § 204.2(c)(1)(vii), 204.2(e)(1)(vii).

[22] Immigration and Nationality Act § 101(f), 8 U.S.C. § 1101(f).

[23] *Id.* § 244(a), 8 U.S.C. § 1254(a).

Publications and Technical Assistance Available from the National Council of Juvenile and Family Court Judges

The National Council of Juvenile and Family Court Judges has several publications of interest to practitioners representing victims of domestic violence.

Family Violence: Improving Court Practice details the policies and procedures necessary to create and maintain an effective court, agency, and community response to family violence. In addition to recommendations concerning criminal and civil courts, policy recommendations and recommendations for court-related agencies, such as law enforcement, prosecutors, court administrators, and children's protective services and treatment providers, are included. 1990. 59pp. $5.

Family Violence: State-of-the-Art Court Programs examines 18 of the best court programs in the United States dealing with family violence. Comprehensive programs, statewide court programs, rural programs, civil protection order programs, and prosecution programs are discussed. Intended to offer practical solutions, the book includes sections on offender accountability, coordinating councils, and legislation and policy development. 1992. 100pp. $15.

The Juvenile and Family Court Journal, State Codes on Domestic Violence: Analysis, Commentary, and Recommendations, an article by Barbara Hart, examines existing state laws with respect to (1) civil protection orders, (2) child custody, (3) mediation, (4) civil damages, (5) social and health services, (6) evidence, (7) battered women defendants, and (8) the duty to protect children. Each chapter includes recommendations for provisions to be included in state codes concerning domestic and family violence. 1992. 81pp. $10.

The Model Code on Domestic and Family Violence was drafted by a multidisciplinary advisory committee comprised of judges, battered women's advocates, attorneys, law enforcement officers, and other professionals. Commentary by Barbara Hart follows each section. 1994. 50pp. Single copies free of charge. Additional copies $10 each.

An *Appendix to the Model Code* contains the Model Code and a variety of resources, including overviews of each chapter of the Model Code; research statistics and articles about mandatory arrest, safety planning, child custody, mediation, rural problems, and funding of family violence legislation; sample forms; protocols for law enforcement, prosecutors, and health care providers; and a listing of state coalitions for domestic violence. $25.

The Family Violence Project distributes specialized information packets on the following topics: child protection and custody; effects of domestic violence on children; coordinating councils; fatality review; legal advocacy; mediation; and supervised visitation centers. It also gives technical assistance to individuals interested in ameliorating family violence, with a special emphasis on child protection and child custody issues. For further information or to order publications, contact the Family Violence Project of the National Council of Juvenile and Family Court Judges, P.O. Box 8970, Reno, NV 89507; (800) 427-3223 (voice); (702) 784-6161 (fax).

---

cation opportunities; and the adverse psychological impact of deportation.[24]

In addition, self-petitioners may submit evidence of the nature and extent of the physical and psychological consequences of battery or cruelty, the effect of loss of access to U.S. courts, the continuing need for medical or psychological counseling that is not available in the home country, and the existence of laws or social customs in the home country that would penalize or otherwise adversely affect the abused party.[25]

Documentary evidence. INS will consider all credible evidence submitted with the petition before reaching a conclusion.[26] Primary evidence, such as medical, police, or court records, is pre-

---

[24] *See In re* Anderson, 16 I&N Dec. 596 (BIA 1978). *See also* 61 Fed. Reg. 13067 (Mar. 26, 1996).

[25] 8 C.F.R. § 204.2(c)(1)(viii), 204.2(e)(1)(viii). *See also* 61 Fed. Reg. 13067 (Mar. 26, 1996).

[26] *Id.* § 204.1(f)(1), 204.2(c)(2)(i), 204.2(e)(2)(i).

ferred to secondary evidence, such as affidavits.[27] The self-petitioning spouse or child must submit documentation establishing (1) a legal relationship to the abuser;[28] (2) the abuser's citizenship or LPR status;[29] (3) suffering from battery or extreme cruelty, as evidenced by photographs, reports or affidavits from police, court officials, medical personnel, school officials, clergy, and social service agency personnel, and even unsupported affidavits from the abused person;[30] (4) good moral character, as evidenced by an affidavit from the self-petitioner and police clearance letter(s) from jurisdictions where the self-petitioner resided for six months or more during the preceding three years;[31] (5) residence with the abuser in the U.S. and current residence at the time the self-petition is filed;[32] (6) good-faith marriage, as evidenced by joint property or leasehold interests, bank accounts, income tax returns, birth certificates of children born of the marriage, and evidence of courtship and marriage ceremony;[33] and (7) extreme hardship, as evidenced by birth certificates of children, medical reports, police reports, and other court documents indicating abuse.[34]

Derivative children. Children of the abused spouse who are unmarried and under age 21 can qualify for derivative status provided they are included on the spouse's self-petition. Children are not required to have been the victims of abuse or to have resided in the United States. They must meet the re-quirements only for immigrant visa issuance abroad or adjustment of status in the United States.[35]

C. Procedure for Filing

The self-petitioner must complete and file an INS form I-360. If the self-petition is being filed together with an application for adjustment of status, forms I-360 and I-485 usually are filed with the INS district director's office with jurisdiction over the applicant's place of residence. If only the I-360 is being filed, it must be mailed to the INS regional service center with jurisdiction over the applicant's place of residence. The filing fee is $80, but low-income persons can request a fee waiver.[36]

D. Employment Authorization

Self-petitioners may qualify for employment authorization if they are filing simultaneously for adjustment of status.[37] Alternatively, self-petitioners who apply for and are granted voluntary departure may obtain employment authorization.[38]

III. Suspension of Deportation

A. Who May Apply

The VAWA also created a new form of relief—suspension of deportation—for abused spouses or children of U.S. citizens or LPRs.[39] Suspension of deportation existed under prior law but was available only to persons of good moral character whose deportation would result in extreme hardship and who had either

---

[27] *Id.* § 204.2(c)(2)(i), 204.2(e)(2)(i).

[28] *Id.* § 204.2(c)(2)(ii), 204.2(e)(2)(ii).

[29] *Id.*

[30] *Id.* § 204.2(c)(2)(iv), 204.2(e)(2)(iv).

[31] *Id.* § 204.2(c)(2)(v), 204.2(e)(2)(v).

[32] *Id.* § 204.2(c)(2)(iii), 204.2(e)(2)(iii).

[33] *Id.* § 204.2(c)(2)(vii).

[34] *Id.* § 204.2(c)(2)(vi), 204.2(e)(2)(vi).

[35] *Id.* § 204.2(c)(4).

[36] *Id.* § 103.7(c).

[37] *Id.* § 274a.12(c)(9).

[38] *Id.* § 274a.12(c)(12). Eligibility for voluntary departure is set forth in *id.* § 242.5(a)(2)(v)–(vii).

[39] Violent Crime and Law Enforcement Act of 1994, Pub. L. No. 103-322, § 40703(a) (adding Immigration and Nationality Act § 244(a)(3), 8 U.S.C. § 1154(a)(3)).

seven or ten years' physical presence in the United States.[40] In a significant change, the VAWA shortened the physical-presence requirement to three years for abused spouses and children. The applicant for this new form of suspension of deportation must be a spouse or child suffering from domestic abuse or the parent of a child suffering from domestic abuse. If a child is not suffering from domestic abuse but his or her parent is, the parent's suspension application may not include his or her children.[41]

B. Basic Requirements

The new provisions for suspension of deportation are available to abused spouses and children who are in deportation proceedings and can demonstrate that they (1) are persons of good moral character, (2) suffered battery or ex-

In a significant change, the Violence Against Women Act shortened the physical-presence requirement for suspension of deportation to three years for abused spouses and children.

treme cruelty at the hands of a U.S. citizen or LPR spouse or parent, (3) would suffer extreme hardship if deported, and (4) have resided continuously for three years' in the United States.[42]

Battering or extreme cruelty. The abuser must be a U.S. citizen or LPR spouse or parent, and the applicant must have been battered or subjected to extreme cruelty in the United States by the spouse or parent. While applicants for this form of suspension of deportation do not have to show that the marriage was entered into in good faith, they are ineligible if they are deportable for having committed marriage fraud.[43]

Termination of the marriage before filing for suspension of deportation does not affect eligibility.

Continuous physical presence. Applicants must have been physically present in the United States for a continuous period of not less than three years immediately preceding the date of the application. While "brief, casual, and innocent" departures are permitted for suspension applicants with seven or ten years' presence, any departures during the three-year period may preclude eligibility for abused spouses and children.[44] Unlike the requirement for self-petitioners, applicants for suspension are not required to have resided with the abuser.

Extreme hardship. To be eligible for suspension, applicants must show that they would suffer extreme hardship if they were deported; the hardship may be to the suspension applicant or the applicant's parent or child.[45] The factors that the immigration judge considers in determining extreme hardship are those that INS considers when adjudicating a self-petition and are described above.

Good moral character. Persons seeking suspension of deportation must prove that they were of "good moral character" during the three-year period required for suspension.[46] It is unclear whether applicants must also show good moral character for the entire time they have resided in the United States.

Deportability. Applicants seeking this form of suspension must be deportable only under certain grounds, such as illegal entry, violation of nonimmigrant status, or smuggling.[47] Applicants who are deportable based on certain criminal convictions, use of fraudulent documents, or for security reasons do not qualify for this relief.[48] On the other

---

[40] Immigration and Nationality Act § 244 (a)(1)–(2), 8 U.S.C. § 1254(a)(1)–(2).
[41] *Id.* § 244 (a)(3), 8 U.S.C. § 1254(a)(3).
[42] *Id.*
[43] *Id.*
[44] *Id.* § 244(b)(2), 8 U.S.C. § 1254(b)(2).
[45] *Id.* § 244(a)(3), 8 U.S.C. § 1254(a)(3).
[46] *Id.*
[47] *Id. See id.* § 241(a)(1), (5), 8 U.S.C. § 1251(a)(1), (5).
[48] *Id.* § 244(a)(3), 8 U.S.C. § 1254(a)(3). *See id.* § 241(a)(2)–(4), 8 U.S.C. § 1251(a)(2)–(4).

hand, deportability due to receipt of public benefits or HIV seropositivity are not bars to suspension under the VAWA.

C. Procedure for Filing

Since abused spouses and children may file for suspension of deportation only before an immigration judge, they must wait until INS commences deportation proceedings against them before they can file for this relief. Unlike the self-petitioning provision, the new suspension statute does not allow parents to include their children in their applications. Abused children have to file their own applications, although they may do so at the same time their abused parent files. Children who are not abused may not obtain status through suspension. Applicants complete and submit form EOIR-40, together with a filing fee of $100, directly with the immigration court. Low-income persons can request a fee waiver.[49]

D. Employment Authorization

INS will grant suspension applicants employment authorization in one-year increments during the pendency of their applications, provided they demonstrate an economic need to work.[50]

IV. Conclusion

By amending serious defects in immigration law, recent legislation and implementing regulations have provided critical relief for immigrant spouses and children who are victims of domestic violence or abuse. The self-petition and suspension of deportation provisions give this vulnerable group important options that they did not have previously and allow them both to leave the abusive relationship and obtain or maintain lawful immigration status. The new law attempts to remove those inequities in prior immigration law that practically encouraged domestic violence and, at a minimum, to put immigrant spouses and children in no worse a position than their U.S. citizen counterparts.

---

[49] 8 C.F.R. § 103.7(C).
[50] *Id.* § 274a.12(c)(10).

Subtitle G—Protections for Battered Immigrant Women and Children

SEC. 40701. ALIEN PETITIONING RIGHTS FOR IMMEDIATE RELATIVE OR SECOND PREFERENCE STATUS.

(a) IN GENERAL.—Section 204(a)(1) of the Immigration and Nationality Act (8 U.S.C. 1154(a)(1)) is amended—

(1) in subparagraph (A)—

(A) by inserting "(i)" after "(A)",

(B) by redesignating the second sentence as clause (ii), and

(C) by adding at the end the following new clauses:

"(iii) An alien who is the spouse of a citizen of the United States, who is a person of good moral character, who is eligible to be classified as an immediate relative under section 201(b)(2)(A)(i), and who has resided in the United States with the alien's spouse may file a petition with the Attorney General under this subparagraph for classification of the alien (and any child of the alien if such a child has not been classified under clause (iv)) under such section if the alien demonstrates to the Attorney General that—

"(I) the alien is residing in the United States, the marriage between the alien and the spouse was entered into in good faith by the alien, and during the marriage the alien or a child of the alien has been battered by or has been the subject of extreme cruelty perpetrated by the alien's spouse; and

"(II) the alien is a person whose deportation, in the opinion of the Attorney General, would result in extreme hardship to the alien or a child of the alien.

"(iv) An alien who is the child of a citizen of the United States, who is a person of good moral character, who is eligible to be classified as an immediate relative under section 201(b)(2)(A)(i), and who has resided in the United States with the citizen parent may file a petition with the Attorney General under this subparagraph for classification of the alien under such section if the alien demonstrates to the Attorney General that—

"(I) the alien is residing in the United States and during the period of residence with the citizen parent the alien has been battered by or has been the subject of extreme cruelty perpetrated by the alien's citizen parent; and

"(II) the alien is a person whose deportation, in the opinion of the Attorney General, would result in extreme hardship to the alien.";
(2) in subparagraph (B)—
(A) by inserting "(i)" after "(B)"; and
(B) by adding at the end the following new clauses:
"(ii) An alien who is the spouse of an alien lawfully admitted for permanent residence, who is a person of good moral character, who is eligible for classification under section 203(a)(2)(A), and who has resided in the United States with the alien's legal permanent resident spouse may file a petition with the Attorney General under this subparagraph for classification of the alien (and any child of the alien if such a child has not been classified under clause (iii)) under such section if the alien demonstrates to the Attorney General that the conditions described in subclauses (I) and (II) of subparagraph (A)(iii) are met with respect to the alien.
"(iii) An alien who is the child of an alien lawfully admitted for permanent residence, who is a person of good moral character, who is eligible for classification under section 203(a)(2)(A), and who has resided in the United States with the alien's permanent resident alien parent may file a petition with the Attorney General under this subparagraph for classification of the alien under such section if the alien demonstrates to the Attorney General that—
"(I) the alien is residing in the United States and during the period of residence with the permanent resident parent the alien has been battered by or has been the subject of extreme cruelty perpetrated by the alien's permanent resident parent; and
"(II) the alien is a person whose deportation, in the opinion of the Attorney General, would result in extreme hardship to the alien."; and
(3) by adding at the end the following new subparagraph:
"(H) In acting on petitions filed under clause (iii) or (iv) of subparagraph (A) or clause (ii) or (iii) of subparagraph (B), the Attorney General shall consider any credible evidence relevant to the petition. The determination of what evidence is credible and the weight to be given that evidence shall be within the sole discretion of the Attorney General.".
(b) CONFORMING AMENDMENTS.—(1) Section 204(a)(2) of the Immigration and Nationality Act (8 U.S.C. 1154(a)(2)) is amended—
(A) in subparagraph (A) by striking "filed by an alien who," and inserting "for the classification of the spouse of an alien if the alien,"; and
(B) in subparagraph (B) by striking "by an alien whose prior marriage" and inserting "for the classification of the spouse of an alien if the prior marriage of the alien".
(2) Section 201(b)(2)(A)(i) of the Immigration and Nationality Act (8 U.S.C. 1151(b)(2)(A)(i)) is amended by striking "204(a)(1)(A)" and inserting "204(a)(1)(A)(ii)".
(c) SURVIVAL RIGHTS TO PETITION.—Section 204 of the Immigration and Nationality Act (8 U.S.C. 1154) is amended by adding at the end the following new subsection:
"(h) The legal termination of a marriage may not be the sole basis for revocation under section 205 of a petition filed under subsection (a)(1)(A)(iii) or a petition filed under subsection (a)(1)(B)(ii) pursuant to conditions described in subsection (a)(1)(A)(iii)(I).".

(d) EFFECTIVE DATE.—The amendments made by this section 8 USC 1151 note.
shall take effect January 1, 1995.

SEC. 40702. USE OF CREDIBLE EVIDENCE IN SPOUSAL WAIVER APPLICATIONS.

(a) IN GENERAL.—Section 216(c)(4) of the Immigration and
Nationality Act (8 U.S.C. 1186a(c)(4)) is amended by inserting after
the second sentence the following: "In acting on applications under
this paragraph, the Attorney General shall consider any credible
evidence relevant to the application. The determination of what
evidence is credible and the weight to be given that evidence shall
be within the sole discretion of the Attorney General.".

(b) EFFECTIVE DATE.—The amendment made by subsection (a)   8 USC 1186a
shall take effect on the date of enactment of this Act and shall   note.
apply to applications made before, on, or after such date.

SEC. 40703. SUSPENSION OF DEPORTATION.

(a) BATTERED SPOUSE OR CHILD.—Section 244(a) of the
Immigration and Nationality Act (8 U.S.C. 1254(a)) is amended—
    (1) by striking "or" at the end of paragraph (1);
    (2) by striking the period at the end of paragraph (2)
and inserting "; or"; and
    (3) by inserting after paragraph (2) the following:
"(3) is deportable under any law of the United States
except section 241(a)(1)(G) and the provisions specified in paragraph (2); has been physically present in the United States
for a continuous period of not less than 3 years immediately
preceding the date of such application; has been battered or
subjected to extreme cruelty in the United States by a spouse
or parent who is a United States citizen or lawful permanent
resident (or is the parent of a child of a United States citizen
or lawful permanent resident and the child has been battered
or subjected to extreme cruelty in the United States by such
citizen or permanent resident parent); and proves that during
all of such time in the United States the alien was and is
a person of good moral character; and is a person whose deportation would, in the opinion of the Attorney General, result
in extreme hardship to the alien or the alien's parent or child.".

(b) CONSIDERATION OF EVIDENCE.—Section 244 of the Immigration and Nationality Act (8 U.S.C. 1254) is amended by adding
at the end the following new subsection:
"(g) In acting on applications under subsection (a)(3), the Attorney General shall consider any credible evidence relevant to the
application. The determination of what evidence is credible and
the weight to be given that evidence shall be within the sole
discretion of the Attorney General.".

§ 1154. Procedure for granting immigrant status

(a) Petitioning procedure

'(1)(A)(l) Any citizen of the United States claiming that an alien is entitled to classification by reason of a relationship described in paragraph (1), (3), or (4) of section

1153(a) of this title or to an immediate relative status under section 1151(b)(2)(A)(i) of this title may file a petition with the Attorney General for such classification.

(ii) An alien spouse described in the second sentence of section 1151(b)(2)(A)(i) of this title also may file a petition with the Attorney General under this subparagraph for classification of the alien (and the alien's children) under such section.

(iii) An alien who is the spouse of a citizen of the United States, who is a person of good moral character, who is eligible to be classified as an immediate relative under section 1151(b)(2)(A)(i) of this title, and who has resided in the United States with the alien's spouse may file a petition with the Attorney General under this subparagraph for classification of the alien (and any child of the alien if such a child has not been classified under clause (iv)) under such section if the alien demonstrates to the Attorney General that—

(I) the alien is residing in the United States, the marriage between the alien and the spouse was entered into in good faith by the alien, and during the marriage the alien or a child of the alien has been battered by or has been the subject of extreme cruelty perpetrated by the alien's spouse; and

(II) the alien is a person whose deportation, in the opinion of the Attorney General, would result in extreme hardship to the alien or a child of the alien.

(iv) An alien who is the child of a citizen of the United States, who is a person of good moral character, who is eligible to be classified as an immediate relative under section 1151(b)(2)(A)(i) of this title, and who has resided in the United States with the citizen parent may file a petition with the Attorney General under this subparagraph for classification of the alien under such section if the alien demonstrates to the Attorney General that—

(I) the alien is residing in the United States and during the period of residence with the citizen parent the alien has been battered by or has been the subject of extreme cruelty perpetrated by the alien's citizen parent; and

(II) the alien is a person whose deportation, in the opinion of the Attorney General, would result in extreme hardship to the alien.

(B)(i) Any alien lawfully admitted for permanent residence claiming that an alien is entitled to a classification by reason of the relationship described in section 1153(a)(2) of this title may file a petition with the Attorney General for such classification.

(ii) An alien who is the spouse of an alien lawfully admitted for permanent residence, who is a person of good moral character, who is eligible for classification under section 1153(a)(2)(A) of this title, and who has resided in the United States with the alien's legal permanent resident spouse may file a petition with the Attorney General under this subparagraph for classification of the alien (and any child of the alien if such a child has not been classified under clause (iii)) under such section if the alien demonstrates to the Attorney General that the conditions described in subclauses (I) and (II) of subparagraph (A)(iii) are met with respect to the alien.

(iii) An alien who is the child of an alien lawfully admitted for permanent residence, who is a person of good moral character, who is eligible for classification under section 1153(a)(2)(A) of this title, and who has resided in the United States with the alien's permanent resident alien parent may file a petition with the Attorney General under this subparagraph for classification of the alien under such section if the alien demonstrates to the Attorney General that—

(I) the alien is residing in the United States and during the period of residence with the permanent resident parent the alien has been battered by or has been the subject of extreme cruelty perpetrated by the alien's permanent resident parent; and

(II) the alien is a person whose deportation, in the opinion of the Attorney General, would result in extreme hardship to the alien.

Zakia CARTER, Petitioner,

v.

IMMIGRATION AND
NATURALIZATION SERVICE,
Respondent.

No. 95–1840.

United States Court of Appeals,
First Circuit.

July 30, 1996.

Alien sought judicial review of decision
of Board of Immigration Appeals (BIA) denying her motion to reopen deportation proceedings based on her claim for protection
under newly enacted battered spouse provision. The Court of Appeals, Selya, Circuit
Judge, held that: (1) alien failed to present
her petition for adjusted status as battered
spouse to Immigration and Naturalization
Service (INS), as required to secure requisite
agency approval of petition; (2) her conviction
for manslaughter stemming from assault and
battery precluded her from establishing good
moral character necessary to qualify for status adjustment based on battered spouse
provision; and (3) her failure to proffer any
evidence on how deportation would work ex-

treme hardship to either herself or her child prevented her from establishing prima facie case for relief in form of motion to reopen deportation proceedings.

Petition denied.

1. Aliens ⟲54.3(3)

On review of Board of Immigration Appeals' (BIA) denial of motion to reopen, the Court of Appeals probes denial solely to determine whether BIA misread law or otherwise abused its discretion by acting in arbitrary or capricious fashion, though denial usually possesses requisite finality to trigger judicial review provisions of the Immigration and Nationality Act (INA). Immigration and Nationality Act, § 106, as amended, 8 U.S.C.A. § 1105a.

2. Aliens ⟲54(5)

In exercising discretionary authority, Board of Immigration Appeals (BIA) is obliged to weigh all pertinent factors, both favorable and unfavorable, exhibit due consideration for weighted factors when tallying equities, exercise independent judgment, and state plainly its reasons for granting or denying relief.

3. Aliens ⟲54(5)

Once Board of Immigration Appeals (BIA) satisfies its obligations in exercising its discretionary authority, it has discretion not only to deny motion to reopen but also to deny hearing on that motion.

4. Aliens ⟲54(5)

Board of Immigration Appeals (BIA) can deny motion to reopen if alien fails to limn prima facie case warranting relief, introduce material evidence that was not previously available, discoverable, or considered at original hearing, or if BIA reasonably determines that equities do not justify application of discretionary balm. 8 C.F.R. § 3.2.

5. Aliens ⟲54(5)

Immigration and Naturalization Service (INS) authorization of petition for status adjustment as battered spouse must occur before Board of Immigration Appeals (BIA) can grant alien's petition for adjusted status.

Immigration and Nationality Act, § 204(b), as amended, 8 U.S.C.A. § 1154(b).

6. Aliens ⟲54(5)

Board of Immigration Appeals (BIA) properly refused to reopen alien's deportation proceedings based on newly enacted battered spouse provision of Immigration and Nationality Act (INA), where she failed to present her petition for adjusted status as battered spouse to Immigration and Naturalization Service (INS), as required to secure requisite agency approval. Immigration and Nationality Act, § 204(a)(1)(A)(iii), as amended, 8 U.S.C.A. § 1154(a)(1)(A)(iii).

7. Aliens ⟲53.2(2)

Petitioner's conviction for manslaughter stemming from assault and battery not only made her deportable under statute providing for deportation of alien convicted of crime involving moral turpitude committed within five years, but also precluded her from establishing good moral character necessary to qualify for status adjustment based on newly enacted battered spouse provision of Immigration and Nationality Act (INA). Immigration and Nationality Act, §§ 204(a)(1)(A)(iii), 241(a)(2)(A)(i), as amended, 8 U.S.C.A. §§ 1154(a)(1)(A)(iii), 1251(a)(2)(A)(i).

8. Aliens ⟲53.10(3)

Petitioner's failure to proffer any evidence on how deportation would work extreme hardship to either herself or her child prevented her from establishing prima facie case for relief in form of motion to reopen deportation proceedings. 8 C.F.R. § 3.2.

———

Joseph S. Callahan, on brief, Fall River, MA, for petitioner.

Frank W. Hunger, Assistant Attorney General, Civil Division, and Philemina McNeill Jones, Assistant Director, Office of Immigration Litigation, United States Department of Justice, on brief, Washington, DC, for respondent.

Before SELYA and BOUDIN, Circuit Judges, and McAULIFFE,* District Judge.

SELYA, Circuit Judge.

Invoking the newly enacted "battered spouse" provision of the Immigration and Nationality Act (I & N Act), 8 U.S.C. § 1154(a)(1)(A)(iii) (1994), petitioner Zakia Carter seeks judicial review of an order of the Board of Immigration Appeals (the Board) denying her motion to reopen deportation proceedings. Discerning no cognizable error, we decline to grant the petition.

I

Carter, a native and citizen of Morocco, was convicted of assault and battery on March 8, 1981. After the victim died, Carter pled guilty to a charge of manslaughter. The state court sentenced her to serve 12–20 years in prison. She was not released from the penitentiary until March 20, 1993.

The Immigration and Naturalization Service (INS) instituted deportation proceedings against petitioner on October 28, 1988 (while she was still incarcerated). In its order to show cause, the INS charged her inter alia with committing a crime involving moral turpitude (for which she was convicted and sentenced to a prison term of more than one year) within five years of her lawful entry into the United States, in violation of section 241(a)(2) of the I & N Act, 8 U.S.C. § 1251(a)(2).[1] Petitioner disputed this charge, denying that the crime she had committed involved moral turpitude.

On March 19, 1990, an immigration judge (IJ) found petitioner deportable. While her

appeal to the Board was pending, petitioner, though still incarcerated, married Dale Carter (a native and citizen of the United States). Following her release, she gave birth to a child, Jamila Carter, on August 22, 1994. Six weeks thereafter, the Board affirmed the IJ's decision and entered a deportation order. See Matter of Carter, Interim Dec. No. 23–200–544 (BIA 1995).

Petitioner subsequently sought a divorce. She then filed a motion to reopen the deportation proceedings. Although the Board previously found petitioner deportable due to her manslaughter conviction, her motion asserts an entitlement to a waiver of excludability premised on her status as a battered spouse.[2] The Board denied her motion on July 12, 1995. Petitioner now seeks judicial review. At the present time, her divorce case is pending, as are certain domestic violence proceedings against her husband.

II

We pause to emphasize the circumscribed nature of our review. The Board originally found Carter to be inadmissible (and, therefore, deportable) because she had committed a crime of moral turpitude (and served more than twelve months in prison) within five years of entering the United States. It denied her motion to reopen for a variety of reasons (most of which related to the absence of a prima facie showing of entitlement to relief).

[1] We inquire only into the Board's denial of the motion to reopen, not its earlier adjudication of the merits of petitioner's ex-

---

* Of the District of New Hampshire, sitting by designation.

1. The statute reads in pertinent part:
 Any alien who (I) is convicted of a crime involving moral turpitude committed within five years ... after the date of entry, and (II) either is sentenced to confinement or is confined therefor ... for one year or longer, is deportable.
 8 U.S.C. § 1251(a)(2)(A)(i). Since the charge under this provision is the only charge that INS pressed, it is the only charge that we discuss.

2. The applicable statute reads in pertinent part:
 An alien who is the spouse of a citizen of the United States, who is a person of good moral character, who is eligible to be classified as an

immediate relative ..., and who has resided in the United States with the alien's spouse may file a petition ... [for relief if]:
 (I) the alien is residing in the United States, the marriage between the alien and the spouse was entered into in good faith by the alien, and during the marriage the alien ... has been battered by or has been the subject of extreme cruelty perpetrated by the alien's spouse; and
 (II) the alien is a person whose deportation would result in extreme hardship to the alien or a child of the alien.
 8 U.S.C. § 1154(a)(1)(A)(iii) (1994).

cludability. *See Gando–Coello v. INS,* 888 F.2d 197, 198 (1st Cir.1989). Though the denial of a motion to reopen deportation proceedings usually possesses the requisite finality and thus triggers the judicial review provisions of the I & N Act, *see, e.g., Baez v. INS,* 41 F.3d 19, 21 (1st Cir.1994); *Goncalves v. INS,* 6 F.3d 830, 831–32 (1st Cir.1993); *Athehortua–Vanegas v. INS,* 876 F.2d 238, 240 (1st Cir.1989), we probe that denial solely to determine whether the Board misread the law or otherwise abused its discretion by acting in an arbitrary or capricious fashion. *See INS v. Doherty,* 502 U.S. 314, 323, 112 S.Ct. 719, 724–25, 116 L.Ed.2d 823 (1992); *INS v. Abudu,* 485 U.S. 94, 105, 108 S.Ct. 904, 912, 99 L.Ed.2d 90 (1988); *Henry v. INS,* 74 F.3d 1, 4 (1st Cir.1996).

[2, 3] The Board's discretion is sprawling, but it does not go untethered. "[A]djudicatory tribunals can exceed grants of discretion—even ringing grants of broad, essentially standardless discretion—in various ways." *Henry,* 74 F.3d at 4. In exercising discretionary authority, the Board is "obliged to weigh all the pertinent factors (both favorable and unfavorable), to exhibit due consideration for the universe of weighted factors when tallying the equities, to exercise independent judgment, and to state plainly its reasons for granting or denying relief." *Bing Feng Chen v. INS,* 87 F.3d 5, 7 (1st Cir.1996). Once the Board satisfies these obligations, however, it has discretion not only to deny a motion to reopen but also to deny a hearing thereon. *See Moore v. INS,* 715 F.2d 13, 16 n. 2 (1st Cir.1983).

III

[4] It is settled that the Board can deny a motion to reopen if (1) the alien fails to limn a prima facie case warranting relief, or (2) the alien fails to introduce material evidence that was not previously available, discoverable, or considered at the original hear-

ing, or (3) the Board reasonably determines that the equities do not justify the application of a discretionary balm. *See* 8 C.F.R. § 3.2 (1996); *see also Abudu,* 485 U.S. at 104–05, 108 S.Ct. at 911–12 (applying this paradigm to the Board's denial of a motion to reopen); *Gando–Coello,* 888 F.2d at 198 (same). Here, the Board had ample justification to deny the petitioner's motion.

[5, 6] 1. *INS Approval.* INS authorization of a petition for a status adjustment under 8 U.S.C. § 1154 must occur before the Board can grant such relief. *See* 8 U.S.C. § 1154(b) (1994) (placing upon the Attorney General or her designee the responsibility to determine in the first instance "that the facts stated in the petition are true and that the [petitioner] is an immediate relative"). In this case, petitioner failed to present her petition for adjusted status as a battered spouse to the INS, and thus did not secure the requisite agency approval.

Approval by the INS is not an empty exercise, but, rather, ensures that the agency has a meaningful opportunity to verify a petitioner's claim that she has been subjected to physical abuse and otherwise satisfies the statutory criteria. Since the INS's imprimatur is a condition precedent to obtaining relief under 8 U.S.C. § 1154(a)(1)(A)(iii), petitioner's failure to comply with this requirement means that she is unable to state a prima facie case. Consequently, the Board's refusal to reopen the proceedings is unimpugnable.[3]

[7] 2. *Good Moral Character; Extreme Hardship.* Petitioner also failed to establish a prima facie case under the battered spouse provision because she did not submit adequate evidence of either "good moral character" or "extreme hardship." We explain briefly.

As to character, the only evidence that petitioner proffered consists of a copy of her

---

3. Highlighting this same deficiency, the INS challenges our jurisdiction on the basis that petitioner failed to exhaust all available administrative remedies in that she neglected to have her petition verified by the INS.. "It is a familiar tenet that when an appeal presents a jurisdictional quandary, yet the merits of the underlying issue, if reached, will in any event be resolved in

favor of the party challenging the court's jurisdiction, then the court may forsake the jurisdictional riddle and simply dispose of the appeal on the merits." *United States v. Stoller,* 78 F.3d 710, 715 (1st Cir.1996) (collecting cases). This is such a case. Hence, we take no view of the government's jurisdictional argument.

prison records, detailing her good behavior and involvement in training programs while she was incarcerated. The Board declined to accept these records as sufficient to show good moral character, and we are not persuaded that the Board's position is arbitrary or capricious.

We note that even appropriate extrinsic evidence of good moral character might well be futile here due to petitioner's conviction. In the deportation case proper, the Board found petitioner's manslaughter offense to be a crime of moral turpitude. The Board's judgments in such matters are not easily dismissed, *see Franklin v. INS*, 72 F.3d 571, 573 (8th Cir.1996) (explaining that since moral turpitude is a "nebulous" concept, courts will only overturn the Board's determination that a crime fits within that rubric if the determination is unreasonable); and, in all events, we think that manslaughter stemming from assault and battery is properly classified as a crime of moral turpitude. *Compare, e.g., Asencio v. INS*, 37 F.3d 614, 615 (11th Cir.1994) (holding that attempted murder is a crime of moral turpitude); *Rodriguez–Padron v. INS*, 13 F.3d 1455, 1458 (11th Cir.1994) (holding that second-degree murder is a crime of moral turpitude); *Gouveia v. INS*, 980 F.2d 814, 815–16 (1st Cir. 1992) (holding that rape is a crime of moral turpitude); *Thomas v. INS*, 976 F.2d 786, 787–88 (1st Cir.1992) (holding assault and battery with a baseball bat to be crimes involving moral turpitude). Accordingly, petitioner's conviction for manslaughter not only would constitute a violation of 8 U.S.C. § 1251(a)(2)(A)(i) but also would preclude her from establishing the "good moral character" necessary to qualify under the battered spouse provision. *See Flores v. INS*, 66 F.3d 1069, 1073 (9th Cir.1995) (holding that petitioner's conviction for welfare fraud precluded her from establishing the "good moral character" required to apply for a suspension of deportation under 8 U.S.C. § 1254(a)(1)).

[8] Relatedly, petitioner neglected to proffer any evidence as to how deportation would work an extreme hardship to either herself or her child. This omission, in and of itself, prevented the establishment of a prima facie case. This is especially true in light of the Board's wide discretion in determining what does and does not rise to the level of "extreme hardship." *See Luna v. INS*, 709 F.2d 126, 127 (1st Cir.1983).

IV

We need go no further. Given the absence of a prima facie case, the Board acted well within its discretion in summarily denying petitioner's motion to reopen.

The petition for review is denied and dismissed. See 1st Cir. R. 27.1.

Illegal
Immigration
Reform and
Immigrant
Responsibility
Act of 1996.

DIVISION C—ILLEGAL IMMIGRATION REFORM AND IMMIGRANT RESPONSIBILITY ACT OF 1996

TITLE III—INSPECTION, APPREHENSION, DETENTION, ADJUDICATION, AND REMOVAL OF INADMISSIBLE AND DEPORTABLE ALIENS

SEC. 350. OFFENSES OF DOMESTIC VIOLENCE AND STALKING AS GROUND FOR DEPORTATION.

(a) IN GENERAL.—Section 241(a)(2) (8 U.S.C. 1251(a)(2)) is amended by adding at the end the following:

"(E) CRIMES OF DOMESTIC VIOLENCE, STALKING, OR VIOLATION OF PROTECTION ORDER, CRIMES AGAINST CHILDREN AND .—

"(i) DOMESTIC VIOLENCE, STALKING, AND CHILD ABUSE.—Any alien who at any time after entry is convicted of a crime of domestic violence, a crime of stalking, or a crime of child abuse, child neglect, or child abandonment is deportable. For purposes of this clause, the term 'crime of domestic violence' means any crime of violence (as defined in section 16 of title 18, United States Code) against a person committed by a current or former spouse of the person, by an individual with whom the person shares a child in common, by an individual who is cohabiting with or has cohabited with the person as a spouse, by an individual similarly situated to a spouse of the person under the domestic or family violence laws of the jurisdiction where the offense occurs, or by any other individual against a person who is protected from that individual's acts under the domestic or family violence laws of the United States or any State, Indian tribal government, or unit of local government.

"(ii) VIOLATORS OF PROTECTION ORDERS.—Any alien who at any time after entry is enjoined under a protection order issued by a court and whom the court determines has engaged in conduct that violates the portion of a protection order that involves protection against credible threats of violence, repeated harassment, or bodily injury to the person or persons for whom the protection order was issued is deportable. For purposes of this clause, the term 'protection order' means any injunction issued for the purpose of preventing violent or threatening acts of domestic violence, including temporary or final orders issued by civil or criminal courts (other than support or child custody orders or provisions) whether obtained by filing an independent action or as a pendente lite order in another proceeding.".

8 USC 1227 note.

(b) EFFECTIVE DATE.—The amendment made by subsection (a) shall apply to convictions, or violations of court orders, occurring after the date of the enactment of this Act.

Battered Immigrants Gain Ally Against Abusers

New INS Rule Lets Spouses, Children Seek U.S. Residence Status on Their Own

By Lena H. Sun
Washington Post Staff Writer

Battered immigrant women and children no longer have to depend on their abusers to become legal, permanent residents of the United States and can now seek legal status on their own, the Immigration and Naturalization Service announced yesterday.

In the past, only U.S. citizens and legal, permanent residents could file applications for their noncitizen spouses and children to become legal residents. Typically, the husband filed the papers for his wife and children.

In domestic violence cases, the husband, already a U.S. citizen or legal resident, often uses his role in the immigration process to keep his wife in the abusive relationship, U.S. officials and representatives of advocacy groups said.

"Foreign-born spouses and children are particularly vulnerable when their ability to remain in this country is controlled by an abusive U.S. citizen or lawful, permanent resident," said INS Commissioner Doris M. Meissner.

In those situations, the abuser "often forces family members to stay in abusive relationships by falsely promising their victims that they will petition on their behalf for permanent resident status in the future, or by threatening their victims with deportation—creating a cycle of continuing abuse," she said.

The new rule, which takes effect immediately, will allow abused family members who otherwise would be eligible for permanent residence to seek legal resident status on their own. The rule implements a provision of the Violence Against Women Act, part of the 1994 crime bill.

Between 300 and 400 immigrants have cases pending under an interim procedure that allowed INS officials to begin accepting—but not acting on—applications a year ago, INS officials said.

Officials and advocacy groups said it is hard to estimate how many others could be affected because immigrant women who are victims of domestic violence traditionally have been difficult to reach.

Leslye Orloff, founder of the domestic violence program at Ayuda, a District-based group that provides legal services to immigrants, said there might be an initial surge of "a couple thousand cases" nationwide.

Under the rule change, the abused spouse or child must be living in the United States at the time; be a person of good moral character; and have entered into the marriage in good faith.

They also must provide evidence of abuse, which may include police reports, medical records, affidavits from school officials and social workers, and "other forms of relevant credible evidence," the INS said.

"Physical abuse and mental abuse is common," said Alakananda Paul, who heads the Asian Women's Self Help Association, a local group that helps women from six South Asian countries, including India, Pakistan, Bangladesh and Sri Lanka.

Many women follow their husbands to the United States, arriving with little knowledge of English and less understanding of U.S. immigration law. Most are financially dependent on their husbands.

One Indian woman in Montgomery County said her husband started abusing her five years ago, when she and their daughter joined him in the United States. He was a permanent, legal resident. More than once, she said, he threatened her with a kitchen knife, saying, " 'I'm not going to give you the green card, and where would you go?' "

The woman, 37, initially was afraid to seek police help but finally sought refuge in a woman's shelter and sent her daughter to stay temporarily with a relative. The woman has since moved three times, but is still stalked by her husband, she said.

Last summer, she filed for permanent residence status on her own; her application is pending with the INS office in Baltimore.

"I think the U.S. government has taken a very good decision because there are a lot of women ... who have been ill-treated by their spouses," said the woman, who requested anonymity for fear of retribution.

Subtitle C—Civil Rights for Women

Civil Rights
Remedies for
Gender-
Motivated
Violence Act.
42 USC 13701
note.

SEC. 40301. SHORT TITLE.

This subtitle may be cited as the "Civil Rights Remedies for Gender-Motivated Violence Act".

SEC. 40302. CIVIL RIGHTS.

42 USC 13981.

(a) PURPOSE.—Pursuant to the affirmative power of Congress to enact this subtitle under section 5 of the Fourteenth Amendment to the Constitution, as well as under section 8 of Article I of the Constitution, it is the purpose of this subtitle to protect the civil rights of victims of gender motivated violence and to promote public safety, health, and activities affecting interstate commerce by establishing a Federal civil rights cause of action for victims of crimes of violence motivated by gender.

(b) RIGHT TO BE FREE FROM CRIMES OF VIOLENCE.—All persons within the United States shall have the right to be free from crimes of violence motivated by gender (as defined in subsection (d)).

(c) CAUSE OF ACTION.—A person (including a person who acts under color of any statute, ordinance, regulation, custom, or usage of any State) who commits a crime of violence motivated by gender and thus deprives another of the right declared in subsection (b) shall be liable to the party injured, in an action for the recovery of compensatory and punitive damages, injunctive and declaratory relief, and such other relief as a court may deem appropriate.

(d) DEFINITIONS.—For purposes of this section—

(1) the term "crime of violence motivated by gender" means a crime of violence committed because of gender or on the basis of gender, and due, at least in part, to an animus based on the victim's gender; and

(2) the term "crime of violence" means—

(A) an act or series of acts that would constitute a felony against the person or that would constitute a felony against property if the conduct presents a serious risk of physical injury to another, and that would come within the meaning of State or Federal offenses described in section 16 of title 18, United States Code, whether or not those acts have actually resulted in criminal charges, prosecution, or conviction and whether or not those acts were committed in the special maritime, territorial, or prison jurisdiction of the United States; and

(B) includes an act or series of acts that would constitute a felony described in subparagraph (A) but for the relationship between the person who takes such action and the individual against whom such action is taken.

(e) LIMITATION AND PROCEDURES.—

(1) LIMITATION.—Nothing in this section entitles a person to a cause of action under subsection (c) for random acts of violence unrelated to gender or for acts that cannot be dem-

onstrated, by a preponderance of the evidence, to be motivated by gender (within the meaning of subsection (d)).

(2) No PRIOR CRIMINAL ACTION.—Nothing in this section requires a prior criminal complaint, prosecution, or conviction to establish the elements of a cause of action under subsection (c).

(3) CONCURRENT JURISDICTION.—The Federal and State courts shall have concurrent jurisdiction over actions brought pursuant to this subtitle.

(4) SUPPLEMENTAL JURISDICTION.—Neither section 1367 of title 28, United States Code, nor subsection (c) of this section shall be construed, by reason of a claim arising under such subsection, to confer on the courts of the United States jurisdiction over any State law claim seeking the establishment of a divorce, alimony, equitable distribution of marital property, or child custody decree.

(5) LIMITATION ON REMOVAL.—Section 1445 of title 28, United States Code, is amended by adding at the end the following new subsection:

"(d) A civil action in any State court arising under section 40302 of the Violence Against Women Act of 1994 may not be removed to any district court of the United States.".

SEC. 40303. ATTORNEY'S FEES.

Section 722 of the Revised Statutes (42 U.S.C. 1988) is amended in the last sentence—

(1) by striking "or" after "Public Law 92-318,"; and
(2) by inserting ", or section 40302 of the Violence Against Women Act of 1994," after "1964".

Act Provides Civil Remedy For Violence

Under the new Violence Against Women Act, victims of gender-bias crimes may bring civil rights suits in state and federal court.

BY JULIE GOLDSCHEID AND SUSAN J. KRAHAM
SPECIAL TO THE NATIONAL LAW JOURNAL

IN SEPTEMBER 1994, the U.S. Congress passed VAWA, or the Violence Against Women Act, the first federal law recognizing and attempting to put an end to gender-motivated violence in the United States.[1] In addition to designating $1.6 billion to stem the violence that plagues many women's lives, the act provides that violent crimes motivated by the victim's gender are discriminatory and violate the victim's civil rights under federal law.[2]

Under that key provision, known as the civil rights remedy, victims of gender-motivated violence now may bring a civil rights suit in federal or state court. They can seek compensatory or punitive damages, declaratory or injunctive relief and attorney fees.

In providing this remedy, Congress recognized that "millions of women and girls who each year become victims of rape, domestic violence and many other crimes are not selected at random...rather, they are exposed to terror, brutality, serious injury and even death because of their sex."[3] In fact, violence is now a leading cause of injury among women. At least 2.5 million women are victims of violent crimes every year,[4] and they are 10 times more likely to be victimized by intimates.[5]

385

The civil rights remedy was designed to complement existing federal civil rights laws, which do not protect women from gender-motivated violence. Before the VAWA's enactment, federal civil rights laws applied only to gender discrimination in the workplace; specific, racially motivated acts of violence; and certain class-based wrongdoing by private individuals.

Federal civil rights laws, which address action taken under color of state law[6] or actions committed as part of a conspiracy,[7] preclude suits by women of any race to redress what may be the most common and damaging form of gender discrimination: acts of violence committed by individuals, including sexual assault and domestic violence. The civil rights remedy recombined elements found in existing civil rights laws to address this pervasive problem.[8]

State civil and criminal statutes, as well as the gender-biased administration of justice that occurs in some state courts, often deny adequate remedies to victims of gender-motivated violence. For example, several states have statutes exempting cohabitants and dating companions from rape laws.[9]

In at least seven states, interspousal tort immunity doctrines bar women who have been beaten or assaulted by their husbands from obtaining a tort remedy.[10] Further, police, prosecutors, juries and judges may subject female victims of rape, assault and domestic violence to a wide range of unfair and degrading treatment, which contributes to the low rates of reporting and conviction that characterize these crimes.[11]

Necessary Federal Remedy

The civil rights remedy, like other civil rights laws, was passed to reinforce state remedies by providing a nationally uniform avenue of redress for victims of gender-based violent crimes. The language of the VAWA clearly states that every citizen is entitled to be free from gender-motivated violence.[12] The civil rights rem-

[SEE 'VIOLENCE' PAGE B10]

Ms. Goldscheid is a staff attorney, and Ms. Kraham is a Skadden Foundation fellow, at the NOW Legal Defense and Education Fund in New York.

['VIOLENCE' FROM PAGE B9]
edy provides that a civil cause of action may be brought
against "a person (including a person who acts under
color of any statute, ordinance, regulation, custom, or
usage of any State) who commits a crime of violence
motivated by gender and thus deprives another of the
right declared in subsection (b)."[13]

Under the act, a plaintiff must prove that the defendant committed a crime of violence and that the crime
was motivated by gender, as both those terms are statutorily defined. Existing law, as well as the legislative history driving the civil rights remedy's enactment, will determine how these elements are proved.

The VAWA defines a crime of violence as an act or series of acts that would constitute a felony under state or
federal law and that involve violent acts against a person or against property if the acts place a
person at risk of physical injury.[14] The
statutory definition is intended to bring
within the scope of the VAWA violent acts
that result in actual or threatened physical
harm, even if those acts constituted a
felony under federal[15] but not state law
and even if the acts ultimately did not result in prosecution or conviction.[16]

The VAWA specifically covers criminal
acts that would constitute a felony but for
the relationship between the perpetrator
and the victim, thereby permitting women
to seek civil redress in states that prohibit
marital rape prosecutions or bar civil suits
against husbands for raping their wives, as
well as states that bar criminal prosecution of sexual
assaults between acquaintances.[17]

The remedy's inclusion of acts that would constitute
a felony under either state or federal law similarly reflects the VAWA's purpose to provide a remedy that
transcends the unique, and often restrictive peculiarities of a state's laws, and provide a more uniform basis
for recovery nationwide. An act or series of acts that
would result in a conviction under the VAWA, such as
committing an act of interstate domestic violence, could
qualify as well.

Spotlight of Suspicion

By its plain language, the VAWA does not require either a criminal prosecution or a conviction to support a
civil rights claim.[18] Consequently, women need not rely
on legal relief from the criminal justice system, which
frequently "shine[s] a spotlight of suspicion on the vic-

tim," and does not provide civil relief.[19] If no criminal prosecution or conviction has resulted, the civil rights action will involve a hearing in which the elements of the felony must be proved by a preponderance of the evidence.

Nevertheless, it will be easier to prove that a defendant committed a crime of violence when the defendant has been convicted of a felony because a conviction likely will establish conclusively this element of proof.[20] From a practical perspective, evidence gained in the course of a criminal investigation may be useful in proving gender-based animus, the second prong of the civil rights remedy.

The second prong of a VAWA civil rights claim requires a plaintiff to prove the connection between the defendant's violent acts and the victim's gender. Although the statute enumerates a two-part analysis to prove gender motivation, the legislative history is clear that this statutory element was drafted with one goal: to ensure that only gender-motivated violent acts, rather than random acts of violence, form the basis for a VAWA recovery.[21]

The legislative history makes clear that gender motivation should be proved in the same manner as existing civil rights violations: by evaluating the totality of the circumstances for such evidence as epithets, patterns of behavior, statements evincing bias, and other circumstantial, as well as direct evidence demonstrating gender-based bias.[22]

Motivating Force

The first part of this gender-motivation element requires a plaintiff to prove that the violent act was committed "because of gender or on the basis of gender, and due, at least in part, to an animus based on the victim's gender."[23] Title VII provides the most useful analogy.[24]

Title VII cases typically are of two types, disparate treatment and disparate impact. The disparate-treatment cases will be more useful under the VAWA because the violent acts targeted by the new law, such as battery, gender-motivated assaults and rape, by definition are more similar to the acts scrutinized in disparate-treatment cases rather than the facially neutral policies and practices more typically addressed in disparate-impact cases.

The second part of the gender-motivation element referencing animus serves to clarify the first part and to ensure that the violent act was linked to the victim's gender. Federal civil rights statutes provide a body of

388

analogous law that have addressed the meaning of animus in the context of class-based discriminatory acts.

The VAWA's legislative history specifically suggests that animus should be interpreted as the term was used in the U.S. Supreme Court's decision in *Griffin v. Breckenridge.*[25] That case involved a racially motivated attack by several white persons on African-Americans and whites believed 'to be civil rights workers. The plaintiffs sued, alleging that the defendants had conspired to deprive ,them of their equal protection or equal privileges and immunities rights in violation of 42 U.S.C. 1985(3).

In construing Sec. 1985(3)'s requirement that the conspiracy be committed for the purpose of depriving any person of their rights, the Supreme Court used the terms "intent," "motivation" and "animus" to determine whether a discriminatory motive propelled the conspiratorial act.[26] Similarly, a showing of discriminatory intent or motive will determine whether a violent act reflects the requisite gender-based animus to state a VAWA civil rights claim.[27]

The statute makes clear, however, that a violation may be established as long as it is based in part on gender-based animus. The statutory language thus establishes that the civil rights remedy can be used in cases in which the violent act was motivated by gender as well as another type of motivation, such as race, age, marital status, religion or sexual orientation.

The precise contours of the civil rights remedy will be defined as litigation unfolds. In the meantime, this landmark federal legislation proclaiming that violence motivated by gender is not merely an individual crime or a personal injury, but is a form of discrimination, marks a significant advance in fighting the epidemic of violence.

(1) 42 U.S.C. 13981 (1994).

(2) The Civil Rights Remedy states:

"(b) All persons within the United States shall have the right to be free from crimes of violence motivated by gender...

"(c) Cause of Action. A person (including a person who acts under color of any statute, ordinance, regulation, custom, or usage of any State) who commits a crime of violence motivated by gender and thus deprives another of the right declared in subsection (b) shall be liable to the party injured, in an action for the recovery of compensatory and punitive damages, injunctive and declaratory relief, and such other relief as a court may deem appropriate..."42 U.S.C. 13981 (1994).

(3) Women and Violence: Hearing Before the Senate Comm. on the Judiciary, 101st Con., 2d Sess. (1990) [hereinafter Hearings 1990] (statement of Helen Neuborne).

(4) Ronet Bachman, U.S. Dept. of Justice, Violence Against Women iii (1994).

(5) Id. at 1.

(6) 42 U.S.C. 1983.

(7' 42 U.S.C. 1985(3).

(8) Hearings 1993, 39 (statement of Prof. Burt Neuborne).

(9) See, e.g., Del. Code Ann. tit. 11, Secs. 774, 775 (Supp. 1992).

(10) Leonard Karp and Cheryl Karp, Domestic Torts (1989; 1993 Supp.).

(11) Hearings 1992, 2 and 70 (1992) (statements of Chairman Charles Schumer and Margaret Rosenbaum); Hearings 1990 (statement of Maria Hanson).

(12) See n.2.

(13) Id.

(14) The civil rights remedy's requirement that the violent act must involve the use, attempted use or threatened use of force or a risk that force will be used, in 42 U.S.C. 3981(d)(2)(A), is reinforced by the requirement that the act fall within the definition of a "crime of violence" under 18 U.S.C. 16 (1994). Echoing the language of the remedy itself, this provision includes offenses that involve the use, attempted use, or threatened use of physical force against a person or property as well as other felonies that involve a substantial risk that physical force will be used against a person or property.

(15) Accordingly, federal criminal offenses can provide the basis for a VAWA civil rights claim even if there is no jurisdictional basis to support a federal prosecution.

(16) See H.R. Rep. 711, 103d Con., 2d Sess. 385 (1994); S. Rep. 102-197 at 43-46.

(17) See S. Rep.102-197 at 45.

(18) 42 U.S.C. 3981(e)(2).

(19) See S. Rep. 102-197 at 44.

(20) See. e.g., SEC v. Gruenberg, 989 F.2d 977, 978 (8th Cir. 1993); Nathan v. Tenna Corp., 560 F.2d 761, 763 (7th Cir. 1977); U.S. v. Private Sanitation Industry Ass'n, 811 F.Supp. 808, 813 (E.D.N.Y. 1992) aff'd 995 F.2d 375 (2d Cir. 1993).

(21) For example, the 1993 Senate Report treats "proof of gender motivation" as a single statutory element. See S. Rep. 138, 103d Con., 1st Sess. 52 (1993).

(22) Id.

(23) 42 U.S.C. 13981(d)(1).

(24) The nearly identical language of Title VII requires proof that the behavior was committed "because of...sex." 42 U.S.C. 2000e-2. Case law discussions applying the Title VII standard interchangeably use the terms "motivated by," "because of," "on the basis of" or "based on" sex or gender, further supports applying Title VII caselaw to prove a VAWA civil rights claim.

(25) 403 U.S. 88 (1971). Hearings 1993 at 6-7 (statement of Sally Goldfarb).

(26) Griffin, 403 U.S. at 100, 102.

(27) Litigation will clarify the contours of "animus" in the context of VAWA litigation, particularly in light of post-Griffin cases such as Bray v. Alexandria Women's Health Clinic, 113 S. Ct. 753 (1993), discussing "animus" in the context of scrutinizing anti-abortion protests. ∎

390

Acknowledgments

National Council of Juvenile and Family Court Judges. "Civil Orders for Protection." In
  Model Code on Domestic and Family Violence (Reno, Nev.: National Council of
  Juvenile and Family Court Judges, 1994): 22–32. Reprinted with the
  permission of the National Council of Juvenile and Family Court Judges.
Pennsylvania Coalition Against Domestic Violence. *Model Full Faith and Credit Statute*
  (Harrisburg, Pa.: Pennsylvania Coalition Against Domestic Violence, 1996):
  1–3.
Court of Common Pleas, Allegheny County, Pennsylvania. "Protection from Abuse —
  Final Order" (Dec. 1994): 1–3.
Klein, Catherine F., and Leslye E. Orloff. Excerpt from "Providing Legal Protection for
  Battered Women: An Analysis of State Statutes and Case Law." *Hofstra Law
  Review* 21 (1993): 801, 848–76. Reprinted with the permission of the *Hofstra
  Law Review.*
Keilitz, Susan L., Paula L. Hannaford, and Hillery S. Efkeman. *Civil Protection Orders:
  The Benefits and Limitations for Victims of Domestic Violence* (National Center for
  State Courts, 1996): 1–17. Reprinted with the permission of the U.S.
  Department of Justice, Office of Justice Programs.
State ex rel. Denise Williams v. *William J. Marsh, Judge,* 626 S.W.2d 223 (Mo.banc. 1982):
  223–37. Reprinted with the permission of the West Publishing Company.
People of the State of Illinois v. *Leland Blackwood,* 476 N.E.2d 742 (Ill. 1985): 742–46.
  Reprinted with the permission of the West Publishing Company.
Alvin D. Blazel v. *Ann Walsh Bradley, Judge,* 698 F.Supp. 756 (Wis. 1988): 756–68.
  Reprinted with the permission of the West Publishing Company.
O'Brien, Mary U. "Mutual Restraining Orders in Domestic Violence Civil Cases."
  Clearinghouse Review, Special Issue (1996): 231–42. Reprinted with the
  permission of National Clearinghouse for Legal Services.
Klein, Catherine F. "Full Faith and Credit: Interstate Enforcement of Protection
  Orders Under the Violence Against Women Act of 1994." *Family Law
  Quarterly* 29 (1995): 253–71. Reprinted with the permission of the National
  Council of Juvenile and Family Court Judges.
National Council of Juvenile and Family Court Judges. "Family and Children." In
  Model Code on Domestic and Family Violence (Reno, Nev.: National Council of

Juvenile and Family Court Judges, 1994): 33–38. Reprinted with the
permission of the National Council of Juvenile and Family Court Judges.

Singer, Mark I., Trina Menden Anglin, Li yu Song, and Lisa Lunghofer. "Adolescents'
Exposure to Violence and Associated Symptoms of Psychological Trauma."
Journal of the American Medical Association 273 (Feb. 1995): 477–82. Copyright
1995. The American Medical Association. Reprinted by permission.

Edleson, Jeffrey L. "Mothers and Children: Understanding the Links Between Woman
Battering and Child Abuse." *Synergy: Newsletter of the Resource Center on
Domestic Violence* 1, no.3 (1995): 4–5. Reprinted with the permission of the
National Council of Juvenile and Family Court Judges.

Thormaehlen, Dorothy J., and Eena R. Bass-Feld. "Children: The Secondary Victims
of Domestic Violence." *Maryland Medical Journal* 43 (1994): 355–59.
Reprinted with the permission of the Medical and Chirurgical Faculty of
Maryland.

Krajewski, Sandra S., Mary Fran Rybarik, Margaret F. Dosch, and Gary D. Gilmore.
"Results of a Curriculum Intervention with Seventh Graders Regarding
Violence in Relationships." *Journal of Family Violence* 11 (1996): 93–112.
Reprinted with the permission of Plenum Press.

Thornberry, Terence P. "Violent Families and Youth Violence." *Fact Sheet 21* Office of
Juvenile Justice and Delinquency Prevention (Dec. 1994). Reprinted with
permission of the Office of Juvenile Justice and Delinquency Prevention.

Davidson, Howard A. "Child Abuse and Domestic Violence: Legal Connections and
Controversies." *Family Law Quarterly* 29 (1995): 357–73. Reprinted with the
permission of the National Council of Juvenile and Family Court Judges.

Family Violence Project of the National Council of Juvenile and Family Court Judges.
"Family Violence in Child Custody Statutes: An Analysis of State Codes and
Legal Practice." *Family Law Quarterly* 29 (1995): 197–227. Reprinted with
the permission of the National Council of Juvenile and Family Court Judges.

"Spouse Abuse — Statutory Presumption in Child Custody Litigation." H. Con. Res.
172, 101st Cong. 2d Session (1990): 5182–83.

Barbara Baker v. *James Baker*, 494 N.W.2d 282 (Minn. 1992): 282–90. Reprinted with
the permission of the West Publishing Company.

American Bar Association Center on Children and the Law. *The Impact of Domestic
Violence on Children* (Aug. 1994): 3–4. Reprinted with the permission of the
American Bar Association, Commission on Domestic Violence.

"Protection of the Family and Dependent Persons." Iowa Code — Chapter 726,
Sec. 726.6.

Treuthart, Mary Pat. "All That Glitters Is Not Gold: Mediation in Domestic Abuse
Cases." *Clearinghouse Review*, Special Issue (1996): 243–50, 252–60.
Reprinted with the permission of National Clearinghouse for Legal Services.

Thompson v. *Thompson*, 218 U.S. 611 (1910): 611–24.

Scherer, Douglas D. "Tort Remedies for Victims of Domestic Abuse." *South Carolina
Law Review* 43 (1992): 543–79. Reprinted with the permission of the *South
Carolina Law Review*.

Meier, Linda K., and Brian K. Zoeller. "Taking Abusers to Court: Civil Remedies for

Domestic Violence Victims." *Trial* 31 (June 1995): 60–65. Reprinted with
the permission of the Association of Trial Lawyers of America.

Christina Giovine v. *Peter J. Giovine,* 663 A.2d 109 (N.J.Super.A.D. 1995): 109–30.
Reprinted with the permission of the West Publishing Company.

Charlene Kunza v. *Curtis Pantze,* 527 N.W. 2d 846 (Minn. App. 1995): 846–51.
Reprinted with the permission of the West Publishing Company.

Women's Law Project and the Pennsylvania Coalition Against Domestic Violence.
Insurance Discrimination Against Victims of Domestic Violence (Rev. July 1997):
1–15.

Wheeler, Charles. "New Protections for Immigrant Women and Children Who Are
Victims of Domestic Violence." *Clearinghouse Review,* Special Issue (1996):
222–29. Reprinted with the permission of National Clearinghouse for Legal
Services.

"Violent Crime Control and Law Enforcement Act of 1994." Title IV — Violence
Against Women — Subtitle G — Protections for Battered Immigrant
Women and Children. Public Law 103-322, 103d Congress, 108 Stat. 1953.
United States Statutes at Large. (Washington, D.C.: GPO, 1995): 1953–55.

"Amendment to the U.S. Immigration Act." Title 8 U.S.C. Section 1154
(a)(1)(A)(iii)(1994).

Zakia Carter v. *Immigration and Naturalization Service,* 90 F.3d 14 (1st Cir. 1996): 14–18.
Reprinted with the permission of the West Publishing Company.

"Illegal Immigration Reform and Immigrant Responsibility Act of 1996." Title III,
Sec. 350 Offenses of Domestic Violence and Stalkings as Grounds for
Deportation. Public Law 104-208, 104th Congress, 110 Stat. United States
Code Congressional and Administrative News (St. Paul: West Group, 1997).
Reprinted with the permission of the West Publishing Company.

Sun, Lena H. "Battered Immigrants Gain Ally Against Abusers: New INS Rule Lets
Spouses, Children Seek U.S. Residence Status on Their Own." *Washington
Post* (March 27, 1996). Reprinted with the permission of the Washington
Post Company.

"Civil Rights Remedies for Gender-Motivated Violence Act." Subtitle C — Civil Rights
for Women. Public Law 103-322, 103d Congress, 108 Stat. 1941. United
States Statutes at Large. (Washington, D.C.: GPO, 1995): 1941–42.

Goldscheid, Julie, and Susan J. Kraham. "Act Provides Civil Remedy for Violence."
The National Law Journal (May 1, 1995). Reprinted with the permission of
the New York Law Publishing Company.

Controversies in Constitutional Law

The Constitution and the Flag (1993)
Volume 1: The Flag Salute Cases
Volume 2: The Flag Burning Cases

Prayer in Public Schools and the Constitution 1961–1992 (1993)
Volume 1: Government-Sponsored Religious Activities
in Public Schools and the Constitution

Volume 2: Moments of Silence in Public Schools and the Constitution

Volume 3: Protecting Religious Speech in Public Schools:
The Establishment and Free Exercise Clauses in the Public Arena

Gun Control and the Constitution
Sources and Explorations on the Second Amendment (1993)

Volume 1: The Courts, Congress, and the Second Amendment
Volume 2: Advocates and Scholars: The Modern Debate on Gun Control
Volume 3: Special Topics on Gun Control

School Busing
Constitutional and Political Developments (1994)

Volume 1: The Development of School Busing as a Desegregation Remedy
Volume 2: The Public Debate Over Busing Attempts to Restrict Its Use

Abortion Law in the United States (1995)
Volume 1: From *Roe* v. *Wade* to the Present
Volume 2: Historical Development of Abortion Law
Volume 3: Modern Writings on Abortion

Hate Speech and the Constitution (1996)
Volume 1: The Development of the Hate Speech Debate:
From Group Libel to Campus Speech Codes
Volume 2: The Contemporary Debate:
Reconciling Freedom of Expression and Equality of Citizenship

Capital Punishment (1996)
Volume 1: The Philosophical, Moral, and Penological Debate Over Capital Punishment
Volume 2: Capital Punishment Jurisprudence
Volume 3: Litigating Capital Cases

Homosexuality and the Constitution (1997)
Volume 1: Homosexual Conduct and State Regulation
Volume 2: Homosexuals and the Military
Volume 3: Homosexuality, Politics, and Speech
Volume 4: Homosexuality and the Family

Environment, Property, and the Law (1997)
Federal and State Case Decisions & Journal Articles

Affirmative Action and the Constitution (1998)
Volume 1: Affirmative Action Before Constitutional Law, 1964–1977
Volume 2: The Supreme Court "Solves" the Affirmative Action Issue, 1978–1988
Volume 3: Judicial Reaction to Affirmative Action, 1989–1997

Domestic Violence:
From a Private Matter to a Federal Offense (1998)
Volume 1: Domestic Violence: Intimate Partner Abuse
Volume 2: The Crimes of Domestic Violence
Volume 3: The Civil Justice System's Response to Domestic Violence